THE URBANISM OF
FRANK LLOYD WRIGHT

FOR BRUCE BROOKS PFEIFFER, WHOSE DEDICATION
TO THE PRESERVATION OF WRIGHT'S ARCHIVES,
UNPARALLELED KNOWLEDGE OF THEIR SCOPE AND
SIGNIFICANCE, AND EXTRAORDINARY GENEROSITY
IN SHARING HIS PASSION AND KNOWLEDGE
MADE THIS BOOK POSSIBLE

THE URBANISM OF FRANK LLOYD WRIGHT FEATURES EXTENSIVE IMAGES FROM THE FRANK LLOYD WRIGHT FOUNDATION ARCHIVES (THE MUSEUM OF MODERN ART | AVERY ARCHITECTURAL & FINE ARTS LIBRARY, COLUMBIA UNIVERSITY, NEW YORK). THE AUTHOR AND PUBLISHER EXPRESS THEIR GRATITUDE TO ALL THREE ORGANIZATIONS FOR THE USE OF THESE IMAGES, WHICH HAVE BEEN NEWLY PHOTOGRAPHED BY AVERY ARCHITECTURAL & FINE ARTS LIBRARY. UNLESS OTHERWISE INDICATED, ALL IMAGES COME FROM THIS COLLECTION. FULL CREDIT INFORMATION CAN BE FOUND ON THE PHOTO CREDITS PAGE.

CONTENTS

III: NEW VISIONS FOR THE CITY CENTER: URBANISM UNDER THE HEGEMONY OF THE AUTOMOBILE

PREFACE AND ACKNOWLEDGMENTS

This study had its origins in my book *The Architecture of Frank Lloyd Wright*, published in 1996. It was conceived and developed as a companion volume to that earlier work. As I was writing the book on Wright's architecture, I became keenly aware of the fact that certain important areas of the architect's larger vision for the design of the human environment were being given short shrift by me in order to focus more intensely on the characteristics and meaning of his individual buildings. Two examples that forcefully came to mind were the project for the 1900–1901 Quadruple Block Plan, which formed the foundation of the architect's concept of the Prairie House, and the extensive urban scheme for the expansion of the city of Baghdad in the late 1950s, which provided the framework for the design of an opera house as well as several other individual buildings. I gave neither urban project its due and soon began to think about how I might. More importantly, I thought long and hard about what this would mean for a reevaluation of Wright's work as a whole. I began research on the architect's various urban design initiatives and taught an extensive series of courses at Harvard, beginning in the fall of 1997, on the subject of Wright and the modern city. This book represents the culmination of that nearly twenty-year effort.

I was honored to present my research over the years in lectures and panel discussions at numerous academic institutions in the United States and Europe. I learned much from the feedback and thank all those who offered their comments and advice. Parts of this book have appeared in essays and articles published in academic journals, collections of papers from conferences, and museum catalogues. Such publications are all referred to in the endnotes and so will not be detailed here. What I do want to spell out here, though, is the important financial and moral support I received for the work in progress in the form of a Harvard University Walter Channing Cabot Fellowship (1996–97), a John Simon Guggenheim Memorial Foundation Fellowship (2003–4), a Graham Foundation for Advanced Studies in the Fine Arts Research and Development Grant (2008), and, for the final stage, a National Endowment for the Humanities Fellowship (2012–13). Such support gave me the freedom to spend significant time at the sites under investigation and at the numerous archives associated with them and with the different planners and architects whose interventions were of relevance to Wright's objectives and proposals.

Among the many individuals whose help was instrumental, I first want to mention Bruce Pfeiffer, Margo Stipe, Oskar Muñoz, and Indira Berndtson, who made the Frank Lloyd Wright Archives at Taliesin West available to me in an uncommonly generous way and who offered invaluable insights and ideas on issues ranging from sources and events to the very reading of complex and often difficult-to-decipher drawings. My appreciation of their work and efforts on my behalf is unbounded. During the production of this book, the Wright drawings were transferred from Taliesin West to the Avery Architectural & Fine Arts Library at Columbia University, where they now are being preserved under a joint stewardship arrangement with the Museum of Modern Art. In a spirit of extraordinary professional support, Carole Ann Fabian, the library's director, agreed to allow this book to be the first to benefit from new digital photography of the Wright drawings; and Janet Parks, the curator of drawings and archives, directed and oversaw the operation with the care, commitment, and passion it deserved. Janet's staff, including Margaret Smithglass and Nicole Richard, were unfailingly helpful

Susan Jacobs Lockhart, a former member of the Taliesin Fellowship who became my partner and then my wife during the period of research and writing, has been an indispensable collaborator, thinking through issues with me and pointing me in directions I might not otherwise have investigated. Among colleagues in the field, no one deserves more credit for helping to develop certain ideas and pin down certain facts and issues than David Van Zanten. Kathryn Smith and Mary Jane Hamilton both willingly shared their knowledge with me on numerous questions, always responding with a dependable and characteristic precision. Hugh Spencely and John Minoprio went out of their way to aid me in understanding their fathers' work. Particularly contributory in various important ways were Amanda Bowen, Mary Daniels, David De Long, Sean Malone, William Whitaker, and Inés Zalduendo. Others who provided important ideas, information, or assistance include, in alphabetical order, Muhannad Albaqshi, Amin Alsaden, Jennifer Beauregard, Anne Biebel, Robert Bruegmann, Rifat Chadirji, Sally Chappell, Peter Christensen, Richard Cleary, Jean-Louis Cohen, Dino DeConcini, Thomas Doxiadis, Andres Duany, Judith Eversley, Brendan Fay, Paul Ford, Heidi Galles, David Handlin, Wilbert Hasbrouck, Michael Hays, Mark Henderson, Elizabeth Dean Hermann, Sonja Hildebrand, Jennifer Hock, Ellen Jawdat, William Jerousek, Cemal Kafadar, J. L. (Hans) Krabbendam, Carol Krinsky, Paul Kruty, Michael Kubo, Amanda Reeser Lawrence, Salvatore Licitra,

Pat Mahoney, Kanan Makiya, Mohammed Makiya, Cammie McAtee, Sally McKay, Jerry Morosco, Beth Murfee, Gülru Necipoğlu, Susan Olsen, Ford Peatross, David Phillips, John Rosenfield, Cole Roskam, Paolo Rosselli, Tom Schmidt, Joseph Siry, Sandra Sokol, Carl Smith, Caroline Spurry, Laurent Stalder, John Thorpe, Dell Upton, Lynda Waggoner, Mark Warren, Amber Wiley, Carol Willis, and Fred Zinke.

I want to thank the following, in particular, for their aid in either accessing documents or acquiring illustrations: Arne Hästesko, Mia Hipeli, Katariina Pakoma, and Timo Riekko, Alvar Aalto Museum, Helsinki and Jyväskylä; Mary Woolever and Stephanie Coleman, Art Institute of Chicago; Stefanie Brown, Laurel Mitchell, and Ray Ryan, Carnegie Museum of Art, Pittsburgh; John Russick, Christine McNulty, Dana Lamparello, and Ellen Keith, Chicago History Museum; Sue Kohler, Tony Simon, and Susan Raposa, U.S. Commission of Fine Arts, Washington, D.C.; Giota Pavlidou, Doxiadis Archives, Athens; Spruill Harder, Al Morales, and Bill Connor, Digital Images and Slide Collection, Fine Arts Library, Harvard University; Josh Tidy, First Garden City Heritage Museum, Letchworth; Arnaud Dercelles, Fondation Le Corbusier, Paris; Zarine Weil, Frank Lloyd Wright Trust, Oak Park; Michael Dosch, Frederick Law Olmsted National Historic Site, Brookline, Mass.; Filine Wagner, gta Archives, ETH, Zurich; Dave Mathews, Harvard University Art Museums; Mary Haegert, Houghton Library, Harvard University; Ed Redmond, Geography and Map Division, Library of Congress, Washington, D.C.; William Creech, National Archives and Records Administration, Washington, D.C.; Andrea Gibbs, National Gallery of Art, Washington, D.C.; Ineke Soeterik and Iris de Jong, Het Nieuwe Institut, Rotterdam; Frank Lipo, Oak Park Historical Society; Marilyn Holt, Gil Pietrzak, and Cindy Ulrich, Pennsylvania Department, Carnegie Library, Pittsburgh; James Quigel, Pennsylvania State University Libraries; Christine Roussel, Rockefeller Center Archives, New York; Art Louderback and Kerin Shellenbarger, Sen. John Heinz History Center, Pittsburgh; Amey Hutchins, Rare Book and Manuscript Library, University of Pennsylvania; Tsering Wangyal Shawa, Peter B. Lewis Library, Princeton University; Sheri Dolfen, Cathy Jacob, Andy Kraushaar, Lisa Marine, Carolyn Mattern, Harry Miller, and John Nondorf, Wisconsin Historical Society, Madison; Stephen Ross and Claryn Spies, Manuscripts and Archives, Yale University Library.

Many of my illustrations were scanned by the extraordinarily talented group at the Harvard College Library's Digital Imaging Services, headed by Robert Zinck. For their patience and care, I thank his front office staff of YuHua Li and Evelyn Santana-Nola. My greatest debt of gratitude for all her expert help on technical matters, photographic and otherwise, goes to Deborah Sears, the Harvard History of Art and Architecture department's incomparable former technology administrator. A generous subvention from the department helped defray the cost of illustrations. No one deserves my thanks more for this and innumerable other forms of assistance over the years than the department's wonderful administrator, Deanna Dalrymple.

Finally, my profound thanks go to Michelle Komie, my editor at Princeton University Press, and Peter Dougherty, its director, for their enthusiastic embrace of this project. Michelle has gone well beyond the call of duty in making the book all that I could have hoped for, and then some. Her intelligence, her strength of mind, and her generosity of spirit have had an enormous effect, not the least on those who have worked under her guidance, like Terri O'Prey, who managed the production side of things, and Luke Bulman, who created the book's beautiful design. Finally, I want to commend Dwight Primiano, the photographer at Avery Library, for work that should set a new standard in the reproduction of Wright's drawings.

ABBREVIATIONS

Journals and Newspapers

AA .... *American Architect*
AAAR .... *American Architect and Architectural Review*
AC .... *American City*
AF .... *Architectural Forum*
AR .... *Architectural Record*
CCB .... *City Club Bulletin*
CDT .... *Chicago Daily Tribune*
CHE .... *Chicago Herald and Examiner*
CST .... *Chicago Sunday Tribune*
CT .... *Madison Capital Times*
ES .... *Washington Evening Star*
IT .... *Iraq Times*, Baghdad edition
JAIP .... *Journal of the American Institute of Planners*
JPH .... *Journal of Planning History*
JSAH .... *Journal of the Society of Architectural Historians*
LHJ .... *Ladies' Home Journal*
NYT .... *New York Times*
PD .... *Pittsburgh Dispatch*
PP .... *Pittsburgh Press*
PPG .... *Pittsburgh Post-Gazette*
PS .... *Pittsburgh Sun*
PST .... *Pittsburgh Sun-Telegraph*
TH .... *Washington Times-Herald*
WA .... *Western Architect*
WDN .... *Washington Daily News*
WP .... *Washington Post*
WSG .... *Wisconsin State Journal*

Books and Manuscripts

Azara .... Pedro Azara, ed., *Ciudad del espejismo: Bagdad, de Wright a Venturi/City of Mirages: Baghdad, from Wright to Venturi* (Barcelona: Departament de Composició Arquitectònica, Universitat Politècnica de Catalunya, 2008).

Burnham and Bennett .... Daniel H. Burnham and Edward H. Bennett, *Plan of Chicago*, ed. Charles Moore (1909; repr., New York: Princeton Architectural Press, 1993).

FLWCW .... *Frank Lloyd Wright: Collected Writings*, 5 vols., ed. Bruce Brooks Pfeiffer (New York: Rizzoli, in association with the Frank Lloyd Wright Foundation, 1992–95).

FLWCW/DG/OC .... Bruce Brooks Pfeiffer, ed., *Frank Lloyd Wright: The Complete Work/Das Gesamtwerk/L'oeuvre complète*, 3 vols. (Cologne: Taschen, 2009–11).

FLWM .... Bruce Brooks Pfeiffer and Yukio Futagawa, eds., *Frank Lloyd Wright*, vols. 1–8, *Monograph* (Tokyo: A.D.A. EDITA, 1985–88).

FLWPS .... Bruce Brooks Pfeiffer and Yukio Futagawa, eds., *Frank Lloyd Wright*, vols. 9–11, *Preliminary Studies* (Tokyo: A.D.A. EDITA, 1985–87).

FLWR .... Bruce Brooks Pfeiffer and Yukio Futagawa, eds., *Frank Lloyd Wright*, vol. 12, *In His Renderings* (Tokyo: A.D.A. EDITA, 1984).

Archives and Libraries

Levine .... Neil Levine, *The Architecture of Frank Lloyd Wright* (Princeton, N.J.: Princeton University Press, 1996).

"Middle East Diary" .... [Anthony Minoprio, Greville Spencely, and Peter W. Macfarlane], "Middle East Diary 1955" (15 June 1955–17 December 1957). Private Collection

Minoprio, Spencely,
and Macfarlane .... [Anthony] Minoprio and [Greville] Spencely, and P[eter] W. Macfarlane, *The Master Plan for the City of Baghdad, 1956: Report* (Ekistics Files, Constantinos A. Doxiadis Archives, Athens).

Mollenhoff and Hamilton .... David V. Mollenhoff and Mary Jane Hamilton, *Frank Lloyd Wright's Monona Terrace: The Enduring Power of a Civic Vision* (Madison: University of Wisconsin Press, 1999).

Yeomans .... Alfred B[eaver] Yeomans, ed., *City Residential Land Development: Studies in Planning. Competitive Plans for Subdividing a Typical Quarter Section of Land in the Outskirts of Chicago*, Publications of the City Club of Chicago (Chicago: University of Chicago Press, December 1916).

AAM .... Alvar Aalto Museum, Jyväskylä

ACCD .... Allegheny Conference on Community Development, Pittsburgh

AIC .... Ryerson and Burnham Libraries, Art Institute of Chicago

CFA .... U.S. Commission of Fine Arts, Washington, D.C.

CHM .... Chicago History Museum

FLC .... Fondation Le Corbusier, Paris

FLWFA .... The Frank Lloyd Wright Foundation Archives (The Museum of Modern Art | Avery Architectural & Fine Arts Library, Columbia University, New York)

HNI .... Het Nieuwe Institut, Rotterdam

HSWP .... Historical Society of Western Pennsylvania (now Sen. John Heinz History Center), Pittsburgh

LC .... Library of Congress, Washington, D.C.

NARA .... National Archives and Records Administration, Washington, D.C.

PDCL .... Pennsylvania Department, Carnegie Library, Pittsburgh

PPC .... Point Park Committee, Pittsburgh

PRPA .... Pittsburgh Regional Planning Association

SJHHC .... Sen. John Heinz History Center, Pittsburgh

WHS .... Wisconsin Historical Society, Madison

INTRODUCTION

The Urbanism of Frank Lloyd Wright must strike many as an oxymoron. When thinking of Wright and the city, one usually thinks of Broadacre City, the plan the architect produced between 1929 and 1935 proposing the disappearance of urban and suburban settlement patterns as they were known. In fact, his first book-length presentation of the project, published in 1932, was titled *The Disappearing City*. Paying no attention to existing cities and avoiding contact with the already urbanized fabric of the country, Broadacre City proposed a continent-wide, decentralized network of continuous, low-density rural communities consisting of predominantly single-family houses and small farms all linked to one another by the automobile, the highway, and new forms of telecommunication. Broadacre City substantiates the stereotypical image of Wright the antiurbanist, whether it be the American frontiersman, the Jeffersonian gentleman farmer, the back-to-nature transcendentalist, or the legatee of Frederick Law Olmsted's organic picturesqueness.

Broadacre City grew out of a dissatisfaction with the congestion of the modern metropolis and embodied a utopianism similar to that which drove many European proposals for new forms of urbanism of the preceding decade. Indeed, Broadacre City was explicitly projected by Wright as an American type of "ruralism" to counter Le Corbusier's Machine Age "urbanism."[1] But it represents only one aspect of Wright's rich and complex output in urban design and was, in effect, more a reaction to events than a direct outgrowth of the architect's own previous work. It should therefore not be taken as characteristic of his thinking on the subject of urbanism nor as the culmination of his work in that area. This study documents, analyzes, and interprets Wright's major achievements in the field of urban design both before and after Broadacre City. It provides, for the first time, an integrated and coherent overview of that production and, in the process, reveals Wright's thinking to be less eccentric and less idiosyncratic than previously thought, though no less radical or consequential.

This book is divided into three parts. The first and third, though unequal in length, cover equal periods of time; the middle section, devoted to the work of the 1920s and its outcome in Broadacre City, marks the transition from a city based on one mode of transportation to that based on another. The first part deals with Wright's designs for the inner suburbs of Chicago done between the mid-1890s and the mid-1910s, at the very moment when, as historian Kenneth T. Jackson has remarked,

"a 'new city,'" aided by the development of the streetcar "and encompassing an area triple the territory of the older walking city, had clearly emerged as the center of the American urban society."[2] This was also precisely when Chicago's downtown commercial Loop was being developed and the issue of city planning as such, including both the old city centers and the new residential suburbs, was first receiving professional attention and formal direction in Europe and America.

Following an analysis of Wright's first attempts, in the 1920s, to tackle the challenges faced by the city center at the very dawn of the automobile age and the singular response offered by his Broadacre City project, the third part looks at Wright's designs for Madison, Wisconsin, Washington, D.C., Pittsburgh, and Baghdad dating from the late 1930s through the late 1950s. These large-scale designs for civic, cultural, and residential/commercial centers reflect, and in some cases predict, the renewal of interest worldwide in the "core" of the city that began in the immediate post–World War II era and gave rise to the new concept of urban design developed in large part as a response to problems posed by redevelopment. The three stages in Wright's urbanism embody the general evolution from turn-of-the-century city and town planning practices to the visionary thinking of the interwar years to the ameliorative, problem-solving efforts of the postwar era.

Wright's engagement with urban design issues began within three years of starting his own architectural practice. In 1896 he was commissioned to design an entire block of twenty-two single-family houses in the Chicago suburb of Ridgeland, later annexed to Oak Park. His solution, the subject of chapter 1, was to create a central garden, entered from one of the short sides, that replaced the traditional alley and thus transformed a service element into a communal amenity. Equally important was the fact that he embraced the underlying grid of Chicago's street system as the basis for the plan, a methodology that would remain critical to his work until the later 1930s. For this reason the origin and meaning of the grid in American land-use ideology and practice will be examined in contrast to the later development of the picturesque approach exemplified by Frederick Law Olmsted and Calvert Vaux's Riverside of 1868–69. It will certainly come as a surprise to many that Wright neither valued the Riverside plan nor embraced the Olmsted-Vaux aesthetic.

More radical than the Roberts block project was the plan

Wright presented in the February 1901 issue of the *Ladies' Home Journal* as the precondition and framework for his revolutionary Prairie House. The concept he called the Quadruple Block Plan, to be discussed in chapter 2, envisioned a complete restructuring of the city's system of land subdivision for the purpose of establishing a new basis for the relationship between community and privacy. Blocks were to be square rather than rectangular and to contain only four houses, each occupying the center of a corner lot created by the quartering of the square. The pinwheeling plan of each house extended into low garden walls connecting one house to the next and enclosing a communal garden housing a shared stable in the center.

In 1903, the same client who commissioned the 1896 project asked Wright to revisit the by then Oak Park site; and this time Wright adapted the Quadruple Block Plan to it. Chapter 3 examines the result as well as the numerous variants Wright developed from it for different block configurations in different areas in and around Oak Park. Though never realized, these projects showed how a modern conception of free-flowing space could be applied to the abstraction of the grid to create an overall sense of dynamic order. Its modernity will be contrasted to the prevailing concepts of the City Beautiful and Garden City that were contemporary with it.

The second Roberts block plan formed the ground for the final project in this series that Wright developed in 1912–13 when the City Club of Chicago, which was holding an international housing competition, asked him to offer a model quarter section of a residential neighborhood of the city containing buildings for commercial, government, and cultural uses as well. Chapter 4 reveals how, in contrast to the picturesque, self-contained village-like Garden City designs of many of the competitors, and the City Beautiful–inspired plans of others, Wright's decentered, nonhierarchical, open-ended plan based on the grid established a powerful continuity between center city and suburban edge wherein the latter appeared as merely the extension, rather than the opposite, of the former.

Following the passage in New York in 1916 of the first ordinance limiting building heights, building uses, and area coverage on a differential basis, zoning became the preferred tool of American city planners. Wright's Skyscraper Regulation project of 1926 for the Loop, to be discussed in chapter 5, took into account both the new zoning regulations of Chicago (1923) and the modern concept of a multilevel city to offer a template for decongestion shared with many other architects

and planners of the period. Notable among these were Le Corbusier, Eliel Saarinen, Harvey Wiley Corbett, and Ludwig Hilberseimer. Broadacre City, the subject of chapter 6, can be seen as an expansion of the City Club design into the rural network of the Jeffersonian grid. More importantly, it will be analyzed as an argument for decentralization as the ideal solution to the problem of congestion. And just as the sequential 1896–1913 designs are analyzed in relation to their contemporary European and American counterparts, Broadacre City is compared and contrasted with the other utopian schemes to which it was consciously addressed. Wright's emphasis on the textual as opposed to visual articulation of the design will serve to highlight its utopianism and place it in proper perspective in the architect's career.

The discussion of Broadacre City as a reaction to the automobile's impact on the city serves to highlight and provide a background for the final phase of Wright's engagement with the city, which began almost immediately after the appearance of Broadacre City and focused directly on the revitalization of the downtown core. Chapter 7 takes up the first of these projects, a civic center for Madison that was designed in 1938 and went through a number of revisions during Wright's lifetime before being posthumously realized in much reduced and altered form in the 1990s. Making use of air rights and modern reinforced concrete construction, Wright projected a theater-like semicircular platform over the railroad tracks along the lakeshore and into the lake itself to define an open-air public forum. Spaces for governmental, cultural, and recreational facilities as well as transportation and parking were accommodated in a series of decks suspended beneath the upper terrace.

This new megastructural concept, combining building, landscape, transportation, and parking in a single, multifunctional symbolic whole, determined the form of both the Crystal City residential/commercial complex for Washington, D.C., of 1940 and the Pittsburgh Point Park Civic Center of 1947. The former, the subject of chapter 8, projected a mixed-use "city within the city" containing twenty-five hotel and apartment towers plus a shopping and entertainment center along with what would have been the largest indoor parking garage of the time. It was, among other things, the architect's modernist response to Rockefeller Center.

The Pittsburgh project, discussed in chapter 9, was situated at the city's historic point of origin. In its first iteration, it took the form of a fifteen-story ziggurat-coliseum, containing a convention hall, theaters, restaurants, and even an astro-dome within the atrium space of its encircling roadway and parking decks. In the scaled-back second version, it became a cable-stayed bridge rivaling in symbolic presence and purpose the contemporary Gateway Arch for St. Louis designed by Eero Saarinen. Both Wright schemes created the very type of modern public gathering place as a space of spectacle that Sigfried Giedion was then espousing in his call for a "New Monumentality."[3]

The 1957 project for a cultural center for Baghdad, the subject of chapter 10, was part of an extraordinary effort by the Iraqi government to modernize the country's capital city through a campaign of commissions awarded to an international contingent of "star architects," perhaps the first of its kind, including, aside from Wright, Alvar Aalto, Le Corbusier, Walter Gropius, and Gio Ponti. Wright's contribution, which incorporated an opera house, a university, museums, crafts shops, restaurants, and a zoo, was the only one with an urbanistic intention. His cultural center, contemporary with that of New York's Lincoln Center, was planned to anchor the new development of West Baghdad. It was placed in a pendant position to the historic core of the city so as to preserve it intact while opening up the old city into a dynamic relationship of past and present, of commercial downtown and residential fringe.

When viewed as a whole, Wright's urban designs show the architect to have been both an innovative precursor as well as a creative participant in the world of ideas that helped shape the modern metropolis. Beginning at the turn of the twentieth century with his radical thoughts on how to expand the traditional city as part of a newly developing suburban ring and ending with a series of remarkable designs for reinvigorating the city center after it had been threatened by the automobile, to which he gave pride of place in Broadacre City, Wright emerges as an urbanist who offers new, always fascinating, and invariably important perspectives on the history of modernism as it attempted to accommodate contemporary patterns of living under conditions often at odds with them.

Throughout the book, Wright's designs will be related to those of his contemporaries. Le Corbusier, Corbett, and Eliel Saarinen, already mentioned, are all well-known figures in the history of twentieth-century urbanism. Others, less celebrated and rarely discussed in books on Wright, will appear, often on repeated occasions and in very different contexts. They include such important figures in the fields of city planning and

urban design as Frederic Delano, Frederick Law Olmsted Jr., Harland Bartholomew, Ladislas Segoe, and John Nolen. In this way, Wright's work will be integrated into the larger picture of twentieth-century urbanism as a whole. And by being discussed in this larger context, the traditional aspects of Wright's urbanism will be revealed just as its radical and inventive ones will be thrown into sharper relief.

Let me add just a few things about scope and methodology before concluding with some remarks on terminology. As a book about Wright's urbanism, it will not examine his designs for individual buildings planned for the city, such as skyscrapers, churches, apartment houses, or cultural institutions, except when larger urban considerations, like zoning, were critical to the design process and speak to the historical significance of the issue.[4] Because of the very nature of the urban design enterprise, which generally undertakes to create schemas or models for future development, more often than not remaining on paper, this book is about projects rather than buildings. In fact, other than the project for Madison, none of the examples discussed ever made their way into built form.

What we will study, therefore, are drawings, models, and texts, some of the first being so rich and stunning in their plasticity as to make one almost forget they exist only on paper. To further compensate for the lack of materiality but, even more, to help clarify the origin and significance of a project, much space will be devoted to establishing and explaining the physical, historical, social, and programmatic contexts. Where an individual building has a limited sphere of action and relations, an urban design, whether for a section or neighborhood of a city or for the city as a whole, must take into account an extremely wide range of factors and, often, an equally wide range of disciplinary approaches. For this reason, at least one-third and sometimes nearly one-half of a chapter will be devoted to the context within which Wright had to work, or planned to transform.

Almost all the words generally used to describe the planning and designing of parts or the entirety of a city, or the professionals involved, are modern. They date to the later nineteenth century at the earliest. The term "urbanization" is thought to have been coined around 1867 by Ildefonso Cerdà, the Spanish engineer responsible for the plan of modern Barcelona, the so-called Ensanche (1858–60).[5] But urbanization is not the same thing as urbanism, just as modernization is not the same as modernism. The term "urbanism," meaning "the study of the physical needs of city dwellers," did not make its appearance until 1889 according to the eleventh edition of *Merriam-Webster's Collegiate Dictionary*, and "urbanist," meaning "a specialist in city planning," not until 1930. The online version of the *Oxford English Dictionary* (2000), which defines "urbanism" as "urban life or character" as well as "urban development and planning," dates its first use in English to the 1880s and its connection to planning to 1929, the latter as an importation from the French. Le Corbusier's book *Urbanisme*, published in 1925, certainly represents a signal event in modern architecture's embrace of the term. Le Corbusier later characterized the "urbanist" as "nothing other than an architect [who] … organizes architectural spaces, fixes the location and use of built containers, [and] connects all things in time and space by a network of circulation."[6]

The American term "city planning," referring to "the drawing up of an organized arrangement (as of streets, parks, and business and residential areas) of a city," according to *Merriam-Webster's*, first came into use in 1900. As the practice devolved in the later 1920s and 1930s into a statistics-driven, economics-based analytical tool geared toward policy decisions, the more inclusive concept of urbanism as a spatial-formal response to the "physical needs of city dwellers," as well as their spiritual and cultural ones, came into use not only as a modern substitute for the discredited City Beautiful idea of "civic design," but also as a delimitation of the concept of urbanism to mean "that part of city planning which deals with the physical form of the city" at any scale.[7] Although most city planners and/or urban designers, from Daniel Burnham and Raymond Unwin to Wright, Le Corbusier, and Nolen, looked to certain precedents for their work in earlier periods, it is quite clear they thought they were engaged in something new and modern.

There is no commonly accepted term, however, for such a thing as "suburban designer" or "suburbanism," nor does one often hear the phrase "suburban planner." This underscores the fact, as most definitions of the modern suburb have maintained, that the suburb was considered an integral part of the city until the proliferation of the automobile in the 1950s and 1960s created the critical degree of economic and social change that separated it to all intents and purposes from the central business district. *Merriam-Webster's* gives as its first definition of the suburb "an outlying part of a city or town" and, as its

second, "a smaller community adjacent to or within commuting distance of a city." For historians of the suburb like Kenneth Jackson, the railroad, streetcar, and even early automobile suburbs were part of a "new" definition of the city itself "as an urban-rural continuum."[8] For Robert Fishman, whose book *Bourgeois Utopias: The Rise and Fall of Suburbia* (1987) remains one of the most trenchant on the subject, the suburb and the city are interdependent, the one incapable of existing without the other. Together they create the modern urban dialectic of living in one place and working in another—the one built-up, densely organized, almost entirely man-made; the other spread out, low-lying, close to nature.[9]

Although the suburb and the city center have much in common, they are also, by intention, at odds with one another in many important respects. At the turn of the twentieth century, the period of suburbia that will interest us most here, people were very aware of this dichotomy. Where living in a suburb prior to the late eighteenth century had generally been a sign of poverty, the reverse was true by the end of the following one. In February 1903, to take just one relevant example, the Oak Park newspaper *Oak Leaves* published part of a sermon by the local Reverend William E. Barton in which he began by saying, "'The suburb is created by the city, and is a reaction from it. It is an effect and a protest.…In the old world, men work in the fields by day and sleep at night in their walled cities; we…reverse this, working in the city by day, and turning it over at night to the hotel population, the policemen and the firemen.'" "'But,'" he continued, "'the suburb must not desert the city, nor believe it wholly bad.…We are out in the fresh air, thank God; we must bring fresh air to the city.'"[10] Progressive architects and city planners beginning at the turn of the century looked for ways to bring the advantages of open space and greenery to the city center just as they tried to provide amenities, usually associated with an urban way of life, to the suburb. Throughout his long career, Frank Lloyd Wright was one of those who worked most imaginatively at asserting the ideal of an urban-suburban dialectic and proposing ways to ensure it as a continuum.

I

SUBURBS IN THE GRID:
THE NEW STREETCAR CITY

ONE

WRIGHT'S FIRST URBAN DESIGN INITIATIVE:
THE DEVELOPMENT PLAN FOR THE ROBERTS BLOCK, 1896

When the nineteen-year-old Frank Lloyd Wright arrived in Chicago in 1887 looking for work in an architect's office, he could not have chosen a better time or a better place. The "metropolis of the Middle West," as it would soon be called by Daniel H. Burnham (1846–1912) and Edward H. Bennett (1874–1954) in their influential *Plan of Chicago* of 1906–9, had become, in large part due to its role as the nation's railroad hub, the fastest-growing major city in the world during the second half of the nineteenth century.[1] Fire had destroyed most of the Loop, the central business district at the edge of Lake Michigan, in 1871; and, as a result of the economic depression that followed two years later, building did not pick up significantly until the beginning of the 1880s. When it did, however, the pace was unprecedented, as was the system of fireproof, steel-frame skyscraper construction developed to create the enormous amounts of office space needed in the restricted downtown area within the bend of the Chicago River.

Just as the city was extending upward, it was expanding outward—in ever-widening rings of suburbs served first by the extensive railroad network and then by the new streetcar system. There were those who directly equated the "'rapid transit horizontally'" with the "'perpendicular transportation'" of the elevator that made the center city skyscraper a feasible proposition.[2] Already in 1873 the *Chicago Sunday Times* congratulated itself that "Chicago, for its size, is more given to suburbs than any other city in the world. In fact, it is doubtful if any city, of any size, can boast of an equal number of suburban appendages."[3] However much this declaration may owe to boosterism, by the late 1880s a good deal of what the *Times* reporter said had been realized. Residential construction, though by no means as publicized or celebrated at

the time or even later as the large-scale building operations in the Loop, was a major factor in Chicago's emergence as a world-class city as well as a major element in architectural commissions. The suburbs of Riverside, Lake Forest, Evanston, Highland Park, Wilmette, Hyde Park, River Forest, and Oak Park are only some of the most well-known and well-heeled.

Wright, who was to live in Oak Park from 1889 through 1909 in a house of his own design, and who was to conduct his practice from a studio he added to the house in 1898, clearly found the suburban environment more in tune with his thinking and more accommodating for combining work and family life than the inner city. Indeed, his first job in Chicago was with the transplanted easterner Joseph Lyman Silsbee (1848–1913), whose architectural practice focused almost exclusively on residential work. Among Silsbee's rare nondomestic works were the Unitarian Church of All Souls in Chicago (1885) and a Unitarian chapel in Wyoming (near Spring Green), Wisconsin (1886), both commissioned by Wright's uncle Jenkin Lloyd Jones. Wright had worked on the chapel during the summer prior to his leaving for Chicago and no doubt got the position with Silsbee through family connections. Be that as it may, he soon showed himself to be an excellent draftsman, delineating in an accomplished picturesque manner a number of the Queen Anne/Colonial designs for houses that Silsbee prepared for clients and for publication.

Wright garnered enough experience and proved himself talented enough that within a year he landed a job with one of the city's premier commercial and institutional firms. Either very late in 1887 or early in 1888 he was hired by Adler and Sullivan (est. 1883) to work on the monumental Auditorium

1.1

1.2

1.1. World's Columbian Exposition, Chicago, Daniel H. Burnham and others, 1890–93. View across Court of Honor from South Canal, with Machinery Building in foreground, Administration Building in center, and Electricity Building in background, by Lewis Edward Hickmott, 1893. CHM

1.2. McMillan (Senate Park) Commission Plan for Washington, D.C., Burnham, Frederick Law Olmsted Jr., and others, 1901–2. Aerial perspective, from southwest, by Francis L. V. Hoppin, 1902. CFA

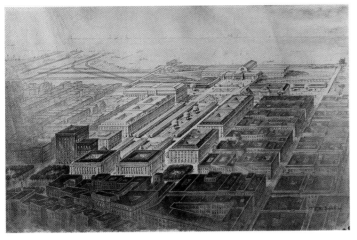

1.3

1.3. Group Plan (civic center) for Cleveland, Burnham, John M. Carrère, and Arnold W. Brunner, 1902–3. Aerial perspective looking north, by Welles Bosworth. From Burnham, Carrère, and Brunner, *The Group Plan of the Public Buildings of the City of Cleveland*, 1903

Building at the corner of Michigan Avenue and Congress Street, along the city's newly improved lakefront (1886–89).[4] By the middle of 1890, the twenty-three-year-old Wright was promoted to the position of head draftsman. In that capacity, he not only supervised work on projects such as the Wainwright Building in St. Louis (1890–91), the Schiller Building in Chicago (1891–92), and the Transportation Building for the World's Columbian Exposition (1890–93), but also was given significant responsibility for the few domestic commissions the firm still accepted.

Wright's training and early design experience were mainly domestic and suburban. Furthermore, neither Silsbee nor Adler and Sullivan were at all involved with large-scale urban problems. The person who helped to create, and then dominated, that newly emerging field was Daniel Burnham, Sullivan's nemesis. By the late 1880s, Burnham and Root (est. 1873) had become the leading commercial firm in the city. When Chicago was chosen in 1890 as the site for the 1893 World's Columbian Exposition, the international exhibition to celebrate the four hundredth anniversary of the "discovery" of America, Burnham was appointed overall director and chief of construction. In that capacity, he oversaw the design and building of what almost immediately came to be viewed as a model city (figure 1.1). The Beaux-Arts classicism of the "White City," as it was called, offered an image of monumental public space in the "grand manner" of the Baroque that contrasted palpably, and deliberately, with the commercially driven development of the real city around it that was based on nothing other than the underlying and relentless street system of the grid. The fair served as the reference point for the first major urban design program in the United States, the City Beautiful movement that emerged by the end of the decade (discussed more fully in chapter 3). In the words of the urban historian Jon A. Peterson, the fair "became a symbol of how great cities might appear as if shaped by civic art."[5]

Realizing the need he would have for a talented designer to aid him in the increased amount and new type of work he expected to issue from the fair's success, Burnham reportedly asked Wright in 1894 to forego his incipient private practice and join his firm. Wright was tempted but declined, thereby giving up the chance for direct involvement in city planning at its very beginnings and at the highest level.[6] Within a couple of years of the fair's closing, Burnham began a study of the south lakefront park and shoreline drive of Chicago connecting

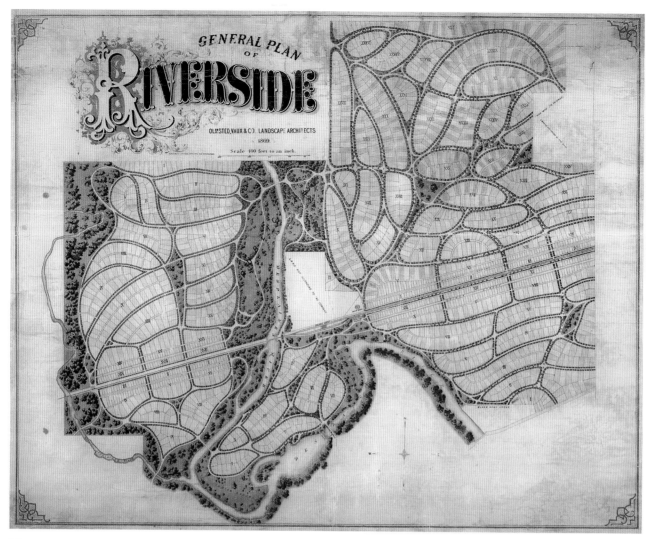

1.4

1.5

1.6

1.4. Riverside, Ill., Master Plan, Frederick Law Olmsted and Calvert Vaux, 1868–69. Courtesy National Park Service, Frederick Law Olmsted Site

1.5. Riverside. View

1.6. Riverside. View of town center, with railroad station and water tower on left and Arcade Building on right

Jackson Park, the site of the 1893 fair, to the downtown Grant Park (1896–97). This would eventually lead to the publication of his and Bennett's *Plan of Chicago* (see figure 3.26).

In the meantime, Burnham, with Frederick Law Olmsted Jr. (1870–1957), led the McMillan (Senate Park) Commission's city planning efforts in Washington, D.C. (1901–2), which Peterson has described as the first implementation of "the comprehensive city planning ideal" of the City Beautiful movement (figure 1.2). Following that, Burnham headed the commission that produced the Civic Center Group Plan for Cleveland (1902–3; figure 1.3), before designing the master plans for San Francisco and the Philippine cities of Manila and Baguio (1904–5).[7] By the end of the first decade of the twentieth century, Burnham was considered such a significant figure in the field that his Chicago plan was featured at the Universal City-Building Exhibition in Berlin in 1910 and the first Town Planning Conference held in London the same year, where Burnham lectured in the section devoted to "Cities of the Future" and was one of only three foreigners invited to speak at the gala banquet.[8]

The Picturesque Railroad Suburb and Its Embodiment in Riverside

Chicago was not only the crucible of city planning in America at the turn of the twentieth century, but also home to some of the earliest and most significant experiments in the area of picturesquely planned railroad suburbs. Lake Forest, on the city's wealthy North Shore, was laid out, most likely by the St. Louis–based landscape architect Almerin Hotchkiss (1816–1903), in 1857 in a naturalistic manner that overrode the mechanical rectilinearity of the grid typical of metropolitan Chicago.[9] Its curving streets and rustic landscaping followed closely the pattern set by the exclusive enclave of Llewellyn Park in northern New Jersey, begun only four years earlier by Alexander Jackson Davis (1803–92) and usually considered America's first picturesque suburb.[10] Much more important for the history of suburban design, however, is Riverside, approximately ten miles west-southwest of the Loop, along the banks of the Des Plaines River. It was planned in 1868–69 by the Boston-based landscape architect Frederick Law Olmsted (1822–1903) in collaboration with his partner Calvert Vaux (1824–95; figure 1.4). Built out over the next forty years, it has come to be seen as the exemplar of the picturesque type by virtue of its unique

combination of architecture, land use, and landscaping.[11]

Olmsted, who had designed Central Park in New York with Vaux during the previous decade, planned Riverside as a model suburb where, as he wrote, "people seeking to escape the confinement of the town" would be greeted by an environment "in which urban and rural advantages are agreeably combined" so that "the special charms and substantial advantages of rural conditions" can be enjoyed without "a sacrifice of urban conveniences."[12] The brochure published by the developer, Emery E. Childs, in 1868 stated that the Riverside Improvement Company intended "to make Riverside in all respects a MODEL SUBURBAN NEIGHBORHOOD" and boasted, paraphrasing Olmsted, that "the improvements now perfected at Riverside combine the conveniences peculiar to the finest modern cities, with the domestic advantages of the most charming country, *in a degree never before realized.*"[13]

To accomplish this, Olmsted and Vaux conceived Riverside as a semi-independent community, having its own limited number of public buildings and commercial establishments yet directly linked to the Chicago business district by railroad as well as by a limited access, landscaped carriage drive called the "parkway."[14] Although the latter was never built, many of the other features in the original plan were eventually realized despite the fact that the firm of Olmsted and Vaux pulled out of the operation in 1870 and the Riverside Improvement Company went bankrupt in the Panic of 1873. As supervisory architect, William LeBaron Jenney (1832–1907), who was involved with Riverside nearly from its beginning and was to become a key figure in the development of skyscraper construction in the Chicago Loop, oversaw the rebound of the community that slowly began in the 1880s, although it never reached the goal of establishing Riverside as a model for Chicago developers.

Of the site's sixteen hundred acres, seven hundred were reserved for public use and meant to be maintained in a natural condition, while the remaining areas, subdivided for the construction of single-family houses, were treated in a sympathetically naturalistic manner. The biomorphically shaped "blocks" were bounded by curving streets that provided for small public green spaces at some intersections (figure 1.5). Although the property lines were drawn in a completely conventional way, creating back-to-back oblong house lots parallel to one another with their narrow ends facing the streets, there was a prohibition on fences and a mandatory 30-foot setback that ensured that the houses would all be more or less centered on their approximately 100-foot-wide by 225-foot-deep lots.

According to Olmsted, the idea was to suggest that the property as a whole "formed … a 'park,' most of the land within which might be divided by lines, mainly imaginary, into building lots."[15] The largest common space was a 160-acre park reserve along the river's edge. The smaller parks dotted throughout were intended to have "the character of informal village-greens, commons and play-grounds, rather than of enclosed and defended parks or gardens."[16] The main landscape feature unifying the suburb and giving it a focus was the Long Common leading diagonally out from the railroad station in a northeasterly direction to form the main internal circulation spine of the community. The railroad station, town hall, resort hotel, and shops were placed at the base of the Long Common so as to create a small-town-like neighborhood center (figure 1.6).

Riverside demonstrated how one could avoid the appearance of rigidity in a residential community and thus differentiate "the secluded peacefulness and tranquility" of the suburb from "the jar, noise, confusion, and bustle" of the city by reference to the naturalistic.[17] With its winding streets, broad expanses of lawn, and open green spaces, the Riverside plan created an image of a rural landscape made domestic. Instead of lining up side by side in regimented rows and facing one another directly across orthogonally laid-out streets, the single-family houses follow a more seemingly naturalistic pattern, allowing for multiple and varying vistas as well as for a critical degree of isolation and privacy. For Olmsted, this "naturalism" and distinctiveness represented a denial of the hard and cold commercialism of the downtown urban core, which was characterized in his view, and particularly in the case of Chicago, by the relentless, monotonous, and mechanical grid. In contrast to "the ordinary directness of line in town-streets, with its resultant regularity of plan, … suggest[ing] eagerness to press forward, without looking to the right or the left," Olmsted described his reliance on "gracefully-curved lines, generous spaces, and the absence of sharp corners" as a way "to suggest and imply leisure, contemplativeness and happy tranquility." The result, he insisted, was "not only informal, but … positively picturesque, and when contrasted with the constantly repeated right angles, straight lines, and flat surfaces which characterize our large modern towns, thoroughly refreshing."[18]

For all its later importance in the history of American architecture and planning, Riverside remained an anomaly in the suburban development of Chicago and, most significantly for us, a cipher for Wright. Completely at odds with the metropolitan grid that extends out from the Loop, the Riverside experiment was never replicated within the inner ring of suburbs and remains to this day entirely uncharacteristic of the area and its flat, prairie topography (figure 1.7). Despite the fact that he lived only a few miles from Riverside and knew it well, Wright never took it as a model for his own planning. Indeed, he rejected it in favor of the very "right angles, straight lines, and flat surfaces" Olmsted considered so uninspiring and antagonistic to the formation of a residential community. In order then to understand the background of Wright's position, which undergirded all his planning thinking up until the 1930s, we must turn to a discussion of the significance of the grid in the United States. In the end, the grid would prove to be more important for Wright than either the classicism of the City Beautiful or the picturesqueness of the garden-type suburb that dominated the professional discourse during his earliest years of practice.

The Ideal of the American Grid

Laid out on a grid in 1830, Chicago followed the orthogonal pattern imposed on the western territories of the new United States by the rectangular land survey system instituted between 1785 and 1796 (figure 1.8). The survey of the western territory of the United States and the subdivision of the land into an allover grid of square-mile sections was authorized by the new federal government in 1785 and reestablished in the Land Act of 1796 (after the earlier Land Ordinance had been allowed to expire in 1789). Growing out of Enlightenment ideals of rational organization, systematic classification, and egalitarian opportunity, the grid defined the topography of the country while at the same time playing a significant role in determining its urban and architectural form.[19] A culture of the grid developed during the nineteenth century into the basic framework of operation for American architects and city planners that went fundamentally unquestioned until the last quarter of the century, when the sense of idealism with which the grid had originally been endowed was

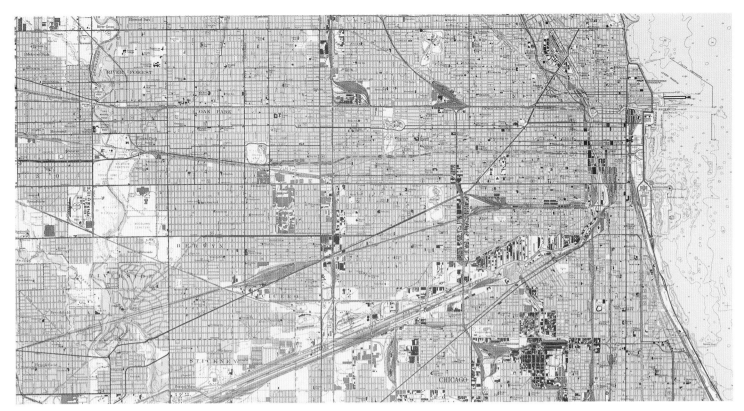

1.7

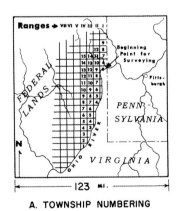

1.8

NUMBERING OF TOWNSHIPS AND LOTS UNDER THE LAND ORDINANCE OF 1785

A. TOWNSHIP NUMBERING

Note: *Ordinance provided for numbering of townships north- ward from Ohio River to Lake Erie.*

36	30	24	18	12	6
35	29	23	17	11	5
34	28	22	16	10	4
33	27	21	15	9	3
32	26	20	14	8	2
31	25	19	13	7	1

← 6 MILES →

B. LOT NUMBERING, WITHIN A TOWNSHIP

Note: *above sequence was adopted as one of several poss- ible under terms of Ordinance.*

1.9

1.7. Chicago. Loop and Western Suburbs. Map of Chicago and Vicinity, Illinois and Indiana, Sheet No. 2 of 3 (Chicago Loop), 1953. Detail. U.S. Department of the Interior Geological Survey. Map Collection, Pusey Library, Harvard University

1.8. Chicago. Original plat, by James Thompson (north is to right). As redrawn in *Industrial Chicago: The Building Interests*, 1891

1.9. System of land subdivision instituted under the Land Ordinance of 1785. From William D. Pattison, *Beginnings of the American Rectangular Land Survey System, 1784–1800*, 1957

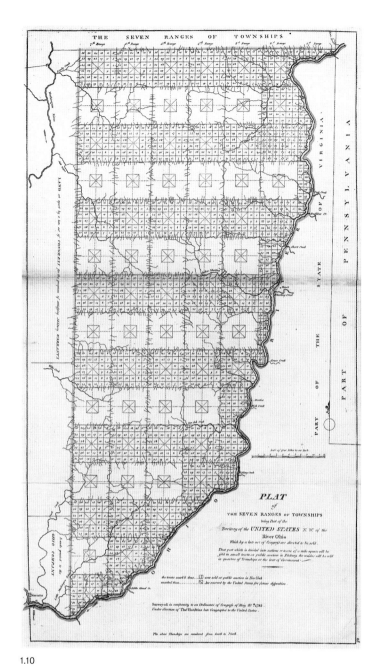

1.10

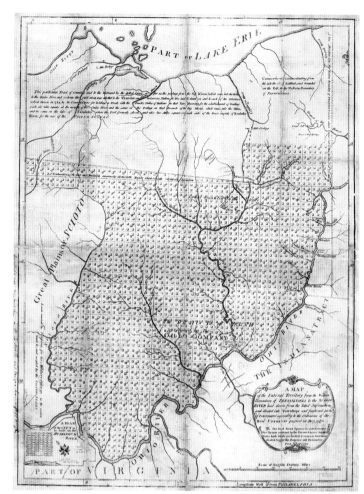

1.11

1.10. U.S. Rectangular Land Survey. "Plat of the Seven Ranges of Townships ... N. W. of the River Ohio," surveyed 1785–87; by Thomas Hutchins, 1788. The Lionel Pincus and Princess Firyal Map Division, New York Public Library, Astor, Lenox and Tilden Foundations

1.11. U.S. Rectangular Land Survey. "Map of the Federal Territory from the Western Boundary of Pennsylvania to the Scioto River [Ohio] . . . Divided into Townships and Fractional Parts of Townships Agreeably to the Ordinance of 1785," by Manasseh Cutler, 1787. LC

compromised by the thoughtlessness and expediency with which it was generally employed.

The concept of surveying and parceling out the land west of the original thirteen states, known as the "national domain," was driven by two fundamental purposes: first, to provide a clear and transparent basis for selling the land in order to pay off debts incurred during the Revolutionary War; and, second, to open up the "national domain" to settlement. In early March 1784, the federal government appointed a Land Ordinance Committee, chaired by Thomas Jefferson, "'to devise and report the most eligible means of disposing of such part of the Western lands as may be obtained of the Indians … and for opening a land office.'"[20] In the wake of a parallel effort by Jefferson, in which he was only partially successful, to divide up the territories west of the Ohio and east of the Mississippi Rivers into fifteen new states defined by straight, north-south and east-west boundaries following continuous baselines and principal meridians, the Land Ordinance Committee he chaired recommended a subdivision of these states according to a strict and abstract orthogonal grid based on a decimal system of "hundreds." Each larger square was to be composed of one hundred one-mile-square lots. Using the measure of the geographical mile, each of these lots would contain 850, or 1,000 reformed, acres. The decimalization of the division of land paralleled Jefferson's concurrent, and successful, effort to decimalize American currency, leading William Pattison to write that "the square-mile lot played the part of penny to the hundred's dollar in a scheme for the minting of land."[21]

Jefferson and Hugh Williamson, the other committee member who may have been equally responsible for its proposals, clearly had simplicity and clarity in mind in dividing up the land so as to make sales and verification of title as easy to understand and transparent as possible. This was part and parcel of the notion of democracy based on freedom of opportunity and open access to land ownership both statesmen held dear. The final piece in this system, that of prior survey, was merely adumbrated in Jefferson's committee report, which was tabled later that year and approved in revised form only the following one, after Jefferson had left the United States to assume the post of ambassador to France. Prior survey meant that no land could be sold before being subject to the orthogonal grid, which, by its abstraction, grouped good land with bad. And this meant that no

purchaser was privileged and everyone would have to take the good with the bad.

Based on the Jefferson-Williamson committee's proposal, the Land Ordinance approved by Congress in May 1785 and, with minor variations and changes, sustained in 1796 determined the shape the American countryside and cities assumed over the course of the succeeding centuries. The decimal division into "hundreds" was replaced by a more traditional division into thirty-six lots or sections (figure 1.9). Each of these was a statute mile square, making each section 640 acres. As a compromise between legislators from the South, who wanted the land to be sold on an individual basis, and those from the North, who wanted it to be sold to communities in the form of "townships," the 1785 ordinance created a system of alternating six-mile-square divisions, half set aside for purchase by individuals and half for purchase by communities. The map drawn in 1788 by Thomas Hutchins, who was charged with carrying out the first phase of the survey (completed in 1787), shows not only the Seven Ranges plotted in the first years of the survey but also the alternation of the two different types of divisions (figure 1.10). The more imaginary map drawn the year before by Manasseh Cutler, a principal in the privately owned and operated Ohio Company, shows another important feature of the ordinance, which was that in each six-mile-square division, four of the thirty-six sections were to be reserved for future government use while one, near the center, was dedicated to educational institutions (figure 1.11).

The 1785 ordinance mandated the concept of prior survey, thus opening up the way to a system of geometric land division that would precede settlement and ultimately lay an abstract, rectilinear net of squares over the entire United States. It also established the concept of sale by public auction, which, at least in principle, made the purchase of land an open affair. In 1804, Jared Mansfield, the surveyor-general appointed by Jefferson when he became president, prepared the groundwork for fulfilling the latter's dream of a continuous, countrywide grid by laying down arbitrary principal meridians and baselines that would ultimately coordinate the square grid lines from the Ohio River to the Pacific Ocean. The accurate surveying and evenhanded distribution of land indicated by the 1785 ordinance and its early stages of implementation have been interpreted as a fundamental basis for the democratic institutions of citizenship and community self-government, creating an environment of transparency

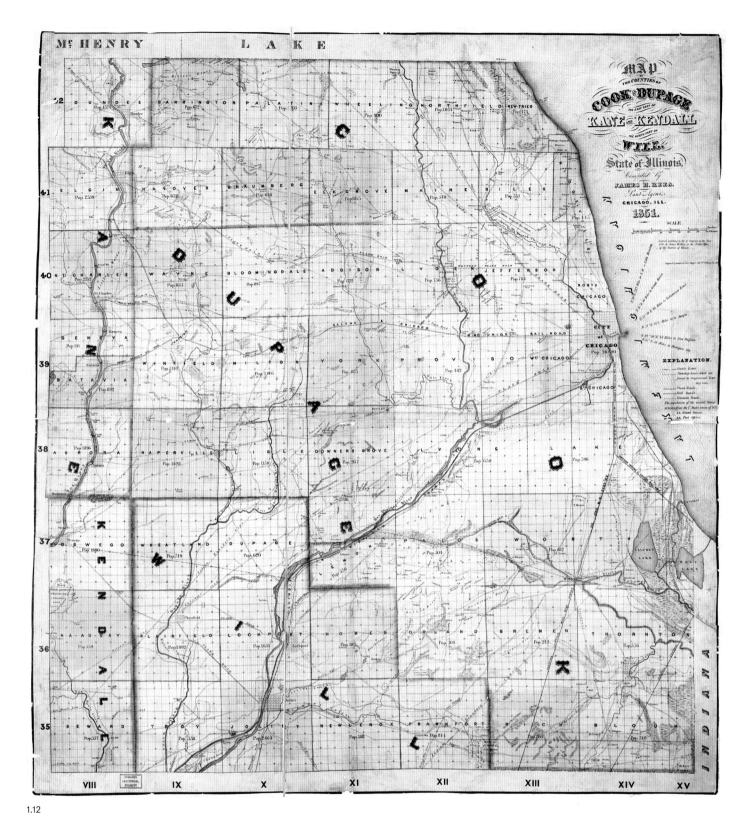

1.12

1.12. Chicago and surroundings. "Map of the Counties of Cook and DuPage, the East
Part of Kane and Kendall, the North Part of Will, State of Illinois," by J. H. Rees, 1851.
CHM

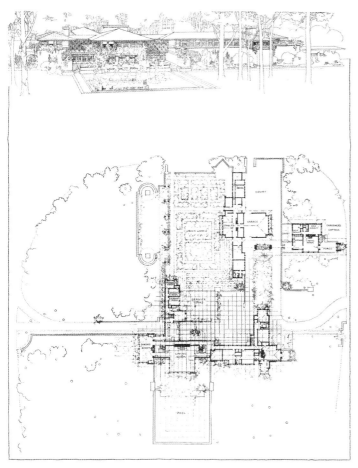

1.13

and egalitarianism that the urban historian André Corboz has gone so far as to characterize as "utopian."[22]

The culture of the grid, as I have called it, directed the layout of cities and towns in the Midwest and beyond during the nineteenth century, more often than not with little or no reference to natural conditions. Chicago, as already noted, was platted in 1830 following the dictates of the grid; and James Rees's map of the area surrounding Chicago shows how the grid had literally blanketed the region and determined its urban planning within twenty years (figure 1.12). In the hands of the real estate speculator and developer, the process of subdivision almost immediately transformed the ideal square block of the eighteenth century into a patchwork of narrow oblong lots separated by alleys, deemed more efficient for house lots and office blocks. The developer soon came to be seen as the one who benefited most from the grid's dominion. By the last quarter of the nineteenth century, the grid, whether in small-town America or its large cities like Chicago, was criticized by architects and others as bereft of beauty, variety, and grandeur and viewed as a mere instrument for profit; and the residential suburbs that were still in large part undeveloped were thought to be condemned from the outset by the rectilinear street pattern imposed by the metropolitan grid. Wright, however, agreed with neither the City Beautiful position calling for the superimposition of a Baroque system of street layout nor the picturesque model dispensing with the grid altogether. Instead, he sought to work with the grid as the fundamental framework of the metropolitan condition and eventually to recuperate for it the sense of idealism and democratic community conferred upon it by the eighteenth-century Land Ordinance.

Wright's Work Prior to 1896

Frank Lloyd Wright was eventually to build two houses in Riverside, one for the Tomek family in 1907 and the other, his grandest domestic work of the period, for the Coonleys, begun the year before and completed in 1909. Neither shows any specific interest on his part in the artificiality of Riverside's naturalism. In fact, quite the opposite is the case (figure 1.13). The strong and insistent orthogonal geometry that rules both designs, in plan as well as in elevation, points to something that will be crucial to our understanding of Wright's urban motivations during this period.[23] He was obsessed with the grid as a planning tool and did all he could to allow it to

ORIGINAL HOME, 1889

PLAYROOM ADDITION, 1895

STUDIO ADDITION, 1898

GARAGE ADDITION, 1911

CHICAGO AVENUE

1.14

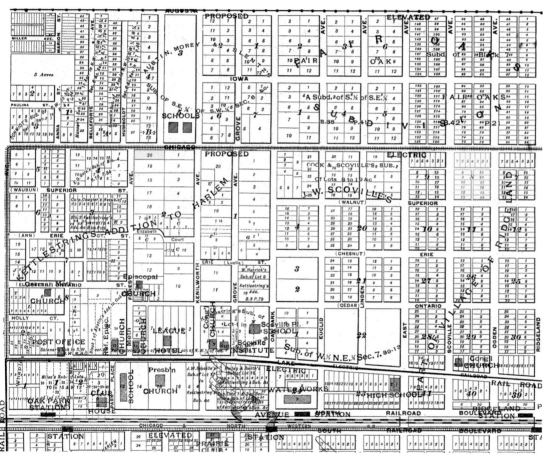

1.15

1.14. Wright House (and later Studio), Oak Park, Ill., Wright, begun 1889–90. Aerial perspective showing changes through 1911, by Ann Williamsen. Frank Lloyd Wright Trust, Oak Park

1.15. Oak Park and Ridgeland, Ill. Plat map, 1894. Detail (Wright House and Studio lot highlighted in green; Roberts block highlighted in yellow)

energize his designs. Far from creating an appearance of rigidity and monotonousness, the grid, as employed by Wright, would make the eventfulness of the picturesque itself seem forced and conventional.

Wright did not arrive at this position right away, however, and the very earliest of his works in the Chicago area are clearly indebted to a picturesque aesthetic. The small house he built for himself and his new wife Catherine in Oak Park in 1889–90 is a perfect example (figure 1.14). The large lot at the corner of Chicago and Forest Avenues was, at the time, at the leading edge of development in the well-to-do though by no means wealthy suburb located eight miles west of the Loop (figure 1.15; colored in green on plan). Situated along Chicago's first railroad line, the Galena and Chicago Union (later Chicago and North Western) Railroad that came through in 1848, Oak Park was initially platted ten years later and began to become popular in the 1870s, after the Great Fire.[24] The area where Wright's lot was located was part of the Kettlestrings subdivision, which dated from the 1850s and was one of the first in Oak Park.[25] Like those that preceded and followed it, the Kettlestrings subdivision aligned with the metropolitan Chicago grid. When Wright purchased the property, there were still farms nearby and views to the west and north over unimproved prairie (his own property had a barn on it). The electric streetcar on Chicago Avenue indicated in the plat map of 1894 began operating between the city and Oak Park in 1895 (the earlier Lake Street line began service in 1891).[26]

Wright set the small two-story house well back from the adjoining streets, more or less equidistantly from each. The main facade was turned toward Forest Avenue, the less busy of the two frontages. Both the ground floor, articulated by projecting bays, and the upper floor, composed of a single large gable, are sheathed in dark, rustic-looking wood shingles. The model for the design was the Shingle Style cottage East Coast architects like McKim, Mead & White (est. 1879) and Bruce Price (1845–1903) had evolved out of a picturesque amalgam of colonial and vernacular sources and adapted for use especially in suburban and resort communities during the earlier years of the decade.[27] Wright emphasized the picturesque aspects by playing the front gable off against the side ones and using the projecting bays and curved brick terraces to give the house a rotational movement. While the gables and front porch were typical conventions for relating building to street characteristic

of the architecture of a suburb like Riverside, the successive views afforded by the corner lot were consciously exploited to reinforce the picturesqueness of the composition. The open corner veranda was as much a place for relaxation as it was an element to attract the eye of the passerby.

Within less than four years, Wright almost entirely rethought his approach to design, not only in a purely architectural sense but also from an urban point of view. These were the years he was working with Sullivan in the firm's office on the top two floors of the seventeen-story Auditorium tower, overlooking the Loop and the lake. It was also the time when the World's Columbian Exposition was being planned and a new sense of urban design was in the air. Much of this excitement about the urban environment comes out in the Winslow House, Wright's first commission after leaving Adler and Sullivan's employ. Designed in 1893 and completed the following year, this masonry structure eschews the picturesque suburban model and bears a radically different public posture from the house Wright built for himself just four years previously and less than a mile away (figure 1.16).

Designed for one of Chicago's leading manufacturers of ornamental iron and bronze, whom Wright met while working for Adler and Sullivan, the Winslow House is located in River Forest, the suburb just west of Oak Park. Winslow purchased the lot from Edward C. Waller, the real estate entrepreneur who owned a sizable tract of land on the banks of the Des Plaines River, where he himself lived in a large Stick Style house designed by Jenney. Winslow was one of the first to build in the new subdivision called Auvergne Place. Located near the entry to the estate, on the east side of the access road that loops through the site, and diagonally opposite Waller's own house, the Winslow House is placed well back from the street and set off from it by a formal stone terrace with a reflecting pool in the middle. A central entrance surrounded by a decorated stone frame projects from the wall plane to highlight the symmetrical composition of the facade. The strong horizontal divisions of tawny-colored Roman brick, textured plaster frieze, and (originally) tiled hip roof establish a clear hierarchical order symbolizing function. Initially intended to have an octagonal pavilion extending into the garden on the right balancing the porte cochere on the left, the house gives the appearance from the street of a self-contained, freestanding, classical block. Only on the garden side, not open to public scrutiny, does the classical order break down and the complex and varied activities of

1.16

1.17

1.16. Winslow House, River Forest, Ill., Wright, 1893–94. Street facade

1.17. Winslow House. Rear (garden) facade

family life make their appearance in the fragmented and discontinuous forms of the rear facade (figure 1.17).

The Winslow House's formal presence on the street has a demonstrable quality of urbanity. It is, in effect, a translation and extension of the palazzo-like Charnley townhouse that Adler and Sullivan built for a tight urban site on the Near North Side of Chicago a couple of years before, when Wright was still working for the firm. The entrance terrace in River Forest, with its reflecting pool, becomes the mediating device between the tight grid of the city and the more expansive suburban situation in which the later building is located. The often commented upon difference between the symmetrical, closed street facade and the asymmetrical, open garden facade can be read as a deliberate distinction between the public and private realms of community and family, of public and private, just as it also can be understood as a residue of the equation of urban and suburban intentions Wright was trying, perhaps still somewhat naively, to effect.

Not surprisingly, it was the Winslow House that caught Burnham's eye and inspired him to hire Wright. Burnham was a friend of Waller's, and the conversation where his offer to Wright was made apparently took place in Waller's house, with the recently completed Winslow House in full view. Although the impression the house made on Burnham would have no issue, the impression it made on Burnham's host, Waller, most certainly did. Between 1895 and 1909, the latter offered the young architect a series of important commissions. Most significantly for us, a number of these were for multifamily dwellings in both urban and suburban settings. In 1895 Waller asked Wright to design two separate housing blocks for moderate- to low-income neighborhoods in West Chicago, both of which were built. Like their counterparts on West Walnut Street, the Francisco Terrace apartments were contained in a two-story perimeter block organized around an open central court (figure 1.18). Access to the upper-floor units was via open corner stairs. Wright expanded the same scheme into a double-block, two-ring version for the Lexington Terraces apartment houses that Waller's son, Edward C. Jr., with Oscar Friedman, commissioned in 1901 and had Wright revise eight years later (figure 1.19). Here a set-back second-floor balcony overlooking the court ringed the interior space in a manner that would become common in European urban social housing of the 1920s.[28]

The two realized Waller apartment blocks of 1895, along with the Francis apartments built at the same time, are particularly significant for us since it was in the following year that Wright received his first commission to plan an entire suburban block of individual dwellings. In 1896 Charles E. Roberts (1843–1934), a friend, neighbor, and fellow Unitarian, asked Wright for designs for a group of houses for a block in Ridgeland, the community just to the east of Oak Park, that he had acquired between 1889 and 1895. Roberts was born in Rochester, New York, and in the early 1870s moved to Chicago, where he invented a method for standardizing and industrializing the manufacture of screws. Within a few years, the Oak Park capitalist and real estate entrepreneur James W. Scoville put up the money to turn Roberts's business into the Chicago Screw Company, which soon became one of the largest manufacturers of screws in the United States. Roberts and his family moved to Oak Park sometime in the late 1870s, and immediately became involved in the Unitarian congregation. Between 1879 and 1904 and again in 1905–6, he was superintendent of the church's Sunday school. A major donor and member of the board of trustees of Unity Temple, he was chair of the building committee in 1905 when Wright was appointed architect. Wright later suggested that it was mainly through Roberts's "force and authority" that the building got built according to his plans.[29]

Roberts and Wright became acquainted early on through their membership in the Oak Park Unitarian church, and Roberts soon became one of Wright's most supportive clients.[30] Already in 1892 he asked the young architect for a house design, although nothing came of this initial contact.[31] Within four years, however, their friendship began to have professional results. In 1896, the same year as the Ridgeland project referred to above, to which we shall presently return, Wright undertook the remodeling of Roberts's Burnham and Root–designed Oak Park house, adding to it, among other things, a stable and a new porch, the latter terminating in semicircular terraces similar to those on Wright's own nearby house. While this work was being done, Wright also produced designs for a summer cottage for the family and a factory for the Chicago Screw Company, neither of which was realized. In 1897 Roberts convinced his friend George Furbeck to have Wright design his family's Oak Park house, which was built that year, and in 1898 Furbeck's brother Rollin followed suit. Two years later Roberts's wife's nephew B. Harley Bradley had Wright build his family's house in Kankakee, Illinois, at the

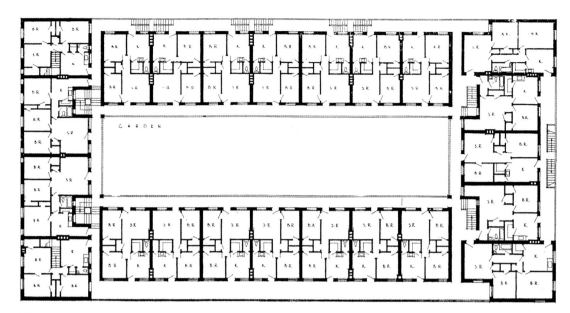

1.18

1.19

1.18. Francisco Terrace apartments, Chicago, Wright, 1895. Plan, redrawn ca. 1940.
From Henry-Russell Hitchcock, *In the Nature of Materials: The Buildings of Frank Lloyd Wright, 1887–1941*, 1942

1.19. Lexington Terraces apartments project, Chicago, Wright, 1901 (revised 1909).
Aerial perspective, antedated 1898

same time as Bradley's brother-in-law Warren Hickox built one on the adjoining lot (see figure 2.23). Roberts's son-in-law Charles E. White Jr. (1876–1936) worked for Wright in 1903–5, during which time Roberts came back to Wright for a second design for the same block for which he had asked Wright to draw up the 1896 plan. That 1903 revision of the 1896 plan will be discussed in chapter 3. The initial development plan is the subject of the rest of this chapter.

Development Plan for the Roberts Block, 1896

The block Roberts began acquiring in 1889 was in the northwest corner of the Village of Ridgeland and is highlighted in yellow on the plat map of 1894 (see figure 1.15; Ridgeland was annexed by Oak Park in 1902).[32] The block is bounded on the north by Chicago Avenue, on the west by Scoville Avenue (called Fair Oaks between 1887 and 1898), on the south by Superior Street, and on the east by Ogden Avenue (which changed its name to Elmwood in 1897).[33] Roberts purchased the western half of lot 4 plus lots 5 to 13 in 1889. In August 1895, he completed the package by buying the eastern half of lot 4 plus lots 1 to 3 and 14 to 19.[34] By that later date the Chicago Avenue streetcar had just begun offering service, which increased the value of the property considerably. The land, however, was unimproved: there were no houses on the block, nor were there sidewalks or street lighting. The 1872 plat made provision for nineteen house lots, with seven facing Chicago Avenue and the rest facing the north-south streets. A T-shaped alley ran through the interior of the site. All the lots were approximately 50 feet wide; numbers 1 to 7 were about 145 feet deep, the rest 172 feet deep. The entire block, including the alleys but excluding everything from the sidewalks to the street, measures approximately 465 feet by 364 feet.[35]

There are over fifty drawings for the project preserved in the Wright Foundation Archives. This is probably close to the number Wright produced. Most of them exist only in the form of prints.[36] They comprise sets for six individual houses plus one overall plan for the block (figures 1.20–33).[37] That plan, which we shall study more closely after looking at the individual house designs, calls for twenty-two rather than nineteen houses and completely reconfigures the plat plan of 1894. Three of the six houses are identified simply by numbers (1, 2, and 4), while one is referred to as a Corner House. All were undoubtedly intended as models, although it is not clear

whether there were to be twenty-two different ones or just the six repeated with variations. Numbers 1 and 2 carry legends that indicate they are presentation drawings, and they are the only dated ones. Number 1 is dated 16 January 1896 and number 2, 20 January 1896. The three other designs for non–corner lots look more like studies than final presentation drawings. Although the Corner House and the general plan have been thought to constitute a separate project dating to 1897, there is no reason to believe that any of the undated sheets are later than 1896 or that more than one project is involved.[38]

The houses are quite modest and look back more to Wright's own house than to the Winslow House or variations of it that were designed or built around the same time (the latter would include the McAfee House project for Kenilworth, Illinois, of 1894, the Devin House project for Chicago of 1896, and the Heller House in Chicago, built in 1897). The proposed Ridgeland houses are all two stories high and average a little less than 2,200 square feet (Wright's own house was originally a little under 2,100 square feet).[39] Houses 1 and 2 are variations of the same almost square plan (figures 1.20, 1.22). A fireplace set two-thirds back from the front wall lies on axis with a bay window projecting out to the street. The sitting room defined by these two elements is entered from a stair hall on the left and leads on the right into a library/dining room that runs the entire depth of the house, leaving space to the rear of the fireplace and behind the stairs for the pantry and kitchen. Upstairs there are four bedrooms.

The main difference between the two designs is the exterior treatment. In the first, the entrance porch makes a right-angle bend in front of the bay window so as to mask the front door from the street (figure 1.21). In House 2, the entrance is head-on (figures 1.22–23). The most distinguishing features, however, are the treatment of the ground floor and the roof. In House 1, the ground floor is brick and is battered at the corners to form a base for the tall, flared gable roof that presents its flat face to the street, with only the dormered bay of the master bedroom to relieve the shingled plane. In House 2, the wood siding of the ground floor is topped by a second-story frieze of windows alternating with golden beige plaster panels, the roof thus presenting a much less exaggerated profile from the side.[40]

Houses [3], 4, and [5] all have slightly more elaborate exterior treatments as well as more movemented plans, the rotational asymmetry of which can be traced back to Wright's own house. The plan of House [3] rotates off the axis leading

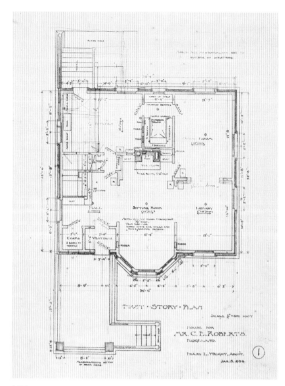

1.20

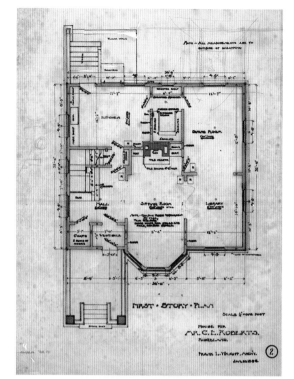

1.22

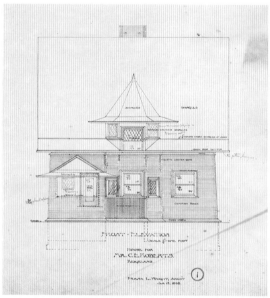

1.21

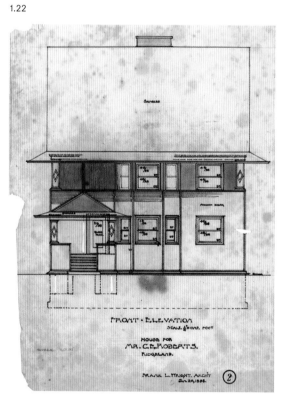

1.23

1.20. First Roberts block project, Ridgeland (later Oak Park), Ill., Wright, 1896. House 1. Plan, first floor, 15 January 1896

1.21. First Roberts block project. House 1. Front elevation, 15 January 1896

1.22. First Roberts block project. House 2. Plan, first floor, 20 January 1896

1.23. First Roberts block project. House 2. Front elevation, 20 January 1896

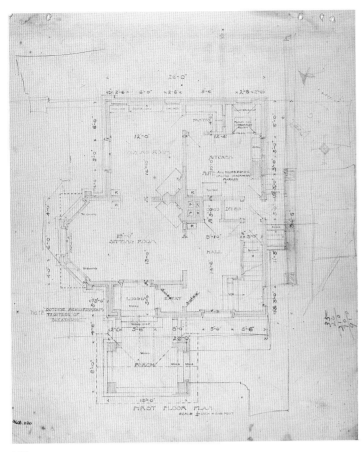

1.24

1.26

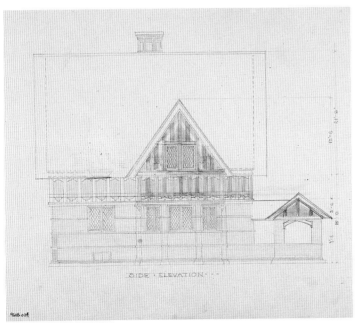

1.25

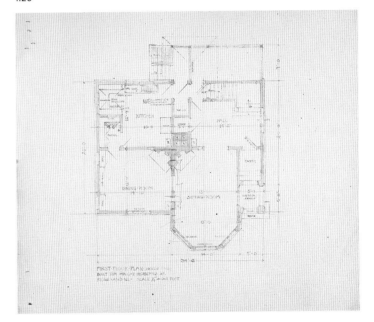

1.27

1.24. First Roberts block project. House [3]. Plan, first floor

1.25. First Roberts block project. House [3]. Side elevation

1.26. First Roberts block project. House 4. Perspective, from street

1.27. First Roberts block project. House 4. Plan, first floor

from the wide street-facing porch around a central fireplace core serving both the bay-windowed sitting room that looks out to the side garden and the dining room in the rear corner (figure 1.24). A complex stair hall arrangement occupying the entire front corner of the ground floor negotiates the winding path from street through porch and loggia to side-facing sitting room. The elevations reveal a more overtly picturesque design than the first two houses, with a wood and plaster-paneled, semi-Tudor upper story sitting on top of a brick lower floor punched into with leaded casement windows (figure 1.25). The side facade containing the service entrance leading to the kitchen area became even more Gothic in feeling when Wright added a multibayed, wooden arched passageway enclosing the ground-level stairs and containing a window seat off the second-floor landing.[41]

House 4 is perhaps the closest in feeling to the Winslow House while at the same time being the most exotically historicizing (figure 1.26). Its tall cubic shape, brick base, and horizontally striated, wood shingle midsection combined with the cutout corner Gothic entrance and delicately paneled Gothic windows give it a Venetian air. The plan, on the other hand, is essentially a simplification of that of House [3]: the side porch has been removed and the street entry incorporated into the body of the house (figure 1.27).[42] House [5] returns to the more Anglo-Gothic interpretation of the Shingle Style used for Houses 1 and 2 while increasing the sense of verticality by the double-height treatment of the bay window facing the street (figure 1.28). The plan, on the other hand, opens up that used for Houses [3] and 4, providing more broadly treated bay windows to both the living and dining rooms (figure 1.29).[43] A fireplace set within an inglenook, much like the one in Wright's own house, becomes almost a separate room around which the rest of the space flows. House [5] is also the only one of the group where the side elevations are identified by their cardinal directions, thus allowing one to understand that the house was planned to face east, onto Ogden Street.

The most interesting and unusual of the six house designs is the one for a Corner House (figures 1.30–31). While its exterior may bear the closest resemblance of all six to Wright's own house, its plan was specifically motivated by its location on the block.[44] As can readily be seen in a preliminary sketch, the plan is based on a rotated square, which provides appropriate emphasis to one of its rear corners (figure 1.32). The diagonals crossing in the center of the symmetrically placed entrance

1.28

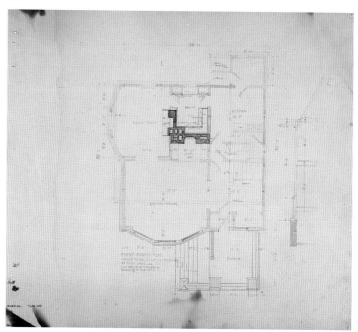

1.29

1.28. First Roberts block project. House [5]. Front elevation

1.29. First Roberts block project. House [5]. Plan, first floor, and partial section

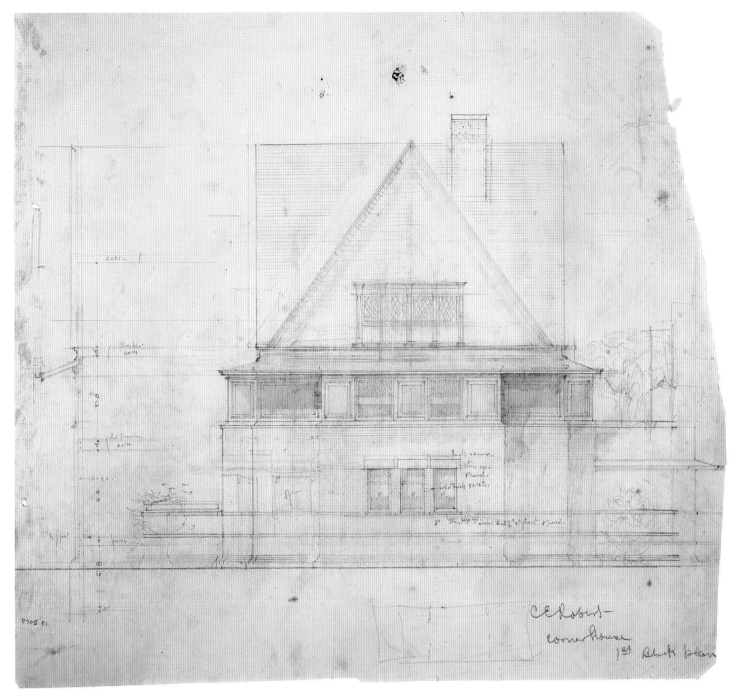

1.30

1.30. First Roberts block project. Corner House. Side elevation

hall lead beyond the splayed sides of the prominent fireplace to stairways in the two corners. The one on the left goes up to the second floor, where the four bedrooms occupy the arms of a Greek cross; the one on the right projects out beyond the kitchen into an angled extension that serves as the house's rear entrance. The front entrance is directly on axis with the fireplace. It is preceded by an open porch nearly the width of the house. The central hall opens on the right into a library and on the left into an equal-sized sitting room. A circuit from the library across the hall and through the sitting room leads into the dining room that backs up to the fireplace and looks onto the rear garden.

The Corner House occupies a special place in Wright's overall scheme for the block. Although the drawing we have for it is not as fully developed as those for single street frontages and privileges one facade over the other, it is clear from the site's development plan that Wright considered the Corner House to be the critical unit in his novel conception of what might constitute the basic building block of the modern suburban community (figure 1.33). Instead of focusing on the picturesque relationship of one house to another or of a group of them to the street they face, the general plan for the Roberts block looked at the problem from the inside out. The opening up of the center of the block and the tying of the four corners to the middle through the design of the Corner House were crucial in this regard, and it is this initial experiment of Wright's in urban design, rather than any of the individual houses in the project, that holds the greatest historical interest for us.

The development plan is a startling piece of historical evidence that throws into the sharpest light the full implications of the 1896 Roberts project and allows us to see, for the first time and in the starkest terms, an aspect of Wright's urban design thinking that is usually more artfully disguised, to wit, the underlying rationality and geometric insistence of the grid.[45] The plan is lightly sketched in pencil over an outline of the block gridded in the form of a graph. The outside border is drawn in black ink, while the interior squares, representing an eight-foot module, are in red ink. The use of graph paper in architectural design goes back to the later eighteenth century. Thomas Jefferson was one of the first to adapt the drafting technique used in the French silk industry to architecture.[46] In the early part of the nineteenth century, the architect Jean-Nicolas-Louis Durand (1760–1834) recommended the

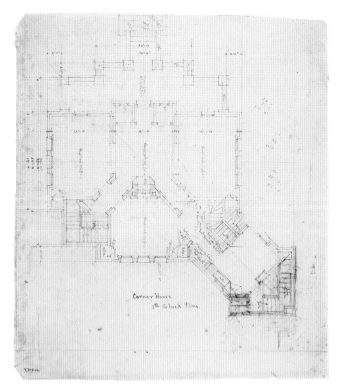

1.31

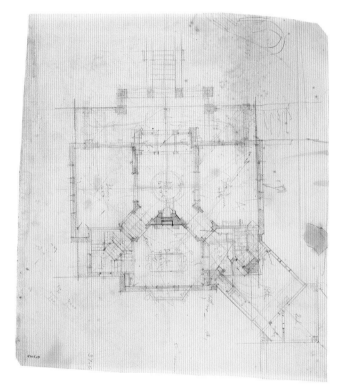

1.32

1.31. First Roberts block project. Corner House. Sketch plan, first floor

1.32. First Roberts block project. Corner House. Sketch plan, first floor

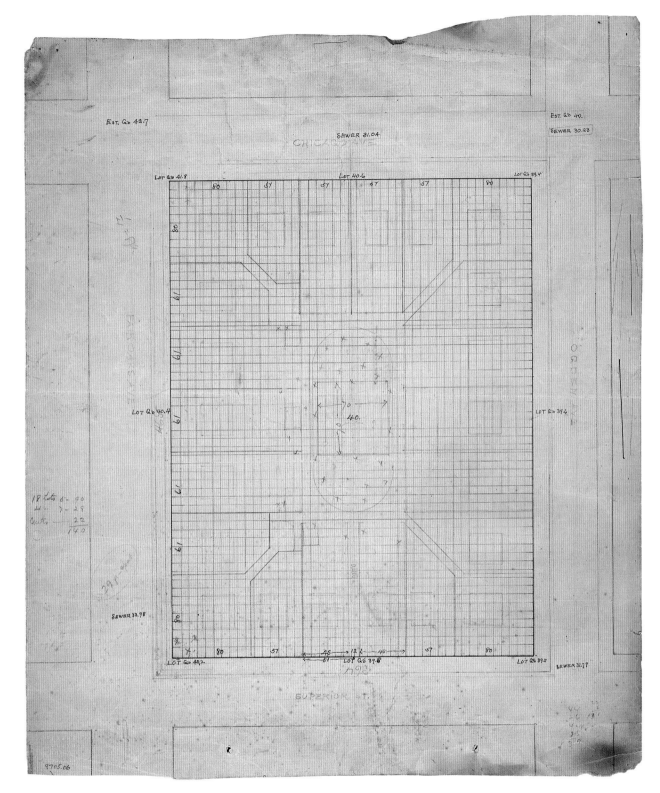

1.33

1.33. First Roberts block project. Development plan

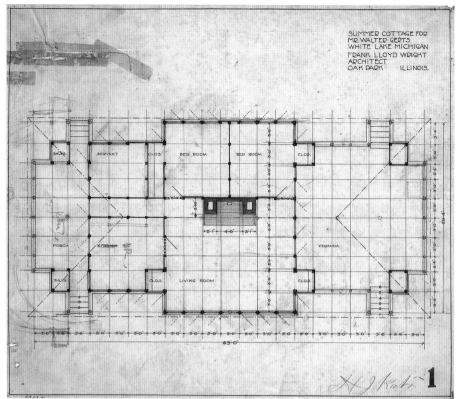

1.34

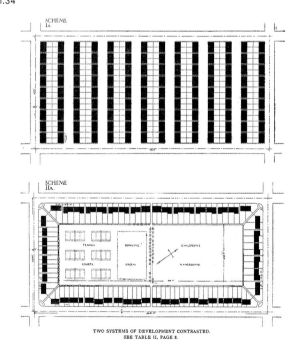

TWO SYSTEMS OF DEVELOPMENT CONTRASTED.
SEE TABLE II, PAGE 8.

1.35

1.36

1.34. Walter Gerts Summer Cottage, Whitehall, Mich., Wright, 1902. Plan

1.35. "Two Systems of [Residential] Development Contrasted," Raymond Unwin, ca. 1912. From Unwin, *Nothing Gained by Overcrowding! How the Garden City Type of Development May Benefit Both Owner and Occupier,* 1912

1.36. Worcester Square, Boston, 1850s–60s

use of the grid to his engineering students at Paris's Ecole Polytechnique as a practical and efficient method for rationalizing and "mechanizing" the process of design.[47] Throughout the rest of the century, however, graph paper was used little, if at all, by architects with any artistic pretensions.

This is Wright's earliest known use of gridded paper. It is unclear whether it was his idea or not. The lot and sewer numbers in ink are not in his hand, but all the indications in pencil, including the house footprints, street names, internal passageways, and shape and dimensions of the central area, are by Wright or one of his staff. Wright is known to have used a "unit system of design" by the early 1900s. An often-quoted letter of 1904 from Charles White Jr., one of the draftsmen in Wright's studio and Charles Roberts's son-in-law, notes that "all his [Wright's] plans are composed of units grouped in a symetrical [sic] and systematic way," adding that this use of the "unit system" is "Wright's greatest contribution to Architecture."[48] Few plans of the period, however, reveal the underlying grid. The Coonley House site plan illustrated in figure 1.13, for instance, was redrawn in the late 1920s to clarify the unit system not represented on the original plan.[49] Some plans, like that for the Walter Gerts Summer Cottage in Whitehall, Michigan, of 1902, do show the grid lines of the module — and in red ink as well (figure 1.34); but they constitute, as White noted, an internal device for creating an integrated structural/proportional system, based on the width of the casement window, that "is consistently carried through every portion of the plan."[50] The grid underlying the Roberts development plan is different. Rather than serving as an abstract compositional tool to control the design and ultimately the construction of an individual building, the grid here materially defines the terrain of a community of houses. It echoes the preexisting grid that governed the platting of the suburb itself and thus makes it clear that Wright conceived the Roberts project in terms of the larger physical and cultural network of Chicago.

Wright's first attempt at group planning was therefore developed in terms of a grid set within the larger metropolitan grid. The scalar relationship of the one to the other mimics that of the city of Chicago to the surrounding counties shown in Rees's earlier map (figures 1.8, 1.12). The innovative aspect of Wright's design lies in the way the architect manipulated his grid to provide a community focus while at the same time offering a more lucrative investment potential for his client. Over the mesh of eight-foot squares, Wright redrew the property lines to allow for a central community space, plus twenty-two instead of the nineteen lots originally platted (figure 1.33).[51] Wright eliminated the alley that ran behind the houses facing Chicago Avenue and drastically shortened and narrowed the one entering the block from Superior Street on the south.[52] Passing between the two middle lots on Superior, this short stretch of alley opens rather dramatically into a large central space a little over one hundred feet in width by two hundred in length (a one-to-two dimension that Wright came to prefer). This public space, which provides access for carriages, is defined by a large oval area planted with trees in the middle of which is a square, seventy feet to a side, devoid of planting, that appears to be a playground area. Some of the lots have small buildings on their internal edges overlooking the central green. These may well be stables. The circulation route around the oval angles out at the four corners to cut through to the service entries of the corner houses, whose lots, only eighty feet to a side, would not otherwise have had access to the central common.

Unlike the conventional subdivision, where all the lots were pretty much the same size and shape and were assumed to relate only to the street they face, the ones in Wright's development plan vary quite considerably in size and shape and relate inward to the communal space — and therefore to one another — as well as outward to the street — and the houses across the street. The lots in Wright's plan vary in shape from square to rectangular to chamfered, and in size from a little over 5,700 to almost 8,000 square feet. The differences, however, are offset by the importance attached to the central public space, which creates a special focus for all the houses in the form of a unique communal gathering place. It is a design idea that appears to be unprecedented in the context of American suburban planning and predicts certain Garden City and Suburb ideas later developed by planners in both England and the United States (figure 1.35).[53] In effect more urban than suburban in character, Wright's plan may have its source in the eighteenth-century London residential square, brought to America in nineteenth-century Boston, where a central garden, often in the shape of an oval, is cut out of the urban fabric and reserved for the communal use of those who own the surrounding townhouses (figure 1.36). Wright's Roberts block transforms that paradigm created for continuous urban terraces into a system for freestanding suburban houses. It could also be read as a disaggregation of the court-yarded urban apartment block type that Wright designed in the same years and its recasting in suburban terms (see figure 1.19).

The thoroughgoing reconceptualization of the suburban block represented by the Roberts development plan might lead one to think that Wright considered it a new type that could be repeated and become a model for the development of the Chicago area. But there is no evidence to support this. The project was short-lived and had no afterlife. Indeed, seven years later, when Roberts went back to Wright to ask him to revisit his plan for the block, the architect came up with what would seem to be, on first glance, a completely different solution (see figure 3.9). Yet, as we shall see in the next chapter, Wright retained many of the ideas worked out in 1896 and merely gave them a different form. Most significant of these would be (1) an unwavering acceptance of the grid as the basic framework for development; (2) the conception of the residential block as a block—not a series of outward-facing street frontages but a unified group of houses connected through the interior of the block to one another; (3) a focus on the idea of community as well as privacy; (4) an effort to transform the much-maligned alley from an interstitial, purely functional and divisive space into one of greater positive value; and, finally, (5) an understanding of the crucial importance of the corner as a means for providing a sense of reflexiveness (and redefined idea of picturesqueness) to a plan based on the grid.

Looked at from a certain distance, and in more abstract terms—as Wright would do over the next several years—the Roberts 1896 development plan contains the outlines of a completely new way of thinking about the residential block in terms of the square geometry of the ideal American grid. First broken down into the smaller square units of the graph paper on which it was drawn, the plan builds up from these units a modular organization that privileges the corners and equates them with the center to which they, exclusively, are attached by diagonal lines. Wright was intrigued by the larger and more consistent pattern that could be abstracted from this and began thinking about how to resubdivide the rectangular grid of the city as it had come to exist into an ideal square scheme where there are only corner lots and where the center becomes the point of communal tangency. From this came his galvanizing Quadruple Block Plan of four years later, published in the *Ladies' Home Journal* in early 1901.

The development of downtown Chicago in the years just before and after the turn of the twentieth century went hand in hand with the growth of the surrounding suburbs. As each element in the city center/suburb dyad grew in size and importance, the tension between them increased proportionately. In the Loop were concentrated not only the commercial skyscrapers and buildings housing government services and offices but also the new department stores and leading civic cultural institutions, including the recently constructed Public Library (Shepley, Rutan and Coolidge, 1892–97), Art Institute (Shepley, Rutan and Coolidge, 1891–93), and Auditorium (Adler and Sullivan, 1886–89). The suburb, by contrast, was almost exclusively residential. The center/periphery distinction became one of work versus domesticity, with the male defining the world of the downtown and the female that of the suburb. Shopping and participation in cultural activities were two of the few reasons for those in charge of the domestic environment to make the trip downtown that otherwise was reserved for the family breadwinner.

Frank Lloyd Wright and his wife, Catherine Tobin Wright, more or less followed this pattern during the first eight years of their marriage. While working for Adler and Sullivan, Wright commuted to the firm's office in the Auditorium Building on the corner of Congress Street and Michigan Avenue. When he opened his own office in 1893, he took space in the nearby Adler and Sullivan–designed Schiller Building (1891) on which he had worked, remaining there until 1897, when he moved first to the recently completed Steinway Hall (Dwight Perkins, 1893–95) and then to Burnham and Root's Rookery Building (1885–88). By 1895, as we read in the previous chapter, the electric streetcar from the Loop passed right in front of the Wrights' Oak Park house. But instead of encouraging the young architect to continue his commuting life, the convenience of a streetcar at his very doorstep provided Wright with an entirely new perspective on how the residential suburb might relate to the downtown business section of the city.

During the year following the development plan for the Roberts block, Wright decided to move his office from the Loop to a studio added to the north side of his Oak Park house, fronting directly onto Chicago Avenue, and to retain a smaller space in the Loop simply for business purposes (see figure 1.14). In the announcement celebrating the opening of his new office in 1898, he gave the following reasons for the relocation of his practice:

THE PRACTICE OF ARCHITECTURE as a profession has fine art as well as commercial elements.

These should be combined to their mutual benefit, not mixed to their detriment.

To develop in a better sense, this fine art side in combination with its commercial condition, the architect should place himself in an environment that conspires to develop the best there is in him. The first requisite is a place fitted and adapted to the work to be performed and set outside distractions of the busy city. The worker is enabled on this basis to secure the quiet concentration of effort essential to the full success of a building project,—the intrinsic value of which is measured by the quality of that effort.

To practice the profession of architecture along these lines, in the hope of reaching these better results, a complete architectural workshop has been constructed at Oak Park, and for purely business purposes, consultation and matters in connection with superintendence, an office has been located in "The Rookery," Chicago.[1]

With this move, Wright initiated a pattern of distancing his architectural practice from the urban center that would only become more, rather than less, exaggerated during the remainder of his long career, first with the construction of Taliesin in rural Wisconsin in 1911 and then with that of Taliesin West in the desert northeast of Phoenix beginning in 1938. In all three situations, one of the compelling reasons, aside from the purely artistic one of being able to work in a "quiet," nondistracting "environment," was the desire to find a way of integrating work with daily family life, in other words, to resolve the split between the realms of the commercial and the domestic that had opened up in late nineteenth-century America with the rapid development of the suburb.

But one should be careful about equating an inner-ring suburb of Chicago, easily reachable by streetcar or commuter rail, with the relatively unsettled areas that Wyoming Valley in Wisconsin and the Sonoran Desert in Arizona represented in 1911 and 1938, respectively. In 1897, Wright realized that the streetcar not only allowed him immediate access to the city center, but also allowed those coming from all parts of the expanding metropolis easy access to him. This of course meant staff as well as clients. The "streetcar suburb," as Sam Bass Warner Jr. called it, established a city of ever-widening boundaries with ever-increasing numbers of nodes.[2] Wright's relocation of his office to Oak Park thus suggested a new role for the suburb. No longer simply the passive partner in the center/periphery, residence/work dialectic, it could, in the architect's view, become a dynamic center itself, combining both living and professional opportunities at a scale more conducive to "their mutual benefit." The Quadruple Block Plan, which he produced during the second year of work in his new suburban locale, laid the groundwork for the urban design ideas that were ultimately to emerge from this perception.

The *Ladies' Home Journal*'s "New Series of Model Suburban Houses Which Can Be Built at Moderate Cost"

Wright's opportunity to rethink his Roberts block plan of 1896 occurred or, rather, was created by him when he was asked in 1900 for a house design to be included in a "New Series of Model Suburban Houses Which Can Be Built at Moderate Cost" that the *Ladies' Home Journal* would publish in fourteen installments beginning with the October issue of that year. It is not known precisely when Wright was contacted, nor how the commission came about, although evidence points to the fact that it may have been his friend and colleague Robert C. Spencer who recommended him sometime in 1900.[3] Wright was the only architect of the group to have two houses in the series, and they were the only nontraditional designs of the lot. The first, called "A Home in a Prairie Town," was published in the February 1901 issue, and the second, "A Small House with 'Lots of Room in It,' " was published in July 1901 (figures 2.16, 2.24).[4] More important for us, Wright was the only architect of the group to design the first of his two houses in accord with a development plan including other houses and, indeed, to use that plan to generate the design of the individual house itself. The Quadruple Block Plan, which Wright offered as a new system for resubdividing the typical suburban plat, was proposed as the "basis" and framework for ensuring that "A Home in a Prairie Town" would not be an isolated single-family house but would be part and parcel of a "prairie community."[5]

The *Ladies' Home Journal* was one of the most widely read magazines in the world at the time and was about to reach the unprecedented circulation figure of more than one million. The person responsible both for its financial success and its editorial content was Edward W. Bok (1863–1930).[6] Bok's life, which he recounted with unabashed self-promotion in the Pulitzer Prize–winning *The Americanization of Edward Bok: An Autobiography of a Dutch Boy Fifty Years After*, first published in 1920, was the classic Horatio Alger story. Born in the Netherlands to an upper-middle-class family that had fallen on difficult times, Bok was brought to the United States by his parents in 1870 in their search for a better life. At the age of thirteen he quit school to start working at the Western Union Telegraph Company. Within just a few years he became the family breadwinner as well as a kind of wunderkind in Brooklyn literary-journalistic circles. While working for Charles Scribner's he continued to write the syndicated column "Literary Leaves," which came to the attention of Cyrus H. K. Curtis, the publisher of the *Ladies' Home Journal*, who was looking for someone to relieve his wife of its editorship. Bok assumed control of the Philadelphia-based magazine in 1889 and ran it with absolute authority for the next thirty years.

Bok's goal for the magazine, as he later wrote, was "to create a national institution of service to the American woman." Compared to other publications of its type, he intended his to be "a magazine of higher standards, of larger initiative — a magazine that would be an authoritative clearing-house for all the problems confronting women in the home, that brought itself closely into contact with those problems and tried to solve them in an entertaining and efficient way; and yet a magazine of uplift and inspiration: a magazine, in other words, that would give light and leading in the woman's world."[7] To these ends he sought out major writers, artists, civic leaders, and public figures of the day. Among those who participated were William Dean Howells, Rudyard Kipling, Kate Greenaway, Charles Dana Gibson, Mark Twain, Bret Harte, Hamlin Garland, Sarah Orne Jewett, Benjamin Harrison, and Theodore Roosevelt. Bok also used the printed page as a platform to mount crusades against the sale of patent medicines, the proliferation of roadside billboards, the domination of the Parisian fashion industry, and the deleterious effects of the electric power industry on such natural landmarks as Niagara Falls. But, as with his refusal to take a positive stand on such controversial issues as women's right to vote, he always maintained a position of moderation that kept the *Journal* well within the bounds of a genteel tradition of Progressive-minded reform.

The raising of aesthetic standards in the domestic environment of the country was one of Bok's most significant preoccupations. He campaigned for reforms in the quality of decoration of Pullman cars on the nation's railroads, describing them as "atrocious," "a veritable riot of the worst conceivable ideas" that, unfortunately, "women of the new money-class were accepting and introducing into their homes!"[8] He made available to his readers, at a cost of ten cents a copy, black-and-white reproductions of works by contemporary artists such as Edwin Austin Abbey, Howard Pyle, and Charles Dana Gibson as part of "a systematic plan for improving the pictures on the walls of the American home." A "cherished dream," which he was able to realize by 1912, was to reproduce "the greatest pictures in the world in their original colors" and make them available at a reasonable cost to "small householders."[9] The artists included Rembrandt, Velasquez, Raphael, Gainsborough, Vermeer, Fragonard, and Titian. Among the most modern were Corot and Turner. Whistler was the only living artist in the group.

By far the most important initiative Bok undertook in the area of aesthetic reform was, in his own view, that of the suburban house. In his autobiography he described his effort to improve the "ugly ... repellently ornate," "wretched architecture of [America's] small houses" as "the signal piece of construction in which he engaged" in his long editorial career. Early on he was able to convince Curtis to purchase the small Buffalo publication *Country Life* in order to transform it into a magazine devoted to "the general subject of a better American architecture, gardening, and interior decoration, with special application to the small house"; but when Curtis shortly thereafter had the opportunity to buy the *Saturday Evening Post*, all efforts went into it and *Country Life* was sold. Undaunted, Bok decided to use the pages of the *Ladies' Home Journal* itself "as his medium for making the small-house architecture of America better."[10] The impact of this campaign of domestic reform was ultimately so far-reaching that Theodore Roosevelt would write that " 'Bok is the only man I ever heard of who changed, for the better, the architecture of an entire nation, and he did it so quickly and yet so effectively that we didn't know it was begun before it was finished.' "[11]

Bok states that when he first asked a number of architects to supply plans and specifications that could be bought by readers at little expense and then turned over to a builder of their choice, his request was met with opposition. One excuse was that "prices differed too much in various parts of the country" to make the idea feasible. More generally it was felt by architects that the "publicity of magazine presentation" represented a " 'cheapening' [of] their profession!"[12] One of those Bok asked, and who refused, was Stanford White (1853–1906). However, the local Philadelphia architect William L. Price (1861–1916), who was later to design Bok's own Tudor-style residence in the Philadelphia suburb of Merion, agreed to join forces. In December 1895, Bok published the first of Price's model houses in the *Journal*. His design for "A $3500 Suburban House" was for a picturesque, half-timbered Elizabethan cottage that did its best, as Price remarked, to adapt the "English precedent" to "the unnatural, speculative ... narrow lots" typical of the American suburb (figure 2.1).[13] Aside from the plans and specifications, the magazine offered estimates from builders in four different areas of the country, all for five dollars a set.

By the beginning of the following year, Bok was describing the Price design as the "first" in "a series of plans and ideas for

2.1

2.1. "A $3500 Suburban House," William L. Price, *LHJ*, December 1895

suburban houses of moderate cost which the Journal proposes to publish." The second, included in the February 1896 issue, was by the Boston-based archtraditionalist Ralph Adams Cram (1863–1942). Set on an isolated lot on the outskirts of town, it was in the Colonial style and was estimated to cost five thousand dollars.[14] The series went through seven more models, including designs by the Connecticut architect Edward T. Hapgood (1866–1915), the well-established New York architect Bruce Price, and the lesser-known Arthur D. Pickering, Frank W. Handy, Ashton Pentecost, and Walter J. Keith.[15] All were for single-family houses conceived of and shown in isolation from any neighbor. Of this group, Bruce Price and Pickering would be asked back to take part in the 1900–1902 series. In the meantime, however, William Price produced, under the anonymous guise of "the Journal's Special Architect," seven designs in a new series launched in July 1897 as "The Ladies' Home Journal Model Homes of Moderate Cost."[16] This campaign was so successful, according to the magazine, that by July 1898 over five hundred sets of plans had been requested and mailed out, of which more than half were actually constructed.[17]

The "New Series of Model Suburban Houses Which Can Be Built at Moderate Cost" that began in October 1900 and ultimately included Wright's two designs was meant by Bok to "set in motion" his "main plan, which … [was that of] placing the best skill of the leading architects of the country within the reach of everybody who wishes to build a pretty country home at a moderate cost."[18] The word "leading" was clearly part of Bok's salesmanship. Of the fourteen designers working either on their own or in partnership with another, only two might conceivably have been described as "the Foremost Architects of New York, Philadelphia, Boston and Chicago," which is how Bok introduced the first two installments.[19] Those two architects were Bruce Price and Wilson Eyre (1858–1944), who were the oldest of the group. The vast majority of the others were in their thirties and even twenties, and their careers were still to be made. Of those who did fulfill Bok's description, even if only partially, were Cram, Milton B. Medary (1874–1929), Elmer Grey (1872–1963), and Wright.[20]

While it is not known precisely what instructions Bok gave his architects, one can ascertain the following based on his own statements and the published projects themselves. All the designs include at least (1) first- and second-floor plans; (2) one exterior perspective, generally taken from the street;

and (3) one or two interior perspectives, usually of the living room, dining room, or entrance hall. Aside from the Eyre design, the penultimate one in the series, all include an itemized estimate of costs falling within a range of five thousand to seventy-five hundred dollars. In addition, the architect was to be prepared to draw up plans and specifications complete enough "that any builder could build the house from them." To this effect, Bok appended to each published proposal (except that of Eyre) an Editor's Note similar to this: "As a guarantee that the plan of this house is practicable and that the estimates for cost are conservative, the architect is ready to accept the commission of preparing the working plans and specifications for this house to cost [X] Dollars, providing that the building site selected is within reasonable distance of a base of supplies where material and labor may be had at the standard market rates." As to the question of program, Bok later wrote that he had but two requirements. First, every servant's room was to "have two windows to insure cross-ventilation" and to be twice the size normally reserved for such rooms. And second, for the "useless" parlor "should be substituted either a living-room or a library."[21]

Each design was accompanied by a descriptive text written by the architect. These vary in length but generally cover the same subjects. First was usually a statement describing the architect's intention and the key factors that motivated his design. This could be anywhere from a single short paragraph to two or three longer ones. Following that, and constituting the bulk of the text, was a discussion of the plans, more often than not in a walk-through manner, focusing on function and how the various rooms interrelate to create a serviceable and comfortable domestic environment. In this context, issues of material finish, furniture, and furnishings usually came up. The construction materials were also clearly stated before the estimate of costs was outlined. Finally, reference to the site, whether it be a specific type of location or not, as well as a discussion of landscaping and the treatment of the contiguous grounds, might be appended at the end or brought to bear on the motivating factors in the design laid out in the beginning.

The opening paragraph or paragraphs are among the most interesting and telling for our purposes. In the very first of the designs in the series, New York–based Bruce Price, noted for his work at the upscale resort suburb of Tuxedo Park as well as more recent institutional and commercial buildings, began by saying that "experience in planning and designing country houses of moderate cost has shown that a symmetrical plan is preferable for many reasons," the most important being the "comparatively inexpensive construction" that results. This preamble was used to justify his choice of style, "which," according to Price, "may be called Georgian" (figure 2.2).[22] The question of style or character, as might be expected, was primary in many of the architects' minds. The Philadelphia firm of Milton Medary and Richard L. Field (1868–1906) claimed up front that their choice of "the Elizabethan period of English architecture" was "best suited to the requirements of the small country house where the intention of the owner is to get away from the formal lines of city architecture" (figure 2.3).[23] The New York architect Arthur D. Pickering (b. 1859), on the other hand, said experience taught him quite conclusively that the "Dutch Colonial" style was the most efficient one for this type of job (figure 2.4), whereas the Milwaukee-based Elmer Grey assumed that some variation on the "Old English" manner would be the most appropriate for a lakeshore setting in the environs "of Chicago or Milwaukee" (figure 2.5).[24]

Although all the architects other than Wright produced designs based on one historical tradition or another, a number of them were less willing to describe their houses in terms of a specific style than in the more general terms of certain time-honored, "traditional values." The Philadelphia firm of Charles Barton Keen (1868–1931) and Frank E. Mead (1865–1940) spoke of their house's wide weather-boarded and shingled design as having an "old-fashioned" and "quaint effect," featuring an "old-fashioned garden ... laid out in front of the porch with quaint, old, low hedges, and flower-plots back of them" (figure 2.6).[25] Cram never specified the medieval sources for his multigabled, half-timbered imagery, simply stating that "the object has been to design a dwelling that should be, above all else, domestic, personal and livable" (figure 2.7).[26] Edwin J. Lewis Jr. (1859–1937), also of Boston and also a Gothic Revivalist, likewise avoided any discussion of the historical origins of his half-timbered design, merely noting that "the owner is a gentleman of moderate means and simple tastes, who has come into possession of a lot of land in a quiet village" where "stone is abundant" and where the desire to be able to look out upon flowers has been the motivation for "an old-fashioned formal garden" (figure 2.8).[27]

"The aim" of the Boston architect William G. Rantoul (1867–1949) was to create "a quiet homelike house with pretty surroundings" (figure 2.9). The "mullioned windows" and

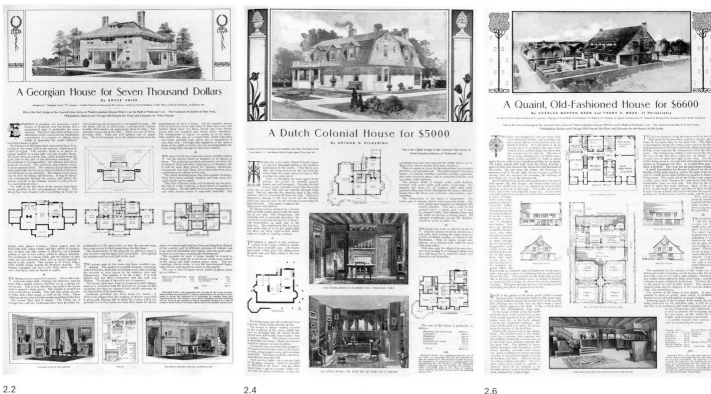

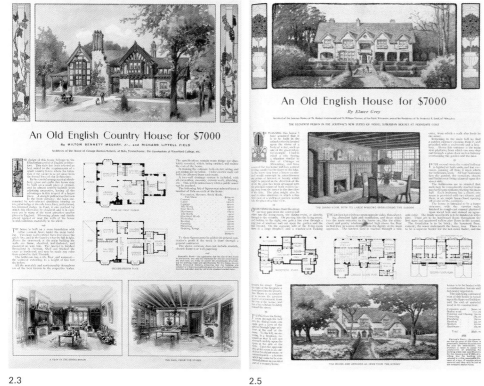

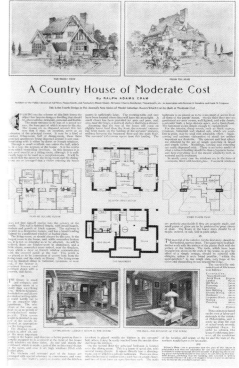

2.2

2.4

2.6

2.3

2.5

2.7

2.2. "A Georgian House for Seven Thousand Dollars," Bruce Price. From "New Series of Model Suburban Houses Which Can be Built at Moderate Cost," *LHJ*, October 1900

2.3. "An Old English Country House for $7000," Milton Bennett Medary and Richard Littell Field. From "New Series," *LHJ*, December 1900

2.4. "A Dutch Colonial House for $5000," Arthur D. Pickering. From "New Series," *LHJ*, May 1901

2.5. "An Old English House for $7000," Elmer Grey. From "New Series," *LHJ*, September 1901

2.6. "A Quaint, Old-Fashioned House for $6600," Charles Barton Keen and Frank E. Mead. From "New Series," *LHJ*, November 1900

2.7. "A Country House of Moderate Cost," Ralph Adams Cram. From "New Series," *LHJ*, January 1901

A Suburban House for $6500
By EDWIN J. LEWIS, Jr.

Architect of the Peabody Association Hotel, Dorchester, Massachusetts; the Baptist Memorial Church, Somerville, Massachusetts; etc.

This is the Sixth Design in the Journal's New Series of Model Suburban Houses of Moderate Cost

A $5000 House for a Family of Three
By Albert Bayne Lawyer

THE TENTH DESIGN IN THE JOURNAL'S NEW SERIES OF MODEL SUBURBAN HOUSES AT MODERATE COST

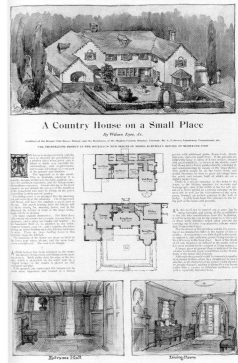

A Country House on a Small Place
By WILSON EYRE, Jr.

Architect of the Bennett Club House, Bolmar; and the Residences of Mr. Stephen Parrish, Windsor, Vermont; Mr. A. J. Drexel, Lansdowne, Pennsylvania; etc.

THE THIRTEENTH DESIGN IN THE JOURNAL'S NEW SERIES OF MODEL SUBURBAN HOUSES AT MODERATE COST

2.8

2.10

2.12

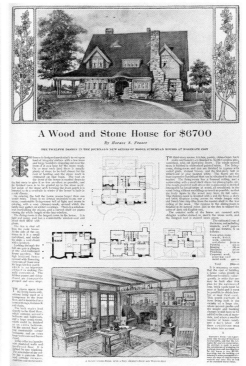

A Stucco Country House for $7500
By WILLIAM G. RANTOUL

This is the Seventh Design in the Journal's New Series of Model Suburban Houses of Moderate Cost

A Wood and Stone House for $6700
By Horace S. Frazer

THE TWELFTH DESIGN IN THE JOURNAL'S NEW SERIES OF MODEL SUBURBAN HOUSES AT MODERATE COST

2.9

2.11

2.8. "A Suburban House for $6500," Edwin J. Lewis Jr. From "New Series," *LHJ*, March 1901

2.9. "A Stucco Country House for $7500," William G. Rantoul. From "New Series," *LHJ*, April 1901

2.10. "A $5000 House for a Family of Three," Albert Bayne Lawyer. From "New Series," *LHJ*, August 1901

2.11. "A Wood and Stone House for $6700," Horace S. Frazer. From "New Series," *LHJ*, October 1901

2.12. "A Country House on a Small Place," Wilson Eyre. From "New Series," *LHJ*, November 1901

"quaint simplicity of English work of two hundred years ago" were employed to give the cottage-like structure a "picturesque" effect.[28] The more limited ambitions, not to speak of results, of New Yorker Albert Bayne Lawyer's (b. 1872) design come through in his text as well as his nondescript drawings. Focusing on cost and program almost exclusively, he said little of style or character, noting that his house was "designed with particular regard for the requirements of a small family" and "planned in a very compact manner, with no waste space, and the exterior treated in a broad and simple style" (figure 2.10).[29] A little more ambitious than Lawyer, Boston's MIT-educated Horace S. Frazer (1862–1931) described his rustic, Old-English-inflected Richardsonian design mainly in terms of materials and site. "This house is designed," he wrote, "particularly to set upon land of irregular surface with a few trees and large boulders cropping out near the front of it as a base for the stone work." To the rear would be "the old-fashioned flower garden" that had by then almost come to be an expected element of the model houses (figure 2.11).[30]

The discussion of site, by contrast, occupies nearly the entire text accompanying the penultimate design in the series, a Mediterranean-inflected, Arts and Craftsy English cottage by the highly respected, very tasteful Philadelphia architect Wilson Eyre. "This house," it begins, "is designed chiefly with the view of showing the possibilities of a modest place when great care is taken to study very carefully the surroundings and requirements and to take advantage of every part of the ground and situation" (figure 2.12). Significantly, neither the total cost nor an itemized budget was supplied, the only case of such in the series. Eyre described, while at the same rendering completely obscure, the approach from the north that ensured that "guests driving to the front entrance do not disturb the privacy of the members of the household who may be sitting on the porch or strolling in their private garden." Against a seemingly impenetrable backdrop of woods, the house—more like a mini-estate than a "model suburban house at moderate cost"—opens onto its own private world. Acknowledging the pretensions implicit in his design concept, Eyre stated that "if the grounds are sufficiently large to allow of it," the enclosed formal garden to the south "could lead down into a flower garden … by means of the steps shown," adding that "all this need not be carried out at once, but by using foresight, and taking all the possibilities of the site into consideration from the beginning, it will be perfectly easy for the owner" to carry out

"some very attractive scheme which may be presented later."[31]

Although stretching the parameters of the program well beyond what Bok had in mind, Eyre's design makes fully manifest the underlying aspirations and assumptions of most of the other projects. Privacy was an overriding issue for a house in the suburbs in almost all the architects' minds. Just four years before, the Boston architect R. Clipston Sturgis (1860–1951) had written, in an important article on "Suburban Homes," that "the first great essential … of a home is privacy," a point that was repeated by the historian Vernon Parrington in his critique of "the lack of privacy" in the typical suburban dwelling, published in *House Beautiful* a few years later.[32] For these two writers, as for almost all the architects who contributed to the *Ladies' Home Journal*, the manipulation of site conditions through orientation and landscape treatment was an obvious way to achieve the desired "essential."

Medary and Field noted how, "by the careful arrangement of shrubbery, grass and paths," their house might "be built on a small piece of ground, and be almost entirely isolated from adjoining properties" (see figure 2.13).[33] Lewis made a point of the fact that the garden porch placed on the rear of his house "forms in summer a pleasant, retired, outdoor living-room, safe from the observation of the passer-by (see figure 2.8)."[34] Grey, for his part, stressed how his "plan has been arranged with the principal rooms of both stories facing away from the street" so as to have a view of a lake, a river, "or a well-kept garden."[35] He, at least, pictured the front of his house with the hedge-bordered path leading in from the street, unlike Eyre who did all he could to isolate his structure from its surrounding environment in order to give the impression that not a single neighbor lived within sight (figures 2.5, 2.12).

It is curious, though perhaps not unexpected, that only one of the designs other than Wright's "Home in a Prairie Town" offered an image of how the house would actually appear in a neighborhood setting. This was the one by Keen and Mead (figure 2.14). All the others showed the building in an isolating, picturesque, rather distant perspective, commanding its own lot. Rarely was the public sidewalk illustrated, and never the access to a stable. By means of a slightly elevated and oblique point of view, the Hughson Hawley rendering of the Keen and Mead design allowed for a panoramic sense of the surroundings. Still, each of the lots was shown to be protected from the street by tall, clipped hedges: the one in the foreground is conveniently undeveloped, and the ones in the background obscured by foliage. The text, however, took up the issue of suburban design in an unusually direct and practical manner. "This house," it begins,

> is designed to fit an average piece of ground in any part of the United States.... The size of the average suburban lot, on which such a house would probably be built, is about eighty feet in width by two hundred and fifty feet in depth. The house stands well back from the street, leaving a space of forty feet between the street-line and the front of the porch. As one faces the house, the driveway or entrance road is on the right, for use in case a stable is desired, and the entrance for servants, the delivery of provisions, etc., is on the extreme left.
>
> An old-fashioned garden is laid out in front of the porch with quaint, old, low hedges.... The entrance from the street is directly in the centre through a high arch of climbing rose-bushes.... The grounds on the front and on each side as far back as the clothes-yard, or farther if desired, are inclosed with a hedge of arbor-vitæ not less than five feet high. This gives not only privacy, but beauty as well, by treating the piece of ground as a whole.[36]

All this was visualized in a site plan, albeit abbreviated, the only one other than the two by Wright and that by George Edward Barton, who provided the final, otherwise unexceptional design in the series, and is better known for his role in the development of occupational therapy than for his architecture (figure 2.15).

Wright's "Home in a Prairie Town" and Its Community Underpinnings

Wright's two designs (figures 2.16, 2.24) are significantly different from the others in more respects than just the matter of style, which has been the almost exclusive focus of discussions of his contributions to the *Ladies' Home Journal* series. Beginning with Henry-Russell Hitchcock's *In the Nature of Materials: The Buildings of Frank Lloyd Wright, 1887–1941* (1942), "A Home in a Prairie Town" has usually been considered the architect's "first Prairie house."[37] Exhibiting all its characteristic features of long, emphatic horizontal lines, deeply overhanging hip roofs, open, interpenetrating volumes, a focal, freestanding fireplace mass, sliding volumes and planes, and an intimate connection with the site, it became

2.13

2.14

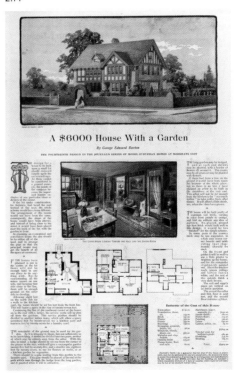

2.15

2.13. "Old English Country House," Medary and Field. Exterior perspective

2.14. "Quaint, Old-Fashioned House," Keen and Mead. Exterior perspective

2.15. "A $6000 House with a Garden," George Edward Barton. From "New Series," *LHJ*, January 1902

the prototype for the site-specific, material-grounded, ahistorical, space-activated concept of domestic design that was to find full expression in later works like the Willits House in Highland Park, Illinois (1902–3), Martin House in Buffalo (1903–6), Coonley House in Riverside (figure 1.13), and Robie House in Chicago (1908–10).

Like most of the authors who followed him, Hitchcock discussed the design of the house itself well before mentioning the fact that it "was not just one house" but "a unit in a middle-class suburban scheme." Following a lengthy description of the house, he noted, "Wright's first [sic] general planning scheme, the 'Quadruple Block Plan,' for a new type of block subdivision neither romantically confused in the tradition of Olmsted's naturalism, nor a mere imposition of equal narrow lots on the helpless soil of the prairie was published with the first *Ladies' Home Journal* house."[38] Instead of saying "with," Hitchcock would have been more accurate to say "as a precondition for," since Wright himself noted in the very beginning of his descriptive text for the first of his two "model suburban houses" that the actual house design was only a "partial solution of a city man's country home on the prairie."[39]

The perspectives Wright used to illustrate the two *Ladies' Home Journal* houses immediately broadcast the fact that something different was at stake in his designs. They would have seemed radically different from the others in the series to even the most visually inexperienced reader of the time. Whereas all of the other views, except for Cram's (which were done in a sketchy vignette style), were rendered in a warm, atmospheric, painterly manner, both the "Home in a Prairie Town" and "Small House with 'Lots of Room in It'" were treated in a crisp, hard-line, starkly abstract manner (figures 2.16, 2.24).[40] Moreover, the two Wright houses are not seen from a picturesque angle nor are they situated at an illusionistically comfortable distance from the viewer (see figures 2.13–14). Rather, they are presented almost head-on, tight up to the front plane of the page, with little or no open space to either side. The street and sidewalk determine the front plane of the image, and the vanishing point in both cases coincides with the stable at the end of the driveway that penetrates the house and connects it to the street. Wright's houses are the only ones in the series to include stables; and, of the others, only the Pickering, Lawyer, Barton, and Keen and Mead designs even picture the street in front of the house. In both of Wright's contributions, the reader is shown precisely how the house and

its outbuildings sit within the surrounding network of streets and sidewalks: in the "Home in a Prairie Town" that takes the form of a site plan and perspective of four similar houses at the top of the page; in the "Small House with 'Lots of Room in It,'" the site plan is limited to one lot only, but that is shown in two possible configurations at the bottom of the page.

Neither distanced from the surrounding environment by an illusion of privacy nor physically isolated from it by a hedged or walled garden, Wright's two houses are viewed as integral aspects of the environment and directly linked to the surrounding cityscape. While their horizontal lines were abstractly meant to express a relationship with the "quiet level" of the prairie, "the low terraces and broad eaves … designed to accentuate that quiet level and complete the harmonious relationship" went further. The houses were meant to appear not only to be "firmly and broadly associated with the site" in a natural sense but seem to grow directly out of its man-made conditions as well. The material of cement would provide a sense of visual continuity. "The curbs of the terraces and formal inclosures," Wright stated, "should be worked in cement with the walks and drives," just as the horizontal planes of the house's exterior walls would be finished in cement plaster. As a "cement construction," the house would not only be "durable and cheap," he wrote, but would partake of the utilitarian character of the suburban infrastructure of streets and sidewalks that frames and supports it.[41]

All of this is consistent with the unique and overriding motivation for Wright's "Home in a Prairie Town." The opening paragraphs make it immediately clear that his interest was not exclusively or even mainly in the issue of style, or character, or type of landscape setting but rather in the way the individual house, as part of a larger grouping, relates to the suburban community and the city to which it owes its origins and on which it ultimately depends for its existence (figure 2.16). Wright's text begins with this historical and sociological observation: "A city man going to the country puts too much in his house and too little in his ground. He drags after him the fifty-foot lot, soon the twenty-five-foot lot, finally the party wall; and the home-maker who fully appreciates the advantages which he came to the country to secure feels himself impelled to move on."[42]

The second paragraph goes to the heart of the issue and directly states the premise for the matrix of the Quadruple Block Plan: "It seems a waste of energy to plan a house haphazard,

A Home in a Prairie Town

By FRANK LLOYD WRIGHT

This is the Fifth Design in the Journal's New Series of Model Suburban Houses Which Can be Built at Moderate Cost

 CITY man going to the country puts too much in his house and too little in his ground. He drags after him the fifty-foot lot, soon the twenty-five-foot lot, finally the party wall; and the home-maker who fully appreciates the advantages which he came to the country to secure feels himself impelled to move on.

It seems a waste of energy to plan a house haphazard, to hit or miss an already distorted condition, so this partial solution of a city man's country home on the prairie begins at the beginning and assumes four houses to the block of four hundred feet square as the minimum of ground for the basis of his prairie community.

The block plan to the left, at the top of the page, shows an arrangement of the four houses that secures breadth and prospect to the community as a whole, and absolute privacy both as regards each to the community, and each to each of the four.

THE perspective view shows the handling of the group at the centre of the block, with its foil of simple lawn, omitting the foliage of curb parkways to better show the scheme, retaining the same house in the four locations merely to afford an idea of the unity of the various elevations. In practice the houses would differ distinctly, though based upon a similar plan.

The ground plan, which is intended to explain itself, is arranged to offer the least resistance to a simple mode of living, in keeping with a high ideal of the family life together. It is arranged, too, with a certain well-established order that enables free use without the sense of confusion felt in five out of seven houses which people really use.

The exterior recognizes the influence of the prairie, is firmly and broadly associated with the site, and makes a feature of its quiet level. The low terraces

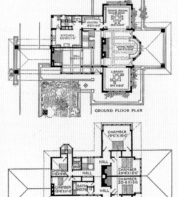

GROUND FLOOR PLAN

SECOND FLOOR PLAN

and broad eaves are designed to accentuate that quiet level and complete the harmonious relationship. The curbs of the terraces and formal inclosures for extremely informal masses of foliage and bloom should be worked in cement with the walks and drives.

Cement on metal lath is suggested for the exterior covering throughout, because it is simple, and, as now understood, durable and cheap.

The cost of this house with interior as specified and cement construction would be seven thousand dollars:

Masonry, Cement and Plaster . . .	$2800.00
Carpentry	3100.00
Plumbing	400.00
Painting and Glass	325.00
Heating — combination (hot water) .	345.00
Total	$6970.00

IN A HOUSE of this character the upper reach and gallery of the central living-room is decidedly a luxury. Two bedrooms may take its place, as suggested by the second-floor plan. The gallery feature is, nevertheless, a temptation because of the happy sense of variety and depth it lends to the composition of the interior, and the sunlight it gains from above to relieve the shadow of the porch. The details are better grasped by a study of the drawings. The interior section in perspective shows the gallery as indicated by dotted lines on the floor plan of the living-room.

The second-floor plan disregards this feature and is arranged for a larger family. Where three bedrooms would suffice the gallery would be practicable, and two large and two small bedrooms with the gallery might be had by rearranging servants' rooms and baths.

The interior is plastered throughout with sand finish and trimmed all through with flat bands of Georgia pine, smaller back bands following the base and casings. This Georgia pine should be selected from straight grain for stiles, rails and running members, and from figured grain for panels and wide surfaces.

All the wood should be shellacked once and waxed, and the plaster should be stained with thin, pure color in water and glue.

EDITOR'S NOTE — As a guarantee that the plan of this house is practicable, and that the estimates for cost are conservative, the architect is ready to accept the commission of preparing the working plans and specifications for this house to cost Seven Thousand Dollars, providing that the building site selected is within reasonable distance of a base of supplies where material and labor may be had at the standard market rates.

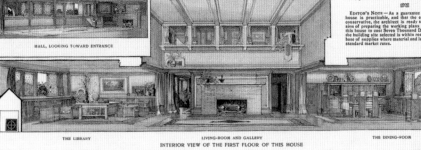

THE LIBRARY   LIVING-ROOM AND GALLERY   THE DINING-ROOM

HALL, LOOKING TOWARD ENTRANCE

INTERIOR VIEW OF THE FIRST FLOOR OF THIS HOUSE

2.16

2.16. "A Home in a Prairie Town," Wright. From "New Series," *LHJ*, February 1901

to hit or miss an already distorted condition, so this partial solution of a city man's country home on the prairie begins at the beginning and assumes four houses to the block of four hundred feet square as the minimum of ground for the basis of his prairie community."[43] The final paragraph of the introduction then offers a brief description of the general plan for the suburban community that states, without equivocation and without any possibility for misinterpretation, that the value of the whole, meaning the community, supersedes its parts, meaning the individual houses that comprise it: "The block plan to the left, at the top of the page, shows an arrangement of the four houses that secures breadth and prospect to the community as a whole, and absolute privacy both as regards each to the community, and each to each of the four."[44] Even the initial paragraph of the central part of the text, which goes on to describe the house itself and ends with an itemized list of costs, is devoted to the group plan. Directing the reader to the bird's-eye perspective to the right of the development plan at the top of the page (see figure 2.19), Wright continued his discussion of the Quadruple Block matrix: "The perspective view [of the four houses] shows the handling of the group at the centre of the block, with its foil of simple lawn, omitting the foliage of curb parkways to better show the scheme, retaining the same house in the four locations merely to afford an idea of the unity of the various elevations. In practice the houses would differ distinctly, though based upon a similar plan."[45]

Almost half of Wright's text regarding "A Home in a Prairie Town" was thus devoted to explaining the prior need for an overall plan to ensure an efficacious subdivision of suburban real estate and to justifying his particular concept for such in terms of the value of community. Set in a box at the top of the page above the title and main body of the article are the plan and perspective of four identical houses forming what Wright called here for the first time the Quadruple Block Plan. Neither the original site plan nor the original bird's-eye perspective still exists. The only other drawing we have that is directly related to the scheme is a half-finished sketch plan annotated with a rather extensive explanatory text (figure 2.17).[46] The sketch helps to reconstruct the architect's thought process, while the marginal note provides information on how the plan diagram could be altered if additional privacy between houses was desired.

Wright's Quadruple Block Plan rejected the conventional oblong-shaped block and related means of subdivision into narrow, deep lots, lined up parallel to one another with the majority having only a single frontage plus access at the rear by means of an alley. In this he predicted strategies for reshaping the residential block later adopted by proponents of housing reform, especially those involved with the Garden City and Suburb movement.[47] In Wright's Quadruple Block Plan the city grid is maintained, but the block is made square and the alley eliminated. The generous, approximately four-acre tract was initially quartered to create four, equal, nearly one-acre corner lots, each having two frontages measuring two hundred feet. Each house was placed just in from the center of its lot, defined by the sidewalks and interior property lines (figure 2.18). The sidewalks establish a crucial datum concentric with the surrounding streets and integral to the coherence of the four separate residences. The cross-axial disposition of the intersecting wings of the T-shaped plan of the houses restates this outer boundary as a virtual interior square forming a communal garden.[48]

As can be more fully appreciated in the aerial perspective (figure 2.19), the internal square-within-a-square is demarcated by low parapet walls that extend from the outer reentrant angles of the wings of one house to the next, thereby connecting one to the other and masking the shared interior garden from the view of passersby. At the very center of this heavily treed compound, whose gardens are apparently undivided by hedges or walls, are four adjoining stables that pinwheel around the point where the property lines meet. These structures, at the very center of the block, are reached by driveways that parallel the houses' entrance walks and create, in the process, space for formal flower beds reaching out to the sidewalk. In concert with the stables, each house is rotated ninety degrees from the previous one, so that none of the main living spaces face in the same direction and each of the four houses has an exclusive street entrance as well as privacy from its immediate neighbors across the internal communal space.

The marginal note on the sketch explains how increased privacy might be achieved. "If greater privacy as a whole were desired," Wright wrote, "the dwellings would move toward the street corners [thereby] enclosing more ground for strictly private uses. The extreme of privacy would be secured by setting the outer walls of [the] houses (exactly) on the street corner [and] training all the principal rooms to the inner ground. A wall would then be built on the inner line of the sidewalk treating the street front in [a] perfectly formal manner—more

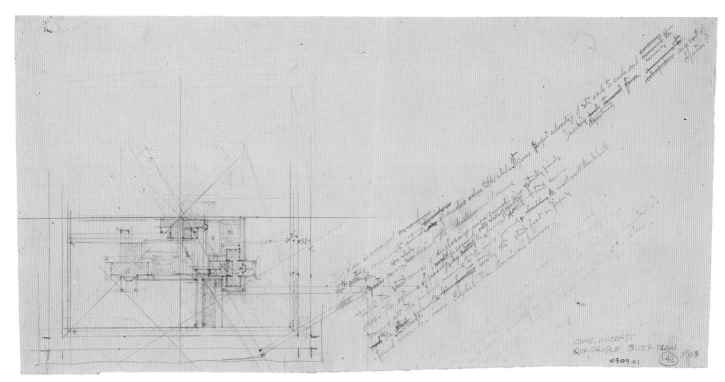

2.17

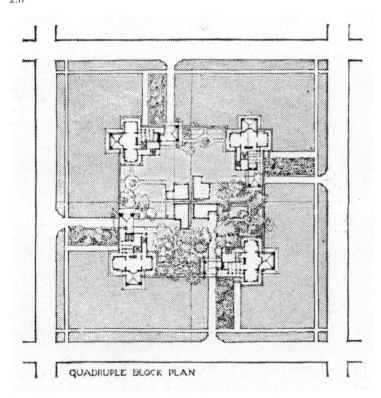

QUADRUPLE BLOCK PLAN

2.18

2.17. "Home in a Prairie Town." Quadruple Block Plan. Preliminary sketch plan, post-dated 1903

2.18. "Home in a Prairie Town." Quadruple Block Plan. Detail of plan

2.19

English than American however." Wright clearly preferred the more even distribution of open and closed, public and private space in the plan as finally drawn and did not see fit even to illustrate what the other possibilities might look like.[49]

On an abstract level, the Quadruple Block Plan is all about framing and quartering, center and periphery, nucleus and edge. The outer square is divided into four smaller squares that in turn allocate one-quarter of their surface area to create the internal square. The movement from center to periphery and the interchange between nucleus and edge are given visual definition by the rotation around the central square. If we focus on the dynamic aspect of the pinwheeling, the plan reads, as might be expected, from the inside out. But when we focus on the underlying and predominant quartering and framing, we are encouraged to read the plan from the periphery to the center, which is precisely how Wright pictured it in the aerial perspective. There, the purpose and meaning of the project become clearer. Each concentric square denotes a degree of movement inward from the public to the private/communal. Within the outer perimeter of the four streets, the sidewalks frame an expanse of lawn that foregrounds the group of houses whose shared walls in turn frame an inner compound fully visible to the inhabitants alone. In providing a sense of shared community through the creation of a common rear garden, the inner court's dense foliage also helps to screen one neighbor from the next while masking the back-to-back stables.

There is hardly a remnant of picturesque planning here. The rectilinearity of the city grid is not only fully acknowledged; it is reified in the enclosed central garden. The street becomes as much a defining edge of the residential block as it was in the buildings then going up in the Loop. If one thinks in terms of a distinction between nature and culture, in which the former is the sign of the suburb and the latter that of the city, as Olmsted might have described it, then Wright's Quadruple Block Plan is clearly a deliberately cultural construct. Designed as a release from and antidote to the "commercial condition" and "distractions of the busy city,"

it becomes its true extension and counterpart through a process of inversion. Where the typical, foursquare, downtown commercial block would surround and open onto a central court or atrium, here the opposite occurs. The central mass of trees contained by the walled precinct of houses is surrounded by the air, space, and greenery of the front lawns and sidewalks. Wright's own design of 1901 for the Lexington Terraces apartments in Chicago provides confirmation of his thinking in these terms (figure 1.19). Two solid-looking perimeter blocks with open central courts combine to create a dense urban fabric tight up to the street yet aerated and light-filled at the core.[50] As the obverse of the downtown urban model, the Quadruple Block Plan maintains an analogous though attenuated adherence to the continuity of the metropolitan grid.[51]

Historical Dimensions of the Quadruple Block Plan

Wright's Quadruple Block Plan lay entirely outside the framework of the responses of the other participants in the *Ladies' Home Journal* series in (1) its presupposition of the necessity for a new type of subdivision of suburban land prior to the designing of any individual house; (2) the type of geometric subdivision it proposed; and (3) the direct impact the ramifications of this geometry had on the consequent house design itself. In all these regards, the Quadruple Block Plan represents a radical solution for suburban development that fully acknowledged the broader implications of the suburban/ urban dialectic. While unprecedented in appearance, the scheme derived logically and organically from the architect's 1896 development plan for Roberts (figure 1.33). The eccentric corner lots and central open space of the earlier design were condensed and imbricated in the *Ladies' Home Journal* scheme to create a new kind of residential space resonating with the urban grid while hearkening back to its ideal, "enlightened" geometric form in the 1785 Land Ordinance (figures 1.10–11).

If the repetitive rectangular units resulting from the orthogonal crisscrossing of lines, with no logical or natural end

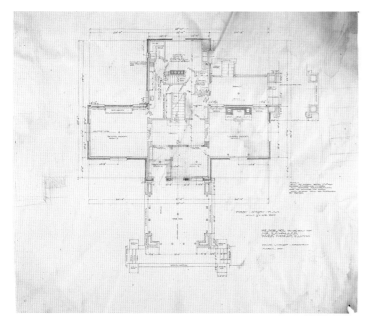

2.20

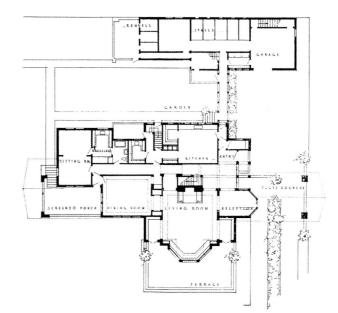

2.22

2.21

2.23

2.19. "Home in a Prairie Town." Quadruple Block Plan. Detail of aerial perspective

2.20. Eckhart House project, River Forest, Wright, 1898. Plan, first floor, March 1898

2.21. Eckhart House project. Elevations, March 1898

2.22. Bradley House, Kankakee, Ill., Wright, 1900–1901. Plan, redrawn ca. 1940. From Hitchcock, *In the Nature of Materials*

2.23. Bradley House. Exterior. Private collection

in sight, is presumably what gave the typical urban grid its mechanical, monotonous, and boring character to many, the square of the modular unit of graph paper can be said to epitomize such a lack of interest or variety. To adopt the square and make it anything other than static was the challenge Wright embraced. The conceptual sketch for the Quadruple Block Plan reveals the intensity with which he approached the problem. It also reveals the interconnected operations of intersecting axes and rotational devices that he employed to give the basic square geometry an unexpected dynamism. The purpose, however, was not merely formal. It was to resolve the tension between the public and the private that lay at the heart of the suburban condition, and which most scholars agree was one of the most important achievements of the Prairie House as it developed over the following decade. The cross-axial articulation of the individual house plans and their pinwheeling, rotational relationship to one another created the connections allowing for both a sense of openness to the street and an unusual degree of separation at the same time. At the heart of the shared communal space were the back-to-back stables that generated the pinwheeling action while providing the fulcrum for each family's private means of transportation throughout the city.

It was through working with the square grid that Wright developed the concept of the Prairie House. The Prairie House should therefore be viewed as epiphenomenal, an effect of the subdivisional techniques of the Quadruple Block Plan. Its typically dynamic, free-flowing, interpenetrating volumes derive from the group plan's cross-axial lines and pinwheeling movement. This perception not only tells us much about Wright's interest in design at the urban scale, but also helps to clarify the history of the architect's use of the techniques of intersecting axes and rotational devices to activate his spaces. Beginning with Hitchcock, scholars have wanted to see the origin of the cross-axial plan—with its "plaiding of interior space" and "composition of inter-penetrating" volumes—in the River Forest Golf Club of 1898.[52] But that structure, as originally designed, was a simple, single volume; it was only in the additions made to it in 1901 that a cross-axiality emerged.[53] A more likely candidate for the origin of Wright's interest in the idea would be his 1898 project for a house for Edward Waller's daughter Rebecca Eckhart (figures 2.20–21). The biaxial symmetry, central stairway, off-axis fireplace, and overall spatial discontinuity combined with the block-like

massing of the exterior, however, reveal the design to be a very conventional interpretation of the concept.[54] It was only in 1900, around the time Wright began planning his first *Ladies' Home Journal* contribution, that cross-axiality would explicitly emerge as a means for activating the interior space of the house in a way that is recognizably and characteristically that of the mature Prairie House.

The cross-axial plan of "A Home in a Prairie Town" takes the shape of a T (figure 2.16). The hall and kitchen occupy the stem, and the interconnected spaces of the dining room, living room, and library, jointed to the stem at the fireplace, form the top bar. The cross-axis implied by the bay window of the central living room is made explicit through the extension of the front porch, while the terraces off the library and dining room expand the space in a lateral sense. Unlike the rather straightforward entrance sequence in the Waller/Eckhart House project, access from the front walk takes a circuitous route that emphasizes the overlapping and sliding aspects of the cross-axial concept. The only other plan comparable to the first *Ladies' Home Journal* design, and which may have preceded it, is that of the Bradley House in Kankakee, Illinois, drawn in June 1900 for Charles Roberts's wife's sister and brother-in-law (figure 2.22). "A Home in a Prairie Town" significantly expanded the cross-axial space, still quite stunted in the Bradley House, to develop its full potential along both major axes.

The Bradley House probably also served as the model for the exterior treatment of the gable-roofed "Small House with 'Lots of Room in It'" (figures 2.23–24). Wright explained his choice of the roof type in the opening sentence of his text accompanying the project. "The average home-maker," he wrote, "is partial to the gable roof." But to put to rest any thought that such a conventional motif was pandering, Wright added that "this house has been designed with a thorough, somewhat new treatment of the gable with gently flaring eaves and pediments, slightly lifted at the peaks, accentuating the perspective, slightly modeling the roof surfaces and making the outlines 'crisp.'"[55] Still, if the second *Ladies' Home Journal* design is to be read as a regression from the first in terms of traditional appearance, as many scholars have suggested, the same can hardly be said about its plan. It took the rotational movement only explicit in the overall Quadruple Block Plan and applied it, for the first time, to the house itself (figure 2.25).[56] The four spaces of entry hall, living room, dining room, and kitchen pinwheel around the vertical axis of the central fireplace. It

A Small House with "Lots of Room in It"

By Frank Lloyd Wright

NINTH DESIGN IN THE JOURNAL'S NEW SERIES OF MODEL SUBURBAN HOUSES AT MODERATE COST

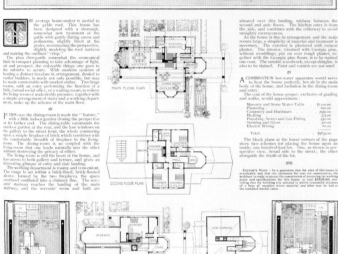

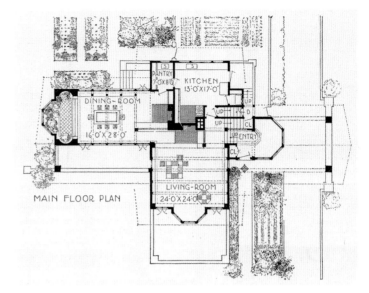

2.25

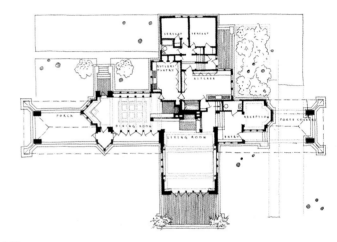

2.24

2.26

2.24. "A Small House with 'Lots of Room in It,'" Wright. From, "New Series," *LHJ*, July 1901

2.25. "A Small House with 'Lots of Room in It.'" Detail of plan

2.26. Willits House, Highland Park, Ill., Wright, 1902–3. Plan, redrawn ca. 1940. From Hitchcock, *In the Nature of Materials*

is the plan that would reappear almost two years later in the Willits House that would symbolize for many the advent of the mature Prairie House (figure 2.26).[57] Like the fully developed idea of cross-axiality, the pinwheel plan represents a condensation of a larger urban concept and a scaling down of the geometrical form initially developed in the first *Ladies' Home Journal* project to impart an interconnectivity and dynamism to a residential community.

The Idealism of the Quadruple Block Plan

The Quadruple Block Plan is the single critical invention of the architect's early years. Out of it grew the Prairie House and the spatial dynamism that characterizes the architect's work after the turn of the new century. As a proposal for suburban development, it offered a radical alternative to the picturesque model, consistent with the urban grid and, as we will see, eminently adaptable to the City Beautiful model. It replaced the easy picturesqueness of Riverside with a new type of individualism and variety derived from the spatial manipulation of the abstract elements of plan and elevation. Perhaps most important, it established a framework for a modern form of residential community situated halfway between the dense urban core and the rural hinterland.

Rejecting the speculative efficacy of the rectangular subdivision of the 1785 Land Survey's square grid, the Quadruple Block Plan returned to its originary geometric form to define an ideal space for the intersection of community and privacy, of the individual and the group. Where the other architects who contributed to the *Ladies' Home Journal* series of "Model Suburban Houses" chose to limit themselves mainly to issues of style, natural setting, and cost, Wright began with the more fundamental question of land use and subdivision. Tackling an issue that would not become part of the conventional planner's mind-set for at least a decade, if not more, he defined the ground of his "Home in a Prairie Town" as a series of spatial coordinates.[58] The "prairie" established "a quiet level," as he put it, an abstract spatial condition. The Quadruple Block Plan in turn offered a form of subdivision that identified real estate not with a retreat or escape into a domesticated nature but with the broader American cultural construct of the myth of unbounded, continuous space.

The unprecedented, fundamentally idealistic character of the Quadruple Block Plan made it difficult for historians and critics through the 1980s to give it the serious consideration it deserves. Donald Leslie Johnson, a student of both Wright's and Walter Burley Griffin's community planning, called the Quadruple Block Plan "undistinguished" and Wright's "efforts in community planning … at best, naive."[59] Gwendolyn Wright, a student of modern American domestic architecture and planning, described the project as more pattern making than community planning, revealing a "conception of urbanity" that was "somewhat narrow and artificial." "Insisting on the need for land and privacy" in a way that was "to become characteristic of middle-class suburbia," the Quadruple Block Plan, in her view, ended up "offering neither independence nor community."[60] The art historian Norris Kelly Smith fundamentally dismissed the plan for not being "a practical one at all"; and Robert Twombly followed suit in calling the project "unrealistic," noting that it "made little sense to real estate agents eager to reduce lot size in rapidly expanding suburbs."[61]

There were some early on, like Grant Carpenter Manson, who saw the project differently and valued it for attempting to place "a maximum number of individual dwellings on an average city block with maximum light and greenery."[62] But it is only since the 1990s that closer attention has been paid to the historical and social significance of the project. David De Long, for instance, characterized the plan as the first example of Wright's "urban-scaled projects" and remarked on the "dynamic unity [that] was achieved there by connecting four separate dwellings through a pinwheel of extended garden walls."[63] Robert McCarter lauded the "paradoxical increase in both density and privacy" along with the "suggestion of multiple spatial and geometrical relationships between the houses … [that] presents the richness and complexity of urban social relations."[64] And Gwendolyn Wright reconsidered her earlier critique to note, in a later commentary, that "the four dwellings formed a cohesive compound" with "abundant land and autonomy for each household, even within the collective enterprise."[65]

But to judge the Quadruple Block Plan in terms of its practicality or efficacy as a realistic solution to suburban land use seems to miss the point of Wright's project, which, as he said, "begins at the beginning." The Quadruple Block Plan was an idealistic reaction to the early stages of suburban development brought on by the advent of the railroad and streetcar and the proliferation of the private horse-drawn carriage. Like other utopian projects such as Claude-Nicolas Ledoux's Ideal City of Chaux (1804), Ebenezer Howard's Garden City (1898; figure 3.31), and Le Corbusier's Contemporary City of Three Million Inhabitants (1922; figure 6.16), it was a *design* on the future, a schema of potentiality. And although it was much smaller and more restricted in scope than the three other utopias just mentioned, it was scalable to the extent, as we will see in the following two chapters, that it could embrace much larger sections of the city fabric than merely a single block. But the single block was the germ of the idea. And as the germ, it contained the basic DNA of the utopian ideal.

In one of the most perceptive essays yet written on the grid as a structuring device, the art historian and critic Rosalind Krauss described the grid in the work of artists and architects as diverse as Piet Mondrian, Agnes Martin, and Wright as a rational, scientific, objective surface masking deeper-seated illusionistic, ideologically charged, and subjective motivations and expressions. She ascribed to the grid a power assimilable to myth. "The grid's mythic power," she wrote, "is that it makes us able to think we are dealing with materialism (or sometimes science, or logic) while at the same time it provides us with a release into belief (or illusion, or fiction)."[66] The explicit rationality of the orthogonal geometry of the Quadruple Block Plan, no less than that of the squared graph paper in the 1896 Roberts development plan, would seem to call for an analysis and judgment on practical and objective terms, yet that is precisely what Krauss's argument and Wright's designs warn us to forego—and, rather, to look beneath the surface for a more ideologically charged expression of belief.

The question then is this: why did Wright reject the conventional subdivision of the square quarter section into rectangular blocks and lots and, against all real estate sense, propose the square itself as the geometric basis for both? There are precedents in American urbanism, such as certain Mormon towns of the mid-nineteenth century, but these are exceptional.[67] One can also refer, as is commonly done, to the architect's early exposure to Froebel training, which could in turn lead to a more abstract, essentializing line of reasoning focusing on Wright's fascination with geometry in general and the square in particular. I would prefer, however, to see Wright's regression to the originary platted square in historically modern terms—perhaps as a form of regionalism, perhaps as a form of purism—but certainly as a deliberate search for something ideal rather than merely instrumental.

The six-mile-square township grid of the original Land Survey reduced in scale even to a four-acre tract had embedded in it the property-based, egalitarian-inspired, democratic impulse of its Jeffersonian model. The Quadruple Block Plan of four such houses thus became for Wright a synecdoche for the township or section itself. The image of four houses pinwheeling around a central block of stables within a larger square recalls the idealizing illustration of square townships in Cutler's early map (figure 1.11). In Wright's plan the square also defines a space for community, while at the same time giving to each of the suburban homeowners a sense of privacy and control over the view. That view and that space virtually extended from the core of the Loop to where the metropolis dissolved into the countryside.

Wright's recuperation of the Enlightenment grid was not a static one. Its rendering bore significant traces of the time during which that grid was implemented, which is to say the period in American history between the taming of the wilderness and the closing of the frontier announced by Frederick Jackson Turner in a celebrated lecture in Chicago during the World's Columbian Exposition, just a little more than seven years prior to the presentation of the Quadruple Block Plan in the pages of the *Ladies' Home Journal*.[68] As revealed in the aerial perspective of the plan, the distinction between individual and community, between outside and inside, is literally rendered as the cityscape-as-closed-frontier, with the former wilderness now contained within as an urban garden. In this way, the individual homeowner is made to sense the dual power of the grid—as an idea for the creation of a condition of privacy within community—and as a daily reminder of the utopian meaning of democratic egalitarianism with which the grid was imbued by its Enlightenment creators.

THREE

There is no evidence in the pages of the *Ladies' Home Journal* following the publication of "A Home in a Prairie Town" that the Quadruple Block Plan had any effect on the way the magazine's editor or readers thought the American suburb should be designed. Public awareness of and reaction to the project in general was hardly any greater. An article that appeared in the *Chicago Evening Post* in July 1901, reprinted the following week in the *Oak Park Reporter*, is the only known mention of the publication. It is significant not just for that fact alone but also because it claimed that the project was to become a reality in the very near future.

Under the headline "New Idea for Suburbs," the story stated that "eight houses will be built in two blocks on plans outlined in a Philadelphia publication by Frank Lloyd Wright of Oak Park." Double the size of the *Journal* scheme, the two groups of four houses each were to be situated north of Chicago Avenue and west of Oak Park Avenue. This would place the pair in block 7 of the Austin, Morey, and Slentz Subdivision, across Chicago Avenue from Wright's own house and two blocks east of it, in an area that had not seen much development up until then (figure 1.15).[1] It was estimated that each house, like the published "Home in a Prairie Town," was to cost between six and seven thousand dollars.[2]

The article called the plan "ideal" and stated that its "object [was] to establish a community where everything will be in harmony and where nothing offensive to the eye shall exist." Noting that "Mr. Wright believes the suburban resident spends too much on his house and too little on his ground," it stressed the importance of the whole over the parts by referring to the project variously as a "community," a "colony," and a "settlement."[3] "The community will be…

a settlement of people desirous of living in the country and in homes that are not an insult to the aesthetic senses." Emphasizing that the architect wanted the completed project to prove above all the feasibility of his concept and thus to serve as "a model" for future planning, it asserted that "the colony in Oak Park will be established" by Wright in order "to show that his ideas are practical."[4]

How real the project was is difficult to say. The article stated that "money sufficient to carry out the plan has been obtained," but we are not told anything more about who the client or clients were (Charles Roberts is an obvious candidate). There is even a suggestion that Wright himself was involved in putting the financial package together and was interested in receiving financial backing. Whatever the case, the story ended on a note of secrecy: "Mr. Wright said to-day that he was not ready to let the public into his scheme, and intimated that when his plans materialized residents of Oak Park and Chicago would be treated to an architectural surprise." It reported, however, that "work will begin in a few days" and that "before fall [that is, in a couple of months] the houses will be ready to be occupied." More cautiously, it added that "Mr. Wright does not expect to have the grounds in correct condition before next spring, when the full beauty of a whole neighborhood built on one artistic plan will be unfolded to all who care to visit Oak Park." To dismiss any thought of local opposition, the article ended by saying that the "residents of Oak Park are pleased with the prospect, for Mr. Wright is held in high esteem by his neighbors."[5]

The article was fairly unspecific in terms of its description of the design, which may either have been a result of Wright's unwillingness to give too much away before work was to begin or of the speculative nature of the project. No doubt relying on the architect for whatever information he felt at liberty to disclose, the reporter began the description by quoting the second, and crucial, paragraph from the *Ladies' Home Journal* text: "'It seems a waste of energy to plan a house haphazard—to hit or miss an already distorted condition—so this partial solution of a city man's country home on the prairie begins at the beginning and assumes four houses to the block 400 feet square as the minimum of ground for the basis of his prairie community.'" The article then went on to quote the phrase about the group design ensuring "'breadth and prospect to the community as a whole and absolute privacy both as regards each to the community and each to each of the four'" before noting a few more specific details of the plan for Oak Park. These included the facts that "parkways will take the place of streets" and that "there will be no alleys in this neighborhood" nor "the discouraging prospect presented by the usual backyard."[6] Fences "will be elminated" and "the wash-tubs and clothes' line which the high board fence is [normally] expected to shield from public view … will be safely stowed away in niches to be built in the basements."[7]

No drawings for this project have been identified, although its double Quadruple Block Plan directly parallels the composition he proposed at more or less the same time for the Lexington Terraces apartments, where a planted walkway, called an "open court," separates the two blocks of living units (figure 1.19). Neither the Chicago apartments nor the scheme for the eight-house "colony" in Oak Park was built. Wright himself never referred to the latter again. Around the same time as he was preparing it, however, he received an inquiry from a developer in Indianapolis who had read the first of the two *Ladies' Home Journal* articles and was interested in knowing more about "the new principle … of subdivision."[8] Nothing came of this either. Undaunted, Wright continued to publicize his idea for abandoning "the stupid system in present vogue" for "subdividing property" that was "founded unthink[ing]ly upon mere *habit*."[9] In the early spring of 1902, when the Oak Park houses were supposed to have been finished, Wright had a mini-retrospective at the Art Institute of Chicago. Within the context of the annual exhibition of the Chicago Architectural Club, he was given an entire gallery to himself as well as a special section in the *Chicago Architectural Annual* that served as an illustrated catalogue of the exhibition.[10] The fifteen-page insert devoted to "The Work of Frank

Lloyd Wright" opened with the two *Ladies' Home Journal* "modern [not model] suburban houses."[11]

The caption describing the "Home in a Prairie Town" said almost nothing about the house itself and was almost entirely devoted to the group plan (figure 3.1). Of "the fifth design in the Ladies' Home Journal series of modern suburban houses," it was stated, "the Quadruple Block Plan and view at bottom of the page shows an arrangement of the houses that gives privacy to each householder securing at the same time a breadth of treatment for the whole that brings many advantages over the present system of subdividing a similar block." Only in the final sentence was it mentioned that "the larger plan at the center of the page shows the detailed arrangement of the plan used as the basis of the group."[12]

The Roberts Block Development Plan Revised According to the Quadruple Block Plan

The closest Wright ever came to seeing the Quadruple Block Plan realized was the following year, when he adapted it to the block for which Roberts had originally commissioned the 1896 scheme. The set of plans for the C. E. Roberts Community Project for Twenty-Four Dwellings, as the highly finished presentation drawings were titled, are dated 1903, although it is known that the project carried on into the following year at least (figures 3.2–4).[13] If a definite terminus ad quem can be established by the fact that Roberts sold the entire block to Joseph Winterbotham in mid-August 1906, it remains unclear precisely when Wright actually began revising the 1896 design.[14] Given Wright's closeness to the client and the frequent interactions between the two, the project may well have been an ongoing affair.

One piece of evidence supporting an earlier date for the revised Roberts scheme is the account given of the origins of the project by Grant Carpenter Manson in his *Frank Lloyd Wright to 1910: The First Golden Age* (1958). Manson, who interviewed Wright, states that the idea of building the Quadruple Block Plan in Oak Park "seems to have originated in the first year of the century as a housing project for Charles E. Roberts, to be erected on a tract of land in Oak Park south of Chicago Avenue and east of Fair Oaks." The reason it was not built at that time, Manson added, was that "it was stopped by the citizens of that area of the town, who objected to it as too radical." Manson (or Wright) may well have been confusing the project in question

THE FIFTH DESIGN IN THE LADIES' HOME JOURNAL SERIES OF MODERN SUBURBAN HOUSES. THE QUADRUPLE BLOCK PLAN AND VIEW AT BOTTOM OF THE PAGE SHOWS AN ARRANGEMENT OF THE HOUSES THAT GIVES PRIVACY TO EACH HOUSEHOLDER, SECURING AT THE SAME TIME A BREADTH OF TREATMENT FOR THE WHOLE THAT BRINGS MANY ADVANTAGES OVER THE PRESENT SYSTEM OF SUBDIVIDING A SIMILAR BLOCK. THE LARGER PLAN AT THE CENTER OF THE PAGE SHOWS THE DETAILED ARRANGEMENT OF THE PLAN USED AS THE BASIS FOR THE GROUP. ▫ ▫ ▫

3.1

3.1. "A Home in a Prairie Town." From "The Work of Frank Lloyd Wright," *Chicago Architectural Annual*, 1902 (catalogue of Fifteenth Annual Exhibition)

with the one announced in the press in July 1901, or even with the earlier 1896 scheme.[15] Still, the account points to the likelihood of recurring discussions.

Further justification for a date earlier than 1903 for the inception of the revision of the Roberts block plan is the letter Wright wrote to the Indianapolis developer S. T. Kendall in September 1901 in response to the latter's request for more information about the "new principle ... of subdivision" outlined in the *Ladies' Home Journal*. Without having "more definite data" about the property owned by Kendall, Wright responded that all he could do was to explain his concept by describing his current project for Roberts. "We are now planning," he wrote, "a system of twenty-four houses to be built at Oak Park, Ill., for Mr. C. E. Roberts on the new principle and have mastered the petty details of subdivision that have arisen." Elaborating further on the program and how it varied from the one for "A Home in a Prairie Town," Wright noted that "these houses [for Roberts] are to cater to the demand for houses to rent at $35.00 per month. The houses are costing $3500.00 each complete." "The germ plan is of course much smaller than the germ plan given in the Journal," he added. "It is different also in many ways [although] the houses are alike except in the matter of color and minor details."[16]

Following these specifics about the new Roberts project, Wright went on to a more general discussion of how one might fine-tune the group planning scheme and what that could achieve. First, he assured Kendall that despite the minimal cost of the houses being designed for Roberts, the Quadruple Block Plan lent itself to residences in every price range: "The houses might range from $3500.00 to almost any sum according to the class you would aim to care for." Yet the plan allowed for certain modern economies of scale: "The houses might be economically heated from a central plant and many economies of construction are possible when handling the houses in groups in this way." The psychological and aesthetic factors noted in the *Journal* text remained critical in his view: "The general aspect of the entire community is free and open without undesirable exposure [and] with more complete privacy in fact than could be had otherwise, owing to the rear court yards and the feature of the single entrance at each side of the block." Wright described the houses as "turn[ing] back to back like soldiers in a hollow square, presenting always the living rooms to the most desirable vistas, and the kitchens and working department countering one on the other." He ended his summary of the scheme by noting that "very little intelligent work has been done in subdividing property, and the architect has been at a disadvantage from the start as he is presented with a fixed condition founded unthink[ing]ly upon mere <u>habit</u>." Like someone totally convinced of an idea nearly to the point of obsession, he declared that "it is inconceivable that the stupid system in present vogue should continue when a precedent of this sort has been established." "The advantages," while they may seem merely "theoretical" at present, were "many" and will, he was convinced, "increase with the work in practice."[17]

Based on this letter, one can conclude that by the late summer or early fall of 1901 Wright was already back at work on a plan for the Roberts block and that this initiative had superseded the double-block, eight-house scheme announced earlier in the summer. In any event, it is clear that the two projects for Oak Park represent ever-diminishing adaptations of the ideal *Ladies' Home Journal* scheme to real site conditions. The lots of "A Home in a Prairie Town" were two hundred feet square each, those in the first Oak Park project would have been no more than one hundred forty feet square, whereas those in the 1903–4 Roberts block scheme were barely eighty feet to a side. Perhaps even more interesting is that at this early, otherwise undocumented stage of the Roberts project, the houses were to be built as rental units rather than offered for sale. Instead of the projected construction cost being somewhere between six and seven thousand dollars per house, as it was for the "Home in a Prairie Town" and the eight-house two-block Oak Park scheme, the Roberts rental houses were to cost only thirty-five hundred dollars, a rather modest price at the time and one in keeping with the cost of those built following Roberts's sale of the tract in 1906.[18]

It is not clear why the 1901 rental scheme came to a halt. Perhaps this was the project Manson was referring to when he said that "it was stopped by the citizens of that area of the town." In any event, by 1903, when the revised plans for the Roberts block were drawn up, the village of Ridgeland had become part of Oak Park and Oak Park itself was in the throes of a major development and expansion with Chicago Avenue serving as a key artery. In 1901, the year before it annexed Ridgeland, Oak Park, which had previously been attached to the township of Cicero, became an independent village. It established its own fire, police, and public works departments in January 1902. Over the next couple of years, streets were

paved, water was supplied to areas previously without, and electric street lighting was installed. By early 1904, street paving and water had come within a block of the Roberts tract.[19] Wright's new "community plan" for Roberts fully exploited the prospect for growth in the newly incorporated eastern section of the streetcar suburb. Instead of the original nineteen lots platted in 1872, which he had increased to twenty-two in 1896 (figures 1.15, 1.33), the plan now was for twenty-four houses, four more than were actually constructed when the block was resubdivided in 1906 and built out over the following few years. As a consequence of this densification, the size of each lot was reduced quite considerably.

There are seven drawings for the final 1903–4 Roberts development plan in the Wright Foundation Archives plus a number of others that were developed either at the same time or shortly thereafter for the same and different sites.[20] Three of the seven are the presentation drawings already referred to (figures 3.2–4). No doubt sensing a determination on his client's part to see the project through, Wright had them done in ink on linen and detailed down to a thirty-second of an inch. The up-to-dateness of the resubdivision concept is graphically highlighted on the sheet of elevations where the letter C in the client's name in the legend block is represented as the handset of a telephone (figure 3.3) and, on the sheet with the partial site plan and sections (figure 3.2), where the north-south arrow is depicted in the form of one of the new electric street lamps. In addition to the presentation drawings are a study for the partial site plan in figure 3.2 (figure 3.6), two sketch perspectives at street level (figure 3.7), and a sketch plan of an individual house (figure 3.8).[21] A half-block plan plus a house plan template used in rendering it were most likely done shortly after the project was completed and can be considered part of its graphic representation (figures 3.9, 3.11). The partial plan in figure 3.2 shows one group of four houses, whereas the slightly later, idealized plan of the upper, or northern, half of the block in figure 3.9 shows twelve of the twenty-four houses.

It is not known whether the houses in this final version of the Roberts block scheme were to be built as rental units or for sale.[22] In comparison with the *Ladies' Home Journal* Quadruple Block Plan, each individual house lot was reduced from nearly an acre to a little more than a sixth of an acre, and the stables in the center of the block were eliminated. The individual houses are all identical. Their design represents the architect's most advanced thinking up until that point in his career. To

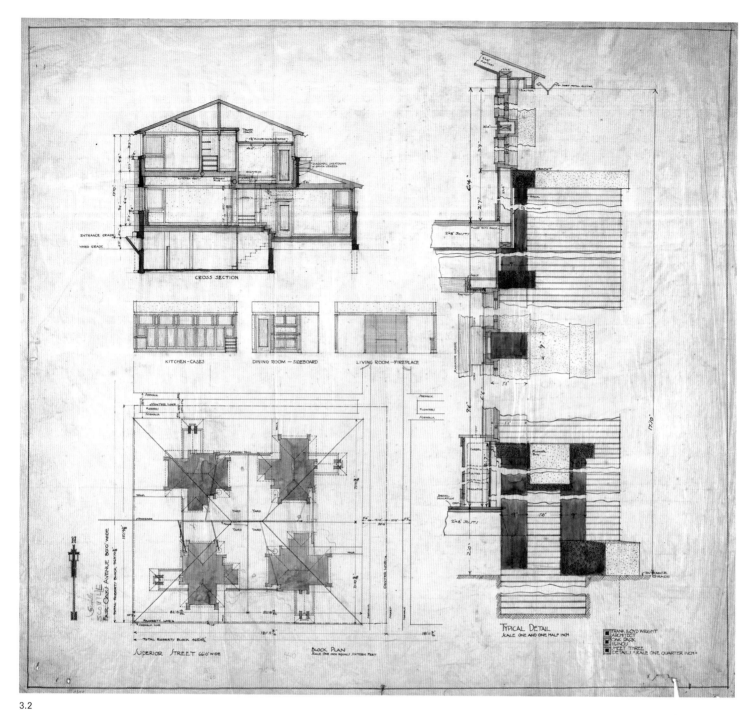

3.2

3.2. Second Roberts block project (C. E. Roberts Community Project for Twenty-Four Dwellings), Oak Park, Wright, 1903–4. Partial block plan, sections, and interior elevations

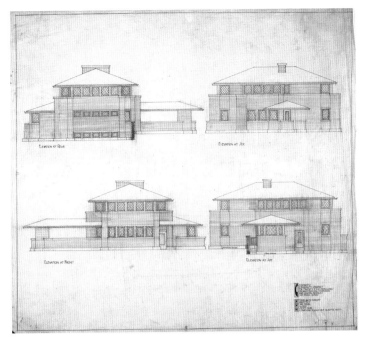

3.3

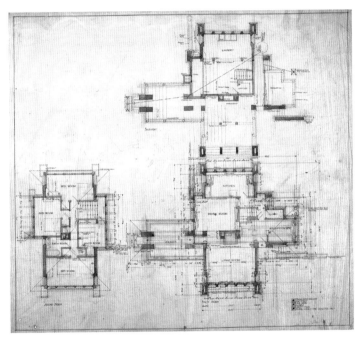

3.4

3.3. Second Roberts block project. House elevations

3.4. Second Roberts block project. House plans

be constructed of exposed brick rather than framed in wood and finished in cement plaster, the houses differed radically in appearance from the "Home in a Prairie Town." Their chunky plasticity, brought out by the structural articulation of deeply cut solids and voids, results from a disaggregation and abstraction of architectural elements that bears comparison with the early stages of Cubist art in Europe (figure 3.3). Their design predicts, in this regard, the Martin House and Larkin Building in Buffalo, both of which were completed in 1906 based on designs worked out in 1904.[23] But more than simply updating the form of the standardized Prairie House unit, Wright was mainly concerned with how the grouped houses would relate to one another in such a compact situation and, especially, how pedestrian and vehicular circulation would work.

The plan of the house is as advanced and inventive as the elevations (figure 3.4). A deep horizontal volume perpendicular to the street from which the house is entered contains the living room on the ground floor and master bedroom above, following the example of the Willits House (figure 2.26) and foreshadowing the 1909 Gale House in Oak Park. A freestanding fireplace, marking the center of the house lot, divides the living room from the dining room, which opens on one side into the reception hall and on the other into a bay partially contained within a sheltered veranda. The kitchen at the rear, facing the central shared garden, has its own side entrance linked to the reception hall. The latter defines a strong cross-axis that slides behind the fireplace mass to extend beyond the dining room into the projecting veranda. This indoor-outdoor space in turn overlaps the living room to provide a rotational dynamic that joins one house to the next in a tight, pinwheeling fashion. The pinwheeling was meant to take care of privacy issues and sight lines.

To give each group of four houses a sense of interconnectedness and seclusion from the public way while at the same time maintaining a continuity with the metropolitan grid, the level of the interior gardens, defined by the parapet wall connecting each of the four houses to the others, was depressed nearly two feet below grade.[24] (This can be seen in the upper-left and lower-right elevations in figure 3.3.) And to provide for circulation through the site given the fact that a number of the houses had no frontage, Wright broke the block down into six miniblocks separated from one another either by pedestrian ways called "esplanades" or by vehicular passages called "courts." Instead of a single multipurpose alley,

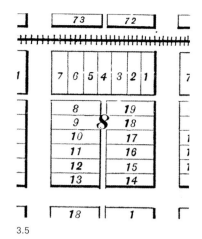

3.5

there was now a finer mesh of different types of passageways offering both greater openness as well as a sense of scale more attuned to the size of the residential units themselves.

While it is significant that, as with the original *Ladies' Home Journal* design, Wright made the Quadruple Block Plan the vehicle for his most advanced architectural thinking, it is even more important to realize how the design of the individual house in the revised Roberts scheme was developed in consequence of and in relation to the group plan as a whole. Most of the architect's time clearly went into the question of site planning. The problem began with one of dimensions. The Roberts block did not lend itself to simple divisions into squares. Each house lot, as shown in the partial site plan of the presentation drawing, measures a little less than seventy-two feet by eighty-two and a half feet (figure 3.2).[25] The divergence from the square is noticeable, at least on the two-dimensional plane of the drawing. At their widest dimensions, the houses were a little over sixty-two by forty-eight feet, which left much less room between one house and the next than in the earlier versions of the Quadruple Block Plan, and no room whatsoever for stables or garages. And since the houses were larger on average as well as more numerous than those in the earlier 1896 development plan, the greater ratio of built space to open space put increased pressure on the need to consider in detail, indeed down to a thirty-second of an inch, the relationship between public and private space and the means of access from one to the other.[26]

Wright's solution, initially, was to place the longer dimension of the house lots paralleling the shorter side of the block.[27] Three pairs of side-by-side Quadruple Block Plans, each measuring a little over 165 feet in breadth and a little under 144 feet in depth, ran from Scoville Avenue on the west to Elmwood on the east and from Superior on the south to Chicago on the north. Although he criticized the convention of the alley and nearly eliminated it completely in the 1896 project, here Wright was forced to retain a semblance of it in order to provide access to the houses whose entrance walks faced the interior of the block. The thirty-six-foot-wide "court," as he renamed the alley, cut between the two pairs of four houses from Superior Street to Chicago Avenue, while the two eighteen-foot-wide "esplanades" planted with flower beds intersected the court at right angles to join Scoville to Elmwood at third points of the block.

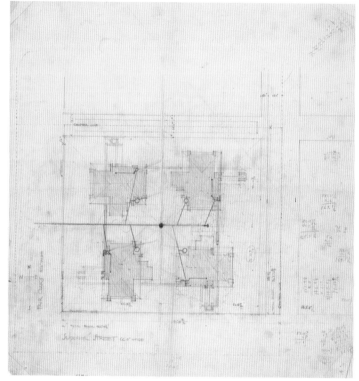

3.6

3.5. Oak Park and Ridgeland. Plat map, 1894. Detail showing block owned by Roberts between 1895 and 1906

3.6. Second Roberts block project. Partial block study plan with sewer lines overlaid

3.7

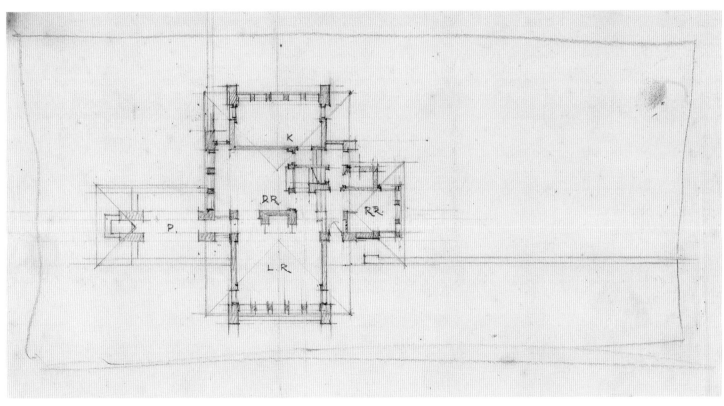

3.8

3.7. Second Roberts block project. Sketch perspective

3.8. Second Roberts block project. Sketch house plan

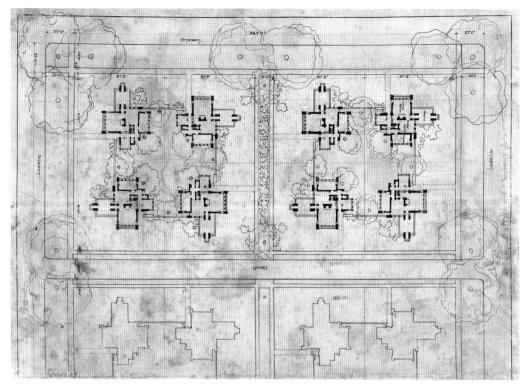

3.9

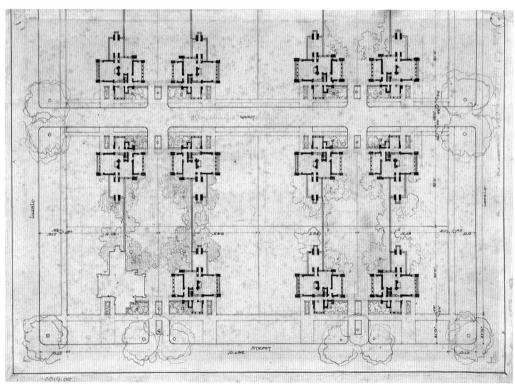

3.10

3.9. Second Roberts block project. Idealized half-block plan

3.10. Second Roberts block project modified. Alternate half-block plan on Roberts
block site

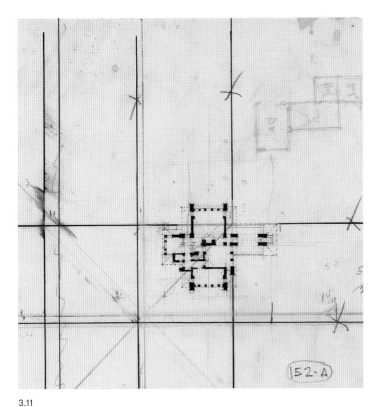

3.11

3.11. Second Roberts block project. House plan template, 1904

The idealized plan showing half the block gives a clearer idea of how this would have worked. Probably drafted shortly after the set of presentation drawings and done like them in ink on linen, though here highlighted with colored washes, this plan also shows Wright's attempt to square up the individual house lots as much as possible (figure 3.9).[28] To do this, he simply reversed the court and esplanades, so that the narrower, exclusively pedestrian passage ran north-south and the two wider private streets east-west. This also allowed the house lots to be increased in size to a near square measuring eighty-seven and a quarter feet wide by eighty-one feet deep. Placing the narrower circulation path on the north-south axis and limiting it to pedestrian movement served to distinguish it from the typically divisive central alley and thus give the block as a whole a greater sense of coherence. By contrast, the wider "courts" cutting through from east to west and providing access for vehicles as well as pedestrians worked to break down the scale of the block and ensure a greater degree of porousness both within and without. The low walls connecting the individual houses of each group of four plus the minimal interior divisions in their secluded central gardens gave to the smallest unit of the group a sense of "community" commensurate with that of the whole.

At the same time as Wright's office drew up the half-block plan with the narrow central pedestrian way and the two wider cross streets, it produced an alternate that departed quite radically from the Quadruple Block Plan concept developed over the previous three years (figure 3.10). For both versions, a tiny house plan drawn in ink on heavy paper, at the same scale as those on the half-block plans, no doubt served as a template to streamline the repetitive drafting process (figure 3.11). In the alternate half-bock plan, the houses no longer pinwheel, nor are they centered in their lots.[29] Instead, they are combined into distinct pairs that are brought up to the sidewalks along the east-west streets and courts. Rather than forming self-contained compounds in the middle of each block, the groups of four here form unities across the space of the internal private streets. Low walls linking the rear verandas of the houses run in a north-south direction to create long internal gardens that continue across the courts through sidewalk cuts and bedded plantings. An even more expansive lawn runs north-south down the center of the block, cut off from public access on both Superior Street and Chicago Avenue by a second low wall that appears to continue around the perimeter of the entire

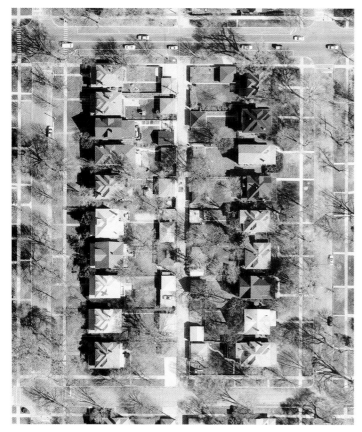

3.12

3.13

3.12. Block bounded by Chicago Avenue (top), Scoville Avenue (formerly Fair Oaks; left), Superior Street (bottom), and Elmwood Street (formerly Ogden; right), Oak Park, as built out in 1906–10. Aerial photograph, 2003

3.13. Scoville Avenue, looking north from Superior Street

block. Each house has a walkway entrance as well as what appears to be a driveway shared with its neighbor, which leads one to suspect that this alternate plan may have been an exercise to see how garages or stables could be accommodated on the site. Four back-to-back structures would easily fit into the walled spaces defined by the two pairs of neighboring houses, while the gardens protected by the outer walls would serve as areas for recreation.

While the alternate site plan is interesting on numerous counts, it is much more conventional in its placement of the houses themselves as well as more direct in its segregation of private from public space without, however, increasing the sense of "community." Based on statements by Marion Mahony Griffin (1871–1961), who along with her husband was employed in Wright's office at the time, it is more than likely that the alternate plan derived in part from Walter Burley Griffin's (1876–1937) input.[30] Wright, as we remember, suggested in the marginal note on his sketch for the *Ladies' Home Journal* project (figure 2.17) that to gain more privacy "the dwellings would move toward the street corners," with "the extreme of privacy" being "secured by setting the outer walls of [the] houses (exactly) on the street corner" and building a wall "on the inner line of the sidewalk." But in rejecting the diagonal movement outward contained in the earlier suggestion, the alternate plan for the Roberts block lost the sense of tension that underlay the interaction of the four houses in the Quadruple Block Plan concept.

Of the two options, Wright clearly preferred the one proposed in the presentation drawings. The reasons seem self-evident when one tries to imagine what the community might have actually looked like. One can get a good idea of this by comparing the perspective sketch of the Wright design with an aerial photograph of what happened to the block after Roberts sold off his holdings (figures 3.7, 3.12). The houses, built mainly between 1906 and 1910, are extremely close together and are exclusively oriented to the street; they turn their backs on one another and their sides to one another as well as to the two main cross streets. The unidimensional, linear pattern of the street facades explicitly denies the bidimensional character of the grid (figure 3.13). And the leftover spaces behind the houses, made up of deep yards butting up against an alley, reinforce the singular aspect of the street condition as a facade. The Roberts Quadruple Block Plan, by contrast, activates the entire space of the block in full recognition of the two-dimensional qualities of the grid in plan as well as its three-dimensional qualities as a latticework in space (figures 3.7, 3.9). It is nonhierarchical, evenly textured, and dynamic in its overall organization. Houses, gardens, and streets are interwoven in a pattern that moves through a graduated sequence of scales from the public to the private/communal, allowing the one to interpenetrate the other and to define the idea of community in dialectical terms—as a grouping of interconnected houses of like-minded neighbors and as a subdivision of the underlying grid.

Wright's Proliferation of the Quadruple Block Plan

Why the project was aborted remains a mystery. Financial issues may have played a part in Roberts's decision. Since Wright's plan called for four houses more than the existing plat, there may have been legal or administrative issues. Possibly most important was the fact that the plan entailed the need for new transverse streets for which someone would have had to pay. It is reasonable to assume that the village of Oak Park would not have welcomed the idea of creating and maintaining additional public ways; but neither the minutes of village meetings nor newspaper accounts suggest that discussions ever got to that point. In any event, whether the result of a further commission from Roberts or his own obsession with the possibility of realizing the Quadruple Block Plan, Wright continued to work on the scheme. Drawings for multiple versions of the idea adapted to different-sized blocks were produced beginning with the two idealized half plans for the Roberts block illustrated in figures 3.9 and 3.10. Seven of these, plus one related to them, are extant.[31] All were done by the same hand (or hands), on exactly the same kind of linen and with the same inks and watercolors as the two Roberts block half-plans. More important, all seven drawings of variations on the Quadruple Block Plan, of which two followed the alternate "Griffin" scheme, made use of the house plan template in figure 3.11 as a means to standardize the design process.[32]

The plans represent designs for blocks of the same width but of three different lengths (the width being almost precisely that of the Roberts block).[33] None of the locations are given, leading one to surmise that they may have been for type-blocks rather than specific sites. There is one plan for an almost square block, 435 feet long by 367 feet wide (figure 3.14).[34] Though close in size to the Roberts block, this one is divided into just

four groups of four houses, each with a court running the shorter way and an esplanade the longer way. Despite the fact that the house lots were increased in size to a little over 100 by 87 feet, there still are no garages or stables. The houses themselves are indicated only in outline. A second plan, for a block 685 feet long by 367 feet wide, was carried to approximately the same degree of finish (figure 3.15). It was to accommodate thirty-two houses with each lot measuring a little under 82 by 79 feet. This time the court ran the longer rather than the shorter dimension; once again, no garages were included.[35]

The final group of plans is also for a thirty-two-house development but for a block 750 feet long. In the most finished drawing of the group, the house lots are nearly square—approximately 87 by 81 feet—and the courts run in the short direction as in the actual project for the Roberts block (figure 3.16). The houses at one end are rendered at ground-floor level whereas those at the other are drawn at roof level. Only the latter Quadruple Block Plans have garages or stables. In order to provide access to two of the houses, the pedestrian esplanade dividing the block down its length was interrupted and replaced by a narrow mews. The standardization of the house type remained absolute, however, since no porte cocheres were added to these eight structures. A partial block plan, without any indication of garages, was produced for this same scheme (figure 3.17), as was one for the same size block and the same number of houses but arranged according to the alternate model of the redrawn Roberts plan (figure 3.18). This alternate design was also drawn showing the entire thirty-two-house development but with the wide court running the length rather than the width of the block.[36]

The one drawing related to the group but not based on the Quadruple Block Plan is also for a block 750 feet long by 367 feet wide (figure 3.19). While the drafting surface and techniques are exactly the same as the other drawings, this one takes a much more conventional approach to the issue of subdivision. Indeed, the plan accepts rather straightforwardly the commonplace system of back-to-back, narrow, deep lots facing opposite streets, divided by a central alley. There are thirty houses in all, fifteen to a street front. The lots are all 50 feet wide by nearly 175 feet deep. Only one side of the block has standardized Wright-type houses. They are appropriately oblong in plan and are almost identical to the Barton House, built on the Martin property in Buffalo in 1903–4.[37] Every other one of these is flipped 180 degrees so that street-facing

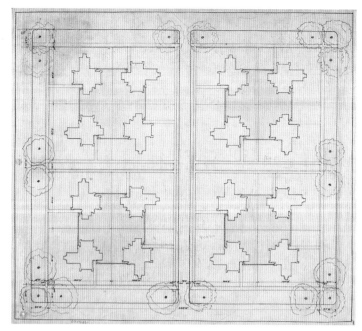

3.14

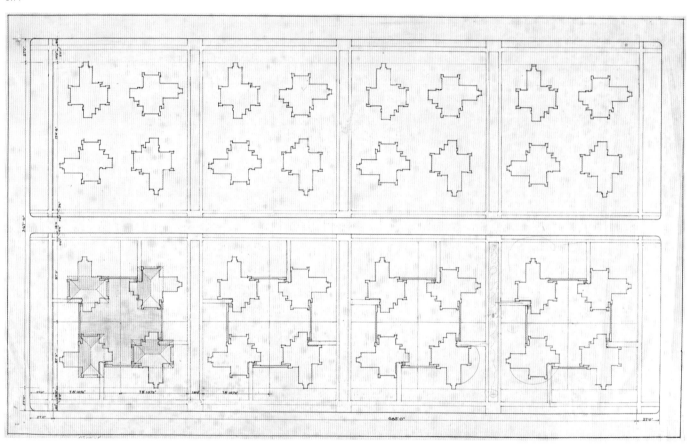

3.15

3.14. Second Roberts block project variation. Sixteen houses on 435-foot-long block.
Plan

3.15. Second Roberts block project variation. Thirty-two houses on 685-foot-long
block. Plan

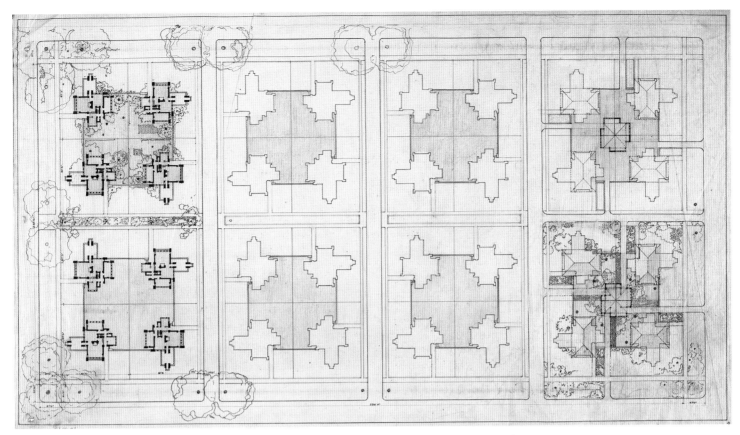

3.16

3.17

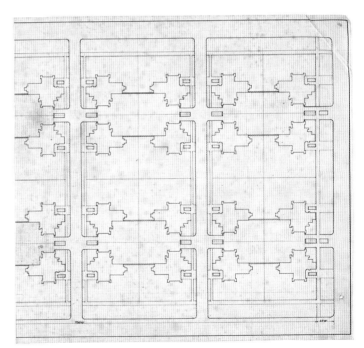

3.18

3.16. Second Roberts block project variation. Thirty-two houses on 750-foot-long block. Plan

3.17. Second Roberts block project variation. Thirty-two houses on 750-foot-long block. Partial block plan

3.18. Second Roberts block project variation. Thirty-two houses on 750-foot-long block. Alternate partial block plan

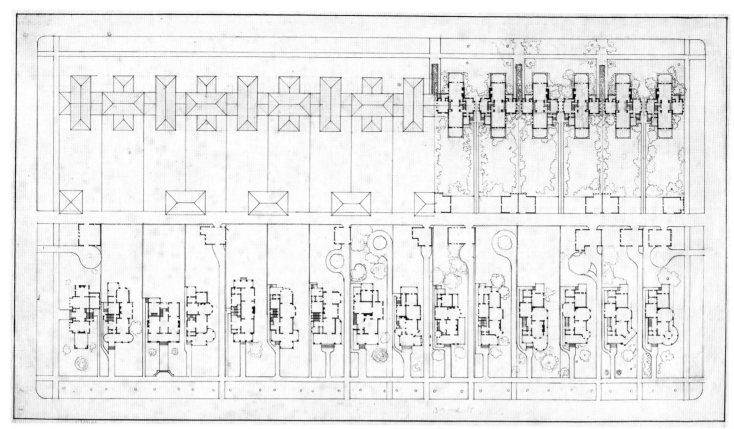

3.19

3.19. Second Roberts block project variation. Row houses and typical existing houses
on 750-foot-long block. Plan

living rooms alternate with ones that face the rear garden, with the reverse occurring with the dining rooms. The houses are arranged in pairs that share walkways from the street as well as attached garages or stables on the alley.

The other side of the block, by contrast, has a variegated collection of houses, no two of them the same. Some have central walkways and others are entered more asymmetrically. Some have garages on the alley, and some do not. Some even have circular drives, either with or without accompanying stables. Each is different from the next in size as well as shape. Were these existing houses, or were they drawn in this picturesque manner in order to contrast with the standardized treatment of the other side of the block? In other words, was the purpose simply to show how much better a row of Wright-designed houses would be than a more conventional one? On the face of it, and taken out of context, this seems like a plausible assumption. But given the other seven drawings in the series, the answer is undoubtedly more complicated, and more interesting. The purpose, I would argue, was to illustrate in graphic terms the normal disconnect between the two sides of a conventionally platted suburban block and how even having Wright-designed houses facing one of the streets makes no difference to the overall effect. In other words, the drawing conveys the message that the Quadruple Block Plan, by its very geometry, has the capacity to transform the typical suburban condition in a fundamental way.[38] It gives a coherence to a block that makes it a community in and of itself and yet, due to the porousness of that geometry to the surrounding neighborhood, it has the inherent ability to integrate that community into the larger metropolitan fabric.

When viewed in relation to the proliferation of Quadruple Block Plans that flowed from it, the 1903–4 development plan for the Roberts block gives powerful evidence of Wright's prescient interest in the issue of suburban land subdivision as well as his nearly obsessive involvement with its engagement in the urban grid.[39] Following the example of the "Home in a Prairie Town," the standardization of the Roberts individual house plan and its replication by means of a template make it clear that Wright was more interested in questions of relationships at the larger scale of urban design than in the individual house plans themselves. That is not to say that the development of the Prairie House type was insignificant for him. But it must always be borne in mind that from the beginning the Quadruple Block Plan served as the matrix for these formal developments

and that its geometry, as a sign of community, became the generative framework not merely for the individual single-family house but, more important, for an accommodation of the Chicago grid to its social purposes.

Suburban Planning in the City Beautiful/Garden City Contexts

Wright would not have the opportunity to develop the full potential of the Quadruple Block Plan as a complete neighborhood community encompassing commercial, cultural, and municipal services in addition to residential construction for nearly a decade. His project for a thirty-two-block-square model Quarter Section for the outskirts of the city of Chicago, produced in 1912–13 and published three years later (see figures 4.28–29), will be the subject of the next and final chapter of the first part of this book—and a fitting conclusion to the early phase of his planning efforts discussed so far. Although Wright's thinking regarding the suburb did not fundamentally change during the intervening years, the field of planning itself witnessed major developments that Wright necessarily took into account in clarifying the novelty and modernity of his own approach. To assess this more fully we must therefore consider the two movements that redirected urban design theory and practice in the first decade of the twentieth century and serve as a foil to Wright's subsequent work, namely, the City Beautiful and the Garden City and Suburb.

It was during the initial decade of the twentieth century, coincident with Wright's invention and various applications of the Quadruple Block Plan, that the first products of the City Beautiful and Garden City movements made their appearance. While antagonistic to one another on a philosophical level having to do with whether one embraced and tried to give order to the modern metropolis or distanced oneself from its problems in favor of a smaller-scaled, alternative model of urban life, the formal devices each proposed were quite compatible in actual practice and were often employed concurrently. While the City Beautiful was essentially an American development, the Garden City and Garden Suburb which soon made cause with it were English.[40] And while Wright knew of the City Beautiful from its very beginnings, since Chicago and Daniel Burnham lay at its source, general awareness of the Garden City and Suburb came more slowly and more indirectly. Its impact in the United States was barely noticeable until the very end of the decade of the 1900s.

Although the City Beautiful movement was responsible for some of the first comprehensive city plans in the world, it is more often than not thought of as focusing exclusively on the city center rather than the periphery.[41] From the outset, however, its emphasis on parks, transportation, and circulation in general meant that it took a regional approach that necessarily included the residential areas typically surrounding the American downtown. For our purposes, the most important evidence for this broad-based treatment of the city as a metropolitan condition is the *Plan of Chicago* that Burnham and his assistant Bennett produced between 1906 and 1909, when it was published by the Commercial Club of Chicago. The ideas embodied in it had been percolating in Burnham's mind for over a decade. More to the point, Burnham located the plan's "origin" well beyond the city center and, more precisely, in a project to connect the city's outskirts with its center. The plan, he stated, could be "traced directly to the World's Columbian Exposition" (figure 1.1).[42] Out of this, he noted, came his 1896–97 scheme for a South Shore Drive and lakefront park and lagoon to link Jackson Park, the fair site, to Grant Park opposite the Loop. And as a direct consequence of that came the commission for the comprehensive city plan.[43]

The *Plan of Chicago* opens with the extraordinary image of an aerial view of "Chicago, the Metropolis of the Middle West," building out from the southwestern tip of Lake Michigan and extending its reach sixty miles to the north, west, and south (figure 3.20).[44] The explanation and description of the plan slowly zooms in through a series of five chapters beginning with a consideration of the city in its regional context and ending with a discussion of the downtown "Heart of Chicago."[45] Probably the most well-known image of the book is the aerial perspective of the civic center, dominating the "heart" and standing out against the distant horizon of endless, nearly invisible western suburbs (figure 3.21). It is an iconic image that has come to symbolize the City Beautiful as such: a dreamlike, otherworldly classical composition, symmetrical and hierarchical, composed of domed and colonnaded buildings, surrounding large-scale public spaces, dwarfing the individual and leading out along interminable radiating diagonals to vistas of yet-to-be-defined places beyond. But to understand more fully the City Beautiful ideal as set forth in the *Plan of Chicago* and especially its engagement with the

3.20

3.21

3.20. Plan of Chicago, Daniel H. Burnham and Edward H. Bennett, 1906–9. Bird's-eye view of city in its regional context, showing connections by radiating arteries, by Jules Guérin. From Burnham and Bennett (frontispiece)

3.21. Plan of Chicago. Proposed civic center. Aerial perspective, by Jules Guérin. From Burnham and Bennett

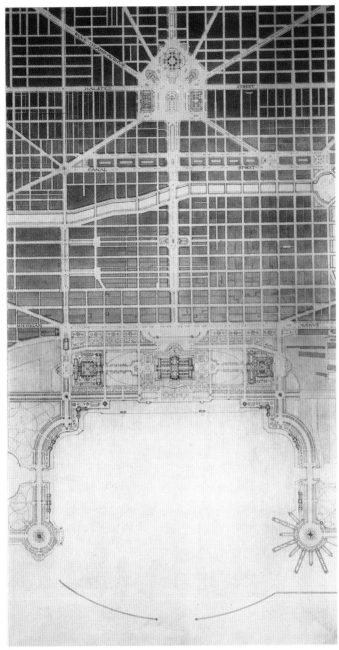

3.22

3.23

3.22. Plan of Chicago. East-west axis through Loop connecting new civic, business, and cultural-recreation centers facing lakefront. Plan. From Burnham and Bennett

3.23. Plan of Chicago. Lakefront with Loop and civic center in background. Elevation. From Burnham and Bennett

3.24

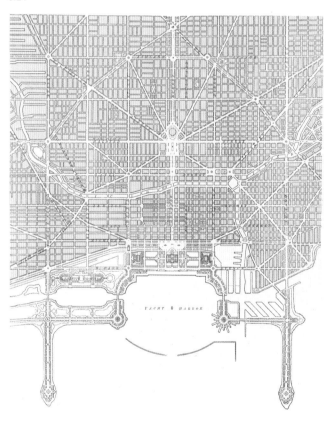

3.25

3.24. Plan of Chicago. Proposed union railroad station and civic center. Aerial perspective, by Jules Guérin. From Burnham and Bennett

3.25. Plan of Chicago. Proposed system of street and rail circulation, including parks and waterways. Plan. From Burnham and Bennett

suburban areas that have been the subject of Wright's work so far, we must not stop at the image of the civic center but work our way back from it to where the plan begins, or rather began.

The civic center was the final element of the plan detailed in the text. It was meant to be impressive, to inspire the virtues of citizenship, and to acculturate the large numbers of Chicago's immigrant population to the values of American life. Celebrated historical examples were alluded to in this cause. The civic center "would be what the Acropolis was to Athens, or the Forum to Rome," Burnham wrote, "the very embodiment of civic life." "Dependent for its effectiveness on the character of the architecture," the buildings were to display, above all, an "attainment of harmony, good order, and beauty." According to Burnham, the "effect" of the towering city hall at the center of the composition "may be compared to that of the dome of St. Peter's at Rome." But "important as is the civic center considered by itself," he added, "when taken in connection with this plan of Chicago," it should merely be read as "the keystone of the arch."[46]

The civic center was in effect just one part of a larger composition that defined the downtown in terms of three major components: government administration, commercial enterprise, and cultural and educational institutions (figures 3.22–23). A cross-axial arrangement extrapolated from the existing city grid enforced the connections among them. A new east-west axis created out of a widened Congress Street ran from the proposed city hall through the commercial Loop to Grant Park on the lake, where it terminated in the domed Field Museum of Natural Sciences. This, in turn, was flanked by symmetrical classical structures devoted to the promotion of the arts and letters. Facing the monumentalized north-south axis of Michigan Avenue, these cultural institutions joined with others along the lakefront to link culture to government as the public expression and beneficial recipients of the vital commercial engine housed in the intermediary section of the Loop.

Where "harmony, good order, and beauty" were the watchwords of the architectural and urban design of the plan, the controlled growth, efficient functioning, and improvement in quality of life of the city as a regional, and ultimately national, economic and cultural force were its overriding goals. Burnham saw that the city's future lay in the movement of population westward and the consequent development of suburbs to employ and house the increasing numbers of people.

The location chosen for the civic center was critical in this regard. Despite the fact that the city had only recently commissioned a new City Hall and County Building from the firm of Holabird and Roche (est. 1883), which went into construction in 1906 and was just two years short of completion, the Burnham plan proposed to move all city, county, and federal buildings from the Loop to a site nearly a mile west of the center of downtown, on the other side of the Chicago River, beyond the proposed union railroad station (figure 3.24). The purpose was to accommodate government functions to the moving "line of density of population." Burnham explained that, although the "proposed center is not far in advance of the growth of the city," "the point selected for the civic center is the center of gravity, so to speak, of all the radial arteries entering Chicago" (figure 3.25).[47]

The civic center was therefore not simply a symbol of the new, well-ordered, and beautified "Heart of Chicago," it was an active force in ordering and directing the city's growth. Diagrams and plans illustrating the *Plan of Chicago* show it as a monumental star-shaped traffic junction overlaid on the existing grid, funneling people and vehicles into and out of the Loop and dispersing them to all parts of the city surrounding the downtown and well beyond even the most distant suburbs (figures 3.26–27). All this is elaborated in the preceding chapter, "Streets within the City," where the focus is on the widening of existing streets and cutting through of new ones to establish a network of "new and enlarged channels of circulation … to accommodate the increasing throngs that choke the narrow and inadequate thoroughfares."[48] A major element in this street plan was a circumferential, planted parkway functioning as an internal greenbelt a little over five miles from the lake at its farthest remove. Not just a pleasure drive, it was meant to connect the northern, western, and southern towns and villages comprising the inner ring of the city's suburbs.

Prior chapters devoted to "Transportation" (mainly railroad) and the "Park System" expand the focus beyond the inner ring road to show how the circulatory and recreational networks, both existing and to be developed, establish links throughout the metropolitan area. The first chapter devoted to the plan itself, titled "Chicago, the Metropolis of the Middle West," lays out the premise of metropolitan development at a regional scale as the scope of the design. And it is here that the suburb and its planning become a major source of

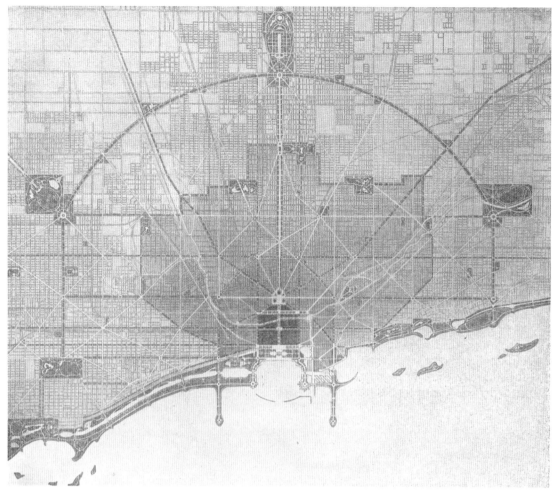

3.26

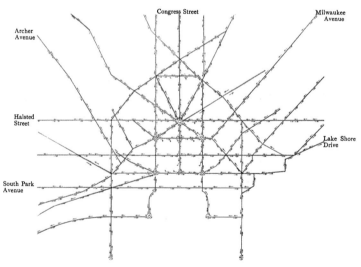

3.27

3.26. Plan of Chicago. Proposed system of boulevards and parks within five-mile-plus radius. Plan. From Burnham and Bennett

3.27. Plan of Chicago. Diagram of existing and proposed roads. From Burnham and Bennett

concern. Burnham stressed the "rapid" and "phenomenal" increase in Chicago's population as a critical reason for the need for a comprehensive plan. This growth, he noted, has found its home in the suburbs and "will necessarily increase as the ground and buildings within the business area of the city become so valuable for commercial purposes as to preclude their use as dwellings."[49] The sixty-mile radius Burnham took as his purview was, he remarked, "no greater than the present suburban electric lines extend, or the automobilist may cover in a drive of two hours."[50]

"Unfortunately," Burnham acknowledged, "conditions near any rapidly growing city are apt to be both squalid and ugly." While "occasionally a suburb grows up at some sightly place on the Lake shore [read Lake Forest], or gathers about some educational institution [read Evanston and Hyde Park]; or a group of people engaged in a common enterprise select a picturesque spot on river banks and there build homes which, by their very relations one to another, indicate neighborliness [read Riverside]," the "community of feeling [that] pervades the place and finds expression in well-shaded streets, broad lawns, and homelike architecture" is rare. "Too often," he continued,

the suburb is laid out by the speculative real estate agent who exerts himself to make every dollar invested turn into as many dollars as possible. Human ingenuity contrives to crowd the maximum number of building lots into the minimum space; if native trees exist on the land they are ruthlessly sacrificed. Then the speculative builder takes matters in hand and in a few months the narrow, grassless streets are lined with rows of cheaply constructed dwellings, and with ugly apartment houses occupying the more desirable sites. In ten years or less the dwellings are dropping to pieces; and the apartment houses, having lost their newness, become rookeries.[51]

Although he provided no specific suggestions in the form of visual material for how new suburbs should be laid out, Burnham devoted a good part of the chapter to general considerations of the subject. His hesitancy in going much further had to do with the fact that more than half the territory involved was not under the jurisdiction of the city of Chicago and that there should be no implication that the prerogatives of independent towns and villages were being undermined. But it is clear that Burnham strongly believed that all new

residential areas as well as preexisting "outlying towns" falling within the metropolitan orbit should be bound "firmly to the central city." To this effect, and "after the English manner," he wrote that "a commission should be appointed to lay out all that territory adjacent to the city of Chicago which is likely to become incorporated in the city at least during the next decade. The plans should be so drawn that as subdivisions are platted the new streets shall bear definite relations to the plan of the city."[52] By this he meant that the Chicago grid should be maintained throughout all new development while at the same time being overlaid with diagonal avenues to facilitate access to the Loop (figure 3.26).[53]

As for those areas falling outside the jurisdiction of the city of Chicago, present or foreseeable, Burnham expressed some optimism regarding how developers might proceed in "creating pleasing conditions" through "thoughtful co-operation." Calling to mind Wright's 1896 Roberts development plan as well as that of 1903–4, he noted that "even the real estate agent is beginning to discover that by cutting off somewhat from the depth of his lots he can get park space that will make his land more available; and by a combination treatment he can secure for a group of houses an enjoyable area of green grass, to take the place of the narrow and ill-kept back yards which are at once unsightly and unsanitary." But this could not be legislated given American property-right laws. Thus, "in every town a public-improvement commission should be formed to bring about the most orderly conditions within the town itself, and especially to act in co-operation with similar bodies in neighboring towns so as to secure harmonious, connected, and continuous improvement."[54]

The process of suburban development, however, should not be limited to the platting and laying out of streets. It should also take into account the various needs of the future community. "Adequate provision should be made for public and semi-public buildings," Burnham noted. "In each town plan spaces should be marked out for public schools, and each school should have about it ample playgrounds." "Next to the school," he added, "the public library should have place; and here again the landscape setting should be generous and the situation commanding."[55] Another important concern of the planner should be the railroad and streetcar stations. The commuter "is interested not only in passing through pleasant scenes on his way to and from Chicago, but he is concerned also in having the railway station in his suburban town conveniently located, constructed simply but artistically, and placed amid surroundings which in themselves are harmonious and appropriate." But it was not enough for such buildings "to present a smiling face to the public," for the larger purpose of suburban planning was the creation of a sense of place and identity for the community through a coordination of all the public structures serving it. "The town-hall, the engine-house with its lookout tower, the police station with its court of justice, and the post-office," Burnham concluded, "all naturally form a group of buildings that may be located about a common or public square, so as to form the suburban civic center."[56] In other words, the suburb should be treated as part and parcel of the City Beautiful.

While it speaks in broad generalities about the public aspect of suburban communities, the *Plan of Chicago* says little about the actual residential fabric that is the suburb's raison d'être. Other than calling for a British-style "commission" to oversee the platting of new streets, the regulation of their widths, and the imposition of "building restrictions … to prevent depreciation of property by the advent of undesirable classes of structures, or the erection of towering apartment houses which keep light and air from adjoining property and the street," Burnham essentially left the process of subdivision and development in the hands of private entrepreneurs and the local citizenry.[57] He counted on their goodwill and enlightened self-interest to achieve the desired goal of a verdant and "home-like" suburban environment that would form an integral part of metropolitan Chicago and allow the city as a whole to live up to "its motto *Urbs in horto*—a city set in a garden."[58]

Burnham's presentation of Chicago as a "city set in a garden" would in no way have been confused by any of his readers at the time with the concept of the Garden City advanced by the social reformer Ebenezer Howard (1850–1928) between 1898 and 1902, first in his short book *To-morrow: A Peaceful Path to Real Reform* and then in its more self-evidently titled second edition, *Garden Cities of To-morrow*.[59] Both Burnham's City Beautiful and Howard's Garden City were aspirational, but whereas the former believed deeply in the historical inevitability and cultural significance of the modern metropolis, the latter denied any such meaning or value to the overcrowded and unhealthy large modern city. Instead of proposing to reform it from within, Howard proposed to abandon the metropolis and replace it with an alternative model of multiple, smaller-scaled communities that,

by "re-distributing the population," would "restore the people to the land" and thereby undo for good the "unholy, unnatural separation of society and nature" that the metropolis enforces.[60] Based on limits and regulations rather than voluntary guidelines, the Garden City substituted a prescriptive program of rules and regulations for the purely advisory tone of Burnham's City Beautiful. These controls would become only more rather than less important for the physical appearance of the environment as the utopic Garden City rapidly devolved into its more practical stepchild, the Garden Suburb.

Howard outlined his urban revolution in a series of striking diagrams to which the relevant parts of his text form extended captions. He introduced his argument for "a third alternative" to city living versus rural existence in a brilliant device he called "The Three Magnets" (figure 3.28). The existing alternatives of "Town" and "Country" were shown at the top, each described by a list comparing its "advantages" to its "disadvantages." At the bottom was the "Town-Country" magnet, "in which the chief advantages of the Town and of the Country" were shown to be synergistically combined and "free from the disadvantages of either."[61] The language immediately reminds one of Olmsted's description of Riverside. In fact, Howard spent the years 1872–76 in Chicago, soon after Riverside was launched, and it has been suggested by Walter Creese that the Olmsted suburb "had a powerful effect on the inventor of the English Garden City."[62]

But Riverside was designed to be a model suburb, not a city in itself—and here is where the innovatory nature of Howard's conception lies. His Garden City was intended to be a fully functional, independent city, albeit unusually small in size. From the outset it was restricted in both physical extent and population. The diagram showing the city, which Howard carefully noted is simply a diagram and not a plan, depicts a circular settlement within a wedge of land totaling six thousand acres, of which the city occupies only one-sixth (figure 3.29). The population was set at thirty-two thousand inhabitants, who would come from all walks of life, including professionals, laborers, and farmers. A more detailed diagram helps to clarify the internal and external relations (figure 3.30). At the center of the city is a garden surrounded by public buildings, constituting the civic center. Six boulevards radiate from this center cutting through a circular Central Park bordered by a "Crystal Palace" serving as an all-season garden and shopping mall. Houses front either on the concentric rings of avenues or

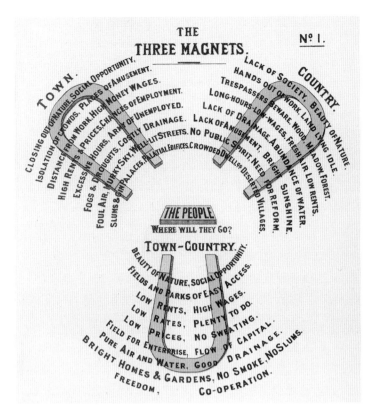

3.28

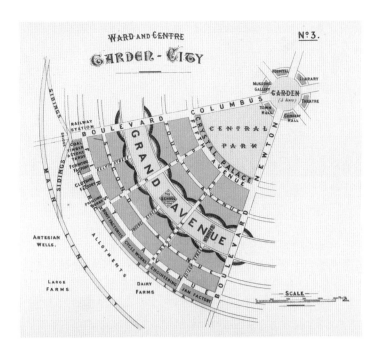

3.30

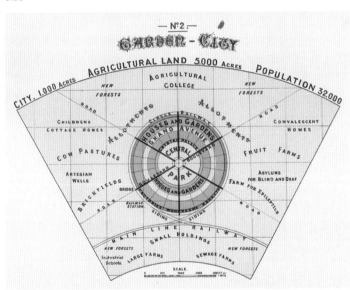

3.29

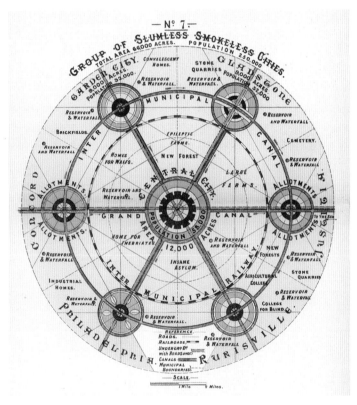

3.31

3.28. "The Three Magnets," Ebenezer Howard, 1898. Diagram No. 1. From Howard, *To-morrow: A Peaceful Path to Real Reform*, 1898

3.29. "Garden City." Diagram No. 2. From Howard, *To-morrow*

3.30. "Ward and Centre Garden-City." Diagram No. 3. From Howard, *To-morrow*

3.31. "Group of Slumless Smokeless Cities." Diagram No. 7. From Howard, *To-morrow*

the radiating boulevards. The "general observance of street line or harmonious departure from it are the chief points as to house-building over which the municipal authorities exert control, for … the fullest measure of individual taste and preference is encouraged."[63]

The double ring of terrace houses lining the Grand Avenue form an inner "belt of green" that provides places for schools, playgrounds, and churches. Beyond the two additional concentric circles of residences, no doubt for the less well-to-do of the population, are the small factories and warehouses serving the economic base of the community. These link up with the mainline railroad, which runs through a much larger greenbelt containing allotment gardens, large farms, as well as various philanthropic and educational institutions. This five-thousand-acre natural area was never to be built on for purposes of expansion. When the total population of thirty-two thousand was reached, an entirely new Garden City would be established next to the first one. In turn, another and another would arise to form a "cluster of cities" surrounding, like satellites, a Central City housing a maximum of fifty-eight thousand people (figure 3.31).[64] Satellites and center would be interconnected by an intermunicipal rail system. When the maximum of six "town clusters" was reached, the conglomerate Garden City would be considered built out and fully occupied, at a population of a quarter of a million inhabitants occupying sixty-six thousand acres. This would have made it a little less than one-seventh the size of Chicago in population but a little more than one-half in area.

The extremely low density was the reformer's dream in response to the overcrowding and congestion of the typical turn-of-the-twentieth-century large city. But it also meant that economic development satisfying the kind of self-sufficiency Howard foresaw would not be a simple thing to achieve. Furthermore, the land "redistribution" was based on socioeconomic principles that were hardly commonly accepted at the time. People would not initially own their own land or houses. The land was to be held for the municipality in trust by a limited-dividend company whose funds were put up by socially minded, philanthropic capitalist types. Inhabitants would pay rent in a system of tenant copartnership in which they were, in effect, shareholders. The rental fees would pay for current municipal expenses and eventually for the purchase by the municipality of the land from the sponsoring limited-dividend company.

The difficulties of realizing this utopian vision became clear almost immediately when the first Garden City was incorporated in 1903 and built beginning in 1904. Letchworth Garden City occupies an approximately four-thousand-acre site about thirty-five miles north of London on the main line railroad leading to Cambridge.[65] It was designed by Barry Parker (1867–1947) and Raymond Unwin (1863–1940), half-cousins and brothers-in-law who had close ties to the Arts and Crafts movement and the circle of social reformers interested in the tenant copartnership idea.[66] Their master plan followed the basic principles of Howard's diagram but interpreted them in architectural and urban terms that substituted for the mechanistic abstraction of the model a classical town plan not unlike the "grand manner" of Burnham and Bennett's Chicago, here relieved by picturesque motifs on the fringes (figure 3.32). At the center is a formal public square and garden containing a monumental grouping of civic buildings. This focal element is aligned on a diagonal axis that connects, via a centrally divided, planted boulevard, the railway station at the northeast to a star-shaped traffic circle at the southwest (figure 3.33). It is a grand concourse scaled, like most of the rest of the town, to vehicular rather than pedestrian movement. Streets radiate symmetrically out from the eighteenth-century-style town center, which is contained and defined by an outer ring echoing the shape of the central square.[67]

Areas beyond the town center are zoned for commercial and industrial uses, mainly along the rail line. Aside from the large house lots lining the main axial boulevard, residential areas are broken down into a number of small, "Old English" village-like groupings at the periphery of the town center but within a greenbelt that surrounds the entire urban fabric and ultimately limits its growth. The residential areas were strictly zoned in terms of density and laid out according to picturesque principles derived from medieval and classical sources, both vernacular and more high-style. Rows of plastered and shingled gabled cottages, some clustered in terraces, others semidetached, and some freestanding, follow curving and winding roads to offer constantly varying perspectives (figures 3.34–35). Cul-de-sacs are employed to create quadrangular groupings that give a sense of intimacy and community. Most houses have private gardens, which, along with the allotment gardens, create a village-like atmosphere recalling the preindustrial era that the Garden City idealized for its "organic" relationship to the land. Their design stands in a schizophrenic

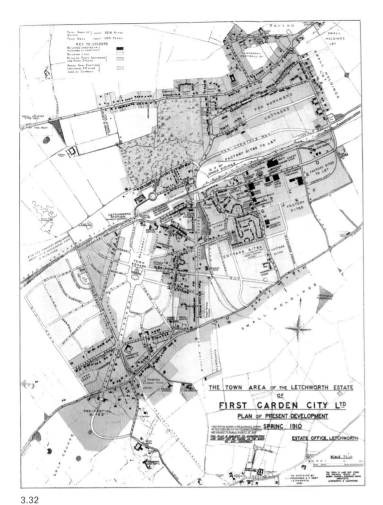

3.32

3.33

3.34

3.35

3.32. Letchworth, Barry Parker and Raymond Unwin, begun 1903–4. Plan, Spring 1910. Letchworth Garden City Heritage Foundation

3.33. Letchworth. Broadway, looking southwest from Station Place toward Town Square

3.34. Letchworth. Garden City Tenants' Cottages, Bird's Hill Estate. Plan. From Raymond Unwin, *Town Planning in Practice*, 2nd ed., 1911

3.35. Letchworth. Attached cottages, Parker and Unwin. From *Letchworth Garden City in Fifty-Five Pictures*, 1911

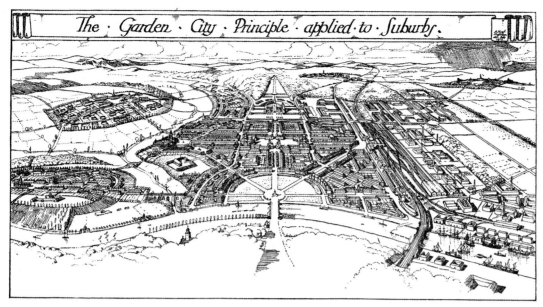

The · Garden · City · Principle · applied · to · Suburbs.

3.36

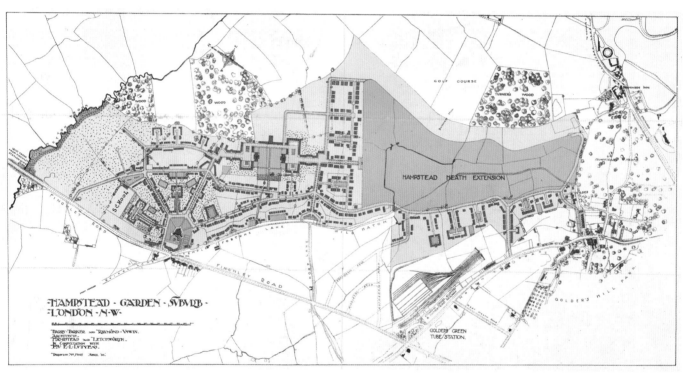

HAMPSTEAD · GARDEN · SVBVRB · LONDON · N·W·

3.37

3.36. Raymond Unwin, "The Garden City Principle Applied to Suburbs," drawn by A. Hugh Mottram, 1912. From Unwin, *Nothing Gained by Overcrowding!*

3.37. Hampstead Garden Suburb, London, Parker and Unwin (with Edwin Lutyens), begun 1905–7. Plan, 1908. Social Museum Collection, Harvard University Art Museums

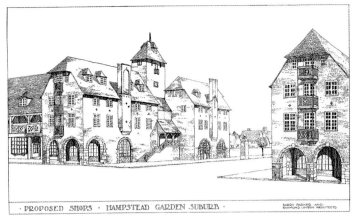

3.38

3.39

3.38. Hampstead Garden Suburb, main entrance on Finchley Road. Perspective. From Unwin, *Town Planning in Practice,* 2nd edition

3.39. Hampstead Garden Suburb. Hampstead Tenants' Quadrangle. Perspective. From Unwin, *Town Planning in Practice,* 2nd edition

relationship to that of the monumental town center. Unwin made this schizophrenia explicit in a subsequent design for the "development of a town by means of self-contained suburbs" in which he translated Howard's Garden City diagram into a City Beautiful–like downtown surrounded by picturesque residential areas and flanked by an industrial park (figure 3.36).

Letchworth attracted enough industry to sustain itself. In its earlier years, it attained a population of around fifteen thousand people, half of what Howard and its founders had projected. But it never was considered successful enough to be widely imitated, and its legacy ultimately lay in the suburban variations on it that made use of its architectural imagery and urban design principles. The devolution from Garden City to Garden Suburb, what the urban historian Anthony Sutcliffe has characterized as "the degradation of the pure garden city idea into the more easily realizable concept of the garden suburb," commenced shortly after Letchworth was begun and at the very hands of the architects and planners responsible for it.[68]

In 1903 the wealthy champion of social causes Henrietta Barnett purchased almost two hundred fifty acres of parkland on Hampstead Heath in the northwest of London in part to ensure its preservation from insensitive development as a result of the extension of the Underground to the area, and in part to make it an experimental planned suburb where a sense of community would be foregrounded and a mix of social and economic classes would be welcomed.[69] An act of Parliament allowed for the establishment of special zoning and building codes overriding local regulations. Hampstead Garden Suburb, as it was called, was laid out beginning in early 1905 by Parker and Unwin. They were joined the following year by Edwin Lutyens (1869–1944) as a consultant, and construction on the site began in 1907.

Since the initial work on Letchworth, Unwin had read (in French translation) Camillo Sitte's (1843–1903) pathbreaking book *Der Städte-Bau nach seinen künstlerischen Grundsätzen* (1889), in which the Austrian architect theorized a design methodology that grounded the picturesque aesthetic of an "organic," preindustrial urban form in clear historically and psychologically definable terms.[70] Lutyens, on the other hand, was just transitioning from his earlier Arts and Crafts phase to the monumental classicism that directed his design of the imperial British capital of New Delhi in India (begun 1912). Like the earlier plan of Letchworth, that of Hampstead Garden

Suburb reveals a fusion of picturesque and classical devices that imparts to the estate an extraordinarily varied yet composed and orderly design (figure 3.37). The tasteful eclecticism of the architecture supports and elaborates this synthesis.

A pair of towered, late-medieval-style structures, based on German models, form an imposing entrance gateway to the estate (figure 3.38). They provide apartments for residents above ground-level stores for commuters returning from London by way of the nearby Underground station. The avenue framed by the two buildings proceeds along one side of a pentagonal public garden from which a number of planted roads radiate into the interior of the community. Single, semidetached, and clustered terrace houses, set back from one another at different intervals, give the streets a varied and movemented line. Every now and then, the street line is broken by an open courtyard or cul-de-sac that creates, as at Letchworth, a sense of group identity for the individual houses or units surrounding them (figure 3.39). Gardens fill out the interiors of the odd-shaped blocks to provide a seemingly continuous greensward between them. Schools and communal recreation areas are dotted throughout. The houses themselves vary, as at Letchworth, from a vernacular late medieval type to an equally heartwarming late Georgian style. An aura of nostalgic well-being separates the present from its industrial, commercial, and crude nineteenth-century origins. While the automobile is accommodated, it seems out of place in what is fundamentally a pedestrian-scaled environment.

The residential clusters and quadrangles follow the natural ridge of the site in an east-west direction and then turn north around what may be the most unusual and interesting part of the plan. This is the Central Square, or common, designed mainly by Lutyens. Raised on a sort of platform and almost entirely grassed over, it is not a civic center based on an urban model but rather a town center derived from a village or country close. Attached houses in an eighteenth-century style articulate its edges, while two monumental churches, one Anglican and one Free, create a formal axis that focuses on a town meeting hall and school at the northern end. This would later become the base of a *patte-d'oie* opening into the large northern extension of the estate.

Hampstead Garden Suburb proved to be enormously successful both as a community for living in a nearby London suburb and as an architectural model for designers around the world. Although a certain amount of tenant copartnership housing for working-class people was provided, the estate ended up attracting a more exclusively upper-middle-class and even upper-class clientele than originally intended. That, however, only attested to the success of the venture and added luster to it as a model to be imitated. Above and beyond the variety and quality of its housing stock, Hampstead Garden Suburb illustrated, from a strictly urban design point of view, how one could give a sense of public space and communal identity to a suburban development attached to yet removed enough from its surrounding environment that it comes to be seen as a perfectly formed world unto itself. In this it appeared to fulfill the very purpose of the picturesque suburb adumbrated in Riverside. In the following chapter, we shall see how that idea was fervently embraced by many American city planners while at the same time being contested by others, notably the strict adherents of a Burnham-derived City Beautiful approach and the more open-ended modern one proposed by Wright.

FOUR

THE QUADRUPLE BLOCK PLAN EXPANDED INTO AN ENTIRE NEIGHBORHOOD SCHEME FOR THE CHICAGO CITY CLUB COMPETITION OF 1912–13

Ten years after working out the details of the Quadruple Block Plan for an actual site in Oak Park, and then adapting it to fit multiple block sizes and configurations, Wright got the opportunity to expand the concept into a full-blown residential neighborhood in metropolitan Chicago. Approximately two-thirds the size of the original Hampstead Garden Suburb, Wright's design for a thirty-two-block area of undeveloped land on the outskirts of the city included housing for nearly five thousand individuals, shops, schools, parks, recreation facilities, buildings for social, cultural, and entertainment uses, plus various structures to house municipal services (figures 4.28–29).

The project was drawn up at the behest of the City Club of Chicago in relation to a competition it initiated in late December 1912 "to extend information and awaken public interest concerning the possibility of developing residential neighborhoods in the unbuilt portions of Chicago and to encourage land owners and capitalists to promote social welfare by developing ideal suburbs."[1] The competition accompanied an exhibition scheduled for the spring of 1913 illustrating Chicago's housing problems and what might be done to solve them. The double event coincided with the city's hosting the fifth annual National Conference on City Planning, the fledgling umbrella group of professionals in the new discipline of city planning. This was the first time a locale west of the Alleghenies had been chosen by the organization founded in 1909, the year Burnham and Bennett published their epoch-defining *Plan of Chicago*.

As we have seen, Chicago was at the forefront of early developments in city planning in America. When Burnham began his study of the lakefront and park system in the mid-1890s, America was only slightly behind initiatives in Europe, where Germany and Austria had established themselves as leaders in the new field of town planning, called *städtebau*, or "city-building." The monumental handbook by Cologne's chief city planner Josef Stübben (1845–1936), *Der Städtebau*, published in 1890, proposed a "scientific" basis for codifying the formal approach to planning associated with such earlier figures as Georges-Eugène Haussmann in Paris. The nearly six-hundred-page text took up a wide range of questions, including zoning, hygiene and sanitation, town extension and housing reform, as well as the legal and political issues that needed to be engaged for their satisfactory resolution.[2]

Camillo Sitte's *Der Städte-Bau nach seinen künstlerischen Grundsätzen* (City Planning According to Artistic Principles), published one year before Stübben's volume, already called to task the rationalist and classicizing approach in favor of a more historically sensitive, spatially varied, and contextually responsive manner that looked to the medieval and Baroque periods for its main precedents.[3] Sitte's ideas would have particular resonance in England where, by the early years of the twentieth century, architect/planners such as Raymond Unwin and Barry Parker gave visual form to Ebenezer Howard's Garden City idea in village-like, preindustrial-style community environments that combined picturesqueness with a classical formality. Their plans for Letchworth and Hampstead Garden Suburb (figures 3.32, 3.37) became models for progressive thinkers in the United States and elsewhere, who often interpreted their small-scale designs and broad-based social concerns as merely a foil to the representational monumentality of the City Beautiful. Indeed, much of the discourse of urban design in America in the early years of the twentieth century turned on the issues of straight versus curved streets and formality versus informality in architectural treatment.[4] The tabula rasa of the suburb, what English and continental planners called "town extensions," became a privileged field for devising formal solutions within the context of providing needed housing for the burgeoning populations of city dwellers.

By the beginning of the twentieth century, the debates and discussions began to be played out in the public sphere as the profession of city, or town, planning emerged on the world stage as a clearly defined and well-publicized discipline. Both the Austro-German journal *Der Städtebau* and the British *Garden Cities & Town Planning* appeared in 1904.[5] The *American City* began publication in 1909, a little over half a year before the British *Town Planning Review* and nearly three years before the Massachusetts-based *National Municipal Review*.[6] Just as important for the dissemination of ideas and sharing of information were national and international meetings, conferences, and exhibitions. The National Conference on City Planning, whose first convention was held in Washington, D.C., in 1909, was preceded by the Cities Exhibition in Dresden in 1903 and the Berlin-Charlottenburg Seminar on City Planning that started in 1908. Three major international events soon after the Washington, D.C., conference solidified the significance of the new discipline. They were the Universal City-Building Exhibition in Berlin in the spring of 1910, the International City-Building Exhibition in Düsseldorf in the early fall, and the first Town Planning Conference held in London in October 1910.[7] Burnham and Bennett's plan for Chicago not only was featured by Werner Hegemann (1881–1936) at the Berlin and Düsseldorf exhibitions; Burnham himself, as we have read, was invited to be one of the main speakers at the London conference, where the Chicago drawings were given pride of place in the exhibition.[8]

George Hooker and the City Club

In 1903, near the very beginning of this surge of interest in city planning, the City Club of Chicago was founded to undertake "'the investigation and improvement of municipal conditions'" by providing a forum for "'those who are sincerely interested in practical methods of improving the public life and affairs of the community'" and "'enabling them to

co-operate more intelligently and effectively for the good of the community.'"[9] A major force in its programming from the beginning was George E. Hooker (1861–1939), the club's founding secretary (1903–8) and later civic secretary, a permanent executive position created for him in 1908. After receiving degrees in the law and the ministry, Hooker served in the American Home Missionary Society. In 1894 he traveled to Europe, living first at Toynbee Hall, the celebrated settlement house in east London, before going on to the continent. There he met Camillo Sitte, an encounter that redirected his future efforts toward the problems of the city and how best to plan for the various needs—physical, social, aesthetic, economic, and political—of its citizens.[10] When he returned to the United States in 1895, he went to Chicago, where he was to live at Jane Addams's Hull House, the most famous settlement house in America and one with which Frank Lloyd Wright was early on involved through his association with the Chicago Arts and Crafts Society headquartered there.

An important aspect of Hooker's municipal reform interests was transportation. In 1896–97 he was appointed secretary to the Chicago City Council's special street railway committee. In 1910 he was made chair of the National Conference on City Planning's Committee on Traction Lines, Railroads and Docks, and, with that, became a member of the conference's Executive Committee. Four years later he authored a study of Chicago's railroad system that built upon the Burnham and Bennett plan while criticizing its lack of provision for through routes to facilitate both interurban and suburban traffic.[11] Hooker's interests in urban planning, however, were much broader than transportation. This made itself evident as early as 1904, when he published a couple of articles in the *Chicago Record-Herald* on recent German town planning. The first was an appreciation of Sitte's ideas and work following his recent death; the second was a more general discussion of "The German Municipal Movement."[12]

Hooker described the "German Municipal Movement" as "remarkable … for its boldness" and "idealism" in "providing for the public and private life of the community." He noted how German cities could buy "outright" the franchises of streetcar companies so as to "get complete control of the uses of the public streets" and thereby "develop transportation in a satisfactory manner." He lauded the fact that the country's municipal governments had "challenged" the right of the landowner "to do as he likes with [his property]" through the implementation and enforcement of "rigid [zoning] regulations." Most impressive, in Hooker's view, was "a law [in many German cities] giving municipal authorities sweeping powers to acquire city land held in small lots by many owners and to rearrange it for more comprehensive building plans." Known as the *Lex Adickes*, after the mayor of Frankfurt who developed the idea, such reparceling was seen by Hooker as a way to overcome "a division of space devised in the interest of real estate sales and fraught with immeasurable prejudice to elastic or ideal building plans."[13] The broad scale of this method predicted the basic outline of the program he would set for the City Club Quarter Section competition eight years later.

Hooker's attraction to the Sittesque approach to urban design, which he viewed as "opposed not only to the dead uniformity of the American checker board type of city, but [also] to the general idea of a hard-and-fast mathematical scheme for a city's street plan," naturally led him to an appreciation of the English Garden City and Suburb as offering its inhabitants an "escape" from the capitalist "conditions which involve the crowding of people into ever smaller, dimmer, and stuffier urban dwellings, in order, among other things, that owners of the land may draw a steadily increasing income from it."[14] In effect, Hooker saw the "idealism" of the Garden City and Suburb as "expressed on the one side in their superior physical aspects as community homes, and on the other side in their violation of so-called business principles" that characterized the "comprehensive"-type planning developed by some German municipalities. By this he was referring to the Garden City and Suburb's "revolutionized land policy" based on limited-dividend companies of copartnership housing having "control administration of the entire site [to] the exclusion of speculation" and to the advantage of the "orderly development" of the site as a whole. In his desire to create better housing conditions for the city dweller, Hooker was not afraid to state his case that the present "situation must be reorganized from a leverage outside itself, and as a *social* necessity, not as a business enterprise."[15]

In his position as civic secretary, Hooker took a lead role in planning exhibitions, directing publications, setting up task forces and discussions, and organizing lectures at the City Club. Subjects ranged from problems of political patronage and corruption to issues of race and health care. After 1909, however, following the publication of the Burnham and Bennett *Plan of Chicago*, city planning and urban design

became increasingly prominent. This new direction was not just a result of Hooker's interest in urban issues but also very much a response to the Commercial Club's publication of the Burnham and Bennett report.[16] One might have expected Hooker to be vitally interested in what the *Plan of Chicago* had to say, but, given his socialist attitude toward planning and his reformist instincts regarding the preeminent importance of housing, one might also have assumed that he would be more critical of the plan than he was. He certainly felt it had its shortcomings, yet he also considered it important enough to warrant the full attention of the City Club and even planned an exhibition centered on the project.[17]

Hooker aired his views on the Chicago plan in an article in the socially oriented journal the *Survey*, published by New York's Charitable Organization Society soon after the Burnham and Bennett book appeared.[18] In general, he applauded the work, noting its broad regional scope as well as its comprehensiveness on other scores. He described it as having "made an inestimable contribution" in offering "a great revelation of the possibilities of improving Chicago" despite certain "deficiencies." While the plan was quite specific in terms of its considerations of the new street network linking the center to the periphery and joining suburban communities to one another, Hooker felt that it did not adequately deal with the problems that existed in the railway system (a point he came back to in his study of through routes four years later). Not enough attention was paid to coordinating the different privately owned lines nor to how the existing tracks and terminals might be redesigned to operate more efficiently. While the recommendations for an expanded elevated loop along with the creation of a streetcar and subway loop, both for passengers and for freight, were praised, the lack of statistical studies to support these recommendations was felt by Hooker to undermine their rationale.[19]

The lack of statistical information along with the general paucity of specific recommendations for a housing policy led Hooker to compare the plan unfavorably with the "scientific planning" that characterized the "established practical art on the continent of Europe" that he had previously written about.[20] In Hooker's view, the Burnham and Bennett plan emphasized the formal rather than the pragmatic, and a rather outdated and inappropriate formalism at that. "It is the formalism of the great master, Le Notre [*sic*], and his followers, as expressed especially in and about Paris, that is referred to for principles of street planning," he commented. "It is Paris whose street plan most conspicuously illustrates the 'round' or 'star' points which characterize the reformed street plan proposed, and the 'circuits' which characterize both that plan and the transportation proposals." The result of this Parisian formalism was an overemphasis on "geometrical symmetry" and "uniformity" that reduced the "stupendous architectural effects" of the individualistic skyscrapers of the Loop to "a uniform sky-line" (see figure 3.14). Hooker regretted the loss of the "splendid and picturesque possibilities which might be realized through a harmonious use of such variety" and concluded that the Burnham and Bennett plan thereby lacked the quality of vitality that characterized "'Chicago construction'" and thus the city's architectural genius.[21]

The aesthetic was important to Hooker. Much of his interest in Sitte was owed to that. But of equal if not greater importance were the social and economic aspects of planning and their role in raising the quality of life for all citizens of a city. Burnham and Bennett's plan was felt by many left-leaning critics to be elitist, favoring entrenched powers and the well-to-do. Hooker was unwilling to go that far. All he said was that "some persons feel that the report should have dealt more directly and at length with questions relating to the improvement of the housing conditions of the common people," but added, "it may be presumed, however, that these matters were regarded as belonging to the more detailed consideration of this whole subject which is anticipated for the future."[22] The editors of the *Survey* gave voice to Hooker's suggestion in stating that it was not that the Burnham and Bennett plan was bad, or even unalterably flawed; it was simply that it was insufficient. The published plan, they wrote, should have been preceded by a much more complete study of the city's inhabitants and their needs in terms of housing, work opportunities, and recreation: "Our suggestion is that the Commercial Club's great design be entitled Volume II, pending the immediate preparation for the 'Survey of Chicago' to constitute Volume I of the 'plan for Chicago.'"[23]

It is impossible to know whether the editors were speaking for Hooker. What is known is that over the next several years he devoted his own energies and those of the City Club to the enterprise the *Survey* outlined. A major piece of this had to do with taking the kind of close look at the suburbs that Burnham failed to do in his emphasis on broad regional concerns and the commercial and representational aspects of the city center.

As already noted, the City Club had considered mounting an exhibition of the Burnham and Bennett plan. When this would have taken place and how it might have differed from the one held at the Chicago Art Institute accompanying the report's publication is impossible to determine, other than assuming that statistics, housing, and the suburbs would have come in for greater attention. The 1913 Housing Exhibition and associated competition for a Scheme of Development for a Quarter Section of Land within the Limits of the City of Chicago were the outcome.

City Club's Housing Exhibition

Hooker believed strongly in the value of exhibitions to spread information about architecture and urbanism and to enlighten a general audience as to how cities could be improved.[24] In late April 1910, in preparation for a proposal he intended to make at the upcoming Second National Conference on City Planning to be held in Rochester, New York, in May, he wrote to the City Club's Committee on City Planning chair, the noted landscape architect Jens Jensen (1860–1951), outlining an idea for an exhibition of what he called "speculative city building." By this he meant "studies of the ideal way in which to lay out and develop given cities" wherein "the principles of city planning could be worked out." While clearly having in mind what Burnham and Bennett had done for Chicago, Hooker added, "this work would of course need to be based on the most thorough research into conditions as they are and into their origin." Elaborating on the contents of the exhibition, Hooker said that it should (1) "present a survey of the historical development of cities … in their physical, political and social aspects"; (2) "contain exhibits of American and foreign cities of the present day in those same aspects"; and (3) "include a purely speculative department, in which there should be plans … showing how those cities should be organized provided they could be entirely rearranged without let or hindrance." For the last, "entirely idealistic" studies, he foresaw a competition in which "the ablest talent … should be invited and large prizes should be offered as inducements."[25]

At the May annual meeting of the National Conference on City Planning, Hooker made a proposal on the part of the City Club that "an exposition of theoretical or speculative city planning" should be held as soon as possible, "the idea being that a given city should be studied with reference to its population, topography and industries, and it should then be determined how to provide for a plan, how that city should be laid out in view of those factors."[26] Later that summer, Hooker returned to Germany, this time with the specific purpose of attending the Universal City-Building Exhibition in Berlin and the related International City-Building Exhibition in Düsseldorf. Organized by Werner Hegemann, both exhibitions featured the Burnham and Bennett plan within the context of German and Austrian projects dominated by the school of Camillo Sitte.[27] Significantly, a competition for the planning of Greater Berlin was held to coincide with the first exhibition, a combination that Hooker lauded and would apply to the Chicago situation three years later.[28]

In late 1910 or early 1911, the City Club's Committee on City Planning, chaired by Jensen, began a "preliminary survey of Chicago," the kind of statistical study the *Survey* had recommended, in preparation, it would seem, for an upcoming exhibition at the club.[29] Indeed a "Civic Exhibit," organized by Edward L. Burchard of the Chicago School of Civics and Philanthropy, was installed at the City Club in January 1912 as part of the opening events celebrating the completion of the club's new building, designed by the firm of Pond & Pond (est. 1886), whose principals were both active club members.[30] Occupying three floors, the exhibition was arranged according to the themes of "THE CITY-PHYSICAL," "THE CITY-CIVIL," and "THE CITY-SOCIAL"; its graphic materials covered subjects ranging from city planning to municipal art, elections, public safety, charities, labor, and housing.[31] Comparative materials illustrating zoning regulations in continental Europe and Garden Cities and Suburbs in England were also included.[32] During the preceding year, attention was focused by Hooker on town planning practices in Britain through a series of lectures dealing with the Garden City movement by such eminent speakers as Raymond Unwin, Thomas H. Mawson, Thomas Adams, and Henry Vivian.[33] The highlighting of this major movement in British planning was apropos, since Forest Hills Gardens in Queens, New York, planned in 1909 as the first American development based on the Garden Suburb concept, was opened for sales to great acclaim in 1911 and formed the subject of a publication in that year by its sponsor, the Russell Sage Foundation (figures 4.3–4).[34]

Hooker clearly saw the "Civic Exhibit" and the lectures on the Garden City and Suburb as preambles to something larger. In commenting on the club's opening exhibition, he

told its members at the end of January 1912 that "we ought to have in this country within the not distant future a real city planning exposition, which should interest the cities of the entire nation and should really bring out, both on the speculative and the practical side, such knowledge in regard to city organization as this country, with assistance from abroad, might be able to produce."[35] The following month is when the club's board of directors authorized the exhibition of the Burnham and Bennett Chicago plan, although this could not have been all that Hooker had in mind.[36] At the club's annual meeting in mid-April, he presented "a matured plan" for what would become the following year's "Housing Exhibition."[37] This comprehensive exhibition not only would include planning initiatives from around the world to complement the Burnham and Bennett project; more important, the 1909 Plan of Chicago would be supplemented by precisely what was lacking in it, namely, a serious investigation of the city's housing conditions combined with a competition to elicit the most advanced thinking about how to plan new residential areas in the growing metropolis.

The year 1913 was the perfect time for such an event since it not only marked the tenth anniversary of the founding of the club but also was when the National Conference on City Planning was to hold its annual meeting in Chicago. Moreover, following a suggestion that Hooker himself had made to the group in 1910, the conference was to exhibit in Chicago the results of a "City Planning Study" initiated in the summer and fall of 1912 in which nine landscape architects or teams of landscape architects and engineers, all members of the conference, were to submit "hypothetical" plans for a suburban development on "a [500-acre] tract in the outskirts of a growing city."[38] The first meeting of the conference's "Planning Study" committee with the participants was held in late November and the deadline for submissions was set for 4 March 1913. With perhaps some sense of rivalry, Hooker moved quickly to get his exhibition and competition in order. Minutes of the City Club's Committee on Housing Conditions of the last week of October 1912 record that Hooker "outlined the plan for the architects' prize exhibit [meaning the competition] to be held in connection with the Housing Committee's exhibit."[39] Some months before, Edward Burchard, who was to head the housing exhibition's Special Committee on Idealistic Housing Enterprise in Europe and America, traveled to various European cities to gather materials for the documentary part of the exhibition. His trip included visits to Letchworth, Hampstead Garden Suburb, Port Sunlight, Bournville, Ulm, Düsseldorf (where he saw Hegemann's Cities Exhibition), Munich, and Cologne.[40]

By late November, the club's president was authorized "to appoint a committee of three to represent the Club in the naming of a jury to judge the proposed competition dealing with housing conditions and particularly as to the best plan of laying out the quarter-section."[41] The jury would eventually be constituted ten days after the competition's scheduled closing date, which was set for 3 March 1913 (one day prior to that of the National Conference on City Planning). The competition program was drawn up by the Illinois Chapter of the American Institute of Architects in December and published on 21 December 1912 under Hooker's name.[42] The opening sentence made it clear that the idea for the housing exhibition came first and that the design competition was planned to be part of it. "The City Club of Chicago," it began, "is preparing to hold a Housing Exhibition to open at the club building March 7, 1913." "As a stimulating and constructive feature of that exhibition," it continued, "it is desired to have displayed plans showing the possibilities, according to the best practice of the present day, for laying out and improving, for residence purposes, areas in Chicago now unoccupied. The City Club has, therefore, asked the Illinois Chapter of the American Institute of Architects to draw up a program … for a competition for plans for laying out, as a residence district, a typical area in the outskirts of the city."[43]

Those interested in entering the competition were asked to notify the club in writing. They would then be invited to a meeting at the club "about January 4, to talk over the competition and any questions which may arise respecting it among those intending to participate." Drawings were to be submitted by the morning of 3 March 1913 and the results to be announced "on or before March 10, 1913."[44] Three cash prizes were to be awarded. The exhibition was a highly publicized event, with articles appearing in the *Chicago Tribune* on each of the three days preceding the announced opening date of 17 March.[45] According to the *Tribune*, however, the exhibition did not open to the public until five days later.[46] The catalogue was not published until late April.[47] Nor were the competition results announced as planned. Whether this was caused by delays in the selection of the jury is not clear, although that may well have been the case.[48] The *Chicago Tribune* did not report

the jury's decision regarding the first prize winner until 17 March; the names of the second- and third-place winners were made public on 22 March.[49]

The exhibition filled all six floors of the new City Club building. The documentary part was divided into four sections. It consisted mainly of photographs, although there were some plans, maps, and a variety of other visual and textual materials. The first section was devoted to "Historical Types of Houses in Chicago" from 1820 to the present. The types included single-family and multifamily houses, row houses, and apartment buildings for different income levels. Statistical data provided information on everything from average population per square mile to percentage of rental versus owner-occupied houses to average value of lots in different parts of the city. The second section, "Current Types of Chicago Dwellings," highlighted the most common types of working-class and lower-middle-class cottages and tenements then under construction. The third section dealt with conditions in the poorest areas of the city and was titled "'Darker Chicago'—Bad Housing in the City." Developed by the Civics Committee of the Chicago Woman's Club in cooperation with the Woman's City Club, the grim photographs in this section illustrated the kinds of slums generally inhabited by "various national and social groups" that are "associated with the worst conditions in poverty, population density, tuberculosis, infant mortality, juvenile delinquency and retardation in school." Among the "Causes of Bad Housing" were shown to be ruthless and unthinking methods of subdivision based on Chicago's "gridiron plan," lack of zoning by use, "inadequate building regulations," and "lack of enforcement of existing health and building laws."[50]

In contrast to "Darker Chicago," the final section of the documentary part of the exhibition, "Idealistic Housing—Europe and America," brought together what Hooker and his colleagues felt were the most socially progressive and aesthetically pleasing examples of the new town planning. Plans of Lake Forest and Riverside were shown at the beginning of the section to illustrate how the "early idealistic planning of suburban towns about Chicago has not been followed by our modern industrial towns, which have instead developed monotony, inconvenience and poor housing by the adoption of the gridiron street system." Among commendable later American examples were Forest Hills Gardens and Roland Park, in Baltimore (begun 1890), plus some Riverside-derived suburbs by John Nolen and others. The main focus of this section, however, was on the products of the Garden City and Garden Suburb movement in England and Germany. As might be expected, Letchworth and Hampstead took pride of place in a display that also included Port Sunlight (begun 1888), Bournville (begun 1893), Hellerau (begun 1908), and Munich-Perlach (planned 1910), among other examples. Low-interest government loans, copartnership societies, unified land ownership, and restricted population density were highlighted as conducive to the realization of such "ideal" results. In addition to these model communities, a final subsection emphasized the adoption in cities like Frankfurt, Cologne, Hamburg, Dresden, and Stuttgart of "The Zone Plan as an Aid to Proper Housing."[51] A projected "zone plan for Chicago" was set alongside these in order to show, in the National Housing Association's John Ihlder's words, how a system of zoning could provide a "constantly better type of housing as the crowded down town district is left farther and farther behind."[52]

Although the bulk of the Housing Exhibition was devoted to surveying existing conditions and "idealistic" solutions, the "theoretical or speculative" projects submitted in the competition to design a suburban subdivision took center stage in terms of public and professional reaction. The more than seventy-five large colored plans and perspectives filled almost an entire floor by themselves near the middle of the exhibition sequence. Almost all accounts in local newspapers featured the competition as the main story. Major reviews in such publications as the *American City, Construction News,* and *Western Architect* never even mentioned the documentary part of the show.[53] Almost all reports emphasized the fact that the competition was not just of local interest but had attracted entries from different parts of the country as well as from Europe.

A total of forty sets of plans were received, three of which were disqualified and two not intended to be competitive.[54] Thirty-eight were included in the exhibition.[55] When the club published the results in late 1916 in the book *City Residential Land Development: Studies in Planning. Competitive Plans for Subdividing a Typical Quarter Section of Land in the Outskirts of Chicago,* edited by the landscape architect Alfred B. Yeomans (1870–1954), who had taken part in the competition, only twenty-six of the projects were illustrated, including one of the two noncompeting designs.[56] This was the project by Wright (the other noncompeting project was by the Stockholm

city planner Per Olof Hallman). Also included in the book was the program, the jury report, the required explanatory texts by the designers, and reviews of the plans by architects William B. Faville, Albert Kelsey, Irving K. Pond, landscape architect Robert A. Pope (also a competitor), and sociologist Carol Aronovici. A special section was devoted to the "Non-Competitive Plan by Frank Lloyd Wright." Filling a little over six pages, it was placed between the projects selected from those who entered the competition and the "Reviews of the Plans."[57]

Despite the fact that the City Club circulated the program "to many city planning experts in other parts of the country and to some extent in Europe," the vast majority of submissions came from architects and landscape architects in Chicago and the Midwest.[58] There were only two from Europe. Both were from recognized Swedish town planners. The prizes were eventually spread out both professionally and geographically, with the first prize going to an architect from Chicago, the second to a landscape architect from Cambridge, Massachusetts, and the third to a town planning partnership from Gothenburg, Sweden. Few if any of the American competitors could be described as major figures in their field. Some, like the Harvard-educated, Cambridge-based landscape architect Arthur C. Comey (1886–1954), who won second prize, would go on to distinguished careers. None, for sure, could be considered Wright's peer. Aside from the two foreign entries, the husband-and-wife team of Albert and Ingrid Lilienberg (1879–1969; 1890–1965) and Per Olof Hallman (1869–1941), who were respected figures in Europe, most of the others were either young or provincial.[59]

Why leading architects in the Chicago area, not to speak of the rest of the country, did not compete, or even submit a noncompeting design as Wright did, is difficult to answer. The only members of the "New School of the Middle West," or Prairie School, who took part were former Wright employees William Drummond (1876–1948) and Walter Burley Griffin. Both were younger and much less accomplished than Wright (Griffin had recently won the competition for the new capital of Australia, at Canberra [1912], but construction was still in the future). Both Griffin and Drummond were important players in the City Club and not disinterested parties to the competition. Griffin had initially been appointed to serve on the jury and had apparently been willing to, despite the fact that he was listed as a consultant to one of the competitors, the "advisory" role being in all likelihood in name alone.[60] Moreover, both Griffin and Drummond were members of the club's Committee on City Planning at the time of the judging, and Griffin was its chair![61]

So what induced Wright to submit a design, even on a "non-competitive" basis? Much had changed in Wright's career and life since the Roberts project was abandoned. On the one hand, he had become both nationally and internationally famous. An important photographic retrospective of his work, including a major text by him outlining his philosophy and method of design, appeared in New York's *Architectural Record* in 1908.[62] This was followed two years later by an even more comprehensive and much more elaborate two-volume German portfolio of his designs (the so-called Wasmuth portfolio) and subsequent "student's edition."[63] The work turned out in his Oak Park studio between 1903 and 1909 was extraordinary. Houses like the ones for the Martins in Buffalo (1903–6), the Coonleys in Riverside (1906–9; figure 1.13), and the Robies in Chicago (1908–10) revealed an original and unusually integrated sense of the relation between structure, materials, and space that set them apart from nearly everything else done at the time. In Europe especially, the larger-scale works like the Larkin Administration Building in Buffalo (1902–6) and Unity Temple in Oak Park (1905–8) were considered pathbreaking.

But by 1909 Wright clearly felt that his career was not progressing in the way he wanted it to and that he was beginning to tread water. Big jobs, particularly things other than single-family dwellings, were not coming his way. He compared the situation to being up against a "dead wall" or on a "closed road."[64] That was when he turned over his practice in Oak Park to the relatively unknown Hermann von Holst and left for Europe with Mamah Borthwick Cheney, with whom he had been having an affair for several years. Instead of reopening his studio in Oak Park when he returned in 1910, he established a base in downtown Chicago before moving the bulk of his work to the house and studio he began building in rural Wisconsin in 1911. Called Taliesin, this new combined residence and office was operational by the beginning of 1912. Wright by no means lost contact with the city, however, and even increased his participation in activities surrounding the emerging intellectual movement known as the Chicago Renaissance.[65]

Nothing illustrates better Wright's ambition to do larger and more challenging things than individual houses than his single-minded pursuit during the years 1912–16 of the commission to design the new Imperial Hotel in Tokyo.[66] More than simply a hotel, it was the multifunctional urban center for activities involving the imperial household with foreigners. Based on contacts in the United States who had influence in Japan, he began corresponding with people at the Imperial Hotel in mid-1912. Without any assurances, he went to Tokyo on 11 January 1913 to lobby for the job. This was just three weeks after the City Club competition opened. Wright stayed in Tokyo into the month of May, during which time he did preliminary sketches and received a provisional go-ahead for the hotel. This means that unless he continued to work on the City Club design while in Japan, he had to have conceived and at least laid out the design between 21 December 1912 and 10 January 1913, after which his office staff at Taliesin could have completed the final set of seven drawings he submitted.[67]

Wright's project was not a retread of earlier ideas but a completely new and fully worked out conception for how an entire suburban neighborhood should be designed (figures 4.28–29). In his critique of the plans published in Yeomans's *City Residential Land Development*, the highly respected Philadelphia architect Albert Kelsey (1870–1950) not only singled out Wright's project for special mention and commendation; he also noted that his "perspectives illustrate his intentions far better than those submitted by any other contributor" and that the "descriptive text comes from a thoughtful mind thoroughly familiar with the splendid effort . . . Chicago is making . . . to better her physical and social conditions."[68] Clearly, this was not a project dashed off in haste. One must assume that Wright had an abiding interest in seeing how his Quadruple Block Plan could be amplified into something more than merely a residential grouping. One must also assume that Wright believed he had something original and important to say in the field of town planning as that impacted suburban conditions. And finally, with his move to Taliesin and then Tokyo, he might have realized that he would never again have such an opportunity to deal with the issues of suburban Chicago that he had been pondering since the beginning of his career.

Still, something had to catalyze Wright into action, given the limited time he had to produce a design. Donald Leslie Johnson suggested that Wright did not voluntarily produce his design but was "solicited" to do so.[69] While Johnson offered no evidence for this assumption, the accuracy of it can now be documented. There are two typescripts in the Wright

Foundation Archives of the explanatory text that was required by the competition program and eventually published in the 1916 Yeomans book (which, it should be noted, was complete and at the press by the summer of 1914).[70] The first is a preliminary draft with changes in Wright's own hand. The second is the final draft submitted for publication and marked up by the editor.[71] Though incomplete, the latter has a note by Wright typed in red ink and pasted onto the bottom of the first page, underneath which is a handwritten addendum by Yeomans, neither of which was included in the published version. They tell the story of what happened to entice Wright to submit a project. Wright's note, which he intended to be included as an asterisked footnote, states:

> This design was submitted because I believe in the work the City Club ~~was~~ is trying to do, and in response to a request ~~from Mr. Hooker~~ that I compete. Because I do not believe in competitions I could not compete, but I could contribute.
>
> ~~Frank Lloyd Wright~~. F. L. W[.]

All the cross-outs and additions appear to be by Yeomans. His handwritten addendum says, "Similar requests were made to a number of architects known to be interested in the problem—Editor." The footnote reference mark was to have come at the end of the suggested title, handwritten at the top of the draft, which says, "Plan submitted by Frank Lloyd Wright (not in competition)*."[72]

This previously unpublished document tells us a number of things: that Wright was requested to do the design; that Hooker himself made the request; and that Wright was not the only architect solicited in this way.[73] While it is not known who else was asked, the relationship between Wright and Hooker suggested by the note provides some basis for believing that Wright not only respected the social activist and reformer but also admired his work enough to find the time, in very constrained circumstances, to produce something that would "contribute" to that work while illustrating his own understanding of its virtues and vices. Wright knew what the civic secretary and City Club stood for and what models they held in high esteem. He had been a member of the club's Committee on City Planning from its creation in July 1908 to early 1910, when he resigned no doubt due to his leaving for Europe.[74] Wright's project, as we shall see, differed fundamentally from all the others in the exhibition. It also differed fundamentally from the Garden City

and Suburb model Hooker had come to uphold. In offering his own way to achieve similar results, the design process allowed Wright to set forth a critique of and alternative to what architects and town planners at the time considered to be the most advanced method of town extension planning developed since the turn of the century. Perhaps in recompense for his effort, and certainly as a mark of respect for it, the exhibition committee showed four drawings of the Wright project rather than the two that were standard for the other participants. And his project was given a space of its own, apart from all the others.[75]

Competition Program and Plans

The program issued just before Christmas 1912 called for "a SCHEME OF DEVELOPMENT for a Quarter-Section of Land within the Limits of the City of Chicago."[76] After a preamble stating that the "competition for plans for laying out, as a residence district, a typical area in the outskirts of the city" was to be part of a larger Housing Exhibition, the text immediately turned to a discussion of the 1906–9 Burnham and Bennett plan (figure 3.26). Noting that "it deals especially with the broad structural features of the city framework and contemplates a long period of time for its execution," the program pointed to the need to think more immediately of "the unoccupied land in the outskirts of the city [that] is being rapidly built up with homes without that intelligent direction which is necessary for the good of the city and its population." "Recreation centers and parks," it continued, "are not being located until population has made them absolutely necessary, and then at large cost for the requisite land. Nor are the essentials for good housing and for neighborhood institutions being recognized."[77] The City Club competition was therefore framed not as a rejection of the Burnham and Bennett plan but as a supplement and a corrective to its long-range, broad-based propositions. It was set out as a pragmatic response to certain existing conditions with goals limited enough in scope so as to have a real possibility of application.[78]

Instead of taking the entire metropolitan region as its canvas, the competition focused on a single, "typical," 160-acre quarter section. "The object," the program stated, "is to extend information and awaken increased interest concerning the matter of laying out, for residential purposes, unbuilt areas in the City of Chicago in an improved manner, showing the essentials of good housing in its broadest sense, the best methods

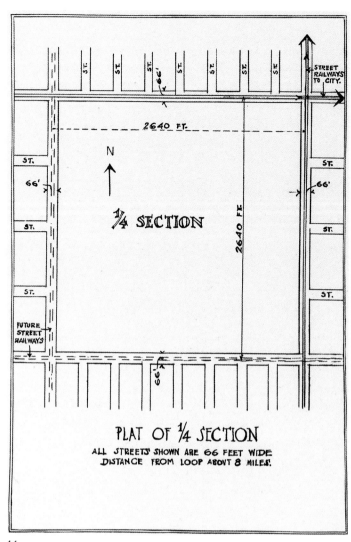

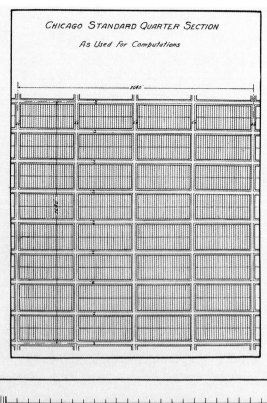

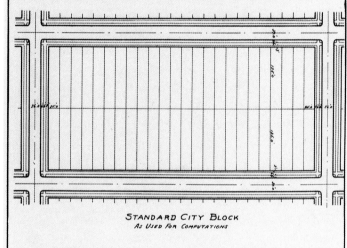

4.1

4.2

4.1. Scheme of Development for a Quarter Section within Chicago, City Club competition, 1912–13. "Typical Quarter Section in the Outskirts of Chicago." Plan supplied with program. From Yeomans

4.2. Scheme of Development for a Quarter Section. "Chicago Standard Quarter Section." Plans. From Yeomans

of subdivision of residential land, the best disposition of space for parks and recreation centers, the most practical width and arrangement of roads, the most convenient location of stores and of public or semi-public grounds and buildings, the most desirable provisions for house yards and gardens and the proper density of population to be provided for."[79]

To encourage a degree of freedom while at the same time ensuring general applicability, the site chosen was purposely "not a precisely located [one], but an imaginary or an assumed site." In other words, it was to be "typical" of the flat, uninterrupted terrain surrounding the city core and extending out from it. The site was illustrated by a simple diagram (figure 4.1) and described as

> compris[ing] a quarter-section of land assumed to be located on the level prairie about 8 miles distant from the business district of … Chicago. The tract is without trees or buildings and is not subdivided. The surrounding property [however] is subdivided in the prevailing gridiron fashion as indicated by [figure 4.1].... It is assumed that within a mile of the site are to be found numerous scattered instances and several groups of ordinary frame and brick houses such as prevail on the southwest, west and northwest outlying sections. Many of the larger industrial plants that are located or are being located west and southwest of the city are distant from ½ mile to 4 miles from the site. Many of these plants can be reached from the site on foot or by [street]car lines, with or without transfer, within twenty minutes.
>
> The site is served by street car lines on two sides, and there is a possibility of street car lines on the other two sides.
>
> The site as shown on the plat is assumed to lie in the southwest quadrant of the city, and is served by street car lines on the east side and the north side. A passenger from the site may, by starting north on one of these lines or east on the other, reach the loop district, by transfer if necessary, in about 45 minutes.

Competitors had the option, if they preferred, of choosing a site in the "northwest quadrant."[80]

Two drawings were required: a plan, approximately three feet square, and a bird's-eye perspective of the entire site or some part of it, no more than twenty inches high by thirty-six inches wide. The plan was to show

> the streets as proposed to be laid out in respect to direction, width, grass plots, fore-gardens, or plantation of trees along

them; the size and arrangement of lots; the location of dwellings upon them; the proper provision of gardens; the provision of public open spaces other than streets; the designation of spaces for the business, recreational, educational, religious, administrative and other social requirements of the prospective inhabitants, and any other features belonging to a proper development of the site as a residential quarter according to the best practicable standards for the location.[81]

Finally, it was stipulated that the "plans are not to provide for a population greater than 1,280 families."[82] A typewritten statement was to accompany the drawings specifying

(1) The number and sizes, in street frontage and superficial area in square feet, of lots for dwellings.
(2) The number of families to be accommodated.
(3) The number of feet of public sewers proposed.
(4) The number of square yards of street pavement proposed.
(5) The number of square yards of sidewalk proposed.
(6) Percentage of total site in streets.
(7) Percentage of total site in other public areas.

In addition, each competitor was asked to supply a discursive text "to explain and discuss … the general purposes, policies or features represented in his solution to the problem."[83]

The program was direct, specific, pragmatic, and dry. It assumed a streetcar suburb with a density and park-like character based on the Garden Suburb. There was no elaboration of issues having to do with quality of life or neighborhood character. Unlike the Burnham and Bennett discussion of the suburban extensions of the city, the focus was not on the local civic center and related public spaces. References to administrative, educational, recreational, and commercial establishments were nominal. There was no discussion of how or if the tract should relate to adjoining ones or how the public transportation system should be integrated. Instead, the program concentrated on what the *Plan of Chicago* left out—the issue of subdivision per se. Priority was given to how streets should be laid out and how the residential lots were to be allocated and designed. What to do vis-à-vis the Chicago grid was thus critical. Anyone who knew Garden Suburb precedents and Hooker's embrace of them would have known where he stood on the issue. "The purely mechanical extension of existing street systems," Yeomans later wrote in his preface to the

4.3

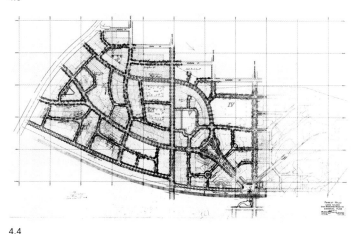

4.4

4.3. Forest Hills Gardens, Queens, N.Y., Grosvenor Atterbury and Frederick Law Olmsted Jr., begun 1909–11. Aerial perspective, 1910. Courtesy National Park Service, Frederick Law Olmsted National Historic Site

4.4. Forest Hills Gardens. Plan, March 1910. Courtesy National Park Service, Frederick Law Olmsted National Historic Site

book, "is giving way to scientific methods of land development based on a careful study of the probable economic, social, and esthetic needs of the prospective inhabitants."[84] The purpose of the competition was to call forth new ideas about how to deal with the very architectural and urban ground of the city.

Numbers and facts were foregrounded and coded. The distance of eight miles gave the problem a particular economic and social cast. It placed the development just beyond the area of recent industrial expansion ("½ mile to 4 miles from the site") and meant that those to be housed would represent a mix of social and economic classes. Some, perhaps half, would not commute to the Loop on a daily basis but work in the factories or shops nearer to the tract. Others, more well-off, would work downtown.[85] The maximum number of 1,280 families was also significant. It broadcast that this development would be not only mixed-income but also considerably less dense than the typically more homogeneous ones. A second diagram published in the book (but not in the program) illustrated what most of the competitors familiar with Chicago would have known (figure 4.2). With narrow deep lots, twenty-five feet wide by one hundred thirty-five feet deep, a quarter section following this pattern would normally accommodate 1,536 families. The City Club was searching for an antidote to the density, uniform repetitiveness, and lack of sense of community in the typical subdivision.

Although Wright had emphasized the importance of rethinking the entire question of subdivision as early as 1900–1901 in his Quadruple Block Plan, he was extremely unusual in doing so at the time. The only hint the program gave regarding the City Club's position on this issue was the reference to recent attempts to avoid "the purely mechanical extension of existing street systems." By 1912, a number of city planners in the United States had come to realize that the indiscriminate and unthinking application of the standard grid throughout American cities had worked against efforts to improve civic and, especially, neighborhood design, but their ideas for change were still quite conventional compared to the English and German examples that the City Club had in mind.[86] To provide competitors with a sense of what could be done, Hooker appended a bibliography to the program "as a convenience and aid to those who shall take part in this study." He also noted that the City Club would offer for sale "a limited number of sets of the [listed] books and pamphlets" and even mail them to those not able to come to the club's offices.[87]

The recommended list of sixteen books and pamphlets, all published between 1904 and 1912, reflected a clear bias in favor of recent town planning in England and Germany. Hooker was quite up front about this, noting that all sixteen titles were devoted to "the progress of the garden city and garden suburb movement, especially in Great Britain and Germany."[88] Among the publications chosen by Hooker, those dealing with England predominated.[89] There were two each about the company towns of Bournville and Port Sunlight, conventionally seen as precedents for the Garden City and Suburb, and three produced by the Co-Partnership Publishers Company in London. Unwin's polemical *Nothing Gained by Overcrowding! How the Garden City Type of Development May Benefit Both Owner and Occupier* (1912) topped the list (figures 1.35, 3.36). But right below it, in the number two spot, was the sole publication related to an American example: the booklet put out in 1911 by the Russell Sage Foundation about *Forest Hills Gardens*, the British/German-influenced Garden Suburb sponsored by the foundation in 1909. With its 142-acre site of previously undeveloped land a little over eight miles from Manhattan as well as its conscious appropriation of European ideas about community design, Forest Hills Gardens represented an almost perfect model from the point of view of someone like Hooker (figures 4.3–4).

Intended to provide housing for a mix of incomes, the Queens community was laid out by Frederick Law Olmsted Jr. and Grosvenor Atterbury (1869–1956) in a picturesque manner that combined methods first employed at Riverside with newer ideas about the grouping of buildings, creation of public spaces, and design of streetscapes learned from Parker and Unwin's medievalizing Sittesque approach. The main Station Square, with shops, office space, and a hotel, forms a gateway to the otherwise self-contained community linking the commuter railroad station to the central park area by a diagonal boulevard that begins at the entrance bridge and then branches off into the curving network of residential streets. A variety of house types, ranging from apartment buildings and row houses to two- and single-family units, were provided and designed, in many cases, to form courtyard-like clusters. In an adaptation of the British system of cooperative ownership to American conditions, building lots were kept relatively shallow and communal gardens and recreation spaces in the interiors of many of the odd-shaped blocks were reserved for the use of abutters.

The projects submitted in the City Club competition offer an excellent overview of the state of the art of planning new residential neighborhoods in American cities just prior to World War I. A careful analysis of the results is thus warranted even if the ultimate purpose was not to create a context in which to understand Wright's contribution in particular.[90] Despite the bias evidenced by the suggested reading list, fewer than half the proposals chosen for illustration in the Yeomans book toed the recommended line. The three prize winners did and were rewarded for their adherence to the Garden Suburb model. Perhaps more significantly, almost none of the competitors used the surrounding grid as a fundamental organizational tool, although some acceptance of it, disguised and reworked, lay behind many of the Garden Suburb–type designs just as it did the more numerous Beaux-Arts-inspired City Beautiful ones. Many of the competitors relied on diagonal axes to offset the rigidity of the grid, while others turned to curved streets to achieve a picturesque effect. The combination of the two approaches in Unwin's "Garden City Applied to Suburbs," illustrated in the suggested reading, offered an acceptable means for compromise (figure 3.36).

The choice of curved versus straight streets was one of the obvious and critical decisions to be made. Another was whether the community defined by the quarter section should be centralized, self-sufficient, and autonomous or open to the surrounding subdivisions and continuous with the rest of the city. Related to this was the decision about whether to place the commercial buildings in the middle of the tract or at its edges, and, conversely, whether the social, educational, and other civic structures should be concentrated or dispersed throughout. On this issue, there was also great variation. Should the school be given a central place, or should that be reserved for a social center or even a municipal building? Should there be one church or many, and should it/they be centrally located or more eccentrically placed? As it happened, churches were generally dispersed and numbered between two and six, although there was one project, aside from Wright's, with only a single church and another with ten.[91]

In considering issues relating to the housing question proper, density was critical in terms of overall character of design. The maximum of 1,280 families set by the program represented a considerable reduction from what was common and followed from practices put in place by advocates of the Garden City and Suburb. The proposals submitted ranged

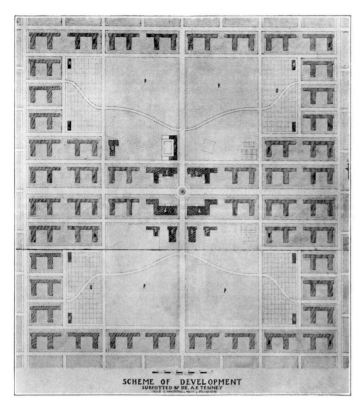

SCHEME OF DEVELOPMENT
SUBMITTED BY DR. A.C. TENNEY

4.5

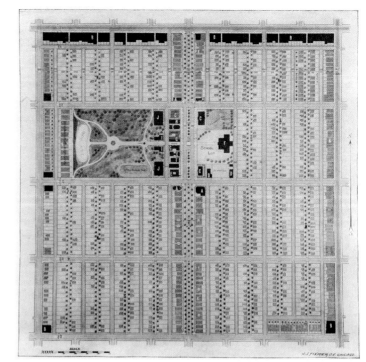

4.6

4.5. Scheme of Development for a Quarter Section, A. C. Tenney, 1912–13. Plan. A=schools; B=churches; C=playgrounds and nurseries; D, E=civic center; F=outdoor bath changing rooms; G=hospital; H=garden tool houses; N=apartment houses; O=apartment houses with stores; P=co-op farms; Q=allotment gardens. From Yeomans

4.6. Scheme of Development for a Quarter Section, H. J. Fixmer, 1912–13. Plan. A=churches; B=stores; C=municipal center; D=police and fire departments; E=YMCA, settlement house, and clubs; F=school and academy; G=office building, studios, and hotels; H=theater; I=public restroom; J=park refectory and gymnasium; K=apartment houses; L=streets and combined streets/alleys; N=semiprivate gardens. From Yeomans

from one that offered accommodation for only 800 families to others, including the three prize winners, that reached or came within just a few of the maximum. A majority provided for somewhere between 1,000 and 1,200 families. House types varied from the traditional American single-family unit to semidetached to more European terrace clusters to larger apartment blocks. Most designs included two or three types, with apartment buildings, if provided, generally being placed along the edges of the site. While the typically narrow and deep lot was surprisingly retained in many projects, a more shallow and wider shape was generally preferred. Some, especially those close to the Garden Suburb ideology, eliminated the private rear yard in favor of a communal garden or recreation space. In general, alleys were also eliminated, although very few designs offered a radical alternative to conventional subdivision practices. Hardly any offered facilities for off-street parking and none, except Wright's, proposed individual garages.

Although the program did not preclude the continuation of the "prevailing gridiron" into the quarter section, it certainly implied that a more imaginative approach was desirable, a point underscored by the jury in "recogniz[ing] the merits of those plans which in the arrangement of streets broke up the long interminable views now so characteristic of Chicago" with its "straight unbroken thoroughfares."[92] One of the four plans, aside from Wright's, based on the grid was by a Chicago physician, A. C. Tenney, who was purely interested in showing how buildings could be scientifically oriented in relation to the sun so as to ensure "a minimum of two hours of direct sunlight to any and every room ... on the shortest day of the year, and adequate shade in the hottest season" (figure 4.5).[93] His three-story courtyard blocks were aligned in a regimented fashion around two large open areas devoted to cooperative farms and allotment gardens that created major discontinuities in the grid.

Chicago civil engineer H. J. Fixmer and Harvard-trained landscape architect George C. Cone (1868–1942), then chief assistant in O. C. Simonds's Chicago office, both accepted the grid as a way to ground more radical innovations in the layout of house lots and the relation of houses to streets. The former described his project as "an engineering rather than an architectural solution of the housing problem" (figure 4.6). Except for the eccentrically placed large park, bordered by all the nonresidential facilities of the community, as well as the north

edge along the streetcar tracks and southeast and southwest corners devoted to shops, the entire site is given over to single- and multifamily houses aligned on north-south pedestrian walks. These are planted to become a "continuous garden tract" intended to "promote sociability and neighborliness." What had been the street is "placed at the rear of the lots, absorbing the customary alley with its various functions, and yet preserving its use as a ... vehicle traffic way." The north-south street/alleys designed to separate vehicles from pedestrians were reserved for local traffic, while the wider east-west streets were bordered by low walls to protect the residents from "through traffic." Such a redefinition of the street and lot within the confines of the grid allowed for "a fuller communal life," in its designer's opinion, "virtually independent of exterior attractions" while at the same time being able to "expand harmoniously, since each 'community' unit ... admits of indefinite repetition" due to the grid.[94]

Cone's proposal was quite similar in terms of its reversal of the roles of street and alley, although he further reduced the number of north-south streets in favor of an unpaved "public greensward or playground" forming a continuous "grass space between the fronts of the houses" (figure 4.7). The reduction in the depth of each lot was justified in his view by the "meanness and wrongdoing [that] flourish in back yards" and the conclusion that front yards "in the city [meaning his reconstituted greenswards] make the best playgrounds." As in Fixmer's proposal, through traffic is channeled along the east-west streets, although Cone placed his community center closer to the middle of the tract and deflected the upper east-west thoroughfare down toward it. Cone was adamant about the value of the grid in helping to prevent "a community consciousness apart from that belonging to the city as a whole" since it had "the advantage of harmonizing with the structure of the city as thus far laid out."[95]

The fourth of the competing proposals to employ the grid as an organizational tool was by the Buffalo architect Albert Sturr (d. 1937), where it is modified to a degree that sets it apart from the other three and, by the overlay of a strong diagonal axis, links it both to the City Beautiful and the Garden Suburb (figure 4.8). The tract is divided into sixteen square superblocks, most of the centers of which are excavated to form quadrangular or octagonal cul-de-sacs. Alleys are omitted and lots are relatively wide and shallow, with much space given over to communal gardens and recreation areas.

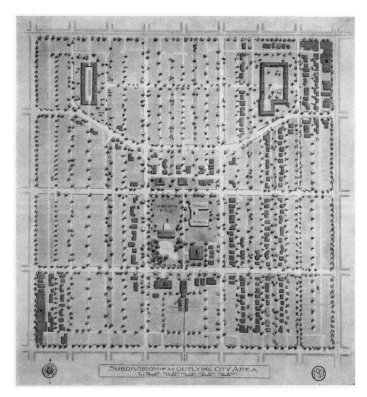

4.7

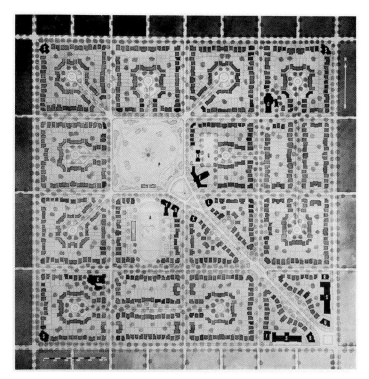

4.8

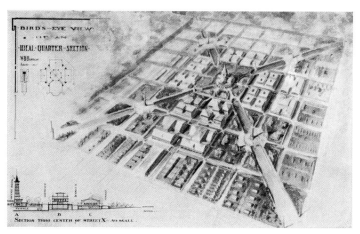

4.9

4.7. Scheme of Development for a Quarter Section, George C. Cone, 1912–13. Plan. D=streets with central parkways; H=two-story cottage; L=central heating plant; M=business buildings; N=large residence lots; O=recreation center; P=streets without sidewalks; Q=barn segregation strips; R=school; S=semipublic buildings. From Yeomans

4.8. Scheme of Development for a Quarter Section, Albert Sturr, 1912–13. Plan. A=athletic field; B=bank; C=church; D=grandstand; E=school; F=fire station; G=playground; K=kindergarten; L=library; O=fraternal orders; P=park; R=police station; S=store; T=park shelter; U=post office; X=public building; Y=YMCA. From Yeomans

4.9. Scheme of Development for a Quarter Section, William B. Hartigan, 1912–13. Aerial perspective and section. From Yeomans

4.10

4.11

4.10. Scheme of Development for a Quarter Section, Hartigan. Plan. A=public or semipublic uses; B=apartment house use; C=public building or commercial use; D, E, F, H=dwellings; G, I=public parks and buildings; A=arcade; B=church or YMCA; C=coliseum; D=dwellings; F=flats; G=gymnasium; H=hotel; L=stable; M=market; S=synagogue or school; X=depressed street; Y=depressed boulevard. From Yeomans

4.11. Scheme of Development for a Quarter Section, Riddle and Riddle, 1912–13. Plan. Shops, markets, and offices line central public square; other business buildings located on diagonal avenues. From Yeomans

Sturr explained his introduction of the "diagonal boulevard [that] leads to a park and to a plaza … forming a social center" as rendering "possible the introduction of many of those features of civic art which are desirable in a residential district." The "grouping" of houses around communal spaces was intended to "suggest and encourage mutual dependence and co-operation" on the Garden Suburb model. While the diagonal boulevard, as in many other designs, was justified by the streetcar intersection at one of the tract's corners, its formal presence also obviously echoed the Burnham and Bennett plan as well as that of Forest Hills Gardens.[96]

As might be expected, the majority of the designs were based to a greater or lesser degree on the City Beautiful ideas that directed the 1909 Chicago plan. One of the most uncompromising in its symmetry, hierarchy, and monumentality was by the Chicago architect William B. Hartigan (1860–1926) (figures 4.9–10). Though he claimed to have treated the quarter section "primarily as a residence proposition," it looks more like the civic center of a midsized American city than a suburban extension of a major metropolis. Four diagonal "boulevards" depressed below street level funnel traffic to the middle, where they tunnel under a municipal office tower rising nearly 150 feet above a public park. Tall apartment blocks surround the main square, while similar-sized public and business buildings lie just beyond them. Ill-defined and ill-differentiated smaller-scale housing is located in the outer corners and along the perimeter of the tract. Just in from the southeast corner, which was no doubt the one where the two streetcar lines crossed, an octagonal "concourse" was dedicated to various community-based facilities.[97]

Few of the City Beautiful–type plans were as doctrinaire as Hartigan's, although the one by the Chicago engineering firm of Riddle and Riddle came close (figure 4.11). In their explanatory text, they directly referred to the Burnham and Bennett plan as an "epoch making … great work" and described their own effort as an attempt to create a "local civic center, subordinate to, but recalling the great municipal center established in the Burnham plan." As in the Hartigan design, a central square at the crossing of two major diagonal avenues becomes the administrative, commercial, and social "meeting place," where shops, markets, and offices surround the more ceremonial public buildings. The Riddles specifically ascribed their use of the intersecting diagonal to the proposed "extension of existing diagonal streets into areas now unimproved" in the

Plan of Chicago, noting that its superimposition of diagonal arteries represents "an attempt to modify in the most direct and practical manner the present gridiron-like arrangement of our streets so as to … give a grateful relief from the interminable vistas and monotonous repetitions of rectangular plans."[98]

The emphatic biaxial symmetry of the designs by Hartigan and the Riddles created self-centered, autonomous neighborhoods, a condition at odds with the very idea of continuity inherent in the grid. One way to overcome this tendency toward isolation inherent in the centralized type plan was to use smaller-scaled elements in conjunction with an overlay of responding curves to create a pattern-like field that could be repeated ad infinitum (figures 4.12–13). According to University of Michigan faculty member Louis H. Boynton (1867–1924), an alumnus of MIT and the offices of McKim, Mead & White and Cass Gilbert, such a "plan for repetition" could be "readily combined with the existing 'gridiron plan'" while "avoiding [its] bad features."[99] Gently curved octagons and half-octagons offering changing points of view punctuated by terminal devices characterize the design submitted by the team of Walter Burley Griffin and Edgar H. Lawrence, an engineer and employee (figure 4.14).[100] Half Renaissance fortified city, half Howardian Garden City, this plan rotates around a central public garden, as in Howard's earlier diagram, from which spoke-like streets radiate to the tract's edges. The closed community is related to the rest of the Chicago grid only by the implied repetitiveness of its expanding geometries. "To seclude the domestic community" from "the external city," Griffin and Lawrence determined that "no streets [were] allowed to pass through without diversion"; but to ensure a connection of sorts with the development's neighbors, all edges were turned to align with the surrounding quarter sections so as to provide "the continuity of the abutting streets."[101] A similar take on the City Beautiful idea of superimposing diagonal lines on the rectilinear grid linking adjoining quarter sections in a larger network was apparently proposed by Wright's other former employee, William Drummond. I say apparently because we have no evidence of what he actually submitted in the competition and only a very elaborate design for a much larger development that Yeomans later published in place of the original project.[102]

A large number of the competitors chose to avoid biaxial symmetry in favor of a singular diagonal geometry that directly related the community to the crossing streetcar lines,

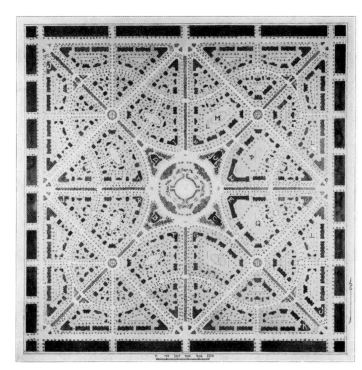

4.12

4.14

4.13

4.12. Scheme of Development for a Quarter Section, Louis H. Boynton, 1912–13. Plan. A=administration building; B=assembly hall; C=church; D=theater; E=school; F=children's clubs; G=office building; H=inn; I=adult clubs; J=stores and flats; K=garage; L=allotment gardens; M=playground; P=athletic field; Q=tennis courts; R=police and firehouse. From Yeomans

4.13. Scheme of Development for a Quarter Section, Boynton. Plan showing potential for repetition. From Yeomans

4.14. Scheme of Development for a Quarter Section, Edgar H. Lawrence and Walter Burley Griffin, 1912–13. Plan. 1, 9–10=stores and shops; 2–7=public service units (post office, bank, etc.); 8=theaters; 11–12=depot and heating plant; 13–24=community and educational units (schools, library, gymnasium, etc.); 25–33=associations (YMCA, YWCA, inn, churches, etc.); 34–36=playing fields and gymnasiums; n.n.: two- and single-family houses. From Yeomans

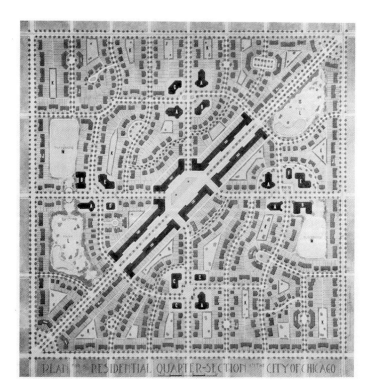

4.15

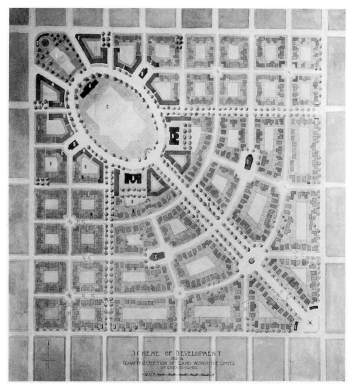

4.16

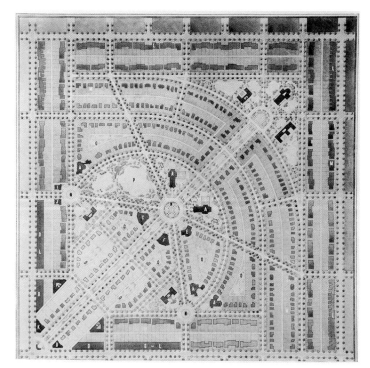

4.17

4.15. Scheme of Development for a Quarter Section, Alfred B. Yeomans, 1912–13. Plan. A=church; B=school; C=lodge hall; D=library; E=auditorium; F=firehouse; G=YMCA; H=stores and offices; I=apartments; J=houses.; K=private park; L=public park; M=playground. From Yeomans

4.16. Scheme of Development for a Quarter Section, Marcia Mead, 1912–13. Plan. A=social hall; B=schools; C=churches; D=firehouse; E=pavilions; F=stores; H=apartments; I=houses; L=playgrounds; N=building lots; O=promenade; P=parks; R=play space or gardens; S=athletic field or plaza. From Yeomans

4.17. Scheme of Development for a Quarter Section, Morell & Nichols, 1912–13. Plan. A=church; B=school; C=social hall or club; D=stores; E=library; F=administration; G=market; H=hospital; I=firehouse; J=police station; K=hotel; L=apartments; M=houses; N=public square; O=play court; P=park. From Yeomans

a tactic already seen in Sturr's project. Some of these plans were more formal in the City Beautiful mode, while others followed the more picturesque lines of the Garden Suburb model. Many, like the one by Alfred Yeomans, combined aspects of both (figure 4.15).[103] Almost all were symmetrical in relation to the bisecting diagonal. Two of the more formal types were those by the New York architect Marcia J. Mead (1879–1967), a recent graduate of Columbia University's architecture program, and the Minneapolis landscape architectural firm of Morell & Nichols (est. 1909; figures 4.16–17).[104] In these, the diagonal forms a major boulevard or parkway leading from a corner gateway to a monumental plaza constituting a civic center. Morell & Nichols specifically stated that their "plan was determined on the general principles governing [the Burnham and Bennett] civic plan." They explained that the angled and curving streets were intended to interrupt the surrounding ones so as to "avoid the monotony of the gridiron system" and "provide variety in the setting of the public and private buildings."[105] Though unflinching in their formality and restrained monumentality, these two designs gave equal evidence of an acquaintance with, and even willingness to adopt, certain ideas of the English Garden Suburb. In addition to providing for individual single-family houses, they made use of terrace housing with varied setbacks forming cottage-like groupings. Mead, moreover, made most of her house lots extremely shallow and allocated the land in the centers of the residential blocks to communally-held gardens and recreational spaces based on the cooperative practices of the English Garden Suburb. While the Griffin-Lawrence proposal also turned the centers of the residential blocks into what were described as "outdoor neighborhood features," neither it nor the Mead design went very far toward replicating the actual designs of Hampstead and Forest Hills.[106]

The majority of competitors that referred directly to English models either for their architectural style and planning methodology or the underlying social and economic principles did so for designs that were generally more formal, diagrammatic, and geometrically organized than their professed prototype. Boynton, for instance, justified this by explaining that the exact bilateral symmetry of his plan allowed him to split the difference, so to speak, between English and American land-use practices: "The east half follows the practice in the English Co-partnership Suburbs, such as Hampstead Garden Suburb, with ample space … for

allotment gardens and semi-public playgrounds, while the west half is divided for the usual [American] real estate development where the lots are sold to individual owners" (figure 4.12).[107] The New York architectural firm of Brazer & Robb (est. 1911) described the houses in their design as "arranged on the English garden principle" with allotment gardens in the center, noting that the design's overall "geometrical, formal pattern" was meant to create an easy "transition" between "the adopted garden suburb treatment" and the "surrounding gridiron" (figure 4.18).[108]

One of the very few integral examples of the Garden Suburb concept of clustered residential units combined with communal gardens and recreation spaces was by the New York landscape architect Robert Anderson Pope (1878–1936). Pope had already established a national reputation for his opposition to what he called the "showy … civic vanity" of the City Beautiful and his support for "the ideal town planning" that could be achieved through "the co-partnership principle" developed in England and Germany.[109] In the text accompanying his design, he openly claimed that one could "predetermine the social life of the community by means of a scientific design." Groups "from six to ten family units" are arranged in clusters forming varied-shaped quadrangles often facing one another across tree-bordered streets (figures 4.19–20). Walkways define the edges of interior gardens and playgrounds while providing traffic-free access to neighbors' houses, schools, community facilities, stores, and streetcar lines.

The number of streets in Pope's project is minimized so as to leave more open green space; and the majority of the streets are angled "in a picturesque manner" in order to eliminate through traffic and, as Pope wrote, to offer an "escape from the monotony of the typical [gridiron] city plan." Even the formal diagonal boulevard is lined mainly with cottage-like terrace houses to emphasize its domestic character as a "central promenade."[110] It terminates in a gymnasium bordering an athletic field and school sites. The gymnasium's medievalizing tower echoes those marking the gateway structures at the tract's entrance. As in Hampstead Garden Suburb, the latter contain ground-floor stores and apartments above. The houses themselves are designed in a variety of late medieval and eighteenth-century styles to evoke the "organic," village-like character of Parker and Unwin's Garden Suburb (figures 3.38–39). One can, in fact, read the Pope plan as a greatly overscaled cul-de-sac, in which the diagonal axis, as in Sturr's

4.18

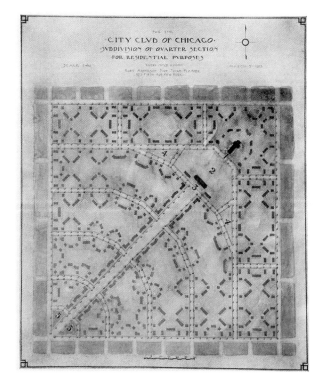

4.19

4.20

4.18. Scheme of Development for a Quarter Section, Brazer & Robb, 1912–13. Plan. A=social center; B=boys' and girls' schools; C=churches; D=dwellings; E=lecture hall; F=field houses; G=garage; H=hotel; I=YMCA; J=theater; L=library; LB=lodge building; M=stores and dwellings; N=pools; O=gardens; P=playgrounds. From Yeomans

4.19. Scheme of Development for a Quarter Section, Robert Anderson Pope, 1912–13. Plan. 1=church; 2=athletic field; 3=gymnasium; 4=schools; 5=stores. From Yeomans

4.20. Scheme of Development for a Quarter Section, Pope. Aerial perspective. From Yeomans

somewhat similar design, functions as a device for organizing a residential community set apart from its surrounding neighborhoods.

Jury Report and Prize Winners

The jury finally selected to judge the competition was made up mostly of outsiders to the City Club organization.[111] The club's only official representative was Jensen. John C. Kennedy, former secretary of the Housing Committee of the Chicago Association of Commerce, was named chair. The other members included the Chicago engineer and town planner John W. Alvord and two Chicago architects, George W. Maher and Arthur W. Woltersdorf. Edward H. Bouton, who was managing director of Forest Hills Gardens before taking over as director of Roland Park, served as a consultant. The jury report listed their five criteria in the following order: (1) "economy and practicality of the plan"; (2) "provision for health and sanitation"; (3) "beauty, including general composition, architecture, originality"; (4) "comfort and convenience of residents"; and (5) "provision for social activities, including education, recreation, business, etc."[112]

The report also spelled out a number of "defects" that would disqualify a project. The first and "most common" was "an over-elaborate system of parks, boulevards, or public buildings which could not be maintained by working people with only moderate means." This was clearly a reproof of the more doctrinaire versions of the Beaux-Arts City Beautiful designs. A second, related to the first, was the "inappropriate[ness] for such a district" of being conceived "on a too monumental scale." A third, which "went to the opposite extreme," was a lack of "originality" combined with "inadequate provision for parks and playgrounds, public buildings and social centers." Fourth was the placement of "the business of the district in the central part away from both [street]car lines." A fifth was the location of "large athletic fields next to residences, libraries, or other buildings where quietness would be desirable." Finally, there was the arrangement of "houses in closed courts, or in a sort of cul-de-sac," which was considered "defective from the standpoint of ventilation."[113]

The issue that raised the largest question in the jury's mind, however, was the grid. Although it was not listed as a "defect," it was incorporated in a larger discussion of street layout. "There was a wide difference in the merits of the street

systems of the various plans," the report began, "and this factor was always considered important." "The jury," it continued, "was not committed to any particular scheme of streets, curved or straight, but favored those plans which provided for easy access to all parts of the district, while at the same time insuring a reasonable degree of privacy, and freedom from through traffic." "We also recognized," the report concluded, "the merits of those plans which in the arrangement of streets broke up the long interminable views now so characteristic of Chicago, and guarded against the clouds of street dust which are likely to sweep through straight unbroken thoroughfares."[114] The grid was thought to work against "beauty" and "originality" and perhaps even "comfort and convenience," although "economy and practicability" might justify its use at some level. In any event, the jury ultimately agreed with Hooker's condemnation of "the dead uniformity of the American checker board type of city" in favor of the model of the picturesque Garden Suburb he hoped would replace it.[115]

The project by Wilhelm Bernhard (1884–1947), a Chicago architect from Dresden who had worked for Olmsted Jr. and for Wright, that was awarded first prize came the closest of any to Forest Hills Gardens and its European predecessors (figure 4.21; figures 4.3–4).[116] Bernhard presented his design not simply as "a mere beautification of existing conditions" nor as "only a civic necessity" but as "a thoroughly rational and practical business proposition," asserting that "whenever town-planning has been properly handled, it has developed a healthy and sound community life, has proved to be profitable, and has shown in dollars and cents that it has fostered the growth of commercial and industrial prosperity."[117] The domesticity of the Garden Suburb was thus opposed to the monumentality of the City Beautiful on "scientific" as well as economic grounds. Although much of the available land was devoted to public use, indeed quite a bit more than in most other projects, Bernhard was able to accommodate the maximum number of 1,280 families by virtue of an extensive use of fairly narrow, twenty-foot-wide lots containing tightly grouped row or terrace houses.

The Bernhard project, planned for the northwest quadrant, was only one of two effectively asymmetrical plans published by Yeomans (the other was Fixmer's; figure 4.6). It was also one of the very few that did not locate the main entrance to the community at the corner intersection of streetcar lines but, instead, established a gateway in the middle of the north-south

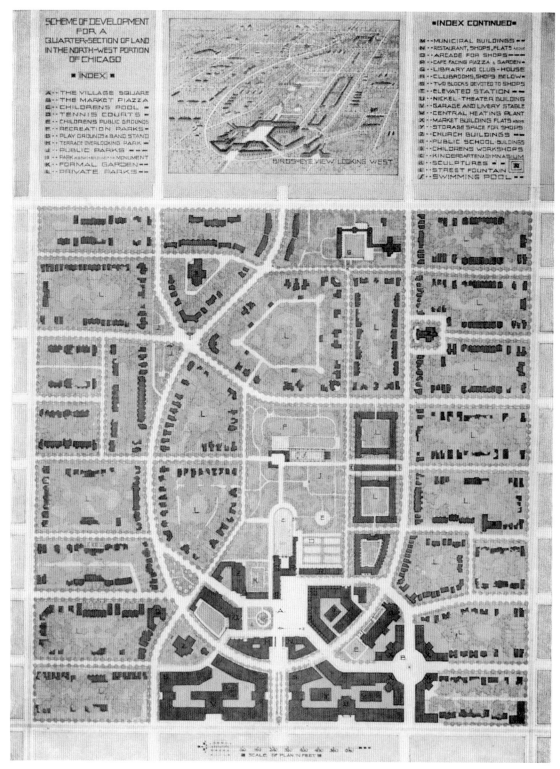

4.21

4.21. Scheme of Development for a Quarter Section, Wilhelm Bernhard, 1912–13 (first prize). Plan and aerial perspective (north is to right). From Yeomans

4.22

4.23

4.24

4.22. Scheme of Development for a Quarter Section, Bernhard. Village Square. Perspective looking toward community center. From Yeomans

4.23. Scheme of Development for a Quarter Section, Bernhard. Attached cottages. Perspective. From Yeomans

4.24. Scheme of Development for a Quarter Section, Bernhard. School. Perspective. From Yeomans

perimeter street (it should be noted that Bernhard oriented his plan with north to the right). Furthermore, the architect assumed that the major form of public transportation would be an elevated railroad line rather than a streetcar and to this end designed a round-arched, two-story station, like the one at Forest Hills, as an integral part of his commercial gateway complex. A short tree-lined avenue leads from the station through nearly symmetrical blocks of shops with apartments above. A public garage and stable is located in the middle of the southern block, while a movie theater occupies a pendant position in the northern one. A circular "market piazza" extends this shopping area further north.

The main avenue from the train station narrows slightly before passing under a triple-arched bridge that opens into the "village square" (figure 4.22). The bridge connects two rather imposing German Secessionist–inflected Prairie Style municipal buildings forming one side of the square surrounded on the others by an office block with arcaded shops on the ground floor, a clubhouse, a public library, a cafe-restaurant, school buildings, plus one of the numerous churches that dot the development.[118] Bernhard described this "community center" as a "mart or exchange for the suburb's civic and business life" and emphasized that, through its location next to the railroad station as well as the nondomestic character of its architecture, "a distinct separation between residential and business parts [of the community] is made."[119] A connection between the two is effected by the public park and recreation areas, which occupy the center of the tract directly behind the cafe-restaurant and clubhouse. Facing the park, on the north side, are two courtyard apartment blocks, reminiscent of Wright's Lexington Terraces design (figure 1.19). Adjoining them, on the west and south, are the large house lots (up to eighty feet wide) for "people in more favorable circumstances" than those destined to occupy the terraces and attached houses "facing the boundary streets ... near the surface car lines."[120]

The central area of the development is contained within a looping ring road that isolates it from the outer residential blocks, protects it from through traffic, and links its wealthier residents to those "of different means" on the perimeter of the tract as well as to the commercial/civic center and railroad station at its base. Most important, the interruption of the surrounding orthogonal geometry of the city declared Bernhard's categorical opposition to the "deadly monotony which has resulted from the obstinate adherence to the gridiron plan."[121]

Likened to a "winding cowpath" by a reporter for the *Chicago Tribune*, the curving street, modeled on the one at Forest Hills, becomes the plan's main feature and key organizing device.[122] Though open-ended, it was never intended to allow the model suburb to be repeated or "multiplied indefinitely."[123] It defines the self-contained character of the community while at the same time providing a certain porousness to the surrounding city grid. In serving as a collector and feeder to the orthogonal system at the edges, it literally turns the grid back on itself and, in the process, dissolves it into a picturesque image of domestic tranquility à la Riverside, Chicago's original answer to the dull uniformity of purely pragmatic land speculation (figure 1.4).[124]

For Bernhard, "a true domestic character" could be achieved only with "the avoidance of unnecessary traffic": "In giving a curved line to the chief streets of the layout, the purpose has been to discourage their use as through streets, and, from an esthetic viewpoint, to avoid the monotony of straight street lines so predominating in this country." The same conflation of the practical and the aesthetic governed the design of the clustered terrace houses on their relatively narrow lots (figure 4.23): "The grouping of houses in larger and smaller units, of which some are set back, some brought forward, will avoid the monotony which the street with a straight line of single houses offers." As in Forest Hills and other Garden Suburbs, the interiors of these blocks as well as those with the larger freestanding houses were set aside for communal use as "private park[s]" for "raising vegetables" and "ideal playground[s] for small children."[125] Unlike the rather monumental Austro-German version of the Prairie Style in the civic/commercial area, here the architecture was appropriately cottage-like, even Arts and Craftsy (figure 4.24).[126]

Bernhard defended his town planning and its architecture as a response to local conditions and as entirely appropriate to them. His purpose he said, in language reminiscent of Wright, was "to give to the architecture an individual character as an outer expression of the inner life of the community." But he also clearly sought to differentiate his development from contiguous tracts so that it could "by no means ... be regarded as a typical model to be multiplied indefinitely." Looking to the example of the Garden Suburb for its conflation of individuality and authenticity—its belief in the organic character of a community as being expressed in the picturesqueness of its forms—Bernhard assumed that "the organically developed suburb, strongly marked by an architecture of its own, able

to impress its individuality on the district, will awaken in its citizens the love for beautiful surroundings, and will express definitely through its individuality the individual life of its citizens."[127]

The jury bought this argument and agreed with Bernhard, noting how his plan gave evidence of a "marked originality" while being "well adapted to the Northwest side of the city."[128] One member of the jury, quoted in *Construction News*, stated that the design would have "'all the charm of a mediaeval city, combined with the practical benefits of modern systematic planning.'"[129] Commentators in the Yeomans publication reiterated this line of thought. San Francisco architect William B. Faville (1866–1946) lauded the plan's "keen appreciation of aesthetic values" and sense of "charm and tranquility." "With its simple and unexpected naïve quality," he explained, the main square, "formal but not too impressive, ... has in it the joy that abounds in the plaza at Venice."[130] In the only dissenting note, Irving K. Pond (1857–1939) opined that the "suggested heaviness" of Bernhard's European-influenced architecture was "of an alien type and not adapted to an American domestic community."[131]

The second-prize plan, by former Olmsted Jr. student and landscape architect Arthur C. Comey (1886–1954), based in Cambridge, Massachusetts, received less enthusiastic reviews from the jury and others (figure 4.25).[132] Albert Kelsey described it as "simple and sensible" and "economical and compact."[133] The jury called it "one of the best balanced in all respects that was submitted."[134] It was in no way particularly unusual. Its major motif, a diagonal axis slicing through the quarter section, was employed by a number of the other competitors. Of all these, except perhaps the one by Yeomans, Comey's proposal was the least formal and hard-edged, in effect, the most naturalistic and picturesque in a Garden Suburb sense of the word. The way the diagonal avenue leading from the community's gateway at the northeast corner splits into two to form a pod-shaped oval containing the school grounds at one end and a public park at the other would have reminded the jury of Forest Hills Gardens (figure 4.4). Other than that, the plan is very much about disrupting the grid to create a sense of local identity and place around the isolated, almost exclusively residential, organic-shaped core.

Comey approached the issue as mainly a problem of housing. There are no civic structures to speak of, just a small

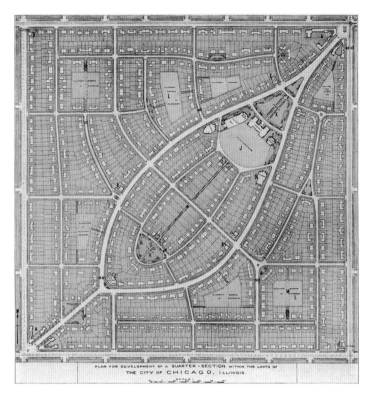

4.25

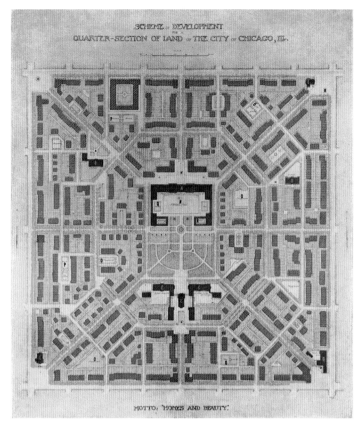

4.26

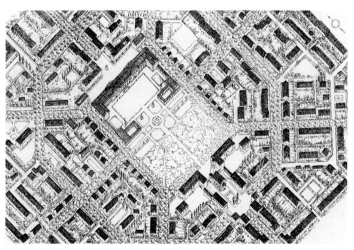

4.27

4.25. Scheme of Development for a Quarter Section, Arthur C. Comey, 1912–13 (second prize). Plan. A=apartment houses; B=stores; C=club or institute; D=churches; E=firehouse; F=library; G=school; H=field house; J=playground; K=parks; L=allotment gardens; M=garden walk. From Yeomans

4.26. Scheme of Development for a Quarter Section, Albert and Ingrid Lilienberg, 1912–13 (third prize). Plan. A=field house, room for lectures and festivities; B=school; C=school, hospital, public buildings; D=restaurant; E=church; N=athletic field; O=playground; P=tennis courts; Q=wading pool; R=swimming pool. From Yeomans

4.27. Scheme of Development for a Quarter Section, Lilienberg and Lilienberg. Axonometric. From Yeomans

clubhouse or institute, a library, the school, a firehouse, two churches, and a modicum of strategically placed stores. Aside from the curving streets and Y-intersections, there is little originality in the subdivision of land. Most of the houses are semidetached, although there are some rows of three to five houses, especially along the perimeter streets, that offer "broken lines [to] permit interesting compositions." About one-sixth of the blocks have communal allotment gardens and playground areas reached by pedestrian walks. The individual, freestanding houses are all in the center, removed from traffic. The few apartment houses are above stores at the diagonal corner entrances. Certain groupings of houses, like those facing the Y-intersections, come closest to what Parker and Unwin did at Hampstead. Indeed, Comey stated that he intended his proposal to serve as a model of how "the essential physical features of a Garden Suburb [could be] adapted to American conditions and ideals."[135]

The third prize was awarded to the accomplished Swedish town planner Albert Lilienberg and his architect wife Ingrid Wallburg Lilienberg for a project that, "of all those having a central social center," was the one that seemed to the jury "to be worked out most successfully" (figures 4.26–27).[136] In other words, it was chosen as a representation of a type—specifically, the type that was most associated with the classical City Beautiful but that could, as the Lilienbergs showed, be realized in the small-scale, small-town terms of the Garden City. The Lilienbergs listed their main objective as satisfying the need for people to "grow up to be healthy and strong citizens, and … be comfortable in their town." To that end, following Garden City and Suburb principles, "the streets have not been made too long, and at the end of them one's eyes will always meet a pleasant view. Streets without any green and streets with grass, trees and fore-gardens alternate with one another. Here and there open spaces are left for small parks and playgrounds."[137]

The plan, which recalls eighteenth-century Scandinavian and German prototypes as well as the central area of Letchworth, is based on a series of concentric octagons inscribed in the square of the quarter section. The streets of the surrounding grid are partially continued into the development; but except for the ones in the middle of each side, they never reach the center. Slightly offset diagonals join the four corners to the main central square, which is half devoted to a public garden, like Letchworth, and half to an athletic field and field house, which also functions as a kind of institute for lectures and

social gatherings, as at Hampstead. Across the park from the field house is an equally symmetrical grouping of buildings for schools, hospitals, and other public services, which flank the main church. Playgrounds, tennis courts, and smaller schools are dotted around the "town," while the corner entrances were intended for shops, restaurants, and additional religious structures.

Planned to house 1,275 families, the same number as Comey, the Lilienberg scheme was certainly the most European, and most urban, of all the designs based on the Garden City and Suburb model. The perimeter streets were lined with rows of attached houses up to thirteen units long. No doubt meant for those of most moderate means, these "solid rows of buildings," as Kelsey noted, "wall off the outside world and its distracting noise and ugliness to the immense advantage of property in the center, toward which all street vistas have been focused upon interesting terminal points."[138] As the blocks become smaller and more irregular toward the center, the groupings of attached and clustered houses take on an increasingly varied disposition, often forming cul-de-sacs and quadrangles in a studied picturesque manner. Instead of alleys, there are village-like pedestrian paths. The mostly two-storied houses are designed in a vernacular *heimatstil* that recalls the work of Heinrich Tessenow, Richard Riemerschmid, Georg Metzendorf, and others involved in the continental European Garden City movement. Surely the most interesting aspect of the design is the diminutive scale, which contrasts manifestly with the analogous City Beautiful projects based on the same "central social center" *parti* (see figures 4.10–11). Yet like them, as well as the two other premiated plans, the Lilienberg project presents an isolated, self-enclosed community that was intended to be a haven and respite from the perceived "monotony" and "ugliness" of the ever-expanding metropolitan grid.[139]

Wright's "Non-Competitive Plan"

The project Wright designed in accordance with the City Club's program was *hors concours* in more ways than the literal meaning of the term (figures 4.28–29). Although it took into account all the requirements and met them as well if not better than any other proposal, it did so in a radically different way from them and at odds with the expressed biases of the club's civic secretary and opinions of the jury.

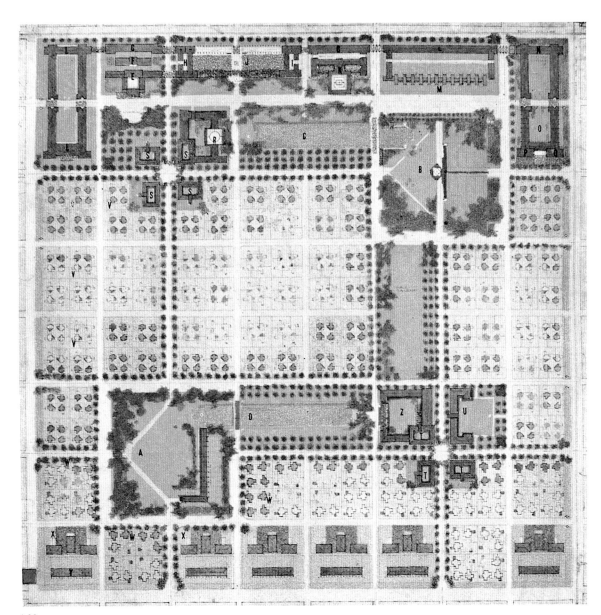

4.28

4.28. Scheme of Development for a Quarter Section, Wright, 1912–13. Plan. A = children's and adults' park and zoo; B=young people's park and athletic field; C=lagoon for aquatic sports; D=lagoon for skating and swimming; E=theater; F=heating/lighting/ garbage reduction plant and fire department; G=stores with apartments above; H=gymnasium; I=natatorium; J=produce market; K=non-sectarian house of worship; L=apartment buildings; M=workers' semi-detached houses; N=four- and five-room apartments; O=stores with arcade; P=post office; Q=bank; R=library, art galleries, museum, and cinema; S=two- and three-room apartments for men; T=two- and three-room apartments for women; U=school; V=seven- and eight-room houses; W=two-flat buildings; X=two-family houses; Y=workers' houses; Z=kindergarten and home economics. From Yeomans

4.29. Scheme of Development for a Quarter Section, Wright. Aerial perspective.
From Yeomans

Wright's plan not only accepted the prevailing condition of the grid, but also made the grid itself the informing concept and driving force of the design. Instead of turning his residential community inward to create a forced sense of neighborhood, a self-contained, village-like environment, he opened it up to the surrounding subdivisions. And rather than offering an abstract pattern of repeatable geometric units as a way of suggesting how the quarter section scheme might expand outward, he developed the existing traffic corridors of the main perimeter streets into continuous connective links.

As already noted, Wright was exceptionally allowed to exhibit four drawings of his project at the City Club. Two were the required overall plan and aerial perspective; the two others were a perspective of a single-family house and an aerial perspective of a grouping of four similar houses (figures 4.30, 4.34). The Yeomans publication also has three site plans for house groupings. Of the seven drawings ultimately included in the Yeomans book, only two were conceived specifically for the project. These were the overall plan and perspective.[140] Unfortunately, neither has been preserved. Four of the five others, however, exist in the Wright Foundation Archives. The view of an individual house is a version of the perspective of the *Ladies' Home Journal* "Home in a Prairie Town" (figure 2.16); and the different site plans are variants of the 1903 Roberts Quadruple Block Plan (figures 4.31–33; see figures 3.9–10). Redrawn as plans A, B, and C, the first has the four houses near the centers of their lots, the second shows them brought out to the sidewalks and grouped in pairs, and the third has them near the outside corners in order to leave place for a four-unit garage in the middle of the shared garden. The final drawing, also lost, is a variant of the aerial perspective of the *Ladies' Home Journal* Quadruple Block Plan (figure 4.34; see figure 2.19).[141]

From this, a number of things become clear. First, given the time constraints, Wright focused his entire effort on what was new in this project, namely, the conception and visualization of the overall scheme for development of an entire suburban community. (This had to be done in less than three weeks.) Second, the Quadruple Block Plan became the module or base unit serving to "discipline," as Wright said, the "practical, economic, and artistic creation of an intelligent system of subdivision" that might be applied in a broad-ranging way to the growing metropolis of Chicago.[142] And third, since the design of the individual residential components of the Quadruple

Block Plan was not the issue, and since the only existing images of them either singly or in groupings dated to the 1900–1901 *Ladies' Home Journal* project, Wright no doubt instructed his office staff to re-create them as best they could. The discrepancy between plans A, B, and C and the perspectives to which they referred was obviously not considered a problem by Wright.

In his explanatory text, Wright took direct issue with the proponents of both the tradition-based British Garden Suburb and the academicism of the Francocentric City Beautiful.[143] An epigraph derived from Thomas Carlyle's *Sartor Resartus* set the stage: "'Fool! The Ideal is within thyself. Thy condition is but the stuff thou shalt use to shape that same Ideal out of.'"[144] The theme of responding to local conditions with local solutions was returned to in the final paragraph:

> Much has been written, said, and done recently in relation to civic planning all over the world. For the most part, what has happened with us in this connection is what has happened to us in individual building: we are obsessed by the old world thing in the old world way with the result that, in this grim workshop, our finer sensibilities are usually handed over to fashion and sham. Confusing art with manners and aristocracy, we ape the academic Gaston [Beaux-Arts City Beautiful] or steal from "My Lord" [British Garden Suburb] his admirable traditions when our own problems need, not fashioning from *without*, but development from *within*.[145]

Bookended between these professions of independence from the two leading approaches to urban design at the time was an argument for "the creation of a new system of resubdivision of the already established blocks of the gridiron" that would be an elaboration and refinement of the existing checkerboard pattern of American real estate development rather than a denial and rejection of it.[146]

To evolve a method of planning for the extension of Chicago's residential neighborhoods from "*within*" meant starting with the grid. Wright laid out this premise without equivocation in the opening paragraphs of his text:

> Accepting the characteristic aggregation of business buildings, flats, apartments, and formal and informal dwellings for well-to-do and poor natural now to every semi-urban section about Chicago, this design introduces only minor modifications in harmony with the nature of this aggregation.

4.30

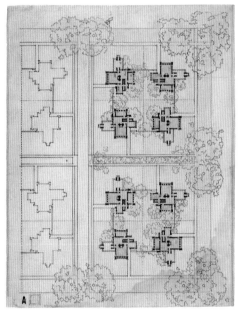

4.31

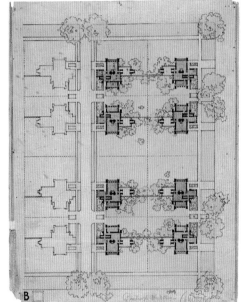

4.32

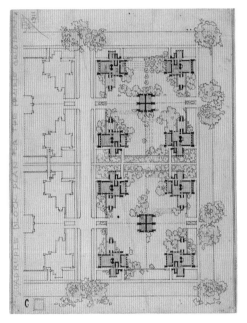

4.33

4.30. Scheme of Development for a Quarter Section, Wright. Typical single-family house of seven to eight rooms. Perspective. From Yeomans

4.31. Scheme of Development for a Quarter Section, Wright. Quadruple Block Plan A

4.32. Scheme of Development for a Quarter Section, Wright. Quadruple Block Plan B, antedated 1904

4.33. Scheme of Development for a Quarter Section, Wright. Quadruple Block Plan C, antedated 1911

4.34

4.34. Scheme of Development for a Quarter Section, Wright. Quadruple Block Plan.
Aerial perspective. From Yeomans

The proposed site locates the given tract upon the prairie within eight miles of the city's center, and so makes it an integral feature of Chicago. The established gridiron of Chicago's streets therefore has been held as the basis of this subdivision. The desired improvements have been effected by occasional widening or narrowing of streets, shifts in the relation of walks to curbs, the provision of an outer border or parkway planted with shrubbery to withdraw the residences somewhat from the noisy, dusty city streets (shelters in which to await [street]cars are features of this parkway at street crossings), the arrangement of a small decorative park system planned to diversify the section in the simplest and most generally effective manner possible, and, finally, the creation of a new system of resubdivision of the already established blocks of the gridiron.[147]

To the diagram of the "typical quarter section" provided the competitors, Wright added four new east-west streets. This established an even number in both directions and thereby emphasized the squareness of the tract itself (figure 4.28; and see figure 4.1). This "resubdivision" based on the square geometry of the Quadruple Block Plan created sixty-four blocks, each approximately three hundred thirty feet square.[148] Some of these were combined to create superblocks for parks and civic and commercial buildings, but the majority were left intact for residential development. The four new east-west streets were allowed to continue through the entire tract unimpeded, as were the complementary four running north-south. The result is a series of squares within squares of varying sizes, pinwheeling around a large and prominent offset square comprising nine blocks of sixteen houses based on the Quadruple Block Plan. The evenness of the overall mesh is defined by the uncolored streets and gray wash of the domestic blocks. Against this recessive ground, the bright green and blue bands of parks and larger buildings form a dynamic, contrapuntal figure that uncannily recalls, in miniature, the Chicago park system as rendered in Burnham and Bennett's plans.[149]

Wright was not the only one to work with rather than against the grid, but only the engineer Fixmer, who presented his design as purely "an engineering rather than an architectural solution," went nearly as far as Wright in emphasizing the interminable, linear aspect of the orthogonal system (figure 4.6). Fixmer created a commercial strip along the northern edge of his development as a link to the surrounding areas as well as a buffer for the community. This

was disaggregated, however, from the civic and social center set well within the confines of the residential blocks. Wright's plan not only unified the commercial and civic structures in a wider linear strip along the quarter section's upper edge; he also connected this band of public activity to a parallel one along the southern edge by means of what he called "the decorative park system" that zigzags through the site. At the opposite extreme from Fixmer's professedly technocratic approach, Wright's plan was determined as much by artistic considerations as by attention to the least programmatic requirement, sometimes even going beyond that as with the provision for streetcar shelters at each crossing.

In direct response to the fundamentally commuter nature of the community, Wright noted that "the inevitable drift of the population toward the business center of the city is recognized in the grouping of the business buildings, more formal dwellings, and apartment buildings, large and small, on the streets next to the [street] railway going to the city's center." In this regard, he acknowledged that "no attempt is made to change the nature of these things as they naturally come." Instead of isolating the quarter section from the surrounding neighborhoods by establishing an internal community center or public square, Wright located his civic and cultural buildings, along with shops and apartment houses, in a continuous strip along the northern edge of the tract adjacent to the streetcar line to the Loop. The nearly solid line of apartment blocks and stores with apartments above, broken only by an open-air produce market bordered by a gymnasium and an indoor swimming pool, were "utilized," in the architect's words, "as 'background' buildings" to screen the rest of the community from "the noisy city thoroughfare." The courtyard apartment buildings at both ends turn the corner to define the two-block depth of the strip development while providing space for such facilities as a post office and branch bank, "where they will be passed morning and evening to and from the city."[150]

The double-block strip at the top of the plan, in which the community's main public buildings were "grouped as features," was treated as part of the overall "park system" running through the site. The civic structures included, in the upper band, a theater, central heating and garbage reduction plant, firehouse, public garage, gymnasium and enclosed swimming pool, open-air market, and the single ecumenical "temple for worship."[151] The theater and nonsectarian "temple" both face an internal street that is entered through the courtyards of the terminal apartment blocks and serves the "park system" as a feeder street. On its south side is a lagoon that connects one of the two large public parks to a courtyard structure containing a branch library, art gallery and small museum, movie theater, boy's club, and branch YMCA. Grouped around this cultural-social center are four small apartment buildings for men, while facing the north side of the public park is a row of semidetached dwellings most likely for workers associated with the service sector of the community.

While serving as a shopping and meeting place for the community as well as a buffer to the main thoroughfare, the buildings along the street connecting the development to the downtown also form a gateway, although one of a very different sort from anything we have seen so far. Following the model of Forest Hills Gardens, Wright's former employee Bernhard used the device of an arched bridge to create a dramatic entrance at the end of the avenue leading from his elevated station. In keeping with the less hierarchical and less centered organization of his design, Wright multiplied the number of bridges to turn the nearly continuous line of buildings surrounding the two northern tiers of blocks into an evenly punctuated, porous wall. "The upper stories" of all the buildings, he wrote, "are carried overhead across intervening streets to give further protection from dust and noise, and to provide, in a picturesque way, economically roofed space for the combination business and dwelling establishments that cling naturally to the main arteries of traffic."[152]

The commercial strip along the northern boundary of the quarter section thus separates the residential community from its neighbors not by a singular, figurative gesture announcing the uniqueness of the development but rather by an extension and subtle "modification" of the typical two- to three-story rows of shops with upper-level apartments that line most suburban main streets. Set against these "'background' buildings," as Wright called them, "banked against the noisy city thoroughfare" are the civic structures and recreational facilities specifically serving the community. The "park system" in which they are located then works its way down through the residential areas of the quarter section. To the east and west of its zigzag path, the exclusively residential blocks bleed into the neighboring communities. Along the southern edge of the tract, however, there is a second buffer zone, less dense and more open than the one to the north. Facing what would

inevitably become another streetcar line into the Loop, the lower band was designed to house "working men and women." Along the street are straight lines of "modest" row houses; and behind them is an "inexpensive type of attached dwelling" that takes the form of two-family houses set perpendicular to one another in groups of threes.[153] Two blocks of duplex apartments for slightly better-off households interrupt this lower band to add both a mix of income levels as well as points of entry into the community.[154]

The most prominent feature of the plan is the zigzagging park. It ties the two main street-facing edges of the tract to one another while providing open access and traffic-free circulation through the residential heart of the community. The figure it makes is a reverse mirror image of dynamic symmetry. The combined library/art museum/movie theater/YMCA that forms the narrow end of the upper band is mirrored in the lower one by a courtyard building housing a kindergarten, domestic science group, and YWCA, right next to which is the public school. Surrounding these latter activities are small apartment buildings for women. A lagoon, similar to the one above, connects this end to a four-block-large park containing a children's playground and zoo. This is diagonally opposite the similar-sized park for "adults and young people [who] are attracted to the less quiet portion of the park [system] near the public buildings."[155]

Bordering the park on all sides but the north are the square blocks of residences. All of these, except for those in the two ranges closest to the southern edge of the development, are based on the Quadruple Block Plan. Wright explained that this "residence park" was "kept as large and unbroken as possible, as it is from the sale of this property that the profit would come that would make the park system possible." Without rethinking in any significant way his more than decade-old concept, he now stressed the economic and social advantages of it in relation to the City Club's interest in the housing question. "The virtue of this plan," Wright stated, "lies in the principle of subdivision underlying its features—the practical, economic, and artistic creation of an intelligent system of subdivision, insuring greater privacy together with all the advantages of co-operation realized in central heating, shorter sewers, well-ordered recreation areas, the abolition of all alleys, fewer and shorter cement walks and driveways, and airiness of arrangement in general with attractive open vistas everywhere. Always there is the maximum of buildings upon a given ground area, dignity and privacy for all."[156]

In addition to the social value of offering "maximum community benefits for all," the Quadruple Block Plan's "entirely new arrangement of the resubdivision of property" had built into its geometry, according to Wright, an aesthetic that would deny entirely the "monotony" of the typical subdivision based on the grid. "Each householder," he noted, "is the only individual upon the entire side of his block.... His windows all look upon open vistas and upon no one's unsightly necessities. His building is in unconscious but necessary grouping with three of his neighbors', looking out upon harmonious groups of other neighbors, no two of which would present to him the same elevation even were they all cast in one mould."[157] As if to forestall any odious comparison with the self-consciously picturesque Garden Suburb, Wright added,

> A succession of buildings of any given length by this arrangement presents the aspect of well-grouped buildings in a park, *of greater picturesque variety than is possible where façade follows façade.*
>
> Architectural features of the various buildings in the general public group [also] recognize and emphasize in an interesting way the street vistas, and nowhere is symmetry obvious or monotonous. The aim has been to make all vistas equally picturesque and attractive and the whole quietly harmonious.[158]

As in his earlier presentations of the Quadruple Block Plan, Wright drew all the houses according to the same design but suggested that variations in elevation and plan were possible and, indeed, to be expected. The standardization that is implied by the concept, however, would bring economic benefit as well as aesthetic order: "Artistically this principle [of subdivision] is susceptible of infinite variety of treatment without sacrificing the economic advantages which the householder gains through commercial repetition." "In skilled hands," Wright added, "these various treatments could rise to great beauty, but, even if neglected, the nature of the plan would discipline the average impulse of the ordinary builder in a manner to insure more harmonious results." Cognizant of the bias of Hooker and others toward the medievalizing character of the Garden Suburb, Wright pointed out that it was the plan concept, not the specific design, that was critical. "Other rhythms in grouping than those suggested here are easily imagined, so that all the charm of variety found in the Gothic colleges of Oxford could easily find its way into the various workings of the underlying scheme." At the same time, taking into account the club's specific concerns for a housing solution for the disadvantaged, Wright maintained that "this plan of subdivision ... is as valuable for low cost cottages as for luxurious dwellings."[159]

In actual fact Wright strictly applied the Quadruple Block Plan concept only to the seven- and eight-room single-family houses that make up the majority of the housing stock, the most "luxurious" of which had the only private garages of any of the published plans (figure 4.34). A modified version of the Quadruple Block Plan was used for the smaller number of five- and six-room duplex apartments. The system of resubdivision, however, allowed for the relatively large expanses of public park area without noticeably decreasing the density of residential development. A comparison with the other projects makes this clear. While the three premiated designs were all meant to accommodate between 1,275 and 1,280 families, almost all others varied from around 800 to around 1,200, with the average being a little over 1,000. Wright's design was planned for 1,032.

A major difference in Wright's thinking, however, is reflected in the fact that he was the only person to include a figure for individuals as well as families. That is no doubt in large part due to the fact that, unlike almost all the others, he provided multiple types of housing based not only on income but also on marital status and gender. In addition to the freestanding single-family houses, there are freestanding duplex apartments, grouped two-family houses, semidetached and attached houses for working-class people, apartments for single men and women, plus larger apartment blocks for families and single people. Whereas Bernhard provided apartments for about 12 percent of his families and Comey only 10, Wright placed approximately two-thirds of his families in apartments, or flats, in addition to the 550 individuals housed that way.[160] All this helps to give his design a sense of the variety and demographic mix more characteristic of an urban situation than of the typically homogeneous suburban development.[161]

Compared to the projects actually submitted in the competition, Wright's design, as David Handlin was the first to point out, was unique in its rejection of the idea of a self-contained, self-centered, homogeneous suburban community.[162] While some have wanted to see in his quarter section scheme the image of an independent "suburban town" based on the University of Michigan sociologist Charles Cooley's Progressivist idea of "self-centered neighbourhoods" offering the alienated city dweller "the urban version of the small-town community," this nostalgic vision characteristic of the proponents of the Garden City and Suburb had no place in Wright's thinking.[163] Wright never thought of the project in terms of a "small-town community." On the contrary, he described its location as "semi-urban" rather than suburban and stated that it was designed as "an integral feature of Chicago."

To that end, Wright adopted the "established gridiron of Chicago's streets" that was "natural," as he wrote, "to every semi-urban section about Chicago" (figure 4.28).[164] Following from that, and "not to change the nature of these things as they naturally come," he sited the various building types in "the location they would naturally prefer." As a consequence, he was forced to contradict one of the most problematic conditions stated in the program, to wit, that two streetcar lines, one going east-west and the other north-south, would intersect at ninety degrees and thus provide a key point of entry and focus for the community. Like the first prize winner, Bernhard, Wright chose to emphasize only one traffic corridor; but unlike his former draftsman, he refused to make a singular and dramatic access point from it into the community.[165] Also, and nearly as important, he created a second edge to his development. The southern band of row houses and multifamily dwellings that parallels the commercial and civic structures on the north wedges the community between the two east-west thoroughfares. This fundamentally eliminated the possibility for self-containment and gave the design an open-endedness that was and is as characteristic of Chicago's inner-ring suburbs as it was uncharacteristic of almost all the other City Club proposals. It mirrors, in effect, the way Oak Park developed in relation to the Loop (figures 1.7, 1.15).

If the rendered plan expresses fully the complex geometric manipulations of the grid that give Wright's quarter section scheme its dynamic symmetry, the aerial perspective provides the image of open-endedness and extensibility that are its direct consequence (figure 4.29). The point of view is low and the perspective forced. This emphasizes in a radical way the linear rather than block-like shape of the design. Between the two east-west bands along the main traffic arteries, and punctuated here and there by the zigzagging "park system," are the gray Quadruple Block Plans. Like the upper and lower strips of collective structures, these bleed off the

edges to appear as if simply cropped from the conurbation of Chicago—and thus allow his neighborhood plan to be perceived as "an integral feature of Chicago." One could imagine similar developments occurring north and south of this one. One cannot help but imagine them continuing east and west of it.[166]

Albert Kelsey, who, as we recall, was "mightily" impressed by the Wright project and described it as the product of "a thoughtful mind thoroughly familiar with" the Chicago context, considered "the accompanying perspectives [to] illustrate his intentions far better than those submitted by any other contributor." His only criticism of the design was "its arterial system," meaning the exclusive focus on the parallel east-west thoroughfares, which Kelsey described as "distinctly bad." He went on to place the rest of the discussion in an urban discourse by relating Wright's strategy of subdivision to the issue of the downtown tall building: "Just as the lofty building is compelling, yearly, smaller and smaller subdivisions of city property in order that a single building may receive proper light and ventilation from all sides, so in semi-suburban residential districts, as suggested by this [Wright's] design, it seems that shorter and wider private lots, in smaller and smaller groups, offer many advantages." "If executed," Kelsey concluded, "the work would not only be individual and artistic but distinctly appropriate if the arterial system were somewhat modified."[167]

If Kelsey's reaction to the strip-like, linear extensibility of Wright's City Club design was problematic, his response to its dependence on the grid was more ambiguous and conflicted. He described the project as a "rectangular scheme . . . without unsightly alleys, but holding somewhat to the established gridiron plan of Chicago."[168] The conditionality of his "but" is substantiated by the general praise he had for projects with "curving streets" having a "home-like" aspect and "pleasant, ever-changing perspectives" in contrast to the "long, monotonous, wind-swept arteries" characteristic of the typical "gridiron plan."[169]

To react positively, without any qualifications, to a design for residential development not rejecting the mundane grid was a rarity at the time. It is therefore interesting to consider the comments of the important architectural critic and editor of *Western Architect*, Robert Craik McLean (1854–1933), who reviewed the Yeomans book in his magazine shortly after it appeared. After recounting the story of the competition and quoting extensively from the jury's report, which described in depth the three prize-winning designs, all of which were illustrated in the article, McLean added a few comments of his own on the Wright project, which he illustrated by its overall plan, the aerial perspective of the Quadruple Block Plan, and the three alternative plans, A, B, and C. McLean also included a long excerpt from the architect's text. The parts chosen were from the opening paragraphs in which Wright explained his reasons for adopting the grid and refusing to contravene its "natural" tendencies. In introducing Wright's explanation, McLean described the architect's approach as one that "seemingly, and wisely, follows the line of least resistance."[170]

Following the "line of least resistance" is a strange way to characterize the work of someone who was usually thought of as a radically innovative, convention-breaking, intensely controlling personality.[171] Obviously, Wright did not resort to the grid out of involition. But why preface "wisely" with "seemingly"? Did that undo the curse of the grid, or did it simply acknowledge Wright's wholesale transformation of it? Wright's use of the grid, though uncompromised by diagonals or curves, was complicated enough as to render it, in actual fact, almost imperspicuous. The strong lateral shearing action of the upper and lower bands, combined with the subtle layering, offsetting, and interpenetration of the different-sized squares, causes the grid to lose visual definition and its diagrammatic geometry to appear to dissolve at the edges. In the City Club project this served to integrate even more completely the quarter section development with its surroundings. By working with and through the Chicago grid, rather than against it, Wright created a dynamic, interactive, indeed *urban* sense of community—a community that was not solely dependent on itself but that deployed its internal resources, energies, and spatial dynamics to establish multiple and diverse relationships both within and outside itself.

The open-endedness and extensibility of the grid deployed by Wright in his City Club project suggest an even wider frame of reference than Chicago and point to the larger meaning the grid had for Wright throughout the earlier part of his career. As we have seen in the projects studied so far, Wright clearly understood the Enlightenment grid to have the kind of "mythic power" that Rosalind Krauss attributed to the form—a power in which the objective and the subjective, the scientific and the ideological are maintained in an equivocatory balance.[172] In the same year that Krauss published her important essay on "Grids" (1979), David Handlin wrote in *The American Home* that, "unlike other architects who despised the grid, Wright attributed a great significance and subtlety to it." That significance and that subtlety were nowhere more in evidence than in the City Club project. There, Handlin continued, "the grid extended out from the quarter section to other parts of Chicago, to roads laid out on the ordinance survey lines and ultimately to the most remote corners of the United States.... The grid had an important meaning in time as well as in space. It had its origins early in American history.... The grid of streets ... joined neighbors [as well as all] Americans from coast to coast. ... Instead of fragmenting a neighborhood, it could be the basis of a community that was much richer and more complex than a version of the self-contained village of the past."[173]

Following Handlin, one can and should read Wright's neighborhood plan as part of a larger continuum, midway between the density of the built-up downtown core and the open landscape of the rural hinterland. This would situate the quarter section's grid within the fabric of American myth and reality—between the taming of the wilderness and the closing of the frontier announced by Frederick Jackson Turner in 1893, the very moment when Burnham and others began to turn their attention to the problems of city planning and urban design and set the stage for the City Club's program. Wright's response to that program represents the culmination of his efforts in this area as well as the most complex of his designs based on the grid formation of the Quadruple Block Plan. His contribution to "the work of the City Club," as he put it, was a kind of swan song to the Chicago suburbs he knew so well. Having moved his residence and practice to Wisconsin and having already planned on spending years overseas in Tokyo, Wright surely knew this would be his last chance to say something large in scale and definitive in scope about an urbanism he had lived, fully experienced, and tried to reshape for twenty-five years—the world that defined his practice from 1889 to 1913. This is the best reason I can think of for his having decided to do the project with only three weeks to spare before departing for Japan, never to return to Oak Park.

II

THE CITY IN QUESTION AT THE DAWN OF THE AUTOMOBILE AGE

Wright went to Tokyo in early 1913 in order to secure the commission for the Imperial Hotel (1913–22), about which he had previously been contacted. A preliminary design was shown at the Chicago Architectural Club's annual exhibition in April 1914. This was further developed by Wright and his staff in his studio at Taliesin in Wisconsin over the next four years and was his main preoccupation during that time. In October 1918 he left for Tokyo to spend most of the next four years supervising the hotel's construction.

When Wright finally returned to the United States in August 1922, he was faced with a new set of architectural and urban conditions. The streetcar suburb and its relation to the downtown were no longer the most exciting issues. The Roaring Twenties had ushered in a new wave of skyscraper construction that was changing the face of the urban core (figure 5.1). The new practice of zoning was coming to be seen as the answer to planning. At the same time, the enormous increase in the use of the automobile posed problems that were unprecedented. Wright was quick to react to this situation, although he was not, as in the 1890s and early 1900s, among the first to do so, nor as unique in his immediate response as he was then.

After placing second in the Chicago Tribune Tower competition of 1922 and receiving accolades from many in the profession for his relatively ahistorical and forward-looking design (figure 5.2), the Finnish architect and city planner Eliel Saarinen (1873–1950) emigrated to the United States, where he took up residence in Evanston, Illinois, the same north Chicago suburb where Burnham had made his home.[1] The year 1923 marked a pregnant moment in Chicago's building

history. The construction of John Mead Howells (1868–1959) and Raymond Hood's (1881–1934) prize-winning Gothic design for the city's main newspaper in 1923–25 highlighted the expansion of the commercial Loop across the Chicago River and into North Michigan Avenue, fulfilling one of the major proposals of the Burnham and Bennett plan (figure 5.3).[2] As part of the second major wave of skyscraper construction in the city, the Tribune Tower and its increasingly tall neighbors fueled the fears of congestion that inspired, initially in New York and then in Chicago, the first concerted efforts to deal with the problem through comprehensive zoning laws and new traffic controls and systems of organization.[3]

Writing in 1923 shortly after his arrival, Saarinen acknowledged that he was rather disappointed with the way Chicago looked—often "dilapidated" and "begrimed with smoke and soot"—especially in comparison with the images of the city in the Burnham and Bennett plan, which he said he had "studied … in all its details" before coming to America. He praised the plan to the skies, calling it a "splendid and grandiose project [that] ought to be adopted in its entirety as a foundation for a rational recreation of Chicago" and for "making Chicago a city beautiful on a truly grand scale." But he expressed one major caveat, the plan's lack of accommodation of the automobile. This was not Burnham and Bennett's fault, however, but just the effect of time. Reviewing in his mind's eye the drawings he had pored over in Finland but could now actually compare with current conditions, Saarinen wrote, "A perspective sketch of Michigan Avenue … arises in my memory.… I see elegant ladies and gentlemen promenading the Avenue in light, colorful costumes, and as a background for the whole, Grant Park in sunny splendor. Instead of finding this, I [now] see the street

5.1. North Michigan Avenue, Chicago, ca. 1926. Foreground right: Chicago Tribune Tower, John Mead Howells and Raymond Hood, 1922–25; foreground left: Wrigley Building, Graham, Anderson, Probst, and White, 1919–22; middle ground right: Allerton Hotel, Murgatroyd and Ogden, with Fugard and Knapp, 1922–24; middle ground left: Water Tower, W. W. Boyington, 1867–69 (National Life Insurance Company Building was to be just behind it). Courtesy of David Phillips Collection

5.2

5.3

5.2. Chicago Tribune Tower project, Chicago, Eliel Saarinen, 1922. Perspective.
From *The International Competition for a New Administration Building for the Chicago
Tribune*, 1923

5.3. Plan of Chicago. Proposed multilevel boulevard connecting Michigan Avenue
to North Michigan Avenue. Aerial perspective, by Jules Guérin. From Burnham
and Bennett

overcrowded with stalled automobiles awaiting their turn to proceed—at least for a space. Thus the picture has changed in fifteen years! And I ask myself, 'What will it be like after another fifteen years has passed?'"[4]

To guide Chicagoans in figuring out how the Burnham and Bennett plan might be updated to deal with the current state of affairs, Saarinen proposed an amendment of his own for the lakefront opposite the Loop (figures 5.4–5). His revision, he stated, was "in a large measure influenced by traffic problems, more especially the solution of the automobile traffic problem."[5] To provide "relief from traffic congestion in the streets" as well as "suitably arranged parking space for present needs and future expansion," Saarinen cut through an entirely new, divided, and limited access motorway running north-south between Michigan Avenue and the lake. Extending the existing North Fairbanks Street to North Lake Shore Drive, where it would connect to Lincoln Park, the nearly seven-mile-long, twelve-lane road, continuing south to Twenty-Second Street, was depressed below street level through most of its length so as to "be free from other vehicle and pedestrian traffic."[6] Beneath Grant Park, it was paralleled on either side by a three-level underground parking garage designed to accommodate forty-seven thousand vehicles and to provide direct pedestrian access to the Loop for office workers and shoppers (figure 5.6).

At both the north and south ends of Grant Park, rising over the roadway and punctuating its extremities, were fifty-seven-story skyscrapers. These disregarded the recently enacted zoning law, which Saarinen no doubt felt justified in doing by virtue of the relative isolation of the towers.[7] The one at the north end of the park, designated for a four-thousand-room hotel, used the air rights over a new central railroad station to create a combined visitor center/transportation hub not unlike the one Le Corbusier (1887–1965) had designed just several months before to serve as the focal point of his ideal Contemporary City of Three Million Inhabitants, shown at the Paris Salon d'Automne in late 1922 (figures 5.7–8). While very different in many respects, the Le Corbusier design issued from a similar intention to adapt the modern city to the scale and speed of the automobile. Like the Saarinen project, Le Corbusier's proposed a multilevel underground complex for rail lines and automobile parking. But instead of depressing the cross-axial, twelve-lane, divided and limited access motorways that intersect in a giant traffic circle under the central

5.4

5.4. Lakefront Development project, Chicago, Eliel Saarinen, 1923. Grant Park, Grant Plaza, and Grant Hotel. Aerial perspective looking northeast. From *AAAR*, December 1923

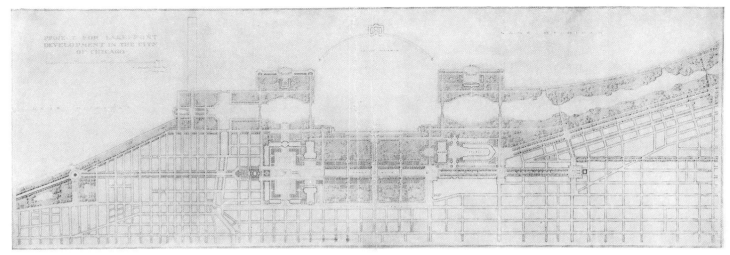

5.5

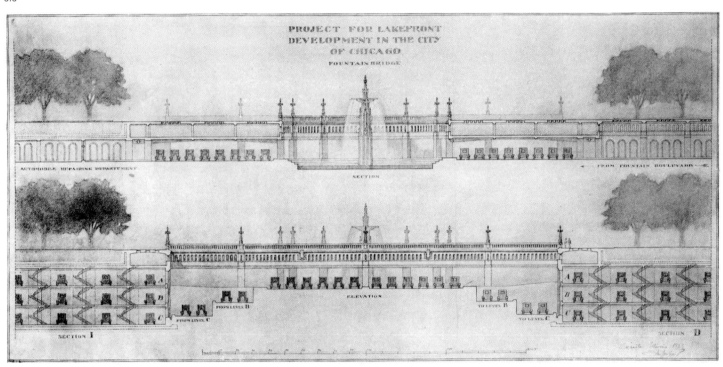

5.6

5.5. Lakefront Development project. Plan. From *AAAR*, December 1923

5.6. Lakefront Development project. Lateral sections through Grant Park. From *AAAR*, December 1923

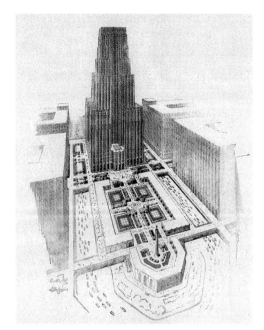

5.7

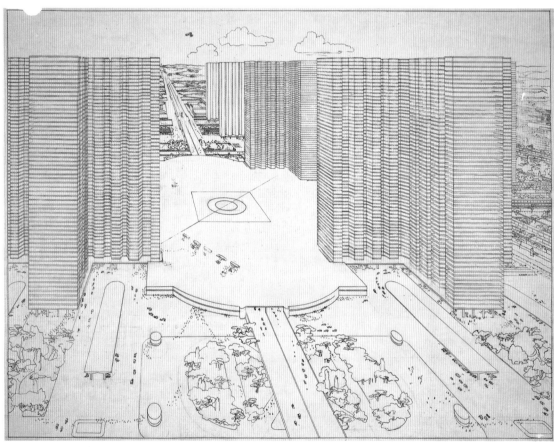

5.8

5.7. Lakefront Development project. Grant Plaza, central railroad station, and Grant Hotel. Aerial perspective from northeast. From *AAAR*, December 1923

5.8. Contemporary City of Three Million Inhabitants project, Le Corbusier, 1922. Central station and transportation hub. Aerial perspective. Reproduced in Le Corbusier, *Urbanisme*, 1925. FLC

platform, Le Corbusier raised the concrete roadbeds above ground level to dramatize the "automobilism" that he believed characterized the modern city. "Motor traffic [*automobilisme*]," he wrote, "is a new factor which will inevitably have far-reaching consequences for the great city" (figures 5.9–10). The tall, sixty-story office towers and lower apartment blocks surrounding the main hub, which also serves as an airport, are spaced out on a quarter-mile street grid generated by the scale of vehicular movement and the purpose to "de-congest the centres of our cities."[8]

Le Corbusier's choice of three million for the number of inhabitants of his Contemporary City was not gratuitous. It was a little more than the population of Paris at the time which, at 2.9 million, was approximately same as Chicago's.[9] The replanning of Paris itself was clearly on his mind and, within three years of the Salon d'Automne, Le Corbusier presented his Voisin Plan for the center of Paris at the international Exposition des Arts Décoratifs held in the summer of 1925 (figure 5.11).[10] As he wrote in a letter to the car manufacturers Citroën, Peugeot, and Voisin requesting funding for the project, "the motor[-car] has killed the large city" and so "the motor[-car] must save the large city."[11] Le Corbusier's solution was similar in certain respects to Saarinen's but much more radical. His idea was to demolish a large part of the historic center of the city—nearly twelve hundred acres in fact—whose street system, he maintained, was incapable of being adapted to the needs and scale of the automobile. Taking the Boulevards Sébastopol and Strasbourg that Haussmann had cut through in the previous century as his north-south axis, he re-created the central railroad station hub of the Contemporary City and surrounded it with widely spaced sixty-story skyscrapers. This area formed a dogleg with a new residential district running east-west, abutting the rue de Rivoli. To open up the city beyond its historic core, Le Corbusier, like Saarinen, thought to create an entirely new, divided, twelve-lane, limited-access motorway doubling and paralleling an existing city street (here the rue de Rivoli and Champs-Elysées). But where Saarinen depressed his below grade, Le Corbusier again elevated his above street level, thereby showcasing the new role the automobile was to play in reconfiguring modern Paris.

The projects for Chicago and Paris by Saarinen and Le Corbusier bear witness to the enormous growth in automobile ownership and use in the years following World War I and the hold this development had on the imagination of architects and city planners. Before Henry Ford built the Model T in 1908, followed by his introduction of assembly line production in 1913, the automobile was a rather rare, luxury item, which it remained in Europe much longer than in the United States. By 1911, there were over 600,000 cars in America and one vehicle for every 169 persons in the city of Chicago. By 1914, that number had been reduced by more than half, and Chicago counted around 30,000 automobiles plus another 10,000 trucks. But the really enormous jump in production and ownership took place between 1914 and 1926. In 1922, for instance, there were almost 10 million private automobiles in the United States, accounting for over 80 percent of the world's supply. This represented nearly a fifteenfold increase in car ownership over a period of less than ten years. Chicago alone had more than 170,000 vehicles, or one per every 16 inhabitants, in that year. That number jumped to 219,000 in 1923, 290,000 in 1925, and nearly 370,000 (including all types of motor vehicles) by 1926.[12]

Frank Lloyd Wright bought the first of his many automobiles in the very early years of the twentieth century. He was one of the first in Oak Park to own a car, where he quickly gained a reputation for his love of driving fast. Soon after the turn of the century, his designs for private houses made the switch from providing stables for horse-drawn carriages to garages for automobiles. The Cheney House in Oak Park (1903–4) was to have included a garage in the raised basement until that was deemed illegal by the authorities, while the Robie House had a three-car garage forming an extended wing of the house. Wright's project for the City Club competition was the only one to provide any private garage facilities for automobiles.

Be that as it may, the city for which Wright was designing prior to World War I was defined by fixed rail traffic, whether streetcar, elevated rapid transit, or steam railroad; and the automobile was still essentially a prerogative of the well-to-do. That all changed by the early 1920s with the boom in automobile ownership and use. According to transportation historian T. C. Barker, "railway passenger mileage" in the United States "reached a peak in 1920" while "ordinary tramway traffic peaked in America in 1926."[13] In a report to the Street Traffic Committee of the Chicago Association of Commerce prepared in 1926 by Miller McClintock (1894–1960), director of the Albert Russel Erskine Bureau for Street Traffic Research at Harvard University and one of the new breed of traffic experts, it was stated that of the approximately 850,000 people entering

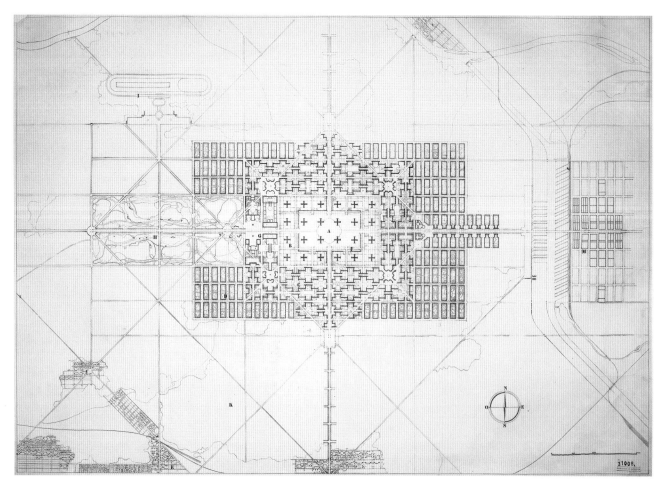

5.9

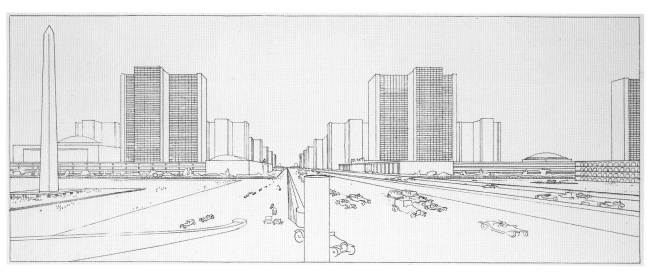

5.10

5.9. Contemporary City of Three Million Inhabitants project. Plan. Reproduced in
Le Corbusier, *Urbanisme*, 1925. FLC

5.10. Contemporary City of Three Million Inhabitants project. Main north-south motorway and skyscraper business district with public service buildings in foreground.
Perspective. Reproduced in Le Corbusier, *Urbanisme*, 1925. FLC

5.11

5.12

5.11. Voisin Plan project for central Paris, Le Corbusier, 1925. Model. FLC

5.12. Congestion of downtown streets in Chicago, ca. 1926. From Miller McClintock, *Report and Recommendations of the Metropolitan Street Traffic Survey*, 1926

the city's downtown area in an average twelve-hour period—a number that constituted more than one-quarter of the city's total population—a little over 33 percent took streetcars, 28 percent took the elevated railway, and more than 19 percent came by private automobile. However, the significant figure for city planners in terms of congestion was that the total number of streetcars going in and out of the Loop was not quite 17,000, whereas private automobiles had by 1926 reached the staggering number of almost 181,000.[14] The report was illustrated with dramatic charts and photographs (figure 5.12).

Wright was in Japan for a good part of this crucial transition from public traction to private motor vehicles. In that country, the automobile was barely in evidence (there were fewer than six thousand at the time Wright arrived).[15] In contrast to such a premodern urban environment, the city where Wright reestablished his American practice must have come as a shock. After returning to Taliesin to put his affairs in order, Wright initially chose Los Angeles as his new base of operations. It was the most automobile-oriented city in the world at the time and, by 1925, boasted one car per every 2.3 persons residing in its sprawling metropolitan area.[16]

Robert Fishman has suggested that living and working in Los Angeles for about a year, between February 1923 and the early spring of 1924, may have influenced Wright's embrace of the automobile as a key factor in urban planning.[17] But whereas Fishman points to the project for Broadacre City (1929–35) as the primary consequence of this, the impact of the automobile as an instrument of both congestion and decongestion became evident in Wright's work much earlier and in more complex ways than has generally been perceived. Chicago, second only to New York in terms of dynamic city growth and change, was the crucible. This time it was to the city center rather than its suburban edges that Wright looked for work. And it was a place now defined as much if not more by the automobile than the soon-to-be outmoded streetcar.

Wright made his intentions clear regarding the focus of his operations in a press conference in Chicago in the fall of 1924 where he announced his decision to "make his home in Chicago [as of] Jan. 1 [1925]." Not only would he live in the city and maintain a downtown office; he would also turn his attention from residential to commercial architecture. The report in the *Chicago Tribune* noted that, although known as the "creator of unique residential architecture," Wright "now ... says he will devote himself entirely to industrial [meaning commercial] architecture."[18] In a follow-up story one month later, the *Tribune* reported that Wright's office/residence would be located on East Cedar Street, on the northern edge of the new North Michigan Avenue development, two blocks from the recently completed Drake Hotel (1919–20) and six blocks north of Water Tower Square, the site of the National Life Insurance Company skyscraper (1923–25) on which he was working at the time (figures 5.1, 5.17). Wright also told the reporter that his office would have an international character, including "a dozen young architects from Japan, Switzerland, Holland, and the United States."[19]

The National Life Insurance Company Building was Wright's first Chicago commercial project during this period. Planned to be one of the largest office buildings in the city, located in the heart of the new North Michigan Avenue business district, it was a major commission that, had it been built, would have provided the architect enormous visibility and recognition. Its design involved Wright in all the current urban issues being faced by the city's architects and planners, namely, congestion, zoning, office building typology, automobile access and parking, and mixed-use development. Wright used the design to rethink conventional strategies for dealing with these problems in ways that intersected with progressive thinking in the United States and in Europe, where a modified version of the project by his young Swiss employee Werner Moser (1896–1970) was soon published in the avant-garde journal *ABC: Beiträge zum Bauen*.[20] It also became the jumping-off point for a much more systematic investigation of the relationship between zoning and traffic congestion in the Skyscraper Regulation project of 1926 (figures 5.35–38), which will be the main focus of the final section of this chapter.

The Skyscraper and the City: From Height Limits to Zoning

The story of the National Life Insurance Company Building precedes Wright's involvement by a few years and charts the development in Chicago from an earlier type of height limitation on buildings to the more comprehensive form of zoning that in many ways subsumed urban planning in the United States following the passage of the New York Building Zone Resolution of 1916, the first such zoning ordinance in the country.[21] The restriction on building heights goes back in modern history to the laws passed in Paris in the 1780s, where the height of a structure was regulated in relation to the width of the street it faced. In America, following the invention and proliferation of the steel-frame tall building, concerns about the effects of excessive height on property values as much as on issues of safety and the quality of the environment led to the institution of restrictive measures as early as the 1890s.

It is hardly surprising that Chicago, the birthplace of steel-frame construction, was at the forefront of this movement, although Boston was the first actually to enact a law limiting building heights. This occurred in 1891, when the state legislature set a flat maximum limit of 125 feet on fireproof structures.[22] In Chicago, discussions that began in the fall of 1891 dragged on for over a year and a half before action was finally taken. Some favored an upper limit of 180 feet, others 160, still others 125; some related the height limit to street width, some called for a single limit, while others allowed for projecting elements like towers, domes, or cupolas as long as they did not occupy more than 15 percent of the building's footprint. When the City Council passed an ordinance calling for a limit of 160 feet, or twelve stories, in late November 1891, the mayor vetoed it. But the matter did not die, no doubt partly as a result of the serious downturn in the economy the following year. A law restricting the height of new buildings to 130 feet, or ten stories, was enacted over a second veto by the mayor in early March 1893 as part of a general ordinance covering all aspects of building within the city limits.[23]

Many cities followed the lead of Boston and Chicago. Baltimore passed a law in 1904 generally restricting heights to 175 feet; two years later Los Angeles set the limit at 150 feet. In 1910 the U.S. Congress established an ordinance for Washington, D.C., imposing a sliding scale of limits based on the width of the street and whether it was designated commercial or residential, the tallest allowable being 130 feet.[24] Such differentiation based upon the width and type of street or predominant use of the district had its source in German zoning laws of the 1890s, which Boston was the first American city to adopt. In 1904 Boston was divided into two districts, one commercial and the other residential, each having its own height limit, the former retaining the 125-foot height, the latter being reduced to 80 feet.[25] This "differential" approach became the basis for the extraordinarily influential 1916 New York zoning law and the 1923 Chicago one that followed it.

But before Chicago arrived at the type of zoning New York pioneered, the height limit for tall buildings in the Loop was reset three times. Economic conditions, concerns over congestion, and a desire to spread out development beyond the area contained by the Chicago River and Lake Michigan determined these revisions. In 1901, the City Council began entertaining ideas for raising the height limit above the 130 feet set eight years before. After considering and actually agreeing to the removal of any upper limit whatsoever, a temporary one of 260 feet was put into place in early 1902.[26] But concerns about congestion as well as the desire to encourage development beyond the Loop led the city, by the end of 1910, to return the limit to 200 feet, or sixteen stories. Towers, domes, and spires not occupying more than 15 percent of the building's footprint could extend the total height to 400 feet.[27] In March 1920, the Chicago City Council raised the height limit back to 260 feet, while retaining a similar allowance for towers, domes, and other ornamental features. It was under this regulation, as Carol Willis points out, that the Tribune Tower competition was conducted and the image of the Chicago skyscraper transformed into something quite different from the typically cubical mass it had been since the late 1880s.[28]

The process of creating a comprehensive zoning ordinance for Chicago began in early 1917, half a year after the New York law was enacted. But Chicago appointed a Zoning Commission charged with drafting the law only in the summer of 1921; and it was not for nearly another two years that the Chicago Zoning Ordinance came into being.[29] The law was approved in April 1923 and took effect in May, the same month Wright made the first set of drawings for the National Life Insurance Company Building, which he published in 1928, well after the project had been canceled, as a theoretical "practical solution of the skyscraper problem" (figures 5.15–17).[30] While Wright did not actually sign a contract for the work until the summer of 1924, the May 1923 drawings were clearly done in expectation of receiving the job, which had previously been given to another firm whose design was rejected by the client, Albert M. Johnson (1870–1948), after receiving major coverage in the Chicago press.

When the city's building height limit was raised to 260 feet in March 1920, the reporter for the *Chicago Tribune* covering the story spoke of the change as "opening the way to a skyscraper building boom."[31] Although many objected to the increase in height, Ernest R. Graham (1866–1936), one of the principals of Graham, Anderson, Probst, and White, the successor firm to D. H. Burnham and Company, spoke in favor

of it.[32] It was his firm that designed the Wrigley Building, which initiated the new wave of construction on North Michigan Avenue (1919–22; figure 5.1); and it was Graham, Anderson, Probst, and White who were commissioned by Johnson in 1921 to design the new National Life Insurance Company headquarters in the very heart of the North Michigan Avenue district. Their project, which heeded closely the revised 1920 regulations, was published under the headline "Chicago's Newest and Greatest" in early January 1922 (figure 5.13).[33]

Johnson, who became president of National Life in 1906 and, by the early 1920s, had turned it into one of the largest insurance companies in the world, began thinking about capitalizing on the development of North Michigan Avenue soon after the Wrigley Building was announced. After contemplating a new headquarters on the corner of North Michigan Avenue and East Erie Street, about five blocks north of the Wrigley site, he finally settled on the east portion of the block between Pearson and Chestnut Streets, facing the Water Tower (the smaller, west portion of the block, facing Rush Street, was occupied by the just completed Quigley Preparatory Seminary; see figure 5.14).[34] Had he been able to acquire it all, the site would have totaled sixty-seven thousand square feet and made his building's footprint the largest in the city. The frontage on Pearson Street was a little over 300 feet, that on Michigan Avenue 214 feet, and that on Chestnut almost 330 feet.

The design by Graham, Anderson, Probst, and White filled the entire site with an Italianate-style, twenty-two-story, 260-foot-high block cut out at the southeast corner of its arcaded upper portion to allow for a tower to rise up to the legal 400-foot limit (figure 5.13). Other than the corner cutout, the block was solid and no doubt had a central light court. The prominent tower, based on Giotto's campanile for the Cathedral of Santa Maria dei Fiore in Florence, addressed the special corner condition of the site. Located at the point where North Michigan Avenue angles to the east, the tower would have been visible from the southern tip of the avenue, between the Wrigley Building and the projected Tribune Tower, and thus made the National Life Building a landmark to rival those other two.

Johnson was unable to purchase the north half of the site from the Potter Palmer estate. He terminated the Graham, Anderson, Probst, and White contract sometime in 1922 or early 1923. Whether this was directly related to the failure to assemble the entire parcel or to a dissatisfaction with the design is not known. What is known is that Johnson had a definite change of heart regarding the type of architecture he would encourage for this " 'large scale' " urban venture, as he put it, " 'to participate in the unmistakable trend to upper Michigan avenue' " and to play his part in bringing into being the " 'great buildings [that] will line the boulevard, making it one of the showplaces of the country.' "[35] For this he hired Frank Lloyd Wright.[36]

It is not known when Johnson first approached Wright. We also do not know precisely what the program called for. Both Johnson and Wright always referred to the structure as an "office building," but the plans from the beginning included a shopping arcade as well as studio and apartment units. This was a novel and forward-looking idea at the time.[37] In his *Autobiography* (1932), Wright stated that he began working on a "study" related to the cantilever-construction, curtain-wall concept of the Johnson "office building" as early as 1920, based on the techniques to withstand the effects of earthquakes he developed for the Tokyo hotel. He added that "Johnson was interested to see how the cantilever principle so successful there could be adapted to skyscraper requirements."[38] In the 1928 *Architectural Record* article in which they were later published, the drawings for the National Life Building are dated May 1923. In his text, Wright stated that he "began work upon *this* study [meaning the actual Johnson design] in Los Angeles in the winter of 1923 having had the main features of it in mind for many years."[39] Wright noted that the plan was "worked out for a lot three hundred feet by one hundred feet, the courts being open to the south," which precisely describes the site on East Pearson Street and North Michigan Avenue, facing the Water Tower, that Johnson had been able to acquire (figure 5.14).[40]

The earliest documentation we have is a letter written by Wright's former employee Rudolf Schindler (1887–1953) from Los Angeles in early February 1924 to his Viennese compatriot Richard Neutra (1892–1970), then living in Chicago, stating that Wright was in Los Angeles, at the Beverly Hills Hotel, working on a project for a skyscraper to be built in Chicago (Neutra would eventually work for Wright between October 1924 and February 1925).[41] Johnson later remembered meeting with Wright at the hotel and inviting him to accompany him to Death Valley to look at the site where he wanted to build a winter lodging. They went there in early March 1924, and Wright began developing the design for the Death Valley

ranch soon after the middle of the month. Johnson also later recalled to Henry-Russell Hitchcock that "about this time, I was contemplating the building of an office building in Chicago for the National Life Insurance Company and I asked Mr. Wright to submit the proposed design."[42]

The first documented meeting of Johnson and Wright specifically to discuss the National Life Building took place at Taliesin on 12 July 1924. It is not known if any drawings were shown to the insurance company executive at this time, although Neutra's wife wrote to her parents saying that Wright was banking "all his hopes" on the occasion and that "for weeks all had been prepared for this visit."[43] A week after the meeting, Johnson wrote to Wright saying "we would like to have you, as Architect, take up a preliminary study" and, to that effect, he sent a contract that Wright duly signed. It was specified that the contract was "not a continuing contract" and that if the client was pleased with the proposal, then and only then would a further contract be issued to "erect a building upon plans designed by you."[44] That never happened and the project died sometime in the latter part of 1925.

Wright's description of the National Life design published in the *Record* and subsequently more or less verbatim in the *Autobiography* stressed the structural and material aspects of the building (figures 5.15–17). It began with a lengthy discussion of the use of sheet-copper in combination with glass to create "suspended" walls as "screens," making "the exterior walls, as such, disappear." It pointed out that the "standardized" facade elements, based on a two-foot "unit system," would be factory-made by modern machine methods and that only the reinforced concrete or steel structure (he left the choice open) would be made at the site. The floors would be cantilevered from the vertical piers, which would be revealed as they rose through the upper part of the building. Throughout, the supporting structure and enclosing screen walls would be kept conceptually and visually distinct from one another. The open floor plan, in combination with the unit-system design of partitions, was meant to allow "any changes to suit tenants." Finally, the cantilevered structural system and use of modern materials, according to Wright, eliminated traditional masonry-derived " 'architecture' " and " '*features*,' " resulting in a transparent, luminous building "one-third lighter than anything in the way of a tall building yet built—and three times stronger."[45]

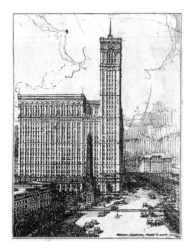

5.13

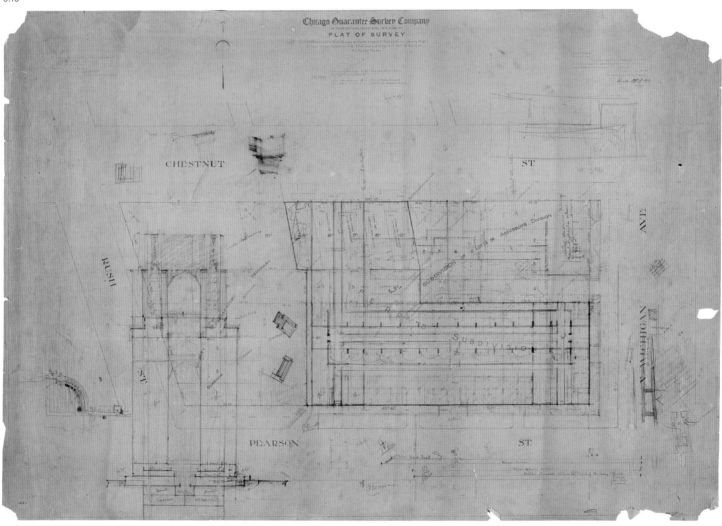

5.14

5.13. National Life Insurance Company Building project, Chicago, Graham, Anderson, Probst, and White, 1921–22. Perspective. From *CDT*, January 1922

5.14. National Life Insurance Company Building project, Wright, 1923–25. Preliminary sketch plan, section, perspectives, and details drawn over 1921 plat map, ca. 1923

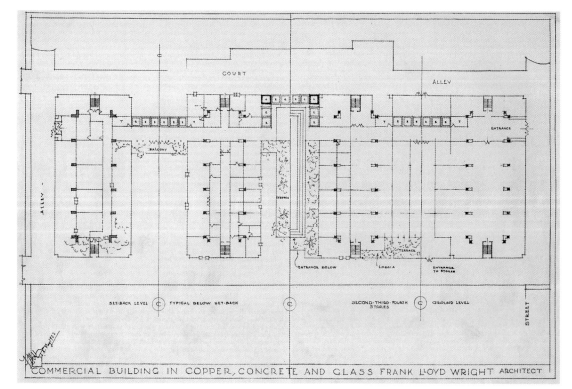

COMMERCIAL BUILDING IN COPPER, CONCRETE AND GLASS FRANK LLOYD WRIGHT ARCHITECT

5.15

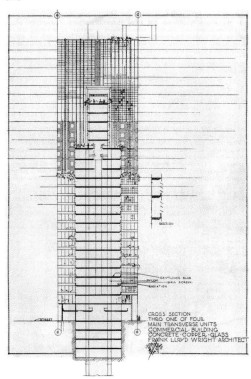

5.16

5.15. National Life Insurance Company Building project (prob.). Plan at four different levels, May 1923. From *AR*, October 1928

5.16. National Life Insurance Company Building project (prob.). Section through one of the four transverse units, May 1923. From *AR*, October 1928

OFFICE BUILDING FOR NATIONAL LIFE INSURANCE CO. OF U.S.A. CHICAGO. A. M. JOHNSON PRESIDENT   FRANK LLOYD WRIGHT ARCHITECT

5.17

5.17. National Life Insurance Company Building project. Perspective from southeast,
1925. Reproduced in *AR*, October 1928. Private collection

There was but a single passing reference, toward the very end of the description, to the building's unusual form, meaning its setback masses and square-faced sawtooth plan. "To gratify the landlord," Wright wrote, "his lot area is now salable to the very lot-line and on every floor, where ordinances do not interfere and demand that they be reduced in area as the building soars."[46] The reference to the impact of the new zoning law of May 1923 is clear, although Wright did not discuss it as a generating principle of design. Nor did he even broach the larger issue that gave rise to such "ordinances," namely, the proliferation of skyscrapers in cities like Chicago. This is especially puzzling since Wright spent a good deal of energy at this time outlining his reasons for condemning the tall building in a series of writings and interviews that would lay the foundation for his future diatribes against what he would call the "tyranny of the skyscraper."[47]

Wright's negativity toward the skyscraper no doubt owed much to his contempt for the ubiquitous eclectic products of the large commercial architectural firms that produced them. One can actually date his initial public statements on this score to the latter part of 1923, right after he claimed to have embarked on the National Life project. The occasion was the Great Kanto earthquake of 1 September 1923, which destroyed much of Tokyo and, most disastrously in Wright's view, the American-style steel-frame buildings that had recently been constructed there. Within a week of the event, he wrote the text "Why the Skyscraper?" that Ralph Fletcher Seymour published shortly thereafter in Chicago with a new, more alarming title, *Experimenting with Human Lives*.[48]

The death and destruction in Japan, Wright wrote, "raise the question WHY THE SKYSCRAPER?—a question from time to time successfully evaded by landlord and commercialized architect—and by false civic pride." "The skyscraper, never more than a commercial expedient," he went on, "is become a threat, a menace to the welfare of human beings." Because of its size and the consequent "congestion that raises ground values and rates to fabulous figures," "the skyscraper has become an immoral expedient, one that demoralizes its neighbors, when it does not rob them [of light and air], compelling them to compete in kind or perish." "The tall steel-frame building we call the skyscraper," he declared, "has no ... scientific, aesthetic, or moral basis for existence." In demanding "the abolition of the skyscraper," Wright joined with those who would use an even more draconian system of height limitations and zoning laws

than so far proposed by any American city. "There seems to be no way to check it," he concluded, "except by radical legislation based upon a radically different conception of what constitutes a modern habitable city."[49]

Over the next month, Wright pursued this line of attack, though not always suggesting the legislative route, in interviews in Chicago and Madison, Wisconsin. He linked the issue of congestion directly to the increased traffic resulting from the massive numbers of people commuting to work in the skyscrapers. "I'll tell you how this traffic problem should be remedied," he said to a reporter for the *Chicago Tribune*: "'Take a gigantic knife and sweep it over your loop. Cut off your skyscrapers at the seventh floor. Spread out your loop. Spread out everything.... If you cut down these horrible buildings you'll have no traffic jams. You'll have trees again.'"[50] To the founder and publisher of the *Madison Capital Times*, William T. Evjue, he said he was "greatly pleased" at the fact that the Supreme Court had recently sustained a state law limiting building heights, and added, "'The skyscraper is an abomination. It is ugly and it is not necessary. It brings congestion where congestion is not necessary in these days of steam, telephone, and speed. The only trouble with your Wisconsin law is that it is too liberal,—125 feet [or ten stories] is too high. Buildings should not exceed seven stories in height.'"[51]

Wright's comments on skyscrapers point in two different, though related directions. The first, having to do with his criticism of the mere expediency of the type and the desire to limit building heights to a maximum of seven stories, aligns him with the most conservative wing of architectural thought at the time. This may be best represented by Thomas Hastings (1860–1929), a graduate of the Ecole des Beaux-Arts and the office of McKim, Mead & White, and architect, with his partner, John M. Carrère (1858–1911), of the classical New York Public Library (1897–1911). In 1926, Hastings described skyscrapers as "'a calamity'" and "'the craziest buildings in New York.'" Calling for "'limiting the height of buildings to not more than eight stories,'" he defended this position by noting that "'there is nothing like it in all Europe, and surely they are not wrong.'" Echoing Wright, he declared that "'a radical revision in building laws is the only remedy for our growing congestion'": "'The time is coming when the skyscraper will be torn down because of high taxes'" and "'every large city will be decentralized.'"[52]

Wright's advertence to legislation as the way to "check" the baleful influence of the skyscraper, a solution he shared with Hastings, is the second point I have in mind and the one more relevant to the work Wright was then doing and would continue to do for several years. Despite his remarks regarding the calamitous nature of the skyscraper, Hastings had in fact designed a number of New York buildings that topped out at well over twenty stories each. These included the twenty-two-story Liggett Building of 1919–20 and the twenty-six-story Fisk Building, finished one year later. He also served as design consultant to his former employee Benjamin Wistar Morris on the twenty-two-story Cunard Building (1917–21). All three, but especially the first, were viewed as pace-setting attempts to deal with the 1916 New York zoning law regarding height limitations.

Wright, as we shall see, was no different from Hastings in his willingness, even enthusiasm, to speak out of both sides of his mouth, as it were, and take on the task of skyscraper design while calling for the disappearance of the type as such. And as with Hastings, a close reading of the applicable zoning provisions would fundamentally direct his thinking about the form of the skyscraper, its relation to its neighbors, and even determine in detail the size and shape of the building's envelope. For this reason, it is necessary to review the Chicago Zoning Ordinance that was instrumental in the development of the National Life Insurance Building and succeeding Skyscraper Regulation project. And because the Chicago law derived directly from the previous New York resolution, we shall look at that first.

Although it would eventually result in the first comprehensive districting plan for an American city, the New York process began with the narrower purpose of simply studying the problem of limiting the height of the city's skyscrapers. But the work of the Heights of Building Commission appointed in 1913 soon made it apparent that the problem was more complex. And so the following year, a Commission on Building Districts and Restrictions was established "to arrest the seriously increasing evil of the shutting off of light and air from other buildings and from the public streets, to prevent unwholesome and dangerous congestion both in living conditions and in street and transit traffic and to reduce the hazards of fire and peril to life." This would be achieved, first, by "divid[ing] the City into districts or into zones" and then "prescrib[ing] the regulation of the height, size and

arrangement of buildings upon different bases in such different districts or zones."[53]

The Building Zone Resolution enacted into law in July 1916 divided the five boroughs of the city into three Use Districts, five Height Districts, and five Area Districts. The Use Districts were defined as Residence, Business, and Unrestricted (meaning essentially factories and warehouses). The Height Districts, which took into account both "the height and bulk of buildings," were defined in relation to a multiplier of street widths ranging from "one times districts" to "two and one-half times districts." The Area Districts were differentiated according to the relationship between building lot occupancy and required open spaces, such as yards and courts.[54]

For architects working in the commercial center of Manhattan, from Wall Street to Fifty-Ninth Street, the regulations on height and bulk were the most important. The "two and one-half times" district was confined to the Wall Street area, where, because of the existing tall buildings, it was thought that any new construction would be unduly prejudiced by a lesser limit. All other office buildings were in a "two times" district. The multiplier, as already noted, related to street width, of which the minimum was set at fifty feet and the maximum at one hundred. All calculations were based on perimeter-block buildings built up to the street line and filling their entire lot. Thus, in a "two times" district, the maximum height of a building on a street one hundred feet wide or more was two hundred feet. This amounted to approximately sixteen stories.

But this was not the whole story. The novelty of the New York ordinance, firmly rooted in the eighteenth-century Parisian law and its allowance for mansard roofs, was the concept of the setback.[55] Any sixteen-story building in a "two-times" district was allowed to go higher by stepping back from the street line one foot in depth for every four feet in height, while the twenty-story building in the "two and one-half times" district had to step back five feet from the street line for every additional foot in height (figure 5.18). The only practical limits were the depth of the lot and the economic advantage or disadvantage of building higher. Finally, in addition to the "setback principle," as it was called, there was a provision for a tower, with no height limit, as long as it did not occupy more than 25 percent of the building lot (figure 5.19). The tower could be square or rectangular in plan and placed anywhere on the building's footprint.

SETBACK PRINCIPLE.

Typical example in a 1½ times district, for streets 50' to 100' wide.

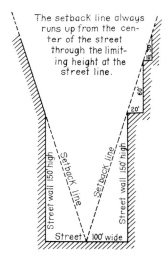

The setback line always runs up from the center of the street through the limiting height at the street line.

5.18

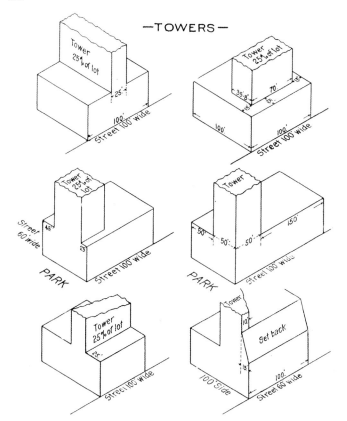

—TOWERS—

5.19

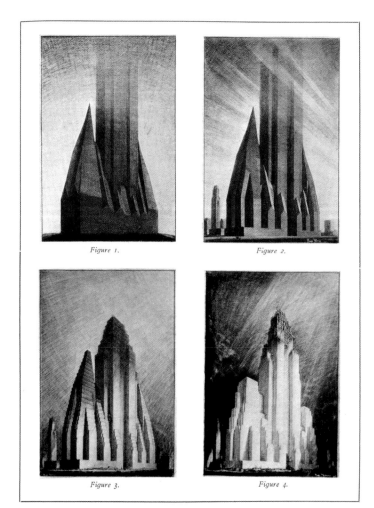

Figure 1.

Figure 2.

Figure 3.

Figure 4.

5.20

5.18. Setback principle diagram for a "one and one-half times" district, New York Building Zone Resolution, 1916. From *Commission on Buildings and Restrictions: Final Report*, 1916

5.19. Towers diagram, New York Building Zone Resolution. From *Commission on Buildings and Restrictions: Final Report*

5.20. "Evolution of a City Building under the Zoning Law" (sequential stages in development of skyscraper design according to the setback principle), Harvey Wiley Corbett and Hugh Ferriss, 1921–22. From *Pencil Points*, April 1923

Of all the provisions of the Building Zone Resolution, the "setback principle" had the most significant influence on architectural design. The editors of *Western Architect* went so far as to characterize the entire document as "the Set-Back Zoning Law."[56] In the years following the law's implementation, the setback device became so prominent and widespread that architects began to speak of it as having established the basis for an entirely new, modern style that was truly American. One of the earliest articles defining the formal opportunities encouraged by the new design principle was written by the New York architect Harvey Wiley Corbett (1873–1954) and illustrated with Hastings's Fisk and Liggett Buildings.[57]

Corbett and his sometime collaborator the architectural renderer Hugh Ferriss (1889–1962) went on to write many articles on the subject, explaining how the use of setbacks changed the way architects designed buildings. These changes included a new emphasis on the vertical rather than the horizontal; the use of continuous channels or "sinkages" to highlight the vertical lines; the disappearance of the traditional cornice and its replacement by the step-back angle forming a continuous and uniform street line; and, finally, the emergence of a sculptural approach in place of the former, two-dimensional "facadism."[58] As a team, Corbett and Ferriss also produced a set of dramatic drawings illustrating sequentially how the setback principle would govern the shaping of the skyscraper's exterior envelope (figure 5.20). These were often published at the time and, as Carol Willis has pointed out, were exhibited not only in New York in early 1922 but also in Chicago, as architects there and elsewhere were working on their submissions for the Tribune Tower competition (June–November 1922).[59]

Chicago architects and critics closely followed the changes in New York and discussed the effects of the new zoning law, especially once the city approved the proposition to create an ordinance for Chicago in early 1920 and then appointed a Zoning Commission to draft it over a year later.[60] Writing in 1921, the City Club's Irving Pond remarked that "the zoning commission of Manhattan," in suggesting the use of setbacks to allow for "light and air," "brought designers to their semi-senses" and "told them almost how to design for beauty." According to Pond, the New York "zoning law has given architects a chance to create beautiful and appropriate buildings" that would be "something modern, born of a new spirit which is neither Greek or Gothic nor Roman or classic renaissance,

but which is intensely of today."[61] In a two-part follow-up, written in early 1923 as a critique of the Tribune Tower competition, Pond noted that although no law imposing "restrictions as to setbacks" was then in force in Chicago, "the setback" as a "form or contrivance" had come to dominate architectural thinking regarding the design of the skyscraper. Pointing to example after example where the principle came into play, and was either overused or misunderstood, Pond constantly returned to Saarinen's second-place project as showing how the setback principle could create a design of "exalted spirituality" embodying "an American ideal," despite its being produced by a foreigner (figure 5.2).[62]

As it happened, by the time the second part of Pond's article on the Tribune Tower competition celebrating the setback principle in skyscraper design was published, the Chicago Zoning Ordinance, based in large part on the New York law, had been approved by the City Council and was about to go into effect.[63] In force as of 12 May 1923, the Chicago ordinance followed that of New York in its basic concept of differential districting. But instead of distinguishing three Use Districts, as the earlier New York ordinance had, Chicago's included four; and instead of defining both Height and Area Districts as distinct categories, the Chicago law combined all aspects dealing with the height, bulk, and lot coverage of buildings into what it called Volume Districts. There were also significant differences in the limits placed on height. The four Use Districts defined by the Chicago Zoning Ordinance were Residential, Apartment, Commercial, and Manufacturing. Volume Districts were defined as five in number. The "5th Volume District," of which the Loop and North Michigan Avenue were the most prominent, had no restrictions regarding lot occupancy or building volume as a multiplier of lot area and thus no requirement for courts or open space. The height limitation in the "5th Volume District" was the least restrictive. In fact, it was more lenient than New York's "two and one-half times district" and was not tied to street width.

In its 1923 ordinance, Chicago's existing height limit of 260 feet was raised to 264 feet. This held true for any street, be it wide, like North Michigan Avenue or State Street, or narrow, like so many in the Loop. Furthermore, the only provisions for setbacks above the 264-foot limit were (1) on the street face of the building, the height defined by a thirty-degree angle for a distance of 32 feet from the upper edge of the wall plane; and (2) on the alley side of a building, a shallow step back within this same angle based on a ratio of one to ten for any part of the wall higher than ten times the distance of the building to the centerline of the alley. This second setback, however, would come into play only after a distance of 55 feet from an intersection.

Like previous height limit laws in Chicago, there was a provision for towers, which could now be fully occupied as functional office spaces. Furthermore, like the New York regulation but unlike the previous 400-foot limit in Chicago, there was no upper limit for such projecting elements. Any tower, dome, or volume of any shape could rise to whatever height desired as long as (1) it did not have a footprint larger than 25 percent of the building block or lot and (2) the volume in cubic feet of any such projection or projections did not exceed one-sixth of the total volume of the building within the 264-foot-high envelope. For Chicago architects then, in contradistinction to their New York counterparts, the calculation of cubic contents was a special factor needing to be addressed.

The National Life Insurance Company Building as an Expression of the Zoning Envelope

The National Life Insurance Company's site was in the Commercial District that extended north from the Loop into a large part of the Near North Side. It was also just inside the same "5th Volume District," whose western boundary, above Chicago Street, followed a zigzag line running northeast to the Drake Hotel at the top of North Michigan Avenue (figure 5.21). The line cuts through the western section of the block bounded by East Pearson Street on the south, Rush on the west, East Chestnut on the north, and North Michigan Avenue on the east, leaving the existing Quigley Preparatory Seminary in two different districts but maintaining the entire parcel Johnson had originally hoped to acquire within the highest density district (see figure 5.14). Even without the northern part of the block, separated from the southern half by an alley, the inclusion of the site in the "5th Volume District," with frontage on both Water Tower Square and the developing area's main north-south axis, made it an extremely desirable location.

Despite its advantages in real estate terms and the fact that it faced south onto an open square containing a famous city landmark, the site presented an awkward, long, and narrow footprint. This was rather unusual in the office building/shopping areas of Chicago where, as the well-established local

architect George C. Nimmons (1865–1947) wrote in commenting on the proposed zoning law, the "form of a hollow square" (see figure 3.24) was preferred by the Chicago Real Estate Board and adopted by them as the model for determining the ideal "earning power of a typical office building." On this basis, on a typical lot of about 160 by 170 feet, "the building," Nimmons said, "reaches its maximum rate of earning at about the twentieth story."[64] A site such as that of the National Life, measuring approximately 100 by 300 feet, was less efficient and less flexible in conventional real estate terms.

Presented with this situation, Wright began on a much more conservative tack than the final design would suggest. Evidence for this is what is undoubtedly the initial sketch, done most likely in the early spring of 1923 (figure 5.14). Drawn over a 1921 plat survey of the site, on the southern three-quarters of the block, is a plan accompanied by a section, two thumbnail perspectives, some details, and numerous marginal notes.[65] The plan shows a modular structure, based on a twenty-foot bay, surrounding an atrium court running the entire width of the building, from east to west. The section to the lower left reveals that the atrium court does not quite rise to the top of the building but only to a height of approximately three hundred and fifty feet. Above is a setback open lantern, containing the heating and ventilating ducts, which rises about another fifty feet. Setbacks on both the front and rear of the building, also visible in the thumbnail sketches, articulate the massing of the structure in terms of its functional spaces and dramatize the extension of the atrium lantern. Offices occupy the floors up to the first setback, at a height of nearly 260 feet, above which studio apartments begin. Though conceived essentially as a thin slab, like the architect's only previous skyscraper project, the Press Building for the *San Francisco Call* (1913), the preliminary design for the National Life Building completely eschews the earlier Sullivanesque structural grid and capping cornice in favor of a play of shifting planes related to one another in a series of setbacks.

While echoing somewhat the profile and vertical emphasis of Saarinen's Tribune Tower, which Wright surely knew through Sullivan's publication of it in the February 1923 *Architectural Record*, the shallow planar setbacks indicated in the thumbnail sketches look forward to the more modernistic designs of such later buildings as Raymond Hood's Daily News Building (1929–30) and RCA Building at Rockefeller Center (1931–33), both in New York.[66] On the other hand, the decision to design the structure around an open skylit court conforms to a Chicago tradition, alluded to by Nimmons, that can be traced back, most famously, to Burnham and Root's Masonic Temple, built in the Loop in 1890–92 as the tallest building in the world. But in contrast to the earlier building's square-shaped court, the one in Wright's preliminary design is oblong, recalling the arcade-like court in the Bradbury Building in Los Angeles (George H. Wyman, 1889–93), which Wright would recently have come to know.

The opening up of the structure to pedestrian movement and activity was a response to the fact that the National Life Building, like the Masonic Temple and Bradbury Building, was intended to have shops and other commercial activities on the ground-floor and mezzanine levels.[67] Whether there were to be entrances for office workers and shoppers from both Michigan Avenue and Pearson Street is difficult to tell. But even more important than the accommodation of foot traffic, at least in the context of urban planning, is the fact that the building was intended to have vehicular access and underground parking. It is unclear how much parking was projected, but one can see, on the left side of the plan, the ramp for automobiles in the space between the proposed building and the neighboring seminary and, in the section, the lower levels devoted to parking. Most intriguing is the cut through the main floor into the lower "automobile roadway," allowing the building's occupants and shoppers to see down into the underground garage.

The integration of parking within an office building was a novel concept at the time. The most celebrated early example of the idea was realized in Chicago a little after Wright's preliminary design for the National Life Building. In order to provide security for its users, the forty-story Jewelers' Building, built at the northern edge of the Loop between 1924 and 1926, was designed with a 572-car garage-tower in its central core. This was serviced by a twenty-two-story automobile elevator that could take a vehicle with its occupants and precious gems and metals directly to any floor from a street-level entrance or an underground one off the lower level of Water Street (now Wacker Drive), which was concurrently being double-decked (1924–26).[68] One of the first buildings to be designed and constructed under the new zoning ordinance, the Jewelers' Building was a textbook example of the application of the law in the city's "5th Volume District." The nearly square base rises to a height of 264 feet beneath the cornice; the central tower above occupies 25 percent of the 162-by-140-foot lot; and

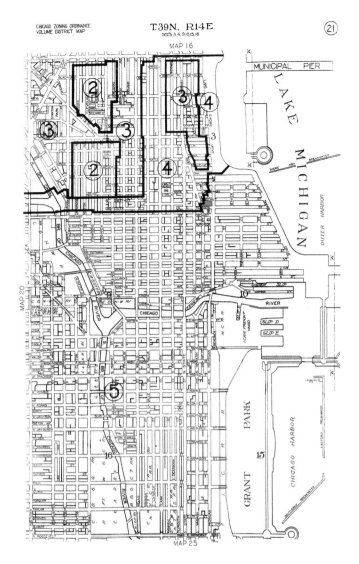

5.21

5.21. Volume District Map of Loop and Near North Side, Chicago Zoning Ordinance, 1923. (National Life Insurance Company Building site indicated in red.) From *Chicago Zoning Ordinance, Passed by the City Council of the City of Chicago on April 5, 1923,* 1923

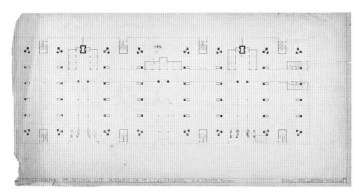

5.22

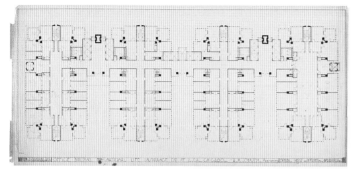

5.23

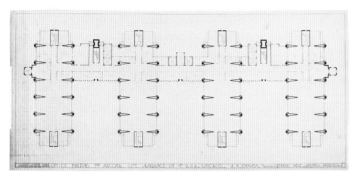

5.24

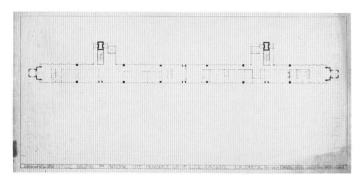

5.25

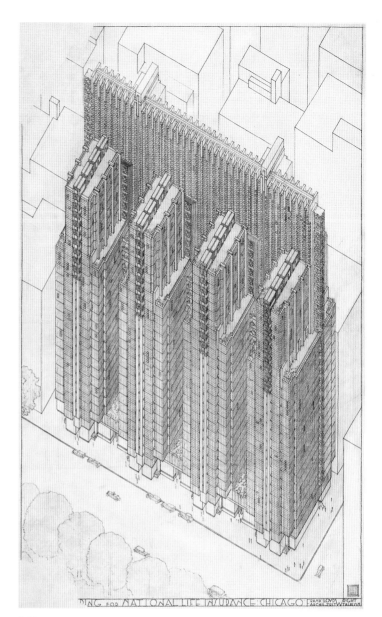

5.26

5.22. National Life Insurance Company Building project, Wright. Plan, first floor, 1925

5.23. National Life Insurance Company Building project. Plan, fifth through seventeenth floors, 1925

5.24. National Life Insurance Company Building project. Plan, twenty-seventh floor, 1925

5.25. National Life Insurance Company Building project. Plan, thirty-second floor, 1925

5.26. National Life Insurance Company Building project. Axonometric perspective from southeast

5.27

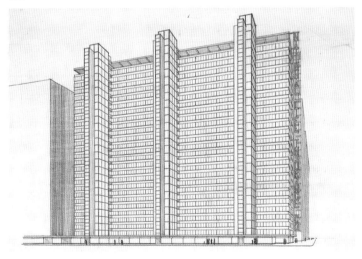

5.28

5.27. National Life Insurance Company Building project. Perspective from east-southeast

5.28. Office Building project, Chicago, Werner Moser, 1924. gta Archives/ETH Zurich

the top of the dome containing the Stratosphere Restaurant reaches a height of over 500 feet.[69]

Wright's final design for the National Life Building lacked the forward-looking accommodation for the automobile of the preliminary project and Jewelers' Building, although it did preserve the radical programmatic combination of living units within a predominantly office building. Its innovative and experimental aspects on the formal level, however, are revealed in the way the plan was organized and how the building's envelope was shaped to respond to the new zoning ordinance, both in its letter and in its spirit. The desirability of reducing bulk and bringing light and air into the commercial areas of the city lay behind the fundamental move Wright made in going from the atrium court *parti* of the preliminary project to a sawtooth plan (figures 5.14–15).

In the project as worked out by May 1923, at the very moment the new zoning ordinance was to go into effect, Wright turned the building inside out, opening up the block and disaggregating it to form three large light courts within the four fin-like wings that project perpendicularly to the south from the flat slab forming the building's tall, thin backbone. To make that openness and sense of transparency part and parcel of the very material being of the structure, Wright forsook the appearance of structural mass conveyed by the planar interlocking of the forms in the preliminary design. The previously solid-looking wall was treated as a "light-giving exterior screen," as he wrote.[70] Pleated, faceted, and folded back over the extruded structural frame, the glass and copper curtain walls reflect the passing clouds and gleam from within in the perspective drawn for Johnson and published in the 1928 *Record* article on the building (figure 5.17).

If the move from preliminary sketch to final design is clear, the different stages in the final design as represented by the drawings in the Wright Foundation Archives are not. There are more than forty drawings. Among these are at least two sets, some with multiple copies, of floor plans at different levels of the building, interior views, and several versions of the perspective published in 1928 (figures 5.22–25).[71] These are all either dated 1925 or form part of the group produced at that time. The draftsmen likely included Neutra and Moser, the latter of whom, as mentioned earlier, produced his own variation on the design (figure 5.28).[72]

In addition to the main group of 1925 drawings, there are two perspectives reflecting a slightly different design (figures

5.26–27). One is an axonometric projection, possibly done to satisfy a client request; the other is a raking perspective from the east side of North Michigan Avenue. Both are less decorated, especially in the lower stories, where, at street level, the continuous plane of glass display windows is made quite conspicuous. Finally, and most revealing of all the sheets preserved in the Wright Foundation Archives is one that is not a drawing of the building but rather an architecturally lettered chart detailing the cubic contents of the structure with the obvious purpose of clarifying its combined height and bulk in response to the Chicago Zoning Ordinance's distinctive focus on volume (figure 5.29).

The set of 1925 drawings, as well as the two additional perspectives, illustrate a thirty-three-story building (including the top-floor space for mechanical equipment) whose fin wings project from the transverse vertical slab four bays south toward Water Tower Square and two bays back to the rear alley.[73] The square-faced sawtooth plan was motivated by the desire to bring natural light into all the building's offices as well as to decrease the bulk of the structure.[74] Such a plan type was hardly unknown in skyscraper construction, although, by the 1920s, and especially in the United States, it had become more generally associated with hotels and apartment houses than with commercial office buildings.[75] Wright's mentor Sullivan used an open U-shaped courtyard plan for the Union Trust Building in St. Louis (1892–93) and Burnham designed the twenty-three-story Dime Savings Bank in Detroit (1910–12) on the same principle. But certainly the most famous office building of the type in the United States constructed in the early 1920s was Albert Kahn's (1869–1942) General Motors Building in Detroit, designed in 1919–20 and completed in 1923 (figure 5.30). Like Wright's National Life project, it has four projecting wings framing three light courts opening onto the street above a two-story base.

In comparison with these, Wright's sawtooth National Life design is much more articulated in terms of function while at the same time being uniquely expressive of the new zoning conditions under which it was to have been built. The thin, thirty-three-story slab forming the backbone, or spine, of the structure rises well above the projecting wings, thus markedly differentiating itself from them in a forecast of the servant-served distinction that Louis Kahn would later describe as fundamental to his conception of modern architecture.[76] In the National Life Building, the transverse slab contains and defines both the vertical and the horizontal circulation routes through the building (figure 5.26). An unbroken corridor or hallway runs east-west through the structure at every floor. At street level, it can be reached from the entrance on North Michigan Avenue and from the three others located between the projecting wings facing Water Tower Square (figure 5.22). The three elevator banks are directly opposite the Water Tower Square entrances, at the rear of the transverse circulation spine. The four wings, which slice through the slab at the twenty-sixth floor, are defined on both their front and rear faces by vertical conduits containing the fire stairs. On the alley side, only the two outer ones rise up to the roof level. They house the elevators serving the apartments occupying the upper floors (figure 5.25).[77]

Like the diagrams Corbett and Ferriss produced to illustrate how the 1916 New York zoning regulations might ideally be interpreted for a masonry-clad steel-frame structure (figure 5.20), Wright's National Life Building design can also be read as a "theoretical" undertaking, but one conceived for Chicago and the modern envelope of a metal and glass curtain wall. The four projecting wings of the sawtooth plan rise to a height of twenty stories, or approximately 200 feet, before they step back ten feet on either side to continue up to the 264-foot limit set by the 1923 ordinance (figure 5.26).[78] At the level of the setbacks, floor-to-ceiling glass doors open onto roof decks like those Corbett later proposed for Rockefeller Center (figures 8.2–8.3).[79] These gardens-in-the-air would have culminated a mounting series of outdoor terraces, beginning at the third-floor level between the projecting wings, and including the balconies on the fourth through eighteenth floors that extend out from the transverse circulation corridor.

As the building rises, a series of less visible setbacks in ever-widening notches also occur on the rear facade in order to meet the requirements of the zoning ordinance regarding alley conditions. Finally, the seven top floors protrude through the lower, perpendicularly set wings to form a crowning element reaching a height of nearly 340 feet while covering an area a little under one-quarter of the building's footprint. Occupying less than the one-sixth total cubic footage allowed, this element substituted a thin modernist plane of shimmering copper and reflective glass for the traditional towers, domes, and cupolas the ordinance was designed to accommodate. Given all the other volumetric manipulations evident in the design, it is clear that far from rejecting or attempting to counteract the zoning ordinance, Wright worked through its stipulated limits to create a building that conformed entirely to the letter and spirit of the law if not to the image its framers had for it.

Despite its elaborate decorative surface and pyramidal setback form characteristic of the more conventional eclectic skyscrapers of the period, it is easy to see how a young European architect like Moser would take Wright's National Life Building project as a basis for his own, more explicitly constructivist variant (figure 5.28). Reversing the servant-served categories to locate the elevator banks in the four projecting towers, Moser foregrounded the mechanical services while reducing the building's profile to an absolutely rectilinear configuration.[80] Wright himself, as we will next see, also moved in the direction of "modernizing" the National Life design in the Skyscraper Regulation project of the following year. But more important in the context of Wright's urbanism is how the later project expanded the National Life Insurance Company's exposition of the effects of Chicago's zoning ordinance on a single building into a multiblock design ostensibly for an entire section of the Chicago Loop that would propose not only a way to counteract building bulk and street congestion but also to provide a fully mixed-use solution of integrated parking, office space, and apartment living in a downtown setting. That the actual location in Chicago is nowhere indicated on the drawings may have to do with Wright's intention to position the design as a purely theoretical solution of a general nature.

Skyscraper Regulation Project of 1926: A Multilevel Superblock Remedy for Congestion

Adherence to the zoning regulations regarding the height and bulk of downtown buildings in the commercial center of Chicago could go only so far in alleviating the problem of congestion that was one of the crucial factors in generating those regulations in the first place. Between 1921, when the Zoning Commission began its work, and 1926, three years after the ordinance went into effect, the impact of increased automobile traffic on congestion in the Loop became increasingly apparent. While observers often vacillated on whether the blame should be placed on the growing quantity and size of skyscrapers bringing more and more office workers into the Loop or on the additional number of automobiles those workers and shoppers were now using to arrive at their downtown destinations, it had become clear by early 1926 that, whatever the cause,

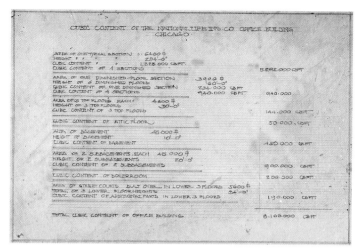

5.29

5.30

5.29. National Life Insurance Company Building project. Calculation of cubic footage

5.30. General Motors Building, Detroit, Albert Kahn, 1919–23. Exterior traffic congestion now pitted vehicles against pedestrians in a most dangerous competition for space that had to be dealt with by new means (see figure 5.12).

In the late fall of 1925, the city asked the Chicago Association of Commerce to undertake "an intensive engineering study of street traffic conditions," for which it hired Miller McClintock. In his *Report and Recommendations of the Metropolitan Street Traffic Survey*, published at the end of 1926, McClintock noted that "the principal motive for the survey has come from the pressure developed by increasing traffic accidents and congestion." "The past few years," he explained, "have witnessed a material increase in the number of traffic movements over the streets. This increased volume of traffic has resulted in a general retardation of street travel and in many locations has caused serious congestion. Injuries and deaths to citizens, through traffic accidents, have reached large figures."[81] If the report's recommendations, such as banning curbside parking and systematizing street signs and signals, were rather banal from a city planning point of view, the statistics on automobile use were startling. As previously noted, the report pointed out that on a typical working day almost 850,000 people entered and left the central business district. Even more disquieting was the fact that, although only about 20 percent of them came by private automobile, the latter outnumbered streetcars and buses by about nine to one (180,486 versus 20,534).[82]

Edward H. Bennett, who, after Burnham's death, became consulting architect to the Chicago Plan Commission, summarized the problem and offered an urban design solution in a series of articles published in the *Chicago Herald and Examiner* and *Chicago Evening Post* in mid-January 1926. The "causes of congestion," he wrote,

> are primarily the volume of traffic and the number of pedestrians due to the size of our city and the concentration of affairs in the center. The great height and consequent volume of the buildings has [sic] been blamed for the congestion, but no appreciable relief in traffic could be expected were they cut to a really low height limit and the area spread [out]. …
>
> Considering the congestion more in detail, we find as principal causes (1) delays due to block intersection interference … [;] (2) narrowness of roadways … [;] and (3) the interference between pedestrians and vehicular traffic.[83]

Reacting negatively to the most recent proposal for a subway to alleviate the congestion, Bennett maintained that "subway transit" would only bring more people into the Loop and thus exacerbate the fundamental problem, namely, "interference between pedestrians and vehicles" on the city's streets. His only recommendation was to create a clear-cut "separation of levels at those intersections" where pedestrians and vehicles converge. Raising the sidewalks to the second floor and ramping streets under one another at intersections would turn "all streets and every street in the loop into channels of easily flowing wheel and pedestrian movement." Bennett's solution was the construction of "raised sidewalks" to separate pedestrians above from vehicular traffic below. He acknowledged that the idea "is not a new one"; that it was proposed "in New York, a year or so ago"; and that "it has been definitely suggested … for Chicago by others not connected with the [Chicago Plan Commission]."[84] Three months later he offered an image of what such a solution might look like when he republished the articles in slightly expanded form as a brochure (figure 5.31).[85]

We can be sure that Bennett's reference to New York was to the scheme for elevated sidewalks and depressed streets developed by Corbett and Ferriss for the Regional Plan of New York and Its Environs in 1923 and published extensively in 1924 (figure 5.32).[86] As for Chicago, the question is more intriguing and the answer less clear. There were those in the city who had called for the double-decking of streets as early as 1922, and a project for converting Madison Street along these lines, sponsored by the *Chicago Tribune* as part of their "Platform for Chicago," was published in the city's major newspaper in the spring of 1923 (figure 5.33).[87] Within the next year and a half many articles on the subject appeared in both the daily and professional press. But one also wonders whether, in referring to "others" in the city "not connected with" the Chicago Plan Commission, Bennett might have had in mind Wright's Skyscraper Regulation project, in which a system of raised sidewalks and through traffic streets was an essential component of a nine-block plan for the downtown that the architect began working on perhaps as early as the end of 1925 but certainly by the very beginning of 1926.[88]

There are six drawings by Wright for the project, all either completely or partially in the architect's own hand. Although some of them have been published, nothing of any significance has been written about the project, which remains one of the least well-known and least understood of Wright's designs.[89]

5.31

5.33

5.32

5.31. Multilevel street project, Chicago, Edward H. Bennett, 1926. Perspective. From *AC*, July 1926

5.32. Multilevel street project, New York, Harvey Wiley Corbett, with Hugh Ferriss, 1923–24. Perspective. Reproduced on cover of *AC*, July 1924. From *AF*, March 1927

5.33. Double-decked Madison Street project, Chicago, 1923. Perspective. From *CDT*, May 1923

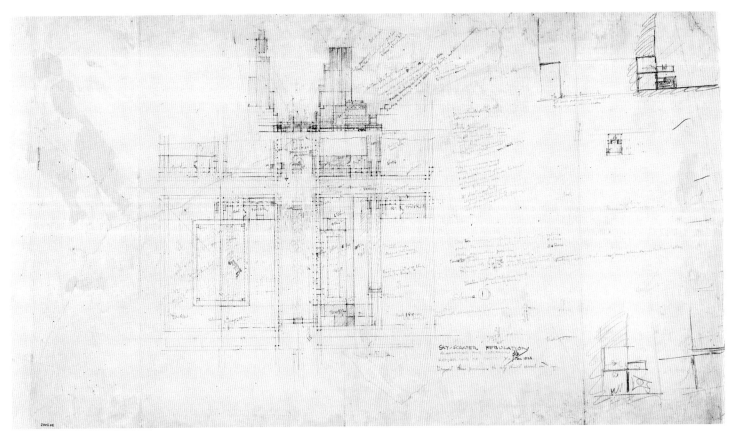

5.34

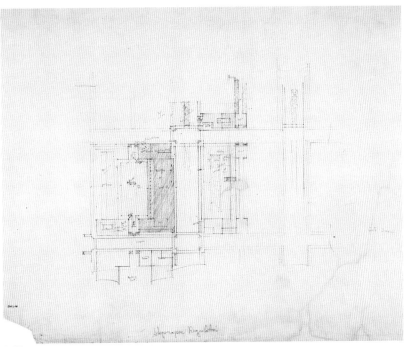

5.35

5.34. Skyscraper Regulation project, Chicago, Wright, 1926. Sketch plan and elevation

5.35. Skyscraper Regulation project. Plan

The first in the series of drawings is a sketch plan showing two full city blocks, approximately 400 by 370 feet each, plus two partial blocks and a partial elevation (figure 5.34). The sheet is crammed with marginal notes explaining in detail the various aspects of the scheme. The architect signed and dated the sheet January 1926 under the title "Sky-Scraper Regulation. Augmenting the Gridiron. Remodeling of the City." To this he appended the phrase "Beyond these provisions the city should spread out—." The second drawing in the sequence is a larger-scale plan showing the same two full blocks plus partial plans of the seven contiguous ones, thus making nine in all (figure 5.35). In this drawing, the main streets, side streets, and alleys are also carefully delineated.

Following these two preliminary plans, the first of which is quite a bit sketchier than the second, are two elevations of two blocks each and a section through a different pair of blocks (figures 5.36–38). The elevations differ from one another mainly in that one shows a couple of blocks separated by a wide, ten-lane street with a median strip, while the other has a narrower street between its two blocks. The one with the wider street has a store sign for the "americ[an] hardware co." accompanied by the date "march 5 1926." The elevation with the narrower street has a series of small sketch plans at the bottom of the sheet, to which we shall return. In the section, the "alley court" on the left, the "avenue" in the center, and the "alley" on the right are all labeled. The sixth and final drawing, which includes a plan, section, and elevation, is a detailed study of a corner intersection showing traffic patterns, both vehicular and pedestrian, plus store locations (figure 5.39).

There is no known client for the project and no evidence of an actual commission. Had Albert Johnson been involved, there would certainly be some reference somewhere. One can speculate, however, about the role of another Chicago businessman, the prominent real estate figure Gordon Strong, who was introduced to Wright in the late summer of 1924 and, after seeing some of the initial studies for the National Life project, asked the architect to design a destination point for a mountain he owned in Maryland, northwest of Washington, D.C. Wright designed an Automobile Objective and Planetarium for the rural site between the early fall of 1924 and the late summer of the following year when, before being put on hold and then abandoned by the client, the project was shown in the Republic Building on State Street, which was one of Strong's numerous properties in the Loop (figures 6.3–4).[90]

Strong owned and/or managed twenty-eight buildings in Chicago by the beginning of the 1920s. He was a member of the Chicago Real Estate Board and Cook County Real Estate Board, the first president of the State Street Council of Chicago, and a former president of the National Association of Building Owners and Managers.[91] He was active in the development of the Chicago Zoning Ordinance as an appointed member of the advisory Citizens' Committee. While he was personally opposed on ideological grounds to the imposition of height limitations, he was outspoken in the mid-1920s in pushing for a multilevel street system for the Loop, writing a letter to the editor of the *Chicago Tribune* in support of the idea and telling the National Association of Building Managers and Owners that "the solution of the problem of downtown congestion in all American cities was the construction of additional street levels."[92] He would certainly have been interested in knowing how Wright might resolve the problem of designing skyscrapers while eliminating the traffic congestion accompanying them.

It is not inconceivable, however, that the Skyscraper Regulation project had no client and was done on a purely theoretical or speculative basis. This was true of Broadacre City, which came just three years later. The problem of dealing with the issue of zoning in the National Life Insurance Building clearly intrigued Wright, resulting, as it did, in a very original proposal, tailor-made for the site. The Skyscraper Regulation design took that solution well beyond the limits of the individual building to embed it in the larger urban context, where many of the issues critical to the quality of life and economic stability of the city not directly addressed by the narrow focus of the zoning ordinance could be taken into account. These issues, all of which Wright's 1926 project engaged, included parking, traffic congestion, mixed-use development, and, finally, the adumbration of a superblock concept for rewriting the zoning code at the scale of the city grid itself. It was to represent, as Wright noted on the initial sketch plan, "the Zoning law and setback ordinances carried to a logical conclusion" (figure 5.35). Among its specific legal impositions were that skyscrapers would be limited to certain corner properties and that all lots designated "skyscraper lots [had] to pay [a] super tax when [a] tall building is built." In addition, all "skyscrapers must devote at least two sub-basements to parking," extending beyond the property line and under the alley behind them.[93]

SKYSCRAPER REGULATION.

5.36. Skyscraper Regulation project. Elevation with wider streets

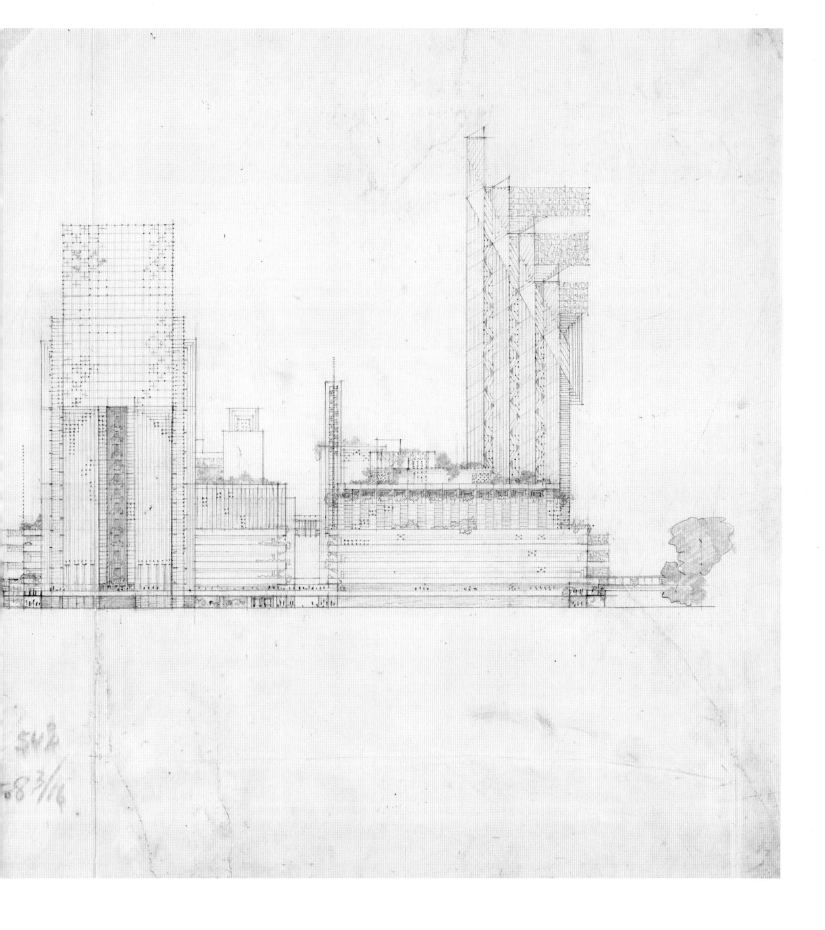

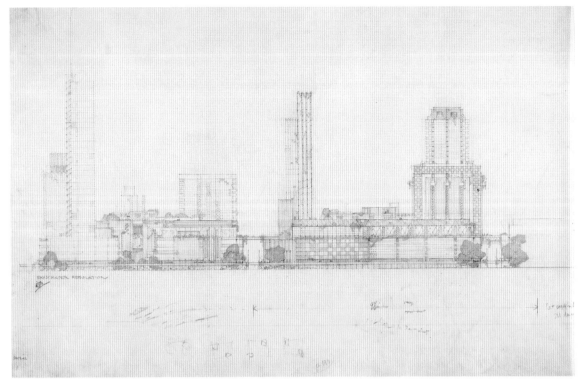

5.37

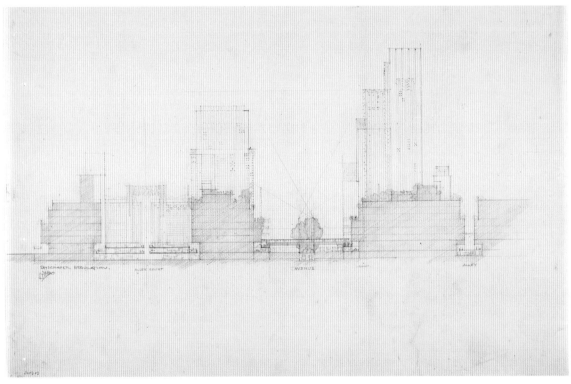

5.38

5.37. Skyscraper Regulation project. Elevation with narrower streets

5.38. Skyscraper Regulation project. Section through wider streets, 5 March 1926
(written on sign)

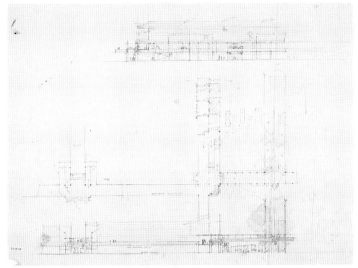

5.39

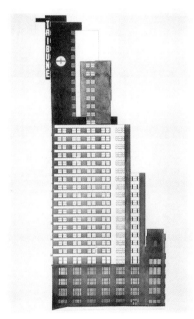

5.40

5.39. Skyscraper Regulation project. Plan, section, and elevation of street corner intersection

5.40. Chicago Tribune Tower project, Knud Lönberg-Holm, 1922. Side elevation. From *L'Architecture vivante*, Fall–Winter 1924

Wright's point of departure for the project was the typical perimeter-block condition of buildings in the Loop. He accepted the ground-level density that such buildings occasioned and made no effort to reduce or interfere with the continuity of the ordinary street-line facade—up to, that is, a certain height, which was considerably lower than what the zoning law allowed and much closer to the height the architect had proposed in the National Life design. An eight-story street-line height defines each block except at alternate corners, where the skyscraper towers rise to heights of 350 feet and more (figures 5.35–37). The street-conforming lower blocks, in conjunction with the lower sections of the corner towers, create courtyards of varying dimensions, some filling up the entire center of a block where the alley has been vacated, others forming a narrow light court parallel to the alley (figure 5.38).

The adherence to the city's grid and the treatment of the block as a whole, with a continuous line of buildings around its perimeter surrounding an open central space, can be traced back in Wright's work to his very first urban design, the Roberts development plan of 1896 (figure 1.33). It was the planning model the architect returned to in the double-block Lexington Terraces apartment house project (figure 1.19). The 1926 revision, however, entails a much greater degree of complexity, both in the perimeter blocks and the central courtyards. In the earlier designs, the central space served a communal purpose exclusively for the residents of the block. In the 1926 plan, the surrounding blocks provide varied types of accommodation for the mixed uses of shopping, apartment living, entertainment, hotel lodging, and commercial office space. While the residential units tend to be grouped in the lower structures around the internal courts and the office space fills much of the surrounding blocks, especially the corner towers, shops line the raised sidewalks of many, if not all, of the streets. An "AMSTERDAM THEATRE" and a "HOTEL EMBASSY" are located amid the stores and office buildings on the street sides of the block (figure 5.37).

The courtyards that replace alleys and fill the entire block become public spaces capable of serving a multiplicity of functions. Much larger than earlier atrium courts or even arcades, they are open to the sky and call to mind the mall-like spaces of later superblock designs like Rockefeller Center (figure 8.2). In the Skyscraper Regulation project, the ground plane of these courtyards is raised to the second floor to form a deck over a two-level parking facility, one floor of which is below grade and the other at street level (there is also below-grade parking and truck delivery access under the remaining alleys). Both the larger and smaller interior courtyards provide secluded spaces within the tightly knit fabric of downtown streets, where light and air and greenery find their place and where restaurants, cafes, and other facilities permit the apartment dweller, hotel occupant, and office worker to relax and congregate without having to confront the surrounding street traffic.

Some of the eight-story perimeter-block buildings are shown as having balconies overhanging the streets below. The buildings themselves have setbacks at the seventh and eighth floors along both streets and alleys, but are flush on the court sides (figure 5.38). A much deeper setback, and even a double one in some cases, provides accommodation for floor-through penthouse units overlooking both courtyard and street. While these manipulations and tweakings of the zoning rules for dealing with height and bulk give the Skyscraper Regulation project a consistency and thoroughness at the fine-grain scale of the more European-type city of seventy- to eighty-foot-high buildings, the location, alignment, and variation in height of the corner skyscraper towers manifest most fully Wright's effort to carry the Chicago zoning ordinance "to a logical conclusion."

The towers, as noted, are located exclusively at the corners. While some retain the stepped-back, symmetrical form of the National Life project, many are composed of more discrete, asymmetrically organized volumetric units, very possibly indebted to some of the European projects for the Chicago Tribune Tower, such as those by Adolf Meyer (1881–1929) and Walter Gropius (1883–1969), Max Taut (1884–1967), and, most specifically, Knud Lönberg-Holm (1895–1972; figure 5.40).[94] Wright's towers vary in height from about eighteen to just under forty stories. More important, their lower sections alternate from a north-south to an east-west alignment, while the placement of the skyscrapers themselves is staggered from block to block, as Wright indicated in the quick sketch drawn at the bottom of the elevation in figure 5.37.

All these subtle shifts and changes were meant to provide light and air to the densely built-up city grid, to which only lip service was paid in the 1923 zoning ordinance. The openness and porousness of the resulting architectural fabric reminds one of the earlier Quadruple Block Plan, just as the dynamic movement of shifting and alternating masses recalls the pinwheeling energies of that concept. Both the earlier and later

conceptions were extruded from and integral with the circulation pattern established by the Chicago grid. But whereas the Quadruple Block Plan, because of its suburban condition, exercised its control over space almost exclusively at ground level, the Skyscraper Regulation project developed its spatial network in a three-dimensional, multilevel system deemed necessary for the much more dense downtown area of the city.

Circulation of pedestrians and vehicles occurs at five different levels in the 1926 scheme. The levels also serve to segregate one type of movement from another: cars and trucks are placed at street level and one level below grade; sidewalks for pedestrians are elevated to the second floor and connect to bridges crossing streets at a level above that; finally pedestrian bridges at the sixth floor cross both streets and alleys to link the courtyarded blocks to one another (figures 5.36–38). Store display windows are located on the second floor, where the raised sidewalks form a continuous arcade-balcony ringing the perimeter-block buildings. In the space below, where sidewalks traditionally were, are delivery lanes for trucks, drop-off locations for taxis, and spaces for short-term parking. Stairs connect the elevated sidewalks to the street level, belowground parking, and subway stations that Wright indicated at the corner intersections. The corner intersections are in fact the critical junctions in the plan, since it is there that the bridges one level above the raised sidewalks carry pedestrians from block to block without their having to cross streets crowded with automobiles, buses, and trucks. Most trucks, in any event, were to be kept off the main streets and confined to below-grade tunnels as in the double-decked Wacker Drive on the northern edge of the Loop that was just being finished.

Apart from its generous provision for parking, Wright's Skyscraper Regulation scheme, at least in terms of its circulation pattern, was nowhere near as novel for its time as the earlier Quadruple Block Plan. Indeed, the futuristic, multilevel aspect of its design had much in common with the most popular new recipe of the 1920s for overcoming traffic congestion and reducing accidents. The idea of elevated sidewalks, like the related one of depressed roadways, went back to the first decade of the twentieth century.[95] In the United States it made a celebrated appearance as *King's Dream of New York*, the frontispiece of Moses King's 1908 edition of views of the city (figure 5.41).[96] This early example attested to the origin of the concept in the turn-of-the-century elevated rail line, the promise of excitement it held for the modern city, and the basic appeal it had to the popular imagination.

The last two aspects highlight the very similar, front-page illustration of the early January 1910 *New-York Tribune* article about the engineer Henry Harrison Suplee's proposal to rationalize New York's circulation system.[97] The image was republished three years later on the cover of *Scientific American* announcing an article by Suplee himself in which he called for the "absolute segregation of foot travel from any kind of vehicles" as the only means to secure "relief" from "congestion" and provide "a free and safe path" for the pedestrian (figure 5.42). The cutaway perspective shows three subsurface levels, the partially exposed upper one for vehicles, and two levels of pedestrian sidewalks. Multiple tiers of bridges connect the sidewalks and buildings that line the street. The drawing would become a template for later projects of the sort.[98]

As Jean-Louis Cohen has shown, the *Scientific American* image had a large reach in Europe. In its wake, a number of important architects and planners produced multilevel, skyscraper city projects. Aside from Le Corbusier's Contemporary City of Three Million Inhabitants, there were designs by Auguste Perret (1922–25), Cornelis van Eesteren (1926), and Ludwig Hilberseimer (1924), among others (figure 5.43).[99] In the United States there was even a very early realization of such a vision, although on a limited scale. This involved the construction of Grand Central Station in New York between 1903 and 1913 and the routing of vehicular traffic to and around it (Warren and Wetmore, architects; Reed and Stem, engineers; figure 5.44). In order to negotiate the problem created by the site astride Park Avenue and potentially blocking through traffic, the architects and engineers planned to tunnel under Park Avenue South from Thirty-Third Street to Fortieth Street, where cars would ascend onto a viaduct over Forty-Second Street, then encircle the station on an upper deck, and finally descend to ground level at Forty-Sixth Street via Piranesian passages cut through the New York Central Building. The deck was built with the station, but the viaduct connecting to upper-level roadways was added only in 1919. The complex, including related hotels, clubs, and office buildings, was completed over the next decade, at the very time the idea of a multilevel city was becoming popular, very possibly fueled by this construction in the center of New York.[100]

Although Harvey Wiley Corbett would be a leading champion of the multilevel city and certainly the best-known

5.41

5.42

5.41. Harry M. Pettit, *King's Dream of New York*, 1908. Frontispiece of Moses King, *King's Views: New York, 1908–1909*, 1908

5.42. Cover illustration for Henry Harrison Suplee, "The Elevated Sidewalk," *Scientific American*, July 1913; originally published in the *New-York Tribune*, January 1910

5.43

5.45

5.44

CROSS SECTIONS SHOWING INCREASED STREET CAPACITY SECURED WITH EACH STEP

5.46

5.43. Highrise City (Hochhausstadt) project, Ludwig Hilberseimer, 1924. Cutaway perspective. Reproduced in Hilberseimer's *Grosstadtbauten* (1925) and *Groszstadtarchitektur* (1927). Ludwig Karl Hilberseimer Papers, AIC

5.44. Grand Central Station, New York, Reed and Stem; and Warren and Wetmore, 1903–13. Terminal City project. Aerial perspective, by Vernon Howe Bailey. From *Harper's Weekly*, 25 January 1913

5.45. Proposal for elevated north-south roadway through center of Manhattan between Fifth and Sixth Avenues, Richard E. Enright, 1922–23. From *NYT*, January 1923

5.46. Multilevel street project, New York, Harvey Wiley Corbett, with Hugh Ferriss, 1923–24. From Thomas Adams, *Regional Plan of New York and Its Environs*, vol. 2, *The Building of the City*, 1931

proponent of the idea among professionals (see figure 5.32), one of the most interesting aspects of the concept was that it was embraced by people from all walks of life and proposed as often in letters to the editor of daily newspapers as it was discussed in journals of architecture and planning. New York and Chicago both participated in this discourse. One of the first professional calls for the "construction of elevated streets" as a means of "eliminating present congestion" came in early 1921 from the architect and city planner Arnold W. Brunner (1857–1925), who collaborated on the Cleveland Group Plan and later worked on plans for Baltimore, Denver, Rochester, and Albany.[101] A fascinating counterproposal by the police commissioner of New York followed in very early 1923. Instead of providing elevated sidewalks for pedestrians, Richard E. Enright called for the construction of elevated highways or "viaducts" to carry motorized traffic along both riverfronts as well as north-south through the middle of the city, between Fifth and Sixth Avenues, by means of a ten-lane road tunneling through buildings at the second- and third-floor levels "from Harlem to the Battery" (figure 5.45).[102] It is just as doubtful that Enright knew of Le Corbusier's slightly earlier Contemporary City of Three Million Inhabitants than the latter knew of this project before designing his elevated east-west highway through the center of Paris in the 1925 Voisin Plan (see figure 5.11).

An idea such as Enright's, despite its adoption by Le Corbusier, gained very little traction in the United States until the late 1930s, and even then only in a much mitigated form. The less intrusive Corbett model of the elevated sidewalk and depressed street rather became the norm. And it was Corbett who gave visual form to the concept in the mid-1920s in numerous publications in professional journals as well as the daily press (see figure 5.32). The scheme Corbett developed in collaboration with Hugh Ferriss in 1923 for the Regional Plan of New York and Its Environs was first published in a copiously illustrated spread in the Sunday edition of the *New York Times* in February 1924. The three-level design, with sidewalks raised to the second-floor level and cross streets depressed under the main north-south avenues, was specifically targeted at the "rival" Enright proposal, which Corbett self-interestedly protested would "necessitate an enormous expense in the demolition of miles of buildings"[103]

Corbett illustrated the "simplicity, economy and permanency" of his proposal for retrofitting New York's street system in almost cartoon-like fashion (figure 5.46). The first stage simply involved the construction of rather temporary-looking steel platforms supported by columns held away from building walls. These would run for only a block at a time and, like elevated train platforms, have stairways at the corners. With the street-level sidewalks removed, traffic would benefit from at least two extra lanes. The next stage entailed connecting these platforms by bridging over streets at intersections so that "the pedestrian thus would pass without interruption from one block to another without a thought of the street crossing and the inconveniences and dangers of vehicular traffic." At the same time, shops would be relocated to the second-floor level and the ground-floor space assigned to additional traffic lanes for deliveries, drop-offs, and short-term parking. Finally, permanent underpinning of buildings would be constructed so as to provide additional depth for truck deliveries. At the same time, masonry arcades would be built at the second-floor level to offer pedestrians elegant shopping streets comparable, in Corbett's view, to "the Rue de Rivoli in Paris." These arcades would continue across intersections on wide, monumental bridges connecting the four corners. Beneath, cross streets would be depressed below the level of the north-south avenues to allow for unimpeded "cross currents of vehicular traffic [that] would thus weave past each other like the lacing of a basket."[104]

Corbett presented the proposal at a major conference on traffic congestion organized by the Regional Plan of New York and Its Environs held in the city in the late spring of 1924.[105] Following that, in the summer of 1924, came the important article "Different Levels for Foot, Wheel and Rail" published in the *American City*, the same journal where Bennett's plan was reprinted two years later. While reiterating much of what was said in the earlier *Times* spread and including the same drawings plus several additional ones dramatizing the existing conditions and efficacy of the proposed solution, "Different Levels for Foot, Wheel and Rail" also contained "an imaginary view of the future city of New York" by Ferriss showing how the multilevel idea might be expanded into a system of superblocks such as Wright was about to propose.[106] A major summation of the scheme with an expanded description and numerous new illustrations was published in *Architectural Forum* in early 1927, but by that time Chicago already had its own versions of the design concept in the projects by Bennett, Wright, and others.[107]

If New York provided the earliest and iconic images of what a future city with multilevel circulation arteries would look like, as well as the first limited realization in Grand Central Station, Chicago witnessed a groundswell of popular interest in the subject in the 1920s due to the worsening traffic conditions in its singularly concentrated central business district and the debate over whether or not to build a subway to ease the burden on Loop streets. An often cited proof of the city's can-do spirit was, in fact, the wholesale raising of its street level in the late 1850s and 1860s to accommodate the construction of the nation's first sewerage system. Between late 1922 and early 1926, at least six letters to the editor calling for elevated sidewalks and eventually depressed cross streets and/or subways were published by the city's leading newspaper, the *Chicago Tribune*. The first of these was signed by "One Who Walks" and one of the later ones by Gordon Strong.[108]

The *Tribune* was not innocent in printing these pleas for a multilevel city. Between 1923 and 1926, the newspaper published more than ten editorials demanding such a program of construction, with titles like "Unstrangling the Loop," "Cut the Knot of Loop Traffic," "A Double Decked Loop," and "The Automobile and the City."[109] The first, "Unstrangling the Loop," was accompanied by the project the paper itself commissioned for double-decking Madison Street, where its offices were located prior to the construction of the Hood and Howells building on North Michigan Avenue (figure 5.33). Significantly, the *Tribune* referred twice in its earlier editorials to Corbett's scheme for New York.[110] The second specifically cited the architect's article in the *American City*, whose cover drawing was more or less copied by Bennett to publicize his own 1926 proposal for Chicago.[111]

Wright's Skyscraper Regulation project for the "remodeling of the city" by "augmenting the gridiron" was part and parcel of the urban planning culture of the period and its deep investment in a city of skyscrapers justified by the new zoning laws and facilitated by a futuristic vision of modern means of circulation. If, in many ways, the project's prismatic glass towers rising freely from a multilevel gridded matrix seem to echo the forms of some modern European examples, Wright's less rigorously abstract design is much closer to Corbett's more conventional one in urban design terms. The section Wright drew showing how the main downtown streets would be bridged over and how the second-level sidewalks would

liberate grade-level traffic can be read as basically a revision of the Corbett diagrams previously published in the *New York Times* and the *American City*. Indeed, when Wright designed the program for the Hillside Home School of Allied Arts in late 1928, the institution that would become the Taliesin Fellowship four years subsequently, he showed his esteem for the New York architect and urban designer by including him as one of the visiting studio critics in architecture in the school's prospectus, a position Corbett shared with H. P. Berlage, Erich Mendelsohn, J.J.P. Oud, Lewis Mumford, and, most notably, Le Corbusier.[112]

In most ways, Corbett was absolutely opposite to Wright—professionally, personally, culturally, and socially. He was an academic and corporate architect and an urban creature, in love with the city and apparently totally uneasy with the idea of spending any significant amount of time outside of it. "The country is lovely," he said in a talk in 1929 at the National Conference on Housing, but then added to much laughter: "I like to move out of this intolerable city of dreadful height—occasionally; once every two weeks, or something of that kind—not otherwise." "People won't stay away from the city" he went on. "They will concentrate as much as they physically can. Our problem [as architects and planners] is to deal with that phase of it. The problems of properly handling the concentrated centers of our city is an infinitely more complicated, difficult one to deal with than the problem of moving out into the open country and planning new districts. It requires more courage and vision."[113]

While Wright may well have disagreed with Corbett's characterization of which environment took "courage and vision" to "deal with" and would certainly make that position a fundamental aspect of his ruralist conception for Broadacre City of 1929—the year of Corbett's remarks—Wright continued to work on the Skyscraper Regulation project into 1930 and add annotations to the earlier drawings for it.[114] What moved him out of the still tradition-based orbit of American urbanism that Corbett, Ferriss, Bennett, Saarinen, and others represented, with their visions of a multilevel city based on a retrofit of the existing perimeter-block grid, and, ironically, into Corbett's "open country" was the confrontation Wright had with the archurbanist Le Corbusier's writings and ideas in 1928 when reviewing the 1927 English translation of *Vers une architecture* (1923). It was no doubt based on this reading that Wright thought of having the Swiss-French architect join his faculty in Wisconsin—and it was also from this reading that Broadacre City emerged.

SIX

DECENTRALIZATION VERSUS CENTRALIZATION: BROADACRE CITY'S RURALIST ALTERNATIVE TO LE CORBUSIER'S URBANISM, 1929–35

If the Skyscraper Regulation project was the product of a commission, then it would represent one of the very few Wright received between 1926 and 1932. As a result of the dearth of work, the architect turned his hand to writing and devoted much of his creative energy to the elaboration of his architectural and urban thought in print rather than graphic or built form. Although it is rarely discussed as such, Broadacre City was a textual construct long before it had any visual reality.

Wright's reason for focusing on writing was in part financial, but it was also driven by profound intellectual and psychological needs. Wright was a very competitive person who openly acknowledged that "the best work I have ever done was the result of provocation."[1] Up until the mid-1920s, he had little concern or fear that any of his peers were capable of producing a more inventive or advanced form of modern architecture. His criticism was directed either at the corporate-type eclectic architects who were dominating the profession and getting all the significant jobs or those who, in his view, stole his ideas and made them more palatable to public consumption.[2] But in the year or two following the Skyscraper Regulation design, Wright realized that there were ideas in the air newer than his own, which it was imperative for him both to engage and to critique. Soon to be imported into the United States under the rubric of the International Style, the "neues bauen," or "new architecture," of Germany, Holland, Austria, and France was most powerfully epitomized for Wright by the work of Le Corbusier, whose seminal book *Vers une architecture* (1923) was reviewed by him after it appeared in English translation four years later with the even more provocative title *Towards a New Architecture*.[3]

Wright began his print-based polemical campaign with a well-paid series of articles in the highly visible mainstream professional journal *Architectural Record*. Between May 1927 and December 1928, he published fourteen pieces under the general title "In the Cause of Architecture." These ranged in subject matter from the role of the machine and standardization in modern design to the issues of style, meaning, use, and expression of materials. The penultimate was the article devoted to the National Life Insurance Company Building and the problem of the modern skyscraper. The topic of urbanism as such did not appear.[4] It was, however, addressed in a piece possibly intended to conclude the series but not published in the journal. Originally titled "In the Cause of Architecture: The City," it was completed in late September 1929 and constitutes the first description of what the architect later called Broadacre City.[5]

Wright's review of *Towards a New Architecture* preceded by precisely one year this first text of his exclusively devoted to the problem of the city. The review appeared in September 1928 in the journal *World Unity*, of which Wright was a contributing editor.[6] Despite the fact that Wright had already begun to be perceived as representing a previous generation of thought and thus merely an outmoded prelude to the more radical European modern movement embodied most prominently in the person of Le Corbusier, his review was surprisingly generous and even laudatory in places, no matter how begrudgingly the praise was bestowed.[7] Complimenting "the talented Frenchman" on being "no sentimentalist," Wright criticized Le Corbusier's buildings for their focus on " 'surface and mass' " effects and for the "stark," reductive form of their machine-inspired shapes. Yet he went on to acknowledge that Le Corbusier was "right" in his praise for the " 'new' beauty" of machinery, correct in his dismissal of the " 'styles,' " and on the mark in "dressing down" the eclectic commercial architecture of New York.[8]

The thrust of Wright's argument was that Le Corbusier's achievement, as new as it might appear and as important as it might be, ultimately rested on the advances he and Sullivan had made—and thus should be understood as part of a continuum. "All Le Corbusier says or means," Wright asserted, "was at home here in architecture in America in the work of Louis Sullivan and myself—more than twenty-five years ago."[9] But he did not, for that reason, devalue Le Corbusier's text or its theoretical consequences either for modern architecture in general or for his own work in particular. Indeed, he praised his rival for giving credence and support to what he and Sullivan stood for, and ended the review on an unexpected and not insincere note of thanks: "Had you [Le Corbusier] not taken it [the lesson furnished by Sullivan and himself], we as a nation might never have been aware of it, never, even, have seen it!"[10]

A backhanded form of praise, yes, but praise nevertheless. Wright even expressed the thought that Le Corbusier's work might not be that distant from his own and that "the French movement may soon lose its two dimensions, 'surface and mass,' within the three that characterize the American work." This suggestion of the possibility for synergy and rapprochement surely helps to explain the fact of Wright's including Le Corbusier on the list of visiting faculty he proposed two months later for the Hillside Home School of Allied Arts, the predecessor of the Taliesin Fellowship (1932).[11] The work and ideas contained in *Towards a New Architecture* so impressed Wright that he ended up recommending that "everyone engaged in making or breaking these United States ... read the Le Corbusier book," those in "universities especially."[12] For his own part, Wright included *Towards a New Architecture* as one of only four texts mentioned by name for the library of his prospective School of Allied Arts. He characterized Le Corbusier's volume in the school's brochure as "of a similar portent" to his own "In the Cause of Architecture" series in *Architectural Record* and of "a similar spirit" to the writings of Viollet-le-Duc, Owen Jones, and Louis Sullivan, all familiar heroes of his.[13]

Towards a New Architecture weighed heavily on Wright's mind. It would compel him to take Le Corbusier's ideas seriously into account, especially as regards the question of urbanism for which the latter had come to be considered the most powerful and imaginative voice in the field.[14] The very term "urbanism," which was by then closely identified with Le Corbusier, was, as the critic Catherine Bauer (1905–64) pointed out in a review of modern French architecture in the *New York Times* in early 1928, as foreign to most American ears as "such terms as 'Esprit Nouveau' [Le Corbusier and Ozenfant's journal in which most of *Towards a New Architecture* originally appeared], 'Futurism,' [and] 'Cubism.' "[15]

Although *Towards a New Architecture* did not provide many illustrations of the author's urban designs and, of these, drawings only collateral to the two major projects for which he was best known at the time, the Contemporary City of Three Million Inhabitants and the Voisin Plan (figures 5.8–11), there was certainly enough descriptive text as well as enough graphic information for Wright to get an excellent sense of the radicality of Le Corbusier's propositions and the "terrifying, pitiless but magnificent" conditions his city plans presented.[16] In any event, it is probable that, by 1929 at the very latest, Wright knew Le Corbusier's book *Urbanisme* (1925) as well, which came out in English as *The City of To-morrow and Its Planning* that year and offered a complete exposition of his urban theory along with full graphic presentations of both the 1922 and 1925 projects referred to above.[17]

Le Corbusier's impact on Wright was not of a simple formal sort manifested in obvious morphological borrowings. Rather, it was as a catalyst, triggering responses in the older architect that can be viewed as implicit in his earlier work—but only in hindsight. And while the result in one case—the form of the skyscraper—paralleled the Corbusian model, the result in the other, more significant one—the idea of the city—took a 180-degree turn, leading to a diametrically opposed solution. The new form of the skyscraper and the new idea of the city were conceived more or less concurrently. But in the fall of 1929, only the former, the skyscraper, was immediately embodied in visual form.

The four apartment towers Wright designed in 1929 for a double corner site in lower Manhattan as an income-producing venture for the Church of St. Mark's-in-the-Bouwerie represent a complete about-face on Wright's part, both urbanistically and structurally (figure 6.1). Although initial discussions with the client began in late 1927, nothing was put on paper until the early spring of 1929, after which the project languished until it was finally aborted the following May. Instead of using a conventional, grid-like structural frame as in the National Life and Skyscraper Regulation projects (figures 5.27, 5.37), Wright designed a cruciform-shaped concrete core from which the floors of the nine levels of duplex apartments were cantilevered and the glass and copper curtain walls hung (figure 6.2). The central core is exposed above the roof line as well as at ground level where, following Le Corbusier's idea of liberating the ground by raising buildings on *pilotis*, the enclosed volumes of St. Mark's Towers are literally lifted off the ground to allow the landscaping of the site to pass under the structure and provide an uninterrupted park-like setting. Instead of maintaining the street line in perimeter-block facades as in Wright's earlier tall buildings, the St. Mark's apartment houses become towers in a park following the model Le Corbusier had established in his urban designs from 1922 to 1925.[18] Le Corbusier published a plan of six such cruciform towers in *Towards a New Architecture* showing the buildings, spaced far apart from one another, rising from their "surrounding parks" with "trees covering the whole town."[19]

The cruciform plan of Wright's St. Mark's Towers is different from Le Corbusier's not only by virtue of its structural form but also because of its dynamic pinwheeling shape based on the thirty-degree rotation of one square within another. For these reasons one could, and usually does, read the St. Mark's plan in terms of Wright's own design history exploiting rotational geometries.[20] More to the point, however, is the self-centered, pinwheel plan as such, which first appeared in the *Ladies' Home Journal* Quadruple Block Plan before becoming a recurrent figure in the architect's work. Why, one wonders, did it take more than a quarter of a century for the architect to apply it to the skyscraper, especially since he had produced within the previous four years two significant projects based on a decidedly conventional, orthogonally gridded model? Since the transformation occurred the year immediately following his review of *Towards a New Architecture*, it stands to reason that Le Corbusier's concept of the tower-in-a-park, raised above ground level, triggered Wright's response to find in his own repertoire a way to create his own version of the concept. By making the cross shape into a structural core similar to the trunk of a

6.1

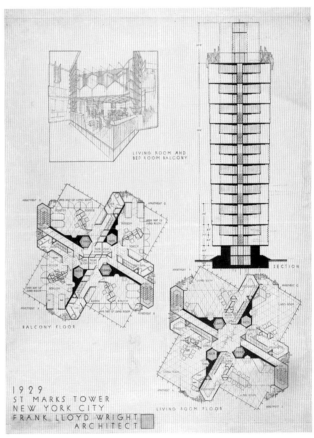

6.2

6.1. St. Mark's Towers project, New York, Wright, 1927–29. Aerial perspective. From *AR*, January 1930

6.2. St. Mark's Towers project. Plans, section, and interior perspective, 1929 tree and cantilevering the floors like branches from it, Wright gave the Corbusian glass box on "stilts" an organic aspect that allowed him to liken his towers in a park to the trees among which they stood.

This is certainly not the first time that the dependence of St. Mark's Towers on Le Corbusier has been observed. When the project was published in January 1930 in *Architectural Record*, the text accompanying the drawings began with the following words: "In this project, Frank Lloyd Wright realizes some of the most advanced aims professed by European architects."[21] More recently, Hilary Ballon has specified that it was Le Corbusier in particular who inspired Wright's design: "St. Mark's shows that Wright carefully studied and learned from Le Corbusier's highrise ideas" as they appeared in his 1922 "*Ville Contemporaine*." "The pedestal base, or pilotis, the freestanding tower, and the park setting," she continued, all "derive from Le Corbusier." Ballon could also have included the idea of duplex apartments, which she earlier noted formed the basic residential unit of Le Corbusier's housing blocks.[22]

But Wright did not remain happy for very long with the idea of building residential towers in the city. While he was still in discussions with his client concerning the St. Mark's project, he wrote the six talks on "Modern Architecture" that he would deliver as the Kahn Lectures at Princeton University in early May 1930. In the fifth, titled "The Tyranny of the Skyscraper," he suggested that it was in the countryside that the skyscraper should, and would, ultimately find its proper home. "The haphazard skyscraper in the rank and file of city streets is doomed," he declared. Any attempt to accommodate it to the city "is no more than an expedient."[23] As the necessity for concentration in urban centers diminishes due to the increased means of mechanical transportation and telecommunications, there will be an "eventual urban exodus," what Wright's friend and supporter Lewis Mumford (1895–1990) had famously called in 1925 the "fourth migration."[24] The "citizen of the near future," Wright stated, "will gradually abandon the city." And so "the tyranny of the skyscraper" would end while the tall building itself, "in the country," no longer a congestion-creating "space-maker-for-rent," would become a new symbol of freedom in which the exurban citizen "might take genuine pride."[25]

Wright had been denouncing the "expediency" of the skyscraper for a number of years, beginning with the pamphlet *Experimenting with Human Lives* (1923). But he had never

before suggested building highrises, especially for apartment living, in the countryside. In the interview he gave to the *Chicago Tribune* in the fall of 1923, in which he spoke of cutting off the tops of all the downtown "'skyscrapers at the seventh floor,'" he said this would be an incentive to "'spread[ing] out your loop.'" "'If you cut down these horrible buildings,'" he added, "'you'll have no traffic jams'" and "'you'll have trees again.'"[26] But Wright was still thinking at this time that the city would not disappear as such, but merely expand and, in the process, break up into multicentered agglomerations. He saw the beginnings of this in Los Angeles, where the "congestion turns to the disadvantage of the city proper by raising various contiguous business centers at the very gates of the city itself."[27]

In late 1927, in the fifth of his series of articles for the *Architectural Record*, Wright began to limn his vision of "The New World." Whether he had already seen a copy of *Towards a New Architecture* by then is not known. In conjuring up his vision of the future, Wright adopted the utopian stance of "looking backward":[28]

> The Classics? A fond professional dream. …
> The Skyscraper — vertical groove of the landlord?
>   Laid down flat wise. A trap that was sprung.
> Churches? We fail to recognize them. …
> Monuments? Abolished as profane. …
> Homes? Growing from their site in native
>   materials, no more "deciduous" than the native
>   rock ledges of the hills, or the fir trees rooted in
>   the ground. …
> The City? Gone to the surrounding country.[29]

In its elliptical form, the statement about the city "gone to the surrounding country" attested to a deeply held belief in the value of rural living but did not indicate in any fashion how that might actually come to pass in a general way.

Once again, it took the reading of Le Corbusier to trigger the formulation of a program, although at first only a program and not a physical design as such. Appropriating Le Corbusier's vision for *The City of To-morrow* and literally co-opting it to turn it on its head, Wright soon described his own "Broadacre City of tomorrow" as the countertype to Le Corbusier's. Rather than "tear down the city [read Voisin Plan] and try to bring the green country in only to build the city up again on its old site," Wright proposed "to let the automobile take the city to the country."[30] If using the term "Broadacre" to qualify (and colonize) Le Corbusier's *City of To-morrow* was perhaps only a "slip," Freudian or not, Wright's description of his plan for a decentralized antidote to the rebuilding of a city core along the lines of the Voisin Plan was consciously meant as a counteraction. Wright pointedly described his proposal as "Ruralism as distinguished from '*Urbanisme*,'" producing a new type of city "without losing a single advantage urbanism can offer."[31]

The Text of Broadacre City and the Confrontation with Le Corbusier, 1929–32

Wright initially laid out the program for his decentralized, automobile-based Broadacre City in the article originally titled "In the Cause of Architecture: The City."[32] Written prior to the stock market crash and finished exactly one month before Black Tuesday (29 October 1929), it was delivered by Wright as the sixth of his Kahn Lectures at Princeton University in May 1930 and published more or less verbatim the following March in *Modern Architecture: Being the Kahn Lectures for 1930*.[33] Because of its publishing history, Wright's Broadacre City has often been read as a reaction to the economic conditions resulting from the Crash rather than as the reaction to Le Corbusier's *City of To-morrow* it was meant to be.[34] The name "Broadacre City" was first used by Wright in the March 1932 article he contributed to the *New York Times Magazine* in response to the one Le Corbusier wrote for the same magazine, two and a half months before, describing his "green city" for "the new epoch of machinery." Wright's piece was billed by the *Times* as presenting "a diametrically opposed program … which he [Wright] sees as the logical development of the machine age."[35]

Wright began his September 1929 article on "The City" by asking a rhetorical question the answer to which underwrote the rest of the discussion: Is the city merely a "hang-over" from the past? Wright's answer was a not unexpected and resounding—yes. What had once made the concentration of people in cities necessary was now counteracted by the new forms of Machine Age transportation and telecommunication which, following Mumford, Wright described as allowing what was previously only able to be accomplished in the centralized city to be done by a dispersed population living in a healthier, more spacious, and more wholesome environment.[36] As a result, "the city, as we know it today," Wright predicted, "is to die." The exacerbation of urban problems brought on by the congestion due to skyscrapers and automobile traffic offered incontrovertible evidence that "we are witnessing the acceleration that precedes dissolution."[37]

Any attempt to redress the evils of the city within the framework of the traditional urban environment was thought by Wright not only to be doomed to failure but also to raise false hopes. (Nor, it should be added, did Howard's Garden City ever seem to enter his mind.) Wright consequently felt it necessary to confront directly and attack from the outset "Le Corbusier and his school" for their plans to redesign the existing city in the guise of "a machine made Utopia" based on a "shallow philosophy accepting Machinery in itself as prophetic." Preferring to refer to his Swiss-French nemesis as an abstract thinker rather than architect, Wright spoke of how "philosophers [i.e., Le Corbusier] draw plans, picture, and prophecy a future city, more desirable, they say, than the one now in travail; the pictures—reducing all to dead level raised to mean height,—geometrically spaced."[38]

The description was no doubt meant to apply to Le Corbusier's Contemporary City of Three Million Inhabitants, with its twenty-four cruciform, glass curtain-walled towers, all the same sixty-story height, occupying the central transportation and commercial hub, surrounded by lower ranges of housing blocks, all the same height and laid out on a modified gridiron plan (figures 5.8–9). "In order to preserve air and passage, this future city," Wright continued in a graphic descriptive passage foreshadowing J. G. Ballard's dystopian vision of the modern metropolis, "relegates the human individual, as a unit or factor, to pigeon-hole 337611, block F, avenue A, street No. 127. And there is nothing at which to wink an eye that could distinguish No. 337611 from No. 337610 or 27643, bureau D, intersection 118 and 9." It is the expression of "a mechanistic system appropriate to man's ultimate extinction."[39]

Perhaps because he was having too much fun, but also because he did not want to limit his criticism to a purely formal analysis, Wright refused to leave the matter of Le Corbusier's projected city there and returned to it a bit later when talking about the problem of "the poor" in terms of the social dimension of housing. Here, he raised the issue of class and money in relation to equality of opportunity. According to Wright, the machine in Le Corbusier's purported "'city of the future'" acted as a social leveler only to produce and enforce "'the common denominator.'" Not fully understanding the economic and social classification of the housing types in the Corbusian scheme, Wright assumed that "the poor man" was to be treated "just as is the rich man,—No. 367222, block 99, shelf 17, entrance K"—"a mechanized unit in a mechanical system"—and thus poverty to be "built in" to the system. "This new city-model," he ironized, "is delightfully impartial, distinguishes no one, nor distinguishes anything except certain routine economies sacred to a business-man's civilization … to be shared with the ubiquitous-numericals who are the 'common denominator' … by the nominators of the system," that is to say, Le Corbusier and the elite group of technocrats for whom the city was designed and who would run its affairs. Everyone else was reduced "to the ranks,—of the poor."[40]

In Wright's counterproject, which is based on even fewer economic specifics than Le Corbusier's, the common denominator would no longer be the poverty bred by the congestion of the city. The horizons of "all 'rich' or 'poor,'" would be expanded by life in the countryside, just as everyone would be afforded the privacy and freedom available almost exclusively to the superrich or superpowerful in the existing city or the "machine made Utopia" of Le Corbusier.[41] Based on the pattern of decentralization he noted as already occurring in metropolises like Chicago and Los Angeles—which were "splitting up … into several 'centers' to again be split into many more"—Wright proposed a radical, multicentered, unbounded, and extensive conception of the city to replace the traditional, hierarchically organized, self-contained urban form.[42] Instead of bringing the "air, space, and greenery" of the countryside to the city, as Le Corbusier proposed, Wright's idea would take "the city … to the country." Clearly setting his own vision in direct opposition to Le Corbusier's, it was at this point in the piece that Wright described his new type of city (in French) as a form of "Ruralisme as distinguished from Urbanisme." Ironically, it became, by inversion, characteristically "American, and … truly Democratic."[43]

Wright allowed that the move to the countryside might not be total at first or even in the foreseeable future. The natural devolution of the city was initially toward a purely "utilitarian" state. As such, and Wright gave no terminus ad

quem for this, the city would be reduced to a six-hour, three-day a week schedule, "invaded at ten o'clock, abandoned at four." The rest of one's time would be lived entirely outside of it. As "the countryside re-absorbs the life of the city," it would eventually offer all the cultural and commercial opportunities the city once did and become "a festival of life." The machine had already made possible the necessary "margin of leisure" for this abandonment of the traditional city, and the infrastructure for such a complete reorganization of human existence was already in place. All that was needed was a realization through design.[44]

The fundamental infrastructural elements allowing for, indeed encouraging, the dispersal of the population from urban centers and their regrouping into new forms of community were the existing highway system and the various new forms of telecommunication, such as telephone, radio, telegraph, and television. Sharing a number of characteristics with the linear city first proposed in the early 1880s by the Spaniard Arturo Soria y Mata (1844–1920) and developed concurrently with Broadacre City by the Soviet planner N. A. Miliutin (1889–1942) and several colleagues, a highway served as the backbone and scaffolding of Wright's proposal. But whereas the typical linear city was based on a purpose-built, single transportation spine, Wright's conception at this point in time was a multidirectional, multifunctional network using the existing "great road systems." The highways were not merely a means of physical movement but also took on the role of place-making that squares and plazas once played in older cities.[45]

The gas, or "'service' station along the high-way" was to act as the driver of this anamorphic urbanism in its role as "advance agent of decentralization." As "the future 'city' service in embryo," Wright correctly predicted it would "naturally grow into a neighborhood distribution center, meeting place, restaurant, rest room or whatever else is needed." Spread throughout the landscape in every direction, such service stations would form "a thousand centers as city equivalents to every town or city center we now have." "Decentralized chain-stores, linked to decentralized chain-service stations" would become neighborhood shopping centers, while "temporary lodging" could be had there in what later would be called motels.[46]

The most significant architectural element that would define these new forms of community center were what

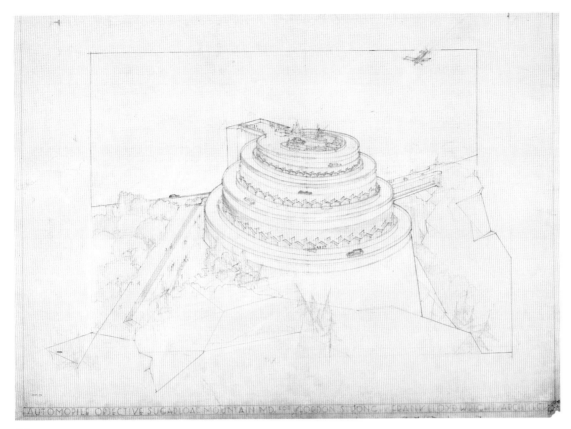

6.3

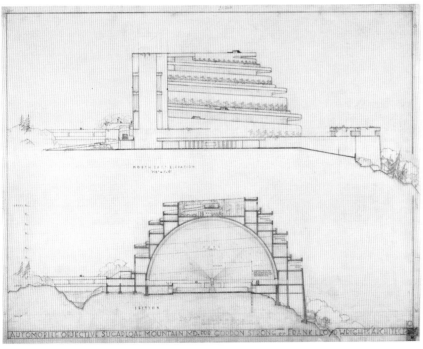

6.4

6.3. Strong Automobile Objective and Planetarium project, Wright, near Dickerson, Md., 1924–25. Aerial perspective, antedated 1923–24

6.4. Strong Automobile Objective and Planetarium project. Elevation and section, antedated 1923–24

the architect called "automobile objectives." Based on the design done for Gordon Strong in 1924–25 for a rural site near Dickerson, Maryland, about an hour's drive from Washington, D.C., such automobile-accessible, multiuse structures would house planetariums, concert halls, theaters, museums, and art galleries, as well as other outdoor facilities on the surrounding "recreation grounds" (figures 6.3–4). One could find entertainment without even leaving one's automobile, as the continuous, double-level helical ramp was meant to afford its users panoramic views of the landscape while their cars ascended and descended the building's external roadway. Such "automobile objectives" were envisioned by the architect as occurring "from end to end of the country."[47]

While the highway and its centers for shopping, eating, recreation, and cultural activities would amply "gratify," in Wright's words, the "get-together instinct of the community," much of the social and intellectual life of the individual would be focused on the single-family house, "the home of the individual social-unit." Defining the bottom-line condition of Broadacre City, as well as explaining in some way the source of the name it would shortly acquire, Wright stated that each family would be given "an acre" as "the democratic minimum" of land. While he did not specify how this would be accomplished nor how the land was to be used other than for residential purposes (there was no mention of farming yet), he did make much of the fact that the private house would become in this new "ruralism" an integrated home entertainment center, complementing and supplementing the ones on the highway. Soon there would be little not reaching each family member "at his fireside by broadcasting, television [and] publication." "The 'movies,' talkies and all," Wright forecast, "will soon be better seen at home than in any hall. Symphony-concerts, opera, lectures will eventually be more easily taken to the home than the people there may be taken to the great halls in old-style and be more satisfactorily heard in company of our own choosing."[48] This domestic environment would provide all sorts of programming, be it for entertainment or education, in the "intimate comfort" of one's own home and with "free individual choice."[49]

Wright had not yet designed the typical house for the minimum one-acre freeholds that would dot the countryside and be called by him, in the later 1930s, the Usonian house.[50] And although he had designed the automobile objective, the most significant building in the cultural life of the decentralized

city, he neither mentioned that fact in the article nor used the project to illustrate the chapter in *Modern Architecture* based on the earlier text. Instead, when it came to choose the single work intended to carry the visual meaning of the final chapter of *Modern Architecture*, Wright decided on a rather minor and idiosyncratic building of the mid-1910s that bears no relationship whatsoever to the subject matter of Broadacre City and is even at odds with it. The drawing is of a project for a "small city house," or urban townhouse, of 1915–16, done as part of the series of prefabricated "American Ready-Cut" or "American System-Built Houses."[51] Why it was chosen over the Strong Automobile Objective is anyone's guess. The more important point is that, even by 1931, when *Modern Architecture* was published, Broadacre City had not yet been designed, and was only a verbal construct.

The apparent lack of interest in the visual—or reliance on the verbal—are indicative of the utopian character of the project. Despite the fact that his "ruralist" vision was deeply grounded in the realities of American land-use development and would eventually appear in many of its aspects in the post–World War II highway culture of the United States, the new type of city Wright described in "The City" did not cohere as an image but only as a descriptive text. It was in fact invisible—as indeterminate in shape as it was boundless in scope. Unlike Le Corbusier's projected cities of the 1920s, where the power of the images was arguably greater than the words accompanying them, in Wright's case it was the text that carried the force of the argument and made the imagination work overtime. Even when the proposal published in *Modern Architecture* was developed in *The Disappearing City* in 1932 and actually called Broadacre City, there was still no visual representation of it. That came only in 1934–35, when a large model, accompanied by smaller ones of individual structures, was built and exhibited in New York, Madison, Wisconsin, Pittsburgh, and Washington, D.C. Wright later often described Broadacre City as being "nowhere unless everywhere," thereby acknowledging both the shapelessness and fundamental imperceptibility of the concept as well as its source in the "no place" that the Greek neologism Utopia can mean.[52]

Beginning in early 1932, with his response in the *New York Times Magazine* to Le Corbusier's earlier presentation of his urban ideas in the same publication, Wright began to flesh out the image of Broadacre City that would lead to the building of the model exhibited and published in the spring of 1935 and by which the design has mainly come to be known. The *Times* article, " 'Broadacre City': An Architect's Vision," was the first publication of the scheme under that name and was illustrated by only a single Wright design. The perspective of one of the St. Mark's Towers was redrawn and labeled "A Design for an Apartment Building in the 'Broadacre City.' "[53] Although the text did not comment on the drawing, in *The Disappearing City*, published later the same year, Wright justified his recycling of the design for Manhattan as "enabl[ing] many to go to the country with their children who have grown so accustomed to apartment life under serviced conditions that they would be unable or unwilling ... to establish themselves in the country otherwise."[54] The use of such a seemingly inappropriate design as the representative image of Broadacre City in its first major public exposition simply underscores the degree to which the project was as yet "nowhere."

Despite the lack of new illustrative material, the article did get more specific about a number of elements critical to the Broadacre City concept. The most considered of these was the highway transportation system. Whereas Wright still spoke in 1929 of the usefulness of the railroad for " 'long-haul' " traffic, with the "luxurious motor-bus" only replacing it over shorter distances, by 1932 he eliminated the railway completely and transformed its vast network of rights-of-way into multilane highways of "six or more" arteries.[55] The former freight trains were replaced by a new type of "low-gravity truck-train" creating a new "swift moving fleet." Grade crossings were eliminated and the new highways received special attention as a form of "noble engineering." The highways would be linked to "systems of noiseless, compact air transport." More practically, they were directly connected with food distribution centers and "roadside markets" close to residential areas. In addition, the same "roadside markets" were now "integrated with groups of three, five and ten acre intensive farm units" as well as with "diversified manufacturing units not far away."[56]

This was the first time that Wright mentioned anything to do with farming in Broadacre City; it is also the first time he actually began to talk specifically about adjacencies and ideas of sustainability. The farm units and the factories were to be located "within a ten-mile radius of the extensive roadside markets," meaning a drive of "ten minutes" by automobile. During that time, "the citizen ... in his car" could listen to the news on the radio "from all over the surface of the globe,"

with this "modern newspaper" resulting in "forests saved and millions of tons of waste paper eliminated." Through the automobile and the radio, especially, the individual family house "would be integrated with all other homes and forms of production or of distribution spontaneously and instantaneously." Another advantage of the "spaciousness" of Broadacre City would be to allow for a proliferation of "the integrated three, five and ten acre farms" providing "a basis for a safe, rich life for the rearing of families ... in architecturally planned association, in surroundings where the nature of the association is recognized and provided for intelligently."[57] Farming would thus exist side by side with other forms of work and recreation, although it was still described as a primary occupation for only some members of the community rather than a more generalized, part-time one for most everyone.

The only indication of density given by Wright in the *New York Times* piece was vague and offered simply in response to Le Corbusier. The latter had suggested 1,000 people per hectare in his preceding article, which Wright said was " 980 too many."[58] Le Corbusier's figure equaled 400 people per acre, Wright's about 8 per acre. This was more than four times sparser than his quarter section project for the City Club but still almost three times denser than the final design for Broadacre City, where the figure would turn out to be a little over 2.5 persons per acre.[59]

In *The Disappearing City*, published about six months after the *Times* piece, Wright upped his critique of Le Corbusier's figure from " 980 too many" to " 990 too many." This now gave Broadacre City a population of about 4 persons per acre, which, like much else in the book, came closer to what the final scheme would involve. But still there were no actual designs. The only illustrations in the book-length presentation were six photographs of existing cities, places, and people (including one of himself). Facing the title page and captioned "The Disappearing City" was a Fairchild Aerial Survey view of Manhattan almost entirely shrouded in smoke and smog. The most telling of the other five, captioned "Find the Citizen," was a similar aerial view of the city, closer in, looking down into its maze of streets and buildings (figure 6.5).[60] The rest showed an aerial view of a Renaissance fortified city (captioned "Futile Pattern. The Present City"), a tangle of railroad tracks leading into a city (captioned "The Feeder for the Old City"; figure 6.6), a rural farming scene (captioned "Beyond the Vortex"; figure 6.7), and the self-portrait. The choice clearly reflected the fact that Wright probably had no idea yet what Broadacre

FIND THE CITIZEN

6.5

BEYOND THE VORTEX

6.7

THE FEEDER FOR THE OLD CITY

6.6

6.5. "Find the Citizen," illustration in Wright, *The Disappearing City*, 1932

6.6. "The Feeder for the Old City," illustration in *The Disappearing City*

6.7. "Beyond the Vortex," illustration in *The Disappearing City*

City might look like or that he had spent any time attempting to give it visual form.[61]

With the Great Depression in full force and Herbert Hoover still president, the early fall of 1932 marked a serious worsening of economic conditions, especially for the working class and farmers, accompanied by a deep sense of anxiety about the future of the country. In response, Wright gave his Broadacre City proposal a more explicit socioeconomic rationale. For the first time in his discussions of his plan for a city of the future, he referenced Thomas Jefferson and his agrarian-based "democratic ideal" as a source of inspiration. The other figure he now invoked was the late nineteenth-century political economist Henry George, whose critique of unearned wealth and consequent poverty resulting from the concentration of land ownership in the hands of the few, led Wright at this time to call for the abolition of all forms of "rent" or "unearned increment" on land, money, and inventions. Upholding the "complete logic" of George's program of "communal ownership by way of taxation of all communal resources," Wright intimated that taxing unimproved land value might provide the basis for his own, still only rudimentarily defined land redistribution program, wherein each family was promised a minimum of one acre as its birthright.[62]

After elaborating on the points made in earlier iterations of his decentralized city, Wright turned his attention first to the problem of housing the poor. Instead of simply condemning earlier approaches that he believed transformed the inhabitant into a mere number and took no account of his or her humanity and individuality, Wright proposed an owner-built housing solution, where a prefabricated, standardized kit of parts would be made available to the factory worker. In possession of an acre and therefore having no rent to pay, the prospective homeowner could start by purchasing bath and kitchen units, then additional rooms, until finally the family was comfortably housed. The garden would not only provide food for the family; it would also give them extra to sell at the nearby roadside market.[63]

The second class of individuals Wright now focused on were the beleaguered farmers. Leaving aside the large "grain and beef-raising areas" as being unaffected by his scheme (a large chunk of the country), Wright called for the transformation of the family farm into smaller, more efficient, more "intensive" operations that would cater to more specialty markets, closer to what today is called niche farming. "Dairying,

fruit growing, truck gardening, raising the rarer meats and fowls, eggs, in all of which freshness is a first condition," he explained, "the little-farmer ... will take the place of the big-farmer by intensive methods" such as the use of greenhouses.[64] Cooperative centers would supply the needed heavy machinery and the farm buildings themselves would be built of integrated component parts, factory-built and standardized, based on a project Wright had undertaken for Walter V. Davidson, whose Buffalo house he had designed in the first decade of the century.[65]

The idea of smaller is better, combined with those of mobility, decentralization, and reintegration, characterized all aspects of the scheme as elaborated in *The Disappearing City*. Factories would be reduced in size, spread out over the landscape, and linked with transportation routes as well as housing communities. Because of the new forms of electric communication, there would no longer be any need for large office buildings in centralized locations. Police and fire departments, district courts, and banks would be grouped in community-sized structures at highway interchanges. Professional offices would no longer be in separate commercial buildings but would become home offices attached to the private house and thus in close proximity to those who might need their services. The large, big-city hotel would become a thing of the past, as groups of cottages would replace them in the countryside in natural settings. A novel addition to the type would be the "hotel on wheels," which could be trucked to different parts of the country as a kind of terrestrial cruise ship. "Motor houses," like the later RV, would serve the individual in the same way.[66]

The list goes on and on. Hospitals were to be split up into small neighborhood "clinics scattered in a spacious garden." Universities would be downsized into small-group learning centers "available for free study" to all. Performances at theaters and cinemas, when not brought directly into the home by radio, could be experienced along with other cultural and entertainment events at the "community center" automobile objectives "scattered over the states." Schools would be broken down into modules for ten to forty students and located in park-like surroundings. There would be nonsectarian churches and also what Wright called "Design Centers." The latter, like his proposed Hillside Home School of Allied Arts that was nearing realization in the about-to-be-inaugurated Taliesin Fellowship, were to serve as schools for the application of industrial techniques to the creation of useful objects à la the Bauhaus. These would be dotted around the countryside in a chain of "style stations or culture centers."[67]

Curiously, aside from the discussion of the prefabricated, self-built concept for workers' houses and farmhouses, nothing was said about the design of the middle- and upper-class single-family house and its setting other than superficial generalities. In fact, more specific details were given about the apartment houses that would be built for those incapable of immediately weaning themselves from the traditional mode of city living. Modeled on "the type proposed for … the small park of St. Mark's on the Bouwerie in New York City," these duplex apartment towers would likewise be arranged in groups of four, totaling thirty-six in all, and occupying thirty acres with integral underground parking.[68]

Whether it was because of the lack of actual, physical designs to illustrate the words or because of the rather futuristic thinking represented by the words themselves, Wright acknowledged in the conclusion to *The Disappearing City* that Broadacre City "may seem to the patient reader … [just] another Utopia." Nor did he try to deny the truth of this. "I am not trying to prove a case," he said.[69] In fact, one could read the book less as a project for the future than as a simple extrapolation from existing conditions. Certainly, the small neighborhood clinics, niche farming establishments, RV-type motor homes, and motel cottage groupings, not to speak of highway-based shopping and entertainment centers, were things either already in place or easily imagined. There was even a greater reality in the picture Wright presented in that he spoke on a couple of occasions, in the plural, of "Broadacre cities" and of the differences that would always obtain between "an inland city" and "a port-city," the latter of which would "be subject to special concentrations."[70] In actually designing Broadacre City over the next couple of years, Wright eliminated much of the scheme's purely imaginary, utopian side while reinforcing its nearly unimaginable comprehensiveness by means of a model that could only be read as a fragment of a uniform, infinitely extensible spatial environment.

The Belated Three-Dimensional Version of Wright's Ruralism, 1934–35

For its first five and a half years, then, Broadacre City existed only in the mind, as a textual construct of words. Wright did not seem interested in providing visualization of it in either drawn or model form. It has been suggested by Kathryn Smith that the impetus for building a model and exhibiting it came from one of his office staff and that even then Wright only agreed "grudgingly."[71] He must have known that such a concrete, physical representation would overdetermine Broadacre City's reception and ultimately limit its capacity for development. He was right. Where the potential for realization was ingrained in Le Corbusier's model of the Voisin Plan (figure 5.11), not to speak of the accompanying drawings that explained in almost scientific detail how things would work, the Broadacre City model fundamentally contradicted the inherent unrepresentability and imponderability of a city that was, by definition, "nowhere unless everywhere."[72]

When Wright finally presented Broadacre City visually, in a series of exhibitions held in the spring and early summer of 1935, he did do so most prominently in the form of three-dimensional models rather than the more abstract one of architectural drawings (figure 6.8). The models included numerous individual structures, ranging from a highway interchange, gas station, theater, and motel cabins to various types of private houses and the St. Mark's apartment tower.[73] These were grouped around the main object of display, a nominally twelve-foot by twelve-foot table-height model of a four-square-mile section of the city itself.[74] Standing plywood text panels highlighting the main concepts of the proposal linked the different elements to one another while creating a path of movement through the exhibition.

Subsidized by Edgar Kaufmann, the owner of Kaufmann's Department Store in Pittsburgh and a leading citizen of the city whose son, Edgar Jr., had joined the Taliesin Fellowship in October 1934, the models were built by the Fellowship in the winter and early spring of 1935 while the group was staying in Chandler, Arizona.[75] The exhibition opened in New York on 15 April 1935 at Rockefeller Center as part of the Industrial Arts Exposition sponsored by the National Alliance of Arts and Industry. After closing one month later, the exhibition traveled first to Madison, where it was shown at the State Historical Society of Wisconsin, before going on to Pittsburgh, where it was included as part of the Federal Housing Administration's "New Homes for Old" exhibition held at Kaufmann's Department Store in late June. In July the exhibition moved to the main courtyard of the Corcoran Gallery of Art in Washington, D.C., after which it made a

6.8

6.8. Broadacre City exhibition, Industrial Arts Exposition, Rockefeller Center, New York, 15 April–15 May 1935. Reproduced in *AA*, May 1935. Fay S. Lincoln Photograph Collection, Special Collections Library, Pennsylvania State University Libraries

final four-day stop at the Iowa County Fair in Mineral Point, Wisconsin.[76]

There is but a single preliminary sketch in Wright's hand for the general layout of the large model (figure 6.9). The sketch is unusual in being in ink as well as having an extensive explanatory text on the rear of the sheet, plus marginal notes on the plan itself. Oriented with the highway to the left, the drawing ostensibly shows the same four-square-mile landmass depicted in the model (see figure 6.10), although no dimensions are indicated and the left border of the plan had to be extended beyond the highway's edge to square up the site. Also, unlike the model, the sketch is not neatly divided into four, one-mile-square sections as per the Rectangular Land Survey system instituted in the 1780s and 1790s (figure 1.10). Only two areas in the sketch are clearly delineated by an orthogonal grid. They are the checkerboard pattern of small house units and subsistence farms occupying most of the upper left-hand corner of the site and the rectangular bands of "little farms" at the bottom and to the right. Otherwise, the site is treated in an uncharacteristically loose and almost picturesque manner, very different from the earlier City Club project (figure 4.28). Curving roads of "fluid traffic" exiting the main highway, with access to the airport, circumscribe three sides of a large park and recreation area in the lower middle before climbing up to the better-class housing district laid out on the slopes of the hill that fills the top right-hand corner of the site.

If the earlier descriptions of Broadacre City left some doubt as to whether its concept was truly that of a linear city, the sketch dispels much of the doubt. There is one main highway indicated, and it is both the feeder for all life in the four-square-mile area as well as the link to other communities connected with it. Obviously, there would be a continuity with lands lying to the top, right, and bottom of what is drawn, but none of that is delineated. The only suggestions are the curvilinear secondary roads that stop at the edges of the site. The baseline highway on the left, as is indicated in the marginal note on the drawing and explained in the text on the rear, appropriates the right of way of the existing railroad line. An eight-lane roadway for automobile traffic lies above a lower deck of six designated trucking lanes. Warehouses were to be located within the substructure of the highway and connected to distribution centers through on- and off-ramps at main intersections. The distribution center shown in

the sketch just to the top of the airport is directly linked to a major "roadside market." Most of the factories are adjacent to the highway, although there are others at the base of the hill near the upper group of small farms. Gas stations, serving as shopping centers, are located along the highway as well as at the two corners, where the hill levels out to the plain occupied by the minimum acre-lot houses and small farms.

Aside from the notation of a theater, art collections, and clubs in the vaguely triangular area of the park anchored at the lower left by the market and defined at its upper right by a lake formed by damming the stream that meanders horizontally through the site, there are no other community or public buildings indicated. (The circular automobile objective is drawn at the upper right-hand corner but not labeled.) The explanatory note on the rear of the sketch, however, which may have been done after the drawing, gives some sense of at least one of the important structures that would ultimately be included in every area serving as a county seat. This is the "official building" of the county government, which was to provide most of the public services, including police and fire protection, garbage collection, and local mail delivery. It would, in fact, do much more than that, for in the final design it was designated as the location from which land, no longer held and sold for speculation, would be distributed by the county architect. Working for the state through the county government, the architect's office would be in the prominently placed skyscraper towering high above a much expanded lake (see figure 6.12).[77]

The model developed from Wright's sketch was built on four 6-foot by 6-foot plywood pieces joined to create the larger unit shown in the spring of 1935 along with the smaller models of individual structures, drawings of earlier building designs incorporated in the project, and the explanatory text panels (figure 6.10).[78] The panel facing the model, diagonally opposite the one headlined by the words "LIVING IN AMERICA," featured the large plan seen in figure 6.11. Its schematic character helps to clarify the model's complexity and will be useful to us as we look at the model in detail.[79] Each of the four 6-foot-square units of the model was meant to equal a mile-square section of the country based on the Rectangular Land Survey. This meant that each of the four squares comprised 640 acres and the entire model, 2,560 acres. With the population for the area represented by the model now set at 1,400 families, and each family averaging five members according to Wright, the

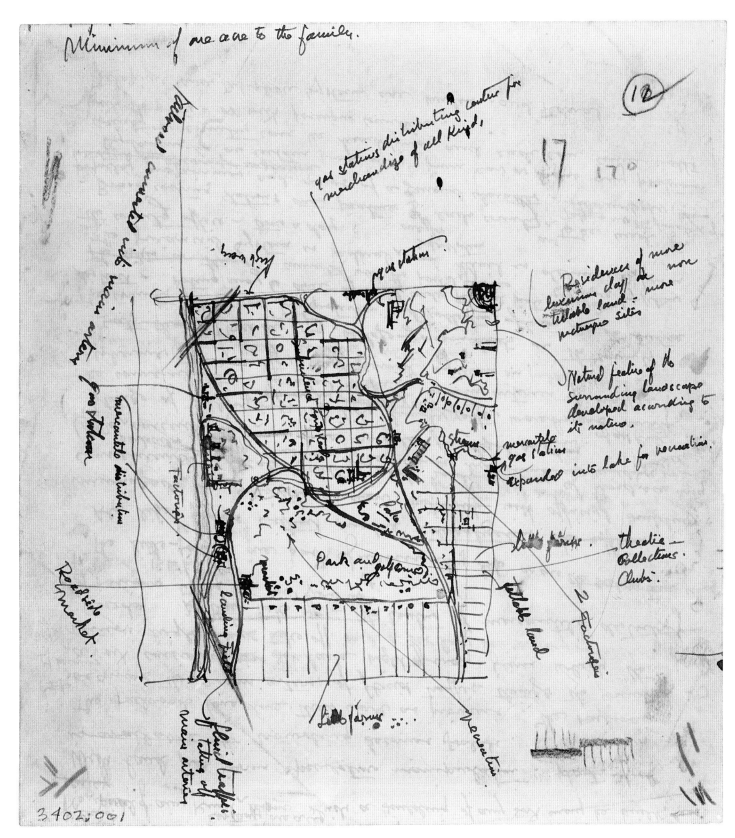

6.9. Broadacre City project, Wright, 1929–35. Preliminary sketch, 1934 (highway on left)

total number of people to be housed and provided for was 7,000. This gave the modeled site a density of a little over 2.5 persons per acre.[80]

There is no remnant of the sketch plan's curvilinear road system anywhere in the model except for the limited area of the hill in its upper left-hand corner. A rectangular, one-acre grid, measuring 165 by 264 feet, more visible perhaps on the plan than the model, underlies all aspects of the final design (figures 6.10–11). The looseness of the preliminary sketch is overridden by a controlling rectilinear order that is firmly established by the dominating baseline of the wide highway and reiterated in the center of the model by a horizontal band introduced as an open landscaped space containing the community's various school buildings. While the middle one of these structures asserts a note of centrality and even cross-axiality, the overall impression is of a strong horizontal banding paralleling the direction of the highway. This substantiates the linear type of planning on which the model was seemingly based.

The horizontal banding corresponds to functional divisions. At the base of the model is the highway with its related facilities for utilitarian and supportive uses. The highway itself has been expanded from two to three levels, with the top level now having twelve lanes of automobile traffic, divided by a wide median strip with a monorail for long-haul intercity travel, which Wright claimed would go at speeds of up to 220 miles per hour (figure 6.13).[81] This above-grade level is crossed by overpasses using a cable-stayed design supported by decoratively detailed, sail-like abutments. The first trucking level, camouflaged by side berms, has two divided roadbeds of three lanes each. The lowest level was reserved for local trucking and deliveries. Both trucking levels connect directly to warehouses and supply and distribution centers.

Immediately alongside the highway, at the lower right, are a number of small factory buildings with workers' residences above (figures 6.10–11).[82] To their left are a large assembly plant connected to service facilities and, to the extreme left, a factory for the building of "aerotors," the name Wright gave to the rotorcraft, an early form of helicopter that he believed would replace normal airplanes. He specified these for use in Broadacre City, which no doubt explains the elimination of the airport shown in the sketch. More small factories with housing are located just above the aerotor plant, between the farm units that border the model on the left up to the center

line and a merchandising mart. Between the latter and a motor hotel, or "automobile inn," on the opposite, right-hand side of the model, are large plots for vineyards and orchards, surrounded by single-family houses.[83]

In the lower middle horizontal band, between the area just described and the zone set aside for the schools, are lots for various-sized houses, ranging from the rather banal single-story, pitched-roof type with subsistence farm Wright referred to as "minimum," or "one-car," dwellings to the more spacious, two-story, flat-roofed types he described as "two-car" and "three-car" houses (figure 6.14).[84] Bordering the main roads beginning at the highway overpasses are houses for professionals of all sorts with their attached home offices. In the right quadrant of this band is the main shopping center and market facility, with its one-story streamlined structures intended for direct automobile access, modeled on recent shopping centers, especially in Los Angeles.[85]

The shopping center/market sits diagonally across a small body of water from an outdoor concert hall and music garden (figures 6.10–11). Together these elements form a node of community activity at the base of the stream that flows through the site to the large lake near its top. Immediately to the right of the lower grouping is one of the examples of the most elegant and spacious house-types in Broadacre City, the "five-car" "house of machine-age luxury" that the architect originally designed for a site in Denver, Colorado, in 1931, a model of which was featured in the Museum of Modern Art's International Style exhibition the following year. In close proximity to this quite palatial dwelling and bordering the right side of the model along the edges of its middle two bands are more small farm units, clearly making Wright's point that these farms were to be understood as integral parts of the community and not simply necessary evils.

As already noted, a broad swathe of parkland creates a horizontal division across the middle of the model. A relatively large building serving as the high school (and probably the small-group-learning version of a college or university) is located between two smaller structures intended for grade schools. The placement of such a school complex in the center of the plan recalls the position schools were given in the different designs in the City Club competition as well as the prominence they had recently acquired in Clarence Stein and Henry Wright's "neighborhood unit" concept developed for the Garden Suburb of Radburn, New Jersey, in 1927–29. The

6.10

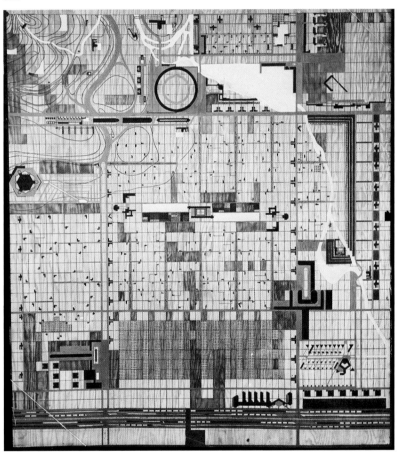

6.11

6.10. Broadacre City project. Model, 1935 (highway on bottom). Reproduced in *AA*, May 1935

6.11. Broadacre City project. Plan (highway on bottom)

school complex acts as a community center and focus. At the same time, it serves to divide the neighborhoods associated with the highway and factories in the lower half of the model from those around the administrative and recreational/cultural facilities dominating the upper half.

Houses, probably of the medium-size variety, occupy the central section of the third band, the one just above the school complex. At the inner right edge, across the stream, the area is contained by rows of planting bordering the park, beyond which are farmsteads. To the left of the house lots and professional offices is the hexagonal ecumenical church, based on the Steel Cathedral project Wright had done for New York in 1927 for the same client that commissioned St. Mark's Towers. In front of that very large structure is a landscaped columbarium and cemetery. And above and closer to the center, starting at the base of the hill, is a one-unit-wide stretch of land containing scientific and agricultural research facilities and an arboretum, zoo, and aquarium. Just below this group is one of the St. Mark's–type apartment houses, and across some more medium-size house lots to the right of that is another "house of machine-age luxury."

A wide, undivided road separates the band just described from the fourth, top one, where the main administrative and cultural buildings of the part of the city represented by the model are located. More or less in the center is a vast circular stadium meant for athletic events. To its right is the large triangular lake formed by damming the stream that runs through the right half of the site. A bathhouse is located at the upper corner of the lake, across from the stadium. Along the hypotenuse of the lake is the design center, modeled on Wright's proposed Hillside Home School of Allied Arts. It was here that young men and women were to be trained in various industries and crafts to create objects of high quality for use in Broadacre City. House-offices for those engaged in the instructional program, like the Bauhaus Masters' houses at Dessau, form a line along the rear of the building, while diagonally across the lake from the design center is the administrative seat of the county government, where all decisions regarding land distribution and design criteria would be made. Where the two low wings of the county building meet, a nearly sixty-story skyscraper rises as if out of the water. Modeled on the corner towers of the Skyscraper Regulation project as revised in the architect's unrealized design for the 1933 Century of Progress Exposition in Chicago,

the tower would have had no other real purpose in the rural surroundings of Broadacre City than to broadcast the fact that this is a city, albeit one different in type from any previously known (see figure 6.12).

In the area just above the county building are structures for light manufacturing, apartments for workers, and small farm units. In the quadrant to the right of these is an administrative building for the local aerotor industry surrounded by sports fields, a baseball diamond, and various clubs. Above and to the immediate left of the stadium, at the base of the hill, are a sanatorium, country club, and hotel, all of which benefit from the more open and exclusive setting that exists there. Along the contours of the hill, with its winding roads, are sites for most of the larger houses, including at least one more "house of machine-age luxury" and a couple of St. Mark's–type apartment towers. There is one grade school serving the children of the area plus a number of water reservoirs. At the top of the hill, actually extending beyond the model through three-quarters of its circumference, is the light-colored, spiral-shaped automobile objective, the main cultural and community center of the automobile-based city (figure 6.15). The roads giving access to it for the crowds that were intended to use it frequently are not shown, although they would naturally follow the section lines marked by the top and left edges of the model. Tourist cabins in the forested area just below the automobile objective on the left were no doubt meant for overnight stays for those coming from a distance.

The lack of main highway access to the automobile objective and the inclusion in the model of both it and the county office building—the two most significant structures in Broadacre City—raise important questions as to how the fragment of the ruralist city represented by the model relates to the larger county and national grid. Or, to put it more simply, what are we actually looking at? The four-mile-square fragment is similar in certain respects to the earlier City Club quarter section in accepting, as the architect said then, "the established gridiron" derived from the 1785 Rectangular Land Survey as the "basis" for the design.[86] But in the earlier project, despite the appearance of infinite extension in relation to the abstract continuity of the underlying grid, it was absolutely clear how the 160-acre neighborhood development fit in with and was served by the city's street pattern and mass transit system.

6.12

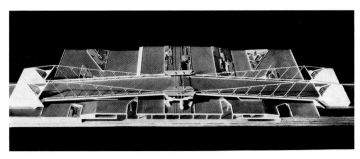

6.13

6.14

6.12. Broadacre City project. Model. Detail looking from top of county skyscraper building toward automobile objective

6.13. Broadacre City project. Model of main highway. From *AA*, May 1935

6.14. Broadacre City project. Models of "minimum" houses, as reproduced in *AR*, April 1935. WHS

In the Broadacre City model, that is not the case. As in his 1912–13 design, Wright spoke of heeding the operative grid, noting that "Broadacre City makes no changes in existing land surveys." In fact, he even went further in saying that Broadacre City's "forms are not mere invention" but rather "conservative **interpretations** of actual circumstances today."[87] It was, in effect, a directed form of extrapolation, taking the ways the American countryside was ordinarily developed and organized and imparting to that development and organization a more artistic, more efficient, and more meaningful order. According to Wright's own calculations, the four-mile-square area of the model was about one-ninth the size of the county its administrative building and automobile objective served.[88] This meant that the county represented by the model's civic center was precisely equal in size to the township established in the 1785 survey as the basic governmental unit of the new western territories, to wit, thirty-six square miles.

The model is thus both intellectually an abstraction and physically a fragment. The fragmentary part of the equation has been commented on in the past but not with much purpose or precision. If we understand the model to represent approximately one-ninth the area of the county its main buildings serve, then the major highway running along its base is probably the only one of its size parallel to it for perhaps one hundred fifty miles, which is the distance Wright spoke of as the feasible "radius" of operations for "all forms of production and distribution" in the automobile age.[89] But this accounts only for major, limited-access, latitudinal roads and not smaller ones or any longitudinal ones. All those are missing. To visualize them following section lines along the other three edges of the model and beyond both undercuts the linear city aspect of the project and forces us to appreciate its multidirectional, boundless character.

Broadacre City Before the Crash — and After

Most scholars have assumed that "the physical form of Broadacre City," as Anthony Alofsin put it, is "inseparable from its ideological content" and that its "ideological content" derives from the architect's response to the stock market crash and onset of the Great Depression thought to have preceded the project.[90] The apprentices who joined Wright in the midst of the Depression and built the model that George

Collins called "a sort of [private] WPA project" were probably an important source for this misreading of history. Cornelia Brierly, who not only was part of the construction team but also helped truck the model to its early exhibition venues, stated that "the Depression was a great factor in stimulating thought that culminated in the ideas for Broadacre City."[91]

As we have seen, nothing can be further from the truth. Broadacre City was conceived before the October crash and its outlines fleshed out well before the effects of the Depression set in. In fact, even as late as 1935, when the model was produced and exhibited, Wright made only a couple of passing references to contemporary social, economic, and political conditions. In the radio broadcast he gave on the opening of the Rockefeller Center exhibition, he spoke of the present "economic, aesthetic and moral chaos" and the "tragic breakdown staring us in the face" but related this more to a lack of "organic form" at work in society than a failure of America's capitalist system. In any event, he did not propose that Broadacre City was designed to solve the current economic problems and even went so far as to assert that "Broadacre City is no mere 'Back-to-the-Land' idea," one of the most popular means seen at the time for dealing with urban unemployment and poverty.[92] As already noted, the only two thinkers Wright alluded to prior to 1935 were Thomas Jefferson and Henry George, and then only in very general terms and almost three years after the concept for his city of the future had been well mapped out. The others like Silvio Gesell, Ralph Borsodi, and C. H. Douglas who offered sympathetic methods for dealing with the crisis were mentioned by Wright only in revisiting Broadacre City in the 1940s and 1950s, and thus well after the fact.[93]

While there is no point in denying the social, political, and economic changes that Broadacre City would have entailed, it is equally if not more important to recover its origins in the city planning debates over congestion, traffic, and zoning in the 1920s in order to arrive at an accurate explanation of its place in the history of twentieth-century urban planning. Broadacre City was, first and foremost, a response to the increased use of the automobile in the 1920s and the congestion this, along with the growth in the number and bulk of skyscrapers, produced in the city by the middle of the decade. Zoning ordinances and design responses, like Wright's own National Life Insurance Company Building and Skyscraper Regulation projects, either resulted or would have resulted in

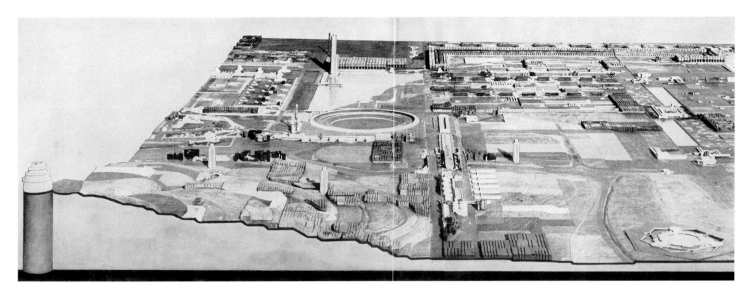

6.15

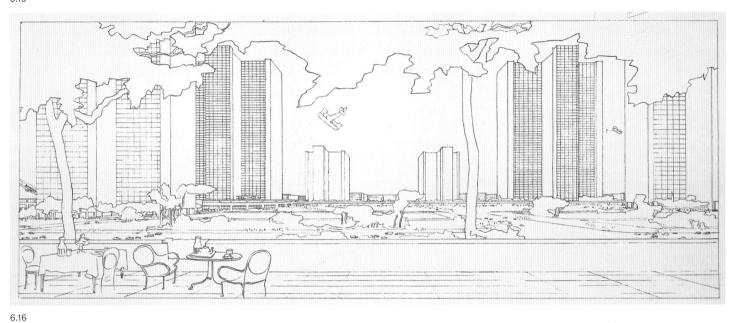

6.16

6.15. Broadacre City project. Model, with automobile objective at lower left. From *AR*, April 1935

6.16. Contemporary City of Three Million Inhabitants project, Le Corbusier. Perspective from raised cafe terrace, looking toward center. Reproduced in Le Corbusier, *Urbanisme*, 1925. FLC

minimal improvements. Wright, like Le Corbusier, realized that a more radical approach was necessary.

Both Le Corbusier and Wright saw the automobile as the solution rather than the problem—but in entirely different ways. Whereas the former sought to open up the traditional city by eliminating its densely packed, congestion-producing, street-defined blocks of living and working quarters to enable automobiles to move freely through the city at the speed for which they were designed (figure 5.10), the latter believed this would never work. "Which would you rather give up first," Wright asked in 1933,

the city or the automobile, if you had to choose between moving away into more ordered green spaciousness to keep your mobilization or remain on "the hard," in the herd, where you must eventually give it up?

You will have to choose before very long. The traffic problem in any busy city is practically unsolvable. Destroying the present city and beginning all over again [read Le Corbusier]—or even [doing] much to modify it [read Corbett]—costs too much to be regarded as a probability. ...[94]

A more sensible proceeding is to *let the automobile* take the city to the country.

The city has today only about one-third the motor car men it will inevitably have. And congestion, as it is, is nothing at all [compared] to what it must become when the city-man is the success he will be if promises are kept. His success means a car. His family and the family of his increase are dreaming of it now and envying the neighbor who has one or two—or three. ...

It is in the nature of the automobile that the city spreads out. ...

The traffic problem will be solved ... by ... Broadacre City. Twentieth century life not only seems likely to dissolve the city into the country—there is no other city possible.[95]

Where Le Corbusier offered a more densely populated yet more open city than before by spacing his skyscrapers and housing blocks at wide intervals and placing them and the roadways that served them in a vast park-like setting, Wright countered this European "*urbanisme*," as he called it, with an American "ruralism" as radical as its antitype. Instead of pastoralizing the city, as Le Corbusier did, Wright citified the countryside (figures 6.15–16). The intention of both

was to break down traditional categories and boundaries. Le Corbusier wrote in the *New York Times* that in his city "nothing of tradition will remain. Everything will be new."[96] Wright spoke of Broadacre City as "a breaking down of the artificial divisions set up between urban and rural life."[97] As much as it was a critique of the traditional city, Wright's Broadacre City was also a critique of the suburb that was an integral part of the American urban condition, the residential half of the bipartite paradigm that had existed since the late nineteenth century and to which Wright had contributed so much.

Le Corbusier's Contemporary City of Three Million Inhabitants and Voisin Plan for Paris and Wright's response in his Broadacre City each, in its own way, represented an attempt, first set forth by Olmsted and then reiterated by Ebenezer Howard, to realize the ideal of combining the "advantages" of city and country life without incurring the "disadvantages" of either. At the same time, both Le Corbusier and Wright sought to advance the discourse about the modern city beyond the limits set by the turn-of-the-century concept of the Garden City (figure 3.31). In that vision, grounded as it was in the downtown/suburb dyad, Howard proffered a solution in the form of a limited-size city-country amalgam. Over and against this rather sentimental aggrandizement of the village into a pseudocity, Le Corbusier sought to bring the advantages of the countryside directly into the existing city, whereas Wright sought to bring the advantages of the city directly into the existing countryside. But while Le Corbusier retained some vestiges of the suburb in the small working-class "garden suburbs" (*cités-jardins*) that lie outside the central section of his Contemporary City, Wright went further by eliminating any distinction between city and country and any hierarchy in the process of urbanization in Broadacre City.[98] In its premodel, purely textual form, this utopic dream found its most faithful expression.

Although it started out as a response to urban conditions in the 1920s and as a rejection not only of the supposed safety valve of the suburb but of the very city center/suburb dyad itself, Broadacre City became over the years in the eyes of most critics and historians the ur-type of the modern sprawling suburb, dependent on the highway and often forming new centers independent of the downtown core. Wright, for his part, continued to elaborate the Broadacre City project in numerous publications that added nothing new to the concept and seemed to support this interpretation. The so-called Usonian houses he began building in great numbers in the later 1930s replaced those in the 1935 model by the time it was refurbished for the architect's one-man exhibition at the Museum of Modern Art in 1940–41. The new images were included in the second iteration of the project, *When Democracy Builds*, published in 1945. Finally, in the drawings updated for *The Living City*, published in 1958, not only were the architect's myriad suburban houses included; so were buildings like the Beth Sholom Synagogue, built in the Elkins Park suburb of Philadelphia in the mid-1950s.

The afterlife of Broadacre City in the 1940s and 1950s, when its images so easily resonated with the advance of suburban sprawl, not only made it seem that sprawl was what the project was about, but also made it seem as if this is what Wright was about. The architect was characterized as someone who hated the city and would have nothing to do with it. The final part of this book challenges that view. Indeed, it was precisely in the years following the making of the Broadacre City model that Wright designed major schemes for giving new vitality to the urban centers of Madison (1938), Washington, D.C. (1940), and Pittsburgh (1947). It is no small irony that these were the very three cities where the Broadacre model was exhibited following its inauguration in New York.[99]

In looking back at Wright's work of the 1920s and early 1930s, we should therefore be cautious of too closely identifying the personal feelings of the architect with the actual work. Wright did have a profound attachment to the landscape and rural life of the countryside — and he loved automobiles. Broadacre City certainly expresses those feelings. The design is antiurban. But that should not be taken to mean that Wright himself was antiurban, and the project should not be taken to indicate that the architect could not or would not respond sympathetically and creatively to a problem of urban design when that was presented to him. In the projects for existing cities to which we shall next turn our attention, Wright showed that he fully understood how the abandonment of the city, as a consequence of the increased dependence on the automobile, made rebuilding the core seem more desirable and more important than furthering the process of decentralization. It may in fact be for this reason that, while Le Corbusier continued after the 1920s

to propose new and often quite different schemes for the redesign of the modern city, Wright never gave much further intellectual or artistic thought to how Broadacre City could evolve. Both *When Democracy Builds* and *The Living City* were simply warmed over versions of Broadacre City, which, in retrospect, seems more an anomaly than representative of Wright's architecture as a whole.

III

NEW VISIONS FOR THE CITY CENTER: URBANISM UNDER THE HEGEMONY OF THE AUTOMOBILE

SEVEN

A CIVIC CENTER MEGASTRUCTURE FOR
THE LAKEFRONT OF MADISON, WISCONSIN, 1938

During the second half of the 1920s—when the final wave of traditionalist skyscrapers in the "setback style" was transforming the American city and a younger generation of European architects was evolving its response to the urban problematic—and the first half of the 1930s—when little building anywhere was going on—Wright had almost no work. The production of the Broadacre City model gave his recently established Taliesin Fellowship something to do. But the year following the exhibition and publication of this project saw Wright's practice take off as never before. Fallingwater, the weekend house for the same Edgar Kaufmann who subsidized the model, went into construction in 1936 and, after completion in 1937, was the subject of the first one-building exhibition at New York's Museum of Modern Art. Following Fallingwater, and in fairly rapid succession, were the new headquarters for the Johnson Wax Company in Racine, Wisconsin (1936–39); the Jacobs House in Madison, Wisconsin (1936–37), the first of many low-cost Usonian houses built over the next decade and a half; and the plans for Taliesin West in Scottsdale, Arizona, and Florida Southern College in Lakeland, Florida, both begun in 1938.[1]

The prominence Wright achieved by this work was broad-based and lasted until his death in 1959. He was featured on the cover of *Time* magazine in January 1938 and had entire issues of *Architectural Forum* devoted to him in January 1938 and January 1948, with "A Selection of Current Work" following ten years later in *Architectural Record*.[2] A significant part of this resurgence and recognition of Wright occurred in the area of urban design. The project for a civic center for downtown Madison undertaken in 1938 was the first of a series of major urban designs produced over the next twenty years, which

sought to bring life back to cities that had suffered under the new hegemony of the automobile. Coming only three years after the publicity surrounding Broadacre City and offering a direct challenge to, even a rebuttal of, its premises and conclusions, the Madison design calls into serious question the narrow reading of Wright as an antiurbanist.

In the Sir George Watson Lectures delivered in London in 1939, Wright spoke of Broadacre City but emphasized that it was not to be confused with the traditional city nor were its principles to be applied to the detriment of existing urban areas.[3] Wright clearly realized that the very forces that led to decentralization were responsible for the erosion of the fabric of the city and the city's growing subservience to increasingly distant and independent suburbs, which had once been dependent on it. To revitalize the urban core entailed a process of counteraction whereby those things that had begun to do most damage, in particular, the automobile, were to be harnessed to create a new structure within which urban life could flourish.

The fact that Wright reentered the arena of urban design in the later 1930s rather than after World War II is of significance and gives the trajectory of his work a certain uniqueness. From the point of view of urbanism, the later thirties was a period of stagnation in both Europe and America. Aside from Albert Speer's (1905–81) work for Hitler and Mussolini's various projects, almost nothing else at the urban scale came near being built in Europe. Modern architects in Germany and Austria began fleeing those countries by the early thirties, while those in France, England, Holland, and elsewhere found little if any opportunity for work. In America, where the modernist impulse of urbanism on the order of Le Corbusier's Contemporary City of Three Million Inhabitants and Voisin

Plan for Paris (figures 5.10–11) had little serious impact until after the war, whatever was done during the New Deal era was still fundamentally dominated by the classical precepts of a City Beautiful movement now watered down and reduced to the essentially pragmatic concerns of professional city planners and engineers less interested in leaps of the imagination than in finding the most efficient and cost-effective solution to a problem. Zoning was often thought to be the panacea. In his initial engagement with urban design in the period, Wright came face-to-face in Madison with a city plan that had been conceived at the height of the City Beautiful movement—indeed, by one of its leading practitioners—before devolving into a pale facsimile of itself under the direction of local political leadership. Willingly working within the established parameters, Wright was able to show what could still be wrung from such a traditional approach by adapting it to modern needs, modern concepts of space, and modern methods of construction.

The project for a civic center on one of the two lakefronts of Madison—first referred to by Wright as Olin Terraces, then as Monona Terraces, and finally as the Monona Terrace Civic Center—was designed in the late summer and fall of 1938 in direct response to government initiatives to construct a new city-county office building and a new auditorium-armory, which would have jeopardized, in certain people's minds, a long-standing plan for a monumental civic center along the axis connecting the State Capitol to Lake Monona. While the Wright design had the immediate effect of deferring the construction of the city-county building and ensuring the cancellation of an independent auditorium-armory scheme, it remained on paper throughout the architect's lifetime.

The Second World War dashed any hope for the implementation of the scheme when it was revived and redrawn by the architect in 1941. In 1954, a referendum in its favor was passed, but by that time a separate city-county building, designed by the Chicago firm of Holabird, Root and Burgee (est. 1945), was in the works. With this central element made redundant, the Wright lakefront project was reprogrammed in 1955 and then downsized significantly in the following years to meet budgetary restrictions. Although still ongoing when the architect died, it was abandoned by the city in 1962 only to be given new life in the 1990s when it was finally built close to what it had looked like at the time of Wright's death.[4] The original project of 1938 is the significant one for both historical and aesthetic

reasons, and it is this one that will be discussed. It was a direct response to the plan for the site developed nearly thirty years before by John Nolen (1869–1937), already one of the country's leading figures in the new discipline of city planning. While never implemented, his plan guided development during the intervening years, and for this reason we shall turn to it first.

Madison's New State Capitol and Nolen's Civic Center Plan, 1905–1911

The impetus to commission Nolen for a comprehensive plan for Madison came from John M. Olin, a lawyer, faculty member of the University of Wisconsin, and the city's leading advocate for park development. Olin founded the Lake Mendota Pleasure Drive Association in 1892 and became its president two years later, when it changed its name to the Madison Park and Pleasure Drive Association. Over the next decade or so, he was instrumental in the creation of parkways on both the eastern and western shores of the lake that borders the city to its north as well as in the establishment of several parks within the city itself. In order to give professional direction to these efforts and plan for future initiatives, in early 1908 he contacted Nolen, one of the most prominent graduates of Harvard's new program in landscape architecture (est. 1900), a major training ground for the emerging city planning profession.[5]

Olin's initial idea was to hire Nolen as the landscape architect for the Madison Park and Pleasure Drive Association and, to make the deal more attractive, to arrange for the university to create a landscape architecture department with Nolen as chair. Although this plan fell through, Olin was able to persuade the city to offer the Cambridge-based landscape architect and planner a part-time position as landscape architect for municipal parks. Nolen visited Madison in April 1908, during which time he lectured on city planning at the annual meeting of the Park and Pleasure Drive Association. Olin convinced him to undertake a master plan for the city, which Nolen began on a return visit in December. With Olin's strong support, he was officially hired by the city to develop the plan.[6] Nolen presented his preliminary recommendations at the next annual meeting of the Madison Park and Pleasure Drive Association in April 1909.[7] His final plan, produced just a little over a year after the publication of Burnham and Bennett's *Plan of Chicago*, is dated August 1910. It was approved by the city the following month and published in early 1911.[8]

Although Nolen is often viewed as someone who combined the data-based efficiency thinking of the City Practical or City Functional with the more genteel aestheticism and classical techniques of the City Beautiful, there is little evidence to support this in his published report of 1911.[9] *Madison: A Model City* follows directly in the line of Burnham and Bennett's *Plan of Chicago* and even exaggerates some of the earlier document's privileging of the representational and visual aspects of city planning over more social and economic concerns. In the concluding pages of his text, Nolen explicitly referred to "the recently published plan for Chicago" as establishing the benchmark for "a new standard of city making" and praised Burnham and Bennett's approach as "big, broad, far-seeing."[10]

Throughout his report, Nolen left no doubt as to what he considered to be the first priorities of planning for Madison. "As a Capital City, Madison should possess dignity and even some restrained splendor; as a University City it should manifest a love of learning, culture, art, and nature."[11] "Beauty," he added, "is the most important element in the control of the people." He justified such an emphasis by quoting Frederick Law Olmsted's statement that "the demands of beauty are in large measure identical with those of efficiency and economy."[12] For precedents and models, Nolen, like Burnham and Bennett, constantly referred to the "achievements of the cities of the Old World." Among these, the smaller lakeside ones in Switzerland were highlighted "as an inspiration and guide for Madison," so much so that Nolen ended his report by grandiloquently assuring the civic leaders: "It is within the power of the people of Wisconsin to make Madison in the future what Geneva is today — a beautiful, well-ordered, free, organic city."[13]

The report is organized in five chapters or sections. The first gives a capsule history of the city, notes its special topographical features, and expands mainly on its special identity as the state capital and site of the state's main research university. The second chapter is devoted to the most important part of the plan: the civic center, its connection to Lake Monona, its link to the University of Wisconsin campus bordering Lake Mendota to the west, and its extended relationship to the city as a whole through a rationalized and beautified street and parkway system. This is the only aspect of the plan that includes designs for buildings and their surroundings. Following the relatively detailed exposition of his project for the heart of the city, Nolen turned in the third chapter to a much more general discussion of the role of the university itself in the future development of Madison, and especially its importance for new efforts in landscape architecture.

In the penultimate chapter, somewhat misleadingly titled "Madison as a Place of Residence," Nolen talked of the need to improve the "inconvenient and ugly" railroad approaches to the city by creating "open squares or plazas" with "fountains or monuments and … important public and semi-public buildings"; the necessity for removing "unsightly poles and wires" from city streets; the importance of "planting and maintaining street trees"; and the value of parks, playgrounds, and "connecting parkways or parked avenues" ideally organized within a "park *system*."[14] When he finally came to the issue of housing as such, he had little more to say than, as "in Europe," it should be "proper" and should afford the advantages of "beauty and opportunity for health and recreation."[15] To achieve this, he recommended rethinking conventional patterns of subdivision and municipal controls on platting, and even suggested a modified version of German zoning regulations.[16] The concluding chapter, titled "The Future City of Madison," which likened the city to Geneva, began with a seventeen-point list of recommendations, starting with those related to the proposed civic center. To this list was added the caveat that the city's first order of business should be to create a "permanent city plan commission … with power and funds to investigate, study and execute comprehensive plans of improvement," which the city ultimately did in 1920.[17]

While similar in almost all essentials to the *Plan of Chicago*, Nolen's *Madison: A Model City* reversed the order of subjects taken up by Burnham and Bennett. The question of residential conditions was demoted to last and the city center, dominated by its civic center, was promoted to the primary area of concern. To underscore this prioritization, Nolen included seven images of his plans for the civic center and its connection to the university, whereas he produced only one other drawing for the entire rest of the report. That was a map of Madison showing the relationship of the downtown to the rest of the region by means of a park and extensive parkway system, the latter encircling both Lakes Monona and Mendota (figure 7.1).[18]

A monumental downtown civic center was typically the focus and major design element in City Beautiful plans. Often these have been criticized as extravagant displays of authority imposed upon the existing urban fabric and extraneous to its previous developmental pattern. In Madison, however, there is

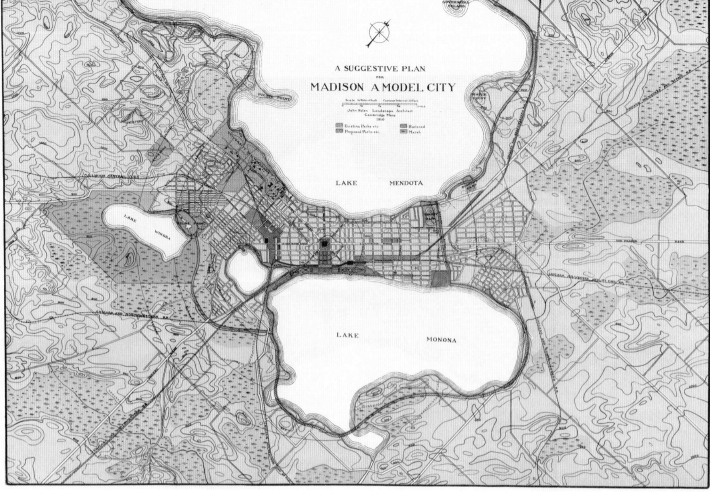

7.1

7.1. Madison, Wis., Master Plan, John Nolen, 1908–9. Proposed circulation and park
system. Plan. From Nolen, *Madison: A Model City*, 1911

7.2

7.3

7.2. Madison. Aerial view, 1885, by Wellge & Co., looking due north. LC

7.3. State Capitol, Madison, George B. Post and Sons, 1906–17. Perspective submitted
in competition, 1906. WHS

a strong case to be made for an "organic" relationship, a word Nolen himself used, between what existed and what he proposed. Indeed, there can be little doubt that one of the main reasons Nolen was hired, quite apart from Olin's particular interest in Madison's parks, was the fact that construction on a new State Capitol had just started and, for a number of years, the city had been debating how to provide it with an appropriate setting.[19]

In 1904, a fire destroyed the mid-nineteenth-century capitol building located near the center of the isthmus, between Lake Monona and Lake Mendota, connecting the city's east and west sides (figure 7.2). The building that replaced it, by the New York firm of George B. Post and Sons (est. 1904), resulted from a competition held in 1906 (figure 7.3).[20] Built between 1907 and 1917, it not only was much larger and more grandiloquent than the previous structure, but also followed a biaxially symmetrical Greek-cross plan that gave full expression to the radial pattern of diagonal avenues that overlays the orthogonal grid of the city center (originally laid out in 1836), and accommodates it to the forty-five-degree shift that occurs at the edge of the university area to the west. By its alignment with the city's overall circulation pattern and, even more, its pivotal location in the narrow isthmus, the new design almost inevitably called for an entourage that would link it with one or both of the lakes from which it was seen to best advantage and which it overlooked.

Four of the building's eight entrances are located on the downtown grid in the reentrant angles between the wings that project on diagonals aligned with the cardinal points. Topped by a nearly three-hundred-foot-high white granite dome, the building acted, as Wright later wrote, "as a sort of wheel with eight spokes radiating from the Capitol dome."[21] Although the building's form does not privilege one facade over another, its architect considered the main entrance to be the one facing Lake Monona, since the outlook in that direction was "the most interesting view."[22] When it came time to decide upon the orientation of the gilded statue of *Wisconsin* by Daniel Chester French that was placed on top of the dome in 1914, it was the view to the southeast, toward Lake Monona, that was selected.

The overriding factor in that decision, however, was not Post's opinion; rather it was the Nolen design for a six-block capitol mall and civic center which, according to the city planner, was intended to establish an "organic relation between

the new Capitol and Lake Monona" and, at the same time, "make the new Capitol what it should be—the greatest permanent work of civic art in the State" (figures 7.4–6).[23] The new "Lake Monona approach to the Capitol," Nolen told the audience gathered for the April 1909 annual meeting of the Park and Pleasure Drive Association, where he first publicly presented his plan, "is certainly unexcelled and probably unequaled in any American commonwealth, and is as good in relation to state needs as the capitol at Washington is to those of the national."[24] The restoration and aggrandizement of the late eighteenth-century L'Enfant plan for the nation's capital, along with the Group Plan for Cleveland's civic center and the Chicago plan, served as models for Nolen (figures 1.2–3, 3.22). All were based on European classical sources employing symmetry, axiality, and geometry to order large-scale compositions of monumental public buildings grouped within and set off by formally landscaped elements.

A major reason why Nolen oriented the civic center toward Lake Monona, rather than Lake Mendota, was the fact that the main railroad stations were located on the south side of the city, and it was from this direction that visitors and state legislators arrived. Also, the distance from the Capitol to the southeastern lakeshore was quite a bit shorter than that to the northwest. It followed a gentle slope before dropping precipitously to the railroad tracks at lake level. A critical problem was thus how to negotiate the nearly fifty-foot drop from the end of Monona Avenue to the lake while at the same time dealing with the railroad tracks that ran along the shore creating both an eyesore and a physical barrier between the lake and the city.[25] Here, the Cleveland plan, whose mall terminated at the lake with a railroad station above lakeside tracks, provided an especially appropriate precedent.

Nolen began by designing what he called "the Great Mall" to extend one thousand feet from Capitol Square, the park immediately surrounding the new Post building, to the bluff at the end of Monona Avenue (figures 7.4–5).[26] The existing street was widened to create a boulevard, divided into three lanes by strips of park planted with double rows of trees. On either side of this mall, as in Cleveland, were tree-bordered lots reserved for the major components of the civic center. The four blocks closest to the capitol building were intended for "public buildings" for government use. Nolen was extremely vague about their functions, noting that "just what these should be it is not necessary now to say." He thought that the two closest to the

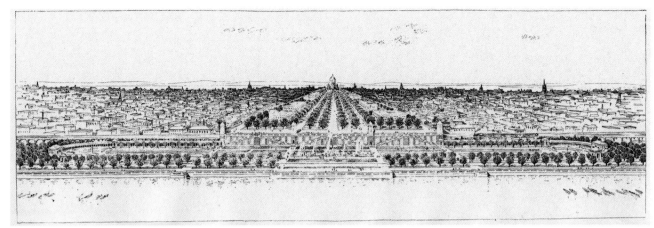

7.4

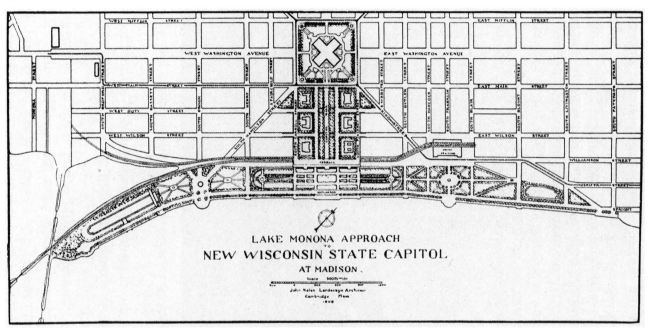

7.5

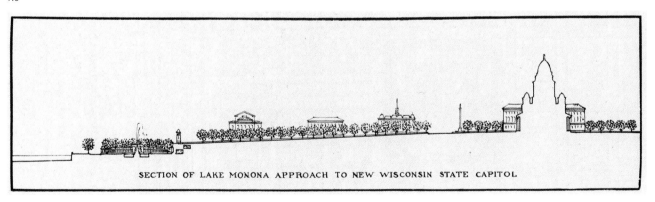

7.6

7.4. Madison Master Plan. Proposed capitol mall and civic center. Aerial perspective.
From Nolen, *Madison*

7.5. Madison Master Plan. Proposed capitol mall and civic center. Plan. From
Nolen, *Madison*

7.6. Madison Master Plan. Proposed capitol mall and civic center. Section.
From Nolen, *Madison*

Capitol "would undoubtedly be required at once by the State," whereas the next two could be built with no definite purpose in mind, leased as "private office buildings," and later converted for government use as needed.[27]

The two sites nearest to the lake were to be used for "semi-public purposes" dedicated to "the pleasure interests of the people," as Nolen genteelly put it. On one side he thought should be "a really fine theatre and opera house," serving as an "educational feature" of the state's Progressive social and political ideals. This was located by him on the west side of the mall. Opposite it he suggested "a much needed hotel," designed with a "character" in keeping with the classicism of the rest of the composition. Benefiting from such a "situation that could scarcely be equaled elsewhere in Wisconsin," the hotel would be "comparable in many ways to the Chateau Frontenac at Quebec."[28]

Unlike Cleveland, the mall area ends not in a building but in a terrace providing a broad promenade along the lakefront and views over the water. Built over the existing, lower railroad tracks, it conceals them from view while at the same time serving as a bridge leading to a mile-long park created by filling in approximately sixty acres of the lake to extend three hundred and fifty feet into it (figure 7.6). Access to this waterfront recreational area is by three pairs of rather steep flights of stairs along the embankment wall. At the base of the stairs is a pool, nearly the width of the mall, with fountains designed to project water high enough so as to be seen from the mall. Formal gardens to either side of this feature terminate in low, classical exedras. Beyond these are additional formal landscape elements articulated by *pattes-d'oie* that link them directly to the city street system through underpasses. Though exceedingly awkward in its relation to the new union railroad station, the plaza on the east would have provided the arriving visitor an immediate visual impression of the interrelationship Nolen hoped to establish between the city and its waterfront.

Nolen referred to the lakeshore extension of his civic center as a "waterfront esplanade," thereby endowing it with a certain international elegance and cachet. He compared his City Beautiful ideal of Madison as a "model city" to European cities like Versailles, Lucerne, and Geneva. He boasted that his plan might prove to "be better than anything of the kind that has so far been done in this country." Most important, it raised the city's status beyond national limits. "In fact," he wrote, "it is not too much to say that this waterfront esplanade

… might equal any similar development anywhere in the world."[29] Most civic leaders of Madison believed, or at least wanted to believe, what Nolen said, and the plan for the civic center he proposed in 1909–10 remained the template for the city's thinking over the next half century and more. Unlike Cleveland, however, things moved slowly, with the result that what eventually was built had very little of the classical appearance of the original design.

Competing Suggestions and Alternatives, 1918–38

As David Mollenhoff and Mary Jane Hamilton have carefully documented, the move to implement the Nolen plan took many years to get under way.[30] During that time certain buildings were built and a number of alternative ideas placed the plan in jeopardy of never being realized as conceived. Almost immediately after the State Capitol was inaugurated in 1917, the private, well-heeled Madison Club, comprising the city's business elite, purchased part of the block at the southeast end of the mall that Nolen had proposed, in its entirety, for a grand hotel commanding views over the lake. With no planning commission to object, the club built its headquarters in 1917–18 on what was arguably the most desirable site in the Nolen plan. Moreover, the three-and-a-half-story brick structure paid no attention to the setback from the future mall that Nolen had prescribed so as to allow for a broad perspective of Lake Monona from Capitol Square (figure 7.7).

In 1918, the Association of Commerce made the first of its numerous proposals for the construction of a civic auditorium. Its idea was quite different from Nolen's "educational feature" of "a really fine theatre and opera house." The Association of Commerce's goal was to provide space for a combined convention hall, auditorium, city hall, and armory. Nothing happened right away, but the program in one form or another remained central to the ensuing debate over the shape and location of the civic center. Nolen's plan, however, was never far from people's minds. Following his recommendation and the nonconforming construction of the Madison Club, Madison created a City Planning Commission in early 1920. And, in 1921, the *Wisconsin State Journal*, one of the city's two major newspapers, serialized Nolen's entire report.

One of the first acts of the City Planning Commission was to draft an ordinance limiting the height of buildings around Capitol Square to ninety feet.[31] Another was to commission

7.7

7.7. State Capitol, Capitol Square, and Monona Avenue, Madison. Aerial view looking
southeast to Lake Monona, showing development up to early 1990s. Top center: Olin
Terrace, Frank Riley, 1934–35; to left: Madison Club, 1917–18; immediately below: U.S.
Post Office and Courthouse, James A. Wetmore, 1927–29; opposite, across avenue:
City-County Building, Holabird, Root and Burgee, 1953–57; above, to right of Olin
Terrace: State Office Building, Arthur Peabody, begun 1929–32

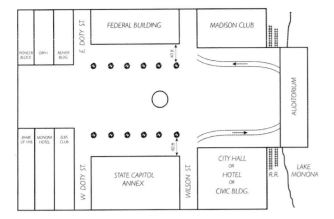

7.8

7.8. Civic Auditorium/Boathouse project for end of Monona Avenue, Association of Commerce, 1925. Plan. Redrawn from *WSJ*, 18 October 1925, by Bill Martinelli

a new city plan to give a more practical and solid grounding to the future growth of the city than that offered by Nolen's. For this they hired Harland Bartholomew (1889–1989), a more nuts-and-bolts city planner of St. Louis who described himself as a "city plan engineer." Trained in civil engineering and an early and recognized expert in traffic and zoning issues, Bartholomew was commissioned to "prepare a major street plan, transportation plan, and zoning ordinance for Madison."[32] His report, submitted in the fall of 1922, was entirely different from Nolen's in style, and even at odds with it. Aside from a number of drawings showing street intersections, grade separations, and street section types, the majority of illustrations comprised maps documenting existing and future traffic loads, zoning uses, and, most important, new and widened streets and highways. Fundamental to his plan for increasing traffic movement and efficiency, Bartholomew proposed augmenting the number of railroad tracks running along the lakeshore at the base of Monona Avenue from four to thirteen and filling the shoreline beyond that to create a four-lane highway that would ring the lake and thus allow for easy commutes from the suburbs.

While he took pains to praise his predecessor for a "report that embodied many splendid suggestions," Bartholomew also noted in the introduction to his own report that "the full significance of city planning is just becoming appreciated" and that "the field of action has been considerably widened" so that "the emphasis is no longer on the 'city beautiful' but on orderliness and comprehensiveness of design." For Bartholomew this meant "a coordinated scheme of streets, street railways, railroads, recreation grounds, and all related civic improvements."[33] It also meant for Madison that Nolen's idea for a civic center running from Capitol Square to Lake Monona fell by the wayside. Bartholomew made no reference to this key element of the Nolen scheme, nor did he allow it to figure in any of his plans.

Instead, following even more closely the precedent established by the earlier Cleveland Group Plan, he chose to place at the foot of Nolen's proposed mall a union railroad station directly above the considerably widened lake-level track bed.[34] The station's location "at the front door of [the] city," Bartholomew claimed, was perfect from the point of view of efficiency: "This site is not only the nearest available one to the Capitol and business district, but with an outer boulevard along the lake shore it will be easily reached from east, west and south Madison without the necessity of traversing the central part of the city." Noting that "the location at the foot of Monona Street [*sic*] is unsurpassed in scenic beauty, and the opportunity is unlimited for making it one of the most noteworthy and interesting views in Madison," he made no mention of the fact that the construction would block those same views from any civic center that might eventually be built on axis with it.[35]

Although Bartholomew's recommendations regarding zoning formed the basis for Madison's first zoning ordinance (March 1927), his idea for a union station at the foot of Monona Avenue had little effect on the thinking of Madison's civic leaders and did nothing to erase the memory of Nolen's civic center.[36] Ironically, it may even have provided an additional justification for Nolen's concept. This came in the form of a renewed call by Madison's Mayor Milo Kittleson and the Association of Commerce for an auditorium to combine a facility for conventions, exhibitions, concerts, and the like with a boathouse. The multipurpose structure was to be sited at the end of Monona Avenue, over the railroad tracks, on filled land in the lake. The scheme for a five- to six-thousand-seat hall that would also include parking for up to eighteen hundred automobiles was published in diagrammatic form in the *Wisconsin State Journal* in the fall of 1925 (figure 7.8). It was positively received and much discussed in the press over the succeeding months.[37]

On the heels of these discussions, the civic center itself began to come closer to some form of realization when, in 1927, the U.S. Post Office and Courthouse (completed 1929) went into construction on the middle block of the east side of Nolen's projected mall (see figure 7.7).[38] Although the design did not fully respect the setback established by Nolen's plan, it was much better in that regard than the Madison Club. Moreover, its sober neoclassicism, rendered in gray granite, followed Nolen's schematic indications for the site in both style and massing. Soon after groundbreaking, the city officially designated the six-block area between the Capitol and the lake as a civic center and later that year secured permission to fill in the lake out to the 350-foot distance specified by Nolen for his lakeshore esplanade and parkway.

Over the next several years, different locations and programmatic combinations were suggested for the auditorium, which continued to create indecision regarding the fate of the civic center. Among these was a variant of an earlier idea, this time to join to the auditorium a combined city-county building, the city part to replace the old city hall and the county part to serve mainly as a new courthouse. Although rejected at first, the concept would return a decade later to inform Wright's 1938 design.[39] In the meantime, the newly designated civic center received its second building with the construction of a State Office Building in 1929–32 on the lakeshore site earlier set aside by Nolen for a theater and opera house. Directly across the projected mall from the Madison Club, it conformed to the shallower setback established by its counterpart, thus constricting forever the outlet of a future mall to the lake. In addition, the stripped classicism of its design gave further evidence of the watering down of the City Beautiful ideal that was only to increase following the Depression and revival of construction with the New Deal (see figure 7.7).

One of the designs submitted for an auditorium in 1929 was the work of James R. Law (1885–1952), a principal in Madison's leading architectural firm, Law, Law and Potter (est. 1914). More important to our story, however, is that Law became mayor of Madison in 1932, in which capacity he served for eleven years, and during which time he helped give city planning in general and the civic center in particular a major boost. In this effort he often worked side by side with Joseph W. Jackson (1878–1969), a business and civic leader who had become infatuated with John Nolen's thinking about Madison's future. As a board member and vice president of the Association of Commerce, Jackson invited Nolen back to Madison to give a lecture in June 1934 on "what <u>can</u> be done and <u>should</u> be done to make Madison ... a truly model City—such as you visualized ... 24 years ago." Jackson hoped Nolen would pick up where he left off in 1910 in order "to make our people <u>think</u> in terms of Madison, A Model City so that they will <u>act</u> to bring it about."[40]

Jackson's not-so-hidden agenda was for the city to rehire Nolen. To this end, he involved Law in the city planner's visit and lecture. For his part, Law saw a major opportunity to move his mayoral agenda forward. This would include the establishment of a new City Plan Commission in early January 1935 to recommend projects for federal Public Works Administration (PWA) funding (Jackson was appointed to the commission's Executive Committee on 28 January 1928). Upon hearing that a friend's son, William V. Kaeser (1906–95), was finishing a postgraduate thesis on a fifty-year "Master Plan for Madison Wisconsin" under Eliel Saarinen's direction at the

7.9

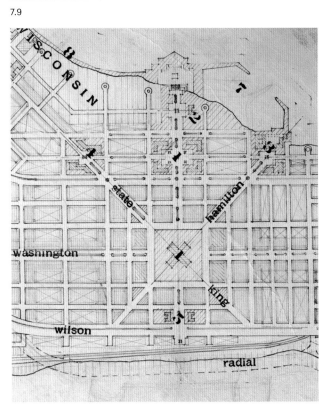

7.10

7.9. "A Master Plan for Madison, Wisconsin," thesis project, Cranbrook Academy of Art, William V. Kaeser, 1934–35 (north-northwest is at bottom). From *AA*, October 1935

7.10. Madison Master Plan, Kaeser, ca. 1936–37. Detail of downtown and civic center. WHS

Cranbrook Academy of Art, Law invited Kaeser to come to the Nolen lecture and tour the city with Nolen, Jackson, and himself.[41] Kaeser had a degree in architecture from MIT, where he was the roommate of William Wesley Peters (1912–91), who, by 1935, had become Wright's chief assistant in the Taliesin drafting room. No doubt thinking ahead to the possibility of hiring Kaeser, Law wrote to him again in December about whether he had thought of incorporating in his master plan a scheme for a municipal harbor, boathouse, and concert hall on Lake Mendota.[42] Law and Jackson had been discussing this idea for some time and would, over the following year, develop a plan for a combined auditorium, convention center, armory, municipal pier, and boathouse on Lake Mendota that would divert much of the impetus for a Monona-oriented civic center to one focusing on the opposite side of Capitol Square.[43]

Most probably at the prompting of Law, Kaeser's thesis project, completed in early 1935, features a civic center, generally based on Nolen's, running from a reduced area southeast of the State Capitol through Capitol Square to an expansive group of buildings and plazas on the northwest, terminating in a large boat basin on Lake Mendota (figure 7.9).[44] As if to minimize, perhaps even to disguise, the divergence from Nolen, Kaeser oriented his plan south-north rather than north-south, so that his Lake Mendota civic center appeared in the same place it did in the earlier design. Kaeser's plan, like Nolen's, extended well beyond the existing city to encompass future suburban growth. He described the organization, in Garden City terms, as a series of rings. An outer grouping of clustered, "satellite" residential communities, bounded by a greenbelt surrounded a ring of "apartment houses and residential developments," which in turn surrounded the "business and commercial sections." At the focal point was the "nucleus [of] a great central governmental and civic plaza or park."[45] As the locus of government authority and cultural activity, the civic center was treated in a grandiose Beaux-Arts manner, whose boulevards, plazas, and public buildings, laid out in symmetrical and radiating patterns, went well beyond Nolen's more restrained design. By rejecting the orientation toward Lake Monona, its domain was further extended to include the university.

Kaeser was invited to lecture on his plan to the Madison City Plan Commission in March 1935, the text of which he had previously published as *City Planning: A Discussion Outlining a System for the Design of a Master Plan of Madison, Wisconsin.*[46] Law, and no doubt Jackson too, must have been very impressed

by Kaeser's project, for not long after the young architect returned to the city and opened his own office, the mayor hired Kaeser on a part-time basis to work on various city projects before appointing him in mid-November to serve on a new City Plan Commission. In 1936 Kaeser was made the unofficial city planner of Madison and was commissioned to draft a set of plans and maps based on the thesis project. Early in 1937 he exhibited his Cranbrook thesis project along with other studies for Madison and its surrounding area at the Memorial Union Gallery of the University of Wisconsin.

The Wisconsin Historical Society preserves a number of unpublished plans drawn by Kaeser in 1935–37 that reveal how he thought to develop his thesis project in his capacity as Madison's unofficial city planner prior to the events of 1937–38 that would set the stage for Wright's intervention.[47] The civic center was a major focus of his energies. One of the most finished, and probably latest, master plans has numbers and a legend that allow us to know more precisely the functions of the different public buildings he envisaged (figure 7.10). Unlike the Cranbrook project, here the existing four diagonals radiating from Capitol Square have been retained, although the two leading due north and west are given a more monumental treatment as divided boulevards. The Post Office/Courthouse is shown mirrored by a similar structure facing it across the divided, southern section of the mall. Together they form a mini-federal center (number 5 on plan). The blocks southeast of Wilson Street along the Monona lakeshore, where the Madison Club and State Office Building are located, have also been retained, although nothing has been done to "beautify" the lakeshore itself other than to preserve the small Olin Terrace that was built in 1934–35 by Kaeser's former employer, Frank Riley, to serve as a terminal feature of Nolen's projected mall (figure 7.7).[48] The railroad tracks, however, continue to separate the city from the lake as they run along the shore to a new central station at the southern corner of the downtown (number 6 on plan).

All state offices have been placed on the Mendota Lake section of the mall, where four L-shaped buildings create, in the middle of that space, a large rectangular plaza (number 1 on plan) that opens into a sequence of smaller public spaces embellished by fountains or statues. These lead down by means of a stepped terrace to a boat basin and harbor. In the block just beyond the four state office buildings, east of the mall, is a rather imposing building meant to serve as the governor's residence (number 2 on plan). The diagonal running north from Capitol Square terminates at the lower end of the boat harbor in a monumental plaza surrounded on three sides by new city and county buildings (number 3 on plan). The corresponding diagonal leading to the university passes through a symmetrically placed monumental grouping housing museums and art galleries (number 4 on plan).

Kaeser's plan to reorient Madison's civic center and develop the Mendota lakeshore was in line with the thinking that Law and Jackson were promoting as part of the city's efforts to attract funds from the federal PWA program for a new city hall and auditorium. The question of where to build new municipal facilities was linked to the larger one of whether and how they could be combined with those for the county government. This, in turn, was connected to the issue of where to build a municipal auditorium and what precisely its function should be.[49] In April 1935 a mayor's advisory committee called for the construction of a convention hall/auditorium, and two months later the Municipal Pier Committee of the Association of Commerce, of which Jackson was vice president, recommended the Mendota lakeshore as the most appropriate location for a municipal pier and recreation center to include an auditorium and convention hall. By September, the city authorized its engineering department to do drawings for the buildings and breakwater.

On the heels of these developments, Jackson renewed contact with Nolen, and by August 1936, the latter agreed in principle to resume work on the Madison plan. No doubt as a direct result of the exhibition of Kaeser's Cranbrook "Master Plan," which opened at the university's Memorial Union Gallery at the beginning of February 1937, Jackson wrote to Nolen suggesting that Kaeser, "who was preparing to be a follower of your footsteps," might serve as a "genuinely helpful" assistant on the Madison work.[50] But this was not to be, for Nolen died only a few days after receiving Jackson's letter.

Jackson had in the meantime conceived of a new organization that would have the funds and wherewithal to develop a comprehensive plan for the city as well the power and influence to ensure its implementation. Between late January and mid-March 1937, when it was formally established, the Madison and Wisconsin Foundation, with Jackson as its founding executive director, was created out of the Association of Commerce "to promote, encourage and aid the general welfare and the fullest material and cultural development of the State of Wisconsin, particularly of Madison, its capital and university city, and the surrounding area."[51] With Jackson at its helm, the Madison and Wisconsin Foundation quickly produced a "31 point-program" outlining its vision for everything from the "construction of [a] convention hall and auditorium" and the "development of lakes and water ways" to "promot[ing] Madison as a research center" and "promot[ing] the welfare of the agricultural area surrounding Madison." First on the list of priorities, however, was to "complete [a] city plan for [the] future physical development of Madison."[52]

By early June 1937, less than three months after its incorporation, the foundation invited the Cincinnati-based, civil-engineering-trained, Hungarian-born city planner Ladislas Segoe (1894–1983) to consider taking on the job left vacant by Nolen's death.[53] Following a couple of visits to Madison including a lecture at the Rotary Club, where he was introduced to Kaeser, Segoe was hired by the newly constituted, semipublic Madison Planning Trust, with Mayor Law as chair, in May 1938.[54] Between mid-May 1938, when he began work, and late December 1939, when the work was completed, Segoe produced fifteen separate reports. They were brought together in two mimeographed volumes titled "Comprehensive Plan of Madison, Wisconsin, and Environs." The first four reports, released in 1938, were "Proposed Regulations for the Subdivision of Land and Platting Procedure," a "Proposed Building Zone Ordinance," and surveys of "The Economic Base of Madison" and "The Population of Madison." Those released the following year included proposals for the "Park and Playground System," "Airports and Aviation," "Railroad Facilities and Grade Elimination," and an outline of the "Functions, … Policies and Procedures of the City Plan Commission." Most relevant to our interests are the reports produced between June and August 1939 on the "Proposed Major Street Plan," the "Location and Grouping of Public and Semi-Public Buildings," and "Parking and Parking Facilities in [the] Central Business District," the last including a "Study of the Need and Possibilities of Establishing Off-Street Parking Areas."[55]

The reports on the "Major Street Plan," "Location and Grouping of Public and Semi-Public Buildings," and downtown "Parking and Parking Facilities" were done well after Wright produced his project for the Monona lakefront civic center. The one on the "Location and Grouping of Public and Semi-Public Buildings," which dealt in large part with the

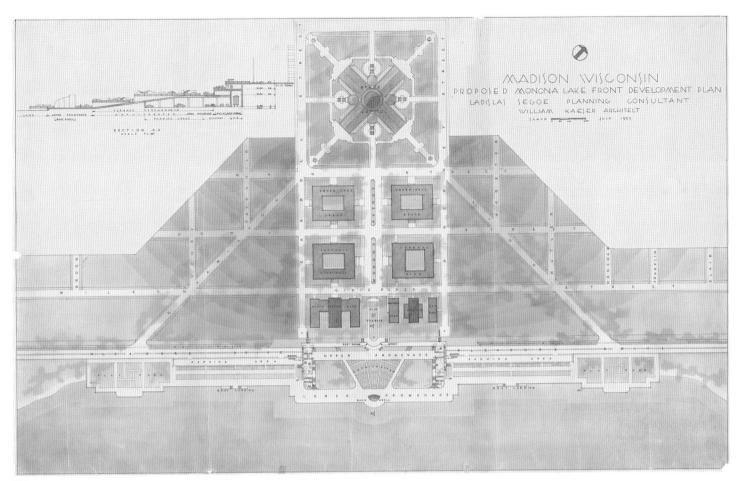

7.11

7.11. Madison Master Plan, Ladislas Segoe, 1938–39. Proposed Monona lakefront development, by William Kaeser. Plan, July 1939. WHS

civic center and auditorium complex, was accompanied by renderings by Kaeser, who had been hired by Segoe specifically to work on those aspects of the comprehensive plan (figure 7.11). The civic center was clearly based on the Wright project, and we shall therefore look at it after studying his. But before turning to Wright's project, we must consider the events that immediately led up to it and, in fact, generated it. These have to do with the continuing discussions around whether to construct a building to house a combined city hall and county courthouse, and if this should form part of a unified civic center containing an auditorium/community center.

Both Law and Jackson favored the idea of a dual city-county building and campaigned for it to be located on the block opposite the Post Office and Courthouse on the Monona Avenue mall. Since at least 1936, they also agreed that an auditorium, perhaps including a convention center, community center, armory, and/or marina, should be constructed on the Mendota lakefront, thus robbing the Nolen civic center of its unified conception. Even before Segoe was hired, Law and Jackson lobbied him to support their desire for a dual city-county building; and in July 1938 Segoe issued a public statement in favor of the joint structure as part of a civic center without, however, alluding to his clients' agenda of a separate auditorium complex.[56]

From June 1938 through the end of October, efforts to move ahead on the two different building projects—the city-county building on the Lake Monona side of the State Capitol and the auditorium-armory complex on the Lake Mendota lakeshore—proceeded apace. While funding from the PWA was sought for both, only the former initiative was successful, but on the condition, which was to prove fatal, that construction begin by the end of the year. Karl Sheldon, of the local architectural firm of Starck, Sheldon, and Schneider (est. 1935), who had earlier been responsible for the State Office Building, produced a design for a twelve-story structure, which was published in the *Madison Capital Times* in the beginning of the third week of July (figure 7.12).[57] Two slightly lower wings projected from a wide central mass topped by a broad tower-like element framed by small corner belvederes. The eclectic style was a restrained kind of early Renaissance classicism that had something of the stripped, modernistic style of New York's Shelton Hotel (Arthur Loomis Harmon, 1924). The design went through a number of changes, reducing the building's size and further simplifying the decoration, before the project

was voted down by the Dane County Board of Supervisors in early November, following the brouhaha created by Wright's intervention in the planning process.[58]

The auditorium-armory complex followed a similar trajectory. Jackson, who was the leader on this, wrote a program in June 1938 for a Mendota "Lake Shore Community Development" to include a naval armory, yacht club, and "additional public recreational facilities," which would "eventually be the complete Madison Community Center, with combined Municipal Auditorium [and] Convention Hall."[59] Early the following month Law appointed a Naval Armory–Civic Building–Boat Harbor Committee to steer the project through. Kaeser was hired as architect. By the third week in July he produced a streamlined design for a one-story Naval Armory and Community Building attached to an esplanade along Lake Mendota and opening onto a boat basin protected by a breakwater. A main feature was a five- to six-thousand-seat auditorium accompanied by ample outdoor parking. When the project was refused funding by the federal government, it died, although the auditorium had in the meantime been returned to Lake Monona in Wright's design.

Wright's Intervention

Nearly half a year before the scheduled November vote by the Dane County Board of Supervisors on the construction of a joint city hall and county courthouse, Wright was asked to produce a counterproject that would maintain the spirit of Nolen's original idea by combining a new city-county building with a civic auditorium on the mall overlooking Lake Monona. When presented by the architect at the November 1938 Board of Supervisors meeting, Wright's concept so impressed enough county representatives that, despite its $2.75 million price tag, the proposal for the Starck, Sheldon, and Schneider building was temporarily defeated, and the idea of a Wright-designed, auditorium-focused civic center on the Monona lakeshore became an issue for Madisonians to grapple with over the succeeding decades.[60]

Despite the fact that Wright was brought up in Madison, had his Taliesin studio and residence not more than forty miles from downtown, and was clearly the most celebrated architect in the state and entire country, he was not commissioned for the civic center job by the powers that be, nor would he ever have been considered a candidate for it. His parents moved to the city in 1878, when he was about to enter the sixth grade, and he lived on the shore of Lake Mendota until he moved to Chicago. Before finishing high school, he enrolled for two terms as a special student in civil engineering at the University of Wisconsin working under Allan Conover, who was just appointed supervising architect of the new Dane County Courthouse, located one block south of Capitol Square. Wright never spent as much time in any single city as he did in Madison, and he knew it well. Between 1893 and 1938, he designed many buildings for the city, a number of which were built. But none was for a government or institutional client.[61] It was not just the modernity of Wright's architecture that put people off; it was also, and perhaps even more, the architect's unconventional lifestyle, beginning with his elopement to Europe in 1909 with the wife of a former client and continuing into the 1930s and after with his establishment of the suspiciously commune-like Taliesin Fellowship.

The circumstances surrounding Wright's engagement are still not entirely clear. In a letter written a couple of weeks after the November Board of Supervisors meeting to P. B. Grove, the contractor for the Madison Jacobs House and a county supervisor, Wright said that the real estate developer, retired electrical contractor, and downtown businessman Paul Harloff had asked him a couple of years before to do a design for the Lake Monona site and then, "about six months ago," recontacted him to see if the previous "offer to make a sketch still held good—taking in the city and county coalition." Wright responded that he "was dreadfully busy—but hated the thought of more office buildings on the Madison streets when the great chance at the foot of Monona lay open." Harloff supposedly replied that "he would raise the [originally stipulated fee of a] thousand dollars" and "if I [Wright] would go ahead, George Steinle [another Madison businessman] would contribute and five other citizens besides himself." Wright added, "I regarded myself as retained by a public spirited group of Madisonians interested in a real development of the Olin pland [sic] for a civic center for Madison. It is a grand but shamefully neglected idea." Wright specified that the first discussions with Harloff took place "two years ago," meaning 1936.[62] David Mollenhoff and Mary Jane Hamilton are less specific, saying it happened "one evening in the mid-1930s," with the follow-up occurring "sometime in the summer of 1938."[63]

The "evening in the mid-1930s" was most probably in 1935 or 1936, when it first began to look like an auditorium,

7.12

7.12. City-County Building project, Madison, Starck, Sheldon and Schneider, 1938. Elevation. From *CT*, 21 July 1938

independent of a city-county building, might be built on Lake Mendota. Harloff was apparently committed to having the auditorium be a part of the civic center at Lake Monona and believed that the city-county building had to be an integral programmatic element. Wright told Grove in the letter quoted above that he and Harloff walked over to the bluff at the end of Monona Avenue and "the possibilities of the site dawned on me then."[64] The renewal of the request for a counterproject must have been in July 1938 and was no doubt precipitated by the announcement at the beginning of the month of the final agreement of the city and county to combine their facilities into a single structure, followed by the publication of the ponderous Starck, Sheldon, and Schneider design for the twelve-story building that would have been completely out of scale with the three-story Post Office and Courthouse directly across the mall from it (figure 7.12).[65]

Between the end of July, soon after the publication of the new city-county building design and the Kaeser Mendota auditorium-armory project, and early September, Harloff wrote six letters to the editor of the *Wisconsin State Journal* and *Madison Capital Times* to garner support for his idea of a building that would extend out from "the end of Monona ave., over the tracks and into the lake." That quotation comes from the first of the six letters, where he noted that with "the recent decision … to build a new joint city hall and courthouse," Madison had "the chance of a lifetime" to "make one grand effort to make up for lost time," clearly referring to the city's inability to give reality to Nolen's vision. Harloff maintained that "the matter of location" of the city-county building was "of the utmost importance" and strongly criticized the projected site opposite the Post Office and Federal Courthouse as "entirely too small" and "prohibitive" in cost.[66]

More to the point, Harloff stated that "for years" he believed that the city hall and county courthouse should be conceived in conjunction with an auditorium and that "the most logical location for a city hall, courthouse and auditorium, combined" would be the site at "the end of Monona ave., over the tracks and into the lake." It would have, in his view, the greatly added benefit of allowing for a "beautiful lake park around it" that could form part of a six-lane "lake shore drive" connecting the downtown to Olin Park to the south and the areas to the north and east. To envisage the possibilities for such a "grand effort," Harloff understood that "the services of an architect and engineer of unusual ability" would be needed.

So as not to seem as if he had decided in advance on Wright, Harloff suggested "inviting the best talent available [to] ask for suggestions accompanied by plans explaining their ideas." A fund of ten thousand dollars, he thought, should be set aside to pay for the drawings.[67]

In his second letter, Harloff reiterated his basic idea for a civic center built in part on landfill. The cost of the filling operation, he claimed, would be less than a third of the price of the proposed Monona Avenue site, not even accounting for what would have to be paid for land for the auditorium.[68] In the succeeding four letters, Harloff added nothing new. Arguing on the grounds of economy, availability of space, and benefit to the park system, he simply repeated his call for a city hall, courthouse, and auditorium complex to be built as part of "the park system in the shape of terraces" at "the end of Monona ave. over the tracks and into the lake."[69] He clearly felt that repeating the same points over and over again would serve to impress on the public the obviousness of his idea, its value for the community, and, above all, its potential for achieving the goals of Olin and Nolen that had been lost sight of for too long.[70]

It is difficult to ascertain how much Harloff's thinking owed to discussions with Wright. While the programmatic concept of a city-county building combined with an auditorium on the landfill site might have been Harloff's, the daring idea for a structure extending out "over the tracks and into the lake" was probably not something an electrical engineer, or even a conventional architect for that matter, might have conceived on his own. Certainly, the vision of a parklike, multiuse structure "in the shape of terraces" must have come from Wright, who, as we shall see, originally called his design for the civic center "Olin Terraces," based on the fact that it stepped down in a series of cantilevered planes from the street-level Olin Terrace that served as a landscaped terminus for Monona Avenue since 1935. In any event, besides creating quite a stir, Harloff's letters to the editor must have brought Wright's name to mind in certain circles, for just five days after the publication of the third letter, indeed the one referring to a structure "in the shape of terraces," Wright was invited in mid-August by the civic-minded, community-service-oriented Lions Club of Madison to give a talk at their regular luncheon on 27 September.[71] The title of his talk, Wright informed them a week before the event, would be "What Madison Needs."[72] This would have left little doubt in anyone's mind that he was going to enter the debate on the city-county/auditorium issue.

Wright most likely did the first studies for the Madison Civic Center project between the time of the Lions Club invitation and the talk itself, meaning mid-August to late September 1938.[73] Harloff went out to Taliesin sometime before 15 September to see the progress Wright had made on the design but "came away with the impression," as he wrote to the architect a little over a week later, that "you were not as greatly interested in my Park and Building Plan as you had been" and wanted to know "weather [sic] or not you really care to do any work on it."[74] Wright told him that he intended to discuss the project in the next several days with William T. Evjue, the publisher of the Madison Capital Times, and Lucien M. Hanks, a Madison banker and old friend, and that he would apprise Harloff of their reactions. There is no evidence that Wright got back to Harloff about the meeting, nor that he informed him of the presentation he was to give at the Lions Club.

Mollenhoff and Hamilton suggest that "Wright's first sketches of [the civic center] were almost certainly done before or during [the] meeting" with Evjue and Hanks, which would mean around a week or so before the Lions Club talk.[75] They reproduce two of the sketches, although there is also a third (on the verso of one of the sheets) that is part of the group (figures 7.13, 7.15, 7.17). The two they reproduce are a site plan and a plan of the structure itself; the third is a section through the site. When Wright explained his scheme to the audience at the Lions Club, however, he showed no visual materials, probably meaning that by that point in time, he had not yet developed the design much beyond the preliminary sketch stage. On the other hand, he did offer a fairly complete description of what his project would comprise, and this dovetailed quite neatly with the ideas Harloff had articulated in his six letters to the editor.

Both local newspapers gave important coverage to Wright's talk. In his piece for the Wisconsin State Journal, staff reporter Russell Pyre opened by stating that Wright's first object was to underscore the fact that Madison was wrong even to consider the Starck, Sheldon, and Schneider project. Instead, it should summon the "civic spirit to build a new county-city building as it should be built." To this effect, "he sketched his concept of a plan" that would create a "new union [railroad] station [and] ... combine it with the courthouse and city hall" in what was "essentially ... an elaboration of the ... Nolen and Olin plans

for development of the Monona ave. approach to the state capitol building."[76] Pyre then went on to describe how Wright pictured his design: "Looking from the [Capitol] square, the development envisioned by Wright would be a flat, park-like expanse, extending out into the lake and connected by parkway and drive with Olin park [to the south]. Underneath the park surface would be the stations [sic] and the civic hall, and ... courthouse buildings, arranged like a 'sweeping circular terrace.' And there would be ample parking space to go with this 'great civic expression.'" All this would be accomplished, Pyre noted, "without cutting off the view."[77]

No mention was made in the article of the auditorium, although it is likely that Wright spoke of it and that it was the reporter who left it out. Nor was any reference made to Harloff, although Wright repeated many of the ideas and phrases from his client's letters to the editor in the same newspaper, down to the point about "'putting the money into a building'" rather than "'into the pockets of property owners.'"[78] But perhaps most important for us, Pyre suggested up front, in his second paragraph, that Wright had every intention of developing his proposal into a set of drawings that would enable him very soon "to offer to the city his idea of what the new building should be."[79] Wright would, in fact, have little over a month to complete the drawings since the meeting of the county Board of Supervisors to vote on the proposed dual city-county building was scheduled to take place on 2 November. In the meantime, the federal government, through the office of the PWA, had granted nearly one million dollars to the city and county to help defray the projected two-million-dollar cost of the new building.

While he may not have been willing publicly to give Harloff credit for any of the ideas that generated his design (which Harloff may or may not have deserved), Wright still considered the businessman his client. Five days after the Lions Club event, he wrote to Harloff, saying, "I am working something up for you and you will have it soon."[80] A little over two weeks later, his secretary notified Harloff that "the plans are ready" but, because of an out-of-town speaking engagement, Wright could not show them to him until the end of the month.[81] The final designs were indeed completed by the middle of October. The text written by Wright explaining the project is dated 15 October. It is titled "OLIN TERRACES. FACTS CONCERNING THE SCHEME: HANGING GARDENS CONSTRUCTED ABOVE THE LAKE."[82] When Harloff went to Taliesin toward the end of the month,

Wright not only showed him the drawings but gave him some to take back to Madison in preparation for the county Board of Supervisors meeting.[83]

Harloff made good use of the drawings. He arranged a meeting with Frank Stewart, chair of the Board of Supervisors, and several other members of the board, to come to his downtown apartment on 1 November, the day before the crucial meeting, to show them Wright's design and, most important, to convince Stewart to permit Wright to speak at the meeting. Wright was not on the agenda, and what he might have to say had nothing directly to do with the main object of the meeting, whether or not to approve funds for the Starck, Sheldon, and Schneider city-county building.[84] As Mollenhoff and Hamilton have explained, Stewart, a small-town businessman from nearby Verona, was personally against the expenditure on the building and, as a forceful chair and leader of the rural county bloc, was the key figure to win over in promoting Wright's oppositional project. As it turned out, Harloff did his job well.

The meeting was extremely contentious. It took more than one session to resolve the issue of whether to go ahead on the joint building. In the first, morning session a telegram to Mayor Law from the PWA confirming that it had agreed to earmark the $186,000 necessary for the purchase of the Monona Avenue site was read. This should have cleared the way for a vote. However, board member Paul Robinson, a Stewart ally adamantly opposed to the Starck, Sheldon, and Schneider building and possibly an attendee at the meeting at Harloff's apartment the day before, first raised legal objections to the filing of the telegram before stating that no vote should be taken without considering "other sites" and consulting "additional architects." More precisely, as reported in the *Capital Times*, "he told board members that he desired to bring in plans for a dual building, designed by Frank Lloyd Wright, before the board pledged itself to build according to the present plans."[85] Robinson surely knew that Harloff had asked Wright to appear at the meeting and that Wright was in town—with drawings—ready to explain his counterproject to the board.[86]

After the legal objections to filing the PWA telegram were disposed of, the first and, as it turned out, main event of the afternoon session was Wright's appearance and presentation of his Olin Terraces design. Robinson requested that the board grant him permission to speak, and Stewart ruled that

he could do so as long as he did not speak to the bond issue for the Starck, Sheldon, and Schneider building and thus "jeopardize a vote on [it]." Stewart allotted Wright fifteen minutes, no doubt knowing full well that what Wright was to present to the board would affect their vote. Not to leave anything unsaid, Wright stayed on after the meeting had concluded its business, and proceeded to decry funding for the proposed building and to elaborate further on his ideas for what the Madison Civic Center should be and where it should be.[87]

Wright began his official presentation by stating, "'I came here to represent the people. I have no interest—no axe to grind outside of the fact that I am a native of this region, and am ashamed of the fact that Madison has never done anything for Madison.'" Pointing to the beauty of the city's situation and bemoaning the blindness of the authorities to take advantage of it, he arrived at his main point, that the site selected for the city-county building was inappropriate in size and unnecessarily costly: "'We don't need another office building. Why spend the people's money to build another congested building in a congested area?'" Instead, the board should think of combining the city and county offices with a civic auditorium and union depot and locate the grouping on filled land at the edge of Lake Monona in what would be a "'dream' building."[88] The complex would be a fulfillment of the Olin-Nolen project to make the city "a model city."

"'Why shouldn't Madison do something to justify its place as the capital city of Wisconsin?'" Wright asked:

'And in so doing, why not take advantage of the nature of the situation—let the lake go to work for it, as it has been ready to do all these years? Present buildings have all been built with their backs to the lake, facing the streets and ignoring the beautiful lake scene.

I suspect that John M. Olin was perhaps the only man—or at least he is the only one I can remember—who had an interest in developing Madison in connection with the lakes. …

His scheme for the development of Monona ave. was a good one, but it was ignored by the city when it permitted construction of buildings that obstructed the view.

Blessings could flow to the city, the state, and to the whole country from this development [of mine], for no other city has anything like the chance that Madison has to take advantage of the lakes.'[89]

To illustrate his points, Wright showed at least two colored perspectives: one taken from a low vantage point south of the site and across the surface of the lake (figure 7.21); the other a bird's-eye view from the northwest looking over the building with the lake in the background, suggesting a vantage point near the top of the capitol dome (figure 7.22). He might also have shown the longitudinal section (figure 7.23), and perhaps even a couple of plans, in order to explain how the various programmatic elements were accommodated and interconnected.[90]

Although Wright's drawings were probably not easy to understand for most of the board members, they surely added a spectacular dimension to his verbal description. All told, his performance was apparently riveting. One newspaper story stated that even the provincial and philistine Stewart became so "suddenly interested in the famed architect" that he decided to give Wright more time to explain his ideas once the meeting had adjourned. It was noted that "no other outsider [at a board meeting] … ever drew such an interesting circle around him after a speech."[91] The immediate upshot was for the board to take a short recess in order to visit the Monona Avenue site. Upon their return, a vote on the Starck, Sheldon, and Schneider building was taken and the bond issue was turned down, thirty-nine to thirty-eight. In light of his success at stymieing the process, and maybe even creating for himself a window of opportunity, Wright took up Stewart's offer to stick around and elaborate further on his "'dream' center … [to those who] pressed around him afterward to find out more about it."[92] This despite the fact, as Stewart noted the next day, that "'he (Wright) was talking about a building we didn't intend to build.'"[93]

The negative vote was attributed by nearly everyone to Wright's last-minute intervention. The *Capital Times* stated that Wright's appearance at the board meeting "was instrumental in defeating plans for the $2,000,000 city-county building." The *Wisconsin State Journal* called Wright's presentation "influential," adding that "the 'dream' civic center planned by Frank Lloyd Wright … was used to help defeat the bond issue, and precipitated a fight between the proponents and opponents of the dual building."[94] The role of spoiler was not far from people's lips. A revote the following evening failed to overturn the negative one, and the Starck, Sheldon, and Schneider building was defeated by a slightly larger margin (42–40). The *Capital Times* reported that "most of the blame for the defeat of the building plans was laid on the shoulders of

Frank Lloyd Wright." "The defeat," it noted the previous day, "was a personal triumph for Frank Lloyd Wright."[95]

Madisonians in general were angry at the decision not to go ahead with the proposed city-county building since it meant relinquishing a nearly one-million-dollar grant from the federal government that would have covered almost half the cost of the structure.[96] They were particularly angry at the Board of Supervisors for allowing the rural interests of the county, a minority in terms of population, to dominate the visible needs of the city. Under pressure from many quarters, including Jackson and the Madison and Wisconsin Foundation, the Board of Supervisors reopened the case of the dual city-county building and ultimately voted to approve the project and bonding for it on 25 November.[97] It was a hollow victory, however. The PWA had canceled its grant a week prior to the final vote. Law was notified to that effect in early December, at which point any idea of proceeding with the building was out of the question.[98]

Wright's role as spoiler did not help his reputation in Madison, nor his case for the city seriously to consider his design in the immediate future. It did, however, serve more than the short-term purpose of preventing a hackneyed building from getting built by revealing, even to those initially unprepared for a message of this sort, what an architecturally imaginative solution could do for a city's urban environment. As noted at the beginning of this chapter, the design would remain on the minds of Madisonians for more than half a century, as the debate over whether to build it continued until a decision was taken in the mid-1990s to go ahead with a pale simulacrum of the original project.[99] Wright himself reworked the design numerous times between 1941 and 1959. It was clearly not just important to him for its location in the city he thought of as his hometown. It was also equally important to him for establishing the parameters and creating the model for the other urban interventions he would undertake in the 1940s and 1950s. And so, if the project started out as a kind of shot in the dark, with a client who turned out to be little more than a go-between, it soon became a self-regenerating one in which the architect, as urbanist, took upon himself the role of promoter/client.[100]

Civic Center as Urban Megastructure

Wright's concept for the civic center must have seemed extraordinary to local citizens, especially when viewed in the context of what had previously been planned and, especially, what had recently been built. The design was intimately related to the site and made the site an integral part of the city's downtown while also linking it to the surrounding area. Instead of separate buildings housing the city-county offices and auditorium, or even a single building combining the different uses, Wright proposed a megastructure conceived as a monumental, man-made landscape providing space for a multiplicity of functions in a series of semicircular terraces beginning at the level of the adjoining streets and descending in layers to the lake (figures 7.22–23).[101] By using the air rights over the railroad tracks and landfill, Wright explained in the text accompanying the design that his "scheme creates new space" and thus had obvious economic and urban advantages. The goal of "creating space rather than investing large sums in more congestion of space by putting more extravagant buildings on the city streets and over crowding with cars the already congested parking places" was just the means. The ultimate purpose was to provide Madison with a civic center that would allow the city, as never before, to enjoy the beauty of its natural setting on a daily and constant basis. "This scheme," Wright wrote, "discovers the lake and … in cooperation with the lake claims the lake for the life of the city."[102]

Wright's plan continued the ground plane of the mall over the tracks, the lakeshore, and the lake, thus incorporating Nolen's idea of a garden or esplanade within the building itself. The streets running down to the lake from the State Capitol were extended into a perforated, reinforced concrete terrace, or deck, a little under one thousand feet wide and four hundred eighty-five feet deep. Only about a fifth of this depth was contained within the limits of the shoreline. Four-fifths of the structure was built over water. Triangular pylons set on pilings driven into the lake bed supported the structure along the inner edge of its circumference, beyond which a roadway deck was cantilevered about a hundred feet. None of the major programmatic elements were visible from the street, the lake, or even the air. All were embedded within the multilayered structure of concrete terraces. This was one of the most complex and unusual designs Wright had devised to date. The conception was sectional, and a visual comprehension of the project entails a spatial translation of the planimetric layers through their sectional disposition. Moreover, as a matter of urban design, the entire conception has to be viewed within the larger context of the city center.

We have very few preliminary sketches by Wright of a conceptual sort. The fact that there exist three for the Madison Civic Center is therefore extremely interesting. Were they produced simply in order to explain the design to Harloff? Or were they drawn prior to the latter's visit to Taliesin, as Mollenhoff and Hamilton suggest, and therefore as a means for Wright himself to visualize the possibilities of the site and program? In either case, they help us reconstruct the very early stages in the architect's thinking about the project. The sketch plan illustrated in figure 7.13 was almost surely done first.[103] While it shows a building quite a bit smaller than what soon came to be (and with four major circular elements rather than three), it established the semicircular shape of the *parti*, a shape derived from the form of an ancient theater and directly responsive to the major programmatic element of the civic auditorium (figure 7.14). The outward-expanding concentric rings are drawn to suggest tiers of seats banking up to the "balconies" indicated on the circumference. The four circular elements along this edge contain the city and county courtrooms; the segments between them provide office space at the lower levels. It is unclear whether the auditorium was roofed over or open-air, like the one Kaeser designed for Segoe more than half a year later (figure 7.11). If the former, the upper surface was to serve as a park and the interior would be accessed by stairs descending to the railroad tracks. Either way, the semicircular auditorium shape was, from the outset, highlighted as the iconic and form-giving element of the civic center.

The sketch section through the site, drawn on the rear of the same sheet, makes it clear that at this very preliminary stage Wright thought of the building as rather dense and rising above street level (figure 7.15).[104] While allowing one to see the building in depth, and in relation to the local topography, the section also gives some sense of how the megastructure incorporated the railroad tracks and made use of the air rights. Perhaps even more important from the point of view of explaining his ideas to Harloff—and this drawing may well have been done for that purpose—the section reveals, and is the only one of the three that could, how the building actually provides for multiple levels of interior space. At the same time it gives an idea of what the construction would entail in terms of pilings driven into the lake bed and the problems posed by cantilevering a good part of the building over the water. The descending terraces or trays recall the structural system

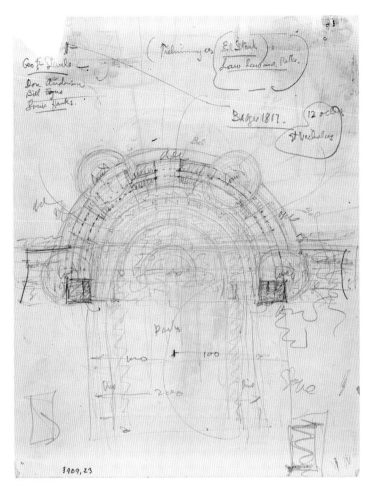

7.13

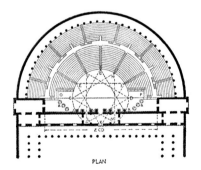

7.15

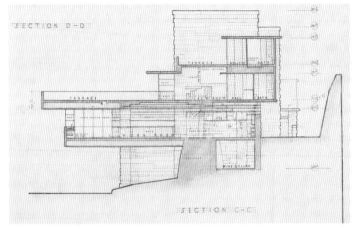

7.16

7.14

7.13. Civic Center project (Olin Terraces), Madison, Wright, 1938. Concept sketch (recto). Plan

7.14. "Roman Theater According to Vitruvius," by Herbert Langford Warren. Plan and section. From Morris Hicky Morgan translation of Vitruvius, *The Ten Books on Architecture*, 1914

7.15. Madison Civic Center project. Concept sketch (verso). Section

7.16. Fallingwater (Kaufmann House), Mill Run, Pa., 1934–37. Section, January/May 1936. Detail

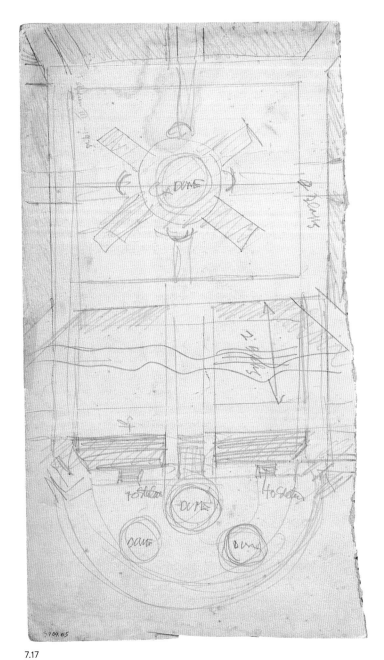

7.17

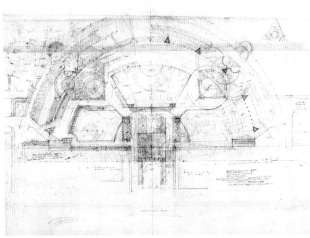

7.18

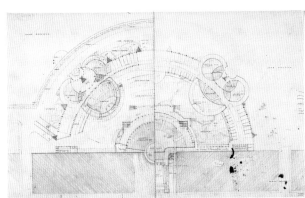

7.19

7.20

7.17. Madison Civic Center project. Concept sketch site plan

7.18. Madison Civic Center project. Study plan, elevation, and sketch section

7.19. Madison Civic Center project. Study plan, different levels

7.20. Madison Civic Center project. Study plan, terraces 3 and 4

Wright had only recently devised at Fallingwater, where a similar section was developed in response to the steeply sloping site (figure 7.16). Although the piers on pilings supporting the deep overhang appear extremely thin, one can imagine Wright describing to Harloff the dendriform columns of the Johnson Wax headquarters, then nearing completion, as the structural model he would employ.

The third sketch, another plan, includes the entire area from the lakeshore to Capitol Square and shows the design, schematically, as it would be developed in the final presentation drawings (figure 7.17). Instead of occupying merely the width of Olin Park, which is to say, the space between the Madison Club and the State Office Building, the design now expanded to fill the entire width of the mall, from one side of Capitol Square to the other. This allowed the structure to be lowered, so as not to rise above street level and thus read, in an extremely subtle way, as a mere continuation of the existing city fabric. As a matter of urban design, this drawing is critical. By rotating the point of view one hundred eighty degrees, Wright demonstrated that his primary focus was on establishing a correspondence between his civic center and the State Capitol and mall to which it owed its existence and of which it was ultimately a dependence.[105]

Capitol Square is drawn toward the top and serves as the determinant figure. A cut, allowing Wright to shorten the distance from it to the lakeshore, reinforces the physical connection he then made by extending the two northwest-southeast streets (Carroll and Pinckney) bordering the square beyond the lakeshore and curving them toward one other to form the outer boundary of his civic center. The resulting semicircle is defined by three domes, the center one over the auditorium being the largest and directly on axis with the capitol building (the other two cover the city and county courtrooms). The triangular relationship of these three domes to one another is also clearly shown as echoing the diagonal geometry of the capitol building and the two avenues radiating from it toward the lake.

Three drawings also exist showing the next stage in the development of the design. One is a plan and elevation done in the manner of a Beaux-Arts *esquisse*, the elevation drawn at the bottom as if directly extruded from the plan (figure 7.18). (There is also a thumbnail section between the two, to the right.) The two other drawings, both also notated in Wright's hand, are plans of the structure at different levels (figures 7.19–20). All three plans show the building as level with the adjoining streets and as wide as the entire mall area extending to the lake from Capitol Square. The divided plan in figure 7.18 offers a transparent view through several terrace levels. It is particularly interesting for the indications it gives of how the structure supporting the overhang was transformed from a series of deep, narrow piers into a more massive set of pylons rising through the upper deck and interconnected below the lowest one by splayed capitals. The two other plans reveal the numerous considerations that went into the development of a circulation system designed to accommodate, and to separate, people arriving on foot, by automobile, and by railroad, either for business or for pleasure.

The two perspectives (figures 7.21–22), longitudinal section (figure 7.23), and plans of the five separate levels (figures 7.24–28) produced by late October must be read through and against one another to fully understand the way the megastructure was intended to serve as a civic center and to be perceived, in Wright's words, both as the "central civic feature of [a] new civic drive extending around Lake Monona to Olin Park" and as "a natural and becoming completion of the capitol-park and the capitol building."[106] People coming by train would enter the structure through a new union station at the lake, or −4, level (terrace 5 on the plans; figures 7.28, 7.21). Elevators and stairs at both ends of the landside platform take the arriving passengers up into the building or out onto the street-level garden terrace (terrace 1; figures 7.21, 7.24). Those coming by automobile along the "new Lake Shore Drive" would enter the structure at the −3 (terrace 4) level (figure 7.27). There, they would have a choice of either parking along the bowed front of the structure overlooking the lake or taking one of the ramps up to additional parking on the −2, −1, and top levels (terraces 3, 2, and 1; figures 7.26, 7.25, 7.24). Cars could also exit directly onto the city streets by ramps at either end of the building on the −4 level, or skirt the structure entirely to rejoin the Lake Shore Drive on the other side by continuing on the multilane cantilevered deck that curves around the front (figures 7.27, 7.22).[107]

Cars arriving from the city could enter the −4 level of the building from the ramps off Carroll Street on the southwest and Pinckney Street on the northeast, but the main point of access from downtown, for both pedestrians and vehicles, was down the center of the Monona Avenue mall. The fountain and water dome over the auditorium provide a point of orientation and a complementary figure to the Capitol dome on axis with it (see figures 7.21–22). In the block between the Madison Club and the State Office Building, where the mall narrows, Wright divided the cars from people arriving on foot. The broad central area is given over to pedestrians. They are led down a double flight of steps to a sunken plaza at the –1 level. There, a loggia serves as the main entrance to the auditorium and gardens that surround it on three sides and are visible through the cutouts in the upper terrace.

The upper terrace itself is largely turned into a perforated parking deck with space for about one-quarter of the forty-five hundred parking places Wright planned for the structure.[108] Parking on this upper level would not be the unceremonious act it normally is. Once out of the car, the visitor could stroll in a park-like atmosphere, looking down into the gardens below, out over the lake, or back to the city center. A planted promenade along the front edge connects two enclosed gardens, at the south and east cardinal points, each of which is enlivened by fountains and water domes marking the location of the city and county courtrooms below. As in the main water dome covering the auditorium, jets of water pumped up from the lake splash down over a transparent, metal-framed glass hemisphere. Through the glistening sheen on the surface could be seen sculptural figures echoing French's gilded figure of *Wisconsin* atop the capitol dome.[109] In 1941, when he renamed the project "Monona Terraces" and partially redrew it, Wright gave even greater transparency to the upper level by removing the solid floor under the domes, thereby transforming them into water-covered skylights for the major spaces beneath them (figure 7.29).[110] Finally, along the outer edge of this terrace, the triangular pylons are carried up into glass towers, fitted out with jets of water and containing lights to animate the space at night (stairs in these towers connected levels –1 through –4).

The three levels below the upper terrace (terraces 4, 3, and 2) contain the three major volumes of the program: a sloped-floor, air-conditioned civic auditorium seating five thousand people; an approximately hundred-thousand-square-foot county building containing one large and two small courtrooms plus offices; and a city building of equal size and accommodations (figures 7.25–27).[111] The –1 (terrace 2) level reached by the main stairway and sunken plaza at the end of Monona Avenue serves as the major public space of the complex. The garden glimpsed through the cutouts in the street-level terrace forms a continuous circuit separating the auditorium from the courtrooms and curved ring of offices that bounds the space along the outer edge and bridges the upper level of both the city and county courts.

The protected garden space is treated in an informal manner with low trees and bushes planted in casual groupings around rivulets carrying the water from the main dome out to the edges, where it is channeled over falls, two levels below, back into the lake (figures 7.22, 7.27). The main foyer of the auditorium is directly opposite an orchestra shell for open-air concerts.[112] While not visible on the plans, there are facilities for eating, drinking, and other forms of refreshment accommodating "several thousand people" at a time. Wright noted that because the garden is on the same level as the "balcony-foyer of the auditorium," the tables ("a thousand" in all) "might be used between the acts in connection with the auditorium-events, or as a general restaurant-rendevous [*sic*] for Madisonians and their guests."[113]

The double-loaded corridor of offices on the –1 level receives direct light from the continuous glass wall facing the sunken garden as well as more shaded light from the glass wall facing the lake under the overhang of the upper terrace. A court between the two ranges of offices open to levels –2 and –3 brings added light into those lower offices, which have only an exterior exposure (figures 7.25–26). What had been the inner range on the level above becomes part of the large covered parking area that occupies the leftover space between the auditorium and the city and county facilities. The two eccentric pairs of three interlocked courtrooms, the ones for the city on the left and the ones for the county on the right, are located on the lowest of these two levels, with their galleries occupying part of the terrace floor above. In the 1941 refinement of the design, the open, three-story space of the courtrooms would have been flooded with light from the glass water domes covering them. Open-air parking with direct access to the courtrooms is provided along the perimeter of the parkway cantilevered over the lake on this level. Along the outer edge of the raised roadway is a landscaped pedestrian path accented by two waterfalls opposite the entries to the courtrooms.

The circular drums of the courtrooms are the only parts of the structure other than the outer pylons to touch the water (figure 7.28). The outermost of the three cylinders in each pair is entirely enclosed in order to contain the holding cells of the jails attached to the city and county courtrooms above. A little more than half of the cells have a view of the lake, while

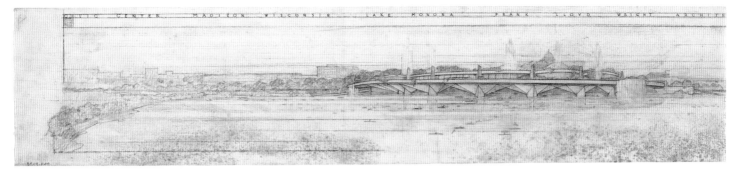

7.21

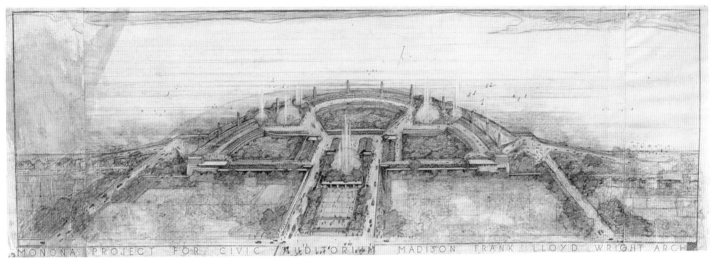

7.22

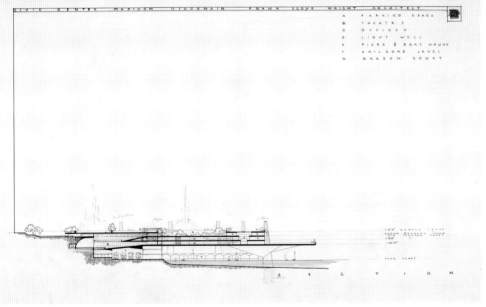

7.23

7.21. Madison Civic Center project. Perspective from south looking across Lake Monona

7.22. Madison Civic Center project. Aerial perspective from northwest. Private collection

7.23. Madison Civic Center project. Section, antedated July 1938

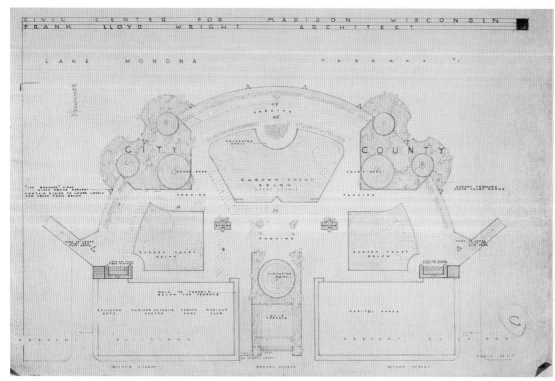

7.24

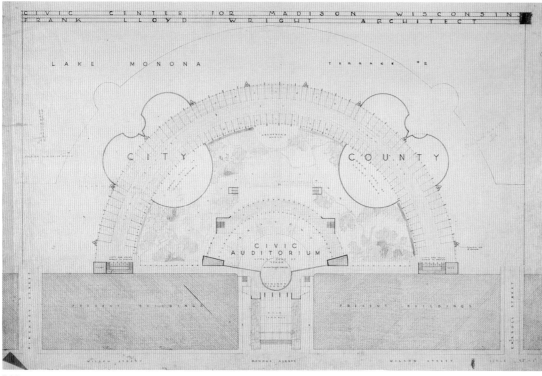

7.25

7.24. Madison Civic Center project. Plan, terrace 1 (street level)

7.25. Madison Civic Center project. Plan, terrace 2

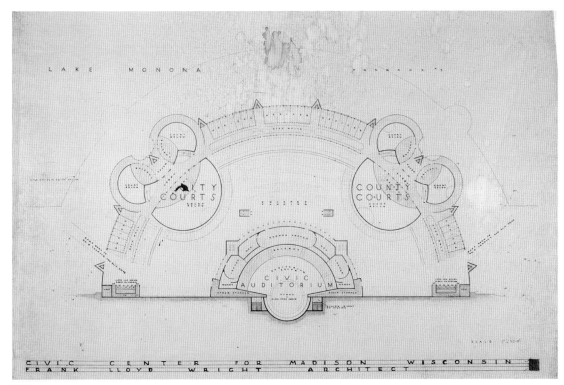

7.26

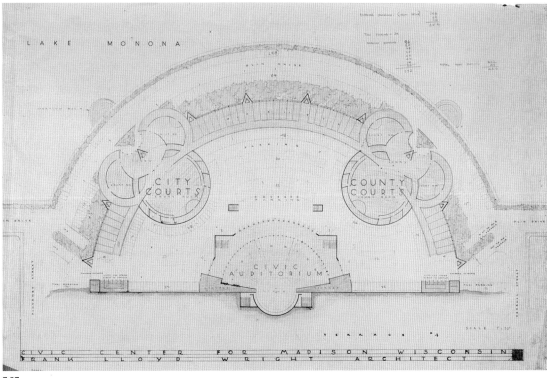

7.27

7.26. Madison Civic Center project. Plan, terrace 3

7.27. Madison Civic Center project. Plan, terrace 4

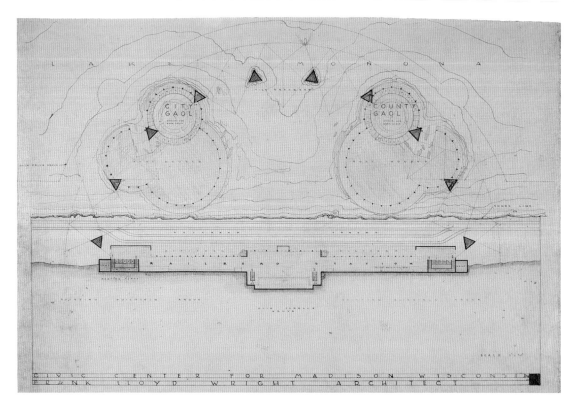

7.28

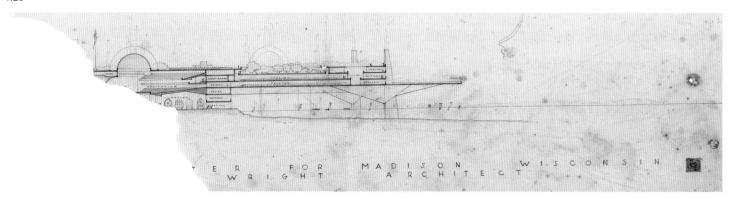

7.29

7.28. Madison Civic Center project. Plan, terrace 5 (lake level)

7.29. Madison Civic Center (Monona Terraces) project, 1941. Section

the others look into the boathouses that occupy the rest of the space created by the interlocking circles. A civic boathouse or marina had been an important aspect of the auditorium-armory proposal for Lake Mendota as well as a significant part of the long-standing effort to beautify the Monona lakefront and use it for a civic center. Wright's project provided slips for five hundred boats. The inclusion of numbers of them in his drawings helps give a sense of life and activity to the design. Boaters, inmates, and jailers alike would ascend to the upper levels of the building by means of the stairways in the triangular pylons at the outer edges of the two smaller semicircles.

A New Type of "Gathering Place" in "the Heart of the City"

One can question Wright's Madison Civic Center design on a number of points, most obviously, perhaps, the dedication of the largest part of the upper terrace to what we today might visualize as a sea of parking, but which at the time probably seemed a truly exciting way to come downtown and experience one of the best views the city had to offer (figure 7.30). The lack of direct access to the water, except for boaters, and the location of the major garden space in a depression are also targets for criticism, although the idea of protecting the garden by a walled enclosure could certainly be justified on climatological grounds.[114] But to take such a utilitarian view of the design is to miss its point—in the same way one would miss the point of Le Corbusier's Contemporary City of Three Million Inhabitants if one were to quibble over the noise, not to speak of the danger, created by helicopters and planes landing in the middle of its main pedestrian plaza (figure 5.8). Both Wright's and Le Corbusier's designs are significant in ways that speak to issues other than the merely practical. Both are paradigmatic of new ways of thinking about urban space and its uses. But where Le Corbusier's project represented a radical tabula rasa, the futuristic image of a not-yet-existing machinist society, Wright's articulated the actual shift about to take place from a tradition-based classical mode of city planning to a modern one. In this, as in many other ways, it was unique for its time.

In certain key respects Wright's 1938 design is quintessentially derivative of the City Beautiful tradition; in others, it is archetypally modern. The symmetry, axiality, deference to existing street patterns, dependence on classical features such as domes and statuary as well as classical models such as the semicircular theater or auditorium, all these carry the weight of a tradition that, in city planning in America at least, went back to the cycle of events initiated by Burnham and others at the World's Columbian Exposition and continued in the projects for Madison by Nolen, Bartholomew, and Kaeser. On the other hand, no traditional architect or city planner would have conceived a single structure, in reinforced concrete, to house the exceedingly different elements of the program Wright developed. Nor would such an architect have designed a building with no facade, no real elevation, and one that was to be entered either from above, through a parking lot and garden, or from the side by means of a highway off-ramp. With its rather Corbusian *toit-jardin* and reinterpreted *pilotis*, the design "creates new space," as Wright said, by means of the fundamentally modern idea of "artificial sites," a series of horizontal planes neither flush with the ground nor clearly dependent on it.[115]

From the beginning, as seen in one of his early conceptual sketches (figure 7.17), Wright intended the scheme to serve as a "completion of capitol-park and the capitol building."[116] This was, in effect, the original impetus of Nolen's civic center mall, and Wright followed its main lines almost religiously. The earlier City Beautiful scheme established Wright's axis of symmetry as well as the idea of bridging over the railroad tracks to create a link between the city and the lake (figures 7.4–6). Like his predecessor, Wright arrayed the major elements of his design on both sides of that axis and equidistant from it, their triangulation mirroring the rotation of the capitol building in relation to the downtown grid. Even the use of water domes was designed to resonate with the building at the origin of Nolen's mall.[117] The perspective of Wright's civic center taken from the south clearly illustrates the intended apposition (7.21). Wright described his civic center as "creating a great concord with the capital [*sic*] as a terminal feature" and, even rather deferentially, as "a becoming foil" for it.[118]

Yet Wright's civic center is not classical in any conventional sense of the word, nor does it project a recognizably City Beautiful image. While echoing certain classical devices and employing certain classical compositional tools, Wright's scheme transformed them and subverted their meaning. Certainly the most obvious example of this is the way the water domes differ from and comment upon the masonry dome of the State Capitol. In the first place, in Wright's project there are seven domes rather than one, thus undercutting the sense of hegemonic power implicit in Post's representation of the Michelangelo model of St. Peter's in Rome. Then, Wright's

EXTENSION AND TERMINAL OF MONONA AVENUE

SEVEN ACRES OF MADE OVER EXISTING RAILROAD TRACKS FOR PARKING.
LAKE WATER THROWN UP INTO MONUMENTAL FOUNTAINS.   MONONA AVE.
CIVIC AUDITORIUM SEATING 10,000, FRONTING OLIN TERRACE.
COUNTY JAIL AND OFFICES, CITY HALL, UNION RAILROAD DEPOT.   COST $17,500,000.

7.30. Madison Civic Center (Monona Terrace) project, 1953. Aerial perspective from northwest

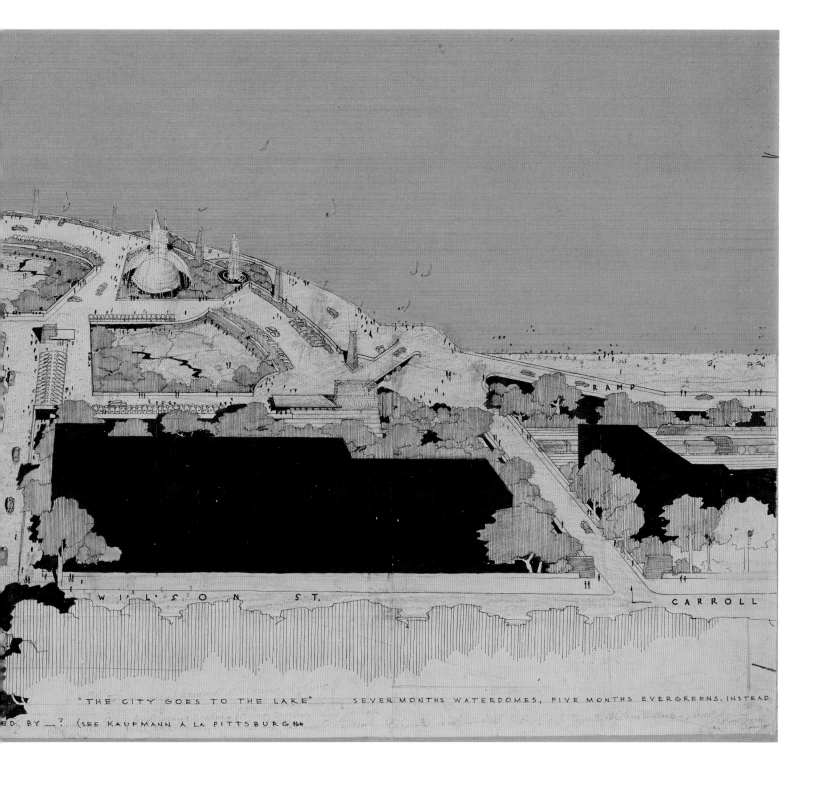

WILSON ST.   CARROLL   RAMP

"THE CITY GOES TO THE LAKE"   SEVEN MONTHS WATERDOMES, FIVE MONTHS EVERGREENS, INSTEAD.

ED BY —? (SEE KAUFMANN À LA PITTSBURG)

domes are pure hemispheres and rise directly from ground level, unlike the stilted Baroque one on the Capitol that towers above the city. In addition, Wright's were to be constructed of glass rather than stone, thus giving transparency to the workings of the government system that a solid dome would have rendered opaque. Finally, the effect of dematerialization would have been further enhanced by the water cascading down the sides of the domes, glistening in the sun and creating rainbow-like effects of light.[119]

The departure from the classical forms of the City Beautiful is even more significant at the level of planning and composition. This can be illustrated most vividly, and most appropriately, by comparing Wright's design to the one produced for the Monona lakefront development by Kaeser to accompany Segoe's "Report on the Location and Grouping of Public and Semi-Public Buildings" released in July 1939 (figure 7.11).[120] In its overall form and concept, the Kaeser/Segoe plan more or less replicated Nolen's project, although it did so by simplifying and attenuating most of the earlier design's elaborate and generous treatment of public buildings and spaces. It also took into account the erosive effect of buildings built between 1909 and 1932. To conform to the diminished setbacks of the Madison Club and State Office Building, the boulevard that Nolen planned for Monona Avenue was reduced to a two-lane street divided by a grass median strip.[121]

More to the point, Kaeser maintained Nolen's concept for the use of the shore as a park and recreation area but in a rather diminished and different form. While the number of railroad tracks was reduced to one, a four-lane "pleasure drive" complemented by parking for six hundred cars greatly limited the amount of landscaped space. In addition, and representing its most radical departure from the Nolen plan, the entire central area of the lakefront development was taken up by a sloping plane containing an amphitheater facing a band shell, with terraced outdoor restaurants bordering it on both sides.[122] This feature was no doubt inspired by Wright's plan, which Kaeser would have known and no doubt carefully studied.[123] Kaeser kept up his friendship with Wright's assistant Peters and visited him often at Taliesin. By 1938, his own architecture had moved from the traditionalism that characterized his overtly classical planning of the mid-1930s to a modified Wrightian aesthetic.

When compared to the watered-down version of the Nolen master plan drawn by Kaeser for Segoe, Wright's clearly represents a radical extension of the former into a modern frame of reference. The section is the key here (figures 7.6, 7.11 [upper left], 7.23). Nolen (and later Kaeser/Segoe) separated the mall-as-civic-center from the landscaped esplanade at lake level by a terrace that steps down to the water. The division is functional and is marked by a clear break in relation to the ground plane. Wright undid the fundamentally classical distinctions between building, garden, street, and roadway. Taking advantage of the modern technique of reinforced concrete construction and use of air rights, Wright combined all four aspects into the new modern type of megastructure. In 1941, he described his civic center as a "landscape feature," "a great terraced park" of which "the inner rooms [i.e., the different functional spaces] ... are not buildings but elements in the park scheme."[124] The landscape design no longer sets off and frames the buildings. Instead, landscape and building become one, integrating transportation, parking, and indoor and outdoor spaces into a singular landscaped structure that presents itself to the city, first and foremost, as what Wright described as a public "gathering place."[125] Specificity of function is incidental to general purpose. In other words, Wright's civic center was created as a coherent urban space from the outset rather than resulting from a composition of separate though related elements.

Among the many novel features of this new conception of a civic center, two stand out for special notice in terms of urban design: the first is the integration of transportation, especially the automobile, in the constitution of the scheme; the second is the emphasis on the creation of a public "gathering place" as a civic form of theater. Wright's focus on transportation was hardly new in the discipline of city planning. From Haussmann through Burnham, Nolen, Corbett, and Bartholomew, issues of transportation served to redefine how a city was organized. In his projects of the late twenties and early thirties, Le Corbusier gave unprecedented scope to the moving vehicle, even designing entire sections of the city in the form of multilayered highways, as in his project for the urbanization of Rio de Janeiro (1929–30) and Algiers (1931–32; figure 7.31). Wright's Madison Civic Center built on those ideas, which he had already considered in his multilevel Skyscraper Regulation project of 1926, but gave them an entirely new dimension and direction by explicitly recognizing the needs of the stationary vehicle as well as the moving one. Rarely considered up until then as a visible feature of urban design, parking became in Wright's Madison project a fundamental determinant of the megastructure's space and form.

Wright's civic center is designed around the needs and desires of people coming to it in cars, parking their cars in it, or driving their cars around and through it. From the lake, it looks more like a highway than a building (figure 7.21). From the air it looks like a city center evacuated of buildings, the sunken gardens having been planted in the place of foundations (figure 7.22). The section could easily be that of a complex transit system (figure 7.23). The major change in the project's design, evident in the move from the initial conceptual sketch as a tightly bounded auditorium-shaped object (figure 7.13) to a more expansive, contextually engaged environment (figure 7.17), resulted from the incorporation of the automobile as a crucial form-determining and scale-giving element.

The railroad was not the issue. It moved in a nineteenth-century, predetermined way on its own restricted path. Wright treated it almost exactly the way Nolen and Bartholomew did. But whereas Nolen fundamentally likened the path of the automobile to that of the train, Wright knew otherwise. He realized that the automobile derived its increasing use and popularity from its individualistic operation and its potential for offering its users a more diverse, immediate, and direct connection to their destination. Here, of course, is where parking becomes the problem. Of the thousands of cars each day that might have to be accommodated, not all would come to the civic center for the same purpose. Those that brought people to work in the city and county offices would be there for the whole day; some would park on a short-term basis, just for a court trial or a meeting; others would come for a business lunch in the garden and others for an evening concert; still others would come for the pure enjoyment of a pleasure drive. Parking, especially for the last group, Wright understood, should be an integral part of that experience, the prelude to strolling around the civic center by the lake.

"The parking problem," Wright wrote in defense of his design in 1941, "has reached the city to stay and grows steadily worse unless something like this project is done to help remedy the situation."[126] Madison civic leaders had considered the problem as early as the mid-1920s, when the idea of building the auditorium on the Lake Monona site was briefly supported by businessmen in part because the filled land would provide parking for hundreds of automobiles.[127] But like most American cities, little of consequence was done until the late

7.31

7.31. Development scheme for Algiers (Obus Plan), Algeria, Le Corbusier, 1931–32. Model. FLC

7.32

7.33

7.34

7.32. Monona Terrace Community and Convention Center, Madison, Taliesin Architects, 1989–97. View to State Capitol

7.33. Monona Terrace Community and Convention Center. View south across Lake Monona

7.34. Theater, Orange, France, 1st century. Reconstruction of interior looking toward *scaena frons*. From Auguste-Nicolas Caristie, *Monuments antiques à Orange: arc de triomphe et théâtre*, 1856

1940s or early 1950s, when the drop in retail sales resulting from the growth of suburbs and shopping centers became apparent.[128] According to Segoe's analysis of the "Parking and Parking Facilities" in Madison, conducted in August 1939, the central area of the city had approximately seven thousand parking spaces.[129] Wright's project would have increased that figure by nearly 65 percent. And it would have done so in a remarkably new, urbanistically inventive, and sensitive way. Large, multistory garages had been built in major American and European cities since the 1920s, but these were almost invariably stand-alone structures devoted exclusively to parking. The Olin Terraces project made parking a critical but not exclusive component of a multifunctional urban center intended to enhance "the life of the entire city," as Wright said, "in the heart of the city," by providing not only automobile access for those coming from the suburbs but also a beautifully landscaped car park in the very literal sense of the term.[130] Its unique design, Wright added, would also result in an "increase in tourist traffic," making the civic center a destination point whose "benefits to the city merchants could be counted a million a year."[131]

The project for the Madison Civic Center thus represents a rejection of the fundamental premise of Broadacre City, that decentralization was the answer to congestion. Solving the parking problem in midsized cities like Madison was one way to decrease congestion on the city's streets while at the same time encouraging people to return to the downtown area and continue to think of it as "the heart of the city." The issue, as Wright now saw it, was not to decrease the amount of traffic — for cars brought economic health and vitality — but to find an intelligent and artistically meaningful way to accommodate it. The integration of the automobile in his solution to the civic center program not only determined most of the larger design decisions, but ultimately affected in a most direct and profound way how the building would be experienced and used.

The question of experience and use brings us to the second outstanding feature of the megastructure's design as a civic center and its transformation of the City Beautiful legacy into a modern form of urban design. The semicircular structure and public plaza of Olin Terraces represent, at the scale of the city, the classical shape of the auditorium within it (figures 7.22, 7.25). By virtue of the geometry of its model, the street-level terrace functions as a double-acting element, focusing the view of those gathered on it, in one direction, toward the Capitol and, in the other, providing a panorama of the lake's expanse (figures 7.32–33). The public plaza thus becomes a kind of outdoor theater in itself in which the city and its environs serve alternately as stage set and backdrop. In classical thought, the city was a virtual stage for human activity and the theater a traditional metaphor for the public space of the city. The design of the ancient theater, reintroduced in the early modern era by Andrea Palladio (1508–80) in his Teatro Olimpico in Vicenza (begun 1579), made such analogies the basis for an architectural illusionism in which the *scaenae frons*, or proscenium, literally replicated the facade of a palace or other important city building and thus made the urban environment coincident with the performance (figure 7.34).

In Wright's Madison design, the theatrical underpins the reality of experience so as to make the latter seem more meaningful within the civic context. From one point of view, the State Capitol and the buildings framing it become a stage set for public gatherings by the lake; from another, the curved parapet of the plaza, punctuated by pylons and fountains, becomes the apron of a virtual auditorium that brings the space of the lake and its distant shore onto the stage of the city. The effect, especially at night, when the pylons were illuminated and the water domes glowing with light, would have been spectacular (figure 7.35). Yet not a single classical element disturbs the abstractness of the actual design. In this modern transformation of a City Beautiful concept, concerts, dining, parking, promenading, and gazing at the city and its natural surroundings would all be part of a new idea of the civic center as gathering place and spectacle. This idea would shortly inform the thinking of Sigfried Giedion, Fernand Léger, José Luis Sert, and others as to how to revive the traditional concept of monumentality in the public sphere without relying on the traditional materials and forms of classical monumentality—just as Wright's identification of "the heart of the city" as the necessary focus of urban design would become the byword of the 1951 CIAM 8 meeting as well as the very title of its published proceedings.[132]

MONONA TER

FRANK LLOYD W

7.35. Madison Civic Center project. Aerial perspective from west at night, January 1955

ACE PROJECT
ADISON WISCONSIN
GHT ARCHITECT

EIGHT

CRYSTAL CITY: A HIGHRISE, MIXED-USE, SUPERBLOCK DEVELOPMENT FOR WASHINGTON, D.C., 1940

When Sigfried Giedion came to the United States in 1938–39 to give the Norton Lectures at Harvard University that formed the basis for his book *Space, Time and Architecture*, his seminal study of the modern movement published in 1941, he made a special effort to see Wright's work in the flesh. On a trip during the winter break between terms, he visited Chicago, Oak Park, and Racine, Wisconsin, where he was able to visit the nearly completed Johnson Wax Headquarters. Later that summer he returned to Wisconsin to see Taliesin. Wright himself showed Giedion around his house and studio. Yet despite the relatively long section in the book devoted to Wright's work and the importance Giedion attached to urban design as the fundamental index of modern society's ability to reintegrate "thinking and feeling" in an expression of a new "unity of culture," he made no mention of the project for the Madison Civic Center that Wright had just finished.[1]

Giedion saw the contemporary civic center as the key element of the modern city. "In the great city of our age," he began the section immediately preceding the book's conclusion, "there will be a civic center, a public place which, like the agora of Athens, the Roman forum, and the medieval cathedral square, will be community focus and popular concourse." "According to the highly differentiated requirements of present-day social life," he continued, "this center will be concentrated in tall buildings freely placed in open spaces, surrounded and defined by greenery. What it will be like in spatial organization and plastic treatment may be largely foreseen in a recent great urban development—Rockefeller Center in New York City (1931–39 [figure 8.1])."[2]

The choice of Rockefeller Center as the prime example of the modern civic center gave the midtown three-block complex, bounded by Fifth and Sixth Avenues and Forty-Eighth and Fifty-First Streets, an iconic status. While extraordinarily influential on the later historiography of modern architecture and urbanism, it nevertheless posed a number of serious problems for Giedion that could not be completely ignored. First was the fact that despite its origin in a proposal to create a new home for the Metropolitan Opera House within an income-producing development, the complex ended up, in Giedion's own words, as "a private enterprise arising from private initiative and carried out as a private speculation." "Obviously," he had to admit, "such a commercial composition does not constitute a civic center." In addition, "it is not surrounded by greenery but instead is confined by the limitations of street and traffic." But perhaps most important from an aesthetic point of view was its symmetrical, Beaux-Arts plan combined with its conventional masonry-clad facades stepping back from the street line following the typical pattern that stemmed from the 1916 New York zoning law. Giedion acknowledged in passing that the site plan reveals "nothing new or significant," that at ground level it would seem to be "entirely conventional," and that it "possesses symmetries which are senseless" (figures 8.2–3).[3]

If Rockefeller Center could still offer the premonition or, as Giedion put it, "the skeleton of a civic center," how, in effect, did it differ from the traditional commercial "downtown district"? "The difference," he answered, "lies in one thing only: in the new scale of city planning inherent in Rockefeller Center, which coincides with the scale of modern bridges and parkways." He meant that the site, though composed of several blocks and many individual building lots, was designed "in coördination as a unit." The relationship of one building to

8.1

8.1. Rockefeller Center (Radio City), New York, Associated Architects: Corbett, Harrison and MacMurray; Hood and Fouilhoux; and Reinhard and Hofmeister, initial phase, 1929–40. Aerial view, ca. 1940. Rockefeller Center Archives

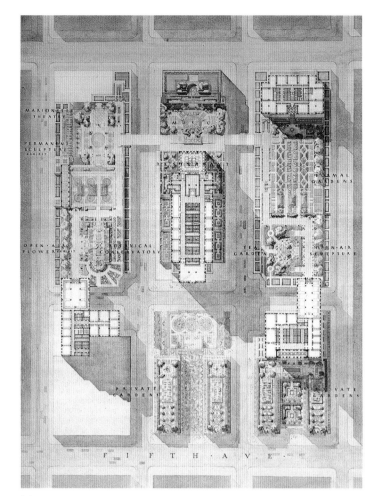

8.2

8.3

8.2. Rockefeller Center. Plan, showing proposed rooftop gardens, 1932. Rockefeller Center Archives

8.3. Rockefeller Center. Perspective, by John Wenrich, 1932. Rockefeller Center Archives

8.4

another was not determined by the "gridiron system" of "existing streets." Rather it was defined by a larger compositional idea that followed the concept of the superblock predicted by earlier European urban designs like those by Le Corbusier, which Giedion discussed in the section just preceding that devoted to Rockefeller Center (figure 5.11).[4]

The physical realization of the superblock concept in Rockefeller Center, despite its all too apparent ties to convention, made Giedion literally dizzy with excitement. Stating that the design of the complex could "be grasped from no single position nor embraced in any single view," he compared its perceptual field to "that which a rotating sphere of mirrored facets gives to a ballroom when the facets reflect whirling spots of light in all directions and into every dimension." The observer in the street is bombarded with "a succession of impressions like visual impulses recorded in time." Using a photomontage of multiple and disconnected views of the structures to illustrate this idea, Giedion compared the visual experience of this "new urban scale" to Harold Edgerton's high-speed stroboscopic photographs and claimed that it expressed the "space-time conception of our period" (figure 8.4).[5]

More popularly known at the time as Radio City, due to the centrality of the RCA (Radio Corporation of America) Building in the complex and the location of the NBC broadcasting studios on that building's lower floors, the twelve-acre, nearly $120 million Rockefeller Center defined for many, as it did for Wright, the relatively new concept of a "city within the city" rather than the civic center Giedion wanted it to be.[6] Indeed, aside from its lack of tall buildings, Wright's Madison design came much closer to embodying Giedion's idea of a "public place" serving as "community focus and popular concourse" and conceived in the terms and at the scale of contemporary bridges and highways (figures 7.21–22). Even more to the point, Wright's subsequent major urban project, the Crystal City residential and commercial complex designed at the very moment *Space, Time and Architecture* was being prepared for publication, advanced a truly modern interpretation of the superblock concept suggested by Rockefeller Center (figure 8.27).

If Wright's 1938 project for Madison gave new form and meaning to the traditional City Beautiful civic center—and can even be seen as a logical extension of the classical type—the unprecedented residential and commercial complex the architect proposed two years later for a nearly ten-acre site at the edge of downtown Washington, D.C., was based on a radically different, more modern idea for the development of the superblock as a mixed-use city within the city. When the project, slated to cost around twelve million dollars, was first made public at a press conference in Washington in early August 1940, the front-page headline in the *Washington Daily News* described it as a "'Radio City' Planned for D.C."[7] Two months later *Architectural Forum* ran a news story calling it a "second and smaller edition of Rockefeller Center"; and when the drawings were exhibited the following month in the Wright retrospective at the Museum of Modern Art, the project was once again compared to Radio City in *Newsweek* magazine. In that same piece, John McAndrew, the show's curator, emphasized that the commission was "the largest architectural job ever given to one man."[8]

While Crystal City was to cost only about a tenth of what Radio City did, and was to contain much less useable square footage, the ground surface it covered was nearly identical. The complex was to consist of 24 twelve- to fourteen-story reinforced concrete structures clad in glass, bronze, and marble plus one taller tower, the whole constituting the largest apartment-hotel in the world at the time. All this would have rested on a plinth containing a high-end shopping center, a large movie theater, as well as a five-story parking garage, the largest then in existence in the United States.[9] In 1942 Henry-Russell Hitchcock, a leading critic and historian of modern architecture, praised what he called Wright's "own version of Rockefeller Center" as an example of "brilliant urbanism," "a model of how the urban ideal might be maintained in the mid-twentieth century." Clearly alluding to Giedion's earlier comments on the New York development, Hitchcock claimed that "here at last is urbanism at the proper scale for the twentieth century." Crystal City, he declared, is "a masterpiece of urban architecture, beside which Rockefeller Center ... appear[s] as [a] timid, half-hearted compromise."[10]

An Obscure Client, a Unique Site, and a Restrictive and Contested Context

Wright's project for Crystal City had a very short but fascinating life, which, it should be noted, shares nothing but its name with the later development in Arlington County, Virginia (begun 1963).[11] Designed during the late summer and fall of 1940, it was abandoned by its client in the early winter of 1941 after

coming up against the restrictive zoning regulations of the nation's capital governing height and land use and the various agencies and personalities empowered to enforce them. To tell the story of the project and reveal its full significance demands a detailed account of the building site's history, the establishment of its innovative program, and the complex design review process that defeated the project.

The announcement in the middle of the summer of 1940 that "something akin to New York's famed Radio City" was being planned for Washington was carried by all four of the city's major daily newspapers and was even the subject of a lead editorial in one of them.[12] The story in the *Washington Daily News* described the real estate transaction for "this only major undeveloped acreage in downtown Washington" as "one of the biggest private real estate deals ever completed here."[13] The editorial in the *Washington Post* two days later, "Work for Planners," cautioned that, with this development, "the heirs of L'Enfant have a tremendous and rapidly increasing responsibility upon their shoulders."[14] The price for the nearly ten-acre site was said to be "close to $1,000,000."[15] According to the reports, the 180-day option to purchase the property (renewable for an equal period of time, though with a penalty) was taken by a "syndicate, composed of local men," headed by Roy S. Thurman (1906–93).[16] The names of the other members of the syndicate were not revealed at the time, nor were they ever made public. When pressed later on in the process by a reporter for the *Washington Evening Star*, Thurman remained evasive, saying that the members of the syndicate had "'a passion for anonymity.'"[17]

Thurman himself was a shadowy figure about whom precious little is known. Wright was apparently so concerned about what he was letting himself in for that he had a confidential background check done on his prospective client before getting too involved in the affair.[18] From this and other scattered sources we are told that Thurman was born in Worcester, Massachusetts, in 1906; that he attended Harvard University (untrue); that he engaged in real estate development in Cambridge, Massachusetts, in the late 1920s; and that he moved to Washington, D.C., around 1930.[19] In 1932, he cofounded with his cousin Sherman F. Mittell the nonprofit National Home Library Foundation "to promote and inculcate in more people the desire to read good literature" and "to make home libraries more easily available to great numbers of our population." This the foundation did by adapting methods of mass production to the publishing of flexible-binding books that were the precursors of paperbacks.[20]

Thurman remained vice president and managing director of the National Home Library Foundation until February 1940, when he resigned to devote his full energy to real estate development. Aside from commissioning Wright for the Crystal City project, he was apparently involved the year before, with Mittell, in hiring the émigré Swiss modernist William Lescaze (1896–1969) to design the twelve-story Longfellow Building (1939–41) that was built on the corner of Connecticut and Rhode Island Avenues to serve in part as the headquarters of the National Home Library Foundation.[21] Yet despite these high-end and, for Washington, quite radical architectural ventures, Thurman apparently did not have a license to engage in real estate development in the District until early September 1940, nor was the bank that supplied the confidential report to Wright able "to state the extent of his operations" or "to estimate income."[22] Photographs of Thurman at the time reveal a nattily dressed, self-confident, ambitious-looking man on the make.[23]

Despite little experience in the complex, restrictive, and highly political Washington real estate field, Thurman seems to have had no compunction about starting at the top. Bounded by Connecticut Avenue on the west, Florida Avenue on the south, Nineteenth Street on the east, and the luxury Wyoming Apartments (B. Stanley Simmons, 1905–11) on the north, the Dean Tract, as the heavily wooded Crystal City site was officially named, stood out as a one-of-a-kind development opportunity (figures 8.5–6). Just a little over a mile from the White House and the main downtown business and shopping district, it had a nearly eight-hundred-foot frontage on Connecticut Avenue, the prestigious main artery connecting the city center to the upscale residential districts lying to the northwest, beginning around Dupont Circle and continuing across Rock Creek Park through Woodley Park, Cleveland Park, and Garfield Heights, out into Chevy Chase and Bethesda in the fast-growing Montgomery County of Maryland (figure 8.7). As the contemporary aerial photograph looking north makes dramatically clear, the Dean Tract appeared to all intents and purposes in 1940 as a natural preserve amid what were by then among the fastest growing urban population and suburban developments in the nation.[24]

The Dean Tract was not the only name by which the property was known, and certainly not the most colorful. The land

8.5

8.6

8.5. Dean Tract (aka Temple Heights), Washington, D.C. Aerial view looking north, ca. 1940. Wooded area in center bounded by Connecticut Avenue on left, Florida Avenue below, Nineteenth Street on right, and Wyoming Apartments above. From Roy Thurman, "Crystal City, Washington, D.C.," prospectus. Roy S. Thurman Papers, Prints and Photographs Division, LC

8.6. Dean Tract (wooded area in left foreground). Aerial view, looking southwest toward Mall, ca. 1940

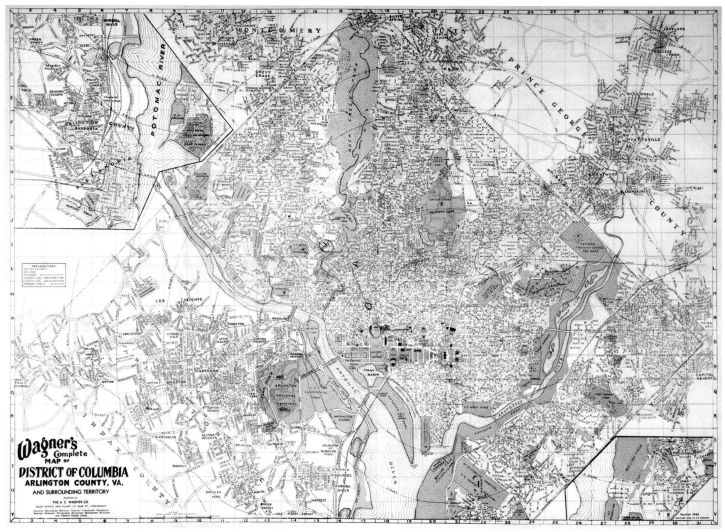

8.7

8.7. Map of District of Columbia, Arlington County, and Surrounding Territory, orig. pub. 1928; rev. 1940. Sites marked by Roy Thurman: White House (circled); to right of it: National Press Club Building (formerly Ebbitt Hotel; circled, with an X); line along F Street extending east to Patent Office; Mayflower Hotel, above and slightly to left of White House (circled); Dean Tract, further up Connecticut Avenue (with an X); Shoreham Hotel, still further up Connecticut Avenue, on other side of Rock Creek Park. Thurman Papers, LC

had a fabled history, which its nomenclature carried down to the present. Within the oak grove on the upper ridge of the steeply sloping site was a particularly grand and important specimen thought to be at least three and perhaps even four hundred years old. The so-called Treaty Oak got its name from the story that it was under this tree, in the seventeenth century, that the European settlers signed the agreement with the local Indians by which they took possession of the territory. Connected to this was the name the "Widow's Mite," by which the property was often referred to early on. As legend goes, the first white settlers of the city deeded the land around the famed oak to the European-born woman who, after spurning the Anacostia Chief Manacassett, whom she had been forced to marry, was condemned by him to remain always under the shade of the tree and, even after he died, never found it within herself to leave.[25]

When L'Enfant drew up his plan for the new capital in 1791, the "Widow's Mite" lay just outside the city's northwest boundary, on the edge of the Wicomico-Sunderland escarpment. Florida Avenue was, in fact, called Boundary Street. Within less than twenty years, however, a house was built on the property by Colonel Michael Nourse, who worked in the Treasury Department. After passing through two other owners and being reduced from sixteen to a little less than ten acres, the land was bought in 1866 by the well-to-do businessman and future District Commissioner Thomas P. Morgan, who, over the next ten years, greatly enlarged the original Federal-style house and called his new estate Oak Lawn. He sold the opulent, mansarded Second Empire structure in 1878 to Edward C. Dean, president of the Potomac Terra Cotta Company, who gave his name to the property his heirs retained until 1922.

In recognition of the value of the Dean Tract as a relatively pristine natural landmark imbued with historical memories, both public and private efforts were made during the first two decades of the twentieth century to preserve it from speculative development. In 1916, Congress moved to acquire the land as a city park, and the Washington Board of Trade followed suit. Around 1921, Bertha T. Voorhorst organized the Woman's National Foundation to purchase the property and preserve its natural beauty by erecting a Temple to Womanhood on it. Finally, in 1922, the Grand Lodge of Masons of the District of Columbia bought the estate for nine hundred thousand dollars from the Dean heirs for the purpose of building a national

United Masonic Temple. As their plans proceeded in fits and starts over the following decade and the vision of a great classical structure rising from the site took hold in their minds, the Masons and others began to call the site Temple Heights. It was a name—as well as an image—that clearly resonated in Wright's mind, as he always referred to his Crystal City design as Crystal Heights.[26] More important, the design the Masons ultimately proposed for the site had significant implications for the viability of Wright's later project.

Before settling on Harvey Wiley Corbett, who would soon be a key figure in the design of Rockefeller Center, the Masons apparently first sought plans from the local firm of James R. Marshall and Frank R. Pierson before contacting Waddy B. Wood in 1922–24.[27] Neither of these efforts bore fruit. Cost was an issue from the beginning. The Grand Lodge began a campaign in 1925 to sell a portion of the property to the federal government for use as a public park. This attempt to defray expenses and reduce their tax burden while also preserving a natural forecourt for their temple lasted well into the following decade. But those responsible for agreeing to the deal, most notably the recently created National Capital Park and Planning Commission (1926; NCPPC), never saw eye to eye with the Masons over price, size, or precise location of the park area.[28] By 1929, however, those discussions took a back seat to more heated ones over the design of the temple and its ancillary buildings in terms of zoning and aesthetics.

It is unclear whether Corbett, who was a Mason and architect of the tower-like, classical George Washington Masonic National Memorial in nearby Alexandria, Virginia (1917–32), had been contacted earlier on by the Grand Lodge of the District of Columbia or whether he was only brought into the process at a later stage. Corbett's first known design for Temple Heights dates from early 1929 and is thus contemporary with his much praised initial project for Rockefeller Center (figures 8.8–10).[29] Despite their entirely different sites, programs, and outward style, the projects for Washington and New York had much in common. Both were grand, symmetrical schemes based on the kind of Beaux-Arts compositional training Corbett had received under Jean-Louis Pascal in Paris. Both create a dramatic processional movement, exaggerated by the renderings of Hugh Ferriss. In Washington, a stark Doric temple, modeled on the Lincoln Memorial, sits atop a multitiered base that steps back as it rises to a height of 180 feet from the highest point of the site (itself nearly 60 feet above

8.8

8.10

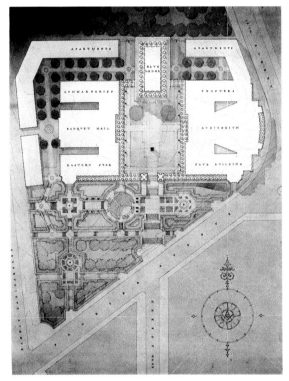

8.9

8.8. United Masonic Temple project, Washington, D.C., Corbett, Harrison and MacMurray (Harvey Wiley Corbett, designer), 1929. Perspective, from south, by Hugh Ferriss. NARA

8.9. United Masonic Temple project, 1929. Plan. NARA

8.10. Symposium (Arts Center) project, Rockefeller Center, Corbett, 1929. Perspective, by Hugh Ferriss

the southern property line). In front is a colonnaded court reached by broad flights of steps beginning near the middle of the Florida Avenue frontage and passing through formal gardens filling out the lower triangle of the site. To either side of the upper court are structures serving the various ritual and administrative needs of the Masons. On the east, these extend into an apartment building wrapping around the rear; on the west, a pair of apartment houses buffer the institutional buildings from Connecticut Avenue and the existing Wyoming Apartments to the north.

Given the classicism of the design as well as the specific references to such respected local models as Henry Bacon's (1866–1924) Lincoln Memorial (1912–22) and John Russell Pope's (1874–1937) Temple of the Scottish Rite (1910–16), it comes as somewhat of a surprise to learn that the Corbett project was not well received by the government agencies that would have to approve it. The issue had to do with height regulations and zoning. As noted in chapter 5, the U.S. Congress passed in 1910 an act regulating building heights in the District relative to the width and type of street the building faced. Structures on commercial streets were allowed a maximum height of 130 feet, whereas those facing residential streets were limited to 85 feet (almost immediately amended to ninety).[30]

Ten years later, following the New York zoning law, Congress established a Zoning Commission for the District of Columbia to create and enforce comprehensive zoning regulations based on the division of the city into Height, Area, and Use Districts.[31] In the ordinance of August 1920, which Harland Bartholomew was instrumental in drafting, Use Districts were divided into Residential, First Commercial, Second Commercial, and Industrial, while the four Area Districts were defined by a maximum permissible lot coverage. The maximum height of buildings in a Residential area was limited to 85 feet, as in the original 1910 ordinance, but the maximum for Commercial areas was reduced from 130 to 110 feet.[32] During the 1920s a number of amendments were made, the most important of which, for our purposes, were (1) the increase in 1923 of the 85-foot Height District to 90 feet; and (2) the allowance, in 1927, for an additional 20 feet in setbacks in a 110-foot district.[33]

The same year the 1910 Height of Buildings Act was passed, a Commission of Fine Arts (CFA) was established by Congress to ensure adherence to the principles of the McMillan Plan (1901–2; figure 1.2).[34] Six years after the passage of the 1920

Zoning Act, the NCPPC was created to expand the oversight power of the earlier commission beyond the Mall area and public buildings to include "'preparing, developing, and maintaining a comprehensive, consistent, and coordinated plan for the National Capital and its environs.'" Under the strong and effective leadership of its chair from 1929 until 1942, Frederic A. Delano (1863–1953), the NCPPC became the ultimate authority regarding new building in the District. Delano, who had been a major force in convincing Burnham to take on the Chicago plan, was also president of the American Planning and Civic Association as well as the uncle of Franklin Delano Roosevelt.[35]

The Dean Tract was zoned for residential use only, with a ninety-foot height limit (figures 8.11–12).[36] Following the principle established by the 1920 ordinance, such residential zoning made no allowance for business use even along a main artery like Connecticut Avenue, thus limiting strip commercial development and preserving a residential character within neighborhoods and across potentially divisive avenues.[37] Corbett's United Masonic Temple clearly violated the ninety-foot maximum height. But since the purpose of the building was neither commercial nor ostensibly speculative, its promoters thought to circumvent the normal procedures by appealing directly to Congress to pass an amendment to the zoning ordinance allowing for an exception in their case. The bill was introduced in late April 1929 by Senator Arthur Capper, chair of the Senate Committee on the District of Columbia and member of the NCPPC. It was passed by both the Senate and the House of Representatives the following March and signed into law by President Herbert Hoover on 29 April 1930.[38]

But that was not the end of the matter. Although Capper justified the zoning exemption based on the fact that "the United Masonic Temple … is to be a monumental structure, of unquestioned scenic value to the Nation's Capital," neither the Senate nor the House nor even the president had the last word on this subject.[39] The final provision of the bill stated "that the design of said building and the layout of said ground be subject to approval by the Fine Arts Commission and the National Capital Park and Planning Commission," a point that Hoover himself felt he needed to explain to the head of the Grand Lodge of Masons when he informed him of having signed the bill.[40]

Both the CFA and the NCPPC had objections to the Corbett project, but it was those of the latter that were most clearly formulated and carried the day. No doubt in response to the

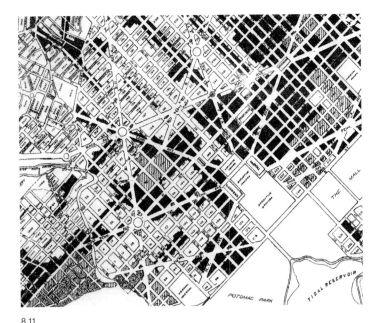

8.11

8.13

8.12

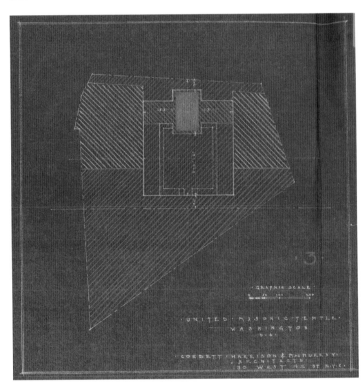

8.14

8.11. Zoning Use Map, District of Columbia, 30 August 1920 (northeast is at top). Detail showing Dean Tract (near upper left), Dupont Circle, and White House and Mall (mid- to lower right). White=Residential, Parkland, or other Public Property; black=- First Commercial; hatched=Second Commercial. Map Division, LC

8.12. Zoning Height Map, District of Columbia, 30 August 1920 (northeast is at top). Black=fifty-five-foot limit; stippled=eighty-five-foot limit (increased to ninety in 1923); hatched=one hundred ten-foot limit. Map Division, LC

8.13. United Masonic Temple project, 1930. Model, from southwest. NARA

8.14. United Masonic Temple project, 1930. Plan showing future buildings, indicated by lighter hatching to left and right of main temple structure. NARA

amendment's proviso that the project needed their approval, Corbett presented it to both commissions soon after the Senate bill was introduced. The NCPPC had fundamentally three reservations. First, and ultimately the most powerful, was the excessive height of the building (figure 8.8). This meant, as Delano noted, "that it called for a special Exception of Zoning Law which made a dangerous precedent."[41] Second, and clearly exacerbated by the first, was an "esthetic one"— the all too obvious resemblance of the temple to the Lincoln Memorial. The "building," Delano observed, "looked like [the] Lincoln Memorial on a Pedestal."[42] Third, and one that it seems members of Congress were not aware of when they voted to approve the exemption for the design, was the inclusion of income-producing apartment buildings that added bulk and density to the already overly built-up site (figure 8.9). The "latest objection," according to Delano, was that "it is proposed to build a lot of apartments to full zoning heights flanking the monumental structure."[43] This gave a mixed-use aspect to the project that undercut and compromised the higher meaning of its monumental, institutional program.

Following the refusal of the NCPPC to approve the design, Delano and Corbett met and corresponded with each other over the next year and a half to see if a compromise could be reached.[44] By early November 1930, Corbett had substantially reduced the scope of his design so that it could be built "within the limitations of the existing zoning regulations" (figure 8.13). The photograph of the model he sent to the commission shows a single structure composed of a central, pedimented, gabled-roofed temple rising above a high base that joins two closed, pilastraded versions of the Lincoln Memorial. Plans, on the other hand, suggested additional buildings to the east and west coming up to both street lines, plus an enclosed forecourt in front of the central temple (figure 8.14). The architect's accompanying letter explained that "the first building which it is proposed to erect at this time is the central Temple at the north side of the tract. This happens to fall in a position which necessitates the removal of the fewest possible number of trees."[45] Despite the reference to the saving of the trees and the expressed desire that "we may still be able to have the advice and counsel of the National Capital Park and Planning Commission in the development of this project," the commission would initially agree to approve only the building of the single, tripartite structure shown in the model.[46] While it later reopened the option of utilizing the "Connecticut Avenue and

19th Street frontage to a limited extent for apartment houses which would … help in the financing," the substantial shrinking of the scheme combined with the onset of the Depression put an end to the Masons' ambition to use Temple Heights as a home for their national headquarters.[47]

Washington, D.C., The "Last of the Romans"

The years 1926–41 represent not only the period when the NCPPC consolidated its power over building in Washington, but also the moment when the McMillan Plan's restatement of L'Enfant's classical vision for the city took its firmest hold. Perhaps the most visible and certainly the largest-scale building operation in the urban core in these years was the Federal Triangle, just north of the Mall, extending from Sixth to Fifteenth Streets between Pennsylvania and Constitution Avenues (1926–37; figure 8.15). Planned under the general direction of Burnham's former assistant Edward Bennett and housing numerous government offices and public services, the individual buildings, though designed by different architects, formed a homogeneous grouping due in part to the common classical style employed but also, just as much if not more, to the continuous cornice lines and consistency of building envelope regulated by the zoning code. Though the site might have lent itself to treatment as a superblock and some of the interior courtyards even suggest the idea, each building was designed as a separate perimeter-block structure addressing the street in a conventional manner. Nor was there provision for anything other than grade-level, mainly curbside parking.[48]

If the Federal Triangle was the most conspicuous construction project of these years, it was neither the most artistically celebrated nor the most controversial. Among the former were the stripped modern classical designs by Paul Cret (1876–1945) for the Folger Shakespeare Library (1929–32) and Federal Reserve Building (1935–37). Among the latter were the Jefferson Memorial (1936–42) and National Gallery of Art (1937–41), both designed by John Russell Pope in a purified classical style, and the proposed Smithsonian Gallery of Art, the uncompromisingly modern design by Eliel Saarinen, Eero Saarinen (1910–61), and Robert Swanson (1900–81) that was awarded first prize in a national competition in 1939. By the time they were finished, or nearly so, the Jefferson Memorial and National Gallery became poster children in the eyes of modern architects for a dying tradition. At a talk in

8.15

8.15. Federal Triangle, Washington, D.C., Edward H. Bennett (chair, Board of Architectural Consultants), 1926–37. View from southeast, 18 December 1937. Dean Tract visible at top center. Dunlap Society Collection, Department of Image Collections, National Gallery of Art

Washington in late 1938, Wright characterized the city's new federal buildings as only meant "'to satisfy a kind of grandomania utterly obsolete'" and called the Jefferson Memorial "'the greatest insult yet.'"[49] Joseph Hudnut (1886–1968), dean of Harvard's Graduate School of Design, organizer of the Smithsonian competition, and professional advisor to its jury, dismissed the National Gallery as the "last of the Romans," maintaining that "the time cannot be far distant" when the "'prevailing style' in Washington to which architecture is chained" will become a thing of the past.[50]

The strong opposition of the CFA to the addition of a modern Smithsonian on the Mall surfaced right away and prevented it from being built.[51] At the same time, the contrast between the embrace of the National Gallery and the rejection of the Smithsonian by the powers that be opened the gates to a public debate that took place in 1940–41 — the very moment Wright's design for Crystal City appeared — over the continued relevance of the classical tradition and the force of authority it should have in the future planning of the nation's capital. While the issue of style was critical and most often was viewed in black-and-white terms, the larger question of urban design, as in the case of Corbett's United Masonic Temple, had more complex underpinnings and ramifications.

No building might have seemed more classical than Corbett's first project for the Masons. The objection to its excessive height and resemblance to the Lincoln Memorial had to do with a more profound understanding of classicism as a means for ensuring an urban coherence and order grounded in a sense of proportionality, hierarchy, and decorum. Corbett's design was thought to upstage the more important buildings on the Mall rather than to defer to them as a private, sectarian commission should. It also involved a mixture of uses that compromised the purity of ideals expressed in its forms, both in an architectural as well as an urban sense. The NCPPC and CFA were willing to work with the idea of a freestanding monumental structure in a park as authorized in the congressional amendment, albeit reduced in height; but they could not accept that the more utilitarian structures along the perimeter, added for purely economic reasons, were coherent with this vision.

The application of fundamentally eighteenth-century principles of classical thought to twentieth-century problems of urban design resulted in extraordinary paradoxes in Washington's evolution as a modern city. The regulations regarding building heights as related to street widths owed their origin to the first such laws in Paris in the 1780s. Why commercial structures in Washington should have been allowed to go twenty feet higher than residential ones despite the fact that streets were often narrower and congestion was much greater in the downtown core is just one such contradiction. And if Paris was the model, as indeed it was, then the zoning of uses on a strictly segregated basis in Washington created a pattern of downtown core versus outlying residential areas that ran counter to the integrated form of the European model vaunted by Delano and others.[52] Moreover, because of the rather draconian height limitations on both commercial and residential buildings, a very non-Parisian, decentralized, and spread-out city was created, which depended on the automobile as much if not more than Los Angeles.[53] According to Thurman, in the prospectus he put together to attract investors to Crystal City, Washington had by 1940 "the highest per capita [automobile traffic] in the world" and the fastest-growing metropolitan population in the United States.[54] His assumption, in hiring Wright, was that only a modern architect could find a way to deal with this situation intelligently. The question Wright's plan would raise is whether the rules were flexible enough to permit his new approach to urban design.

Commission, Program, and Design

In the prospectus he produced in 1940, Thurman explained the reasons why he thought the project represented the right program in the right place at the right time with the right architect as designer.[55] In the section titled "Washington Needs Crystal City," he began with a demographic review that, he claimed, entirely removed investment in "such an enterprise from the uncertain or speculative category." Of prime significance was the tremendous population growth the city had witnessed over the previous decade. Thurman pointed to an increase of 36 percent since 1930, which "led the big cities" throughout the country.[56] Even more critical to the assured success of the venture was the special "character and earning-power of the … residents and … visitors" the nation's capital attracted. It was a stable, well-to-do, white-collar market that could only grow larger. With no significant "industrial or commercial" base, "the City, residentially," Thurman asserted, "is, always has been, and surely will be essentially a community of Federal employees and … those who visit it for (a) conducting the manifold phases of business with the growing scope of Government agencies; and (b) the enormous number of pleasure visitors — 'sightseers' and 'conventionites' included." To these two main groups were added "(a) a liberal element of Diplomatic representation, approximately constant in numbers and spending power; (b) a distinctly Social or retired class, which chooses the City for its prominence, prestige, and general appeal as a residing point ... ; and (c) significant groups of 'business representatives' — lawyers, etc. — domiciled in Washington because their clients' needs demand it."[57]

Thurman described "the stable, Federally-employed element [as] a back-log of the most regular and dependable buying power in the World" and called their "collateral spending power" crucial to his thinking. "Many Government employees are in relatively high brackets....They can live in select quarters, frequently do, and, if not residing in such a place, patronize it liberally by way of entertainment." The same was true for the "well-to-do non-Government resident in Washington." "He or she, often the latter, prefers the quarters and entertainment facilities of an Apartment-Hotel to the responsibility of house-establishment. Any Social Counsellor in Washington," he added, "will confirm the tendency towards entertaining and living in desirable community quarters, versus private domicile."[58]

The demographic analysis justified, in his view, a project for a high-end residential complex, combining a hotel with apartment buildings based on the apartment-hotel model. The need for integrated services and commercial and entertainment facilities would be further reinforced by the site analysis that followed the detailed discussion of the current state of the hotel and apartment house market. Thurman remarked that "transient hotel accommodations in Washington are notoriously inadequate" and that this is "a chronic condition." "Conventions galore pass up Washington," and this will only get worse as the city becomes even more "of a World-Center than it is now." He noted that the average age of hotels with more than one hundred rooms was over twenty years and that the newest hotel in the city, which was twelve years old, could "by no stretch of the imagination ... be called 'first class.'" The apartment-hotel situation was even more in need of remedy. "No place in the Country presents the anomaly of Washington," where there is an almost unheard-of "vacancy-rate in upper-bracket in-town establishments [of the apartment-hotel type] of about 3%." To reinforce this point,

he noted that the "prominent" Shoreham Hotel in neighboring Woodley Park, on Connecticut Avenue about a mile north of the Dean Tract, "recently erected an annex of 200 rooms, unfurnished, and all were leased ... before completion."[59] The site was circled and marked with an X on the map Thurman included in his promotional brochure (figure 8.7).

Within the larger context of Washington, the project's site on Connecticut Avenue — halfway between Dupont Circle and Rock Creek Park — was as ideal as one could find for a residential-commercial development of the scope and size Thurman envisaged. Not only was the Dean Tract "located in the heart of the metropolitan area of Washington, D.C.," it was also the only remaining large piece of property "'close to the center of the downtown area'" that was still "'undeveloped'" (see figure 8.15, top center). While "dense and populous development has occurred" since the early 1920s "extending in every direction from each boundary-line of the Tract," Thurman emphasized the arterial connection to the well-to-do residential communities to the northwest as being the most significant. "About a mile further distant" along Connecticut Avenue, "two of the City's largest and best known hotels (Wardman Park and The Shoreham) are situated. Beyond, for more than eight miles," he added, "are apartment, commercial and dwelling areas, utilizing virtually all available land." Thurman pointed out that the Dean Tract was especially valuable since "there [wa]s practically no land available on [Connecticut] Avenue" aside from it. Moreover, "there [we]re no vacancies on Connecticut Avenue at present" for store rentals.[60]

The commercial link was critical to Thurman's conception of Crystal City and the value he placed on the Connecticut Avenue location. This was brought out in his analysis of the retail and entertainment potential for the project. He began the section "Review of Commercial Occupancy Situation" by recalling that "Washington's so-called downtown 'shopping district' was for many years concentrated in the five blocks on F Street between Ninth and Fourteenth Streets" but that during the 1920s "there commenced a general trend of the commercial development of the Northwest section of the city." At the center of this activity was Connecticut Avenue: "previously an exclusive residential street, [it] rapidly advanced as the 'Fifth Avenue' of the city." It was a story of transformation from residential to commercial use. The "better-class retail establishments" looked to relocate there mainly for two reasons. The first was "the wish to escape from a highly congested area which made it impossible for patrons to visit their establishments by automobile"; the second was the desire "to escape proximity to the cheaper type of retail establishments … which had invaded F Street."[61]

But Connecticut Avenue, as Thurman noted, had not yet reached anywhere near its full commercial development potential. "The many exclusive shops that would naturally seek Connecticut Avenue locations" were thwarted in their efforts because existing "buildings were old and inadequate" and "new construction did not keep pace with the rapid enhancement of [the avenue's] realty values." Even more crucial to his thinking about what would make Crystal City unique—and profitable—was the lack of attention so far given to solving the problem of "the tremendous automobile traffic in the city" and harnessing it to serve the needs of shopping. Up to the present, he wrote, "the average Connecticut Avenue property" suffered from a lack of "convenience to automobile shoppers, and the absence of adequate parking space."[62]

Crystal City would thus not be a residential community exclusively, but would also contain a "Shopping Center" planned for ease of automobile access, with "ample and convenient parking space for 1,500 cars." To bolster his analysis of the situation, Thurman noted that already "the owners and managers of a number of the better Connecticut Avenue stores … have requested consideration as prospective tenants" while "substantial interest also has been displayed by out-of-town enterprises."[63] The program, or "Projected Development of Tract," outlined in the promotional prospectus, defined the four principal elements of the complex as the following:

(a) A major apartment hotel of the order of 2500 rooms

(b) Comprehensive store and shop quarters, in the general direction of a Shopping Center

(c) A moving picture theatre with a capacity of 1100 seats

(d) Large-scale garage and parking facilities to accommodate the clientele of the foregoing—1500 car capacity.[64]

These, Thurman explained, were decided upon "after eight months of careful survey and professional consultation," which began with the "negotiations for acquisition of the Tract"—thus placing that moment sometime in February 1940.[65]

Wright's views, as we will see, were clearly reflected in the final program as enunciated in the developer's marketing booklet, although Thurman stated that Wright was chosen as architect only once decisions had "been reached on

the broad plan of development" and that the architect "accepted the commission to execute the designs conforming to the plans projected." The choice of Wright, according to Thurman, was based on his "renown" as "the world's greatest living architect."[66] Although he never gave any indication in the prospectus that the project had zoning issues, Thurman undoubtedly thought, quite naively, that an architect of Wright's stature and talent would ensure approval: "It was the considered judgment of the sponsors of the project, that of importance equal to its commercial success and of essence to this prime aspect, regard must be had for the cultural and aesthetic phase, indelibly associated with Washington, the Nation's Capital, and rapidly becoming the World's Capital. FRANK LLOYD WRIGHT was therefore selected."[67]

The first indication of what Thurman had in mind for Crystal City can be gleaned from the newspaper reports of the press conference he gave on 9 August 1940 announcing his purchase of the option to buy the Dean Tract. The story in the *Washington Post*, echoed in the *Times-Herald*, stated that the development would include "a hotel, several apartment houses, a park-and-shop center, garages, a motion-picture theater and an auditorium."[68] The *Washington Daily News* and *Evening Star* added "an athletic center."[69] The term "park-and-shop" would have had special resonance in the Washington area. As Richard Longstreth has written, Park and Shop was the brand name of a new type of drive-in shopping complex that made its appearance in Washington in 1930 as the first of a projected chain of multiunit, automobile-accessible strip malls, five more of which were built between 1935 and 1938 (figure 8.16).[70]

Located on Connecticut Avenue in Cleveland Park, just north of the Shoreham and Wardman Park Hotels, the basically one-story Park and Shop (there was a partial upper floor for storage) was arranged in an L shape around a parking area facing the corner. Being on the northeast corner of the intersection, the complex could attract and easily receive those driving home from work. Crystal City had a similar orientation, and Thurman obviously thought about the attractiveness of his "shopping center" to commuters. But the Park and Shop stores were fundamentally of a convenience variety, whereas Thurman was projecting elegant specialty shops and nationally known anchor stores. The term "park-and-shop center," if it was in fact used by Thurman in the August press conference, was never employed by him elsewhere. Whether the term

8.16

8.16. Park and Shop, Connecticut Avenue, NW, Washington, D.C., Arthur B. Heaton, 1930. View from southwest, along Connecticut Avenue. Theodor Horydczak Collection, Prints and Photographs Division, LC

"shopping center" came from Wright is not known, but he became involved with rewriting and developing the program by the second or third week in August, shortly after receiving the commission from Thurman.

Thurman initially contacted Wright the day before the press conference announcing the future development. In a telegram sent to the architect on 8 August 1940, he wrote, "I expect to be in Milwaukee within the next few days and would apreciate [sic] hearing whether it would be convenient to visit you for purpose of discussing most unusual large scale development project approximately heart of Washington DC."[71] Wright responded positively, and Thurman spent part of the weekend at Taliesin, before visiting the Johnson Wax Headquarters. The following Monday (12 August), he wrote to Wright from Chicago thanking him for a "most pleasant and inspiring day at Taliesin" and sending him a couple of the news stories about the "acquisition of the site" that were published after he left Washington. He reported that he was "stopping here in Chicago for a few days at the request of Montgomery Ward, who want to talk about location in our new development." He ended by saying that he would send a memorandum of under-standing on his return and that, "in the meantime," he trusted that Wright will have "given no little thought to the form and visualization that this great project will take."[72]

Thurman sent Wright the promised memorandum on 16 August along with additional news stories and an aerial photo-graph of the site (probably figure 8.6).[73] He may also have sent, if he had not already left it with Wright at Taliesin or mailed it a few days later, a handwritten note listing the main elements of the program. Under the words "Group Idea" are the follow-ing items:

1. Transient Hotel—approx—1000 Rooms
2. Residential Apts. 1 & 2 Rooms light housekeeping
3. Non housekeeping Apts 1 Room
4. Garage—1000–1500 car cap.
5. Theatre—1000 seats
6. Stores[74]

The list was vague on several points. This would become a problem for Wright in developing a design that satisfied Thurman's economic criteria. The number of stores was not indicated, while the capacity of the garage left a wide margin for interpretation, not to speak of the type of structure the term "garage" was meant to signify. There was no indication of how many apartments the complex was to contain. But most glaring was the lack of any reference to the strict zoning regulations of the District. Thurman never appears to have apprised his architect of them or even discussed them with him until it was too late.

The memorandum of agreement that Thurman sent to Wright on 16 August was nearly as vague as the program. It stated that the architect was "to prepare designs, layouts, prospectives [sic] and whatever detailed plans, specifications, etc." might be "required in conducting negotiations with sources of financing the projected development." In other words, Thurman did not yet have the financial means to proceed with the project and Wright's designs were to be used as part of the fund-raising effort. To make the job seem worthwhile, Thurman specified to Wright that "if such negotiations materialize you are to be the designated architect for the entire undertaking, including supervisory services," at a fee of 10 percent of the construction costs.[75]

Wright signed and returned the memorandum on 19 August despite misgivings about his fee and the commission in general.[76] Before he could "start to lay out the ground plans," he urged Thurman to send him "the programme in detail of what you would like to see on the property in order to give you the needed return on your investment."[77] If Thurman sent Wright a more detailed program at this time, we have no record of it (unless it is the "Group Idea" referred to above). A couple of days later, Wright's secretary, Eugene Masselink, apparently sent Thurman "a beginning of something which Mr. Wright has written for you according to your suggestion," and asked him to let the architect know if this was "the sort of thing you want."[78]

Whether or not Wright received a response with more specific information, which seems unlikely, he went ahead with the preliminary planning. On 27 August he wrote to Thurman to say that he was sending what he characterized as "a pan-out of the buildings," adding, quite pointedly, that he felt "like the lady who played the piano for her own 'amazement.'"[79] The "pan-out," or "layout" as he described it elsewhere in the letter, was a verbal description of the design rather than a sketch or drawing.[80] Wright distinguished the number and types of rooms in the "Hotel" from those in the category he called "Separate Apartments" but noted that "there is no break between Hotel and Apartment" and that "any portion" of the former could become "apartments of any one of the

classes" Thurman indicated he wanted. That said, the hotel, at this point in Wright's thinking, comprised 1,230 rooms, all with baths. Two-thirds of them were medium size and one-third large. The latter all had working fireplaces and corner windows. There were 138 apartments, of which a little under one-third were studios and the rest one-bedroom units.

As far as one can tell, the complex was composed of a series of linked tower units based on the so-called Grouped Apartment Towers project for Chicago of 1930, in which the slightly earlier scheme for St. Mark's Towers was reworked into a more continuous urban fabric by joining the separate structures into pairs linked by elevated glass bridges (figures 8.17, 6.1). As a precedent for a self-contained residential complex of tower buildings surrounding a landscaped garden court serving both a permanent and a transient population, Wright may have had in mind Tudor City, the recently completed multi-highrise complex in New York City, built in 1925–32 (figure 8.18).[81]

The preliminary section, labeled "Temple Heights," probably represents something close to this early stage in Wright's thinking (figure 8.20). In describing the hotel proper, Wright referred in his "pan-out" to rooms being located in three "upper towers," one or two "entrance towers," "lower south [and north] terraces," as well as one much larger structure. The latter, along with the entrance towers, contained fourteen floors of rooms, which meant that their total height, including the ground floor and upper setbacks, was anywhere from sixteen to eighteen stories (the interfloor height was only eight feet nine inches).[82] It is unclear whether the apartments units were in separate towers or shared space with the "transient" hotel. Ten "attic studio apartments" were to be "between stacks," meaning they occupied the setback spaces between the protruding concrete cores of the tower structures.[83] In deference to the monumental character of the Washington context, the buildings were clad in white marble, verdigris bronze, and glass rather than the copper and glass of the New York and Chicago prototypes.

Directly related to the hotel was a thousand-seat banquet hall; twelve private dining rooms; a cocktail lounge, bar, and lobby-promenade; an off-street tunnel access and waiting area for taxis; an indoor-outdoor dining terrace seating one thousand; and an expansive "central oak garden" with "flower terraces and fountains." The other, more commercial aspects of the complex were accommodated in a series of terraces

8.17

8.18

8.17. Grouped Apartment Towers project, Chicago, Wright, 1930. Perspective, looking along East Pearson St. toward Lake Michigan

8.18. Tudor City, New York, H. Douglas Ives, 1925–32. View from north end of Tudor City Place, ca. 1930. Irma and Paul Milstein Division of United States History, Local History and Genealogy, New York Public Library

forming the plinth on which the hotel and apartments towers stood. These additional facilities included a movie theater seating eleven hundred; an underground nine-lane bowling alley; a thirty-thousand-square-foot art gallery and museum; and seventy-two shops, the majority of which were to face Connecticut Avenue with the rest fronting Florida Avenue. All the shops had reserved parking in a covered "rear drive" that was connected with the multistoried covered parking for moviegoers, hotel guests, apartment owners, and visitors. The total number of parking spaces, calculated at two hundred square feet per car, amounted to fourteen hundred.[84]

Flexibility was as important a consideration for the public areas as it was for the private spaces. Taking into account the convention trade as well as local cultural events, Wright noted that the private dining rooms were "suitable for small lecture rooms" while the banquet hall could double as a concert hall. Particularly sensitive to the topographical features of the site, Wright noted that he had "managed to save the better part of the oaks" on the property, which now formed the upper-level "oak tree gardens" at the center of the scheme. He specifically remarked on the fact the "immediate surroundings are all blotted out" by the height of the plinth "so that all upper terraces and most room exposures open to the South" would have a "view of [the] Washington Monument and [the] Potomac" (see figure 8.6). When looked at—rather than from—the hotel would appear to be made of "an irridescent [*sic*] fabric" and have a "crystalline character." This led Wright to "suggest" to Thurman that he change the name of the development from "Temple Heights to Crystal Heights."[85] And this is the way Wright labeled all future drawings and how he always referred to the project, although no one else, aside from Thurman at times, followed his lead.[86]

It is probably the case that Wright did not have any drawings ready to send Thurman at this time. In any event, he wrote that before he sent any visuals he wanted firm "assurance" that no "'lessee'" could change the design to suit his or her own preferences.[87] Thurman responded to Wright's verbal "layout" by saying he would send comments shortly but wanted to know the "earliest date" he might "expect [a] perspective and initial sketches which are vitally necessary presently." Wright stuck to his guns regarding visual materials and responded that he first needed Thurman's "criticism and amplification" of the programmatic "layout."[88] On 5 September, he wrote to Thurman saying he would bring the "preliminaries" with him when he came to Washington in a fortnight "if" the developer's "corrections and approval" of the "layout" reached him "soon."[89] The Washington trip was for the press conference to unveil the design.[90]

Obviously concerned about the growing lack of communication, Thurman sent a telegram to Wright the next day saying that he was "amazed and happy. Crystal Heights it is." He promised "no interference from lesse[e]s that would alter or shade any part of the mosaic" but noted that he could not "presume to make corrections without knowing" more precisely Wright's calculations of "areas, cubage, etc." He did, however, make one important observation. Assuming that Wright's "hand-out" (Thurman's term for Wright's "pan-out" or "layout") made use of the entire property, he stated that the design was not dense enough and would have "to utilize [a] larger proportion [of the property] to provide for [a] much greater number [of] housekeeping apartments." "Your setup as I now figure it," he added, "indicates the necessity for more revenue to carry our brave new world." He ended by urging Wright to proceed on the "basis" of the "present plan but [to] allow for the extensibility that may be financially necessary." To discuss the issue further, he offered to go to Taliesin the following weekend.[91]

Wright's response to the suggestion of enlarging the buildings' footprint was a kind of stonewalling. He wrote that the idea of leaving so much of the site in its natural state was precisely "to increase [the] quality of [the] area for revenue" by endowing it with a unique sense of spaciousness and "elegance" that would ultimately prove profitable. Still, he would look over the plans with Thurman if he came to Taliesin on the weekend of 14–15 September. Thurman wrote back to Wright two days later in a rather hard-nosed, noncommittal fashion. First, he agreed that Washington could certainly "support an institution such as your conception of Crystal Heights." "The hotel business, including the 'carriage trade,' is excellent here" and "the city has very little in the way of elite accommodations."[92] But that was not the fundamental issue as far as he was concerned. In the short run, he had to think purely in terms of economics. Since he still had not seen any drawings, Thurman had no real conception of what Wright was thinking and how different it would be from what he originally had in mind for the site.

"Our original proposition for the area," Thurman admitted to Wright, "was sufficiently different from your 'pan-out,'

more particularly in contemplating a vastly larger apartment and residential treatment, [as] to leave us puzzled." "The economics of a venture such as this," he continued, "are beyond our control" and "must be regarded on the basis of a reasonably assured return on a prudent investment." Although he was not ruling out the fact that Wright's design might "conform to these orthodox financial standards," he needed "for our bankers bullet proof pro formae." He therefore asked Wright to send "thoroughly reliable figures on construction cost." In the meantime, he would attempt to obtain "equally reliable figures on operations cost and earnings." "With the understanding that this question of figures in the finality will be the deciding factor," he demurred on the trip to Wisconsin saying that his time would be more profitably spent in Washington.[93]

Wright promptly acceded to Thurman's request for increased density by adding "seven hundred single apartments" and "twenty pent house apartments," saying he could also add one hundred twenty more "if pressed." He sidestepped the issue of construction cost estimates by stating that the means of "extreme standardization" employed would "greatly reduc[e] costs [while] conserving space." As an example of this, he referred to his plan to use two thousand "identical one piece bath installations." Fearing a real problem up the road, however, he implored Thurman to come to Taliesin that weekend, maintaining that it was "unwise [to] proceed further until you take a look."[94] A day or two after sending this note, Wright received the confidential report he had requested about Thurman in which he was told in no uncertain terms that "Mr. Thurman ... has evidently not been a very successful operator!"[95]

It is doubtful Thurman went to Taliesin to see the drawings before Wright was to deliver them for the Washington press conference, originally scheduled for 21 September, but delayed until the 24th. On 18 September, Thurman reminded his architect that he was "anxiously awaiting the finished perspectives and sketches which you undertook to have ready for the 21st."[96] Thurman also asked for a separate "floor plan of [the] single towers showing [the] division into the smaller one story apartments," a complete set of the original plans for St. Mark's Towers, and a sketch of the site "showing only [the] coverage of stores, garages and theatre." Finally, he requested that Wright send the construction cost estimates for St. Mark's as a basis for "making more accurate estimates of our potential construction costs."[97] In all likelihood then, Thurman's first view of Wright's proposal for the Dean Tract came no more than a few hours before the Washington press corps got to see the two perspectives the architect brought with him to Washington in late September (figures 8.27–28).[98]

The drawings for Crystal City were done in September and early October 1940.[99] Sixteen are preserved in the Wright Foundation Archives, of which four are duplicates rendered in a slightly different style.[100] The series consists of two preliminary sections through the site (figures 8.20–21); two overall sketch plans (figures 8.22–23); site plans at the hotel entrance, mezzanine, and lobby levels (figures 8.24–26); a floor plan of a double-unit tower; elevations of the Connecticut and Florida Avenue frontages (figures 8.29–30); a perspective of the Connecticut Avenue frontage (figure 8.28); and an aerial perspective of the complex from the south (figure 8.27).[101] In addition to the drawings done by the Wright office, there is also a topographical survey plat of the tract produced by Corbett, Harrison and MacMurray in 1930, at the time Corbett was working on the United Masonic Temple (figure 8.19).[102] None of the Wright drawings are precisely datable, nor is the sequence absolutely clear.[103] What we know for sure is that the two perspectives (figures 8.27–28) were finished prior to the 24 September press conference since they were published in the local newspapers at that time.[104] We also know that Wright sent off the final group of drawings to Thurman on 10 October 1940.[105] Unfortunately, the extant drawings do not present a complete enough picture of the project to allow for a detailed reading of all its elements, in particular the planning and disposition of the interior spaces.

Although Wright knew Washington fairly well, we have no evidence that he had seen the actual site prior to the commission, nor that he visited it before the public presentation of the design in late September.[106] This means that, as in so many cases during the last two decades of his career, he worked primarily from photographs and topographical survey plats. The ones supplied by Thurman were of high quality and would have been more than adequate (figures 8.5–6, 8.19). The earliest drawing, which predates Wright's naming the project "Crystal Heights," must be the preliminary sketch section through the site's north-south axis (figure 8.20). As in the Madison Civic Center, the design proceeded from the sectional possibilities of terracing out and down from the highest elevation to create a platform or plinth with a stack of decks beneath (figures 7.15, 7.23). But where the lakeshore site had an

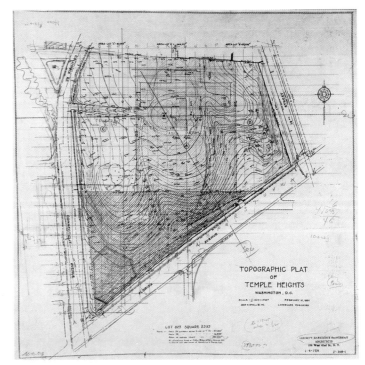

8.19

8.19. Dean Tract (aka Temple Heights). Topographical survey plat, Corbett, Harrison and MacMurray, 12 February 1930

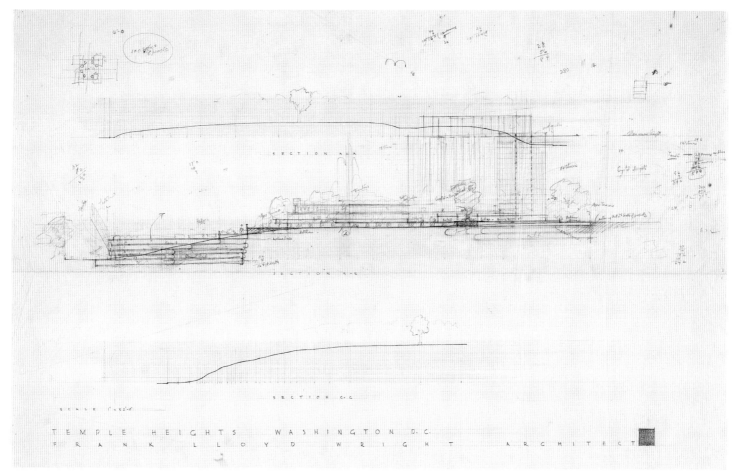

8.20

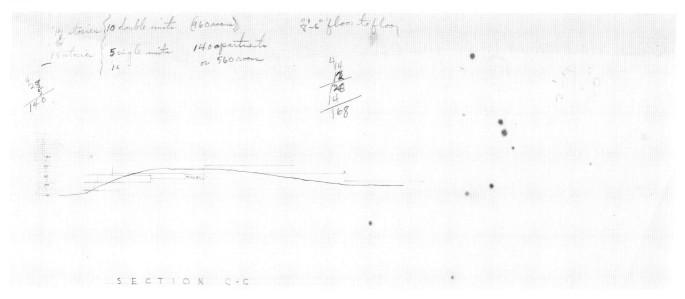

8.21

8.20. Crystal City project (titled "Temple Heights"), Washington, D.C., Wright, 1940.
Preliminary section along north-south axis

8.21. Crystal City project. Preliminary section along north-south axis

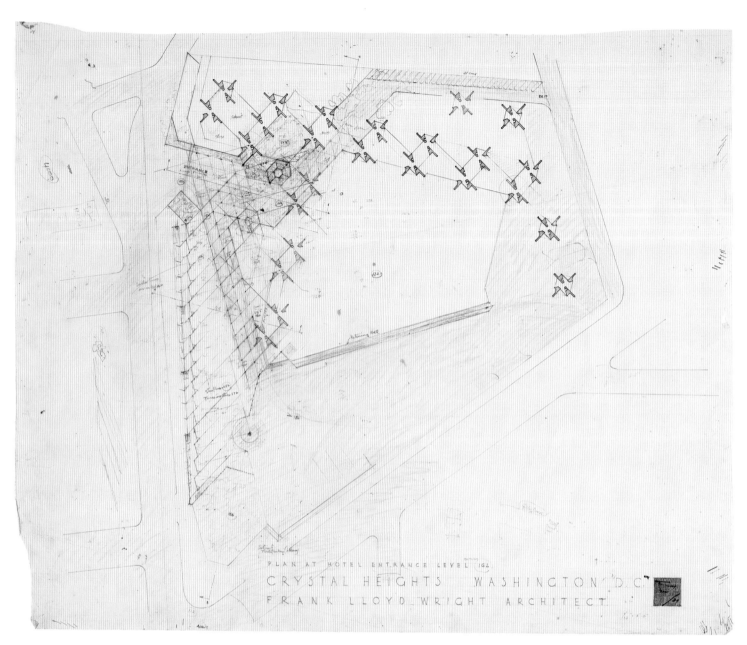

PLAN AT HOTEL ENTRANCE LEVEL 162
CRYSTAL HEIGHTS WASHINGTON D.C.
FRANK LLOYD WRIGHT ARCHITECT

8.22

8.22. Crystal City project. Sketch site plan, hotel entrance level, antedated
December 1939

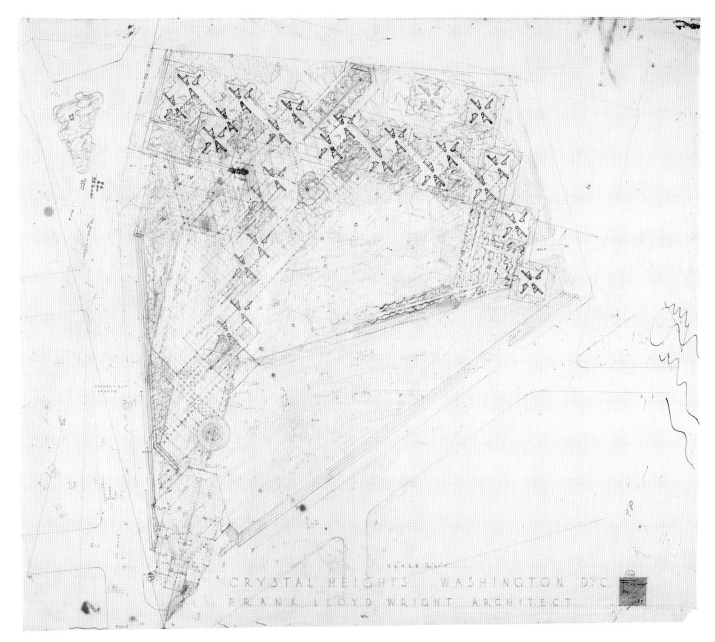

8.23

CRYSTAL HEIGHTS   WASHINGTON D.C.
FRANK LLOYD WRIGHT ARCHITECT

8.23. Crystal City project. Sketch site plan, hotel lobby level, antedated
December 1939

almost sheer drop of approximately fifty feet, the similar difference in level in Washington followed a more gradual slope. This led Wright to a somewhat different solution. Here he placed the main group of buildings on the relatively flat upper level, where the Dean House and Treaty Oak were located (the celebrated tree appears in the middle of the group). A lower wing extends south from this group following the contours along Connecticut Avenue to define the western edge of the garden-forecourt preceding the hotel/apartment buildings. A later sketch plan, containing more tower units than are indicated in the preliminary section, shows how the structures conformed to the upper plateau, defined more or less by an east-west line running from the corner of Florida Avenue and Nineteenth Street to the middle of the Connecticut Avenue frontage (figure 8.23).

The sketch plan also allows us to visualize more clearly the degree of restraint with which Wright approached the questions of building density and site coverage. Almost half the truncated, wedge-shaped site appears to be devoid of buildings. Moreover, nearly half the upper plateau is devoted to a garden preserving much of the original oak grove, with the tower grouping essentially forming a frame for it. The connection with the Madison project can be seen in the way this upper plateau is extended into the man-made terraces that take up the difference in height from upper to lower levels by projecting the garden-forecourt of the hotel/apartment buildings into the arrow-shaped portion of the site where Connecticut and Florida Avenues converge five levels below. The infill band of shops and parking that wraps around the two avenue frontages creates a continuous base for the complex (figures 8.29–30). In effect, as in Madison, Wright conceived Crystal City in terms of a plinth mediating changes in elevation while integrating automobile access and parking with buildings and gardens.

As mentioned above, the marginal notes on the "Temple Heights" preliminary section correspond to Wright's earliest thinking about the program as revealed in his late August "pan-out." It is difficult to tell from the sketch, however, either the number of towers or their exact heights (figure 8.20). There is even some indication that Wright may have been thinking of an atrium court within a more blocky structure—as he was to employ six years later in the Rogers Lacy Hotel project for Dallas, Texas (1946–47)—rather than the staggered line of linked towers that soon emerged. There is also an indication of a ground-level entrance drive along the rear, which was

later replaced by a tunnel connecting Connecticut Avenue to Nineteenth Street. A "maximum height" line is drawn, but the number 196 next to it cannot possibly refer to the building height at roof-garden level. There is one indication that the structure is fourteen stories high with a setback of three stories, while another note refers to a sixteen-story building with a similar setback. The former would total approximately 160 feet (including a 32-foot setback) and the latter approximately 180, the height the United Masonic Temple had been granted by Congress (but rejected by the NCPPC). The related preliminary section in figure 8.21 clarifies the issue of number and heights of buildings at this early stage of the design by noting that there were to be ten double-unit structures, each twelve stories high, plus five single-unit towers, each fourteen stories high. The total of 960 hotel rooms in the double-unit towers and 140 apartments in the single-unit ones, however, provided considerably fewer hotel rooms than Wright specified in his "pan-out."

Although he must have developed the plan to a near final stage by the time his office produced the two perspectives, Wright apparently did not bring the site plans with him to Washington, nor did he or Thurman refer to them in the press conference. Though not large, the perspectives are quite dramatic and give as good an idea as we have of the architect's fully developed conception of the project. The more informative of the two is the aerial perspective from the south, which shows how the hotel and apartment towers form a continuous, serrated, amphitheatric backdrop to the oak garden contained in its embrace, and how the terrace from which the towers rise projects south and west to the edges of Florida and Connecticut Avenues into the long horizontal lines of a five-story parking garage and shopping center (figure 8.27). The other perspective presents a rather jazzy view along Connecticut Avenue, showing the rear complex of towers growing out of the extended base of shops arranged in terraces and terminating, at the lower end, in the movie theater and, at the upper, in the hotel entrance tunnel (figure 8.28).[107]

Both perspectives "blot out" the immediate surroundings, to use Wright's words, and highlight the new scale and autonomy of what the *Washington Times-Herald*, in its report on the press conference, described as "a city within a city." In its front-page story, the *Evening Star* called Crystal City "a mammoth apartment hotel and shopping center structure of the most modern type." The *Washington Post* headlined it as

8.24

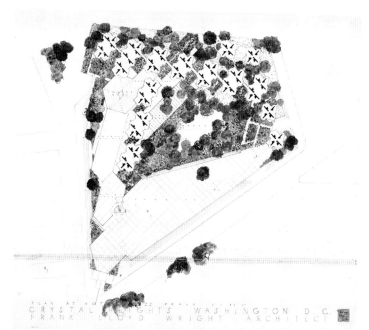

8.26

8.25

8.24. Crystal City project. Plan, hotel entrance level

8.25. Crystal City project. Plan, hotel lobby level

8.26. Crystal City project. Plan, hotel mezzanine level, antedated December 1939

8.27

8.28

8.27. Crystal City project. Aerial perspective from south, antedated December 1939

8.28. Crystal City project. Perspective of Connecticut Avenue frontage, antedated December 1939

a "City of Future on Temple Heights" and described Wright's design as "a self-contained community of hotel, apartments, theater, shops, ballroom, cocktail lounge and garages." Despite the enormous size of the development, the *Star* also noted that the project "would only consume about a third of the 10-acre tract" and that the buildings "would use to full advantage the natural slopes and woodland on the property," ensuring that the legendary Treaty Oak "would be preserved."[108]

The arc of buildings that cups the open space of the oak grove at the upper end of the site is composed of twenty-one towers forming a single megastructure. Wright described this part of the design in the press conference as "'21 buildings in one.'"[109] (The plans as finally worked out show twenty-five towers, four of which are independent, freestanding structures [figure 8.24].) All the reports following the press conference agreed that the twenty-one towers contained a total of twenty-five hundred units, meaning that Wright had by then added almost a thousand to the number in the original "pan-out."[110] Despite obvious visual evidence to the contrary, the height of the tallest tower was said to be 135 feet.[111] The actual fact is that almost all the towers at this stage were sixteen stories (including ground floor and setbacks), making them approximately 140 feet high; and the main tower structure was twenty-seven or twenty-eight stories (including ground floor and setbacks), making it somewhere between 245 and 260 feet in height.[112]

The two elevations Wright's office produced within the next couple of weeks clarify the number of towers, reduce their height, and give the best sense of how the plinth was to function (figures 8.29–30).[113] Although the actual drawings do not conform exactly to the figures marked on them, the average tower is noted as being twelve to fourteen stories high, which, given the interfloor height of 8 feet 9 inches, makes them anywhere from 105 to less than 125 feet high. The single tall tower is variously marked as twenty or twenty-four stories, making it either 175 or 210 feet high, the former figure just within the limit Congress allowed for the United Masonic Temple. The plaited and interlinked vertical towers rise from the six-story terraced plinth that steps back at an angle from Florida Avenue and diminishes in height until it almost levels with the street at the point where Connecticut Avenue splits off from Columbia Road at the northwest corner of the site. The main entrance to the complex is located at this point of divergence, where there is a small triangular plaza containing an equestrian statue of

Gen. George B. McClellan by Frederick MacMonnies (1907; see figure 8.5).[114]

The central part of the plinth, which emerges through the upper terrace level as the oak garden, is left in its natural state (figure 8.25). Tunnels excavated behind it allow taxis entering from Connecticut Avenue to deposit passengers at the lower-level hotel lobby before exiting onto Nineteenth Street at the northeastern corner of the site (see figure 8.24). The tunnels also circumnavigate the central earth mass to permit apartment owners and shoppers to access the four levels of covered parking and top level of open-air parking that fill the main part of the plinth. While the shops along Florida Avenue appear to be accessible exclusively from within the parking structure, the ones facing Connecticut could also be reached on foot by ramps from the street. A special entrance for moviegoers' parking was placed just off Connecticut Avenue, on Florida, and signaled by a tall tower angled over the sidewalk. Cars could exit the parking structure farther up Florida Avenue as well as along Nineteenth Street.

To create a network of tunnels within the plinth and thus eliminate the need for new streets to provide grade-level access to the interior of the site, Wright adapted the modern concept of the superblock to the Dean Tract. It is no doubt in part for this reason that reporters spoke of the projected complex as "a city within a city." And while the idea of an integral movie theater was not entirely new for residential areas of the city, covered parking linked directly to stores was.[115] Newspaper stories stressed the "novel 'tunnel' connections" that "will facilitate the movement of cars within Crystal City" and provide access to "parking facilities for as many as 1,500 cars." "The stores on successive levels," it was pointed out, were designed "to form a complete shopping center," something the city had never seen before, especially at this scale.[116] As if to give a sense of reality to what surely seemed quite visionary, one article reported that, according to the developer, "already more than 50 of the nation's smartest stores have applied for store space in the building."[117]

Zoning Issues and Review Process

As might be expected, the September public presentation of Wright's project received even more ample coverage in local newspapers than Thurman's August press conference. All the reports were exceedingly positive and upbeat, no doubt

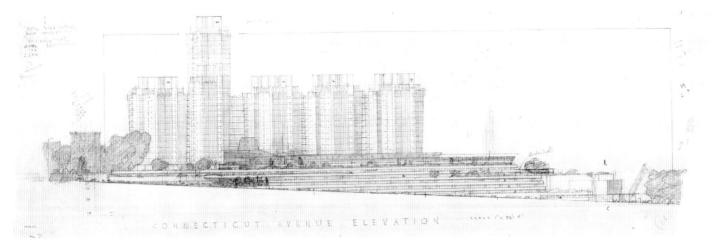

CONNECTICUT AVENUE ELEVATION

8.29

FLORIDA AVENUE ELEVATION

8.30

8.29. Crystal City project. Connecticut Avenue elevation

8.30. Crystal City project. Florida Avenue elevation

reflecting the optimism expressed by the developer and his architect. But one cloud did appear on the horizon. Several of the news reports mentioned the fact that the project violated the zoning regulations and that this would have to be resolved before anything could proceed. The story in the *Times-Herald* put it bluntly: "A variance from zoning regulations must be obtained to permit such construction, and Thurman said the application with the Board of Zoning [A]djustment will be filed within 10 days." The report in the same newspaper the day before was more ominous in noting that the project could proceed only "when and if the Board of Zoning Adjustment can be induced, cajoled or persuaded to grant a variance from the 90-foot [residential zone] height restrictions."[118]

Neither Wright nor Thurman gave any indication that they thought zoning would be a problem, and both maintained that construction would start in three months. It is not clear how seriously Thurman had looked into the zoning issue prior to setting out the parameters for the development, nor is there any evidence that he told Wright about any of the height and use restrictions.[119] Thurman himself seems to have been unaware either of their full extent or of the possibility that the earlier congressional approval of a 180-foot height for the same site might no longer apply. He also seems to have thought that the recently created Board of Zoning Adjustment (BZA) would have a voice in the matter, and that this would play to his advantage.[120] In any event, it was no doubt quite impolitic for him to have presented the project publicly prior to consulting with the authorities. It was equally as impolitic for Wright to have declared to the press that he and his client were going to break the mold of Washington and bring "modernity" into the nation's capital against the forces of tradition. "'We feel Washington has a sufficiency of the deadly conventional,'" Wright chided the reporters. "'There is plenty here of the commonplace elegance,'" but there would be "'none of that for us.'"[121]

Since most previous accounts of Crystal City have assumed that its demise was the result of its anticlassical appearance, it is important to look closely at the zoning issues that were the real cause of its undoing. After the United Masonic Temple project fell victim to the NCPPC's strict interpretation of the District zoning ordinance, a more clearly defined and even more stringent means for its enforcement had come into existence. In late June 1938, a new Zoning Act was passed transferring the police power from the elected District commissioners to the appointed Zoning Commission itself.[122] In addition, a Zoning Advisory Council and a BZA were established to aid the commission in its work. The former was composed of representatives designated by the NCPPC, the Zoning Commission, and the District commissioners, "all of whom," it was emphasized, "shall be persons experienced in zoning practice." Their job was to examine any "amendment of any zoning regulation or map" and to instruct the Zoning Commission as to whether or not to accept it. Since spot zoning was greatly frowned upon, an amendment to the zoning regulations or map, as occurred in the case of the United Masonic Temple, remained the ultimate recourse for developers.[123]

The BZA, one of whose five members came from the NCPPC and one from the Zoning Commission, was created to provide some wiggle room, albeit very little. It was empowered to entertain appeals to "make special exceptions to the provisions of the zoning regulations in harmony with their general purpose and intent." It was clearly stated, however, that the board "shall not have the power to amend any regulation or map." And while it could "hear and decide ... requests for special exceptions or map interpretations," the only situation where these were specifically indicated had to do with "undue hardship" caused by the "exceptional narrowness, shallowness or shape of a specific piece of property ... or ... exceptional topographical conditions." A variance might then be granted, but only if it was assured that this would be "without substantial detriment to the public good and without substantially impairing the intent, purpose, and integrity of the zone plan as embodied in the zoning regulations and map."[124]

The 1938 Zoning Act professionalized the zoning authority at the same time as it clarified the procedures for appeal for exceptions to the regulations. In the process, it gave a more precisely defined role to the NCPPC and consolidated its power in the process. It was now represented on both the new Zoning Advisory Council and the BZA. Its general concern for maintaining the image and integrity of the McMillan Plan was now effectively written into the zoning regulations. No longer confined mainly to practical matters like height, lot occupancy, and use, or even more broadly conceived concerns for safety, health, and prosperity, the 1938 Zoning Act referred to the need "to lessen congestion in the street" and "prevent the undue concentration of population and the overcrowding of land." Perhaps most expressive of the concerns of the NCPPC was the prescription regarding preservation of neighborhood character and integrity. All future zoning regulations and changes to existing ones, it was stated in the second paragraph of the document, "shall be made with reasonable consideration, among other things, of the character of the respective districts and their suitability for the uses provided in the regulations, and with a view to encouraging stability of districts and of land values therein."[125]

Thurman apparently consulted informally with staff members of both the Zoning Commission and the Zoning Advisory Council soon after the September press conference and was told that "an application for [a] zoning change to fit [the] project … would be ineligible for affirmative action." Instead, "a change in the substantive law," meaning an amendment to the zoning statute similar to the one the Masons got from Congress, would be required. As a result, Thurman wrote to the District commissioners asking them, first, if this was an accurate assessment and, second, if that was the case, whether the commissioners and the Zoning Commission would "give sanction to legislation amending the legislation of 1930."[126] He also met with the Corps of Army Engineers Colonel David McCoach, who was one of the three District commissioners and chair of the five-member Zoning Commission.[127] Following that meeting, Thurman sent Wright a copy of his letter to the District commissioners and told McCoach that he "conferred" with his architect "and impressed him with the necessity of our adhering to the statutory and regulatory requirements of the District, even though it might be necessary to depart somewhat from his first conceptions." Thurman asked Wright to send copies of the drawings "plainly indicating the height limits to which he felt each of the main building units could be accommodated."[128]

In a letter of 10 October written to accompany the complement of drawings he was sending, Wright told Thurman that he had "marked the heights of the various units in Crystal City as you requested."[129] This no doubt referred to the two elevations illustrated in figures 8.29 and 8.30, both of which show buildings well over the 90-foot limit for residential districts, including one over the 130-foot limit for commercially zoned areas.[130] To arm his client with a new argument that might sway the authorities to overlook such violations, Wright emphasized that this was not a typical perimeter-block development but rather a superblock, which should therefore not be constrained by regulations that apply only to building heights measured at the street line:

> All the units are set back from the property line seventy feet to the center of the unit and the units are only forty two feet in diameter. The tall single unit stands back 128 feet from lot line on both sides to center of shaft. Same diameter as other units. The shadows from the various units practically fall on our own ground.
>
> The heights will mostly be seen as slender glass obelisks rising through the mass of big trees culminating in the white marble shafts of the ventilating system.… We are not building buildings on a street front but setting them up in a private park.[131]

To this he added,

> We have been so liberal in the parking provision needed in the capital city for so many years (we are practically the first to do anything about it) that authority will no doubt be happy to favor us if favors are needed. But I don't see where we need anything more than a fair-minded interpretation of existing conditions. If the councel [sic] granted a height of 180'0" to one enterprise on that property [United Masonic Temple] there should be no occasion to deny it to one infinitely more humane and serviceable to Washington.[132]

Wright ended by saying that he wished Thurman "luck if you need it. But suspect you will find generous cooperation, as you should, for a super-class construction such as we propose."[133]

With the completed and marked set of preliminary drawings in hand, along with his architect's justifications, Thurman wrote to McCoach on 15 October asking for another meeting in order to show him the "sketches." These, he told the commissioner, indicated the "heights of the several units which," he pointed out, are "interconnected" and thus "effectually constitute one continuous structure." To make a case for reconsideration, Thurman stated that he was not asking for "a zoning change or building permits" but only for "the cooperation and guidance of the Commission." Rather brazenly, Thurman stated that, based on the notations on the drawings, "the height problems which formerly confronted us had been removed." What he may have been referring to is a blueprint of the Connecticut Avenue perspective, now in the Library

CRYSTAL HEIGHTS WASHINGTON DC FRANK LLOYD WRIGHT ARCHITECT
FOR ROY S THURMAN

8.31

8.31. Crystal City project. Blueprint of Connecticut Avenue frontage perspective, with pencil marks eliminating upper part of tallest tower and lines indicating everything above 130 feet as "out," ca. 20 December 1940. Thurman Papers, LC

of Congress, that has a horizontal line drawn through the tall tower at the height of the others and scribbling across the tower with the note "Out" (figure 8.31).[134] He said he hoped, all the same, that "a concurrence in this view by the authorities would assume some flexibility with respect to regulations as pertaining to measurement from sidewalk levels, in view of the peculiar slope and terrace conditions here prevailing." In other words, he was suggesting that, by considering the site as a superblock and the twenty-five towers as a single building, the regulations as written for perimeter-block structures should not apply. Finally, he made it clear that he was still holding out the hope that the exemption the Masons had gotten for a 180-foot structure would be applicable despite "some question as to whether" this would be true. He maintained, in any event, that no "new legislative remedy" would be necessary if Wright's design was considered a single structure topping out at no more than 180 feet in height.[135]

Before the Zoning Commission could hold a hearing, McCoach informed the NCPPC of the project. They immediately weighed in on the matter since their approval, along with that of the CFA, was mandated by the 1930 congressional amendment in favor of the Masons' proposal. In their monthly meeting held on 17–18 October chaired by Delano, the commission's director of planning, John Nolen Jr. (1898–1986), described the problems raised by the Wright design and called for a preemptive decision based on zoning violations. He noted that a height of 180 feet was being proposed for the "apartment house" and that this raised two important questions: whether the 1930 amendment passed in favor of the Masons "applies to this proposed development" and "whether the Zoning Commission and this Commission would support the developers in any request for special legislation to allow them to go to the additional height and to undertake other things not permitted under the existing Regulations."[136] The "other things" obviously referred to the commercial uses. This was the first time the question of mixed use came up.

Nolen Jr. informed the members of the NCPPC that the legal staff of the District commissioners had "ruled that the Act of 1930 does not apply to this development." Furthermore, he said that McCoach told him that even though it was "his feeling that the Zoning Commission would reply negatively to lending their support to the waiver of any provision of the Regulations," he "would like to have the Commission's

recommendations on this matter." Without looking at the drawings or even discussing the particulars of the project, the NCPPC voted unanimously to send a letter to the Zoning Commission "expressing great concern about the proposed legislation" and urging it "to go on record as being opposed to any special legislation that will permit exceptions of the nature now proposed on the Dean Tract by the developers of the Crystal City development." In addition, it was unanimously voted to oppose "the use of this property for the purpose indicated," meaning a mixture of residential and commercial, and to oppose "any legislation permitting this type of development."[137]

No reference in the discussion was made to the question of style or even to the architect. Whether these were deliberately avoided may never be known. What is clear from the outset is that the argument against the project would be made in terms of the zoning regulations and that any attempt to undermine them would be counteracted with determination and preemption. The NCPPC never wavered in its opinion over the next three and a half months. During this time Thurman tried different strategies, all of which proved ineffective against the two fundamental zoning violations of the project: the excessive height and the mixture of commercial and residential uses. Whether Thurman would have proceeded had he known of the unflinching opposition of the NCPPC is not something that can be ascertained by any documentary evidence. What we do know is that, incredible as it may seem, he gave no indication of being fully cognizant of the zoning regulations or of being able either to deal effectively with the authorities or to communicate with his architect the kinds of obstacles the project faced and the kinds of compromises that might have to be made.

Thurman was informed of the NCPPC's "unfavorable reaction to his proposal" by the head of the Zoning Commission, who told him that he would need "special legislation … to cover his project."[138] Passing this news on to his architect, Thurman finally acknowledged to Wright that the project ran afoul of the "zoning height regulations in the District." However, he misstated to what extent, since he claimed that the district in which the Dean Tract was located allowed for a 130-foot height (rather than 90), including a 20-foot setback. On the other hand, he said that he was "advised by friends on Capital [sic] Hill that we can optimistically expect legislation to embrace the heights we contemplate."[139] Whether there was any truth to this is impossible to establish. Thurman also made rather light of what would turn out to be the real stumbling block, which was the development's mixed-use aspect and the consequent need for a fundamental change in the zoning map from Residential to Commercial. More or less in passing, he said to Wright that "meantime, the vital point is the change of zone to permit our shops, theatre and garages." To bolster the application to the Zoning Board for such an unusual spot zoning request, he asked his architect to set down in writing "all of the arguments that you can muster in support of this great project" and to be prepared to come to the hearing to present them in person.[140]

The Zoning Commission eventually heard the Crystal City case in its meeting of 26 December 1940. This was preceded by a renewed spate of publicity around the project due to its being featured in the Wright retrospective that opened at the Museum of Modern Art on 12 November 1940 and ran through 5 January 1941. *Newsweek* magazine headlined its review of the exhibition "Wright Goes to Washington with a $15,000,000 Surprise" and began the piece thusly: "Amid the stately and solemn Roman columns, Greek temples, and classic colonnades of the nation's capital, a gleaming 25-towered copper [*sic*] and crystal streamlined apartment development might be as shocking as a burlesque show in Sunday school. Next spring Washingtonians are due for just such a shock" with the building of "the first Washington job of the 71-year-old dean of modern architects."[141]

One can only imagine how such talk was greeted by the conservative members of the NCPPC. Indeed, shortly after the *Newsweek* article, Nolen Jr. notified Delano of the upcoming Zoning Commission hearing on Crystal City, saying: "The matter is of such importance that I think the [National Capital Park and Planning] Commission should make a definite recommendation to the Zoning Commission, not on the specific merits of the plan, but on the question of excessive height, density of development and intensive commercial use close to a high-value residence district."[142] In fact, an effort was made to preempt any possible success for the Wright project when the NCPPC presented to the Zoning Commission in early December a proposal to rescind the 1927 amendment to the Zoning Regulations allowing for the additional twenty feet in setbacks in commercial districts and thus restrict all buildings in the city to a maximum 110-foot height. This meant that even if Thurman was able to convince the Zoning

Commission to change the designation of the Dean Tract to commercial, he could only build up to 110 feet. Thurman's lawyer was present at the meeting and convinced the Zoning Commission to defer a decision on the matter so as not to prejudice unfairly its future consideration of the Dean Tract project and "make the development of that tract of land impractical at least under any theory on which the owners are now proceeding."[143]

The NCPPC continued to apply pressure on the Zoning Commission to refuse what it called just "another case of spot zoning," the worst possible infraction, in its view, of zoning principles.[144] A week prior to the planned hearing, it voted to record "its objection to the change in zoning to permit the proposed Crystal City development" and, in opposition to the proposal before the Zoning Commission, to submit "suggestions for the amendment of the Regulations by which areas of considerable extent like this under consideration might be developed as a unit without doing harm to the surrounding property and the zoning plan."[145] The concept of the "community unit plan," which Nolen Jr. would later offer as a way to subvert and derail Thurman's idea for Crystal City, came out of this.[146]

To arm Thurman and his lawyer, James Wilkes, for their confrontation with the Zoning Commission at the end of the month, Wright produced a three-page letter on 19 December outlining his conception of the highrise, mixed-use development and defending its merits against the conventional architecture and planning of Washington and, especially, the city's restrictive zoning regulations. Wright began, somewhat cantankerously, by stating that whereas "in certain areas of the city it may be well to limit the height of construction," a law limiting "construction to 110 feet, regardless" could only be considered a "'totalitarian' act" unfit for a "great democratic nation." Then, more "seriously" as he said, he made the point that his project had nothing to do with the type of conventional perimeter-block building for which such laws were created. How, he asked, can a "law that would wisely enough restrict a building standing on the lot line of a street, apply to a building rising from among the oak trees of a park … ?"[147] His twofold argument was clear: 1) the project had to be thought of as a single building, not a group of buildings; and 2) the building rose freely out of its park-like setting and thus bore no intrinsic relation to the street from which all height limitations were calculated.

Wright went on to make the point about the architecture's contemporaneity as an appropriate expression of its time. Whereas most Washington monuments, he wrote, "are only expressions of the grandeur that was Greece and the glory that was Rome," his design "can be called worthy of our time and place and life," making ample use of "our unprecedented material and scientific resources." He also stressed the "noble" and "dignified" appearance of its architecture as being fitting to the classical traditions of the city and compared his crystalline towers to the Washington Monument, pointedly adding that the project's "taller crystal shaft sets so well back from the street fronts on all sides that it would not be visible competition for anything in the city." "No collateral interests are threatened," he added, "because the building is entirely removed from lot lines or streets and stands free in a great mass of its own foliage." Instead of being an "exploiter of the streets for revenue only," the multitowered building maintains "the natural benefits of its site" for the pleasure of "the citizen."[148]

As a final point, Wright turned to what he thought might be his strongest suit, the issue of parking. Parking was, as Delano stated in the Zoning Commission meeting of 4 December where he lobbied for the rescission of the additional twenty-foot setback allowance, the major problem resulting from the congestion produced by tall buildings: "Is it not self-evident that if we permit buildings to be built which will accommodate thousands of individuals, some provision must be made for the vehicles in which they travel? It is not the moving vehicle that is bothering us; it is the vehicle that is standing still while the driver or owner is inside the building."[149] Wright, who was informed by Thurman of the proceedings of the 4 December meeting, sought to turn Delano's critique to his own advantage. "Our contribution to the parking problem of Washington in itself ... should entitle us to the small distinguishment we ask. Were demands made upon other property owners to provide such parking facilities for their own people the demand would do more for the beauty and dignity of future Washington than to mow all down regardless to one hundred and ten feet in height and leave 'the monuments' still standing in a turmoil of disorganized traffic." Offering such a "benefit" to the city, Wright concluded that he could not but believe that "the municipality ... will help rather than hinder the project."[150]

Wright did not attend the 26 December Zoning Commission hearing. Thurman did not himself speak and had his legal representative make the entire presentation. Wilkes began by describing the hardships imposed by the site—its topography, its depth in relation to surrounding streets, its residential zoning—which made it necessary to come up with a plan that "developed [the site] as a unit." He stated that Wright's design created "in reality ... one building unit" that involved "only a 20% coverage of the area," if one did not count the space devoted solely to parking. Its "angular formation" would allow for "plenty of light and air," while its minimal footprint "preserves as much of the natural beauty as it would be possible to preserve in ... the development of this tract." It was also considerably less dense than was possible as of right: "Without making any application to this zoning body there could be erected on this area approximately four thousand living units as against this proposal which would call for [only] 2500."[151]

The lawyer emphasized that the generous amount of parking offered "one of the outstanding advantages from a public viewpoint" and was consistent with Delano's concern that critical to any design for the Dean Tract should "particularly [be] ... the provision for the parking of a number of cars." Wilkes did not mention the shopping center. On the critical issue of the need for rezoning from residential to commercial to allow for the increase in height, he said the architect had "abandoned" the tall 180-foot tower and that the developers were only asking to be able to go from 110 to 130 feet (see figure 8.31). Finally, to make the case that this was not actually an example of "'spot zoning,'" he pointed out that the Dean Tract would "not constitute a First Commercial island" in an otherwise residential neighborhood since the block across Florida Avenue, just to the south, which "runs right up to it," is already zoned "First Commercial" (see figure 8.11).[152]

A number of people spoke in favor of the project, saying its impact would only be beneficial to the neighborhood. Surprisingly, many fewer spoke against it. But one of those who did was Nolen Jr. He stated that he was appearing on behalf of the NCPPC "to record its objection to the proposed change in zoning." The issue, he asserted forthrightly, was "the maintenance of the [District's] comprehensive zone plan." "If you spot the map with a new commercial district," he remarked, "it would break [the] area down as the kind of residential neighborhood that it is now." Furthermore, based on the commission's discussions concerning an alternate strategy, he proposed a solution that would prove to be a Trojan horse. Claiming that "the Commission is sympathetic ... to a comprehensive development of this tract for some legitimate purpose that ... would not involve a change in the zoning map," he stated that "we have in mind the type of thing that they have in [the] St. Louis ordinance [drafted by Harland Bartholomew] where it provides for a community unit plan." Such a "community [unit] plan," he continued in carefully imprecise terms, allows one "to do things that the ordinary regulations wouldn't permit [one] to do on a community wide basis, but at the same time are not rquired [*sic*] to change the zoning which begins the process of breaking down the neighborhood." He abruptly ended by saying that a letter explaining this concept was on its way to the Zoning Commission.[153]

Thurman's team was clearly taken by surprise and agreed, all too quickly and naively, to continue the discussion on the basis of Nolen Jr.'s suggestion. Wilkes stated in his closing remarks that "the problem [of Crystal City] is unique and whether it is worked out on the basis of the new regulation by Mr. Nolen or on the basis of a qualified zoning [of] it for commercial use, we are not concerned one way or the other."[154] The story in the *Washington Post* the next day shared Wilkes's optimism—and naiveté. Under the headline "Nolen Offers Plan to 'Save' Crystal City," the lead said: "Dream of the $15,000,000 'Crystal City' was a step nearer reality yesterday when the city planner for the National Capital Park and Planning Commission suggested an amendment to the zoning code which would permit erection of the development without changing the basic zoning of the property." Nolen Jr.'s "suggestion of a solution," the article added, "came as a surprise to the zoning commission as well as the promoters themselves."[155] The wolf in sheep's clothing would emerge only in the next week or so.

Based on its having received the NCPPC's draft proposal for the application of the "community unit plan" to the Dean Tract, the Zoning Commission, on 2 January 1941, officially deferred action on the Thurman request for a zoning change and set a date at its first meeting in February to hear arguments relative to the new proposal.[156] In the press coverage of this decision, it was revealed for the first time that a "community unit plan" specifically precluded any form of mixed-use development. "Neither business nor theaters would be permitted in residential sections under the proposed new 'community unit' classification," the *Washington Evening Star* reported. Only "drug stores, barber shops and similar businesses ...

inside hotels or apartments" would be allowed. In consequence of this, the article stated that the Zoning Commission asked Thurman to "eliminate the proposed Connecticut Avenue business front" from the scheme so as to allow the negotiations to proceed.[157] The final draft of the proposal also stated, in what would be the final blow, that "the height of the buildings [in such a 'community unit'] shall be no greater than that permitted in the zoning height district in which the property is located" and that the NCPPC would have to be consulted "first" for its opinion of any specific application.[158]

Thurman sensed that the endgame was at hand. According to Hilary Ballon, his option on the Dean Tract was to expire a few days prior to the scheduled February meeting and, without a decision on the zoning issue, he could no longer maintain his financing.[159] Moreover, Thurman finally seems to have become aware of the ruse to which he was being subjected. Consequently, he wrote an extremely strong letter to McCoach demanding an immediate hearing on his pending request for a zoning change from residential to commercial and blaming the NCPPC, and Delano in particular, for undue influence in delaying the process. What is more, he released the letter to the press, which published excerpts from it. Thurman was quoted as saying that the Zoning Commission's " 'non-action flows directly from the viewpoints expressed by the National Capital Park and Planning Commission, a body ... no more entitled by law to control or dominate decisions of the Zoning Commission than would [be] any private citizen.' " Beyond that, he said that he was " 'charging the Zoning Commission not only with undue domination by the [National Capital] Park and Planning Commission, but also with being absolutely under the dictatorship of Mr. Delano.' "[160]

Under these circumstances, McCoach was more or less forced to hold a hearing to entertain Thurman's request. This occurred on 14 January, and, needless to say, the request for the zoning change was denied.[161] This, of course, still left open the possibility for the Zoning Commission's acceptance of the NCPPC's "community unit plan," but that would be irrelevant to the plan for Crystal City. Thurman publicly accused McCoach and the Zoning Commission of "crass stupidity, blundering and mental myopia" and called their decision "moronic."[162] It was at this point that he released to the press the letter Wright had sent to him in December, prior to the 26 December Zoning Commission hearing, explaining the Crystal City design and celebrating the benefits it offered to the District of Columbia and the contributions it would make to the city. The letter was published in the *Times-Herald* on 18 January under the headline "A Genius Fights with the D.C. Government to Save His Crystal City: But the Pillars of Ancient Rome Are Against Him." It was accompanied by a lengthy, informative, and critical article titled "Wright's Blistering Tongue Is a Terrible Weapon."[163]

Thurman sent Wright the *Times-Herald* pieces the day they appeared along with a letter of capitulation, acknowledging the effectiveness of the "community unit plan" ruse. We can no longer "be misguided by the note of willingness on the part of [the] authorities to make concessions that would make the 'City' possible," he wrote "with utter disgust and dismay." "Their idea of concessions is complete emasculation, no shops, no theatre, in fact nothing on Connecticut Avenue, and the building heights not to exceed 110 feet, which of course makes the idea of 'Crystal City' impossible."[164] The issue, he told the *Times-Herald* reporter, was economic. The development has "'got to pay. It must make money or it won't be built. And it must have the stores if it is to make money. If we can't have the stores, the whole thing will be dropped, abandoned.'"[165]

The NCPPC presented its amendment to the zoning regulations regarding the general establishment of "community unit" plans in the 6 February 1941 hearing of the District Zoning Commission. Apparently, no one opposed the idea, nor did Thurman or anyone representing him speak at the meeting.[166] The Zoning Commission decided against adopting the "community unit" amendment and to defer action "indefinitely" on the Crystal City project.[167] Why the "community unit" plan died such a premature and inconsequential death can probably be explained by the fact that, despite its seemingly "community wide" intention, it was never meant by Nolen Jr. or Delano or anyone else on the NCPPC to serve any other purpose than to undermine the scheme for Crystal City. When that goal was achieved, the need for the amendment disappeared as rapidly and as surreptitiously as it had surfaced in the first place.

"Urbanism at the Proper Scale for the Twentieth Century"

As already noted, historians have generally assumed that it was Crystal City's modern appearance that was the cause of its rejection by the conservative watchdogs of Washington's architectural patrimony. But as we have seen, the issue was more complicated. Undoubtedly, as in the case of the slightly earlier

Saarinen, Saarinen and Swanson design for the Smithsonian Gallery of Art, style played a part in the decision-making process. But style was inextricably linked, especially in the nonmonumental parts of the nation's capital, to the zoning regulations that grew out of the classical tradition and effectively underwrote its continuing influence, no matter how stripped, abstract, or generic the outward forms of the architecture had become. For the NCPPC to condemn the Crystal City project on the basis of its infractions of the zoning ordinance was therefore both an explicit and narrowly defined legal maneuver as well as an implicit and broadly conceived critique of the anticlassical, modern type of urbanism the project embodied.

It was the unprecedented modern scale of the project, which so impressed Henry-Russell Hitchcock, as well as the self-contained, mixed-use character of the development that undoubtedly lay at the core of the difficulties Crystal City posed to traditionalists. Scale more than mere size underlay the prejudices of those in Washington, like the members of the NCPPC, who considered it their duty to protect the city against inappropriate and immoderate interventions. It is interesting to note in this regard that the only building in Washington to which Wright compared his design was the Washington Monument, a singular object whose enormous scale distinguishes it from the traditionally proportioned buildings that surround and frame it. By comparison with a slightly later project for an apartment/apartment-hotel complex on the same Dean Tract, which was described by one of its designers, Pierre Ghent, as "in keeping with Connecticut avenue 'styles and traditions'" and which the NCPPC approved in early 1945 (figure 8.32), Wright's Crystal City made manifest the "new scale of city planning," beyond the framework of the traditional street and related to "the scale of modern bridges and parkways" that Giedion wanted to believe was realized in Rockefeller Center.[168] Hitchcock, by contrast, was more accurate in describing the Wright project for an autonomous city within the city as a bolder, uncompromised version of the "urban ideal" only "timidly" and "half-heartedly" suggested by the New York complex (figures 8.1, 8.27).

Wright conceived the entire nine-and-a-half-acre site of the Dean Tract as a superblock, burying internal circulation routes in tunnels within a multilevel, wedge-shaped plinth. Designed in reinforced concrete like the bridges and highways its forms and scale recall, the plinth served in part as the artificial datum for a megastructure of angular towers, whose glass, bronze, and marble curtain walls were hung off the edges of floors cantilevered from reinforced concrete structural cores. As Wright pointed out in his attempt to justify the inappropriateness of the city's zoning regulations based on conventional perimeter-block buildings, the apartment and hotel components of his complex constituted a single, multifaceted structure related not to the street but to the large wooded park within which it was set (figure 8.25). It occupied only the northern, upper part of the site, leaving an expansive outdoor terrace for public gathering and short-term parking above the shopping center, movie theater, and main parking areas contained within the wedge-shaped space produced by the sectional design responding to the sloping terrain.

As a self-contained urban center providing generous public spaces along with shopping and parking facilities within a large residential and hotel complex, Crystal City presented a close approximation of Giedion's ideal environment for "present-day social life," a "center," as he put it, "concentrated in tall buildings freely placed in open spaces, surrounded and defined by greenery."[169] Wright himself described the residential component of his project as "entirely removed from lot lines or streets and stand[ing] free in a great mass of … foliage"—"a building rising from among the oak trees of a park."[170] The concept of residential towers in a park-like setting was a quintessentially modern one going back, as we have seen, to the 1920s. The integration of parking and a shopping center to service more than the community housed on the superblock site was new, and was what made Crystal City a veritable city within the city rather than a mere residential development, like New York's Tudor City. For this reason, the comparison with Rockefeller Center, despite the fundamental differences in program and architectural design, was and is relevant.

The traditional massing, symmetrical organization, and masonry envelope of Rockefeller Center's buildings are entirely consistent with the essentially perimeter-block thinking underlying its general plan, a point even Giedion had to acknowledge (figures 8.1–2). Disruptions in this organizational pattern are minimal though consequential in providing public space for activities not necessarily linked to the basically corporate and commercial venture that determined the project. These involve mainly a planted promenade linking Fifth Avenue to a new three-block-long north-south private street at the intersection of which was eventually located a below-grade

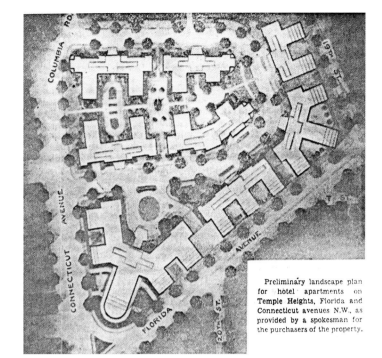

Preliminary landscape plan for hotel apartments on Temple Heights, Florida and Connecticut avenues N.W., as provided by a spokesman for the purchasers of the property.

8.32

8.33

8.32. Apartment house and apartment-hotel project, Dean Tract, E. Burton Corning and Raymond G. Moore, with Pierre Ghent, ca. 1945. From *ES*, January 1945

8.33. Rockefeller Center. View along Fifth Avenue from north, showing International Building, Palazzo d'Italia, British Empire Building, and La Maison Française, September 1955. Rockefeller Center Archives

ice skating rink. The architects took advantage of existing public transportation, reached by an underground network of shopping arcades, to connect the complex to the rest of the city and metropolitan area. The automobile, on the other hand, played no major role in the design.[171] Nor did the architecture at street level alter or upset the scale of the surrounding neighborhood (figure 8.33).

Wright's Crystal City represents an intervention in its neighborhood fabric of an entirely different sort. It is both less consistent in scale, materials, and style with its immediate neighbors than Rockefeller Center and, at the same time, more deliberately and self-consciously adjusted to the scale and needs of the larger, regional context. At the microscale, so to speak, the project forms a separate and distinct neighborhood unit, operating on its own urban terms and offering its inhabitants and visitors a different type of experience of space, light, and movement from what they would otherwise have in the city (figure 8.27). The design provides a coherent expression of civic identity extending well beyond what might be characteristic of an individual apartment house, or even group of apartment houses, yet remaining more limited than what might characterize the city as a whole or any of its suburbs. The automobile is an integral part of this. It is not left on the street, outside the complex, but is the primary means by which one accesses the complex. Though not physically underground, the parking garage literally underpins the whole, serving as the foundation and plinth, in both a concrete and metaphorical way, for the essentially transient inhabitants of Crystal City.

The parking garage as plinth also supports the design's major public space, the expansive terrace extending south from the grove of trees contained within the faceted arc of glass towers. This generous raised plaza serves as a forecourt to the apartment and hotel towers at the same time as it provides a gathering place for people visiting the restaurant, shops, or cinema on their way to or from the city proper and its suburbs. The angled tower at the intersection of Connecticut and Florida Avenues acts as a combined landmark and commercial sign. The plaza, with its shimmering, resplendent backdrop, establishes the macroscale of the project. Functionally, it has a demonstrably metropolitan presence. Symbolically, it does too. From its height one could see down to the Mall, with the Capitol to the southeast, the Lincoln Memorial directly south, and, most significantly, the Washington Monument just beyond the ellipse of the White House (figure 8.6). From the

beginning, Wright envisaged his buildings as referencing and complementing the Washington Monument. "It will belong more with the Washington monument than anything they have down there," he said. Describing his towers as "slender glass obelisks … culminating in … white marble shafts," Crystal City was "conceived as a Washington monument to modern progress and achievement."[172] The amphitheatric grouping both directs the gaze to the central figure in the L'Enfant plan and echoes its shape against the horizon of the modern city's expansive ring of suburbs (figure 8.27).

Wright's "city within the city" that he called Crystal Heights literally and figuratively occupies a place halfway between traditional center city and suburb. Opposing the policies of Frederic Delano and the NCPPC that called for a spread-out, low-profile, homogeneous fabric of clearly differentiated uses, Crystal City proposed a truly urban form of height and density and diversification at the edge of suburbanization. In this regard, it stands at the threshold of a long line of urban/suburban hybrids that attempted in the years following World War II to revitalize city life while accommodating the automobile. From Boston's Back Bay (later Prudential) Center, designed by a consortium of architects, including Walter Gropius, Pietro Belluschi, and Hugh Stubbins (1952–53), through La Défense on the outskirts of Paris, designed by a team including Robert Auzelle, Paul Herbé, Robert Camelot, Jean de Mailly, and Bernard Zehrfuss (begun 1958–64), one can see reverberations of the fundamental concept of Wright's design—a plinth devoted to parking and supporting, in turn, a new type of public space, removed from the surrounding city streets for the very purpose of creating a new sense of urban place.

NINE

THE POINT PARK CIVIC CENTER
AND TRAFFIC INTERCHANGE FOR THE
HEART OF DOWNTOWN PITTSBURGH, 1947

The civic center and monumental highway interchange that Wright planned for Point Park in Pittsburgh in 1947 was the most ambitious urban program he tackled until that time. The two schemes he did culminated his efforts to revitalize the American city through the creation of new forms of public space and community gathering places in tune with modern social, political, and economic conditions. As in the civic center for Madison and the Crystal City development for Washington, though to an inordinately greater degree, the automobile was called upon to do precisely what it had been accused of undoing—to give coherent urban form to contemporary civic institutions and public life.

The site on the western tip of Pittsburgh's Golden Triangle known as the Point, at the edge of the downtown business district where the Allegheny and Monongahela Rivers join to form the Ohio River, was and still is one of the most spectacular of any American city. It was also one of the country's most blighted and neglected historical cores (figures 9.1–2). Working in good faith from an overdetermined program, Wright's initial response to the redevelopment program was deemed too vast and impractical (figure 9.26). As in the case of Madison, a scaled-back scheme was requested, though here almost immediately (figure 9.55). Not long after that was also rejected, the city proceeded to build a previously planned historic park and adjacent commercial development, called Gateway Center, in what was the first major instance of urban redevelopment in postwar America and the leading edge of the city's so-called Renaissance (figure 9.64).[1] In an article devoted to "Pittsburgh Renascent" in November 1949 just prior to the start of construction, *Architectural Forum* declared that "the biggest real estate and building story in the U.S. today is Pittsburgh."[2] While Wright's ideas did not play a physical role in that story, they have their source in its conception and are an important element in its elaboration.

The Point: Historic Significance and Early Ideas for Restoring the "Heart" of the City

According to *Fortune* magazine, Pittsburgh in 1947 was still "the steel capital of the world," although that was to change almost immediately once the upsurge in production for World War II came to an end.[3] From the Civil War through the 1920s, Pittsburgh was a manufacturing powerhouse and one of the richest industrial cities in America. Coal and iron, steel, glass, aluminum, oil, and processed foods made great fortunes for the likes of Andrew Carnegie, Henry Frick, H. J. Heinz, and the Mellons and made such companies as U.S. Steel, Gulf Oil, Mellon Bank, Alcoa, Westinghouse Electric, Pittsburgh Plate Glass, and Heinz's 57 Varieties among the most profitable in the world. The singular and unchecked focus on economic production and development also resulted in one of the dirtiest and most polluted urban environments in the nation. Flooding from the rivers that bound the Golden Triangle on two sides compounded the problem, posing a constant threat to people and property.

Like many of its Midwest Rust Belt counterparts, Pittsburgh fell on hard times during the Depression, from which it only temporarily recovered during the war emergency years. In the later 1930s and into the following decade, programs were initiated for smoke and flood control to start the process of bringing the city back to health. But these had to wait for implementation until the end of World War II when some of the

9.1

9.1. Pittsburgh. Aerial view from west, 1930s. SJHHC

9.2

9.2. Pittsburgh. Aerial view from east (downtown), ca. 1930. PDCL

city's most prominent civic, financial, cultural, and business leaders realized that Pittsburgh's industrial base had irrevocably eroded and that a new ground had to be laid for the city's future. In this perspective, environmental concerns would go hand in hand with urban redevelopment.[4]

The trend toward out-migration of business and people to the suburbs and beyond led to a concerted effort, in the words of Park H. Martin (1887–1972), one of the prime players in the redevelopment process, to "deter decentralization of the Triangle." To that end, it was generally agreed that it was imperative to "save the core" of the city, the Golden Triangle, and "rebuild the City from the heart out."[5] The "heart" was the nearly sixty-acre Point. And it was this derelict warehouse and disused train yard area that was selected, in the words of John J. Grove, another important figure in the Renaissance, to be "the spring board to the rebuilding of the Golden Triangle" as a whole.[6]

The Point marked the foundational site of Pittsburgh, the spot where, in the eighteenth century, the British defeated the French and established the basis for English, and eventually American, control over the Ohio River Valley and lands to the west. The historian John William Oliver, who became chair of the history department at the University of Pittsburgh in 1923 and later played a significant role in promoting the restoration of the Point as a historical landmark, described the site as "sacred ground." Recalling its nineteenth-century designation as "The Gateway to the West," Oliver characterized the Point as "the most significant historical spot in America, this side of the Appalachian Mountains," and ranked it with Plymouth Rock, Bunker Hill, Valley Forge, and Williamsburg as "one of America's greatest shrines."[7]

Hyperbole maybe, but the facts go a long way toward explaining the enthusiasm Pittsburghers felt for celebrating and restoring this degraded historic site. The so-called Forks of the Ohio represented a strategic location in the battle between the French and the English in the mid-eighteenth century for control of trade routes and land between Canada and the port of New Orleans. A few years after a French expedition from Québec established its presence in the area in 1749, the governor of Virginia sent the twenty-one-year-old George Washington to the Forks to order the French to leave and to choose a site for a British fort. The small Fort Prince George, built at the Point in 1753–54, was almost immediately taken over by the French, who dismantled it and used the materials

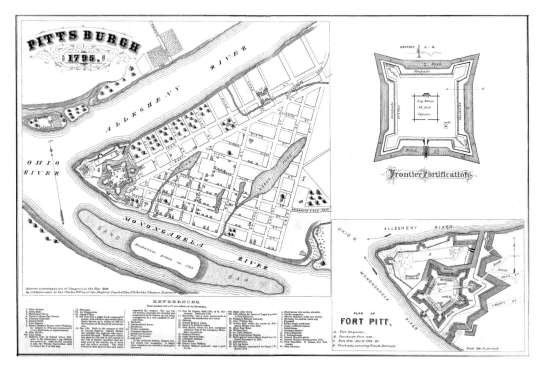

9.3

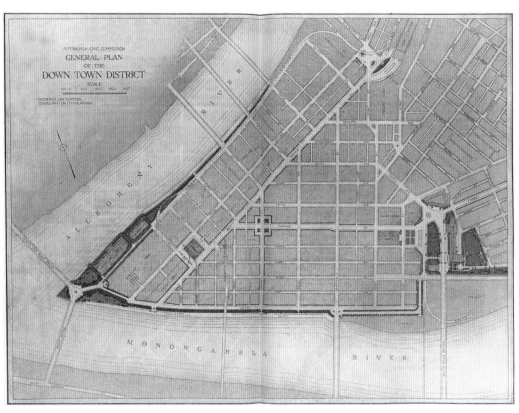

9.4

9.3. Pittsburgh in 1795. Plan, by A. G. Haumann, 1869. Forts Pitt and Duquesne at Point, where Allegheny and Monongahela Rivers join to form the Ohio, also shown in insets on right. Archives Service Center, University of Pittsburgh

9.4. Pittsburgh Master Plan, Frederick Law Olmsted Jr., 1909–10. Plan of downtown area showing proposed civic center at far right. From Olmsted Jr., *Pittsburgh: Main Thoroughfares and the Down Town District. Improvements Necessary to Meet the City's Present and Future Needs*, 1911

9.5

9.5. Pittsburgh Master Plan. Proposed civic center. Olmsted (with Wilhelm Bernhard), 1909–10. Aerial perspective from north. From Olmsted, *Pittsburgh*

to build their own, much larger Fort Duquesne near the tip of the Point. Four years later the British returned and destroyed the French outpost, replacing it with Fort Pitt. Named for the British secretary of state, after whom General John Forbes also named the settlement between the two rivers, the five-bastioned structure was the largest and most expensive built in the colonial era (figure 9.3).

Fort Pitt was tested only once, in the Indian rebellion led by Pontiac in 1763–64, at which time three brick blockhouses were built to aid in fending off the attackers. As the threat from both Native Americans and the French receded, the fort was allowed to disintegrate and was eventually dismantled. Only one of the blockhouses remained as a physical reminder of the pre-Revolutionary events that took place at the Point. During the Revolutionary War, however, the Point continued to play a noteworthy role. In 1778, George Rogers Clark was commissioned by the governor of Kentucky to lead an expeditionary force against British outposts north of the Ohio River. Clark used the Point as the staging ground for what was to make him known, correctly or not, as the "Conqueror of the Old Northwest." Twenty-five years later, in the late summer of 1803, Meriwether Lewis set off from Pittsburgh Point on the expedition across the continent that would be the first to chart the geography, flora, fauna, and indigenous populations of the West.

From the 1830s on, the Point gradually lost its appeal as a place of residence and business as the population of the city shifted toward the higher ground to the east, eventually establishing the upper part of the Golden Triangle as the commercial center of Pittsburgh and suburban neighborhoods like Squirrel Hill, Shadyside, and Oakland as places for well-to-do residential communities and educational and cultural institutions. In the second half of the nineteenth century, the Point was increasingly turned over to factories, warehouses, and especially yards and depots of the proliferating railroads servicing the city's industrial expansion. The area was also surrounded by wharves dedicated to the shipping trade. But perhaps most significant in terms of future attempts to deal with it from the point of view of urban design, in the 1870s bridges were built from the tip of the Point across both the Allegheny and Monongahela Rivers (figures 9.1–2). The Union Bridge (1874–75; rebuilt as Manchester Bridge, 1911–15) connected the Point to the North Side, and the Point Bridge (1876–77; rebuilt 1924–27) joined it to the city's South

Side. In the process, they established a nearly impenetrable barrier, both visual and physical, between the Point and the river and landscape to the west.

The history of reclaiming the Point began in the later nineteenth century when the Western Pennsylvania Exposition Society constructed an Exhibition Hall, Music Hall, and Machinery Hall on the strip of land between the railroad yards and the Allegheny River. On the grounds surrounding the three structures were all sorts of entertainment facilities, ranging from a Ferris wheel and roller coaster to a boardwalk and a pier for boat rides. Until all the facilities shut down in 1916, the society's buildings were, in the words of Robert C. Alberts, author of *The Shaping of the Point: Pittsburgh's Renaissance Park*, "the hub of Pittsburgh's social and cultural life."[8]

The Exposition Society's fairgrounds, along with the adjacent railroad yards and warehouses, were incorporated in the first comprehensive plan for the city that considered the Point in relation to the development of the downtown business area and overall system of traffic circulation for the city and its growing suburbs. Commissioned in 1909, Frederick Law Olmsted Jr.'s vision for Pittsburgh dealt "primarily," as he wrote in the introduction to his 1911 report, "with certain problems of remodeling in the down town district, and with the improvement of the main thoroughfares between this, the heart of the city, and the more important outlying districts."[9] While the bulk of the report was devoted to recommendations for street widening and new boulevards, upgrading the waterfront, and increasing the number of parks and playgrounds, special emphasis was placed, in typically City Beautiful fashion, on the creation of a new civic center linked to a riverside parkway encompassing the Point (figure 9.4).[10] But whereas Nolen, in his Madison plan, took his cue for the central placement of his civic center from the existing State Capitol, Olmsted Jr. chose an eccentric site for Pittsburgh's—one he admitted to be "unpromising and unattractive"—at the southeastern extremity of the Triangle (figure 9.5).[11]

The proposed civic center, whose towered city hall design was developed in a free classical style by Wilhelm Bernhard, then working for Olmsted Jr., faced south over the Monongahela River and north and west toward the city. The landscaped plaza served mainly as a monumental approach from a bridge meant to form a new gateway to the city from the South Side. The riverside boulevard going west along the Monongahela River linked the government complex to the Point before returning east along the Allegheny to create a traffic loop around the Golden Triangle. The awkward, disjointed grids of the downtown were not altered. Nor were the freight yards in the prime location of the Point disturbed, despite Olmsted Jr.'s acknowledgment that at this place "all the most inspiring associations of the city are chiefly concentrated" and that "poetically, this spot, at the meeting of the rivers, stands for Pittsburgh."[12]

Instead of recommending the displacement of the Union and Point Bridges converging at the apex of the Triangle, Olmsted Jr. simply suggested rebuilding both "in a dignified and monumental way" and erecting on the spot, "around which turned the frontier struggles of the war that gave America to the English-speaking race," a traffic circle on the model of a classical *rond point* with a sculptural element in its center.[13] Linked by a short boulevard to the railroad yards, this system of arteries, bordered by trees and plantings, was intended to "nobly form the Point into a great monument." Aside from the entirely conventional set piece of the traffic circle, Olmsted Jr. offered no prescription for how "the Point ... left pocketed beyond the freight yards" and "forgotten and disregarded by most Pittsburghers" could be integrated into the rest of the city and do anything else than provide for the smooth flow of vehicles.[14]

Two years after the plan's publication, the newly constituted Pittsburgh Art Commission took the "improvement" and "beautification of the Point" as one of its main objectives.[15] In 1913 it commissioned Edward Bennett to develop a design for the Point to create a coordinated approach to the two bridges while at the same time making the surrounding land into a park "for the people's benefit, both in the way of providing recreation grounds and art culture."[16] Bennett's plan envisaged a raised stone concourse connecting the two bridges, providing ramped access for traffic to Water Street on the Allegheny shore, and tunnels for pedestrians leading from a classically laid out park on the city side to a smaller one at the apex of the Point, overlooking the confluence of the rivers. It also called for the eventual demolition of the Exposition Society buildings, whose lease was to terminate in just over twenty years.

The essentially cosmetic Bennett plan was received quite favorably but was never implemented. In fact, no thought was given to the recreational or memorial use of the area until the end of the next decade, a period during which a number of other events took place that would affect the later course of action. In 1918, a group of bankers, industrialists, and business leaders, led by Richard B. Mellon, Howard Heinz, and the department store owner Edgar J. Kaufmann (who was to commission Fallingwater from Wright sixteen years later), formed the Citizens Committee on the City Plan, which produced a number of reports in the early 1920s and, in its later incarnation as the Pittsburgh Regional Planning Association (est. 1938; PRPA), sponsored the project for the Point that would form the basis for what was eventually constructed. In 1924, the new Point Bridge was begun. The following year plans were put forth by the Department of Public Works and the recently created City Planning Commission (1918) to transform Water Street and Duquesne Way, the two riverside streets meeting at the Point, into multilane highways. They would form a ring road with a new Crosstown Thoroughfare encircling the Golden Triangle and connecting it to the outlying suburban areas by the bridges at the Point and the new Liberty Bridge and Tunnel, approximately where Olmsted Jr. had planned his gateway-civic center (1921–28).[17]

Following discussions in 1928 regarding the building of a new city hall, the appointment of a presidential commission to establish a monument in Indiana to George Rogers Clark, and the upcoming question of the renewal of the Exposition Society's lease, proposals for the Point became more common, more grandiose, and more linked to the historical memories associated with it. The first two were dedicated to the exploits of George Rogers Clark. In late 1929, a plan for a public park surrounding a large, temple-like city hall was proposed by H. D. Sterick. It featured a restored Blockhouse plus a tall shaft, terminating in a beacon of light, dedicated to George Rogers Clark, rising from the apex of the Point between the two bridges.[18]

A very similar concept, developed the following year by the Allegheny County Planning Commissioner A. Marshall Bell in collaboration with local architect Edward B. Lee, was sent to Pennsylvania Senator David A. Reed in response to his call for the establishment of a memorial at the Point to Clark and others who made Pittsburgh "the Gateway to the West" (figure 9.6). The thirty-four acres allocated for a National Memorial Park and Pioneer Museum was almost exactly what later would be developed as the Point Park site. Around a large classical structure housing either a city hall, assembly hall, or "commercial museum" exhibiting the products of the city's industries, Bell and Lee designed a recreational park including sites for a

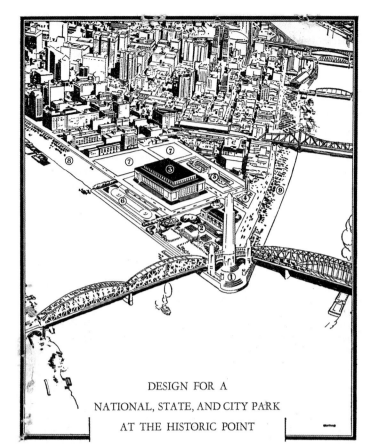

DESIGN FOR A
NATIONAL, STATE, AND CITY PARK
AT THE HISTORIC POINT

9.6

9.6. National Memorial Park and Pioneer Museum project, Pittsburgh, A. Marshall Bell and Edward B. Lee, 1930. Aerial perspective. SJHHC

water park and boat landing, memorial buildings, grade-level parking, and garages for over six thousand automobiles. The Pioneer Museum was dedicated to the "Conquest of the West," symbolized by an enormous illuminated monument to Clark growing out of an arched abutment connecting the two bridges and leading to a west-facing viewing platform.[19]

The Reed bill was not approved by Congress, and the Bell and Lee project died with it. The project was revived for a brief moment in 1934–35 when the city was considering a proposal by the Exposition Society to demolish its existing buildings and construct a multipurpose civic center on the Point site, to include a concert hall, convention center, and exposition facilities.[20] When the Pittsburgh City Planning Commission, under its newly appointed chair Frederick T. Bigger (1881–1963), rejected the idea based on fears of traffic congestion, the Exposition Society hired one of the leading local architectural firms, Janssen and Cocken (est. 1921), to work with the St. Louis–based Harland Bartholomew on a design that might win the authorities over.[21] Although that effort failed, the collaboration between W. York Cocken (1874–1964) and Bartholomew continued over the next several years under somewhat different auspices and with an entirely different program, resulting in a plan for the Point that would have important ramifications for the future.

In August 1935 the Historic Sites Act approved by the U.S. Congress expanded the functions of the National Park Service to include an Advisory Board on Parks, Historic Sites and Monuments. Four months later St. Louis's Jefferson National Expansion Memorial was designated the nation's first Historic Site, leading to the demolition of the city's thirty-eight-acre warehouse district along the Mississippi River in 1940–41.[22] More than ten years before the competition that opened in 1947 and would result in Eero Saarinen's Gateway Arch commemorating Thomas Jefferson as author of the Louisiana Purchase and sponsor of the Lewis and Clark expedition, thus symbolizing St. Louis's role as the "gateway" to the West, Bartholomew produced a grandiose City Beautiful design for the site in 1935. It is not surprising that he was engaged by the Historical Society of Western Pennsylvania (HSWP) when it decided to promote a plan for the Point in Pittsburgh to rival St. Louis's.

In the early spring of 1937, the HSWP, headquartered in Pittsburgh, passed a resolution to promote a "national historic park at The Point" to commemorate the "epochal events"

there, "which belong imperishably to the history of not only America but the world." These events were described as (1) the initial phase of George Washington's "glorious career" wherein he succeeded "in wresting Fort Duquesne from the French and [thus] making Pittsburgh the strategic outpost of the nation then coming into being"; and (2) the defeat of the French by the British in 1758 "in the momentous Seven Years' War" that ensured that America would remain "an Anglo-Saxon civilization."[23] It was specified that the park would include "the sites of Fort Duquesne, Fort Pitt, and the Block House."[24] In designating the project as the George Washington Memorial Park, the HSWP claimed the name of the first president of the United States, in contrast to St. Louis, which had to settle for that of the third.

By the beginning of the following year, the HSWP entered discussions with the National Park Service. It also began collaborating with the Lower Downtown Business Men's Association, whose interests would be served by a park at the Point. As president of the HSWP, Frank C. Harper said that "something must be done to arrest the property depreciation in the lower part of the triangle" and a national memorial park would be "one of the most practical and least costly of the solutions."[25] In a joint venture with the businessmen's group, the HSWP released its plan for the Point in January 1938.[26] As developed by Cocken and Bartholomew and published probably later that year, the memorial park was conceived as a formal, symmetrical piece of landscape architecture. An axial allée leads from a memorial fountain at the base of the triangular site to a vague indication of a reconstructed Fort Duquesne at its apex (figure 9.7).[27]

The two most significant, far-reaching, and prescient aspects of the scheme have to do not with historical memorialization but with parking and vehicular circulation. To counteract possible flooding, the park level was raised two stories. As seen in the section, this allowed for the introduction of a double layer of parking capable of accommodating seven thousand automobiles. Even more important was the removal of the two bridges from the Point's apex and their displacement eastward. This idea, which fundamentally altered the relationship between the park and the rivers as well as the traffic connections between the park and the city and its outlying suburbs, had been suggested by the Citizens Committee on the City Plan in 1935 but rejected by the City Planning Commission, which continued to oppose any

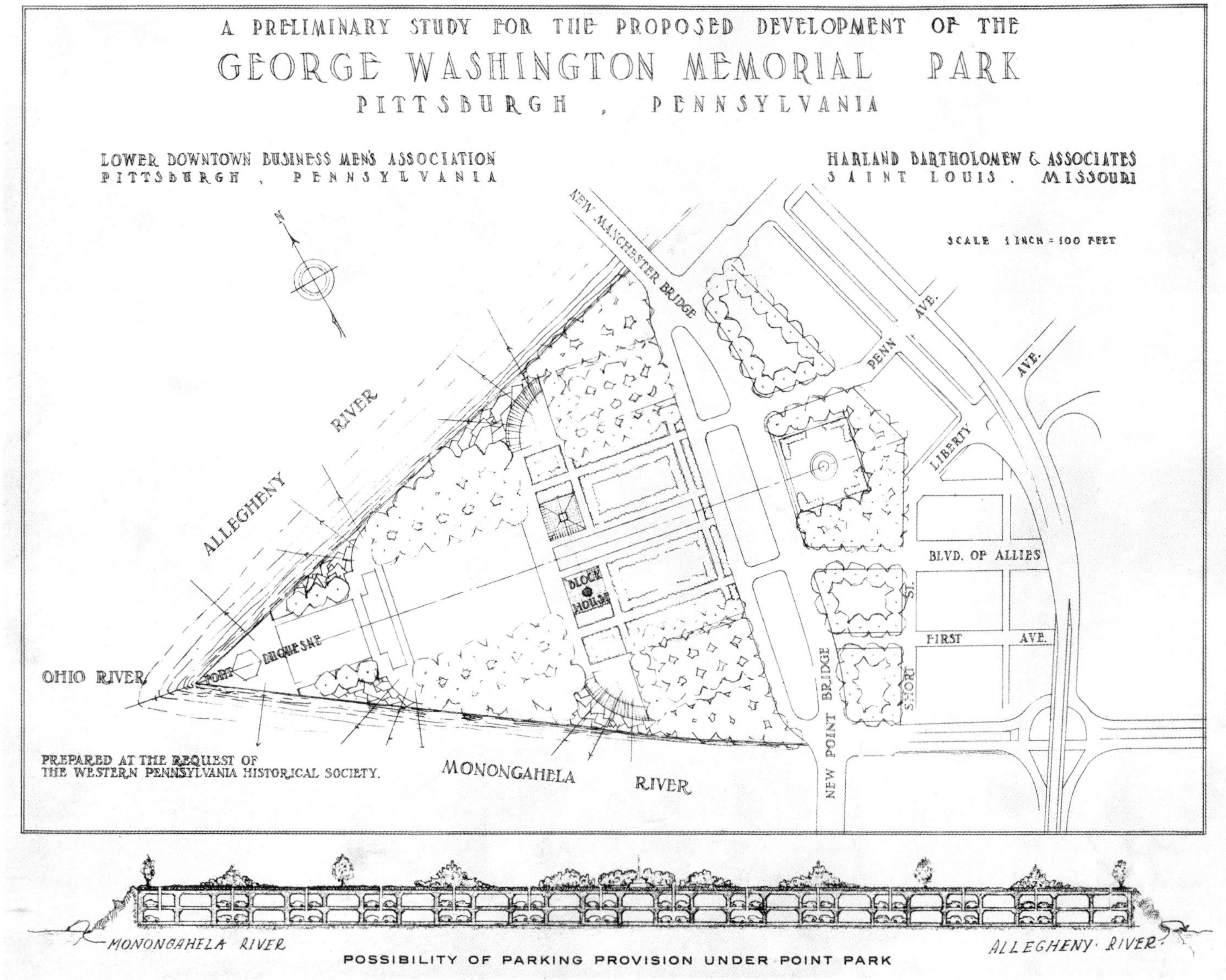

A PRELIMINARY STUDY FOR THE PROPOSED DEVELOPMENT OF THE

GEORGE WASHINGTON MEMORIAL PARK

PITTSBURGH , PENNSYLVANIA

LOWER DOWNTOWN BUSINESS MEN'S ASSOCIATION
PITTSBURGH , PENNSYLVANIA

HARLAND BARTHOLOMEW & ASSOCIATES
SAINT LOUIS . MISSOURI

SCALE 1 INCH = 100 FEET

NEW MANCHESTER BRIDGE

PENN AVE.

LIBERTY AVE.

ALLEGHENY RIVER

BLVD. OF ALLIES

BLOCK HOUSE

POINT DUQUESNE

OHIO RIVER

FIRST AVE.

SHORT ST.

NEW POINT BRIDGE

PREPARED AT THE REQUEST OF
THE WESTERN PENNSYLVANIA HISTORICAL SOCIETY.

MONONGAHELA RIVER

MONONGAHELA RIVER

ALLEGHENY RIVER

POSSIBILITY OF PARKING PROVISION UNDER POINT PARK

9.7

9.7. George Washington Memorial Park project, Pittsburgh, W. York Cocken and Harland Bartholomew, with E. N. Hunting and Don H. Morgan, 1938–39. Preliminary plan and section. From Lower Downtown Business Men's Association and Bartholomew & Associates, "A Preliminary Study for the Proposed Development of the George Washington Memorial Park, Pittsburgh, Pennsylvania," ca. 1938. SJHHC

radical alteration of the road and bridge system throughout the decade.[28] The interchange between the two bridges in the Cocken-Bartholomew plan was elevated above the park as a raised boulevard connecting the new Point and Manchester Bridges and offering a kind of terraced overlook.

The HSWP's plan for a George Washington Memorial Park, conceived as it was in collaboration with the Lower Downtown Business Men's Association, reveals how closely intertwined economic, historic, functional, and recreational concerns were. It also makes abundantly clear how critical the issue of parking was for the business community and how seriously the traffic problems resulting from Pittsburgh's unique topography of rivers, hills, and ravines would impact any design for the site. One of the main reasons the National Park Service was brought into the situation was to help defray costs. But it was soon realized that its participation was not without serious downsides and that a state park funded by a novel form of cooperation between private and public sources would prove to be more suitable.

In mid-1938 the National Park Service's Advisory Committee approved in principle the concept for the George Washington Memorial Park and provided funds for an archaeological study of the site. Conducted between 1939 and 1942, the excavations uncovered some of the original walls of Fort Pitt, six feet below street level. While this might have been exciting news to the historical community, it only added to the problems of working with the National Park Service. As Alberts has explained, the Park Service demanded that the topographic conditions that obtained in the period to be memorialized, that is, the eighteenth century, would have to be accurately reproduced. This meant that the park would have to be lowered below flood level and high flood walls constructed around the entire site, thus precluding views of the rivers. In addition, the Park Service would reconstruct all or parts of the historic forts, with the result that the park would be largely contained within the forts' walls. Furthermore, no traffic considerations could interfere with the newly exposed historical elements. Finally, perhaps the straw that broke the back of the project, the city had first to acquire all the property within the historic boundary and deed it outright to the federal government before being assured of congressional approval for the project. The city did not have enough money to do this, and the idea of a National Historic Park was soon transformed into that of a State Park.[29]

The Pittsburgh Regional Planning Association and the Moses Plan

To find a way out of what was increasingly looking like an impasse, and to achieve some consensus or at least compromise on the traffic planning issues that stymied the HSWP's proposal to dismantle the Point bridges and move them upriver, a newly constituted PRPA (1938), under the proactive leadership of Howard Heinz and its young, progressive, and charismatic executive secretary, Wallace K. Richards (1904–59), made a number of moves to develop a new approach regarding funding, planning, and administration. The PRPA, like its forebear, the Citizens Committee on the City Plan, was not a government body but rather a group of civic-minded business, financial, educational, and cultural leaders who took it upon themselves to collaborate with elected officials and appointed agencies to improve the economic and cultural conditions of metropolitan Pittsburgh and better the quality of life of its inhabitants.

One of the PRPA's first steps was to hire Robert Moses (1888–1981), parks commissioner of New York City and chair of the Triborough Bridge Authority and New York State Council of Parks, to analyze conditions in Pittsburgh and make recommendations for its future planning. In tapping the most renowned and powerful figure in the country at the time in terms of a practical vision for the solution of large-scale urban issues, especially those having to do with traffic and parks, this move seemed to signal a major breakthrough, but the results of Moses's intervention turned out to be far more mundane and uninspiring than expected. From the beginning of discussions over his possible employment, things took a negative turn.

Heinz approached Moses on behalf of the PRPA in the early fall of 1938. According to John F. Bauman and Edward K. Muller, the organization's hope was to have Moses produce a "regional highway system modeled on New York City's, with riverside drives, tunnels, and a New York City Triborough-like bridge gracing the Point."[30] Moses delayed for more than a year. When he finally accepted the job he was quite blunt, saying that he was doing it only for the money and for the very limited purpose of serving as a "'diagnostician'" of the "'traffic problems vitally affecting the business district'" and not with the goal of offering a global solution to the city's planning needs.[31] He arrived with a team of seven New York associates in mid-August 1939 and stayed for ten days. Among

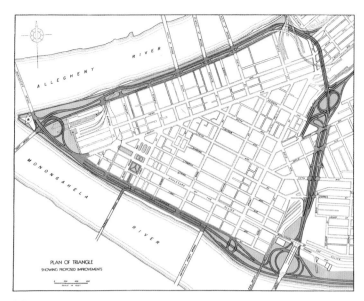

9.8

the "experts" were the architect Aymar Embury II (1880–1966) and landscape architect Gilmore D. Clarke (1892–1982), both classical and traditionalist in orientation (Clarke was chair of Washington's Commission of Fine Arts). The team published its findings in an *Arterial Plan for Pittsburgh* in November 1939.[32]

Moses stated that his brief was "to investigate the arterial problem of Pittsburgh with particular reference to the improvement of conditions in the Triangle," but that "this, of course, necessitated a study of the entire arterial problem of Pittsburgh and its suburbs" due to "the movement of industry out of the city and the growth of various suburbs."[33] The report analyzed and offered recommendations for proposed traffic routes in both the inner city and outlying areas (figure 9.8). These included double-decking Water Street (begun seven months before he arrived); double-decking Duquesne Way; building the Pitt Parkway (later Penn-Lincoln Parkway) to link the soon-to-be-completed Pennsylvania Turnpike with the Golden Triangle and points south and west via the improved Water Street; converting the Wabash Railroad Bridge, the one closest to the Point on the Monongahela, for automobile and bus use; and cutting through a north-south Crosstown Thoroughfare to ring the Golden Triangle. But it was the Point, the idea to create a park there, and the traffic problems resulting from its position at the center of all roads leading into and out of the downtown area that occupied the largest part of Moses's text.

Moses began his analysis of the Point by dismissing the importance of its historical remains. He straightaway challenged the claims for the George Washington National Memorial, even mocking their efficacy. "The relics and historical associations," he said, "should be regarded as comparatively unimportant in the solution of present and future city planning problems."[34] In Pittsburgh, history had effectively already been obliterated to make way for modern needs: "Construction of the Point and Manchester bridges at the site of old Fort Pitt has determined that traffic rather than history must be the decisive factor in the reconstruction of the apex of the Pittsburgh Triangle and in the establishment of Point Park."[35]

Moses dismissed the idea of removing the two obstructive bridges and ridiculed the notion as "fantastic." "The suggestion that these bridges be removed," in obvious reference to the Bartholomew-Cocken plan, "is apparently based on the assumption that this would facilitate federal reconstruction of

9.8. Pittsburgh Traffic Plan, Robert Moses and others, 1939. Plan for Golden Triangle. From Moses et al., *Arterial Plan for Pittsburgh*, 1939

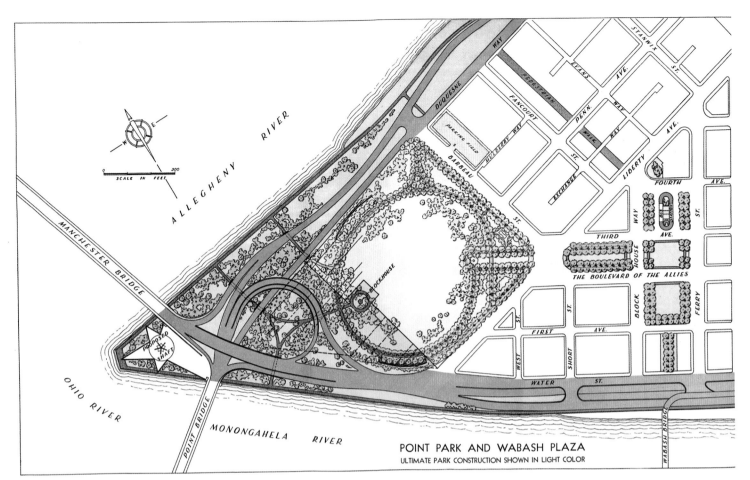

9.9

9.10

9.9. Pittsburgh Traffic Plan. Proposed Point Park and Wabash Plaza, by Moses with Gilmore Clarke and Aymar Embury. Plan (Wabash Plaza is to right). From Moses, *Arterial Plan*

9.10. Pittsburgh Traffic Plan. Proposed Point Park. Aerial perspective looking east. From Moses, *Arterial Plan*

the entire tip of the Triangle as an incident in the restoration of historical Fort Pitt. It is hard to believe," he continued, "that anyone would take this idea seriously even though the National Park Service has shown a polite interest in it." He concluded by warning that "the game of dressing up modern public improvements as historical monuments is played out. This was a quaint and ingenious device calculated to solve local problems at federal expense. The fact is that the era of easy money and federal largesse of this kind is over and that the planners of the future Pittsburgh may as well be realistic about it."[36] Nowhere was Moses's no-nonsense, hard-nosed approach to urban planning as a traffic problem more in evidence than here. As he wrote later in the report, "you can't make an omelet without breaking some eggs."[37]

Moses's plan for Point Park "rest[ed] on the theory that the two bridges will stay" and that a "free flow of traffic … must be provided in place of present street congestion."[38] To this end, he recommended the elimination of all streetcar lines within the Point and all "obtrusive, unnecessary and obsolete structures" such as the disused railroad facilities and "disgraceful old Exposition buildings." In addition, he called for limited-access ramped connections from the bridge interchange to the new double-decked Water Street and Duquesne Way forming the two shoreline highways of the ring road around the city center.[39] Only when all the traffic considerations were taken care of should thought be given to "establish a landscaped area to be known as Point Park."[40]

Despite Clarke's participation, nothing was said about what the park would look like or how it would function in relation to the city. All we have to go on are the plans and perspective in Moses's report. These distinctly recall Olmsted Jr.'s earlier proposal (figures 9.9–10). Easily half the site is taken up by roadways. A complex interchange links the two bridges to Water Street and Duquesne Way, virtually cutting off access to the rivers from the landscaped oval occupying the rest of the site. At the inner edge of that oval, in a grove of trees, is the Blockhouse, "raised to the new elevation of the proposed park" and given "a place of dignity and honor in the plan." "Any attempt to restore … Fort Pitt," however, was ruled out as "impractical and undesirable."[41]

Moses stated that "the waterfront should be reclaimed."[42] His main gesture in this regard was the pair of narrow paths that lead from the oval lawn to the rivers through the maze of highway overpasses. An equally narrow walkway provides access along the two shorelines to the Point's apex, where there is the obligatory monumental shaft. Designed by Embury in the guise of a modernistic lighthouse, its materials of Pennsylvania black granite, steel, glass, and aluminum were intended to "represent a tribute of the modern City of Steel to old Fort Pitt and symbolize the meeting of the Allegheny and Monongahela rivers in the Ohio."[43] The five-pointed column emerges from a truncated fluted base that grows out of a distorted five-pointed foundation, the geometry meant no doubt to recall the effaced Fort Pitt bastions.

Ambiguities and paradoxes abound in the Moses team's design. Despite the intention to restore a close relationship between the city and its riverfront by means of landscaping, the orientation of the proposed park is to the city's downtown rather than its waterways. In fact, the single innovative element in the design is an urban mall that connects the landscaped oval at its eastern edge to a plaza on the site of the Wabash Railroad Terminal, which Moses proposed to demolish. The plaza was to serve as a monumental approach to the repurposed Wabash Bridge as well as the location for a new bus terminal while forming, in Moses's words, "an integral part of the Point Park plan."[44] Yet despite such an explicit move toward linking the park with the downtown and the inevitable traffic this would bring, not to speak of the park's imbrication in the larger highway system proposed for the metropolitan area, the plan offered nothing in the way of much-needed parking facilities.

Moses acknowledged that "automobile parking is one of the Triangle's most vexing problems" while saying, in the very next breath, that "to some extent it must be regarded as insoluble." Placing the number of cars entering the Triangle that actually "park there at any one time" at sixteen thousand, he maintained that "it would be quite impossible at any reasonable expense to provide adequate, convenient and properly administered public parking facilities." And since "it is unlikely that additional privately-owned parking buildings will be constructed," he rather mindlessly concluded that "we can offer no complete answer to this problem" other than the assumption that the "provision for smooth arterial travel" on major limited-access roads "will take a good deal of pressure off the secondary street system."[45]

The "free flow of traffic" governed Moses's thinking on not only how Pittsburgh as a whole could be helped but also how its Point Park should be conceived and developed. It was not just that the Point was to be given over to a traffic interchange and the park take up the leftover space in the spaghetti of overpasses, the park was to find its main value as a thing to be seen and experienced from a moving vehicle. In the final pages of his report, Moses criticized the proposition that had been floated for designing a highway connecting the new Pennsylvania Turnpike to points west, south, and north entirely bypassing the downtown area. Instead, he supported the alternative project, which ultimately came to fruition, of using the Water Street improvement as the key link in his proposed Pitt Parkway skirting the downtown along its southern edge before diverging at the two Point bridges. His reasons were not entirely operational or purely functional. "We can imagine no better advertising of Pittsburgh and no more interesting experience for a motorist than to follow the route [through the city] which we have recommended. It will carry visitors not only past Frick and Schenley parks [in Oakland] . . . , but will afford a remarkable close-up of operating steel plants, and in the case of those who proceed beyond . . . to the Manchester or other bridges across the Allegheny River, will enable the visitor to see the Triangle itself, the Blockhouse and the beginning of the Ohio River, without getting into crosstown traffic."[46] And by this reasoning would obviate the need for any new parking.

The Moses report was received with polite disregard. Pittsburgh's mayor, who supported the National Park Service effort, asked the City Planning Commission to review the report's findings, and the Allegheny County Commissioners asked their Planning Commission to do the same. It is unclear whether Bigger ever officially submitted the City Planning Commission's opinion. Park Martin, the planning engineer for the Allegheny County Department of Planning, found little that was new in Moses's suggestions and nothing much that was particularly controversial. He concluded, rather sardonically, that the "report greatly lends support to most of the major projects [already] under consideration by the Board of County Commissioners." As a traffic engineer himself, he was more than ready to agree with Moses that "the historical importance of the Point should be regarded as comparatively unimportant in the solution of present and future City planning problems" and that the park itself should be "subordinate to the traffic movement in the Point area."[47]

The 1945 Griswold-Stotz-McNeil-Richardson Development Study for Point State Park

Moses's champion, Howard Heinz, died in early 1941, and Richard King Mellon took over the leadership of the PRPA. He was extremely keen on moving the Point Park agenda forward but had to wait until the end of the war for that to happen.[48] By the summer of 1945, the PRPA commissioned a Point Park Development Study from a team of four local practitioners, including a landscape architect, preservation architect, traffic engineer, and civil engineer specializing in bridge construction.[49] Their preliminary design, produced in the fall of that year, became the basis for the final realization of the park—and for Wright's counterproposal.

The landscape architect, who served as the group's leader, was the classically trained Ralph E. Griswold (1894–1981). He was superintendent of the city's Bureau of Parks, had worked on the National Historic Park project, and was about to begin a study for the PRPA of the siting for a new State Office Building in the Point Park area. A winner of the Rome Prize in 1920, he did the landscaping for Clarence Stein and Henry Wright's Chatham Village on Pittsburgh's South Side in the mid-1930s and would later work on the restoration of the gardens at the University of Virginia (1948–64) and the landscaping of the Athenian Agora for the American School of Classical Studies in Athens (1953–60). The architect was Charles M. Stotz (1899–1985), a traditionalist whose career was mainly devoted to historic restoration and who had collaborated with Griswold on the National Park venture. The traffic engineer was Donald M. McNeil (1905–83), who served as traffic engineer of Pittsburgh from 1932 to 1952. George S. Richardson (1896–1988) was the civil engineer whose early, long-span George Westinghouse Memorial Bridge (1930–32) and West End–North Side Bridge (1930–32), both in Pittsburgh, set records for their time. He eventually designed the Fort Pitt Bridge (1959) and Fort Duquesne Bridge (1963–69), which replaced the Point and Manchester Bridges, and his firm engineered the steelwork and erection of Saarinen's St. Louis Arch.

The PRPA's program, formulated in mid-August 1945, called for a strategy that would "successfully combine three major plan factors,—the highways, the rivers, and the Fort sites to the satisfaction of the traffic, aesthetic and historic viewpoints." In considering "the vitally important needs of the living city," the development of the Point Park should "study"

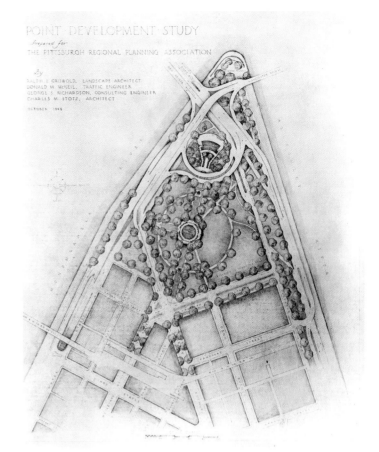

9.11

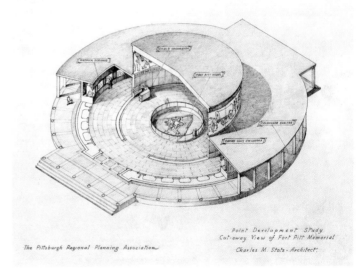

9.12

(1) "the over-all future development of the entire Triangle"; (2) "an efficient solution to the traffic at the Point"; (3) "the importance of river commerce and future river recreation"; (4) "accessibility of [the] park to citizens working and living in the Triangle, including ease of pedestrian circulation and adequate facilities for off-street parking"; and (5) "potential development of properties fronting on the Park."[50]

The PRPA emphasized that the project should "give tangible recognition ... to the outstanding historical significance of the site to the region and nation" and "recognize, in [an] appropriate manner, the fact that the Ohio River is born at the apex of the Triangle and was the pioneers' open road to the development of the West." Furthermore, it should specifically include (1) "restoration of historical structures"; (2) "appropriate treatment of the Block House"; (3) a "historical museum or Fort Pitt Memorial"; (4) "restaurant and concession facilities"; (5) "off-street parking facilities"; (6) a "boat basin"; and (7) "public comfort facilities."[51] Last, it was pointed out that, given the nature of the PRPA as a volunteer and purely advisory body, any proposal should be thought of merely as "a <u>study</u>, ... not a final plan," "<u>an incentive to action</u> ... of possible value in the preparation of the official plan for the Point Park."[52] As it turned out, because of the influence of the PRPA and, especially, the Allegheny Conference on Community Development (ACCD) that it spawned, the Griswold-Stotz-McNeil-Richardson "<u>study</u>" became the blueprint for the "official plan."

The team of architects and engineers produced two separate schemes by late October 1945. One maintained the existing bridges at the Point; the other recommended moving both upstream, pretty much where they were placed in the Cocken-Bartholomew George Washington Memorial Park project. According to those involved, the Griswold-Stotz-McNeil-Richardson team started by leaving the bridges in situ but soon realized that this would make it impossible to achieve the desired results, whether from a historical, aesthetic, or strictly functional point of view. Before adopting the more radical approach of moving the bridges, they got permission from Richards and Mellon to proceed with both schemes; and Richards and Mellon convinced Governor Edward Martin to support the one with the displaced bridges when he included the Point Park project in the fifty-seven-million-dollar "Pittsburgh Plan" he proposed to the state legislature in late October.[53]

9.11. Point Park Development Study, Pittsburgh, Ralph Griswold, Charles Stotz, Donald McNeil, and George Richardson, 1945. Scheme B, October 1945. Plan. SJHHC

9.12. Point Park Development Study. Schemes B and A. Fort Pitt Memorial, by Stotz. Cutaway aerial perspective. SJHHC

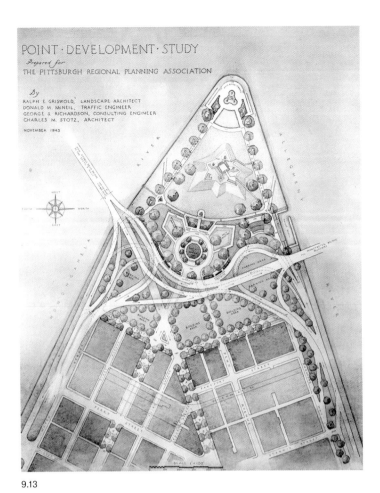

9.13

9.15

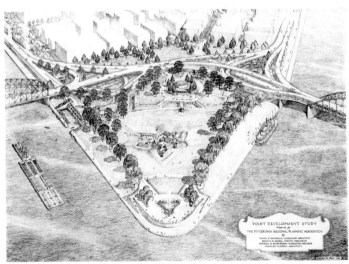

9.14

9.13. Point Park Development Study. Scheme A, November 1945. Plan. SJHHC

9.14. Point Park Development Study. Scheme A. Aerial perspective looking east. SJHHC

9.15. Point Park Development Study. Scheme A. Aerial perspective looking west. SJHHC

9.16

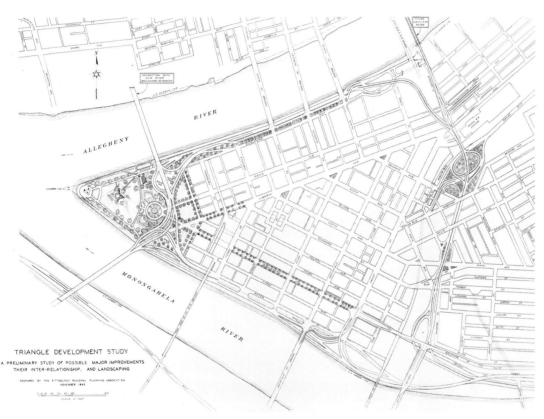

TRIANGLE DEVELOPMENT STUDY

A PRELIMINARY STUDY OF POSSIBLE MAJOR IMPROVEMENTS
THEIR INTER-RELATIONSHIP, AND LANDSCAPING

PREPARED BY THE PITTSBURGH REGIONAL PLANNING ASSOCIATION
NOVEMBER 1945

9.17

9.16. Pittsburgh Point. View from Fort Pitt Bridge looking north

9.17. Point Park Development Study. Scheme A. Triangle Development Study Plan,
November 1945. SJHHC

The plan that maintained the bridges in situ was called Scheme B, while the other was referred to as Scheme A, no doubt to indicate the order of preference.[54] Scheme B followed the Moses plan (figure 9.11). Little effort was put into something that was deemed undesirable and would mainly be used as a foil to the preferred solution. As in the Moses plan, the traffic interchange between the two bridges occupies a good third of the site, leaving a small area at the apex for a terrace overlooking the meeting of the three rivers. The existing Point Bridge was doubled in width to accommodate the traffic expected when the Penn-Lincoln Parkway and Fort Pitt Tunnel through Mt. Washington, leading to a new airport (begun mid-July 1946) and points south, were finished.

Within the circular highway interchange is a restaurant with a curved glass facade. East of it a larger, landscaped circle defines the main open space of the park, as the oval did in the Moses design. It contains a baptistery-like, colonnaded structure (figure 9.12). Intended to serve as a Fort Pitt Memorial, it features historical dioramas on its ambulatory walls and colored glass historical scenes in the clerestory. In a depressed well in its center is a small-scale model of Fort Pitt. The memorial structure defines the main axis of the park leading from the apex through the restaurant and Blockhouse to the junction of Barbeau Street, Liberty Avenue, and the Boulevard of the Allies. A refreshment stand terminates a cross-axis to the south, while the area to the northeast, along Barbeau Street, is indicated as a possible building site or parking area. The area between the park and Short Street is not included in the scheme, thus giving the park a ragged edge toward the city.

Scheme A, while barely more inventive in terms of design, is more fully developed and much richer in historical detail (figures 9.13–15). Instead of following Moses's proposal, this one recalls that of Cocken and Bartholomew (figure 9.7). The Point and Manchester Bridges have been relocated, though not as far upstream as was earlier proposed. The intention was to move the actual Manchester Bridge and to demolish and rebuild the one over the Monongahela. It was to be redesigned as a double-decked structure, with the lower level connecting to the city's South Side and the upper level, as part of the projected Penn-Lincoln Parkway, entering the new Fort Pitt Tunnel through Mt. Washington. Cars coming north from the airport would thus have a dramatic view of the Point and downtown area at the moment they emerge from the tunnel onto the bridge (figure 9.16).

As in the Moses report, a plan of the Golden Triangle showed how the new traffic interchange at the Point would tie in with the proposed ring road around the city's downtown (figures 9.17, 9.8). A comparison of the two allows one to see clearly the benefits the PRPA's team felt were to be gained from moving the two bridges. For one thing, it made the interchange design more fluid and space-saving. For another, it opened up the possibility for the park to have full access to the rivers. However, it placed a major obstacle between the city and the park, namely, the multilane elevated highway crossover with its on- and off-ramps. There was apparently no win-win solution.

One of the big winners in Scheme A was the historical component. By moving the two bridges back from the tip of the Point, the team could think about restoring parts, if not all, of the two forts. A drawing with the archaeological information gleaned from the federally sponsored excavations superimposed over Scheme A, however, reveals the problems that would be faced in any attempt to reconstruct either fort accurately and in its entirety (figures 9.18, 9.13). Once the bridges were moved east, the outlines of Fort Duquesne were revealed, although the structure's relation to the original shoreline as well as its grade elevation were no longer the same as before. Even more problematic is that three-fifths of Fort Pitt was obliterated by highways and a good part of its outer walls was outside the park's boundaries.

In deciding to reconstruct Fort Duquesne in its entirety—though historically inaccurately—and to restore only parts of Fort Pitt, while moving those parts to create a composition framing the memorial building—Stotz justified his archaeological impressionism in the following way: "The literal restoration of either Fort Duquesne or Fort Pitt with relation to the original shore line and the original grades is difficult or impossible to accomplish; the restoration of Fort Pitt in its entirety would occupy too much land to be practical; in addition the restoration of Fort Pitt would immensely complicate and [sic] efficient solution of the complex traffic problem."[55] Since "Fort Duquesne may be restored completely … except for the maintenance of exact grade elevations and relation to shore line," this is what Stotz proposed, despite the defining significance of those elements for such a primitive fort as this. The "unusual character and quaint intimacy" of the structure, it was claimed, would have "greater appeal for the average visitor than the larger and more monumental" Fort Pitt. Still, "because of the sentimental and popular interest" in the latter structure, Stotz decided to turn two of its bastions into "promenade areas," symmetrically framing his Fort Pitt Memorial, and place a "scale model of the fort" inside the memorial.[56]

The major historical elements in Scheme A create a processional backbone for the park and symmetrically order the space along a central axis leading from the highway overpass to where the rivers meet. Picturesqueness and a concern for views and recreational use predominate and often supersede serious historical considerations. Griswold noted that the main terrace on which Fort Pitt Memorial sits "was not an attempt to restore Fort Pitt" but "merely an adaptation of the ramparts on the down-river side as … the setting of the … Memorial" and a place to "stop for a view of the park." "The bastions," he acknowledged, "have been moved … a few feet from their original locations in order to balance them on the Memorial." The original Blockhouse can be seen from the middle of Fort Pitt Terrace "against a panoramic view of the three rivers," while, "for park purposes," the building "has been made directly accessible from the Terrace by means of ramps which of course were not there originally." Finally, because the terrace overlook "is close enough to the business section to be used for noo[n]time relaxation by Downtown workers and shoppers," Griswold acknowledged that "the idea of restoring the stark barren[n]ess of the old parade grounds, devoid of trees or beauty of any kind, has been abandoned as incompatible with modern park use. Instead of a literal restoration … there are tree shaded walks and lawns where benches can be placed for rest and enjoyment of an attractive landscape."[57]

The only other building of significance in the park is the proposed restaurant, which was intended to be a "modern high class" establishment (a refreshment stand is located under the highway overpass near the entrance from Penn Avenue). Removed from its location within the highway interchange in Scheme B to a space nearer the Allegheny River, the restaurant now adjoins a boathouse and yacht basin to the north and "commands a fine view of the park, Fort Duquesne and the Allegheny waterfront." Just below the restaurant's outdoor dining area is a pedestrian path that runs between the Fort Pitt Terrace and the Blockhouse, connecting them to waterfront promenades. Where the two promenades meet at the Point's apex is, in Griswold's words, "the climax of the entire scheme," marked by a "monumental Fountain of the Three Rivers."[58]

The fountain's trilobed design was intended to be "symbolic … of the merging of the Monongahela and Allegheny

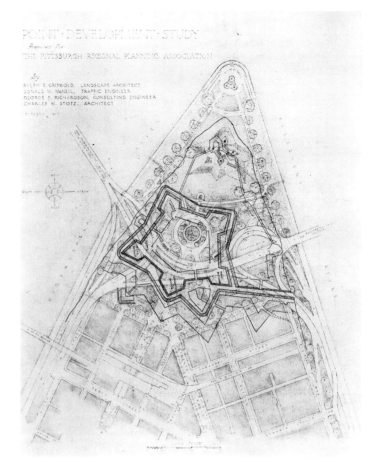

9.18

9.18. Point Park Development Study. Scheme A. Plan with outlines of Forts Duquesne and Pitt superimposed, October 1945. SJHHC

to form the Ohio River, the geographical feature which first attracted George Washington's attention to the strategic importance of the Point." The Ohio River Terrace surrounding the fountain was to provide "a magnificent unbroken view of the origin of the Ohio River, the unique view which more than any other identifies Pittsburgh in the eyes of the world" (figure 9.15).[59] The unadorned character of the landscape treatment, which apparently was something much desired by Mellon, was intended to speak to the "dignity" of the spot and "preserve the traditional simplicity typical of the pioneers who first settled here."[60] For Griswold it was the purity of the landscape articulated by the manipulation of natural elements that carried the meaning of the site. "It is intended," he wrote, "that the grandeur of this natural setting as symbolized in the Three Rivers Fountain will inspire visitors with proper reverence for the epoch making events which have characterized the Point in the history of the nation."[61]

The focus of Scheme A was westward, away from the city. The complex highway and bridge connections created a barrier between the city and the park that the team of designers tried to deny, claiming that "in fact these structures will be quite inconspicuous." "From the full length of Penn Avenue and the Boulevard [of the Allies]," they said (but did not attempt to show visually), "the Fort Pitt Memorial will be clearly visible in tree framed vistas and it will also be seen from Liberty Avenue at the Boulevard intersection. Visitors may walk or drive directly into the park from any of these three major streets," they added, "and circulate around the Memorial or ... stop for a view of the park from the Fort Pitt Terrace."[62]

In reality, much of the later restudy of the design would be devoted to making a visual connection between the city and Point Park that was sorely compromised by the tangle of elevated highways and bridge approaches in Scheme A. Not only was the park cut off from the downtown, the section of the park to the east of the bridge interchange was barely designed and essentially treated as leftover space. The three odd-shaped blocks to the west of Barbeau and Short Streets were indicated merely as "building areas," while the spaces between the bridges' on-/off-ramps were cursorily designated as "parking areas" (figure 9.13). It was noted that "the kind of buildings that may be attracted to [the three indicated building areas] could form a transition between the business section and the park with benefit to both," but nothing was said about the areas set aside for parking.[63] The preliminary cost estimate for demolition and construction at the thirty-six-acre site, exclusive of land acquisition, was put at a little under sixteen million dollars. This was about a third more than the Moses plan, exclusive of his Wabash Plaza add-on.[64]

The Allegheny Conference on Community Development and Edgar Kaufmann's First Overture to Wright

Following the governor's announcement of support for the PRPA's Scheme A, the city's mayor, who had been a strong proponent of the National Park venture, lent his backing to it. Predicting that it would exert "a tremendous drawing power ... on auto tourists throughout this entire region," Cornelius Scully emphasized the economic advantages of the scheme. To exploit even further the park's attractiveness as a tourist destination, he suggested restoring Fort Pitt completely and having "a detail of soldiers stationed there and a sunset gun fired daily." And for the urban betterment of the city, he called for a development of apartment houses and "smart shops" on the street facing the park.[65] The historian John Oliver and Clarence Macartney, the distinguished and popular pastor of downtown Pittsburgh's First Presbyterian Church, both seconded the mayor's call for the restoration of Fort Pitt. But "'in addition to the restoration,'" Macartney declared that "'some great building ought to be erected near The Point, a building which would be useful as well as ornamental, one which would house great conventions ... [and] would let the traveler know ... that this is Pittsburgh.'"[66]

The Griswold-Stotz-McNeil-Richardson plan, absent a complete restoration of Fort Pitt or a landmark convention hall, was presented to the public through wide press coverage on 15 November 1945. Perspectives of Scheme A were illustrated along with a photograph of a model.[67] Although the model gave physical reality to the scheme, some of the newspaper reports were quick to point out that these were merely "tentative and wholly preliminary plans" meant to serve as only a "'starting point' for City, County, State and Federal officials who will determine what form the park is to take."[68] The story behind the story was the change in leadership of the Point Park project from its preliminary development stage under the PRPA to its elaboration and realization under the Planning Association's sibling organization, the ACCD.

Created in the early spring of 1943 as the Allegheny County Conference on Post-War Community Planning, the objective of this citizen's group, as stated in its foundational document, was "to stimulate, coordinate and channel citizen support and activity leading to research, analyses and detailed programing of post-war development within the Pittsburgh-Allegheny region all to such purpose that … the citizens of the region may possess themselves of the opportunity to live, work and play in a manner befitting a democratic society."[69] Support for projects and programs deemed valuable was to be garnered through "educational means" such as public relations, collaboration with government officials and agencies, and private subventions by its members. Its original Citizen Sponsoring Committee included Richard K. Mellon, H. J. Heinz II, Edgar Kaufmann, Mayor Scully, and the two figures most responsible for the conception of the nonprofit corporation, Robert E. Doherty, president of the Carnegie Institute of Technology, and Edward R. Weidlein, president and director of the Mellon Institute for Industrial Research.[70]

While concerning itself with such issues as smoke and flood control, highway and bridge improvement, better housing and recreation facilities, increased parking, and urban redevelopment legislation, a major thrust of the organization's efforts from the beginning was the creation of Point Park as not only an urban amenity but, even more, as a catalytic agent in the renewal of the city's downtown in response to the specter of decentralization.[71] As the organization deemed most appropriate to carry forward the Point Park piece of the governor's Pittsburgh Plan, the conference agreed to take on the job in late October 1945 and officially did so on 14 November, the evening prior to the press coverage of the new plans.[72]

The ACCD immediately announced the formation of a Point Park Committee (PPC) to oversee the project. Among the group of twenty-eight members were Kaufmann, Griswold, Stotz, Heinz, Mellon, Oliver, the former mayor, Scully, and the mayor-elect, David L. Lawrence, who was to prove instrumental in the realization of the park and surrounding redevelopment area.[73] The inclusion of Griswold and Stotz as the only two design professionals signaled the fact that despite the reminder by the conference's executive secretary, Richards, that their Scheme A was "not to be considered a final plan, nor in any sense an official one," it would be difficult, if not impossible, to criticize it openly or avoid using it as a key reference.[74]

At its initial meeting in late December, the PPC established three subcommittees (later called Study Committees) to oversee the specific areas of Historical Significance, Highways and Traffic, and River Commerce and Recreation.[75] To these was added a fourth, Architecture and Design, when the PPC reconvened in mid-January 1946. The Study Committee on Historical Significance was chaired by Oliver and included Macartney and Stotz; the Study Committee on Highways and Traffic was chaired by Charles F. Chubb, head of the Greater Pittsburgh Parks Commission, and included McNeil; the one on River Commerce and Recreation was chaired by William B. Rodgers, a river transportation executive, and included Griswold. Finally, the newly created Study Committee on Architecture and Design was placed under the chairship of Kaufmann.[76] The Committee of Architecture and Design was the smallest of the four and the only one with no professional member.

A major piece of business transacted at the second meeting of the PPC was the revision of the "objectives," or program, for the park set forth by the PRPA the previous August. The most significant changes had to do with the promotion of architecture and design as such and the foregrounding of their expressive potential for creating something unique. Following the charge to "give tangible recognition … to the outstanding historical significance of the site" and its role in "the development of the West," the list of seven "structures and facilities" in the earlier program was eliminated and its place taken by a directive "to study intensively the architecture and design, the general theme, considered appropriate for a Point Park, and to endeavor to aid the official agencies of government to secure plans, and finally to construct a park that will be an outstanding and unique example of civic development."[77]

This was the first time any such statement regarding the value of artistic creativity and originality was made in the context of the future Point Park, and it was clearly Edgar Kaufmann, a champion of modern design and especially Wright's architecture, who was responsible for it. To reinforce this new perspective, the program now stated that it was urged upon all those involved "to recognize the unique opportunity afforded Pittsburgh to secure, at long last, a nationally significant park and to leave no effort unexpended to build it."[78] One can certainly ask whether these textual additions were the result of Kaufmann's unhappiness with the Griswold-Stotz-McNeil-Richardson project and his fear that it was in the pipeline be built.[79] Events certainly bear out this conjecture.

On a practical level, things began to move rather fast and in ways that would influence and constrain any major new architectural initiative. By the end of January 1946, the precise boundaries of the site were defined by a municipal resolution and an official committee to oversee the implementation of the project was put in place. Condemnation of property and acquisition of land began by mid-July. By late August the Pennsylvania Department of Highways authorized engineering studies of the interchange adjoining the proposed new Point Bridge and the section of Penn-Lincoln Parkway that had just gone into construction. And by the beginning of November, George Richardson was awarded the contract to proceed with design studies and working drawings for the Point interchange and new Point Bridge.[80]

One of the most important developments, however, resulted from an unexpected incident. This was the fire in late March 1946 that destroyed the Wabash Terminal as well as eleven nearby warehouses, comprising an area of twelve acres. Out of this serendipitous appearance of unencumbered land contiguous with the proposed park almost immediately came the idea for a major urban redevelopment project, the first of its kind in the United States, that would help pay for the park and related improvements as well as provide clear evidence of the project's potential for reviving the economic and social life of the "core" or "heart" of the city.[81] Although it soon turned into the commercial development called Gateway Center, devoted almost exclusively to office buildings, the added real estate was originally conceived as an upscale residential community, with some office buildings as well as shops and cultural facilities, including a "civic auditorium" that might form the nucleus of a new "civic center" in the area.[82]

Within two months of the fire, the ACCD set up a Point Redevelopment Committee and, by the beginning of July, a recommendation was made to the mayor to establish an Urban Redevelopment Authority, which the city did by mid-November and of which Kaufmann was one of the five original board members.[83] At the same time, the Point Redevelopment Committee, to which Kaufmann was asked to be an advisor, began negotiations with the Equitable Life Assurance Society of the United States in New York to convince them to be the main investor in the redevelopment of the twenty-three-acre parcel running from river to river between the eastern edge of Point Park and Stanwix Street (figure 9.19). The negotiations over the next three and a

half years were successfully concluded in early 1950 when Equitable signed a contract with the city.[84]

While these activities to help make Point Park a reality were going on, still more countersuggestions for enriching the PRPA's Scheme A were being proposed. In the 17 January 1946 meeting of the conference's PPC, where Kaufmann made his plea for a major effort to secure a truly significant work of architecture at the Point, the idea of "considering the various proposals for buildings such as a Town Hall or Symphony Hall within the Point Park" was referred to the conference's Steering Committee.[85] Several months before, Fritz Reiner, the renowned conductor of the Pittsburgh Symphony Orchestra, told a reporter for the *Pittsburgh Sun-Telegraph*, in an interview printed on the front page of the newspaper, that he was in favor of building "an art and industrial center" in the park. Echoing Clarence Macartney's thinking, he said it should be an "'artistic memorial hall,'" like the San Francisco Opera House, which could be used for orchestra and opera as well as conventions and industrial exhibitions.[86]

At the same time as such additions to Point Park were being recommended, similar ones were being made for the redevelopment area beyond its eastern boundary. This served to create some confusion in people's minds. First, there was the suggestion for a civic auditorium to anchor a cultural center in the twenty-three acres being planned by the new Point Redevelopment Committee. And following the announcement of the mayor's plan to establish an Urban Redevelopment Authority, Charles J. Graham, chair of the conference's Point Redevelopment Committee, said that his "'chief desire'" for the area under consideration for redevelopment was "'to get something like the New York music hall [Carnegie Hall] there. A hall where we could hold operas, concerts, and the like.'" In the same newspaper article that reported this, the governor-elect, James H. Duff, revived an ongoing project of the PRPA in saying that he would "urge the construction of a new state office building in the area" (eventually built on the corner of Liberty Avenue and Short Street in 1957).[87]

Making a further potential inroad on the simplicity of the program followed in the Griswold-Stotz-McNeil-Richardson plan for Point Park was the publication in 1946 of a "Parking Study of the Pittsburgh Central Business District" commissioned by the PRPA the year before. The report presented an alarming picture, declaring that while the city may have begun to control the flooding from its rivers, it was nowhere near solving the problem of the flood of automobiles entering the city on a daily basis: "A flood is rolling towards Pittsburgh. A Traffic flood," the report began. "Pittsburgh streets today are as great a potential menace as the Monongahela and the Allegheny Rivers would be without their giant Federal system of flood-preventing dams. The City must prepare to control its approaching traffic-floods by building a series of reservoirs,—by constructing a planned system of off-street parking facilities." The "Triangle," it noted, is "the focal point of the activities of the Pittsburgh area" and therefore "the traffic capacity and efficiency of the Triangle," it underlined, "must be increased by every available means—the most essential of which is the provision of adequate off-street terminal storage facilities." The document recommended the provision of over twenty-five thousand parking spaces in thirty-two facilities, twenty of which were to be newly constructed four- to five-story garages, with an estimated price tag of over thirty-six million dollars. The report also called for a ban on all curbside parking unrelated to shopping and deliveries and the establishment of a public Parking Authority.[88] The latter, the first in the nation, was created in August 1947.

In anticipation of these new initiatives, suggestions, and statistics, the ACCD decided that Kaufmann's Study Committee on Architecture and Design should not move too quickly in its search for a creative architectural solution to Point Park. Although Kaufmann "felt that it would be possible for his committee to begin preliminary study ... of a general theme which would motivate and inspire the architectural aspect of the Point Park" and secure "the finest possible plans [for] ... a park that would be of national and even international significance," the "consensus" of the committee as a whole was that it "would [only] be in a position to begin intensive work when the recommendations of the other three study committees had brought into clearer definition the land area available for park development, the location of highway and transportation facilities and the historical elements to be memorialized."[89]

The Architecture and Design Committee did not meet until well into the spring of 1946 due to Kaufmann's wintering in Palm Springs, California (where Richard Neutra was designing a house for him and his wife). No doubt wanting to make sure that decisions regarding the reconstruction of historical elements and the design and location of bridge approaches and the highway interchange would not be made irrespective of their impact on future architectural considerations, Kaufmann

sent a letter from Palm Springs to be read at the mid-April meeting of the PPC outlining in much greater detail than previously his hopes and dreams for the park. It was meant to serve "purely as a personal statement," he said, given the fact that his committee had not yet "receive[d] the green light" to produce a set of recommendations.[90]

Kaufmann described his "program" for the park quite differently from the way Oliver, chair of the Historical Significance Committee, and others had up until then. Instead of relating the park exclusively to the historical events that transpired at the Point in the eighteenth century, Kaufmann proposed a vision for the site "based on personal freedom and world responsibility." Starting out by saying that "Pittsburgh has been so busy as one of the oldest and greatest centers of heavy industry in the world that it has had little time to worry about finding proper symbols for its existence," he stated that now "the opportunity to create such a symbol is at hand: the new project for a Point Park.... It is here where man and nature can work together to produce something unique." It was not by looking back to the past but rather by looking to contemporary "industrial civilization in which Pittsburgh has played a central role" that the forms might be found to symbolize the "hope there is today for both peace and international cooperation on a world scale" and the "research and experimentation" that the "tremendous productivity" of the modern world has fostered. Point Park, Kaufmann underlined, should represent "a focal point in the progress of human civilization so far as western culture and industry have been able to further it." It was therefore "especially important that the Point Park should not be conceived and executed primarily as a memorial to the past." While "it is ... fine and necessary to recall the early structures that stood in this area, and ... rebuild them so far as possible," what is "most important is that the park should symbolize the same spirit of foresight and adventuresomeness which made this past history possible, and which made Pittsburgh a symbol of industrial enterprise." "No mere museum for relics will achieve this [goal]," he warned.[91]

To accomplish his larger goal was a tall order. His answer was predictable, at least to those who knew him well: "Only the most foresighted park planner and an architect worthy of the name genius could thus continue the traditions which make the Point a shrine. If Pittsburgh has the foresight to grasp this opportunity, to erect at the Point a symbol worthy of our own past and dedicated to the promise of the future, then we can know that we have lived up to our true duty."[92] True to his word, and without apparently consulting the other members of his committee in advance, Kaufmann soon asked the only architectural "genius" he knew whether he would be willing to take on the assignment. When Frank Lloyd Wright came to Pittsburgh for a lecture on 17 May 1946, he spent the following day with Kaufmann at Fallingwater, where Kaufmann offered him the job. Wright, who was deeply hurt by Kaufmann's having commissioned Neutra to design his Palm Springs house, declined, saying, "You have offered me a generous job working with you on the rehabilitation of a portion of Pittsburgh. And it looks like a real work in more than one sense. But, E. J., I cannot take you up.... [Y]ou will never, as a Patron of the Arts, be in a position to help me with one hand and hurt me with the other, because I shall never trust my work to you again."[93]

Kaufmann refused to give up, in either his request for Wright's involvement—which eventually proved successful—or his attempt to convince the other members of his committee to perceive the future park in the light he did—which proved unsuccessful. After taking time to digest Wright's rejection and before planning his next overture, Kaufmann once more laid out to the members of the Architecture and Design Committee the points he thought they should keep in mind. Sensing that he might have been alone in his lack of enthusiasm for the Griswold-Stotz-McNeil-Richardson plan and his idea for a world-class design representing contemporary conditions, he began by saying that "in the absence of anyone coming forward with another idea," he would reiterate what he previously suggested as a "theme ... to symbolize the two greatest ideas of our time," namely, the "freedom gained ... by intelligent use of machines" and the "responsibility of world cooperation and peace." After repeating his admonition that Point Park should not be a monument to the past but "should symbolize the same spirit of foresight and adventuresomeness" that "made Pittsburgh a symbol of industrial enterprise," he suggested that "all of this could perhaps be covered by a theme called 'The Free Culture of the United States.'"[94]

Kaufmann saw the power in such "a comprehensive theme" to inspire "those to whom we might turn to develop the architectural possibilities of the Point Park" and "to excite their imagination." He concluded by saying that "if a theme of great conception can be evolved, I am sure that the genii of the architectural world would attempt to express it" and that the result could form the basis of a major fund-raising effort: "Through this means we could probably go forth to secure funds from the government as well as our own State—yes, and even all the States to the west of us that really look upon this section as the gateway in our early history to their development."[95]

There is no evidence that the other members of his committee either were interested in these thoughts or believed they had any relevance to the issue at hand, be it in terms of architecture or fund-raising. Kaufmann, however, would not be deterred. He proceeded to reopen discussions with Wright the following month, when he visited the architect toward the end of January 1947 at the latter's winter headquarters in Arizona.

Wright's Engagement with Pittsburgh and the Point Park Enterprise

Except for their momentary falling-out over the hiring of Neutra, Edgar Kaufmann and Frank Lloyd Wright maintained a close, warm, and mutually respectful relationship from the time they first came into contact with one another in late 1933 or early 1934 until the department store owner's death in 1955. By the fall of 1934 Kaufmann began discussing with the architect the possibility of a number of commissions. One was for a planetarium and parking facility for a vacant lot next to the downtown department store. Another was for Wright to serve as an adviser to the recently established Allegheny County Authority, which was in charge of overseeing the construction of certain major, federally funded Public Works Administration projects, including several bridges, highways, a tunnel, and riverfront improvements. After visiting Wright in November 1934 at Taliesin, where his son was an apprentice, Kaufmann reiterated his offers to the architect and urged him in early December 1934 to come to Pittsburgh to see the sites in question and meet the people responsible for the urban program.[96]

Wright made the trip in the latter part December, during which time he was also taken by Kaufmann to the site in the Allegheny Mountains, about two hours south of the city, where the family had a weekend cottage they wanted to replace with a more significant structure. On his return to Arizona, Wright wrote to Kaufmann saying he did not think the idea of working with the Pittsburgh architects and authorities he met was a feasible one. On the other hand, he was excited about the prospect of the weekend house, which he had already begun designing in his head and which would be built between 1936 and 1937 and called Fallingwater.[97] The commission for the planetarium dragged on, to no avail, until the following spring.

But one other outcome of this early interaction between Wright and Kaufmann, though less important architecturally than Fallingwater, would prove to have a more lasting effect on the architect's relationship with the city of Pittsburgh and his reputation among its professionals and civic leaders. During their discussions over jobs and fees, Kaufmann agreed to subsidize the construction and travel of the Broadacre City model (figure 6.10). In Pittsburgh, it was included as a major piece of the Federal Housing Administration exhibition "New Homes for Old," installed in Kaufmann's Department Store in June. Not satisfied with the general critique of the American city that Broadacre City represented, Wright wrote an article specifically targeting Pittsburgh, which he published as an op-ed piece in the *Pittsburgh Sun-Telegraph* soon after the exhibition opened. Titled "Broadacres to Pittsburgh," the article was unrelenting in its criticism of the city's having "ignored all principle in getting itself born" and having exploited and destroyed its natural surroundings. "'In spite of the river' ought to be a Pittsburgh slogan," Wright railed, "'to hell with the hills' thrown in for full effect." His conclusion was certainly one that rang true to many: "Pittsburgh is obsolescent and … slowly dying." But his solution was provocative, to say the least: "In all probability the town will have to be abandoned, because a rusty ruin, to tumble into the river, keeping the waters still stained with oxide of iron for another half century."[98]

When he returned to the city to close the exhibition at the end of June, Wright compounded his "bad boy" behavior in interviews to the press. The *Pittsburgh Post-Gazette* quoted him as saying that the highly regarded Oakland cultural center "'isn't culture'" at all and that its buildings are just rehashes of the past. Taking particular aim at the brand-new Cathedral of Learning by Charles Klauder (1925–37), Wright described the unique skyscraper addition to the University of Pittsburgh campus as "'the most outrageous instance of the fruits of the capitalistic system.'" When asked how he would go about rebuilding the city to improve it, he said, "'It would be cheaper to abandon it … and build another real one.'"

"'This is a disappearing city; nothing comes out of it.'" It is just a "'jumble of buildings.'"[99]

Wright's remarks this time raised the hackles of many. The highly respected local architect Henry Hornbostel struck back, castigating Wright's criticisms as a "'senseless condemnation'" that only "'stimulates cheap notoriety.'"[100] Upon returning to Taliesin in Wisconsin, Wright felt compelled to explain away his words, although he could not bring himself really to apologize. In a missive titled "Frank Lloyd Wright to Pittsburgh," he fundamentally blamed the press, saying that he was "truly sorry that in answering the questions Pittsburgh 'publicity' required me to answer I was represented as resentful or sensational." He explained that his "criticisms of Pittsburgh [were] given in the short hand of epigrammatic humor" but could not refrain from adding that they "were nevertheless the sound sense of an architect extended in a friendly way to a friend": "When Pittsburgh asked me what I thought and felt about its buildings it got the truth. And I hope it will think it over without resentment because no offense was meant."[101] It is unclear why Wright wrote this halfhearted disclaimer unless it was at the suggestion of Kaufmann. In any event, it was not published, and even if it had been, it probably would not have lessened the resentment that lasted well into the following decade and surely affected how Wright's Point Park project would be received.

During the next five years Wright visited Pittsburgh a number of times on his way to the Fallingwater site and did a number of small projects for Kaufmann, all of which remained unrealized except for Kaufmann's own department store office (1936–37). It was not until the spring of 1946 that Kaufmann again approached Wright about doing something in the city, when, for a second time, as we read, Wright turned the offer down. This time, however, Kaufmann refused to give up. Following his attempt in late December to convince his fellow committee members at the ACCD of the need for an inspirational theme and a genius architect to carry it out, Kaufmann, as already noted, visited Wright at Taliesin West in late January 1947, at which time he and Wright "discussed rather informally," as Kaufmann later put it, "the possibility of developing a plan as well as sketches for the Point Park."[102] With a sizable fee of twenty-five thousand dollars, to be paid directly to the architect by the Edgar J. Kaufmann Charitable Trust, Wright agreed to take the job.

From Palm Springs, Kaufmann immediately began corresponding with Wallace Richards in order to gather the information that Wright needed to proceed with the design. What was eventually conveyed by Kaufmann to Wright in the way of a program proved critical to the conference's ultimate dismissal of the Wright project. We do not know precisely what Kaufmann requested from Richards, although we know that Wright had asked for materials showing substratum conditions, flood levels, and river elevations.[103] Richards responded to Kaufmann, on 31 January 1947, saying that it took him some time to get the substratum report but now he had everything Kaufmann wanted "with the exception of the amount of square footage that Federal agencies might require." He was able to affirm that "the state office building requirements are set at 80,000 square feet and the design of the building should include an office for the governor ... as well as a cabinet room."[104] What this means, of course, is that Kaufmann, acting in part in his capacity as a member of the Urban Redevelopment Authority and advisor to the Point Redevelopment Committee, considered the site for Wright's design to comprise not just the Point Park's thirty-six acres but the entire fifty-nine acres that included the area for redevelopment.[105]

Kaufmann relayed this information to Wright on 7 February along with what appear to be some of his own thoughts for additional programmatic elements.[106] After reporting that "the [Federal] Government would need for their offices ... at least 100,000 square feet" while "the State office building requires 80,000 square feet," Kaufmann added a "Community Fund Trust Agency" that "will need about 100,000 square feet." But even more important, he introduced several other structures to the list of requirements that would either take up much of the space occupied by the park's historical features or have to be located in the area slated for redevelopment. These included, first and foremost, a building to house "the Civic Opera," an institution that was a particular favorite of Kaufmann's. Kaufmann wanted it to be designed for outdoor performances but to be able to be "closed up for inclement weather." It was to seat ten thousand people. There was also to be a small theater seating about one thousand and an even smaller one with three hundred seats. There was to be a "Sports Arena" with a minimum seating capacity of fifteen thousand and an "Exhibition Hall for the Industrial" containing approximately one hundred thousand square feet. Finally, Kaufmann expected that there would be a significant parking component since he sent along with the letter and other visual materials a copy of the "Parking Study of the Pittsburgh Central Business District" published the previous year.[107]

Not satisfied that he had given his architect enough to consider, Kaufmann sent Wright another letter less than a week later with "additional thoughts for the project." These included "a moving picture theatre, a radio and television station, a hotel, from two to three hundred rooms, a landing platform for the future helicopter or other planes which can land on a limited area, [and] a bus terminal for twenty-five to thirty busses at a time loading and unloading." As if this was still not enough, Kaufmann ended by suggesting that the railroad tracks on the Allegheny River side of the proposed park area, scheduled for removal, should perhaps be retained and redesigned for passenger service.[108] Not only had Kaufmann thus taken extraordinary liberties with what the ACCD and the Urban Redevelopment Authority envisaged for the Point; he had made it impossible for his architect to distinguish clearly between the two different parts of the site, that is, the part set aside for a state park and that for commercial redevelopment. In addition, by suggesting the retention of the railroad tracks, he had given Wright the impression that nothing was sacred — that anything and everything was possible.[109]

It is questionable whether Wright put any thoughts on paper until he returned home from a trip to Pittsburgh on 8 March 1947 to study the site and meet with the members of the ACCD's PPC and Study Committee on Architecture and Design.[110] This visit was preceded just two days before by that of a group of representatives of Equitable Life, the effect of which would ultimately undermine any possibility of Wright's fulfilling the civic program for the expanded Point site laid out by Kaufmann. The group of four Equitable executives came away from their visit with significant concerns regarding the profitability of the combined residential-commercial development city officials were proposing.[111] They subsequently sent Robert W. Dowling (1896–1973), president of New York's largest real estate and investment firm, City Investing Company, and Andrew J. Eken (1882–1965), of Starrett Bros. & Eken, planners and builders of numerous insurance company housing projects, to advise them on the feasibility of redeveloping the twenty-three-acre site adjacent to the proposed Point Park to include "a great garden apartment project." Dowling and Eken concluded that such a downtown area was inappropriate for residential use and that Equitable should only consider developing it for commercial office space. The city's agreement to

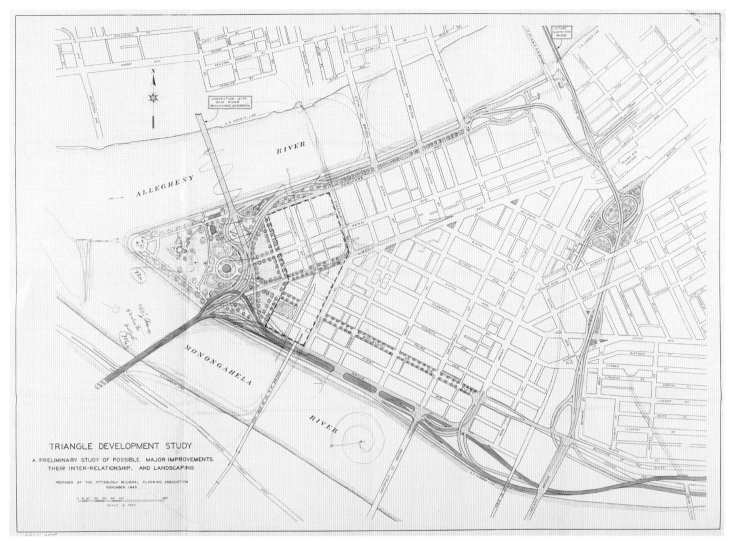

TRIANGLE DEVELOPMENT STUDY

A PRELIMINARY STUDY OF POSSIBLE MAJOR IMPROVEMENTS
THEIR INTER-RELATIONSHIP, AND LANDSCAPING

PREPARED BY THE PITTSBURGH REGIONAL PLANNING ASSOCIATION
NOVEMBER 1945

SCALE IN FEET

9.19

9.19. Point Park Civic Center project, Pittsburgh, Wright, 1947. First scheme.
Preliminary notations by Wright on Griswold-Stotz-McNeil-Richardson Scheme A
Triangle Development Study (dashed red line indicates twenty-three-acre redevelop-
ment area)

go ahead on this basis led the editors of *Architectural Forum* to declare, "That morning [in Pittsburgh, when Dowling and Eken toured the Point] was born the most revolutionary new idea for business district redevelopment since the planning of Rockefeller Center."[112]

Two of the three newspaper reports on Wright's March visit led with references to the architect's remarks about Pittsburgh twelve years before, when he suggested it would be better to abandon the city than to rebuild it. The one in the *Pittsburgh Press* made the comments seem even more sensational by claiming that Wright had wanted to "tear down its buildings."[113] The same report also noted, however, that in the architect's lunch meeting with the representatives of the ACCD at the city's prestigious Duquesne Club, he "made a blanket apology for his past remarks." Saying he was "'sorry [he] made them,'" Wright characterized Pittsburgh as "'a dynamic town … coming into a new era.'"[114] He was clearly trying to please.

Wright's day in Pittsburgh included a site visit of the Point as well as a survey of it from the top of Mt. Washington, on the South Side (see figure 9.1), and from the city's West End, across the Ohio River. Not much more is known about what transpired. According to a later account, one of the "civic leaders" at the occasion said that Wright "'was told that Pittsburgh should have a place like Tivoli (Gardens), in the heart of Copenhagen.'" "'We were thinking of something to attract great crowds of people,'" he added, "'not just once or twice in a lifetime, but time and time again.'"[115] This ties in with a number of the earlier suggestions for Point Park already discussed. At the Duquesne Club lunch, according to Park Martin's recollection of the event, Wright "asked for a free hand" in developing his overall "conception," and the PPC agreed to give him "full latitude to prepare [his] concept and treatment of the Point Park in whatever scale of magnitude [he] conceived."[116] In return, Wright "agreed, to prepare also … a study of a very simple treatment of the [Point Park] area keeping in mind the historical value of the site."[117] Just a few days after the event, however, Kaufmann remembered things differently. One of the two schemes was to be "for the Point Park proper" and the other "for the Point Park plus the twenty-three [redevelopment] acres."[118] This was such an important difference that it is difficult to know how the recollections could have been so at odds with one another or what may have motivated such a divergence.

Wright remembered the occasion still differently, tending to forget the agreement regarding a second, more "simple" scheme. He later claimed that in addition to the design for Point Park, which he "was to project in sketch form," he also suggested to those present two other possible schemes: a "housing project" for "the high ground across the river," opposite the Point, and "a tall shaft rising from the river" at the base of Mt. Washington that would take people up to a "hill top country club." These, he felt, would create a synergy working to the "great advantage" of "Pittsburgh as a whole," although no one else seems to have thought these schemes worth pursuing.[119] Neither Wright nor Kaufmann, nor Martin, nor anyone else involved in the project ever mentioned a budget, or at least there is no record of any such conversation.

Wright apparently showed no drawings and gave no specific indications of what he had in mind. There are no minutes of the lunch meeting, so one has to rely on press reports to get a sense of the general feeling or atmosphere and how Wright's presentation was received. Martin, a transportation engineer by training who had worked in the Allegheny County Authority for a decade before becoming executive director of the ACCD, acted as the conference's spokesperson. According to the story in the *Pittsburgh Press*, he simply reported that Wright "had been retained in an 'advisory' capacity for the proposed Point Park."[120] Beyond that, Martin's reaction was extremely guarded. To the reporter for the *Pittsburgh Sun-Telegraph* he said, "'Since the Point Park is a state project, financed by the Commonwealth and under its jurisdiction, state engineers and architects, in co-operation with the local authorities and civic groups working through the Allegheny Conference, will have the final responsibility and decision for the over-all park plan.'" To the reporter for the *Pittsburgh Press*, he said more ominously, "'We will take his [Wright's] plans for what they are worth.'"[121] The plans were expected to arrive in Pittsburgh in two months, but, as that time neared, Wright suggested to Kaufmann that a group from the ACCD come to Taliesin West to see them prior to any formal presentation in the city.[122]

Design and Reception of Wright's Point Park Civic Center

Wright probably began working on the drawings for Point Park just before the middle of March 1947. At this stage he gave no thought to the "simple treatment" but only worked up the project done with "full latitude" and at a "scale of magnitude" appropriate to visualizing his overall

9.20

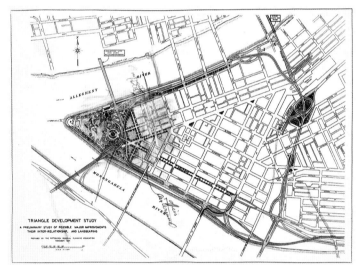

9.21

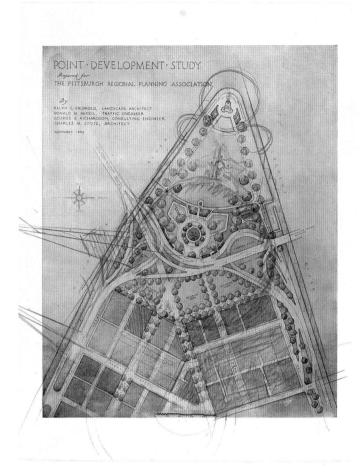

9.22

9.20. Traffic flow map of Pittsburgh, Bureau of Traffic Planning, November 1944

9.21. Point Park Civic Center project. First scheme. Preliminary notations by Wright on Griswold-Stotz-McNeil-Richardson Triangle Development Study

9.22. Point Park Civic Center project. First scheme. Diagram drawn over Griswold-Stotz-McNeil-Richardson plan of Scheme A

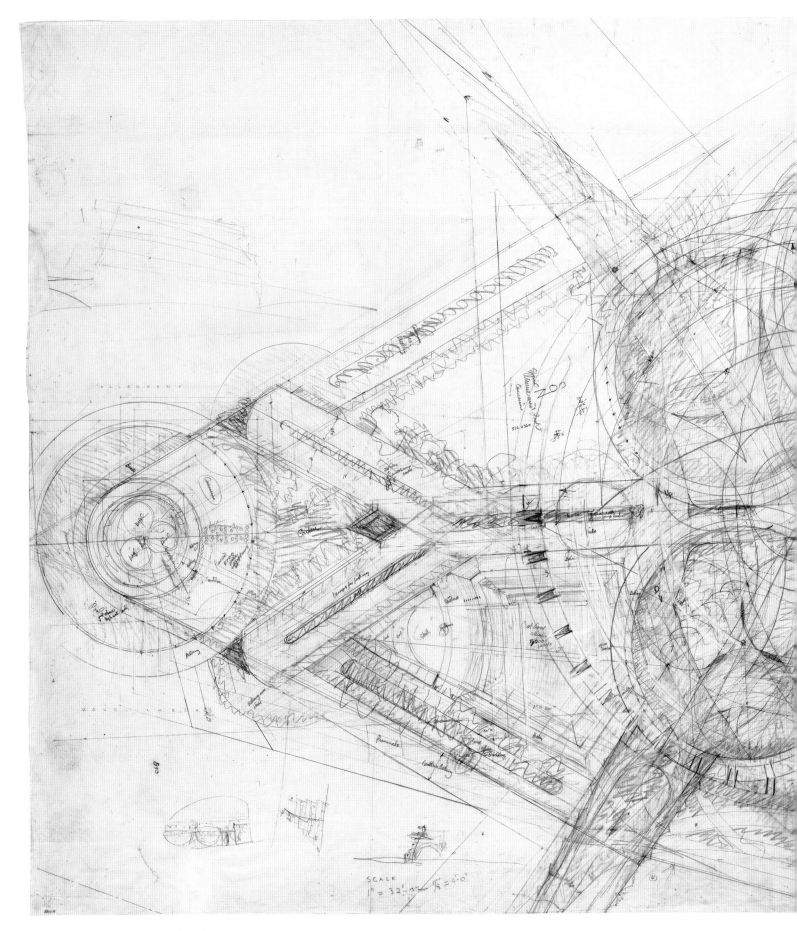

9.23. Point Park Civic Center project. First scheme. Sketch plan drawn over city street plan

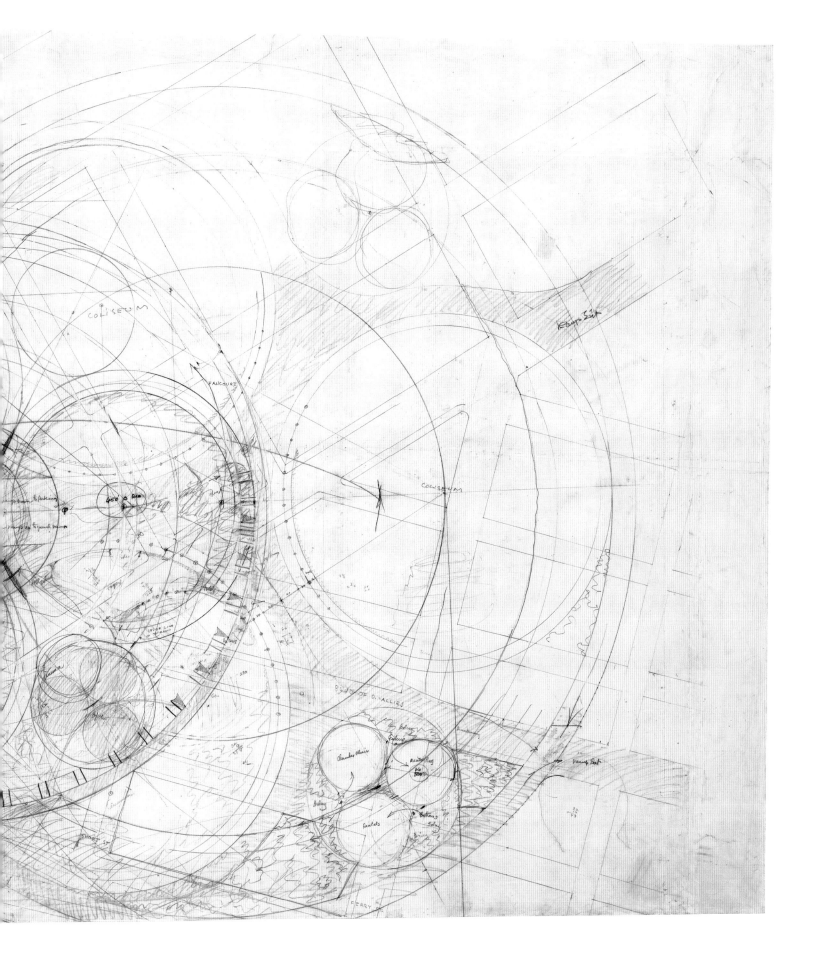

"conception." Furthermore, it was not just for the thirty-six-acre park site but "for the Point Park plus the twenty-three acres" slated for redevelopment that Kaufmann remembered as being one of the two options the architect was to consider.

Since there is no record of any discussion regarding program other than the desiderata Kaufmann had outlined to Wright, we can only assume that these constituted the official program that led Wright to conceive the complex as a civic center. We also have a good sense of the documents the architect had to work with, since a number are either preserved in the Wright Foundation Archives or are referred to in correspondence. Before the architect's visit with the ACCD committees in March, Kaufmann sent Wright a map of the Point area indicating street elevations; blueprints of two of the pier abutments of the existing Point Bridge showing substratum conditions; two aerial photographs of the Triangle and Point, one taken from the east and the other from the west; a map of the twenty-three-acre redevelopment area showing existing buildings and their heights; and the 1945–46 "Parking Study of the Pittsburgh Central Business District," which contained numerous maps, plans, and charts.[123]

Wright also received either from Kaufmann, Martin, or Richards several other important documents. Among those in the Wright Foundation Archives are a map showing the traffic flow through Pittsburgh produced by the city's Bureau of Traffic Planning in 1944 (figure 9.20); the Griswold-Stotz-McNeil-Richardson Scheme A plans for Point Park and for the overall development of the Triangle, both of which have overdrawing by Wright (figures 9.21–22); a large colored version of their plan for the development of the entire Triangle, with the redevelopment area outlined in red (figure 9.19); a chart showing the number of floods in Pittsburgh since 1900, which may have come with a copy of Donald McNeil's 1945 "Report on Point Development Study for Pittsburgh Regional Planning Association: Traffic Analysis"; a colored plan of the northern section of the proposed Crosstown Thoroughfare; and a map of proposed new roads published in the ACCD's 1945 "Report No. 1 on Major Highway Projects in the County of Allegheny."[124] In addition, Wright obtained a copy of the Moses *Arterial Plan for Pittsburgh* from Moses himself, with whom he shared the speakers' platform at a conference on "Planning Man's Physical Environment" at Princeton University just two days prior to the 8 March Pittsburgh visit.[125]

The number, size, and degree of finish of the drawings Wright's office produced for the Point Park project in little over six weeks speak forcefully of the seriousness with which the architect viewed the job as well as the sense of confidence he had in its actually getting built. There are more than fifty extant drawings for this first phase of the process alone (with an equal number for the later, scaled-back version). Many of the drawings are between six and eight feet wide by three to three and a half feet high. One of the preliminary sketches is almost eight and a half feet wide (figure 9.23); almost all the plans of the main structure were split along the central east-west axis of the site so as not to be too unmanageable to handle (figures 9.29–34).

All the preliminary or preparatory drawings reveal that Wright proceeded directly from the givens of the site, the program, and, in particular, the development study the team of Griswold, Stotz, McNeil, and Richardson produced eighteen months before. He also made, as that earlier design did, the problem of automobile traffic the overriding cause for most formal decisions. But unlike the 1945 Scheme A, Wright gave nearly equal importance to the parked as to the moving car and no importance whatsoever to the historical remains at the site. While the Griswold-Stotz-McNeil-Richardson solution was a traditional landscaped park, featuring a series of historical incidents, framed and embraced by a highway interchange, Wright's solution was a traffic interchange and parking facility extruded into a megastructure, part building and part park. It was also, programmatically, much more than an elitist memorial park designed essentially in relation to the downtown business community. Planned to provide "all civic enterprises of a cultural nature for the citizens of Pittsburgh," Wright's Point Park Civic Center was deliberately and consciously intended to offer "entertainment for the urban multitudes" coming from far and wide.[126]

Five preliminary studies by Wright have come to light. In addition to the large sketch referred to above, which has previously been published (figure 9.23), there are four much less well-known items consisting of copies of the Griswold-Stotz-McNeil-Richardson plans with notations and/or overdrawing by Wright. At least three of these are possibly earlier than the large sketch, while the fourth is probably later. Two of the earlier ones color code the loop road system around the Golden Triangle, differentiating the purely local thoroughfares from the double-decked Water Street that skirts the Monongahela before crossing the proposed Fort Pitt Bridge. Color is also laid over the parks through which the roads pass. The larger of these plans (figure 9.19) has the twenty-three-acre redevelopment area outlined in red. The smaller of the two (figure 9.21), which has rubbed out pencil marks over that area, also gives evidence that Wright was not too happy about the exact location of the proposed Fort Pitt Bridge. Lines next to it indicate that he wanted to crank it east about thirty degrees to make it perpendicular to the shoreline, like its complement on the Allegheny side. These may seem like minor points, but they reveal the fact that Wright made no fundamental changes to the officially sanctioned traffic and redevelopment proposals. In removing the bridges from the Point, displacing them upstream, and demolishing everything on the Point up to the eastern boundary of the redevelopment area at Stanwix Street, Wright was simply following what had previously been decided rather than devising on his own, as many historians have claimed, such drastic interventions in the urban topography of the city.[127]

One of the most interesting of the Griswold-Stotz-McNeil-Richardson plans with overdrawing by Wright is that of Scheme A for the park itself (figure 9.22). Using red pencil, Wright boldly superimposed on the earlier design an outline of what he planned to do. In the center of the triangular site is a large circle encompassing the highway interchange, Fort Pitt, the Blockhouse, and most of the area between the interchange and the redevelopment site, which the circle in part overlaps. Almost tangent to the Monongahela and Allegheny shorelines, the circle incorporates the bridge approaches. These link up with an integral riverside parkway, or promenade, system indicated by lines drawn entirely around the Point. The Point itself is prominently outlined by a large circle in the center of which is a smudge, probably indicating a fountain in more or less the same spot as the Griswold-Stotz-McNeil-Richardson trilobed one. Appended to this circle, on the upstream edges, are two half circles, echoing and expanding on the underlying design. A narrow structure, terminating in a lozenge, points from the main circle to the circles at the apex, while a large courtyarded structure balances the composition at the northeast corner of the redevelopment area. This latter element is linked to the North and South Sides of the city by new bridges, while the proposed Fort Pitt Bridge is cranked almost sixty degrees to the east.[128]

As in the Moses plan, which Wright had on his drafting board at the beginning of the design process, the circular form,

like the earlier oval, serves to mediate the city's two differently aligned grids that collide at the Point (figure 9.9).[129] But Wright's circle, which at this stage was nearly double the size of Moses's oval, was not simply a landscape architect's way of filling a void.[130] In addition to its purely formal function, it had a symbolic meaning that related directly to the road system it incorporated. The circular design, when elevated into the third dimension, was based on the helical community cultural and entertainment centers Wright had specified for Broadacre City on the model of the Strong Automobile Objective and Planetarium (figures 6.3–4, 6.15). Conceived as a "gathering place" for visitors arriving by automobile, the curved planes of its reinforced concrete structure were appropriated from the vocabulary of highway engineering. Superimposed on the highway interchange designed by Griswold, Stotz, McNeil, and Richardson, Wright's sketch diagrams his civic center proposition as a "newly spacious means of entertainment for the citizen seated in his motor car" at the same time as it rationalizes the complex road system at the Point in the geometric form of a monumental traffic circle.[131]

The most remarkable of the preliminary sketches is the one that measures four and a half feet high by almost eight and a half feet wide (figure 9.23). Drawn over a greatly enlarged plan of city streets, including the Griswold-Stotz-McNeil-Richardson highway interchange, its sheer size in combination with its explosive energy bear witness to the ambitiousness of Wright's urban project. Like a painting by Jackson Pollock, it records a sequence of gestures not from the wrist but from the whole arm. The first of these outlines a gigantic circle whose midpoint is well to the east of the one finally designated for the civic center's main structure. This allowed the projected megastructure to have a diameter of over seventeen hundred feet, or about a third of a mile, and therefore to encompass all fifty-nine acres of the park and redevelopment area combined. Outlined within this enormous circle are three smaller ones, labeled "coliseums." In their interstices are groupings of three, yet smaller circles. The ones at the lower right-hand corner are indicated as containing recital halls and a room for chamber music concerts.

Wright took advantage of the drawing's size to lay out in scale and at multiple superimposed levels the various individual spaces that would be required to fulfill the program Kaufmann gave him. The large circle that corresponds more or less with the one in the diagrammatic sketch in figure

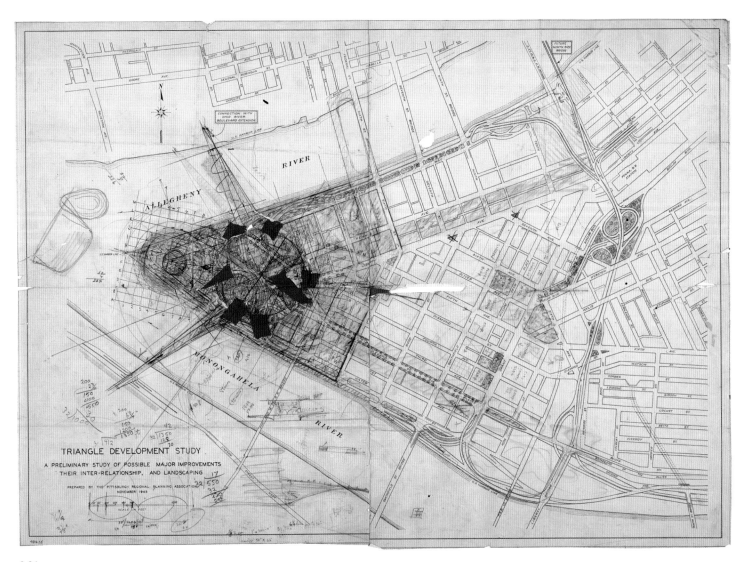

9.24

9.24. Point Park Civic Center project. First scheme. Sketch plan drawn over Griswold-Stotz-McNeil-Richardson Scheme A Triangle Development Study, with section cut out and retaped

9.22 contains three circles tangent to one another and to the outer circumference of the framing figure. Between them are smaller circles, the one in the lower right corner designated for cinemas. In the center, overlapping the tangent circles, is a final circle. The three tangent circles are arranged so that the two toward the apex of the Point are on axis with the new bridges, shown as perpendicular to the shorelines. The circle facing downtown aligns with the main east-west axis of the design. The axis is articulated by a bar-like structure that forks in a sixty-degree angle to embrace a circular figure equal in width to the tangent circles within the main structure. The apical circle, which has a fountain in its center, is surrounded by an inner ring designated for concessions, including a five-thousand-seat restaurant-buffet, and an outer ring containing a swimming pool. In the triangular spaces above and below the forked bar are a zoo (above) and an outdoor concert hall (below). Finally, and perhaps most significant in terms of the historical memories associated with the site, the diamond-shaped element in the crook of the forked bar, which was located farther west in the sketch in figure 9.22 and partially rubbed out, is here highlighted and placed so that it more or less occupies the same position that the similarly shaped westernmost bastion of Fort Duquesne once did. Indeed, in the final project, a five-hundred-foot lighted tower, designated as a "memorial to Fort Duquesne," would rise from this base.[132]

While not all the programmatic elements are denoted on the plan, the indications regarding traffic patterns are fairly specific, with connections between the bridges and the city streets and with proposed underground parking areas indicated by up and down ramps. This concern for linking the civic center to existing and future traffic conditions generated the final preliminary sketch we have (figure 9.24). It is a collage that consists in part of drawing and notations over the Griswold-Stotz-McNeil-Richardson study plan for the entire Triangle and in part of a circular section of that plan that has been cut out, used as a ground for a fairly precisely drawn plan of the civic center, and then replaced and taped onto the original sheet. The bridges are left in their positions on the underlying plan. A grid has been drawn over the circular figure at the apex. There are thumbnail sketches showing how the bridges would join the spiral building forming the main structure of the complex. There are calculations mainly regarding dimensions. And, perhaps most important, there is coloring over the area Wright seems to have considered within his

purview. The main circular building overshoots the designated park site as it did in figures 9.22 and 9.23, but here the area to the east, up to Market and Sixth Streets, is shown as part of the overall conception for the project, which goes even beyond the boundary of the redevelopment area. And a green stretch of park or boulevard between Penn and Liberty Avenues runs from the proposed Point Park Civic Center through downtown to the proposed Crosstown Thoroughfare, where it splits off from its crossing over the Allegheny River to join the Duquesne Way parkway following the river frontage back to the Point.

In his description of the project accompanying the final plans, Wright pointed out the main ideas that generated his design. Some of these have already been referred to, but they are worth repeating in the context of the drawings for which they were intended to serve as a verbal explanation. First, steel and glass, modern materials that Wright noted, in line with Kaufmann, were "special Pittsburgh products," were exploited to create a "newly spacious means of entertainment for the citizen" at the scale of America's new automobile culture. Like the "wide spans" and "sweeping ramps" of modern bridges and highways, the "building-scheme" was to be experienced first and foremost by the "citizen seated in his motor car." No longer the "troublesome burden it has now become to the City," the automobile would be transformed by this civic center into a "pleasurable" means by which to reengage with urban culture and society. And because the project did not call just for a park but had facilities for both outdoor and indoor activities, it could be used during all seasons of the year.[133]

"Entertainment for the citizen" was the watchword of the design. Wright came back to this theme time and again. And the citizen was not merely one of the lucky few who worked downtown. The project, he emphasized, was planned as "natural entertainment for the urban multitudes." "Direct contact of the site with the Allegheny and Monongahela rivers" was to feature as an important part of the experience, but the "entertainment" was to involve an even greater immersion in the various possibilities for urban cultural activities. "All civic enterprises of a cultural nature for the citizens of Pittsburgh are amply provided for," Wright wrote. These ranged from the more highbrow forms of grand opera and symphony concerts to the middlebrow ones of light opera and summertime pop concerts to movies, sports events, swimming, and taking the children to the zoo, aquarium, or planetarium. And while

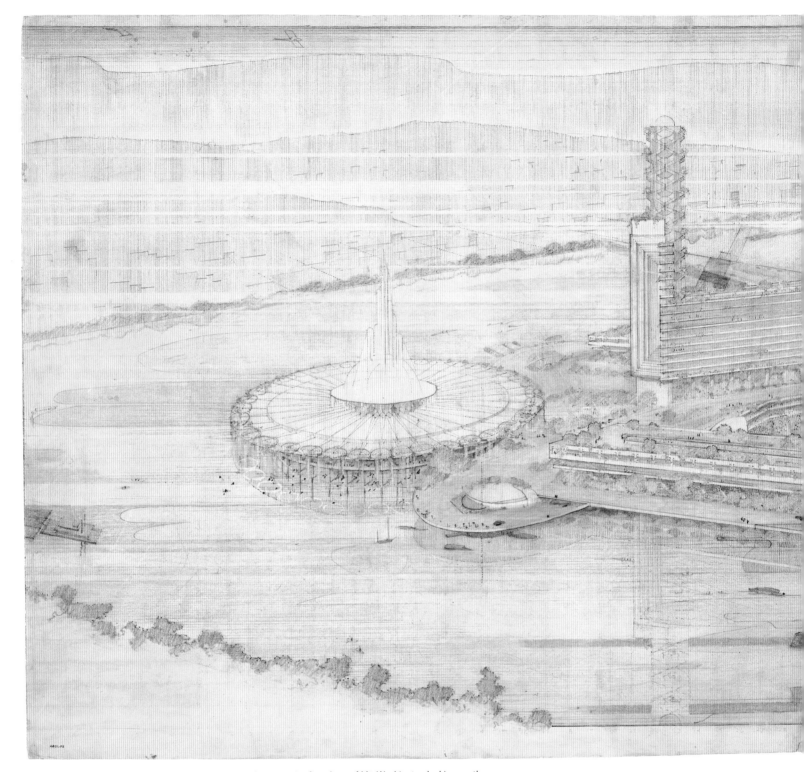

9.25. Point Park Civic Center project. First scheme. Aerial perspective from base of Mt. Washington looking north

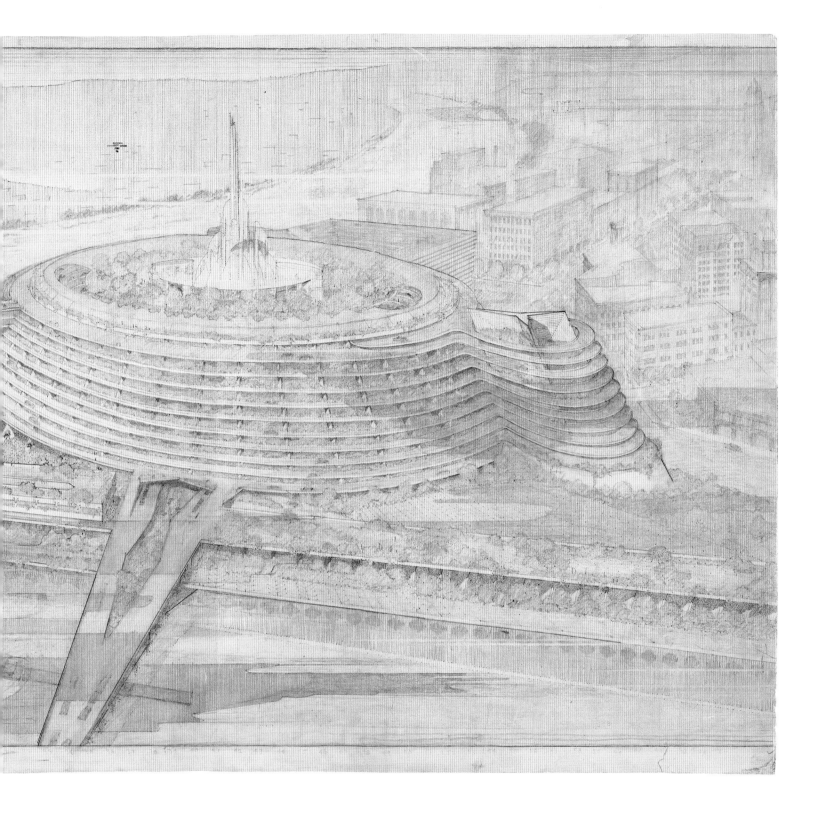

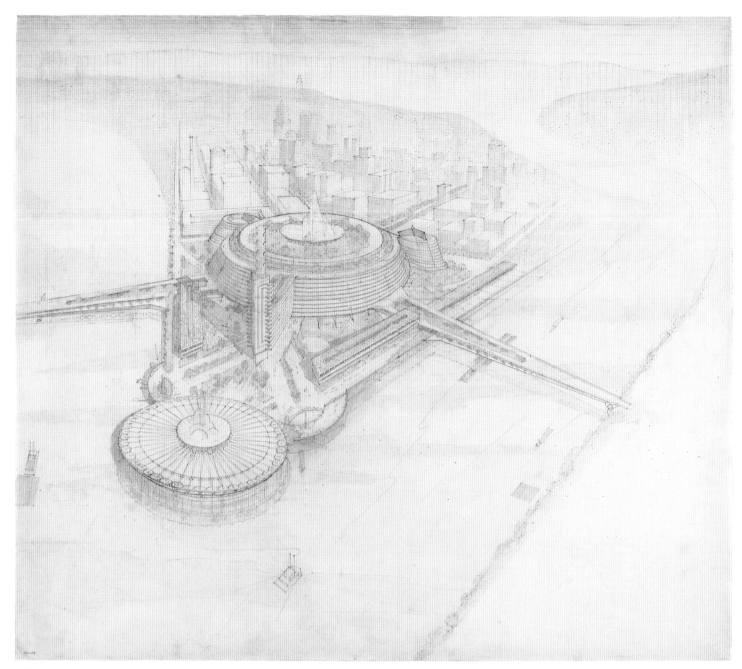

9.26

9.26. Point Park Civic Center project. First scheme. Aerial perspective from Mt.
Washington looking east-northeast

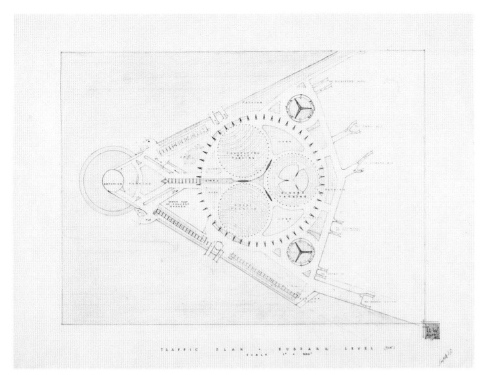

9.27

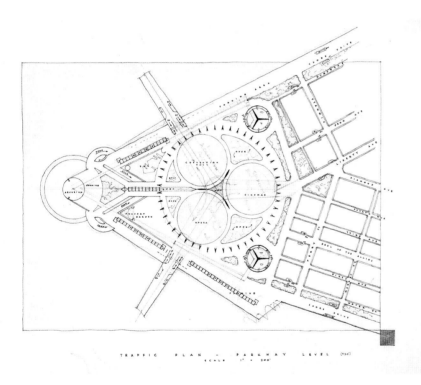

9.28

9.27. Point Park Civic Center project. First scheme. Traffic plan, sub-park level (datum 714'), 20 April 1947

9.28. Point Park Civic Center project. First scheme. Traffic plan, parkway level (datum 730')

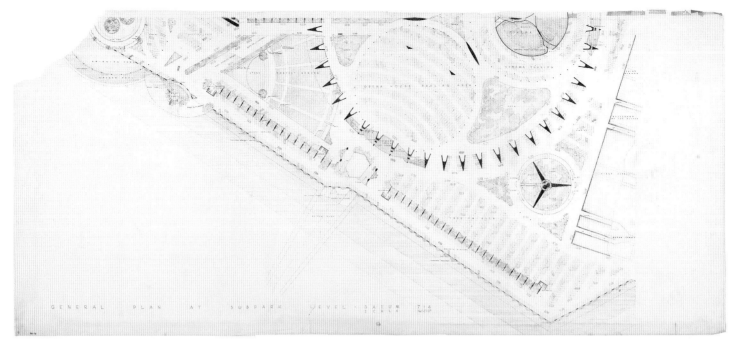

9.29

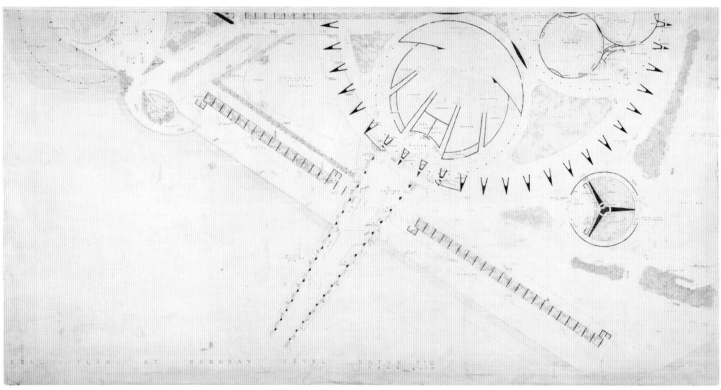

9.30

9.29. Point Park Civic Center project. First scheme. Half plan, sub-park level
(datum 714')

9.30. Point Park Civic Center project. First scheme. Half plan, parkway level
(datum 730')

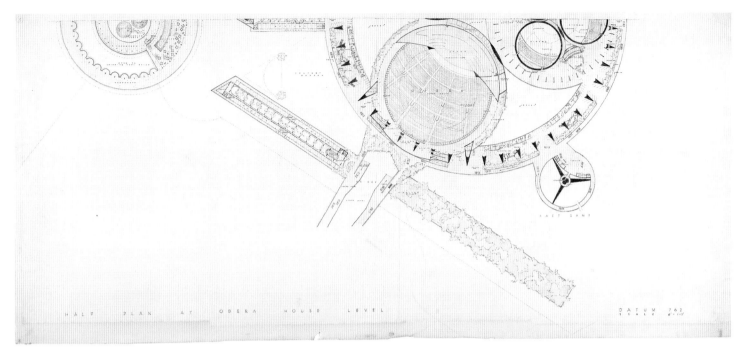

9.31

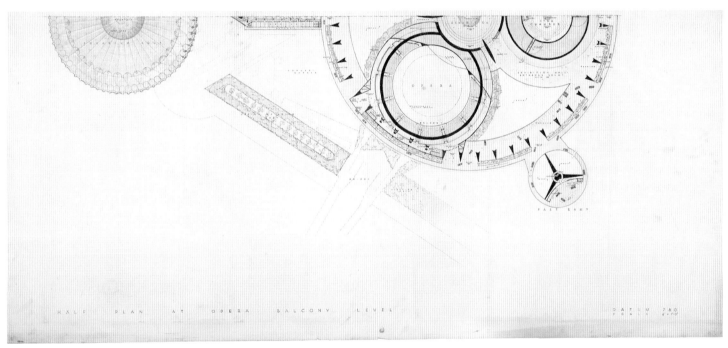

9.32

9.31. Point Park Civic Center project. First scheme. Half plan, opera house level (datum 762')

9.32. Point Park Civic Center project. First scheme. Half plan, opera house balcony level (datum 780')

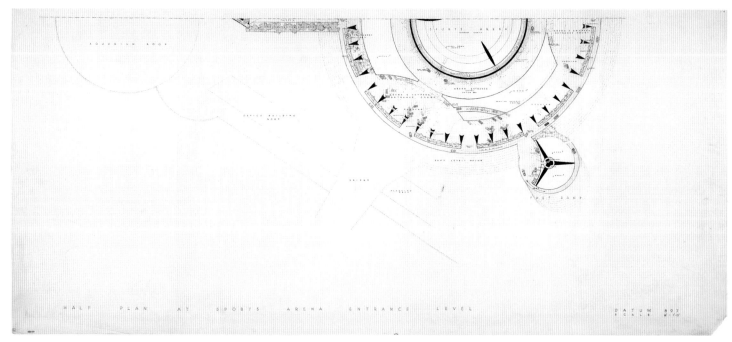

9.33

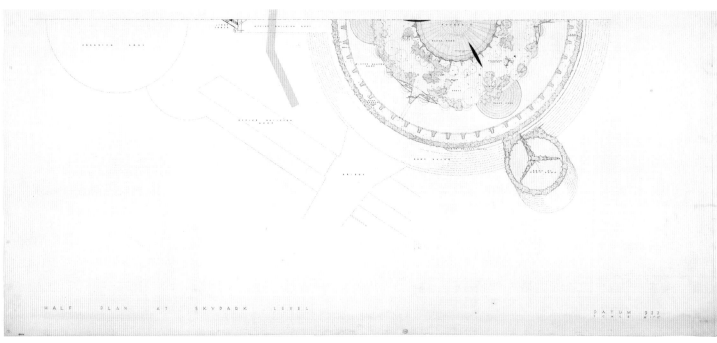

9.34

9.33. Point Park Civic Center project. First scheme. Half plan, sports arena entrance level (datum 897′)

9.34. Point Park Civic Center project. First scheme. Half plan, sports arena skypark (roof) level (datum 922′)

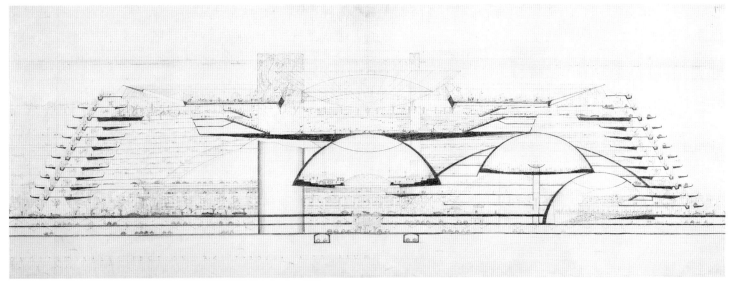

9.35

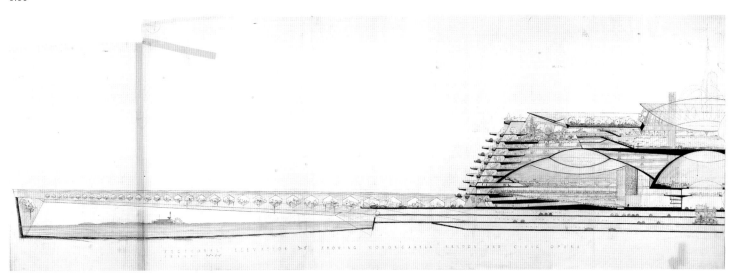

9.36

9.35. Point Park Civic Center project. First scheme. Longitudinal section of main structure along east-west axis

9.36. Point Park Civic Center project. First scheme. Half-section of main structure along northeast-southwest axis (paralleling Monongahela Bridge), showing elevation of bridge and interior of opera house

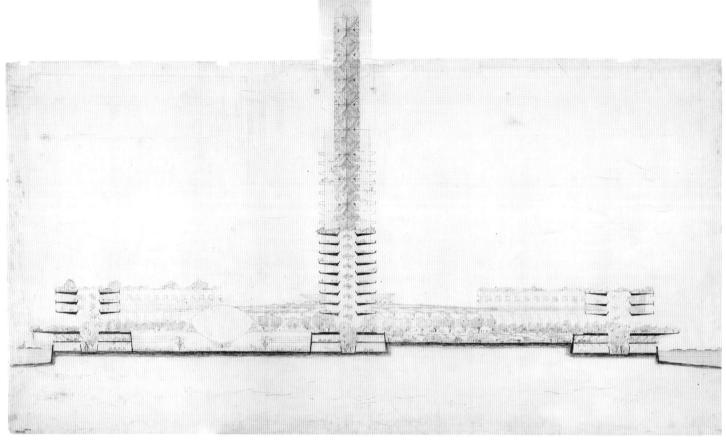

9.37

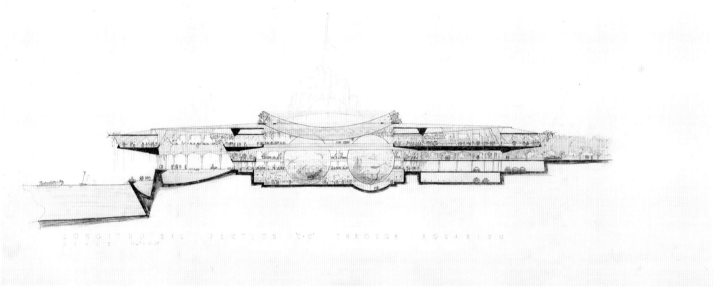

9.38

9.37. Point Park Civic Center project. First scheme. North-south section through lateral office buildings, tower, concert garden, and zoo looking west

9.38. Point Park Civic Center project. First scheme. Longitudinal section through aquarium and restaurant at apex of Point

there was to be a major convention hall and industrial exhibition space for the business community plus office space for government agencies at the federal, county, and state levels, all of which would help pay for the project, it was the facilities for the "average" citizen to which Wright gave special attention. Both inside the main structure and outside in the surrounding gardens were "several hundred commercial concessions" ranging from "hamburg stands, candy, [and] soft drinks to flowers, books, curios, infinite gadgetry and personal services." Predicting the malls that were to become popular in the decades to follow, Wright wrote that the atrium space of the main structure would "resemble a county fair."[134]

And just as in later malls, automobile access and parking were the fundamental basis for the large-scale, wide appeal of the concept. Numbers figured prominently in Wright's description. The sports arena was to have twenty thousand seats; the opera house, anywhere from ten to twenty thousand; the convention hall, space for twelve thousand five hundred; and the restaurant at the Point, space for fifteen hundred people. Each of these venues was to have its own enclosed parking adjacent to it. Much of the short-term parking was to be on the ramp serving as the access route leading directly from the bridges or city streets to the place in the megastructure where the activity was located. The parking for the upper-level sports arena, for example, was eleven to twelve stories above the ground. The ramp that formed the outer structure of the building was designed to accommodate three thousand moving vehicles at a time.

Overall, there were to be ninety-two acres of parking, almost all of it enclosed, either aboveground or belowground. This would have provided enough new spaces to satisfy the demand of the 1945–46 "Parking Study" for the *entire* downtown area. The total number of people the design could accommodate just in its main structure, "seated in audience or in cars on ramps," was 123,000, which was about one-fifth of the city's population at the time.[135] Perhaps realizing how such numbers might alarm the civic leaders who were thinking more of a memorial park than a concrete parking lot, Wright ended his description with the following words: "The entire scheme is arranged with adequate trees, shrubs, grass, and gardening, all of which taken in connection with the broad expanse of flowing river-surface render the whole architectural mass gentle and humane."[136]

While we have the verbal description that Wright prepared for the representatives of the ACCD who went to Taliesin West at the beginning of the second week of May 1947 to review the design, we have no firm evidence of which drawings he showed them. He must have presented a fairly large number due to the size and complexity of the project. There can be little doubt that at least one and perhaps two aerial perspectives were among them (figures 9.25–26). He may also have shown at least one of the two so-called traffic plans, which are the only ones that include the entire site (figures 9.27–28). To give a sense of the different major venues such as the opera house and convention hall, Wright probably brought out the plans of the south half of the main structure since those represent the more complete of the half-plan sets (figures 9.29–34). To reveal how all the interior spaces interconnected with one another and how they accommodated the various functions, he would certainly have presented the several sections taken through different parts of the site (figures 9.35–38). Among these is one through the proposed bridge spanning the Monongahela, which constitutes the only real elevation we have (figure 9.39). Complete with hot-air balloons and a blimp hovering above, the festive civic center, seen from the base of Mt. Washington, is reflected in the river.

The most striking feature of the project by virtue of its size and distinctive shape is the circular structure occupying most of the eastern part of the site (figures 9.25–26). It is drawn in stark and dramatic contrast to the "jumble of buildings" forming the nondescript skyline of the city's downtown business district, with the distant tower of the Cathedral of Learning standing out against the hills. Like its model, the Broadacre City community center, this ziggurat structure is composed of a helical ramp providing automobile access to the various programmed spaces within it. Here the ramp also leads to a rooftop garden, called a "skypark," in the center of which is a towering fountain and around the outer circumference of which, a level below, is a glass-enclosed winter garden.

The ramp winds through approximately eleven turns to reach a height of a little over 175 feet above street level. The total height of the structure is nearly 250 feet, dwarfing most of the nearby office blocks. The ziggurat decreases in width from about 1,220 feet at its base to about 900 feet near its top.[137] Appended like ears to its city side are two narrower ramped structures for speedier access to the upper levels; while projecting toward the apex of the Point is a thin ten-story office block ending in the 500-foot-tall shaft dedicated to Fort Duquesne.

If the circular ziggurat is the most conspicuous element of the design, it is also evident, especially in the aerial perspective in figure 9.26, that it does not stand alone but is the nucleus of a widespread tentacular structure that reaches across both rivers to link the central building with the regional highway network (figure 9.20). The ziggurat is in fact, both physically and metaphorically, the extrusion, in the form of a building, of the interchange between the two new bridges, which are shown as integral aspects of the overall conception. Whether viewed as extended legs or stabilizing outriggers, the multilevel, open-decked tubular bridges read as supports for the building, which in turn floats above them and receives its main influx of visitors through the arterial connections they form.

Traffic and parking were the main generators of the ziggurat's design. The two new bridges are critical to the organization and functioning of the structure. Their multilevel design differentiates between trucks, cars, and pedestrians as the bridges angle down from the opposite shores to funnel vehicles into the building (figure 9.36). Just before reaching the ziggurat, the double-height roadbed splits into a series of internal ramps that provide for through traffic, truck deliveries, long-term underground parking, as well as vehicles and pedestrians visiting the building and wanting to avail themselves of the short-term parking facilities along its circumferential spiral ramp (figures 9.28–30). The section in figure 9.36 shows the four levels coming off the bridge: the top one entering the spiral ramp at street level, the one below at the first underground parking level (figure 9.27), the next one down at the second underground parking level, and the one farthest down descending into the tunnel that runs under the entire ziggurat (figure 9.35), to handle through traffic headed either for the other bridge or for the downtown city streets (figure 9.28).

Wright's presentation perspectives privilege the view of his Point Park Civic Center from across the river, either at a distance—from the top of Mt. Washington (figure 9.26)—or closer up—near the spot where visitors arriving from the south (and airport) would get their first dramatic glimpse of the Point upon emerging from the Fort Pitt Tunnel (figures 9.16, 9.25). In these images, the architect certainly captured the hope, earlier expressed by Macartney, that "'some great

building ... erected near The Point ... would let the traveler know ... that this is Pittsburgh.'"

The approach to the civic center and park from the east, while less comprehensible as a single image, would have been equally spectacular and enticing, although in different ways. The two shoreline drives, Water Street on the south and Duquesne Boulevard on the north, both continue straight into the park, passing under the new bridges and alongside floating boat basins before arriving at the aquarium-restaurant-entertainment pavilion at the Point's apex. Along the way there is ample parking plus continuous views out over the rivers (figures 9.30, 9.28). For automobiles and pedestrians entering the complex from the downtown city streets, the two narrow "fast ramps," as Wright called them, frame the composition as a kind of gateway. Automobiles could use them to go directly to an event in the main structure, or proceed along a number of roads around the ziggurat, or even enter directly the space itself. The section along the main east-west axis in figure 9.35 shows cars sharing the ground-floor space of the atrium court with pedestrians, and masses of trees in the landscaped inner courts. Pedestrians enter the site more or less the same way as the cars but have a much greater freedom of choice as to which path to take into the main structure. The lowest level of the encircling ramp is raised on *pilotis*-like fins, leaving the ground level entirely unenclosed and accessible by foot around most of its perimeter (figures 9.28, 9.26).

While appearing massive and monumental from the outside, the civic center's main structure is in fact quite open, porous, and filled with light and air (figures 9.35, 9.39). Indeed, unlike the Mesopotamian ziggurat from which it ultimately derives its spiral form (via Renaissance reconstructions of the legendary Tower of Babel [figure 9.40]), and unlike Wright's own earlier adaptations of the model (figure 6.3), the Pittsburgh ziggurat is not solid. It maintains only the exterior skeleton of the form surrounding an atrium court, thus creating a new form of ziggurat-coliseum hybrid (figures 9.41, 9.25). The encasing reinforced concrete ramp is cantilevered from both sides of the angled fins. The shallower projection to the outside was meant for moving traffic (on a one-way system of alternating levels) and the deeper trays facing the interior for short-term parking. Light and air penetrate the mounting horizontal layers while a continuous skylight encircling the space, just inside the topmost parking level, allows daylight to enter from above.

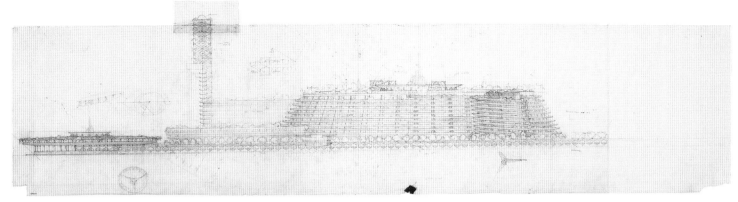

9.39

9.40

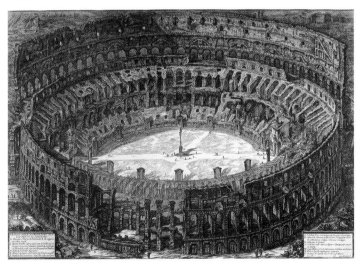

9.41

9.39. Point Park Civic Center project. First scheme. South elevation, with section through Monongahela Bridge

9.40. Pieter Brueghel the Elder, *Tower of Babel*, 1563. Kunsthistorisches Museum, Vienna

9.41. Giovanni Battista Piranesi, *View of the Flavian Amphitheater, Known as the Colosseum* (built 72–80). From Piranesi, *Verdute di Roma*, 1776. Harvard University Art Museums

Within the atrium space are domed shells containing the main programmatic elements. The three most significant are the 10,000- to 20,000-seat opera house, the nearly equally spacious convention hall, and the triplex cinema, with approximately 4,500 seats in all (figures 9.28, 9.31). The opera house and the convention hall are located at street level and have their own dedicated parking beneath as well as on the contiguous ramps; the three back-to-back movie theaters begin below ground level, where they are surrounded by parking (figures 9.29, 9.35). Suspended above and in between the domes covering these spaces are two other domed shells, supported by the three lens-shaped piers that form the independent internal structure of the building and contain the heating, ventilating, and utility ducts. Above the cinemaplex is a planetarium, a relatively small space, with banked perimeter seating (figures 9.32, 9.35). It is reached by a ramp leading down from a curved bridge that links the outer ramp to an exhibition hall for arts, crafts, and industry, which floats above the center of the atrium.

Directly above the exhibition hall, which opens to the space below by means of a glass dome inset in the floor, is the single largest venue in the structure in terms of square footage. This is the twenty-thousand-seat sports arena or stadium, which occupies four levels just below the roof garden and glass-bottomed fountain (figures 9.33–35). Planned to be used for major sports events featuring the Pittsburgh Steelers football team and the Pittsburgh Hornets hockey club, the space could, according to Wright, also be converted into a skating rink or circus (the section in figure 9.35 shows a hockey game in progress). The glass dome over the playing field is encircled by a clerestory, which in turn looks out on the expansive roof garden surrounding the dome (figure 9.34). Within the central glass bowl is a fountain, while the garden itself has a helicopter landing pad as well as moorings for dirigibles and hot-air balloons (figures 9.25, 9.39). Wright noted that the "excitement" provided by the dirigibles and balloons could be increased by the addition of "parachute jumping."[138] The outer edge of the roof garden is composed of a sloping plane of glass that brings natural light into the lower, two-level annular winter garden that runs close to the outside perimeter of the structure. Concession stands for fast food, drinks, amusements, and games, along with all sorts of other shopping and entertainment facilities, line the outer edge of the winter garden as they do much of the length of the ramp, giving to the atrium

space a lively, down-to-earth, commercial quality that Wright likened both to a "county fair" and a "street fair."[139]

Trying to imagine the experience of this ziggurat-coliseum is not easy. Wright's descriptions emphasize the fluidity of movement from vehicular to foot traffic and the lack of distinction between the spaces for the two. Cars and people coexist at all levels and in all places. Wright assumed that much of the time spent in the building would be in one's "motor car" and believed that this was "a pleasurable use of that modern implement." He stressed the immediate access to parking for each venue and characterized the "scale" resulting from the incorporation of the automobile at every level as consonant with the provision of "entertainment for the urban multitudes." Though enormous and even cavernous compared to the typical later twentieth-century mall that in one way or another is modeled on it, the main building of the Pittsburgh civic center is nowhere near as enclosed as its successors. Not only does light flood the space from above; it also penetrates through the continuously open horizontal planes of the surrounding ramp. As it winds around on itself, this four-and-a-half-mile-long "street in the air" allows people to look across the space and feel a sense of the community they are part of at the same time as it affords panoramic views of the city and surrounding landscape.

While many visitors to the civic center would go exclusively to the main building for a specific event, many others, attracted to it as a destination point, would use it as a place from which to investigate the rest of the complex and take advantage of its facilities. Still others, like those working in the state, county, and municipal office buildings, might only enter it on an occasional basis.[140] All these other elements are located to the west of the bridges and ziggurat-coliseum. Wright designed three separate units to contain the required office space. Just to the west of the two new bridges are identical, low, two-story structures raised above grade-level parking on piers. Running from the bridge abutments to the boat basins, they are designed around open interior courts, like the lakeside office buildings in the Madison Civic Center, and have continuous balconies along both front and rear facades (figures 9.26, 9.31, 9.37).

Between the two low office blocks and the tall, slender office bar connecting the main building to the Fort Duquesne memorial tower are the outdoor concert garden in the depressed triangle to the south and the zoo in the opposite location on the north. Between them is the ten-story bar, designed to give each office double exposure by means of a central light court on one side and a balcony and view of the river on the other. Rising above its roof garden is the tower, which includes another eight or nine stories of offices. Its angled prow mimics the shape of the westernmost bastion of Fort Duquesne that once existed at that location. Out of it rises a geometrically faceted shaft five hundred feet high. The "light-shaft memorial to Fort Duquesne" was to be mainly glass and to be "equipped for light concerts and broadcast music."[141] Combining references to the Point's eighteenth-century significance with the city's subsequent industrial prowess, the structure would have functioned as a latter-day Eiffel Tower, broadcasting the message of the civic center's role in the rebirth of the city and expressing Kaufmann's vision of a civic symbol in modern materials and form (figure 9.25). Moreover, this precursor of a "son et lumière" show as a permanent feature of a public forum would have given life to the site at night when the downtown was normally dark and quiet.

The most playful, entertaining, and family-oriented part of the civic center was reserved for the site's apex. Here, Wright placed a wide, low circular pavilion overhanging the shoreline so as to be in direct contact with the water (figure 9.38). Partially enclosed in glass and roofed by a festive, tentlike construction topped by another glass-bottomed fountain, the central galleried space under the dome is devoted to an aquarium and an insectary. The aquarium physically places the viewer within the watery domain. At the lowest level a band of water with fish swimming in it encircles the space. But even more dramatic are the two giant glass spheres in the center that allow the visitor to see the most dangerous of the "sea monsters," as Wright wrote, "from below" while looking up to the pendant insectary.[142] At the same level as the aquarium floor is a swimming pool encircling the structure, and just below it, almost at river level, is an overflow pool and outer walkway. An open, upper promenade deck affords views of the rivers on three sides. On the rear, facing Fort Duquesne Tower and the civic center megastructure itself, is a partially cantilevered restaurant with table seating for one thousand people and counter service for five hundred more.

All this would have been extremely difficult to visualize in reality and make sense of by anyone looking at it for the first time, especially by someone not well versed in modern architecture. Wright's design for Point Park and the redevelopment area contiguous with it heeled pretty closely to the program Kaufmann gave him (the amount of office space was actually less than Kaufmann requested). It also spoke to many of the ideas that had been suggested by others during the public debate on the issue over the years. But it came as a shock to the members of the ACCD who visited Wright with Kaufmann at Taliesin West on 7–8 May 1947 to preview the design.[143] We know that Park Martin and Wallace Richards went; there was the possibility that Heinz would join the group on his way to Australia, but it is not known if he did.[144] None of the group except Kaufmann seems to have been prepared for the expanded program and site that Wright understood to be his mandate. Two weeks before, Wright had sent Kaufmann the "captions" of the drawings giving dimensions, square footage, and other particulars. He also said, "When you see the drawings you will get the thrill of your life."[145]

If, as Griswold later recalled, Kaufmann had worked out the project with Wright "without saying anything to anybody," hoping "to spring up a great surprise on the committee—with Frank Lloyd Wright's gorgeous solution of the whole problem," he was sorely mistaken.[146] We have no record of what Richards thought, but we do know how disturbed, even appalled, Martin was by the design. He later described it as "a huge domed affair that looked like a gigantic beehive" and its author, Wright, as "a little crazy."[147] Martin was put off by a number of things, and his dumbfounded reaction to what he saw clearly colored his memory of the presentation. He claimed that when Wright was asked "how he proposed to handle the traffic to and from the bridges," the architect merely "shrugged his shoulders" and said it would be a problem for "the engineers" to worry about. He was aghast at what the project might cost ($150 million, he guessed) and stated that Wright showed no concern on the matter. He was especially worried about the size and scope of the proposed construction since it encroached on the twenty-three acres being reserved for redevelopment and it completely obliterated the historical remains of the two forts and Blockhouse and thus the rationale for the "Point Park which the State by that time was committed to build."[148]

Kaufmann's reactions are unrecorded, although many of those associated with the ACCD implied in later commentaries that he was less than enthusiastic (at least one even claimed "embarrassed") by what he and his architect had wrought.[149] There is no known correspondence between Kaufmann and Wright immediately following the visit. Silence reigned until three weeks after, when Martin finally wrote to the architect outlining where things stood with the conference's executive committee. He said nothing about what he thought of the project. Instead, he told Wright that any idea regarding the use of the area slated for redevelopment should be immediately dropped and all plans done so far "kept confidential." The executive committee, he said, was "deeply concerned" that "if any question should arise as to the ultimate usage of the area beyond its original conception [for commercial redevelopment]," negotiations then in process with property owners and the redevelopers could be compromised and "jeopardize the entire project." He added that the ACCD was never actually in a position to agree, as it had two months before at the Duquesne Club, to Wright's request for "a free hand" in developing his own "conception of a plan." "We [we]re considerably ahead of ourselves in giving you the assignment," he wrote, without any apology. But, he reminded the architect that he had also agreed to produce "a study of a very simple treatment of the area keeping in mind the historical value of the site." Without any further reference to the project he and others had just seen, Martin urged Wright to turn his attention to the "simple plan idea" as soon as possible.[150]

As one might imagine, Wright was outraged by the deception he had suffered: how was he to have known that the redevelopment area was out-of-bounds and that the goal of a monument symbolizing the "spirit of foresight and adventuresomeness" was not actually written into the ACCD's program? Still, he kept his feelings in check so that something might yet come of the venture. After drafting the beginning of a response to Martin on a rather personally sarcastic note, Wright wrote to say that he agreed "to go on investing more 'libido' in the cause if only I can understand more clearly what you mean by 'the Historical value of the site.'"[151] To Kaufmann he wrote a month later saying that he felt that no one else in the ACCD was interested in what he, Wright, had to say—or was even listening: "So far they have shown a singular indifference."[152] The reaction to a second scheme he produced by the beginning of December would be similar. No doubt this was because, though simpler, it was by no means "simple."

Wright's Second Scheme for Point Park and Its Dismissal

Martin's way of informing Wright about the historical importance of the Point was to send him a copy of the "Report of the Study Committee on the Historical Significance of the Point Park Project" that Oliver had presented at the same mid-April

1946 meeting of the PPC where Kaufmann had proposed a park looking toward the future rather than "conceived and executed primarily as a memorial to the past." Oliver saw the significance of the Point, and therefore the park, in essentially historical terms. Calling it "sacred ground," he intoned that "through this river-gate poured the tide of conquest, of trade, and of ideas which made America." "Our mission under God," he concluded, was to serve "as keepers of the gate." To do so meant (1) preserving the Blockhouse "in its present location"; (2) erecting "a replica of Fort Duquesne as set forth in the [Griswold-Stotz-McNeil-Richardson] Plan"; and (3) building the proposed Fort Pitt Memorial Museum in conjunction with a "restoration of two bastions" of "Old Fort Pitt."[153] All this left little room for much else.

Wright's response to Martin on 15 June 1947 was a classic of its kind:

> While reading the fulsome [Oliver] report . . . which you have just sent me I could not rid myself of the feeling that some practical joke was being played on me.
>
> I kept seeing the famous black-robed widow of "Campo Santo," white handkerchief in hand weeping, still standing in that famous cemetery, beside her dead husband. When he died she had an effigy made of him dressed just as he stood at their wedding and placed in a large glass case—meantime leaving a bequest to have an effigy of herself in deep mourning (white lace handkerchief in hand) made and placed in another glass case beside him when she died. She wanted the public to see her affectionately mourning him beyond the grave.
>
> And of course this foolish attempt to preserve the old fort is in no better case.
>
> Such stupid things do occur but would only add to Pittsburgh's present lack of human grace a note of bathos no self-respecting community should tolerate nor self-respecting architect should accept.
>
> As I see it, Pittsburgh needs no such Historian.
>
> Pittsburgh needs imaginative creative sympathy for the living and I am eager to do something constructive and joy-giving for Pittsburgh people. I thought that was my commission. Am I then mistaken and is this pathetic bathos which you say should have been given me at the start the true situation?
>
> But if among you there is sufficient interest in a future for Pittsburgh, not turned toward the grave, . . . but facing toward the recreation of a happy life for her citizens now and in future,

9.42

and I am so commanded, I will work.
   … Otherwise I am hamstrung.[154]

Martin took a full month to respond, attributing the "long delay" to the need to confer with Kaufmann, who was severely ill and recuperating in Canada.[155] More or less stonewalling the architect, Martin wrote that "the only thing I can add that might clarify the request of the Conference for a simple study and plan of the Point Park area is that the [Oliver] report of the Committee on Historical Significance of the Point was submitted to you in response for your request for some definition of what was meant by historical significance." "It is not my idea," he added in an unusually personal voice, "that either Fort Pitt or Fort Duquesne need to be the dominant factor in any such simple study as you would make, but we do feel that recognition should be given the historical background of the Point." As if to cut short any further debate on the question, he said "in conclusion that I can add nothing to the fact that we are asking for a simple treatment of this area."[156]

The day before Martin sent this letter, Kaufmann wrote to Wright asking him to go ahead with the project while at the same time acknowledging it might prove to be an endgame. "I appreciate there is for the moment a dormant spell," perhaps referring to his own removal from the scene of action, "but I am trying to use my intuition and a little bit of my head as to when we should crack. The time has not yet come." "Work on this simple plan," he implored Wright. "I think that will satisfy the appetite of some of these boys."[157] Though clearly not presented with the most favorable of circumstances, Wright agreed to revisit the project "pretty soon."[158]

By a curious coincidence, Wright conceived and began developing his second, reduced scheme for Pittsburgh in the form of a gateway-like monumental bridge at the same time the competition for the Jefferson National Expansion Memorial in St. Louis was nearing the end of its initial phase and Saarinen's Gateway Arch for the city's riverfront was about to be chosen as one of the five finalists (figure 9.42). Less than two months after the St. Louis decision was announced (26 September 1947), Wright told Kaufmann that his new plans were done and asked him "how and where" they would be reviewed.[159] Indicating that it was not now a top priority for the ACCD, Kaufmann informed the architect that an "immediate presentation [was] not likely."[160]

Three weeks later, however, Martin wrote to Wright saying that he had arranged for himself, Richards, and Richardson,

9.42. Jefferson National Expansion Memorial (Gateway Arch), Eero Saarinen, St. Louis, 1947–1965. Competition design, 1947. Perspective. Eero Saarinen Collection, Manuscripts & Archives, Yale University

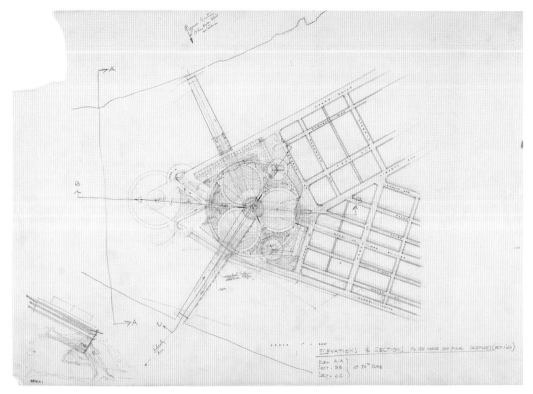

9.43

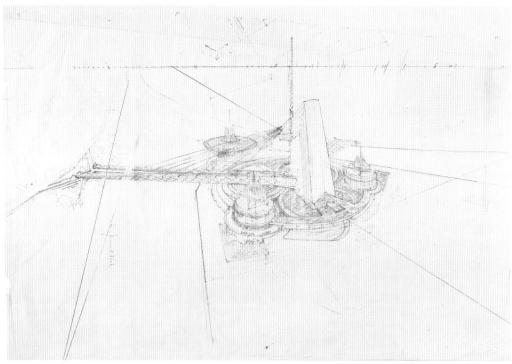

9.44

9.43. Point Park Civic Center project. Second scheme. Site plan (possibly for version with state, county, and municipal office buildings), 1 October 1947

9.44. Point Park Civic Center project. Second scheme. Sketch aerial perspective from south-southeast

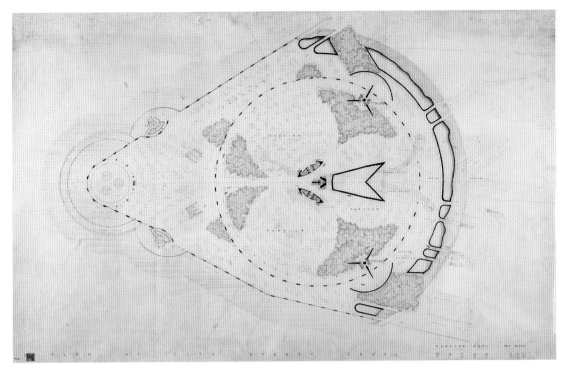

9.45

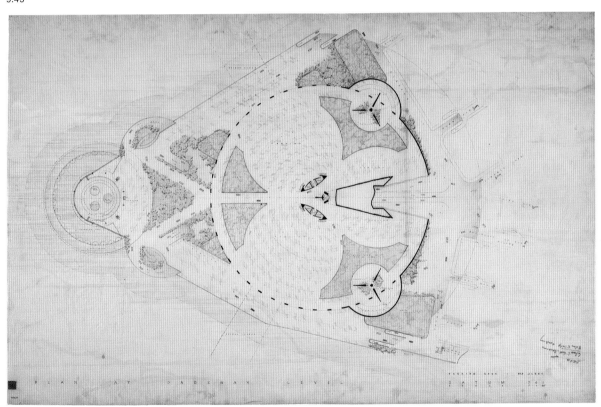

9.46

9.45. Point Park Civic Center project. Second scheme. Plan, city street level
(datum 730'), 20 October 1947

9.46. Point Park Civic Center project. Second scheme. Plan, parkway level
(datum 741')

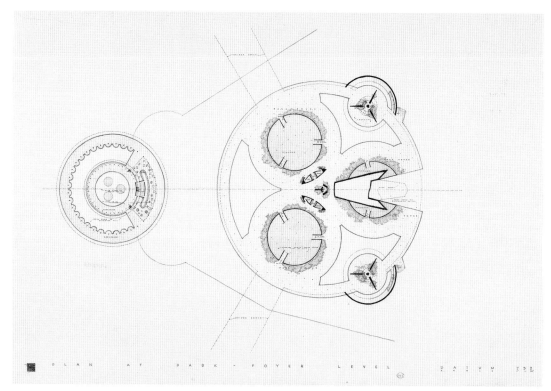

9.47

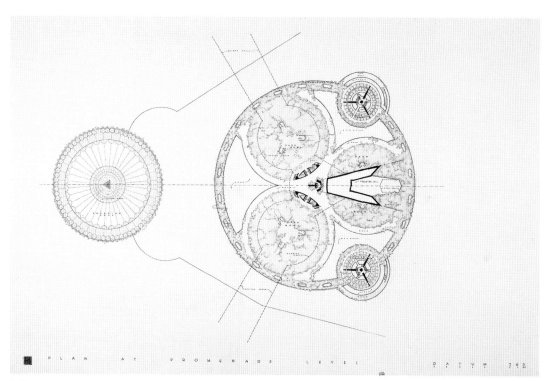

9.48

9.47. Point Park Civic Center project. Second scheme. Plan, park foyer level (datum 752'), 20 October 1947

9.48. Point Park Civic Center project. Second scheme. Plan, promenade level (datum 763'), 20 October 1947

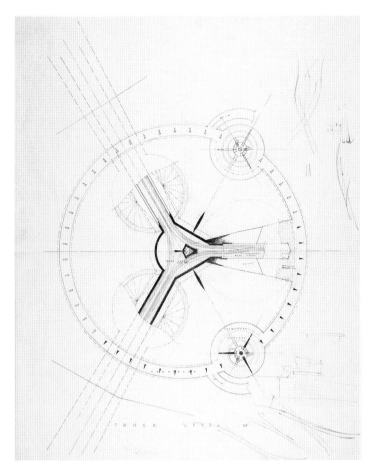

9.49

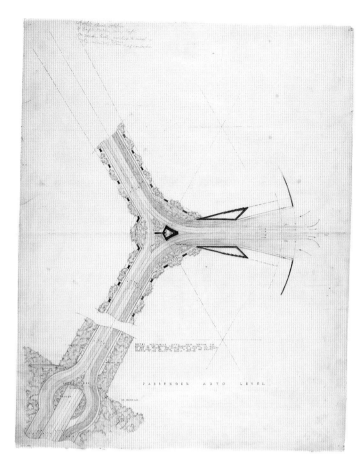

9.50

9.49. Point Park Civic Center project. Second scheme. Plan, truck level (datum 752')

9.50. Point Park Civic Center project. Second scheme. Plan, automobile level (datum 814')

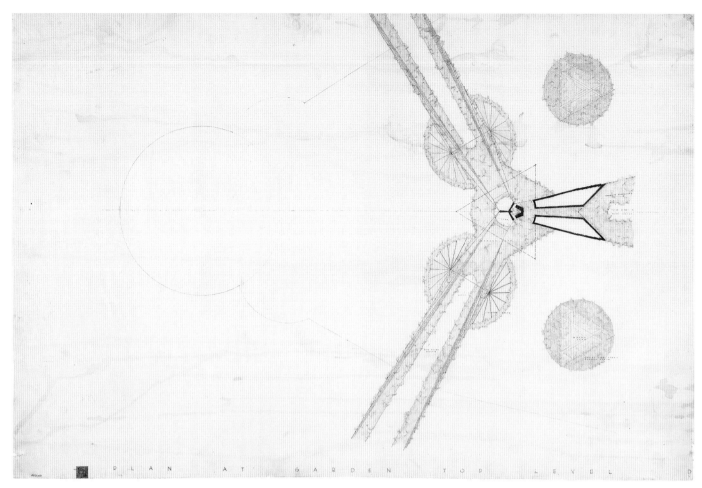

PLAN AT GARDEN TOP LEVEL

9.51

9.51. Point Park Civic Center project. Second scheme. Plan, garden top level (datum 851'), 20 October 1947

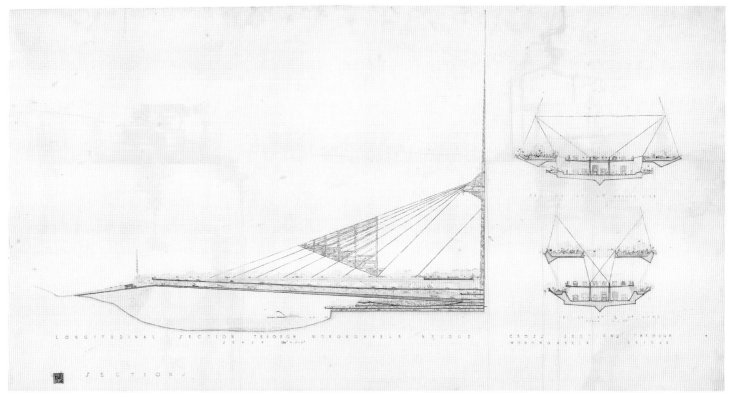

9.52

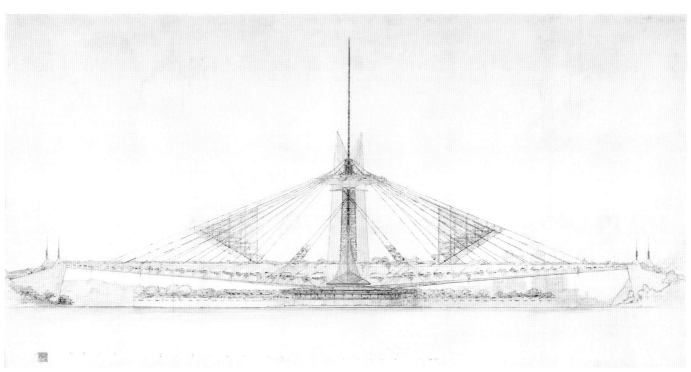

9.53

9.52. Point Park Civic Center project. Second scheme. Lateral half-section through Monongahela Bridge, with separate sections through bridge

9.53. Point Park Civic Center project. Second scheme. West elevation, 20 October 1947. Carnegie Museum of Art, Pittsburgh: Purchase gift of the Women's Committee, Carnegie Treasures Cookbook Fund, 86.24

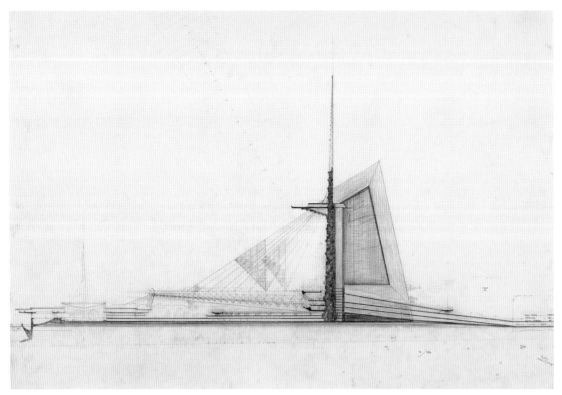

9.54

9.55

9.54. Point Park Civic Center project. Second scheme. Longitudinal section along
east-west axis

9.55. Point Park Civic Center project. Second scheme. South elevation

the engineer who was at that very moment designing the traffic interchange and new bridges for the Point, to come to Arizona to "inspect the [new] drawings." Without even showing the courtesy to ask Wright what time might be convenient, Martin requested the architect to confirm the dates of 4–5 January 1948. Wright responded coolly in the affirmative to the proposed dates and asked rather testily why "the gentlemen with the money-power composing (as I thought) my client" were not also coming.[161] If the architect received an answer to this question, we have no record of it. In the event, neither Kaufmann nor Heinz nor any of the "money-men" joined the conference's executive director, executive secretary, and consulting engineer on this critical occasion. Furthermore, two days before the arrival date, Martin informed Wright that the group would be coming for one day only (4 January).[162]

For this second phase of the design, which was restricted to the park site itself, Wright produced approximately the same number of drawings as for the first. But except for a couple, the drawings are less spectacular. They are also smaller. While the design process probably began toward the end of the summer of 1947, most of the drawings were done in October and early November. Instead of taking to heart Martin's admonition to consider seriously the historical remains at the site, Wright again ignored that aspect of the program. In fact, rather than starting from scratch, Wright simply took the earlier plan, reduced it in size to fit the smaller thirty-six-acre park site, and redrew it more or less to scale (figures 9.43, 9.27). Only when elevated into the third dimension does it reveal the changes he effected, namely, the elimination of the ziggurat-coliseum; the substitution of a double-span, cable-stayed bridge with a central anchor for the two cantilevered roadbeds; and the transformation of the twin "fast ramps" into small, vertical office buildings (figure 9.44).

According to Richard Cleary, the design schematically illustrated in the aerial perspective in figure 9.44 was not the first one the architect conceived when he returned to the drafting board.[163] There is, indeed, a rather undistinguished and incomplete project, consisting of a central, thirty- to thirty-five-story office tower plus two lower office blocks intended to house state, county, and municipal agencies. While the scheme maintained the aquarium/restaurant/swimming pool group at the apex along with the two multilevel cantilevered bridges, the tunnels for through traffic were eliminated. It is not certain, however, that this design predated the one shown to the

representatives of the ACCD in early January 1948.[164] In any event, it was certainly no match for the spectacular imagery and programmatic shift represented by the fully developed second scheme for Point Park (figures 9.53, 9.58).

Wright's "simple plan" shifted the focus of the earlier civic center from an interior experience as a partially enclosed space to an exterior one for the pedestrian and driver. At the same time, and in consequence of this, most of the important civic and cultural venues were eliminated. What did not significantly change, however, was the prominent role played by traffic considerations, meaning the bridges and the highway interchange between them, the regional road network, and the city streets. But now, instead of being hidden aboveground in the helical central structure or belowground in tunnels, the road system is fully exposed across the entire breadth of the site as a monumental overpass in the form of the double-span, cable-stayed bridge. This is anchored to a nearly five-hundred-foot-high steel, glass, and aluminum tower terminating in an observation deck and topped by a slender broadcast antenna reaching a total height of one thousand feet (figure 9.55).

As Cleary has shown, Wright's move to a cable-stayed design for the bridge was at the leading edge of contemporary technology.[165] The adoption of the concept allowed the architect to concentrate all the main structural elements at a central point and thus open up the rest of the space in a dizzying array of levels to the free movement of people and automobiles. The wedge-shaped, sail-like tower, which Wright cunningly called a "bastion," also served a focalizing role in representational terms (figure 9.44, 9.57).[166] It compacted into a single, predominant form the two distinct symbolic ones of the earlier ziggurat-coliseum and "light-shaft memorial to Fort Duquesne." The second scheme transformed the underlying remains of Fort Pitt into a combined phantasmagoric entrance into the city and observation post for surveying the historic gateway role that the city played in opening up the American continent to exploration and settlement.

The "bastion" tower aligns with the east-west axis of the site and forms one of the three spokes that radiate from the hub of the central traffic interchange, the other two being the bridges spanning the Monongahela and Allegheny Rivers (figures 9.43–44). Traffic crosses the rivers on a double-deck system that segregates trucks on a lower level from passenger vehicles and pedestrians above, with the outside lanes being reserved for pedestrians (figure 9.52). After rising in tandem from the opposite shores, the two vehicular roadbeds gradually descend into the central mast but at differential degrees. The lower truck lanes take the steepest grade (figure 9.49); the automobile traffic a median course (figure 9.50); while the pedestrian walkways slowly separate from their connection with the automobiles to follow an almost level path to a raised garden surrounding the tower, high above the ground and rivers (figure 9.51).

Within the hollow of the "bastion," through traffic takes a 120-degree bend to begin its ascent to the opposite bridge, whereas those commercial and passenger vehicles wishing to enter the city are funneled down steeply sloping ramps, under the cover of a raised garden, to the main streets that converge on the Point and its underground parking facilities (figures 9.54, 9.57, 9.44–46). The circular garden concealing the ramp down to street level is one of three such circular platforms set inside the larger circle surrounding the "bastion" and forming a multilayered landscaped setting for it. The centers of the three inner circles are aligned with the radiating spokes of the traffic arteries. The two circles located under the bridge approaches are designed as parks in the air, raised above two lower levels of parking and a third platform labeled the "park foyer" level (figures 9.47–48). A walkway around the outer circumference of the "foyer" connects the two office buildings facing the city to the public areas of the civic center, while recessed stairs lead up through the base of the two circles facing the Point into shallow, landscaped "park bowls." Shown on some drawings with amphitheatric terracing or seating, these saucer-like spaces were no doubt intended to serve as venues for outdoor concerts, performances, and the like. They are covered by canopies hung on cables from the upper bridge supports (see figure 9.55).

Much more than the drawings for the first scheme, those for the second stress the movement of people, their interaction with the landscape—both constructed and natural—and the interrelationships between the monumental forms of the design and the existing cityscape. Instead of creating an enclosed and somewhat forbidding-looking world in contrast to and distinct from the city beyond, the second scheme visibly invites the outside in while building upon, as it were, the industrial landscape of the "city of bridges," as Pittsburgh was called. The elevation looking east from the Ohio River pictures the downtown scene through the gossamer veil of cables supporting the new bridge, which read like the outstretched

wings of a giant transparent bird or butterfly (figure 9.53). In closer-up views, people are everywhere in evidence (figure 9.56). They fill level upon level of the space and use the various vantage points provided to look out onto the gardens, the rivers, and, especially from the observation deck high up on the "bastion," the extraordinary panorama of the valley defined by the surrounding hills.

While foregrounded in a way it was not in the earlier design, the engineering of the second scheme also serves a powerful representational purpose. In this regard, it bears meaningful comparison with Saarinen's design for the St. Louis Arch, although Wright's engineering takes a much less traditional shape and results in a more complex form of imagery (see figure 9.42). The deep indentation in the splay of the central tower, whose inclined angle expresses the anchoring role the structure plays in the stayed-cable support of the bridges, serves to focus the view from the city on the central element of the project, which marks the Point as the gateway to the west and frames the vista in its open wings (figure 9.57).

The "bastion" is both frame and figure at once, something to look at, through, and from. It extrapolates a form of eighteenth-century military defense in the guise of twentieth-century bridge technology on the very site where those two cultures come together in Pittsburgh's history. And it announces that cross-cultural marriage from afar in a symbolic form meant to broadcast and celebrate the city's emergence from its blighted and depressed recent past. Seen from the east, or city side, it projects an image of industrial progress and movement forward (figure 9.57). That sense of dynamism is amplified and restructured in the view from the west, where the design becomes a new icon for the city, different from but analogous to the St. Louis Arch or Paris's Eiffel Tower (figure 9.53). From this perspective, and especially as Wright presented it in a dazzling night view (figure 9.58), the bastion-bridge complex seems to rise up from the formerly derelict Point like a bird about to take wing and carry the city beneath it, with it. Wright often made reference to the legendary story of the phoenix rising from the ashes, and such an image may well have been in his mind when he revisited the project for Point Park. The spectacular night rendering, which at least one of the visiting ACCD representatives loved, conveyed to the fullest the architect's recipe of "planned centralization" for reviving the city in the form of an entertaining "good time place, a people's project."[167]

9.56

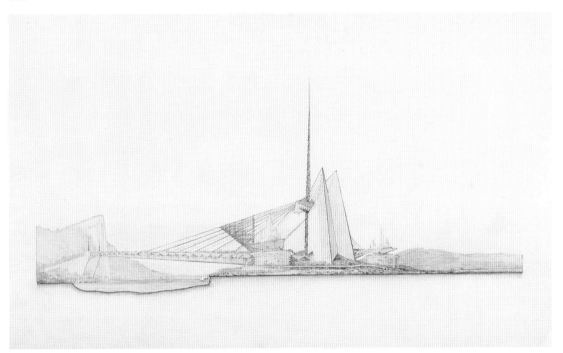

9.57

9.56. Point Park Civic Center project. Second scheme. Detail of south elevation

9.57. Point Park Civic Center project. Second scheme. Perspective from southeast

9.58. Point Park Civic Center project. Second scheme. Perspective at night, from southwest

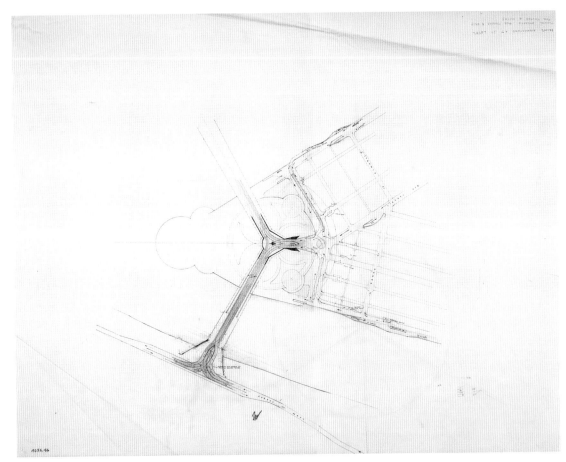

9.59

9.59. Point Park Civic Center project. Second scheme. Traffic diagram

Both Richards and Martin reported to Kaufmann on their January meeting with Wright soon after returning to Pittsburgh. The reports differed markedly in tone although both ultimately were less than reassuring about any positive outcome. Richards, who was described by colleagues as an "inspiring" person, "an idea man" who "knew art" and "had that very important ingredient of boldness of imagination: the ability to dream," was "impressed" with Wright and the "very wonderful visit" the group had.[168] Martin, by contrast, the "practical, realistic," "hard-nosed engineer" and "very smart operator," told Kaufmann that, though the visit was "very pleasant" and the new scheme "dramatic," there were still many, in fact, too many unresolved problems.[169] It was Richards who called the night perspective of the second scheme "as fine a rendering as I have ever seen" and the project itself "even more beautiful" than the first. Referring to both designs, he said that what Wright "has conceived for the Point is magnificent," although he worried out loud about any thought of its realization. "One of the great modern tragedies," he declared, "lies in the fact that in an era which has produced new materials, fresh points of view, and a genius like Wright, there isn't the social or economic mechanism to bring about the new architecture that should exist."[170]

Richards's pessimism and Martin's explicitly negative opinion were in large part prompted by the extremely critical remarks made by George Richardson during and after the January meeting with Wright.[171] Both Richards and Martin referred to Richardson as needling Wright on the question of cost and pointing out that the architect really had no idea what the figure would be and, moreover, did not seem to care. Martin stated that Richardson believed that "the engineering" was impossible and "could not be carried out." Finally, and perhaps most pertinent on a practical level, was the fact that Richardson, who was hard at work designing the very bridges and traffic interchange Wright had made the key to his revised scheme, claimed that Wright's new proposal was "entirely inadequate" when considered "in relationship to the requirements of the Triangle and the Penn-Lincoln Parkway." Because the two bridge spans directed traffic headed for the city into a single exit where "everything was brought into the end of Liberty Avenue," Richardson told his two colleagues that Wright's "proposal simply could not be considered."[172]

It is difficult not to interpret Richardson's participation as a serious conflict of interest. He was, in fact, so far along in his studies for the new bridges and interchange that he received the contract for the job within a little more than a month of the meeting with Wright.[173] It does not seem, however, that either Martin or Richards thought Richardson's involvement a problem. Quite the contrary. When the two of them were ready to suggest how "some of the elements" in Wright's proposal might be extracted and used "with certain modifications," Martin cautioned Kaufmann: "It is Mr. Richardson's opinion that the time required to reconcile all views on treatment of the Point Park would seriously affect his work, and he proposes to continue along the line he has been working on. It is his opinion that the time element is extremely important if he is to complete his work and contracts are to be let for the construction of the interchange and bridges during [the present governor's] term of office."[174]

Perhaps in deference to Kaufmann's personal relationship with Wright, both Martin and Richards came away from the second Arizona meeting with a proposal that might have allowed the Architecture and Design Committee chair the option of offering the architect a consolation prize. Of the two, Richards was more specific about what might be "salvaged."[175] Knowing Kaufmann's particular interest in the Civic Light Opera, Richards said he thought "that serious consideration should be given to the possibility of taking his [Wright's] concept for an aquarium, building it below the surface level of the park, and placing above it the Civic Light Opera. The stage would be at the Point where a massive fountain could rise from the rivers behind the stage so that prior to the performance and after it there could be a display of water and color and music."[176] Apparently following up on an idea that came from Wright himself when it became clear that the first scheme was completely out of the question, Martin suggested that a "modification" of the scheme might be "adapted" to a site on the North Side, across the Allegheny River, where the ACCD had earlier discussed the possibility of locating a park and civic center.[177] In any event, both Richards and Martin suggested that Wright bring the two sets of plans to Pittsburgh when Kaufmann returned from Palm Springs. Not wanting to raise too many expectations, however, they did not propose a public presentation. Rather, the thought was for Wright to present "his plans . . . quite confidentially to a small key group of interested people" before they "decide what other steps should be taken."[178]

After receiving the letters from Martin and Richards, Kaufmann visited Wright at Taliesin West to hear for himself what had transpired. He spent several days with him at the end of the first week of February, following which he wrote a long letter to Richards outlining what he thought should be done, without knowing that by then things had progressed so far in other directions that any serious consideration of the Wright projects was beyond the range of possibility.[179] Kaufmann acknowledged the importance attached to Richardson's criticism of Wright's proposed traffic pattern and cost estimates. He said that he asked Wright to do drawings, which the architect did, to show that Richardson was incorrect in claiming that the scheme was "'inadequate'" and would have forced all vehicles coming into the city "'into the end of Liberty Avenue'" (figure 9.59). He also said that he considered Richardson's comments on cost "not impressive or conclusive."[180]

As for what should be done regarding the proposed presentation by Wright in Pittsburgh of his two sets of plans, Kaufmann told Richards that he asked Wright to "break these projects up into a series of projects." One reason was to make them more understandable, since "it is impossible," as Kaufmann wrote, "to ask any group of men to digest these comprehensive things in one bite." The other was strategic in that Kaufmann felt that "the entire development could be done in stages," with each stage being financed separately and by different agencies and from different sources.[181] He listed for Richards eight possible components (all apparently drawn from the second scheme) more or less in order of priority: (1) "the bridges and the bastion"; (2) "the extension and development of the Park itself in relation to the projects"; (3) "the Garden Promenade on top of the bridges"; (4) "the development of the Point itself by either the aquarium-fountain idea of Wright's or your [Richards's] suggested idea of an aquarium and above it an outdoor auditorium with fountains"; (5) "the development of the water front for water sports and wharves"; (6) "the building of one office building for State purposes"; (7) "the building of another office building for Federal purposes"; and (8) "a radio tower attached to the face of the bastion, which would go up 1000 feet."[182]

Nothing came of this move by Kaufmann, nor was Wright ever invited to Pittsburgh to present the two schemes to the "small key group of interested people." Between mid-March and June 1948, Kaufmann made a final, "third effort" to get a design for the Point that might be acceptable to the ACCD.

This was simply the "outdoor arena" component to house the summer performances of the Civic Light Opera, but it failed as well.[183] Events had begun to outpace Kaufmann and Wright and to breathe new life into the Griswold-Stotz-McNeil-Richardson project that was waiting in the wings and that probably everyone but Kaufmann knew all along would eventually be built. Equitable Life bought its first parcel of property in the redevelopment area at the end of January 1948, just a few days prior to Kaufmann's visit to Taliesin West; and the state awarded Richardson the contract for final plans for the new Fort Pitt Bridge and highway interchange by the end of the second week of February.[184]

On 9 August 1948, Wright was officially informed by Martin that the Point Park project was moving ahead without him. Richardson's "highway interchange plan," he said, "has been completed and is now before the interested groups for study." He added that it would be "some time before the treatment of the Park is taken up for further discussion." At Kaufmann's behest, he asked that Wright send his various "studies … of Point Park," which Kaufmann wanted for his "own personal files."[185] And when the latter asked Wright a couple of months later if he would agree to allow the drawings to be included in an exhibition of civic improvements planned for Pittsburgh to be held at the Carnegie Museum, he spoke of the project entirely in the past tense: "I believe it would be an excellent opportunity for a great many more Pittsburghers than just those in the Allegheny Conference to see your interpretation of what Pittsburgh should have done."[186]

Point State Park and Gateway Center in Light of Wright's Civic Center

What was done between 1949, when operations went into high gear, and 1974, when Point State Park was finally inaugurated, was more or less what had been planned by Griswold, Stotz, McNeil, and Richardson prior to Wright's appearance on the scene. During the first half of 1949, Richardson worked out the final design for the highway interchange, heeding the criticism of the PPC's new Subcommittee on the Plan for Point Park, chaired by none other than Kaufmann, who urged Richardson to reduce the bulk of the "above-surface structures" that created a "barrier between the Park and the rest of the Triangle."[187] The scheme, approved by the governor later that year and constructed in the early 1960s, with important modifications suggested by the landscape architect Michael Rapuano (1904–75), Gilmore Clarke's partner, streamlined the original 1945 plan (figures 9.60–62).[188] The main roadway was widened but condensed into a straight, single-height structure crossing the park farther to the west, directly over the remains of Fort Pitt and necessitating the removal of Stotz's Memorial Museum. The on-/off-ramps were also streamlined, and the park area between the elevated road and the streets bordering the redevelopment area was enlarged.

As might be expected, the commercial redevelopment project moved forward on a faster track than the State Park. Equitable Life announced its decision to build the first three office towers of Gateway Center on a superblock in the north-eastern quadrant of the twenty-three-acre area in late 1949. Wholesale demolition of the Point began in the late spring of 1951, and the shiny chrome-alloyed steel-curtain-walled, cruciform-shaped buildings, designed by Eggers and Higgins (est. 1937), with Robert Dowling and Andrew Eken as consultants and Clarke and Rapuano as the landscape architects, were completed in 1952–53 (figure 9.63). Not only did Dowling, Equitable's advisor on the project, work out the basic plan of the three buildings, he also was responsible for giving the project its catchy name, which capitalized on "'the center's strategic location'" and appropriated to itself the site's "'historic'" significance. Dowling described Gateway Center as being "'the equivalent of Rockefeller Center, but far more modern.'" The modernity came from the Corbusian tower-in-the-park idea it adopted, which "'released [it] from the strait-jacket of closely adjacent sidewalks and streets'" (figure 6.16).[189]

The three twenty- to twenty-four-story Equitable towers set the stage for the rest of the redevelopment project. This was completed over the following decade with a series of structures including the State Office Building (1957), Pittsburgh Hilton Hotel (1959), and Gateway Towers luxury apartment block (1964), all facing the soon-to-be park. Between 1952 and 1954, plans for the park itself were finalized. As part of the earth-moving and grading operation, which began in early 1953, further archaeological work uncovered important elements of Fort Pitt, which would be included in the final design of the park. The river wall, wharves, and river walk were done first. The Fort Pitt Bridge was completed in 1959 and connected to the new Fort Pitt Tunnel the following year. The highway interchange and Fort Duquesne Bridge were completed between

9.60

9.61

9.62

9.60. Point State Park, Griswold, Stotz, McNeil, and Richardson, with Michael Rapuano and Gordon Bunshaft, 1949–74. Plan. SJHHC

9.61. Point State Park. Perspective from park entrance on Commonwealth Avenue, looking west. SJHHC

9.62. Point State Park. Perspective from far side of highway "portal," looking west. SJHHC

1963 and 1969. The Fort Pitt Museum, removed from its original location in the center of the fort to the partially reconstructed Monongahela Bastion abutting the Fort Pitt Bridge, was built between 1964 and 1969. And it was in that year that work began on the demolition of the old Point Bridge, with that of the Manchester Bridge occurring in the following two years. The 150-foot-high fountain at the apex was constructed and put into operation in 1974 in time for the dedication of the park (figure 9.64).[190]

The Point State Park as built differs only in certain details from the 1945 preliminary study prepared for the PRPA and adopted by the ACCD as its guiding document. A transverse elevated highway divides the park as it did in the earlier scheme but this time with a more declarative geometry and leaving relatively less space on the downriver side (figures 9.60, 9.13). The entrance area from the new Gateway Center was aggrandized and given a classical, Roman feeling (figure 9.61). The formal, semicircular path leading to the arched opening surrounds a green that reveals, below grade, the recently excavated remains of Fort Pitt's northeast Music Bastion. The wide greensward passing under the arched "portal" that supports the highway provides a view straight through to the fountain at the Point's apex (figure 9.62). This sense of openness and unobstructed vista was accomplished in large part through the displacement of the Fort Pitt Memorial Museum. It was further enabled by the decision not to attempt a reconstruction of Fort Duquesne but simply to trace its outlines on the ground in stone. The greater overall simplicity of the final plan was also in part the result of the elimination of any structures for entertainment or recreation, such as the earlier restaurant and boating facilities.

Point State Park is almost purely a landscape affair. The historical mementos, such as the Blockhouse, the scattered reconstructed remains of Fort Pitt, and the surface tracing of Fort Duquesne, are discreet and marginal to the park experience. Griswold remarked that visitors "will see the outline location" of the two forts, "but above all, they will behold a beautiful panoramic landscape of rivers, forests and hills." A principle that guided his collaboration with Stotz, in particular, was that Point Park was "not a place to crowd with buildings—it was a place in which to avoid architecture."[191] The idea was to re-create a natural environment as nearly as possible untouched by human intervention, something completely at odds with Pittsburgh's own history and raison d'être.

9.63

9.63. Point State Park site and Gateway Center, Eggers and Higgins, with Robert Dowling and Andrew Eken, and Clarke and Rapuano, 1949–53. Aerial view, 1952. SJHHC

9.64

9.64. Point State Park and Gateway Center, ca. 1974. SJHHC

The "green oasis" was to provide "something of the serenity that once characterized these lovely shores" and "the three God-given rivers converging at the Point": "Native trees will be grouped naturalistically sim[u]lating the forests that [once] covered the river banks," thus forming "symbolic … groves of trees like the clearing for a pioneer enterprise" (figure 9.60).[192]

In opposition to Kaufmann's program calling for a celebration of the city's industrial might and contribution to modern thought, Griswold maintained that his understanding of Point Park revealed that "there was no ancient culture and almost no man-made beauty to revive," and thus "it was necessary to return to the only real beauty in Pittsburgh's heritage — the beauty of an unsurpassed natural setting." "In this evaluation," he pompously wrote, "the designers were following the Biblical wisdom of, 'rendering unto Caesar the things which are Caesar's and unto God the things that are God's.'"[193]

In marked contrast to Wright's desire to "see something done on the Point for Pittsburgh's … citizens' greater enjoyment" in the way of a unique "civic-entertainment-resource," the Griswold-Stotz-McNeil-Richardson park, once it took care of the traffic issues, turned its back on the daily life of the city's average citizens and especially any connection with those living in the suburbs (there was hardly any provision for parking, for one thing).[194] Griswold described his team's rather precious concept for the park as refusing to counter the "decentralizing" trend then in progress by bringing more people in automobiles to the site.[195] When asked "what use was going to be made of the Park," Griswold offered an elitist, genteel response. The park was not about "hav[ing] any 'attractions.'" "The attraction at the Point," and the only one in his view, "was being able to walk along the edge of the river and watch the boats or watch the current, or the water." While not the only audience, for sure, the only one he specified was composed of "business men with brown bags for their lunch, [who will] go down there and sit because it was an open space. You could see the sky, the rivers and the hills and it [would be] a delightful experience to go down there and have lunch on one of those benches."[196] Even the constant roar of ten lanes of trucks and automobiles passing overhead would not affect the abstracted, indeed alien, experience of nature: "Here no automobiles may disturb the leisurely pleasure of a quiet stroll."[197]

In 1958, in one of her first important critiques of the super-block planning that characterized postwar redevelopment in American cities through its tendency "to decentralize" the downtown and "deaden it" by eliminating all sense of "individuality or whim or surprise," Jane Jacobs (1916–2006) cited Pittsburgh and its Gateway Center as one of the prime examples of this mistaken approach. After rhetorically asking "what will the projects look like?" that follow this model, she replied, "They will be spacious, parklike, and uncrowded. They will feature long green vistas. They will be stable and symmetrical and orderly. They will be clean, impressive, and monumental. They will have all the attributes of a well-kept, dignified cemetery."[198] That Jacobs's comments might serve as a description of the Griswold-Stotz-McNeil-Richardson design for Point State Park should come as no surprise, since the park was not only elaborated as an extension of the space and environment of Gateway Center, but also made possible by the economic stability the redevelopment project brought to the Golden Triangle.

Jacobs believed that "it is not the nature of downtown to decentralize" but rather "to become denser, more compact." The goal of urban renewal should be to recapture "the life that makes downtown worth fixing at all."[199] In her view, that could be accomplished only by giving new value to the traditional street. While Wright's plans for the Point Park Civic Center certainly did not adopt such a premodern approach, and while his designs would no doubt have upset Jacobs no end, his desire to bring a sense of liveliness and excitement back to the city center by emphasizing, and even exaggerating, the density and activity that traditionally characterized the downtown oddly aligned with the thoughts expressed by one of the earliest and most significant critics of urban redevelopment.[200]

Wright too was appalled by the plans for Gateway Center and, especially, by the instrumental role Equitable's advisors, Dowling and Eken, played in the planning process. His own initial impulse to use the entire area for an entertainment- and culture-oriented civic center precluded Point Park from devolving into a mere stage or forecourt for the commercial venture. Even his scaled-back second scheme did as much as possible to bring attention to the park structures' iconic and civic role and thereby deny a sense of continuity with, or subservience to, the area slated for commercial redevelopment. Wright described Dowling and Eken to Park Martin as "the two worst characters in the urban building field today." "These men represent," he went on, "the worst, most piratical tendencies in all modern city-building. … The one is a canny profit-hunter, the other the sycophant of any profit-hunter that will hire him as expert." "What they have 'set up' for the Point is the worst civic crime I know," namely, "to exploit Point Park" itself "for their own fortune."[201]

If Wright was appalled by Dowling and Eken's concept for Gateway Center, he would have been equally dismayed by the idea of a park mainly catering to downtown businessmen and wealthy residents of the nearby luxury apartment towers. Wright planned the park for the "urban multitudes" as a community center providing space for government agencies at all levels and offering all sorts of "civic enterprises of a cultural nature for the citizens of [greater] Pittsburgh." When interviewed for the *Pittsburgh Sun-Telegraph* in 1949, he described his first scheme, "his favorite," as a form of "'planned centralization'" that "would hold a third of Pittsburgh's population."[202]

Wright clearly saw his project in terms other than the traditional City Beautiful-type civic center. Instead of forming a group of buildings designed for the conduct of government affairs and the pursuit of certain fairly prescribed cultural activities, his was a permanent kind of fairgrounds raised to the level of serious civic purpose. It was a place where the entertainment of the "multitudes" would go hand in hand with the daily business of federal, state, and municipal agencies, and where an engagement in highbrow pleasures like opera and art could take place cheek by jowl with business conventions, commercial and industrial exhibitions, and shopping and eating (both sit-down and fast food). Furthermore, the radius of influence was infinitely greater than the earlier type of civic center. No longer merely serving a settled urban population, Wright's Point Park Civic Center, in both its initial and scaled-back versions, was to be a regional destination point, acting as a magnet to bring the ever-expanding masses of suburbanites back to the city and to reidentifying with it. The automobile, the very agent of dispersion of people and disintegration of the urban core, was called upon to create a place of convergence and a sense of cohesion in a new type of civic forum foreshadowed by the Madison project.

The Point Park Civic Center as permanent indoor-outdoor fairgrounds was to be a dynamic, lively environment where citizens would actively engage in communal pursuits and events. The architecture was intentionally spectacular and was meant to create a place of spectacle. The tower in the second scheme rivaled the Eiffel Tower in height and, like it, offered not only an extravagant feat of engineering to look at but also a sensational view of the city and its metropolitan environment

from the altitude of its observation deck. The five-hundred-foot-high glass shaft in the initial scheme, intended for public displays combining light and music, became the central actor in celebrations of public holidays and other such events.

The prime symbolic figure in the original design was the atrium megastructure, where the architectural hybrid of Roman amphitheater and Mesopotamian ziggurat transformed the very act of congregating into a participatory spectacle of social significance. The continuous ramp of the exterior gave visible form to the crowds of people converging on any one of the individual halls or arenas and, by its reference to the legendary Tower of Babel, gave a mythic dimension to the modern idea of constant movement and progress that Victor Hugo attributed to the form in *Notre-Dame de Paris* (1831–32), the book of his that Wright most often quoted.[203] But whereas the interior of the Tower of Babel was impenetrable and its builders were ultimately forced to abandon their task due to their inability to communicate with one another, the interior of the Pittsburgh megastructure would have created an open amphitheater where people are constantly in view of one another and the exterior landscape and engaged with one another and the world beyond in the construction of a new civic identity at the vital "heart" of the city. This was not a celebration of the eighteenth-century origins of that "core" but rather, as Kaufmann had hoped, a place to produce collectively the activities and events substantiating the renewal of the city's historic energy and force.

Point Park Civic Center and the "New Monumentality"

While both of Wright's designs for Pittsburgh's Point Park differ greatly from the Madison Civic Center in their abandonment of its residual City Beautiful planning and dissolution of the grid underlying that, the Pittsburgh projects clearly trace their theatrical and spectacular form of space and experience to the earlier design. In embracing the dynamics and diversity of the city and harnessing the automobile to that centralizing end, the earlier and later projects provide a forum for public gathering and communal activity in which the metaphor of the city as stage and the building as theater play a crucial role. The spectacle engages the users with the surrounding cityscape and landscape and, most important, with one another. This social dimension directly links these designs with the so-called search for a new monumentality that

9.65

9.65. Civic Center project, St. Dié, France, Le Corbusier, 1945–46. Model. From Siegfried Giedion, *Architecture, You and Me*, 1958

dominated a very significant body of thinking about architectural design and meaning in the immediate postwar period in America and in Europe.

Wright's extension and transformation of the City Beautiful civic center into fully modernist expressions of public space and form between 1938 and 1947 occurred at a crossroads in the history of twentieth-century architecture and urbanism. In America, the Depression put an end to the last remnants of the City Beautiful approach, except perhaps in Washington, D.C., where it hung on until the 1950s. In Europe, the fascist regimes employed an even more bombastic classicism to embody their political programs in monumental forms for public gatherings. As a result European modernists, unlike Wright, shied away from anything approaching such formal urban settings at the time. Indeed, they did not begin to think seriously about how to renew the "heart of the city" through a program of large-scale civic centers until the end of the last years of the war and its immediate aftermath.[204] But when they did, the idea of the spectacle would play a major role in how the "core" as civic center was interpreted.

The change in thinking is revealed with clarity in the writings of José Luis Sert (1902–83) and Sigfried Giedion, both leading figures in CIAM (Congrès Internationaux d'Architecture Moderne). When Wright's admirer and supporter Lewis Mumford was asked by Sert at the end of 1940 to write an introduction to his CIAM manifesto *Can Our Cities Survive?* (1942), Mumford refused, saying that " 'the four functions of the city' " that defined the CIAM program " 'do not seem to me to adequately cover the ground of city planning.' " " 'Dwelling, work, recreation, and transportation are all important,' " he acknowledged, " 'but what of the political, educational, and cultural functions of the city … ?' " " 'The organs of political and cultural association are, from my standpoint, the *distinguishing* marks of the city.… I regard their omission as the chief defect of routine city planning; and their absence from the program of the C.I.A.M. I find almost inexplicable. Unless some attention was paid to this as a field, at least, for future investigation, I should therefore find it very difficult to write the introduction that you suggested.' "[205]

It is not known if Mumford had Wright's project for Madison in mind when writing his response. Sert eventually added to the final pages of his text some reference to the importance of the civic center for the life of the city and further developed his thoughts on the subject in his article "The

Human Scale in City Planning," published two years later. But it was mainly in the writings of Giedion and his championing of the role the civic center played in Le Corbusier's project for the reconstruction of the war-ravaged city of St. Dié in eastern France (1945–46) that this fundamental aspect of urban design found its way into the European modern movement (figure 9.65). Though hardly visible in the St. Dié civic center—where government office buildings as well as cultural, shopping, and entertainment facilities are freely disposed around a large open square segregated from vehicular traffic—the festive atmosphere of the recent world's fairs in Paris (1937) and New York (1939–40), with their fireworks and sound and light extravaganzas, offered Giedion a prime model for how to revive a sense of community space and symbolism.

In a seminal article, "The Need for a New Monumentality," originally published in 1944, Giedion described the two worlds' fairs as "great spectacles capable of fascinating the people" with their "waterplays, light, sound and fireworks."[206] Over the next few years, he directly related this idea of spectacle to the revival of the civic center. "Civic centres will originate when cities are not regarded as mere agglomerations of jobs and traffic lights" but when "community life is closely connected with a sense for leisure and relaxation." "Those who govern," he added, "must know that spectacles, which will lead the people back to community life, must be re-incorporated into civic centres … [and these] newly created civic centres should be the site for collective, emotional events, where the people play as important a role as the spectacle itself, and where a unity of the architectural background, the people and the symbols created by artists will arise again."[207]

While it is inconceivable that Giedion would have suggested Wright's civic centers as models, the designs for Pittsburgh and Madison arguably fulfill Giedion's criteria for a meaningful solution to the problem of the city "core" more aptly than anything Le Corbusier or Sert produced at the time. The St. Dié concept, which immediately became Giedion's type-solution and, in turn, the prime one for modern architects, was generated by a compositional ideal of open, multidirectional space in which individual building volumes are disposed in relation to one another without resort to classical axes or formal symmetries. Freedom of movement, multiplicity of choice, and a sense of the aleatoric trump any hint of the kind of concerted action and processional direction that would generally support the kinds of

social rituals and spectacular displays that Giedion had in mind.

The problem was how to give permanent form to a vision and experience of the impermanent. Giedion sought to capture and express the "sudden spontaneous applause" of the crowd, the unfolding of "collective emotional events" of people in "symbols [created] for their activities and for their fate or destiny, for their religious beliefs and for their social convictions." To do this, the architecture of the civic center had to make a place "where the people play as important a role as the spectacle itself, and where a unity of the architectural background, the people, and the symbols created by artists, will be achieved."[208] In contrast to the Corbusian paradigm of dispersed volumetric objects, Wright's civic centers for Pittsburgh and Madison condense their symbolic force into singular, unitary megastructures that function visually as superforms and experientially as directional templates for collective movement and activity. Moreover, instead of merely serving as neutral platforms for what Giedion spoke of as the "great spectacles capable of fascinating the people," the Pittsburgh and Madison civic centers have the spectacular built into their designs. Visitors moving through their spaces and taking part in events staged there become agents in the construction of the symbolic form signifying the city's role in the life of the individual and the collectivity. This performative aspect became an especially powerful factor in Wright's final urban design, the 1957 cultural center for Baghdad that is the subject of the last chapter.

TEN

PLAN FOR THE EXPANSION OF BAGHDAD ANCHORED BY A CULTURAL CENTER, 1957

The projects for Madison and Pittsburgh were both tradition-al civic centers in the American meaning of the term going back to the beginning of the twentieth century, that is to say, a single unified urban design combining public buildings for government and cultural purposes. The Pittsburgh project, however, placed the government facilities in such a subsid-iary position and focused attention to such a degree on the elements devoted to the arts and entertainment that it could almost be called a cultural center in the sense that term ac-quired in the 1950s and 1960s when centers for the arts became all the rage in municipal planning in America. Lincoln Center for the Performing Arts in New York, whose planning began in 1956 under the direction of Wallace Harrison (1895–1981), was only the most important and celebrated example of a type that soon came to be seen as a most appropriate driver of urban re-newal and development.[1] Wright's design for a cultural center for Baghdad, meant to anchor the recent westward expansion of the city, followed immediately on the heels of New York's Lincoln Center and thus represents one of the earliest exam-ples of the type that came to such prominence in the last third of the twentieth century.

Wright did not need Lincoln Center as a model. In late 1954, when it seemed possible that the project for the Madison Civic Center might be realized if it could eliminate the gov-ernment facilities made redundant by the Holabird, Roche and Burgee City-County Building about to go into construction, Wright reprogrammed his original design, shoehorning it into a smaller structure containing only cultural facilities. The new project for Monona Terrace, produced between December 1954 and February 1955, contained a large performing arts auditorium, a smaller theater, an art gallery, an exhibition

hall, plus two hotel towers. Compelled to downsize the project even further for financial reasons, Wright redrew the cultural center a number of times. Still, it was rejected in June 1957 on a trumped-up legal technicality having to do with height limits along the lakefront. Wright clearly associated the Madison and Baghdad projects in his own mind. On "reading in the news-paper that … the Wisconsin State Legislature [wa]s going to kill the Monona Terrace project," he remarked to the Taliesin Fellowship that "since we have lost the Terrace, maybe we can get in Baghdad." This was on 23 June 1957, while he and his staff were completing the Baghdad drawings, approximately six weeks before they were to be sent off.[2]

Baghdad, from Round City to Ribbon City

Despite its location in what is often referred to as the "cradle of civilization"—the Fertile Crescent of ancient Mesopotamia lying in the desert flatlands between the Tigris and Euphrates Rivers—Baghdad is nowhere near as old as Paris or London. In fact, in its modern history as the capital of Iraq, a na-tion-state founded in 1921, it is not even as old as Pittsburgh or Madison. Like the country of which it is part, the city is very much a twentieth-century construct. Its modern streets and roads, bridges, public edifices, and infrastructure were built over a rather unassuming settlement that dated back to the middle ages but that had nothing to do with the original, short-lived palatine city created in the eighth century.

The site where the Tigris and Euphrates Rivers converge was chosen by Abu Jafar al-Mansur, the second Abbasid Caliph (r. 654–75), as the ideal location for the administrative center of his regime. It occupied a strategic position on the east-west

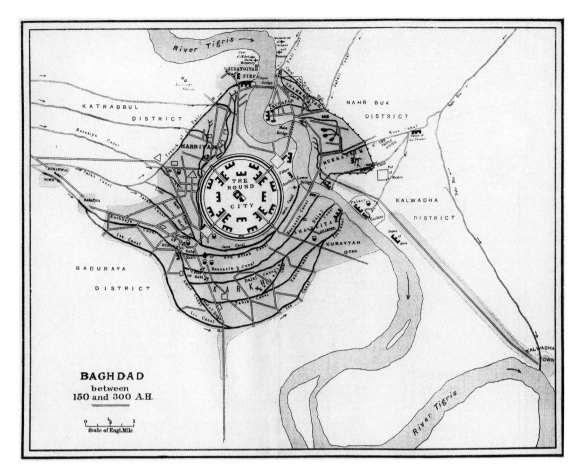

10.1

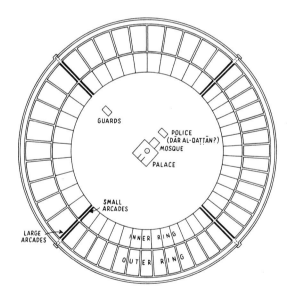

10.2

10.1. Round City of al-Mansur (Baghdad), 762–66. Site plan. Reconstruction by Guy Le Strange. From Le Strange, *Baghdad during the Abbasid Caliphate*, 1900

10.2. Round City of al-Mansur. Plan. Reconstruction by Jacob Lassner. From Lassner, *The Topography of Baghdad in the Early Middle Ages*, 1970

trade route from Asia to the Mediterranean and on the north-south pilgrimage route to Karbala, Najaf, and Mecca.[3] The city was created virtually ex nihilo between 762 and 766 and is, according to the Middle Eastern architectural historian K.A.C. Creswell, "one of the most remarkable examples of town-planning that have come down to us" (figure 10.1).[4] According to literary sources, the fortified city was laid out on the west, or right, bank of the Tigris, northwest of the present city center, as an enormous circle over a mile and a half in diameter. Built of mud brick, with four gates oriented to the cardinal points, it was thought to represent an image of the cosmos (figure 10.2). Al-Mansur called his Round City the "City of Peace," in reference to paradise. Concentric walls defined the residential quarters within the rim of a wheel at whose center stood the royal palace and mosque.[5]

Baghdad reached its cultural zenith, it is commonly thought, during the reign of Harun al-Rashid (r. 786–809). The tales of the *Thousand and One Nights* are a lasting reminder of this period. Already by that time, however, much building had taken place outside the Round City. By the middle of the tenth century, the government officially shifted its headquarters to the left, or east, bank of the Tigris, to the area later known as Rusafa, which still forms the commercial heart of the city (figure 10.3). What remained of al-Mansur's city was soon destroyed by floods. The Round City was to be relegated to archaeological interest and play no part in the later city planning of Baghdad until Wright referred to it in his plan for the city's expansion on the west bank in the 1950s. The existing city was sacked by the Mongols in 1258 and by Timur the Lame in 1393 and 1401. From a population estimated at nearly 1.2 million at the height of its power, the number was to drop to less than twenty thousand by the seventeenth century, when Baghdad fell under Ottoman rule.[6]

Baghdad remained a backwater throughout most of the following two centuries. Few changes occurred in the urban fabric of the much reduced city, dominated as it was by the traditional pattern of abutting two-story houses separated by meandering alleys occasionally relieved by a mosque or market. One of the only significant changes was the partial demolition of the medieval city walls between 1869 and 1872 by the progressive Ottoman governor Midhat Pasha. This would eventually allow for the expansion of the city eastward, although at first the walls were replaced by a dike, or bund, to mitigate the effects of the annual flooding of the river. Another

change was the planning of the first modern street, the New Street (1915–17), which established a relatively wide and nearly straight cut through Rusafa, more or less aligning with the existing River Street (figure 10.4). Rashid Street, as it was later called, was the first of four parallel streets that would form the circulation backbone of the twentieth-century downtown, the other three being, in their order from the Tigris, Queen Aliyah (later Jumhuriya and Khulafa) Street (1954–58), King Ghazi (later Kifah) Street (1936–37), and Shaykh Umar Street (1944) (figure 10.5).

Though laid out by German engineers under the Ottoman governorship of Baghdad, Rashid Street was completed only after the British occupation of the city following the defeat of the Ottoman Empire in World War I. From 1918 until 1958, British politicians, economists, architects, engineers, and city planners would play a predominant role in the shaping of Baghdad's physical fabric. The modern nation-state of Iraq, with its capital in Baghdad, was created as a British mandate at the San Remo Conference in 1920. A limited constitutional monarchy, modeled on Britain's, was established, and the Mecca-born Faysal, one of the two sons of Sharif Husayn, a direct descendent of the Prophet Muhammad who had led the Arab Revolt in 1916, was chosen in 1921 to assume the throne.[7] In 1932, a year before Faysal died, Iraq was admitted to the League of Nations as an independent state.

Independence, of course, is a term open to interpretation. Iraq remained a client state of Britain throughout the duration of the Hashimite dynasty. Faysal was succeeded by his son Ghazi in 1933. When the latter died in a car accident six years later, his son was only four years old. Until the British-educated Faysal II came of age in 1953, Iraq was ruled by his uncle, Abd al-Illah, as regent. Under the system in place until July 1958, when a revolution led by the military toppled the regime, the monarch remained answerable not only to a highly unstable, constantly fluctuating coalition of wealthy landowners and tribal chiefs but in more important ways to its British patrons. The 1930 Anglo-Iraqi Treaty, or Treaty of Preferential Alliance, ensured Britain's "advisory" role in the new nation's affairs. Set to expire in 1957, it was replaced two years before that by the Baghdad Pact, in which Iraq continued to serve pro-Western, Anglo-American interests as a critical factor in the so-called Northern Tier containment of Soviet communism.

Under Britain's direction, Baghdad began to spread north and south along the east bank of the Tigris in a ribbon-like

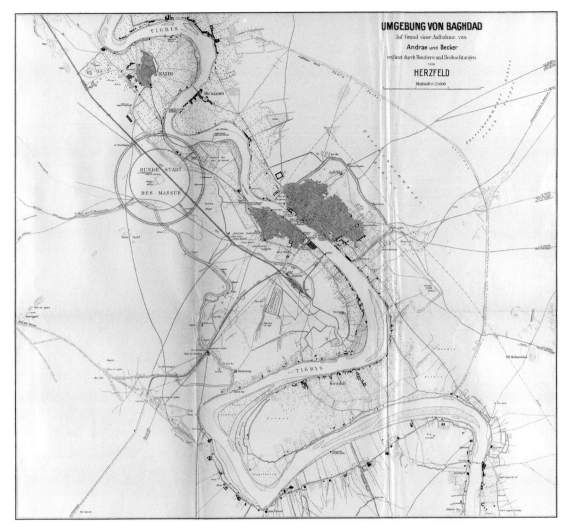

10.3

10.4

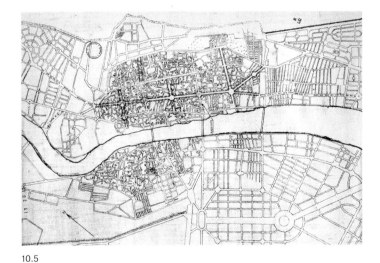

10.5

10.3. Baghdad, 1917. Plan, showing outlines of former Round City. From Friedrich Sarre and Ernst Herzfeld, *Archäologische Reise im Euphrat-und Tigris-gebiet*, vol. 2, 1920

10.4. Baghdad, ca. 1932. Aerial photograph of Rashid Street, in Rusafa, looking northwest. Prints and Photographs Division, LC

10.5. Baghdad, late 1957 or early 1958. Plan, showing new construction and planned extension of Khulafa (now Jumhuriya) Street and proposed development of West Baghdad between Central Railway Station and Tigris River (northeast is at top). FLC

fashion. Its architecture and local planning initiatives conformed to the pattern established by such other English colonial enterprises as imperial India. Indeed, the architect responsible for much of the development between 1918 and 1950 had worked for Edwin Lutyens in his New Delhi office in 1913–16. James M. Wilson (1887–1965), who later formed a partnership with the Liverpool-trained Harold C. Mason (1892–1960), served as director of public works through much of the 1920s, while Mason served as government architect well into the 1930s.[8] Either separately or together they designed and oversaw the construction of a wide range of public buildings, entirely new in programmatic terms to Baghdad. These included the College of Religion at the projected Al il-Bait University (1921–24); the Royal Law Courts, Women's Hospital, Royal Hospital, and Royal Medical College (1922–27); and the Public Library and Baghdad Airport (1931). These buildings were generally designed in a classical manner often overlaid with local, Islamic detail considered appropriate to the context and reflective of the Iraqi-British alliance. All but the airport were located on the east bank of the Tigris, and most were north of the former city walls delimiting Rusafa.[9]

Wilson and his colleagues transformed the northern extension of the downtown commercial area into a kind of government center containing important educational and cultural institutions as well. To house the growing population of middle-class professionals and bureaucrats, the new neighborhood of Waziriyah was laid out on Garden Suburb lines. Detached buildings for residential and institutional use were set back from curving streets, modeled on the squares and circles of Georgian London, to create a new form of open urban space (figure 10.5). These same Garden Suburb ideas were extended to the southern side of the left bank, where gridded street layouts, interconnected by wide avenues dotted with public squares and circles, provided green and airy sites for residences for the middle and upper middle class, many of whom were foreign, in the new neighborhoods of Battawiyin, Saadun, and Alwiyah.[10] By the 1950s, this development extended into the Karada Peninsula to the southwest, facing the area on the river's west bank where the Royal Palace and, eventually, the new Parliament Building and post–World War II government center were located (figure 10.6).

The major trend already observable by the 1930s, which would only grow in significance in the final years of the Hashimite dynasty and have the greatest impact on Wright's

thinking, was the development of the west bank of the city to compete with that of the east. Ever since the abandonment of the Round City and the creation of Rusafa as the economic and administrative center of Baghdad, the area facing it across the Tigris, called Karkh, had remained relatively undeveloped. The building of Baghdad Airport by Wilson and Mason, begun in 1931, and the transfer of the British Embassy in the same year from Sinak (just south of Rusafa) to a riverside site in Karkh, were early signs of things to come.[11] In the early 1930s, it was decided to move the Iraq (Archaeological) Museum from Rusafa to a new, much larger site, at the southern edge of Karkh, close to the existing West Baghdad Railway Station, in the Salhiya section of the area. The German architect Werner March (1894–1976), who was to design Berlin's infamous Olympic Stadium in 1936, was chosen for the project. Nothing was done until 1940–41, however, when a replica of the Assyrian Gate of Sargon II's Palace of Khorsabad was erected at one end of the site and a cast of the seventh-century BCE basalt Lion of Babylon at the other. The museum itself was only built between 1957 and 1966, based on a revised design of 1951–57.[12] By then, a new Royal Palace and Parliament Building, both designed by the Bartlett-trained John Brian Cooper (1899–1983), who replaced Mason as government architect in 1934, were rising along the western bank of the Tigris to the south of the Queen Aliyah (later Jumhuriya) Bridge, which was opened in early 1957 to create a new connection between the two sides of the river (figure 10.7).[13]

The large and opulent 1950s Royal Palace and Parliament were the last significant buildings erected in Baghdad in the British-colonial classical style—symmetrical, columniated structures discreetly inflected with Islamic detailing. They were not, however, the most prominent of the type in the new western development of Baghdad. That honor went to the new Central Baghdad Railway Station begun by Wilson and Mason in 1947 and completed in the early 1950s.[14] This was the architects' swan song, and a most powerful one at that. It not only dominated its surroundings but also established a focus for later city planning efforts, including Wright's. Located between the airport and the incipient Iraq Museum, it had little to do with railway architecture and followed in plan and overall conception the abstracted, Orientalized classicism of Lutyens's Viceroy's House in New Delhi, the grandest of all monuments to British Imperial power (figure 10.8). At its center, over the booking hall, is a seventy-foot-diameter saucer

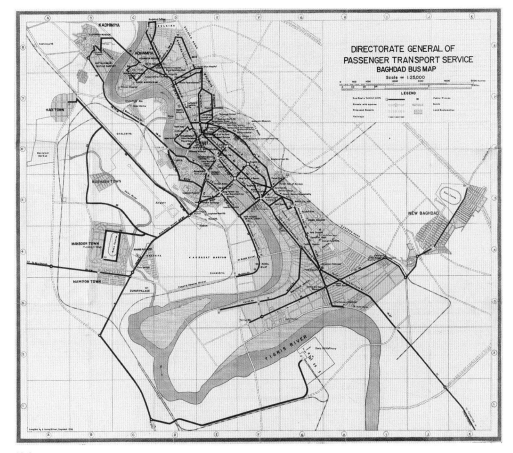

10.6

10.7

10.6. Baghdad, 1957. Bus Map. Map Collection, Pusey Library, Harvard University

10.7. Parliament Building, Baghdad, J. Brian Cooper, 1951–57. Aerial view showing Iraq Petroleum Company headquarters on al-Mansur Street in left foreground. From *Iraq Petroleum Magazine*, March 1958

10.8

10.8. Central Railway Station, Baghdad, James M. Wilson and H. C. Mason, 1947–54. Aerial perspective showing projected plaza and Baghdad Airport to upper left (Wilson and Mason, 1931). From the *Builder*, April 1949

dome derived from the Roman Pantheon. Wings extending to the south create a monumental forecourt centered on a tall colonnade contained by clock towers treated in a modernistic, Art Deco fashion. An enclosed courtyard on the southwest provides offices for the national railway administration, while a symmetrical one on the northeast was left open as a separate pick-up and drop-off point.

Only an urban intention of the most monumental sort could explain such an unusual design for a railroad station. As an article in the *Builder* explained, "the railway building, which is a terminal station, occupies a very important architectural position in the replanning of Baghdad. In front of it there is designed a large piazza from which runs one of the main axial roads of the new development."[15] The article added that the bird's-eye perspective of the station, which shows the new airport to the left, gives an indication of the architects' urban scheme. An undated, partial plan of the city reveals the full extent of their larger program and the degree to which it followed the City Beautiful ideas of Lutyens going back to the earlier part of the century (see figure 10.5).[16] A mall extends southeast from the oval plaza, through a grid of large blocks, down to a circle from which its continuation angles out toward the river in the direction of the soon-to-be-completed Parliament and Palace buildings. The Central Railway Station, the Parliament-Palace complex, and a projected government center north of the latter triangulate what the *Iraq Times* described in 1956 as the "amazing" revival in "Baghdad West" of the glory of the "famed Circular City."[17]

The Minoprio-Spencely-Macfarlane Master Plan, 1954–56

Wilson and Mason's urban vision for West Baghdad was never realized, despite the fact that the city witnessed a major investment in buildings and infrastructure in the 1950s along with the promise of relief from the threat of annual flooding. Oil was the key to this newfound wealth. The British-controlled Iraq Petroleum Company was created in 1925, but Iraq lagged behind other countries in the region in the exploitation of its fields. In 1950, as production increased, Iraq renegotiated its agreement with the company to increase its profits substantially. Following the nationalization of the oil industry in Iran that year and the fifty-fifty split in profits Saudi Arabia negotiated with Aramco, the Iraq Petroleum Company agreed in 1952 to give Iraq an equivalent deal.

Iraq's revenues increased dramatically, almost quadrupling from $32 million in 1951 to $112 million in 1952. (They reached $237 million by 1958.) To manage these enormous sums, the government created a semiautonomous Development Board in 1950, which received 70 percent of the annual oil revenues by 1952. Its object, according to its enabling legislation, was to create "'a general economic and financial plan for the development of the resources of Iraq and the raising of the standard of living of her people.'" "'This plan,'" the legislation continued, "'shall define a general programme of the projects to be undertaken by the Board and shall include in its scope but not be limited to projects in water conserving, flood control, irrigation, drainage, industry and mining as well as projects for the improvement of communications by river, land and air.'"[18] Although investment in new public buildings in Baghdad would come only after 1956, it was the board's Wadi Tharthar reservoir and diversion project, including the Samarra barrage on the Tigris north of Baghdad, undertaken in 1952 and completed in 1956, that set the stage for the capital's redevelopment and expansion.[19]

The municipality of Baghdad and the national Development Board did not generally work hand in hand. Soon after the Central Railway Station was finished, the municipality, on its own, hired a professional town-planning firm from London, Minoprio & Spencely and P. W. Macfarlane, to develop a master plan for the city. While eschewing Wilson and Mason's City Beautiful approach in favor of a more functionalist orientation, their modernism was mitigated by a conservative, middle-of-the-road philosophy recalling Raymond Unwin's compromise between classical design principles and Garden City ethics and aesthetics so evident at Letchworth.[20]

Well known in the Middle East for their work in Kuwait (beginning in 1951), Minoprio & Spencely and P. W. Macfarlane were commissioned for the Baghdad project by the municipality's new lord mayor, Fakhruddin al-Fakhri, in late 1954.[21] The work was completed in March 1956. The twenty-four-page *Master Plan for the City of Baghdad, 1956: Report*, delivered the following month, was accompanied by an approximately three-foot-square colored plan, drawn over a survey map of the city. The plan depicts an urban area extending about twelve and a half miles in a north-south direction and nine in an east-west one, the entire ovoid-shaped city surrounded by a "rural belt" (figure 10.14).[22]

For the next two-plus years, the Minoprio-Spencely-Macfarlane team continued to provide detailed studies of specific areas of the city and to consult with the group of internationally famous architects including Wright, Le Corbusier, Alvar Aalto (1898–1976), Willem Dudok (1884–1974), Gio Ponti (1891–1979), and Walter Gropius, who were commissioned by the Development Board to design signature buildings.[23] The coup d'état of 14 July 1958 that toppled the monarchy effectively ended the British town planners' work. Their master plan, however, remained the "official plan" until at least 1963, notwithstanding the fact that Constantinos Doxiadis (1914–75) produced a rival one in 1958–59 and José Luis Sert was contacted about redesigning the projected civic center in 1960–61.[24] The revolution also put a temporary halt to the architectural commissions the planners were overseeing, only a few of which were ultimately realized in anything like their originally intended form.

Charles Anthony Minoprio (1900–1988), who went by his middle name, and Hugh Greville Castle Spencely (1900–1983), who went by the name Greville, formed a partnership in 1928 after graduating from the University of Liverpool's School of Architecture, where they studied town planning, in the first-of-its-kind Department of Civic Design, with Charles H. Reilly and Patrick Abercrombie.[25] Their work in the 1930s consisted mainly of country houses for the well-to-do, as well as some workers' housing, done mostly in a restrained, elegantly detailed version of the "new tradition," as Henry-Russell Hitchcock would have described it.[26]

The two partners began to get the town planning commissions for which they were trained soon after World War II when Great Britain launched a major effort at reconstruction. At the beginning, Minoprio took the lead and full credit for the jobs. The first was a survey and master plan of the town of Chelmsford, done in 1944–45.[27] The focus on traffic flow, parking, and creation of a new civic center and limited-sized residential areas based on the Garden City "neighborhood unit" concept—all designed within a perimeter-block aesthetic following existing street patterns and picturesque principles—laid down the fundamental lines Minoprio and Spencely would follow in their later work.

Their big break came with the commissions for the New Towns of Crawley and Cwmbran, two of the fourteen publically funded Garden City–like initiatives established by the New Towns Act of 1946 to alleviate the overcrowded conditions of existing cities. They were one of only two architecture and planning firms to design two New Towns in the initial phase of the program. The master plan for Crawley New Town, south of London, was done in 1947–49, again under the name of Minoprio alone.[28] That for Cwmbran New Town, in Wales, was produced in 1950–51, by which time Minoprio and Spencely had associated themselves with Peter W. Macfarlane for his expertise in surveying, zoning, and legal issues.[29] Crawley was the much more important of the two and, as it was built out over the succeeding decades, fulfilled most standards by which the New Town ideal was judged.

Crawley New Town was planned for a population of fifty thousand on the site of a small country town in a location benefiting from the industrial base of nearby Gatwick Airport. The existing street pattern played an important role in the Minoprio-Spencely design. The planners' primary aim, as they stated, was to provide, as would be the case in Baghdad, "a framework of roads and zones upon which the more detailed planning of the town can be based." This took roughly the form of a self-contained oval, organized "on a ring and radial pattern."[30] Two outer rings of residential "neighborhood units" were arranged around the town's civic center and main shopping area (figures 10.9–10). Ring roads surrounded the center and inner residential ring while the "rural belt" around the outer residential ring provided insurance against sprawl. Each of the residential neighborhoods was planned for a diversity of housing classes and types; and each was to have as its local center "a modern and more urban version of the English village green around which may be grouped a church, a primary school, some shops, some service buildings, one or two inns," and so on.[31]

With its array of public and commercial buildings, the town center was designed as an extension of the existing High Street (figure 10.11). Many of the shops on the slightly irregular street were restored and provided with rear car parks. As the main north-south artery leading from the railway station, the High Street defines the western edge of the area of shopping blocks (with internal car parks) that was located between it and the new east-west Boulevard, containing the main elements of the civic center.[32] The Boulevard, which harks back to the one designed by Unwin for Letchworth (figures 3.32–33), terminates in a classical *patte d'oie* embracing an art center containing an art gallery, museum, concert hall, and theater. In its ample provision for parking and its system

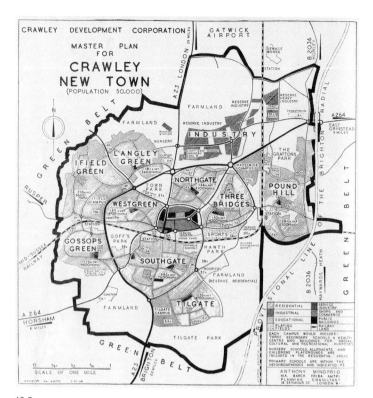

10.9

10.11

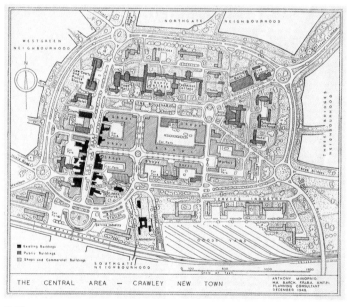

10.10

10.9. Crawley New Town Master Plan, Anthony Minoprio [and Greville Spencely], 1947–49. Overall plan. From *Journal of the Town Planning Institute*, January–February 1949

10.10. Crawley New Town. Plan of town center. From *Journal of the Town Planning Institute*, January–February 1949

10.11. Crawley New Town. Perspective from shopping area to civic center. From *Town and Country Planning*, Winter 1948–49

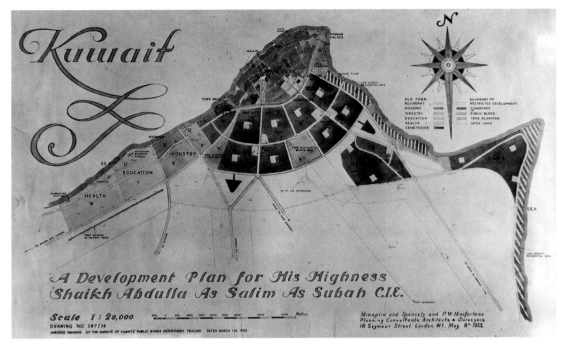

10.12

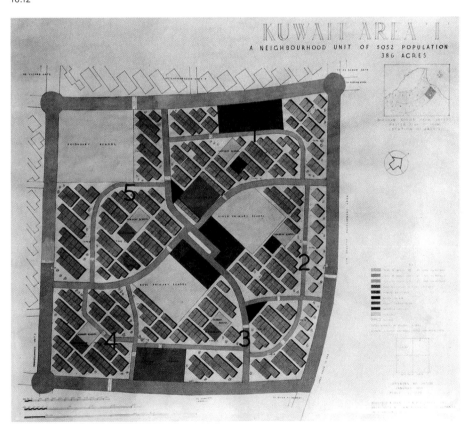

10.13

10.12. Kuwait City Master Plan, Minoprio & Spencely, and P. W. Macfarlane, May 1952.
Private collection

10.13. Kuwait City. Plan of Neighborhood Unit I, 1954. Private collection

of broad streets and roads flowing around numerous traffic circles, the Crawley plan showed how one could accommodate the automobile in a modern town plan without giving up a traditional street pattern in favor of a more radical superblock/tower-in-the-park solution. This same conservative approach would guide the firm's work in the Middle East, first in Kuwait City and a couple of years later in Baghdad.

Based on their work at Crawley, in particular, Minoprio, Spencely, and Macfarlane were hired in April 1951 to produce a master plan for the capital of Kuwait as a major element of the oil-rich British protectorate's project to establish a socialist welfare state on the model of its Laborite guardian.[33] The final plan, accepted in May 1952, was largely implemented by 1967, when it was superseded by one by Colin Buchanan. The old city, facing the Persian Gulf, was partially demolished in order to be redeveloped for government, civic, and commercial uses as well as new residential sections to the northeast (figure 10.12). Ringing this core opened up by a network of new streets and wide avenues is a double arc of superblocks meant in part to house those displaced from the city center. Each block forms a neighborhood unit centered on such communal facilities as schools, playgrounds, shops, and mosques; and each is connected to the downtown by a grid of limited-access highways (figure 10.13). While their self-containment, internal focus, and picturesque street arrangement recall the Garden Suburb–derived plans for the Chicago City Club competition of nearly forty years before (figures 4.15–17), the automobile-based design of the overall conception bears comparison with the nearly contemporaneous Brasilia (1956–60).

Minoprio, Spencely, and Macfarlane were much luckier in Kuwait than in Baghdad, where the political conditions and scale of operations were decidedly more challenging. The planners approached the Baghdad commission not only as a way to give shape and coherence to a strung-out, "scattered" city, as they described it, but equally as a way to provide its people with essential and much-needed housing and social services that would allow the city to achieve the "status [it deserves] as the capital of a strategically placed, rapidly developing Middle East country with a great economic future."[34] Their self-stated goals went well beyond the brief they received from the municipality in early December 1954, which focused on circulation, zoning, and the siting of public buildings. Their "instructions," they said, were to "deal with"

(a) *The Main Road System*, including the principal existing roads and bridges and any new major roads or bridges considered necessary.
(b) The areas recommended for different kinds of *Land Use*, such as Housing, Industry, Commerce and Open Space.
(c) *New Buildings*, such as Schools, Shops or Clinics, or Car Parks.[35]

Although the colored plan submitted with their *Report* (figure 10.14) made it graphically clear that these three desiderata were treated front and center, the text of the *Report* evinced another, more socially progressive set of priorities. It began not with the "Road System" but with a discussion of "Future Population and Housing Proposals." It stated that "the provision of new roads for traffic circulation will solve what is essentially a mechanical problem; but the provision of new homes, the clearance of slum areas, and the relief of over-crowding is, above all, a human and social problem. However mechanically efficient the town may become, however imposing may be its new buildings, unless housing conditions can be drastically improved, it will be but a façade and a sham, hiding a canker that will one day manifest itself in social unrest and dissatisfaction." The new housing would be accompanied by "such social facilities as up-to-date schools and amenities like parks and playing fields."[36]

The housing problem was made only more pressing by the population statistics the planners presented and the impact urban renewal of the downtown areas of Rusafa and Karkh would have on exacerbating the situation. Based on the 1947 census, they estimated the current population within the metropolitan area covered by the master plan as a little over 675,000. Providing for growth over a fifty to sixty-year period, they stated that the plan was intended to accommodate another 790,000-plus persons, thus serving a population of nearly 1.5 million by around 2010. Aside from the increase due to in-migration and better health conditions, the number of people living in the "central areas" would be reduced almost ninefold as a consequence of wholesale clearance and redevelopment (figures 10.17–18). The plan called for a reduction of the downtown population from well over 275,000 to less than 34,000. This meant that nearly a quarter of a million people "will have to be settled in areas on the outskirts of Baghdad zoned for residential development," the majority to the east but a good number also to the west.[37]

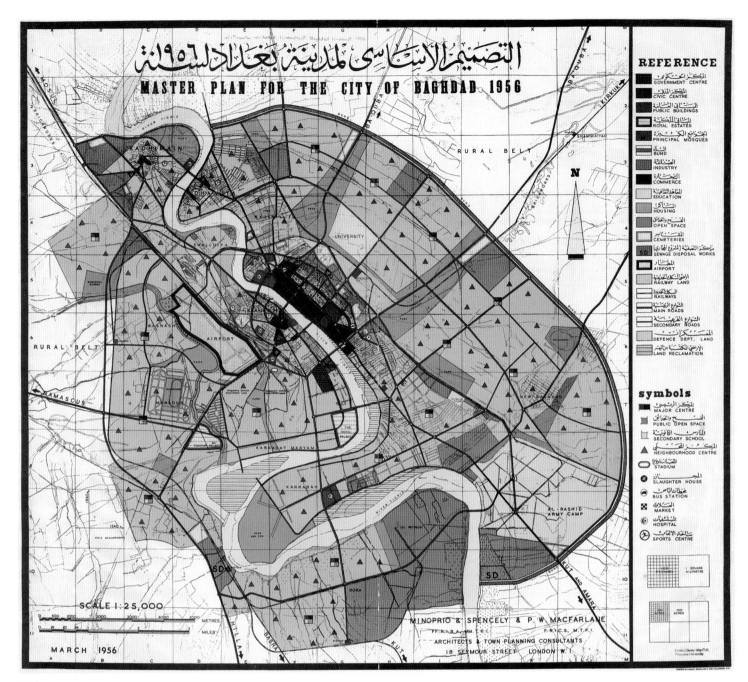

10.14

10.14. Baghdad Master Plan, Minoprio, Spencely, and Macfarlane, 1954–56. Map and
Geospatial Information Center, Peter B. Lewis Library, Princeton University

One can read in this echoes of Haussmann and Moses, mitigated by Garden City/New Town idealism. Rather than allowing those who would be uprooted and displaced from having to fend for themselves, Minoprio, Spencely, and Macfarlane stated that "the Municipality should undertake the social obligation of their rehousing." This would prevent further "hardship" and ensure that "civic improvements will [not] become associated in the public's mind with dispossession of homes … [and thus] give planning a bad name."[38] The new housing stock occupied all the areas on the plan in light brown, the color of the mud-brick commonly used in residential construction.

As in Kuwait City, the housing was arranged in "neighborhood units of varying size" averaging ten thousand residents per unit. These were "bounded but not intersected by traffic roads." Each was to have its own "neighborhood centre," indicated by solid, equilateral triangles, "where the necessary service buildings are grouped, such as shops, clinic, library, public hall, and probably mosque, to meet the community's needs." Each neighborhood unit would have a primary school and public open space, "including playing fields" for children. The "desperate need" for greenery and public gardens would be met by numerous new parks bordering the neighborhood units as well as by the larger centers between neighborhoods, indicated by red, blue, yellow, and green squares, where secondary schools serving multiple neighborhood units were located.[39]

Following the lead-off section on housing, the *Report* dealt next with the "Rural Belt" that would entirely surround the city "to prevent the continuous outward spread of development … in the form of ribbon building" and thus preserve the new "compact" shape the planners gave the city.[40] Next came the section on "Transport," which covered mainly proposals for new and improved streets and roads but also bus, air, and railway service. "Congestion" demanded a modern street and road system with adequate parking facilities. As the master plan shows, the existing streets running through and around the downtown commercial and administrative center were interconnected by a series of traffic circles at major junctions and extended where necessary. They were also widened to a consistent degree and some made into divided avenues.

New bridges were proposed to link Rusafa and Karkh on an east-west grid that ran through the older areas of the left and right banks and extended into the newer residential ones, especially on the east. Karkh itself was now defined by a continuous

street that looped around to the west to connect the new railway station and related public buildings with Rusafa. The larger grid in the newly developed eastern area curved around to follow a projected outer bund that defined the edge of the "rural belt," while at the same time crossing the river on bridges connecting the outlying residential neighborhoods on both banks. While the grid of the street network on the east bank had a clarity, that on the west broke down and followed a rather erratic, ad hoc course. Of great importance to its designers was the "riverside boulevard … proposed for the whole length of the river on the East Bank." An important part of their push for a major increase in open space, it was intended to provide "amenity use of and … public access to the Tigris," something which they felt was sorely lacking in the existing city.[41]

Next in the explanatory text came "Industry, Shopping and Commerce." Here strict zoning was the byword. Industrial areas, indicated on the plan in purple, were generally located at the edges. Only the light industrial workshops, mainly on Shaykh Umar Street at the edge of Rusafa, were retained in close proximity to the city center. In any event all the areas zoned for industry were to remain free of other uses, especially housing. Shopping and other forms of commerce were confined to the areas shown in blue in downtown Rusafa and Karkh. Neighborhood centers would have only what amounted to convenience stores "to meet an essential local need."[42]

Following directly from the discussion of the downtown commercial area came the chapter devoted to the "Civic and Government Centres." These two entirely new additions to the urban landscape would entail major amounts of expropriation and demolition. The purpose was to provide the municipal and national governments with needed public buildings "grouped together" rather than "scattered about the town" as they presently were.[43] The seventy-two-acre civic center was located toward the southern end of Rusafa, between the new Queen Aliyah and existing King Ghazi Streets, with a spur crossing Rashid Street to the river. Although things would change after the plan was submitted, the complex was initially projected to contain, among other institutions, the city hall, main post office, ministry of justice, police courts, and public library (figure 10.15).

Across the river, south of the projected Queen Aliyah Bridge and directly opposite the new Parliament Building was the "imposing Government Center," a seventy-acre site where the state government ministries (other than Justice) would be housed (figure 10.16). Al-Mansur (now Haifa) Street, running between the Parliament and the new center, already contained a number of foreign embassies and had earlier been laid out by Wilson and Mason "for formal use for processions."[44] The buildings of the civic center, rather than the government center, however, would become the greater focus for the Development Board program after 1956.

Next in the planners' explanatory text came a rather loosely knit chapter dealing with "Land for Special Purposes." It included discussions of existing and new mosques, markets, hospitals, fire stations, main slaughterhouse, defense department land, cemeteries, and a crematorium. All these establishments were separately indicated on the colored plan, as were the schools that took up much of the discussion of buildings for "Education" in the next chapter of the *Report*. After calling for the need for the establishment of a "single education authority," the text returned to the subject of the vital need for nursery and primary schools in each "neighborhood unit" plus secondary schools to be shared by several of these residential units. This preceded a discussion of the grouping of the "now widely scattered" existing colleges and their development into a full-fledged "University Centre."[45]

On his visit to Baghdad in June 1955, Minoprio was informed of the government's intention to establish a university. The site then under consideration was the tip of the Karada Peninsula.[46] The planners debated the location with the authorities over the following months and into the next year and a half. While acknowledging "the particular advantages" of the peninsula—"with its date palm groves and long river frontage"—as a "magnificent site for a group of University buildings," they concluded, at the time the *Report* was submitted, that it was "a little far from the centre of the city."[47] They thus chose to locate the new university to the north of Rusafa, near the existing college buildings, just beyond the railway tracks leading to Baghdad East Station (it is shown on the plan in yellow).[48]

This allowed them to devote the tip of the Karada Peninsula to one of the two metropolitan parks planned for the city (although they continued to refer to it as "the alternative site for the University"). What recommended it as a park were "its wonderful display of greenery, its date palm groves and the presence of the river, which bounds it on three sides," all of which "make it a real oasis of beauty, offering opportunities for mental refreshment and quiet that it is

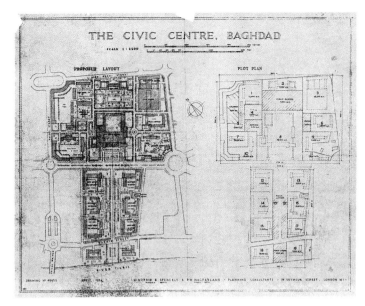

10.15

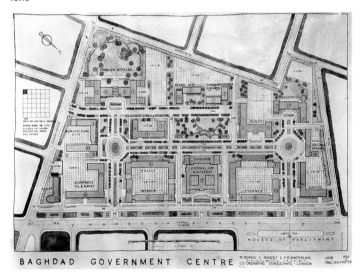

10.16

10.15. Civic center project, Baghdad, Minoprio, Spencely, and Macfarlane. Plan, April 1956. AAM

10.16. Government center project, Baghdad, Minoprio, Spencely, and Macfarlane. Plan, June 1958. Private collection

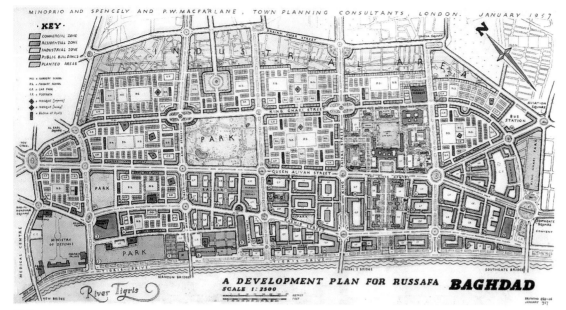

10.17

10.18

10.17. Rusafa development project, Baghdad, Minoprio, Spencely, and Macfarlane.
Plan, January 1957. Private collection

10.18. Baghdad in July 1957, showing demolition and street construction in vicinity of
proposed civic center. Photograph taken or acquired by Alvar Aalto. AAM

so essential a great city should provide for its inhabitants." "Its primary importance … as a green lung for the city" could be supplemented, they said, by the addition of "a zoological gardens and restaurant."[49] These comments were made in the succeeding chapter of the *Report*, which dealt with "Open Space" and included discussions of the need for playgrounds, extensive tree planting, the riverside parkway, and two projects that relate, as we shall see, to the Wright and Le Corbusier commissions. The first called for the "reclamation of river land," in particular, the Umm al-Khanazir Island between the Karada Peninsula and Karadat Maryam; the second described the need for a "major sports centre and stadium," which the planners proposed to locate at the north end of Karadat Maryam, diagonally opposite the Central Railway Station (see figure 10.14).[50]

The final section of the text, titled "Public Utility Services and Flood Protection," laid out plans for sewage and refuse disposal works and water and electricity supply. It concluded with contingency plans for a new outer bund on the east bank in case the flood protection measures promised by the Samarra Barrage and Wadi Tharthar diversion project were judged inadequate by the municipal drainage authority engineers.[51]

The colored drawing that served as the iconic document of the Minoprio-Spencely-Macfarlane master plan at first gives the appearance of a rather low-key, pragmatic, and abstract solution to the problems posed by the city's future development. The masses of light-brown housing and the crisscrossing red lines of streets and roads create an impression of overall evenness that belies the plan's major novelty and contribution to the reinvention of the city's shape. There are no bold gestures, no obvious expressions of pomp or show that might have issued from either a more explicit representation of the monarchical state or from a more radical modernist urban vision.[52]

The city is taken at face value, from a presentist point of view. The rival planner Raglan Squire (1912–2004) complained that it merely "accepted the situation as it exists."[53] The plan itself is drawn over an aerial survey map. The *Report* makes no reference to history other than to note certain mosques "as among the finest architectural features of Baghdad" and to remark unfavorably on the "few important public buildings … scattered about the town … [that] date back to the Turkish period."[54] Neither the Round City of al-Mansur nor the later history of Ottoman and British occupation were referred to, although we know from other contexts that the planners were

aware of Baghdad's originary design and felt some concern for preserving "'the Arab character of the town.'"[55]

Yet the imposition of an almost entirely new urban fabric, literally on top of the existing city, could be considered as bold, or at least as disruptive, as anything Haussmann or Moses did. Indeed, when one looks at the detailed "Development Plan for Rusafa" produced in January 1957 to give more specific information on how the city's center was to be reconfigured, the wholesale destruction of certain parts of Paris or Manhattan certainly comes to mind (figures 10.17–18). And in the same way that Haussmann and Moses showed little regard for existing context and traditional street patterns, the Minoprio-Spencely-Macfarlane scheme implanted a totally foreign, European system of geometrically arranged streets enclosing perimeter blocks of buildings over an area that had been characterized by a jigsaw puzzle of adjoining houses separated by winding alleys. The latter configuration remains visible in the "industrial area" at the top of the detailed plan, just below Shaykh Umar Street, like an underlay left to show what "progress" had been projected.

The boldness of the plan lay neither in novel urban gestures nor in the wholesale remaking of the past that was fairly taken for granted at the time as an inherent part of the redevelopment process. Rather, it lay in the overall shape the city was made to assume. Instead of adhering to the loosely defined pattern of ribbon development that had typified Baghdad's growth along the east bank of the Tigris during the first half of the twentieth century (see figure 10.6)—a pattern that in many ways replicated London's historical growth along the north bank of the Thames—Minoprio, Spencely, and Macfarlane consciously gave to the Iraqi capital what they called a "compact" shape intended to counteract the city's "tendency for scattered development" in "untidy ribbons."[56] The Haussmann connection seems all the more relevant here since the "compact" image Minoprio, Spencely, and Macfarlane imparted to Baghdad explicitly recalls that of pre–World War II, intra-muros Paris, a somewhat irregular ovoid divided more or less in half by a river and growing out in rings on a radial pattern from a dense, contained central core (figure 10.19).

If in fact Paris did serve as the model, it did so for a specific and pragmatic purpose. Whereas Baghdad had "naturally developed," according to the planners, "along the Tigris … in a north-south direction," "future north-south expansion,"

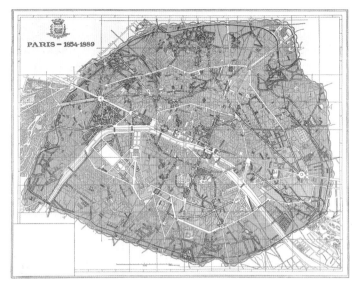

10.19

10.19. Paris. Map showing changes under Georges-Eugène Haussmann, 1854–69. From Burnham and Bennett

they agreed with others in authority, "is not desirable." "By scheduling for residential development large areas on the east side of Rusafa and west of Karkh," as well as new government and cultural uses on the west, "we have aimed," they stated, "at creating a future town of more convenient shape, with as much new development as possible located near to the main centres of employment."[57] In this proposal for a new biaxial pattern of city growth, the Minoprio-Spencely-Macfarlane plan ratified and gave concrete form to the idea for the expansion of the city to the west that had begun earlier in the decade and would become the major thrust of urban thinking by its end.[58]

Development Board Commissions for Signature Buildings

Minoprio, Spencely, and Macfarlane's work did not cease with the submission and acceptance of their master plan. They were appointed "Co-ordinating Architects for the Government and Civic Centres" in February 1957 and continued to produce more detailed "development plans" for Rusafa and Karkh and the nearby suburbs of Khadimain and Adhamiya as well as updated plans for the civic center. In addition, soon after their plan was submitted, they were placed in charge of site selection for new public buildings and the drawing up and conveying of their programs to the invited architects. In this intermediary role, they formed a bridge between the municipality and the Development Board.[59]

The Development Board's first six-year plan (1951–56) emphasized what economists call "social overhead capital." The bulk of the funds were spent on infrastructure: flood control, irrigation, and water storage projects to harness the country's agricultural potential. Transportation and communication, industry, and construction were given lower priority. In response to political pressure against this long-term, trickle-down approach, which was felt by many to help only the rich landowners, the board modified its philosophy in its next effective six-year plan (1955–60), which was budgeted at $1.4 billion. Investment in transportation and public building now amounted to a little under half the budget, with that portion being divided nearly equally between the two sectors.[60]

To maintain its authority and counter the constant threat of insurrection, the government was looking for "widespread and visible benefits quickly."[61] Urban areas, particularly Baghdad, where dissension was most likely to occur, were targeted for housing, health, education, and welfare projects, as well as for civic and cultural buildings. Money was allocated in the 1956–57 budget for the Iraq Museum, the new Parliament Building, the Royal Palace, a national library, and a Hilton hotel. Over the next few years, there would be funds set aside for an opera house, an Olympic-sized stadium, a gallery of modern art, a new law courts building, and a campus to house the new Baghdad University. Beginning in April 1956, a Development Week was celebrated each spring, at which time the latest projects were announced and those just completed were dedicated with great fanfare by the king.

At first there seemed to be no general policy or direction in the building program. The Development Board adopted a number of ongoing projects, like those for the museum of antiquities, Parliament, and the Royal Palace, which were already in the hands of rather undistinguished architects: the first being carried out by the German Werner March, who had been in charge of the job since 1932; the latter two by J. Brian Cooper, who served as the official government architect in the 1930s. The first signs of a change in direction came in 1955 when the board reached out to Le Corbusier and to Constantinos Doxiadis.[62] The former was asked in June 1955 for a design for an Olympic Stadium and sports complex, although he was given only a very sketchy program and no specific idea of where the site would be. A year later he was told that the site was being discussed with the city's planning consultants and that he would receive notice of it in due course.[63] We know from the diary Minoprio, Spencely, and Macfarlane kept of their visits to Baghdad that, in late May-early June 1956, they advocated for moving the stadium site further south from the Central Railway Station, where it was shown on the master plan. The letter from the minister of development telling Le Corbusier of these discussions and an impending decision is dated 23 July. Based on a misunderstanding that surfaced only a year and a half later, when Le Corbusier visited Baghdad, it appears that he may never have been informed of the relocated site.[64]

Doxiadis, who had been the administrator of the Marshall Plan in Greece, was recommended to the Development Board by the International Bank for Reconstruction and Development. He was commissioned, four months after Le Corbusier, to design a large-scale housing and community development program not just for Baghdad but for several cities throughout Iraq as well. The seven-volume housing report he submitted in August of the following year was partially implemented over the next few years, but the projects undertaken were never considered part of the board's signature building program by internationally renowned architects that officially began in December 1956 when Le Corbusier was contacted once again and his earlier commission confirmed.[65]

The decision to move ahead full-steam with the Corbusier stadium was taken by the Development Board on 15 December 1956. The architect was sent a letter to that effect ten days later.[66] Following this action, things progressed rather quickly. On 29 December, the board decided to ask Wright to design the city's Opera House and Aalto its Gallery of Fine Arts, specifically for modern and contemporary art.[67] They also apparently asked Oscar Niemeyer (1907–2012) to participate in the program. The letters went out on 15 January 1957, although the one to Aalto did not get to him until April. Wright responded almost immediately and enthusiastically. Niemeyer, a committed communist, refused the offer to work for a repressive, anticommunist, Baghdad Pact–member government.[68] He was the only foreign architect to do so.

On 21 January the Development Board voted to ask Dudok to design the city's Law Courts and Directorate-General of Police Building, the latter to include a separate structure to house the Divisional Police Headquarters. When informed of this on 2 February, Dudok was told that the buildings were to be in the new civic center and that, since this "development" would involve "several Consultant Architects," the board "appointed a Co-ordinating Architect [Minoprio, Spencely, and Macfarlane] to help the different Consultants in keeping in touch with each other's plans and for the sake of getting [a] harmonious and acceptable general appearance for the Centre as a whole." Dudok gladly accepted the board's offer two weeks later.[69] Aalto was the only other member of the newly appointed architects whose project was in the civic center. He and Dudok would correspond on numerous occasions with each other and with Minoprio, Spencely, and Macfarlane; and Dudok even planned one of his Baghdad trips to coincide with the planners' presence there.

Although Ponti later claimed that he received the commission for the Development Board and Ministry of Development Building at the same time as Wright and Aalto, all available evidence points to the fact that this took place only a week after Dudok's appointment.[70] No doubt because the Development Board itself was the client, Minoprio, Spencely, and Macfarlane were never consulted on the very prominent site, just north of the Parliament Building and northeast of the proposed government center, parallel to the on-ramp of Queen Aliyah Bridge (see figure 10.28).

The final Development Board project, that for Baghdad University, which was ultimately given to Walter Gropius and The Architects Collaborative, was awarded more than seven months after Ponti's. Both Ellen and Nizar Jawdat, whose father served as prime minister between mid-June and mid-December 1957, had studied with Gropius at Harvard and discussed with him as early as 1954 the possibility of his getting work in Baghdad. The following year they specifically referred to the university but said the commission would have to await the completion of the Minoprio-Spencely-Macfarlane master plan.[71] Things took much longer than that, for the Development Board did not officially award the job to Gropius and TAC until early September 1957.[72]

After the various architects responded and their terms for employment were accepted by the Development Board, they were invited to Baghdad to discuss their projects, see the sites allocated to them, and receive a preliminary program. Wright was the first to make the trip, arriving on 20 May 1957 and leaving on the 25th.[73] Aalto was next. He arrived on 11 July and departed on the 18th.[74] Ponti visited Baghdad a month after Aalto, in mid-August.[75] Dudok arrived on 4 October and stayed for nearly two weeks, during which time he met with both Minoprio and Spencely at least five times, in addition to his other official visits.[76] Gropius went to Baghdad for a week, between 2 and 10 November. He overlapped with Le Corbusier, who arrived on the 9th and left on the 12th.[77]

Three of the six architects—Wright, Aalto, and Dudok—received additional commissions while they were in Baghdad. They were also the architects whose site allocations were most discussed by and/or with Minoprio, Spencely, and Macfarlane. After meeting with the Development Board, Wright received the commission to design a new Central Post and Telegraph Building in downtown Baghdad. Often confused with the later Aalto commission for a new Directorate General of Posts and Telegraph Building, to be located in the southwest corner of the civic center, Wright's building was to replace the existing Post and Telegraph Office on Rashid Street, east of the civic center.[78] Wright also came away from his nearly weeklong visit with an understanding that he had been promised the Baghdad University commission as well as one for an art gallery.[79] But the most important outcome of

the Wright trip was a requested change in the site for his opera house. This will be dealt with in detail later in this chapter.

On his visit a month and a half after Wright, Aalto was informed not only that he would be given an additional building, the Directorate General of Posts and Telegraph, but also that it had been decided to locate his Gallery of Fine Arts in the civic center.[80] The museum was added to the civic center by Minoprio, Spencely, and Macfarlane only after the original Aalto commission was awarded and once the center itself had been reduced in size, cleared of many of its administrative buildings, and reconfigured into a simple rectangular shape (figures 10.15, 10.20).[81] Indeed, one of the reasons for Aalto's new commission was that his Posts and Telegraph Building was meant to join with the Fine Arts Gallery in creating an urban composition on the center's west side, anchoring the King Faysal Street frontage at the corners of King Ghazi and Queen Aliyah Streets.

Dudok benefited from a similar urban consideration when he too was commissioned for an additional project on his visit to the city in October. Because of its intended location in the civic center next to the Law Courts and Police Headquarters buildings, Dudok was asked to design a building to house the registry of deeds, or Land Settlement and TAPU Departments.[82] He, like Aalto, was told to communicate directly with Minoprio, Spencely, and Macfarlane to ensure what Minoprio hoped would be "a harmonious result" for the civic center.[83] Over the course of the next year, the three principal players in the civic center design corresponded with each other on a regular basis. Minoprio, Spencely, and Macfarlane provided the two architects with updated programs taking into account the various changes the authorities continued to suggest.[84] They also provided Aalto and Dudok with the latest versions of their civic center plan.

Wright was the first of the "star architects" to complete his project. The drawings for the initial commissions for the Opera House (plus several other buildings accompanying it) and Post and Telegraph Building were finished in June and July 1957 and submitted the following month.[85] Dudok informed the Development Board in mid-April 1958 that he had completed the designs for his three buildings but wanted to come to Baghdad to present them in person. Aalto completed the drawings for his two buildings a little later that month and took them to Baghdad in mid-May. Le Corbusier drew up his Stadium and sports complex between March and May 1958

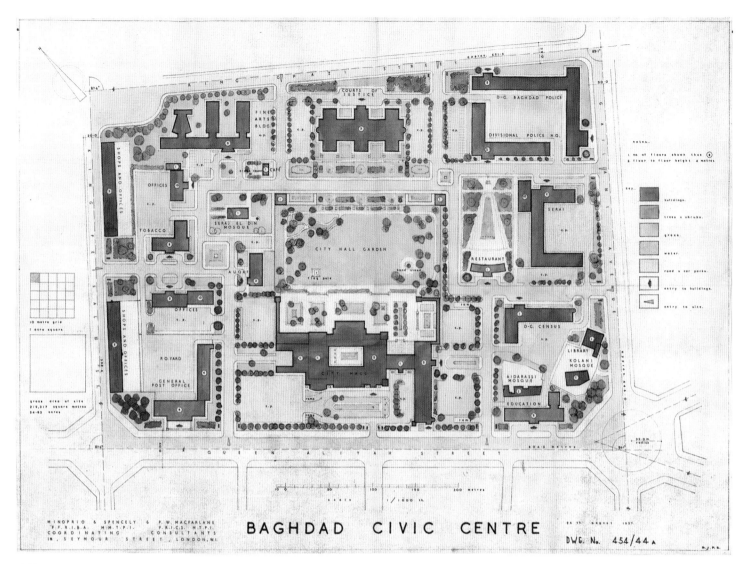

10.20

10.20. Civic center project, Minoprio, Spencely, and Macfarlane. Plan, August 1957.
HNI

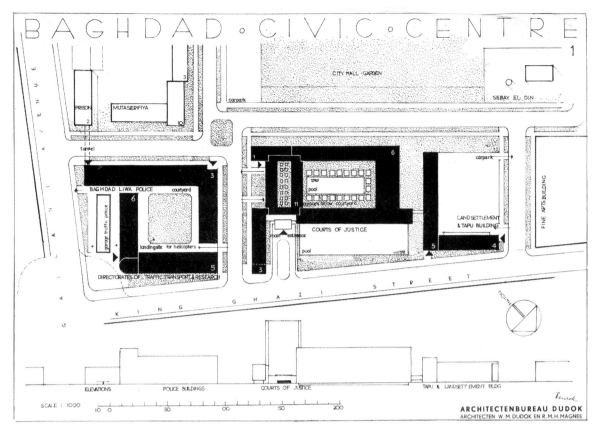

10.21

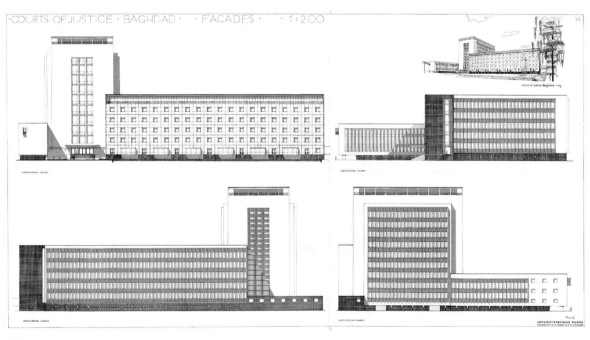

10.22

10.21. Law Courts, Land Settlement and TAPU Building, and Police Headquarters
projects (for civic center), Baghdad, Willem Dudok, 1957–58. Site plan. HNI

10.22. Law Courts project. Elevations and perspective from north. HNI

10.23

10.23. Law Courts project. Sketch perspective showing ideas for polychrome decoration. HNI

and had his associate Georges-Marc Présenté deliver the project in Baghdad on 6 June. Both Gropius and Ponti turned their designs in only after the July 1958 revolution.[86]

Because of the location of their projects in the civic center, Aalto and Dudok worked more closely with Minoprio, Spencely, and Macfarlane than any of the other architects did. Their designs were in significant ways influenced by the framework the planners created for them. Minoprio, Spencely, and Macfarlane sent both architects copies of their March 1956 master plan.[87] The Aalto Museum also preserves a copy of the original civic center plan of April 1956 (figure 10.15) as well as numerous drawings of the revised design showing the final locations of his two buildings (figure 10.24). The Dudok Papers preserve several versions of the operative civic center plan, one of which is a striking rendering in color dating from August 1957 (figure 10.20).

The August 1957 plan was a basically symmetrical, classical composition of picturesquely arranged structures of various shapes and sizes arrayed around a central, slightly asymmetrical garden. In a memorandum accompanying the drawing, the planners described the "layout" as "an informal one ... [that] envisages about 15 new public buildings, varying in height, design and architectural detail, placed in a park-like setting." The central, north-south axis was defined by the two "largest" and most important buildings, the city hall facing Queen Aliyah Street and the Law Courts facing King Ghazi Street. The three corner locations unencumbered by buildings needing to be preserved were where the General Post Office, Fine Arts Gallery, and Police Headquarters were placed. They were to serve as key "access" points while also defining the "civic" character of the composition. The building footprints, the planners noted, were "merely an indication of possible shapes of approximately the correct size." The hope was that though ultimately "varying" in form, they would be given a unity by being "faced with stone."[88]

Dudok created a movemented composition of his three buildings that was quite different from the rather static Minoprio-Spencely-Macfarlane diagram (figure 10.21). His Law Courts, which now shared the central location with the Land Settlement and TAPU Building, replaced the classical, pavilion-type suggestion by the planners with a pinwheeling, dual-courtyard design creating an asymmetrical outline in plan and a dynamic composition of varied volumes in perspective (figure 10.22). But Dudok did not depart completely from the Minoprio-Spencely-Macfarlane template in that his plan for the two structures accommodating the Police Headquarters adopted their interlocking Ls scheme, the only difference being that he brought the northernmost block in from Gailani Avenue so as to open up the corner and provide access to the parking garage. All Dudok's buildings were rendered in a severe, classicizing form of modernism, featuring punched windows, clearly defined structure, and framing edges. As suggested by the planners, the buildings were clad in stone, to which Dudok intended to give a rich and coloristic aspect. In order to "assist in renewing the splendour of this city, which had such a reputation for brilliance in the past," Dudok proposed "to cover the outer walls with white-marble strips, set with panels filled with gilt mosaics and to frame the windows with azure mosaics" (figure 10.23).[89]

Like Dudok, Aalto worked closely in accord with the Minoprio, Spencely, and Macfarlane plan. He too had a copy of the March 1956 master plan as well as several of the civic center itself. He used one of the latter as a basis for sketching out preliminary ideas for his two-building composition on the west side of the superblock (figure 10.24). In the final site plan, the now-named General Post Office has a modified L-shaped footprint that echoes the Minoprio-Spencely-Macfarlane scheme and mirrors the Dudok Police Headquarters diagonally across from it (figure 10.25). The two main wings of the five-story structure surround a skylit court containing the public and mail sorting halls. The outward-facing facades are defined by continuous window bands and ceramic tile spandrel panels separated by columns that flare out toward the top to support a cornice recalling the one in the Dudok Law Courts (figure 10.26). The columns create a shaded portico at ground level while the "capitals" supporting the cornice suggest the image of date palms. The ceramic tiles would have been semicircular in section and laid vertically in a manner characteristic of Aalto's work in Finland and elsewhere. The main difference is that here the tiles were dark blue in color, which Aalto believed was more appropriate to the local context than either the white or black he more commonly used.[90]

The blue tile revetment and flaring, palm-like columns were also employed in the Fine Arts Gallery to create a sense of continuity between the two otherwise very different designs (figure 10.27). Based on a plan-type he had developed for earlier museum projects in Estonia and Scandinavia, Aalto here used the closed, box-like shape containing the galleries in echelon, raised one story above ground level, to define the northwest corner of the civic center while offering a colorful screen to the view from the open court of Dudok's Land Settlement and TAPU Building and the projected city hall garden beyond them.[91] An amphitheatric shape, again common to many Aalto designs, projects above the roofline announcing the community function of the building and the existence of a roof garden for sculpture. The flaring capitals of the columns of the roof garden support a parasol-like structure providing shade and a place to congregate, as in the rooftop spaces of the typical Baghdadi house.

For the Olympic Stadium and sports complex, Le Corbusier apparently had only indirect interaction with Minoprio, Spencely, and Macfarlane, who, as noted previously, were independently involved in the selection of the site. The location was indicated on their March 1956 master plan as well as on a detailed drawing done by the planners at about the same time, showing it on the west bank between the Central Railway Station and the proposed government center (figure 10.14). Both plans are preserved in the Le Corbusier Archive, although there is no evidence the architect received them before his November 1957 visit to Baghdad.[92] What is known is that at that time, Le Corbusier realized that there was an error in the two plans and that his site was farther to the southeast, much closer to the projected government center (figures 10.28–29). This was actually where the British planners had ultimately decided the stadium should be, according to a note in their "Middle East Diary" of late May 1956.[93] Although they never got around to amending the plan, the authorities who took Le Corbusier to see the site obviously knew of the change.[94]

The actual site was in fact better than the original one, although Le Corbusier was still unhappy with it and would have preferred something on the river.[95] Yet despite his ordinarily large urbanistic ambitions, he apparently accepted what he was given and tweaked the site only slightly to adjust his plan's orientation to align on a north-south axis. The northern boundary was the projected main street leading to the recently completed Queen Aliyah Bridge linking the southern part of the west bank with the east. Le Corbusier divided the site into four main areas treated as "large islands" between which would "flow" the masses of spectators and participants in what he called a "hydraulic of crowds" (figure 10.30).[96] At the top, or north, was the fifty-thousand-seat Stadium. To the southwest of it was a grouping of fields for different sports. Below the

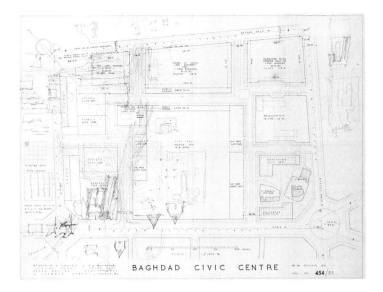

10.24

10.26

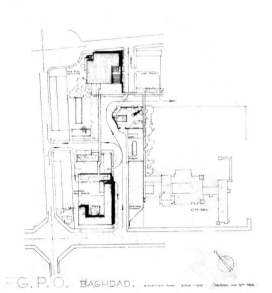

10.25

10.27

10.24. Fine Arts Gallery and General Post Office projects (for civic center), Baghdad, Alvar Aalto, 1957–58. Sketches over Minoprio, Spencely, and Macfarlane site plan of October 1957. AAM

10.25. Fine Arts Gallery and General Post Office projects. Site plan, May 1958. AAM

10.26. General Post Office project. Elevation on Queen Aliyah Street. AAM

10.27. Fine Arts Gallery project. Elevation toward Land Settlement and TAPU Building and city hall garden. AAM

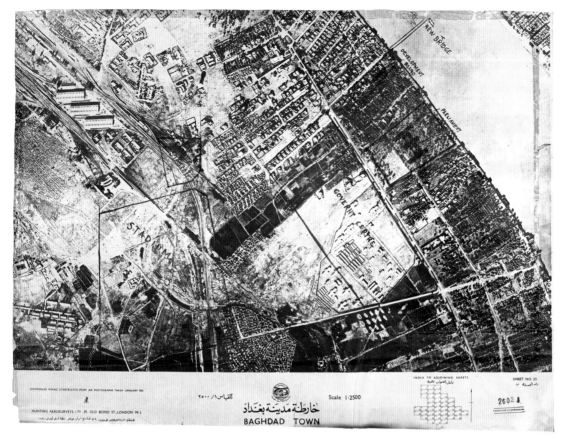

10.28

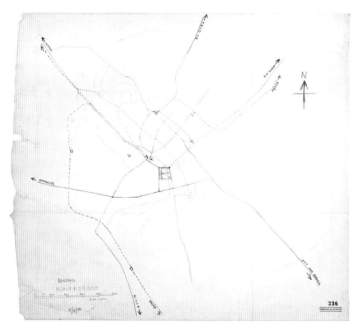

10.29

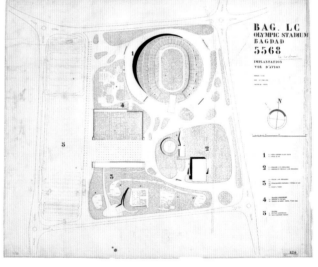

10.30

10.28. Olympic Stadium and sports complex project, Baghdad, Le Corbusier, 1957–58. Site indications of Stadium, government center, Development Board Building, and Parliament drawn on 1951 Hunting Aerosurveys aerial photograph. FLC

10.29. Stadium and sports complex project. Sketch site plan in urban context, 5 May 1958. FLC

10.30. Stadium and sports complex project. Plan, 5 June 1958. FLC

10.31

10.31. Development Board and Ministry of Development (later Economic Planning Board and Ministry of Planning) Building, Baghdad, Gio Ponti, 1958–62. Model, from southeast. Archivio Gio Ponti, Milan

latter and to the east was the indoor gymnasium for thirty-five hundred spectators, accompanied by an open-air, circular amphitheater for basketball, tennis, and other sports. Along the southern edge of the site was the area for aquatic sports and games, with three main swimming pools contained within boomerang-shaped bleachers. And to the west across a planted boulevard was a large area reserved for off-street parking.

The stadium, the driving force of the commission, occupied much of Le Corbusier's attention. Its design was based, as he himself remarked, on the project he did a little over twenty years earlier for a hundred-thousand-seat stadium for alternate sites on the outskirts of Paris.[97] A major concern for the Baghdad version was the excessive sun and heat, especially during the summer. To deal with this, Le Corbusier placed the majority of the stands on the west side under an elegantly curved protective canopy. Literally hundreds of drawings were devoted to figuring out the precise curvature of this detail as well as the precise angle of the stands themselves to ensure unobstructed viewing from all sections. Of similar concern to the architect was the landscaping plan, since he intended the site to be used as a public park, open at all times, even in the evening.

The Ponti Development Board and Ministry of Development Building, constructed for the Economic Planning Board and Ministry of Planning in 1960–62 under the succeeding revolutionary government, was sited and designed without any apparent input from the city's master planners (figures 10.31, 10.28). This was certainly to be expected given the semiautonomous status of the client. The building is composed of two distinct elements, a six-story block for the board attached to a taller, ten-story slab for the ministry offices. The two units slide by one another in a modernist way and are joined only at their ends by a circulation link. Most of the ground level is given over to an expansive portico providing protection from the sun both for pedestrians and their vehicles.

Ponti described the portico as the fundamental "idea" behind the building's design. It revealed, he said, that the structure derived not from any inauthentic adoption of "local stylistic motives" but rather from the "climatic conditions of Baghdad" and from "that climatic local reality only."[98] In fact, the taller building was closely based on Ponti's recently completed Pirelli Building in Milan (1956–58). Cladding the Baghdad version in grayish-blue ceramic tiles, the architect followed Aalto and Dudok in believing that such a coloristic

10.32

10.33

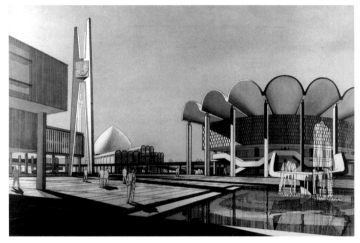

10.34

10.32. Baghdad University, Walter Gropius and The Architects Collaborative, design begun late 1957. First scheme. Site plan, 1958. 1=campus center; 2=teaching space; 3=student residences; 4=individual housing; 5=sports facilities; 6=elementary school; 7=infirmary; 8=service facilities; 9=entrance; 10=shopping center. From *AR*, April 1959

10.33. Baghdad University. First scheme. Perspective of student residences. From [The Architects Collaborative], *Report on the University of Baghdad Designed by The Architects Collaborative, Cambridge, Massachusetts, U.S.A.*, n.d.

10.34. Baghdad University. First scheme. Perspective of campus center, with auditorium, clock tower, and mosque in background. From *Report on the University of Baghdad*

move would bring a welcome and appropriate "gay note" to "the townscape."[99]

The campus for Baghdad University, designed by Gropius and The Architects Collaborative (TAC) beginning in late 1957 and partially constructed during the Qasim regime based on a revised scheme of 1960–62, was the largest Development Board commission as well as Gropius's biggest up until that time. As previously noted, the site suggested by the Minoprio, Spencely, and Macfarlane master plan in the northern part of the city was rejected by the authorities in favor of the alternate one they proposed at the southwest tip of the Karada Peninsula. Land there began to be expropriated by March 1957, just a couple of months before Wright arrived to incorporate the university project in his cultural center and nearly six months before the commission was given to Gropius and TAC.[100]

The initial Gropius-TAC design, done well after Wright's, grouped several separate residential colleges around a common administrative and teaching center (figure 10.32). The system was not unlike the one Gropius knew at his own institution of Harvard, where widely distributed individual "houses," the residential colleges, all share the same teaching, research, sports, and administrative facilities. Gropius's firm by this time was considered expert in not only campus planning but also in the correlation of physical design with issues of institutional organization. The creation of a framework for the first comprehensive university in Iraq was the major challenge they faced, and it was this that Gropius noted first in the publication of the project in *Architectural Record* in early 1959.[101]

The preeminent architectural challenge, however, was for Gropius, as for Ponti, the "climate." "A major problem is to counteract the excessive heat from May to September, often considerably higher than our blood temperature," he remarked. One solution was air-conditioning; the other was to place the buildings "around patios of various sizes" and "close enough to overshadow each other" (figure 10.33).[102] Despite their scattered disposition in a suburban, picturesque manner, the residential colleges were designed in imitation of the tight-knit housing blocks of the urban center of town (see figure 10.4). Although the forms and materials were entirely different from their vernacular mud-brick prototypes—and, like Aalto, Dudok, and Ponti, used colored glazed tile as revetment—a more explicit allusion to Islamic architecture was evident in the mosque just off the central plaza. If its arcaded portico echoed that of the neighboring auditorium-theater in a characteristic late International Style way, its onion dome clearly spoke a local sign language (figure 10.34).[103]

Wright's Baghdad Visit and Expanded Opera House Commission

The project that Wright developed out of his original commission for the Baghdad Opera House was entirely different from anything the other five "star architects" proposed. While all except Le Corbusier made an effort to create a contextual relationship with the city by means of formal elements such as colored tile revetments and shaded roof gardens or patios in what was considered at the time to be a "regionalist" adaptation of modernism to non-Western or local conditions, Wright proceeded differently.[104] Instead of avoiding direct historical references and allusions, he embraced them as he had never before. But even more divergent than this was his transformation of the commission for a single building into an urban plan for the city.

Whereas the other architects limited their scope to the building or buildings assigned to them, on the sites allocated to them, Wright expanded his opera house scheme into what he called a Plan for Greater Baghdad. It is no doubt for this reason that Minoprio, Spencely, and Macfarlane were solicited by the Development Board to comment specifically, first, on Wright's own choice of site and, subsequently, on the project itself. It was the only one of the international projects that they were asked to review. In early June 1957, before Wright had even completed his design, Minoprio discussed Wright's proposed site change with Mahmoud Hasan, director general of the Development Board's Second Technical Section, and submitted his response in writing. In late September, Minoprio and Spencely were asked to look at the actual drawings that, they noted, included bridges connecting the island to the east and west banks. A few days later, Spencely was shown more of Wright's drawings, which impressed him as "fantastic."[105] One might have expected an architect of Le Corbusier's urbanistic vision and accomplishments to have offered a design taking the entire city into account. It is therefore all the more telling about Wright's lifelong engagement with the issues and problems of urban planning that it would be he who would do so in what he must have suspected would be his last such opportunity.[106]

Before Wright arrived in Baghdad in late May 1957, he knew only that he had been commissioned to design an opera house and that the site was "'two acres in the middle of the city.'"[107] It was not in the civic center but diagonally opposite it in Karkh, on the newly developing west bank of the city. It was an unbuilt lot just south of the British Embassy, where the British Trade Fair was held in 1954 (see figure 10.36).[108] It faced al-Mansur Street, then the main north-south artery in Karkh, and was about 150 yards from the river, directly north of the King Faisal I Bridge that linked Karkh to Rusafa. Throughout 1955 and early 1956, it was considered for a museum, the new national library, as well as for an opera house. The museum idea was soon discounted, and by late 1956 Minoprio, Spencely, and Macfarlane concluded that the site would be "very suitable" for the opera and that the library would be better in the civic center. For a time, a location in the government center was mooted for the opera, but ultimately the Trade Fair site remained the one upon which everyone seemed to agree.[109] That is, everyone except for Wright.

There is no record of Wright's reaction to the location when he was taken to see it. However, an article in the *Iraq Times* of 21 May 1957 detailing his first guided tour of the city records the following: "Mr. Frank Lloyd Wright, internationally-known American architect, now in Baghdad to design the Opera House, is visiting different parts of the city, the museum, the Abassid [sic] Palace, the [Karada] site where Baghdad University will be built and other places to see which site is most suitable for the project." More important, it goes on to say that Wright "is not limiting himself to design an opera house only but a sort of cultural centre suited to Baghdad's historical and cultural background as well as its character." It added that he had already had "several talks on the project with the executive members of the Development Board, top-ranking engineers and others."[110]

One can only assume that during the tour Wright was told about the original, eighth-century Round City, something of the subsequent history of the city's move to Rusafa and, more recently, of the city's expansion west and south from Karkh on the right bank. One can also be quite sure that he was informed, if he had not been earlier, about the Minoprio, Spencely, and Macfarlane plan, which included the proposals for the reclamation of Umm al-Khanazir Island in the river, just northwest of the Karada Peninsula, and a zoo near the future university site (see figure 10.14). It was probably at this time, or in his prior meetings with the Development Board's executive members, that he was given copies of the 1956 master plan and aerial photographs of the city done by the British firm of Hunting Aerosurveys in 1950–51.[111]

It was from the air that Wright discovered the site that he preferred. Accounts differ, however, as to precisely when and how this occurred. Some claim that it was while his plane from Paris was circling over the city in preparation for landing that he spotted the island, popularly called Pig Island, that was slated for reclamation. Others, much more reliable, state that it was on a subsequent flight over the city taken specifically for the purpose of scouting out possible sites.[112] The conclusion to the story is less ambiguous. When Wright observed that the island was a "cleavage right between the city and the university," he realized that it was the key to his scheme for a cultural center linking the east and west banks of the city at the southern extremity of recent development. In two meetings with the young Faysal II, at least one of which was attended by his powerful uncle, Abd al-Illah, the architect requested and received the island site for the Opera House and for a cultural center to accompany it, including the University on the east bank facing the island.[113]

Wright's attitude toward how he might ultimately integrate aspects of Baghdad's past and present history in his design was predicted in the talk he gave to the Society of Iraqi Engineers approximately halfway through his stay in the city.[114] His presentation was something between a rant and a plea. It was a rant against the materialism and commercialism of modern Western society and its increasing impact on the Middle East. It was a plea in its nearly missionary zeal to encourage local architects, engineers, and government officials to study their own culture and history and look to the spiritual values they embody for lessons in moving toward the future.[115]

Wright began by laying out his own role as a critical one in relation to a narrow interpretation of development, as material progress, on a purely Western model. "I thought that I might be able to do something useful not only to develop but to preserve the characteristic beauty . . . [of] the Middle East," he declared. This preservationist impulse, he stated in his opening remarks, was to counteract the "materialist" influence of the "West" that he "hope[d] will never reach Iraq." If modern Western "commercialism" was to be defeated, a "rejuvenation" of the "ancient spirit of Baghdad" was needed. This he saw embodied in the "vigor" and "strength" of early Sumerian art and the climactic period of "Harun Al-Rashid" and the "tale[s] of the Arabian Nights." Throughout the talk, Wright exhorted his audience not to "sell out" to the West but to look "deep" into "your [own] inheritance" and make sure that it is "preserved in whatever you build for the future."[116]

As to what he himself might do, Wright spoke mainly in similar generalities. In noting that every nation has its own genius loci ("a genius of itself"), Wright remarked that "an architect should not come in [to Baghdad] and put a cliché [to work]." "He must come in and see the beauty that was, understand the character of nature that made it beautiful and try by every means in his power to keep it alive"—"not imitating it, not trying to reproduce it as it was," but by recapturing, rejuvenating its "spirit." Crucial to being able to achieve anything of the sort, Wright saw two fundamental problems needing to be addressed. The first, which was beyond his or any single architect's power, was the establishment, as Minoprio, Spencely, and Macfarlane had already recommended, of "a building code that is wise and adapted to circumstances." The second, which he referred to more than once and which would ultimately be foregrounded in his proposal, was the increasing presence of the automobile and the traffic hazards that presented. "In five years you are going to be overrun by motor cars," he predicted, comparing their potentially devastating effect to that of "the atom bomb."[117] The two specific problems he outlined were thus strictly in the domain of urban planning.

On his departure, Wright left the Development Board with a written "proposition" of what he intended to produce in addition to the designs for the Opera House and Central Post and Telegraph Building. He was "aware," as he put it shortly after, "of the ambiguous circumstances as I found them in Baghdad" and was thus under no illusion that the "proposition" would be accepted easily or in full.[118] In the cover letter written to the board in early August, accompanying the drawings for the large cultural center at the heart of a Plan for Greater Baghdad, Wright openly expressed doubts about the successful outcome of his efforts.

Apparently, Wright had originally been unaware of the number of other international architects involved. He wrote that he now realized he "had come too late to save [the country] ... from the invasions of the Proffesional [sic] Architects of the West" and that "committments [sic] had been made which would make my efforts unlikely to succeed." He had also become "aware," he said, of the likely criticism of him and

his work expressed by some of the "architectural advice as you have already received," probably referring to the Jawdats and Rifat Chadirji (b. 1926), champions of Gropius and Le Corbusier. Perhaps in direct reference to Gropius's impending hiring, for which the Jawdats had been lobbying, Wright implied to the board that "your plans ... will be exploited by competitions already set up by yourselves." Still, he told the board that he hoped to be able, at the very least, to "plant in your imaginations" a vision that "would make of Baghdad and Iraq a modern mecca for travelers and a place in which to find in modern terms the strength and beauty of ancient-culture—alive today."[119] Like the civic centers for Madison and Pittsburgh, the Baghdad project was thus not only a visionary one but, in all senses, a speculative one as well.

It is quite conceivable that Wright started working on his proposal before leaving Baghdad, since the two earliest drawings we have were done on copies of the Minoprio, Spencely, and Macfarlane master plan (figures 10.35–36). In any event, he promptly applied himself to the task on his return to Wisconsin, for the bulk of the approximately ninety drawings he and his staff produced were completed in three weeks, which is to say, by the end of the third week of June 1957. The rest were done by the end of the following month. While many of the drawings are "fantastic," as Spencely noted, they are also much more sketchy, picturesque, and decorative than the generally hard-line ones the other architects submitted.[120]

Wright sent the drawings to the Iraqi Embassy in Washington, D.C., in early August.[121] They were accompanied by the letter to the minister of development and Development Board quoted above along with a multipart explanatory text. The text, pieces of which were subsequently extracted and edited for publication in the May 1958 Architectural Forum spread on the project, included sections on the overall premise and urban concept of the design, the Opera House, the island bridges and connected King Faisal Avenue, and Baghdad University.[122] Drafts of the texts sent to the minister of development, read in conjunction with the drawings they were meant to explain, help us understand Wright's intentions and interpret the results.

Wright conceived the Baghdad project in city planning terms and started with the urban situation of southwestern Baghdad as his canvas. The designs for the Opera House and other structures included in his final plan were an outcome of the larger urban investigation undertaken, much as the

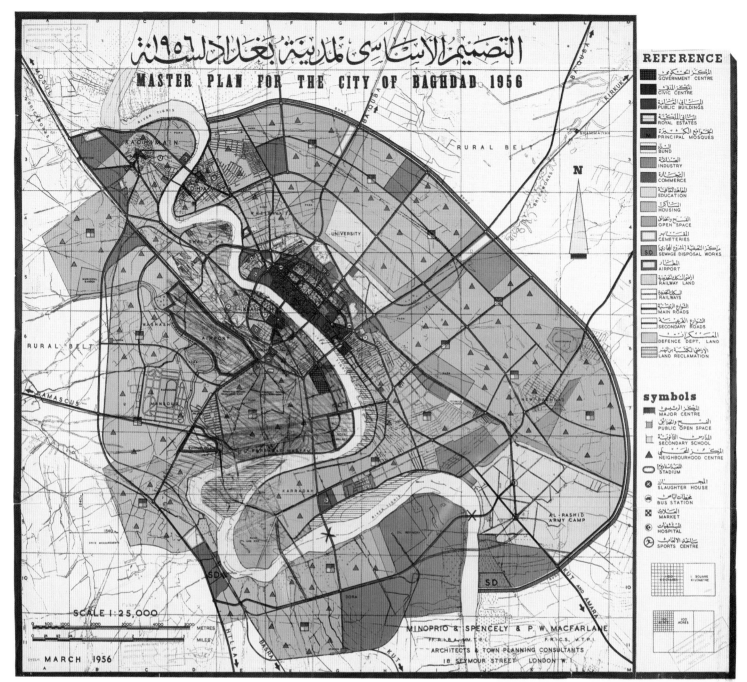

10.35

10.35. Plan for Greater Baghdad project, Wright, 1957. Preliminary sketch over
Minoprio-Spencely-Macfarlane 1956 master plan

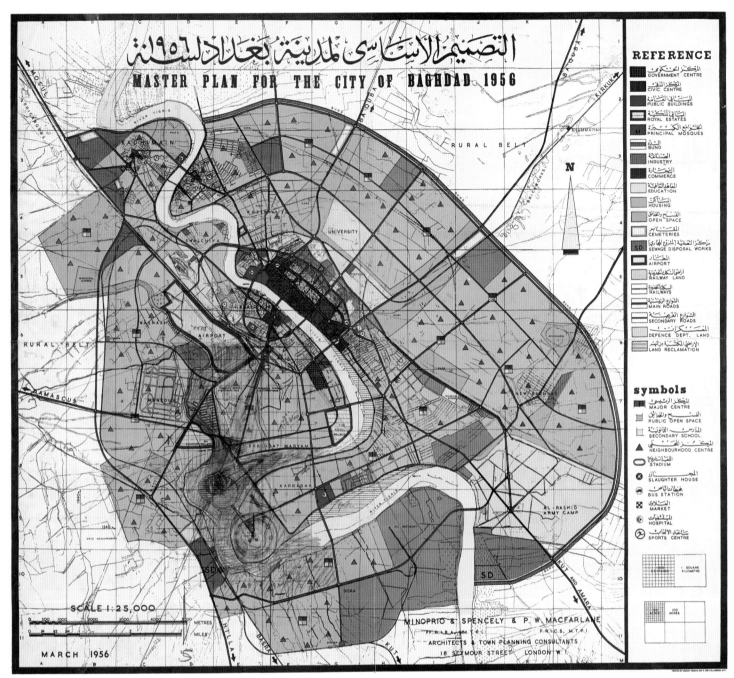

10.36

10.36. Plan for Greater Baghdad project. Preliminary sketch over Minoprio-Spencely-Macfarlane 1956 master plan. British Trade Fair site Wright was originally given is truncated red ovoid bordering the west bank of the river, northeast of the Museum.

Quadruple Block Plan and Prairie House were extrusions of the Chicago grid. In Baghdad, however, it was not the grid but the circle, embedded in the memory of the city's first plan and transformed by Wright into the spiraling three-dimensional form of a ziggurat, which he considered to be the appropriate solution for the "most pressing architectural problems today," namely, "traffic" and "parking."[123]

The geometry of the Baghdad project recalls that of Pittsburgh, as does Wright's design methodology. As in Pittsburgh, where the architect initially sketched his ideas over the existing Griswold-Stotz-McNeil-Richardson plans for the Golden Triangle and Point Park (figures 9.22–24), in Baghdad he took the Minoprio-Spencely-Macfarlane master plan as the point of departure. In what is no doubt the first of these two emended plans, Wright used colored pencils to mark with hatch lines the large area of the west bank he wanted to consider (figure 10.35). This went from the neighborhood of Shalchiya (now Atifiya) north of Karkh to Karadat Maryam in the south. It was bordered on the west by the railroad yards, the airport, and a band of parkland running south from the airport and around the grounds of Zuhour Palace to the river, just above Umm al-Khanazir Island that Wright had been promised by Faysal. The land on the right bank just below the palace grounds and the tip of the Karada Peninsula were also included in this extensive area slated for redevelopment in what the *Iraq Times* had called a year before the new "Baghdad West."[124]

To erase the "cleavage," as Wright described it, between the river's west and east banks at the city's southern end, and to deal with the traffic that would be directed to his proposed cultural center, Wright whited out Minoprio, Spencely, and Macfarlane's main east-west cross-street through Karadat Maryam and extended the western north-south artery over the island and into the Karada Peninsula, creating an elongated, hexagonal traffic-flow pattern. At least one of the two bridge stubs in the Minoprio-Spencely-Macfarlane plan connecting the island to the city streets was also whited out. Next to the one arriving from the west bank, Wright drew a new bridge curving over the island from one bank to the other. Within the bend of the bridge he lightly sketched three circular forms, as well as an elongated oval shape along its outside. He also sketched the beginnings of a large circle over the British town planners' projected park and zoo. From its center at the proposed *patte d'oie*, a diagonal avenue led to the bridge's on-ramp.

The second of the two emended master plans streamlined the traffic patterns and focused more on the combined building/parking structures with which Wright would populate his cultural center (figure 10.36). The relationship to the river, and to water in general, was also highlighted by the extensive blue hatching defining the combined island/peninsula site. The main change in the pattern of vehicular circulation was the creation of a long diagonal avenue cutting northeast through the center of the west bank and connecting the bridge crossing the island to the main square between the Central Railway Station and the bus station opposite it. It then picked up the line of the Minoprio-Spencely-Macfarlane avenue that passed in front of the Iraq Museum site, through downtown Karkh, and across Mamoun Bridge into central Rusafa.

The diagonal thoroughfare, which Wright would name King Faisal Boulevard, provided an entirely new axis for the west bank that offered the possibility for extensive commercial and residential development. At its northern end, leading to the Central Railway Station, it formed a triangle intersecting with the Damascus Road going west and with its projected extension east to the Royal Palace. When it reached the riverside parkway proposed by Minoprio, Spencely, and Macfarlane, King Faisal Boulevard took a 120-degree bend to cross Umm al-Khanazir Island in a single line to the top of the designated park/zoo on the Karada Peninsula, where Wright now drew a large circular shape indicating the University.

On the island, buildings and parks were now equally more defined. A smaller circle drawn in red, no doubt the Opera House, was contained within the cutout of a circular green park, later to be called by Wright the Garden of Eden. The island itself began to assume a shape defined by the drawn structures and parkland. It was also visually connected to the center of the west bank by the Washash Channel, which replaced the green park strip Wright retained from the Minoprio-Spencely-Macfarlane plan in his first sketch. Wright no doubt thought that opening up the partially blocked watercourse would make it available for recreational purposes, thus anticipating a plan the municipality proposed several months later.[125] He connected it to a lake abutting the airport, which was now indicated as a city park, a suggestion that was earlier contained in the British town planners' report.[126]

A third sketch, which also echoes the preliminary drawings for Pittsburgh quite closely, was drawn in large strokes of red pencil over a collage of two sections of the Hunting

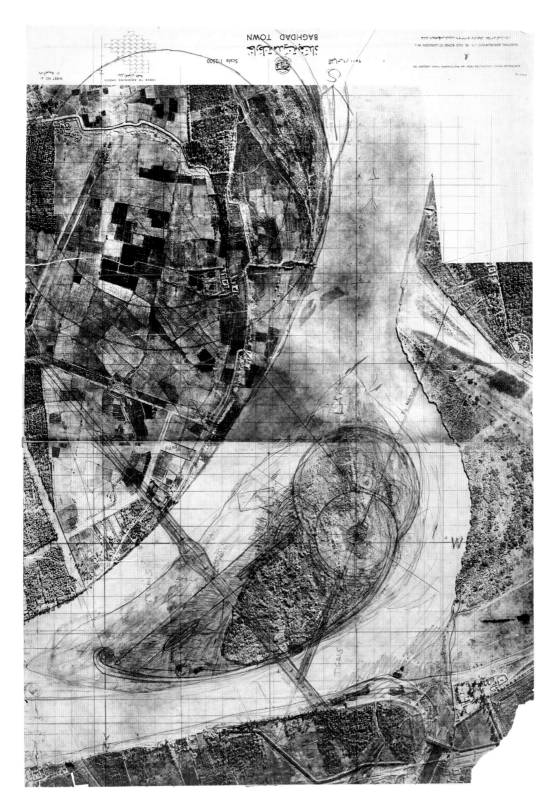

10.37

10.37. Plan for Greater Baghdad project. Cultural center and University. Preliminary
sketch plan over conjoined and inverted 1951 Hunting Aerosurveys aerial photographs

Aerosurveys photographs of the island/peninsula area. The combined images were inverted to place the south at the top as it would be in all Wright's later plans for the project (figure 10.37).[127] Using a compass and ruler, Wright drew the outlines of the bridge, the University, the Opera House and its connected garden, plus a number of the other structures he hoped to build on the island. The island itself was reduced in size and given a streamlined, germinal shape reflecting the flow of the river around it. It had a large circular head projecting downstream with a tail spinning out from the Opera House and narrowing to a point on the upstream side. A single bridge crossed over the inner channel of the Tigris from a park on the southern bank of the western shore. Before it reached the island, it split to send one arm at an angle toward the Opera House while the principal arm carried on straight, over the main channel of the river, to arrive tangent to the outer circle of the University.

The bold strokes of this sketch reveal the new scale of the automobile that Wright imparted to his urban intervention, on the model of Pittsburgh, in the otherwise tight-knit, small-scale fabric of Baghdad. The "new space-scale of time measurements brought in by the automobile" was the only "foundation of sane urban planning [today]," Wright explained to the Development Board, echoing Giedion.[128] The roadway network of the bridge and its direct connections with the circular structures that included multiple levels of parking serving as a base or frame for buildings responded, as Wright explained, to the need to deal effectively with the traffic and parking problems. The large circles of the Opera House and University represented, in effect, earthworks, or "earth-mounds" as Wright called them, based on the "ancient Ziggurat" of Mesopotamian culture. He described its "rejuvenated" form as "a plausible plastic means of absorbing and harboring the motor [car] and accommodating effectively motor traffic"—"a new way of using ancient means to give safe free approach to all buildings … as well as spacious parking and free exit."[129]

Even before Wright worked out the final shapes of the island and bridges, he had begun sketching the various structures that would be included in the overall design. There is at least one such preliminary drawing in the Wright Foundation Archives. It is a very large plan on two separate sheets of tracing paper that were originally taped together (figure 10.38). The island is shown in a form recalling that in figure 10.35.

One bridge goes straight across the narrow upstream end but does not align with the center of the university circle, a terminal condition that was fudged and whited out for the moment. A shorter, single-lane bridge crosses directly over to the Opera House, which is not separated from the Garden of Eden but is surrounded by it. The combined opera and garden are both contained within a three-level spiral ziggurat.[130] Occupying the downstream edge where the garden would later be placed is a small circular "casino," or open-air restaurant pavilion, like those typical of the Tigris banks closer to the city center.

An angled wedge connecting the Opera/Garden of Eden to the larger bridge abutment contains a park with a small, open-air amphitheater at its wider end. Between it and a building housing an Archaeological Museum is a triangular Grand Bazaar bounded on the east by circular kiosks. Bulging out from the shore of the triangular section upstream from the main bridge is a lens-shaped contemporary Art Gallery bordered by an outdoor sculpture park. Finally, at the northeastern tip (lower left) of the island is a tall spiral "turret" dedicated to Harun al-Rashid. It and the nearby Art Gallery are the most well-defined of the various structures indicated.

The final plan for the urbanization of West Baghdad culminating in the new cultural center was illustrated in three colored drawings. The plan and aerial perspective of the cultural center proper are quite well known and have often been reproduced (figures 10.40–41). By contrast, the general plan that shows the cultural center within its larger urban context has never, to my knowledge, been previously published (figure 10.39). It is critical to our understanding of the urban dimension of the project. It was drawn directly from the Minoprio, Spencely, and Macfarlane master plan, whose street system and zoning it replicates (figure 10.14), while it simplified the modifications to the master plan that Wright had sketched in figure 10.36.

The plan for West Baghdad takes in the entire southwest part of the city up to and including Karkh and much of Rusafa. As in the earlier sketch, the key element is a diagonal divided boulevard that links the cultural center, with its allied university campus, to the railway/bus station transportation hub at the heart of the newly developing area of the right bank opposite the historic core of Karkh. The new diagonal artery runs through what was a completely undeveloped section of the city reaching over to the proposed government center and Royal Palace group along al-Mansur Street. The area in question amounted to almost four hundred acres. While it was temporarily being used by the Defense Department, Minoprio, Spencely, and Macfarlane had suggested in their *Report* that it be zoned for residential development. They further noted that it "will become a most sought-after residential area which should be laid out as a whole."[131]

While we have no indication of how Wright might have organized neighborhoods within the street matrix his plan defined, we can say something about how he thought to give the district a kind of City Beautiful character in linking it to his cultural center by means of a park system reminiscent of Boston's Emerald Necklace, Nolen's Madison plan, and Chicago's park system begun by Olmsted and elaborated by Burnham (see figures 7.1 and 3.26).[132] Where Minoprio, Spencely, and Macfarlane had divided the undeveloped area into two distinct sections separated by a thin strip of parkland, Wright kept the residential area whole but reduced it in size so as to expand the park. Reaching over to the restored Washash Channel that now led to a lake, Wright transformed the airport grounds into a major continuation of the park north. This much enlarged park would thus serve as a central park for West Baghdad as a whole.

The cultural and educational center itself might usefully be compared with the Oakland district of Pittsburgh, where, beginning in the early part of the twentieth century, the main educational and cultural buildings of the city were grouped in City Beautiful fashion in a location at an equal remove from downtown as Wright planned for Baghdad. There are two major differences, however. First, Wright envisaged a much more popularly oriented entertainment center than Oakland's; and second, to ensure accessibility, he provided direct and easy approaches by automobile and an abundance of parking. This was to be an automobile-oriented cultural center. It is almost as if he translated the initial scheme for the Pittsburgh Point Park Civic Center onto the Oakland site—and incorporated the University of Pittsburgh and Carnegie Mellon into it (see figure 9.26).

The final plan for the Baghdad cultural center, dated 20 June 1957 (figure 10.40), differs little programmatically from the sketch in figure 10.38. On the reshaped island, the Opera House, which now was also to serve as a civic auditorium, is separated from the Garden of Eden, which it overlooks. The restaurant/theater casino that previously projected out from the downstream shore was moved to the lower, upstream part

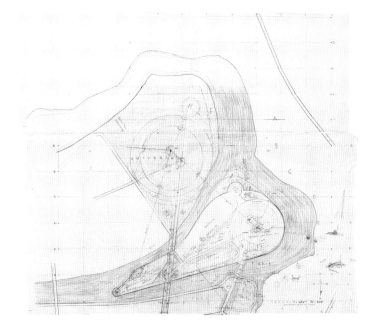

10.38

10.38. Plan for Greater Baghdad project. Cultural center and University. Preliminary sketch plan (north is at bottom; drawing is on two sheets originally taped together)

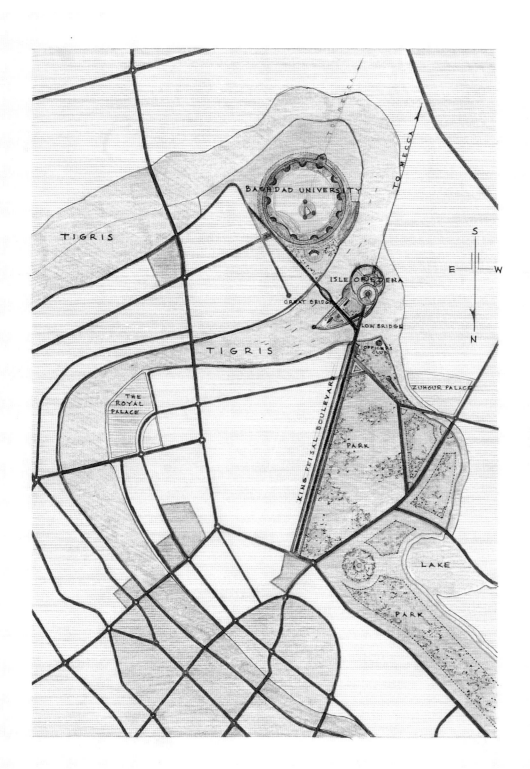

10.39

10.39. Plan for Greater Baghdad project. General urban plan (north is at bottom)

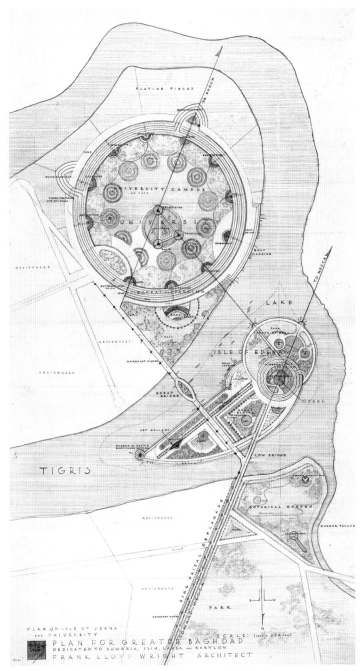

10.40

10.40. Plan for Greater Baghdad project. Cultural center and University. Site plan (north is at bottom), 20 June 1957

of the island, made available by the straightening of the main bridge leading to the University. While the contemporary Art Gallery and Archaeological Museum remained more or less in their same positions, the commercial Grand Bazaar was greatly increased in size and given a more central position in the composition. Spherical merchant kiosks now bounded it on two sides (figure 10.42). A boat landing and helicopter pad were included; planted promenades connecting the various parts of the center were added; and a beach was created on the inner side of the island, facing the botanical garden set in the spur of mainland between the access boulevard and the waterway skirting the Zuhour Palace grounds.

The aerial perspective of the complex further shows how the commercial kiosks were extended out from the island to the University and north up King Faisal Boulevard to create a continuity between the city and the cultural center through the popular pastime of shopping (figure 10.41). The perspective also shows the whole scene as a beehive of activity, with cars moving toward and through it, people congregating everywhere, and masses of boats circling the island and heading up the Washash Channel.

Under the "Crescent Arch": Symbolic and Performative Aspects of the Baghdad Project

Wright's plan for the southwestern expansion of Baghdad, anchored by a new cultural center and university complex, gave coherence to the Minoprio-Spencely-Macfarlane master plan as it gave meaning and focus to the city's development on its right bank. When the *Iraq Times* reported in July 1956 on the projected growth of the city in the direction of the mainly undeveloped areas of the west and southwest, it headlined the article by saying that this would give the city a "significance worthy of ancient times." The writer explained that "Baghdad West ... was in the Abbasid times an extensive city covering all the area between Khadimain and Daura along the river, and almost reaching Abu Ghraib to the west." Its administrative and cultural center was "the famed Circular City," now, like most of the rest of West Baghdad, reduced to "a few old-fashioned and intricately patterned quarters where there [a]re more dead ends than lanes."[133]

Wright referred to the original Round, or Circular, City of Baghdad more than once in explaining his project to the Development Board. He wrote in the foreword to his cultural

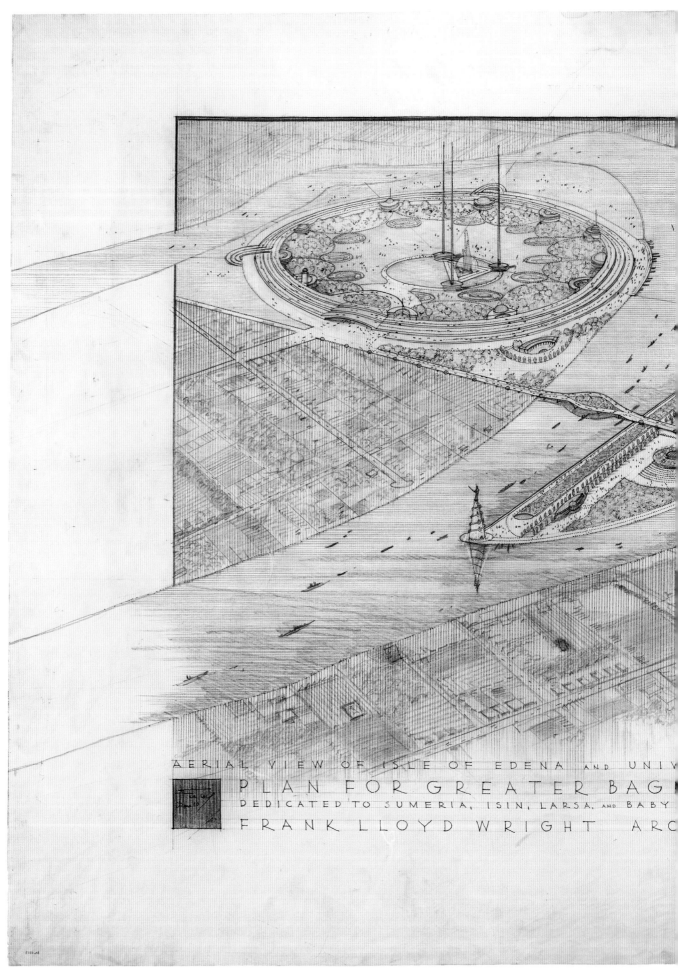

AERIAL VIEW OF ISLE OF EDENA AND UNIV

PLAN FOR GREATER BAG

DEDICATED TO SUMERIA, ISIN, LARSA, AND BABY

FRANK LLOYD WRIGHT ARC

10.41. Plan for Greater Baghdad project. Cultural center and University. Aerial perspective from north, 20 June 1957

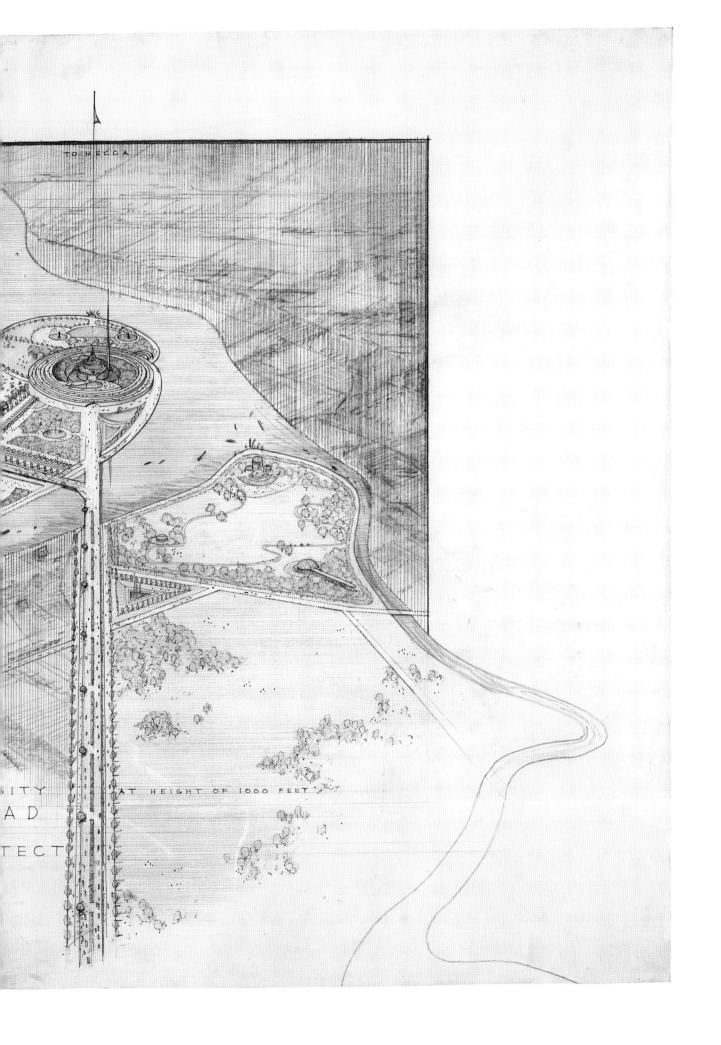

TO MECCA

SITY AT HEIGHT OF 1000 FEET

AD

TECT

center proposal dominated by the circular Opera House and University that "it is worth [noting] here that the original city of Bag[h]dad—built by Harun al Rashid [*sic*—]was circular and walled." In the cover letter to the board, he linked the reference directly to other memorable aspects of Baghdad's history in saying that his project was intended to "glorify IRAQ—its people and history" through its references to "the great circular city of Harun al Rashid [*sic*—]the romance of the Thousand and One Nights—[and] the story of Adam and Eve in the Garden of Eden."[134]

The fact that Wright attributed the Round City to Harun rather than to al-Mansur only points to the degree to which the early history of Baghdad was little known at the time other than to a specialist, archaeologically informed audience. None of the other international architects referred to the Round City at all, nor, as noted, did Minoprio, Spencely, and Macfarlane. If he really did his homework, Wright could have known it through Creswell's *Early Muslim Architecture* (1940) or even Guy Le Strange's *Baghdad during the Abbasid Caliphate* (1900); but it is much more likely that he was told about it while touring the city. This would explain the confusion over which caliph actually was responsible for the construction.[135]

The circular layout of eighth-century Baghdad, as interpreted by Wright in the plans for the University and the Opera House, linked his overall design directly to the origins of Baghdad as the administrative and cultural capital of the Abbasid Caliphate. It also established a geometric framework around which to develop a themed environment alluding to the larger history of the city and nation, going back to biblical times and taking into account both the ancient history of Mesopotamia and the later development of Islamic culture. In comparison with the Opera House, the University was large enough to approximate in both size and diversity of parts the original city plan. It is possibly for this reason that Wright held to the importance of including it in his project despite the fact that it was never officially commissioned and, most important, that some with close ties to the government, namely the Jawdats, were strongly lobbying for their former mentor, Gropius, to be awarded the job.

Wright's Plan for Greater Baghdad is an essay in archaeourbanism—retrospective, imaginative, and reconstitutive all at once. It mirrors, with elegant symmetry, the original plan of al-Mansur's Round City in another time and at the opposite end of the city (figures 10.1, 10.3, 10.40). The circular University and its satellite island in the Tigris become a new urban node at the edge of the existing city, a magnet for future development on the model of its original counterpart. Like the City of Peace, it serves as a social condenser in the form of an ideal landscape of paradisiacal significance.

As in his civic centers for Madison and Pittsburgh, Wright designed the University not as a collection of individual buildings but as a megastructure (figures 10.40, 10.43; see figures 7.21, 9.25). In Baghdad the broad, low, circular earthwork that constitutes the infrastructure and perimeter wall of the campus is a three-level spiral road taking its form from what Wright believed to be that of the Mesopotamia ziggurat.[136] The curvilinear path serves for access, vehicular communication from one part of the campus to another, and parking. The various departments, or faculties, are plugged into this "curriculum," as Wright punned the vehicular network, by clipping onto its internal circumference.[137] New ones could be added or functions interchanged whenever necessary, although the location on the axis to Mecca was reserved for the faculty of religion and, as originally designed, culminated in a pointed, horseshoe-shaped dome similar to that of the Khadimain Mosque (figure 10.43).[138] The central space of the campus, which is left free of traffic to become a pedestrian park, contains a pool with fountains surrounded by radio and television broadcasting studios. Their tall antenna towers call attention to the fact that Iraq was the first Middle Eastern country to have broadcast television. The towers also bear witness to the underlying importance of the production and circulation of images in the cultural center design.

Wright's Baghdad University does not simply resemble al-Mansur's Round City in its superficial form but is a reinterpretation of the earlier design at the more fundamental levels of structure and meaning. In the original city plan, the interstitial space of the concentric walls provided living quarters for the royal city's inhabitants (figure 10.2). These were arranged in sectors according to tribal groupings and separated by intermediate streets. Located around the inner circumference of the thickened wall, comparable to Wright's vehicular ramps, were accommodations for the different government officers and members of the royal household. This inner ring, added after the initial stage of construction, can thus be likened to Wright's additive and interchangeable faculty buildings lining the inner edge of the transportation loop. Finally, the royal palace and mosque, with the latter's dome defining the open

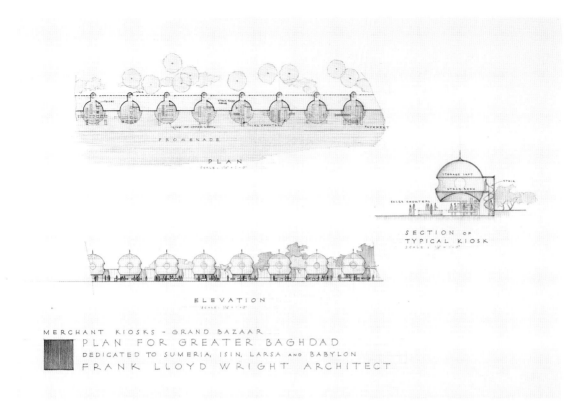

10.42

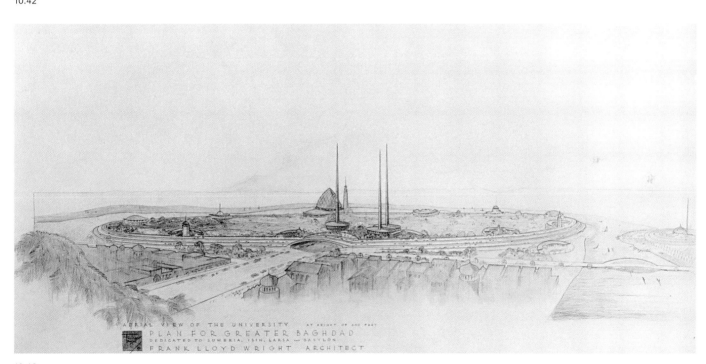

10.43

10.42. Plan for Greater Baghdad project. Merchant kiosks in Grand Bazaar. Plan, sections, and elevation

10.43. Plan for Greater Baghdad project. University. Perspective (showing faculty of religion prior to erasure of dome and minaret), 20 June 1957

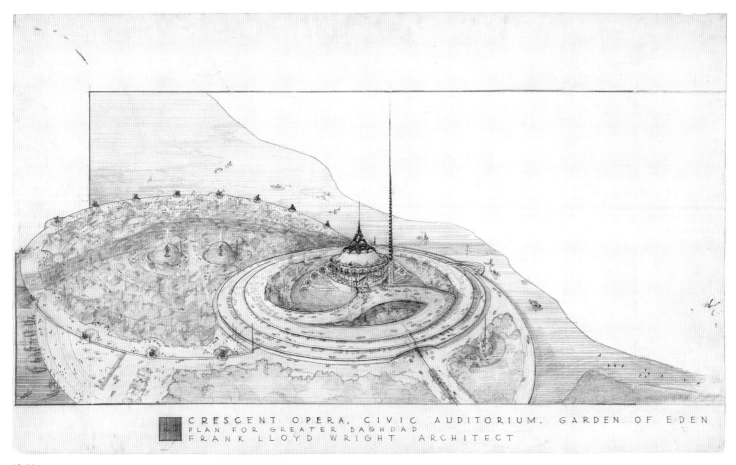

CRESCENT OPERA, CIVIC AUDITORIUM. GARDEN OF EDEN
PLAN FOR GREATER BAGHDAD
FRANK LLOYD WRIGHT ARCHITECT

10.44

10.44. Plan for Greater Baghdad project. Opera House and Garden of Eden. Aerial
perspective looking south

HAROUN AL RASHID
FRANK LLOYD WRIGHT ARCHITECT

10.45

10.45. Plan for Greater Baghdad project. Harun al-Rashid Monument. East elevation

center of the Round City, were translated into the towered broadcasting stations where communication and dissemination of information, rather than entrenched power and tradition, are given preeminence (figure 10.40).

The central focus, coherence, and singularity of the City of Peace are thus transformed at the megastructure's core to create an image of modern Baghdad that refers to the past while being grounded in the present. The conflict between the religious focus of traditional Arab education and the secular humanism guiding the new university toward a more modern approach to scholarship was only one aspect of contemporary cultural policy highlighted by Wright's design.[139] Another had to do with a more explicitly political discourse. Iraq, like Egypt, was caught between two historical cultures, the one ancient and pre-Islamic, the other medieval and Islamic. A modern regime had somehow to balance these two legacies. Wright's conflation of al-Mansur's Islamic capital for the Abbasid Caliphate with the Babylonian and Sumerian ziggurat allowed him to express the idea of a modern Islamic culture supported and served by a unique, originary civilization.[140]

The Opera House and its island site condensed and elaborated the ideas introduced in the University (figure 10.44). The name Wright gave to the polliwog-shaped island provides the first clue. He called it Edena in reference to the marshland south of Baghdad where the biblical Garden of Eden is believed to have been located.[141] Eden thus joined Sumeria/Babylon and Baghdad in Wright's scheme to encompass the three historic horizons of Iraqi culture.[142] As the representation of the legendary site of the beginning of the world, Eden almost had to be an island—autonomous, embryonic, omphalic.

At the northern tip of the Isle of Edena, facing the old city, Wright placed a monument to Harun al-Rashid. Made of gilded sheet metal over a steel frame, it was to rise to a height of three hundred feet on a spiral base representing a procession of camels (figure 10.45). The substructure was modeled on the minaret of the Great Mosque at Samarra, the town about sixty miles north that was built in the ninth century to replace Baghdad for a brief interregnum as the Abbasid capital. This highly unusual form of the minaret has most often been connected with the earlier Mesopotamian ziggurat and may have served as a model for popular images of the biblical Tower of Babel (see figure 9.40).[143] For Wright, it became a perfect vehicle for introducing, at the tip of the Isle of Edena, the theme of cultural continuity developed throughout the design.

The avenue leading from the statue of Harun to the Opera House at the head of the island is treated as a cultural mall. On the near side of the cross-axis is the lens-shaped museum for contemporary art. Beyond that is a long, red-brick, clerestoried building with a high battered base, devoted to the display of Mesopotamian sculpture. In between these two structures, filling out the protuberance of the island, are lines of domed kiosks forming a shopping bazaar and casino, set aside for eating, drinking, and popular entertainment. Like the *kazinu* on Abu Nuwas Street lining the southern section of the Tigris's east bank, the one on Edena, along with the bazaar, was intended to bring to the island aspects of daily life in contemporary Baghdad and provide a commercial vitality to the scheme.[144]

The focus of Edena is the building for the opera that generated the entire project (figure 10.44).[145] Perhaps to remove from the structure some of its elitist connotations and certainly to give it a greater multifunctionality, Wright transformed it into a flexible hall that could be expanded from approximately sixteen hundred seats to anywhere from five thousand to seventy-five hundred. As a result, it could also serve as a civic auditorium for conventions, public celebrations, and large political gatherings.[146] This redefinition added a national dimension to the program, while the idea of a multiuse auditorium led Wright to revisit the Adler and Sullivan Auditorium, on which he had worked when he first joined the firm's Chicago office (figure 10.46).

The Baghdad Opera House is one of the most elaborate, symbolically charged buildings Wright designed and demands a close reading of its various elements before one can understand how it was meant to relate to and inform its immediate context. King Faisal Avenue provides a direct axial approach to it, continuing under it in the form of a tunnel that opens onto a vista across the Tigris in the direction of Mecca (figures 10.39–41, 10.47). The building is a circular structure surrounded by an alabaster colonnade and topped by an openwork, gilded metal crown containing a statue of Aladdin. The tentlike pavilion rises out of a circular pool. It is stabilized by flying buttresses that take the form of incurving half-arches. Wright called these "crescent arches" or "crescent rainbow" arches (figures 10.47–48). The pool is surrounded by a garden, which in turn is surrounded by three spiraling roadways raised on banked earth.

The ground-level tunnel under the main structure leads to a planetarium, on the domed ceiling of which floats the floor

of the theater (figures 10.48–49). The surrounding ziggurat takes cars through three revolutions, where there is parking for almost two thousand automobiles, before depositing attendees at the front entrance. This is marked by a tall, tapered antenna symbolizing the Sword of Muhammad. Entrance to the nearly circular, bowl-shaped auditorium is through a delicate arcade illusionistically representing tied-back curtains (figure 10.50).

The interior space is shaped by interlocking spherical surfaces (figures 10.47–49). The *cavea*, or auditorium proper, forms a shell angling down toward the stage.[147] The proscenium arch, by reflection, starts a rippling action in the opposite direction that spreads over the seats in an expanding series of curves. The model was the Chicago Auditorium (figure 10.46). The earlier ceiling design, derived from acoustic calculations, can be read as representing the movement of sound waves in space. Wright emphasized the representational aspects of its translation in Baghdad both in instrumental and in anthropomorphic terms. He said it was "like a great horn" that "carries sound as hands would if cupped above the mouth."[148] The outermost arch served as a track for sliding screens to close off the rear of the theater when not needed, a provision for flexibility also indebted to the Auditorium.

But there is one significant way in which the ceiling of the Baghdad Opera House is different from that of the Chicago theater, and this is what carries the full impact of the building's representational charge. In Baghdad, the largest arch, the one farthest removed from the proscenium, continues beyond the outer walls of the building into the surrounding pool (figures 10.44, 10.48). One immediately thinks of Le Corbusier's 1931 project for Moscow's Palace of the Soviets, echoed in the auditorium of Gropius and TAC's 1956 Civic Center project for Tallahassee, Florida (figure 10.51) — as well, perhaps, of the McDonald's "golden arches," introduced three years earlier in Phoenix.[149] But Le Corbusier's and Gropius's giant parabolic arches were the actual structure from which the roof of the hall was hung. They were never meant to be seen from inside. In the Baghdad project, the arch reads as an integral feature of both the interior and exterior spaces of the building.

The externalized arches of the Baghdad Opera House were in part intended to carry the image of sound into the environment, across the actual threshold of hearing, as a "poetic extension of the acoustic principle involved," as Wright put it.[150] This highly imagistic interpretation of the program of an opera house brings to mind Jørn Utzon's prize-winning entry in the Sydney Opera House competition of 1955–57, whose exposed, interlocking concrete shells similarly look as if they were designed to project and resonate sound across Sydney harbor (figure 10.52). There is good reason to believe that Wright knew the Sydney design since the competition results were published in the months between the Baghdad commission and his visit to the city.[151] Though comparable in certain respects to Utzon's solution, Wright's is much more *operatic* in that his does not simply take music and the natural environment into account but includes all the narrative and historical components that are part of the *gesamtkunstwerk* that opera uniquely represents. The key to this conception is the "crescent arch," which functions as a synecdoche for the design as a whole.

In referring to the arch as a "poetic extension of the acoustic principle involved," Wright meant the phrase to be taken literally as well as figuratively. At the simplest level, the arch is the external efflorescence of the proscenium and stage. But it is not just that. Its traceried design contains a series of roundels depicting "sculptured scenes" from the *Thousand and One Nights*. These celebrated tales, which date back at least to the ninth century, were a national folk literature that had particular relevance for Baghdad since many of the stories were set in Harun's court. Wright had always been drawn to them as a source of imaginative and didactic force. In the project for the Baghdad Opera House they became an ideal framing device for his larger narrative.[152]

The tales of the *Thousand and One Nights* are recounted by Shahrazad to King Shahrayar in an attempt to ward off her death at his hands. Having been the victim of adultery, Shahrayar swore to sleep with a different woman each night before killing her. To cure the king of his misogyny and thus spare her young women compatriots, Shahrazad volunteered to become one of his victims. The ruse was to tell him stories each night that had to be continued the following night and thereby forever stave off the fatal consequence. So enraptured was Shahrayar with Shahrazad's storytelling that he let these trysts go on long enough—a "thousand and one nights"—to fall in love with her and marry her.

The *Thousand and One Nights* symbolizes the power of art and illusion even over life and death. Of particular significance in the context of an opera house for Baghdad, it inscribes the world of the imaginary in the lunar path of the night. Wright's

10.46

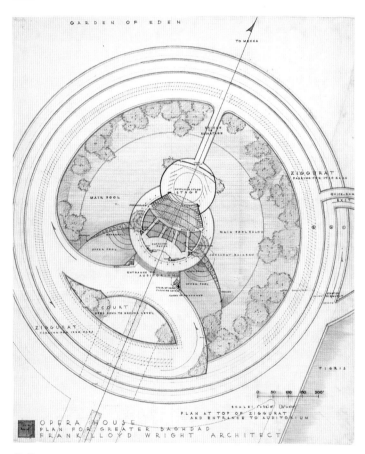

10.47

10.46. Auditorium, Chicago, Adler and Sullivan, 1886–89. Interior, ca. 1890. Courtesy David Phillips Collection

10.47. Plan for Greater Baghdad project. Opera House. Plan, entrance level

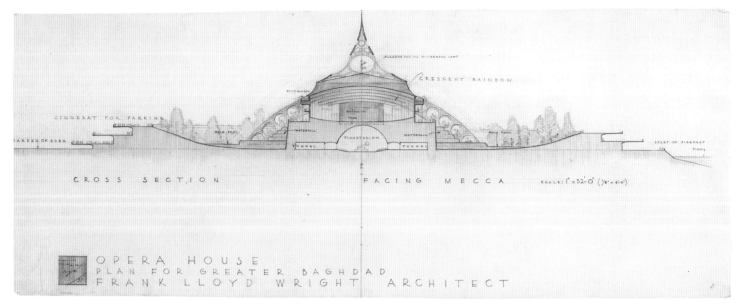

10.48

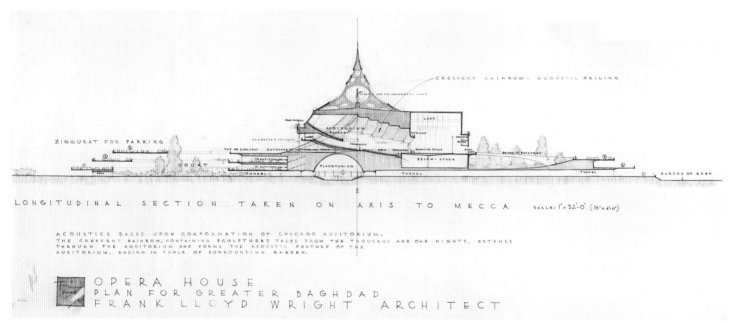

10.49

10.48. Plan for Greater Baghdad project. Opera House. Lateral section

10.49. Plan for Greater Baghdad project. Opera House. Longitudinal section,
20 June 1957

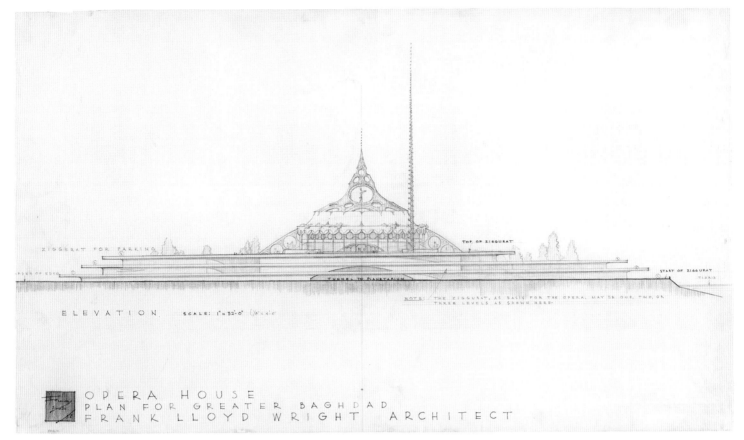

ELEVATION   SCALE: 1"=32'-0" (⅛"=1'-0")

ZIGGURAT FOR PARKING

TOP OF ZIGGURAT

START OF ZIGGURAT

TUNNEL TO PLANETARIUM

NOTE: THE ZIGGURAT, AS BASIS FOR THE OPERA, MAY BE ONE, TWO, OR THREE LEVELS AS SHOWN HERE.

OPERA HOUSE
PLAN FOR GREATER BAGHDAD
FRANK LLOYD WRIGHT ARCHITECT

10.50

10.50. Plan for Greater Baghdad project. Opera House. North elevation, 20 June 1957

10.51

10.52

10.51. Civic Center project, Tallahassee, Florida, Gropius and TAC, 1956. Aerial perspective. Detail of auditorium. From [Walter Gropius], *A Civic Center for Tallahassee, Florida. The Architects Collaborative, Cambridge, Massachusetts*, 1 August 1956

10.52. Opera House, Sydney, Jørn Utzon, 1955–73. Model, 1955–57

"crescent arch" frames this nighttime activity. Time is suspended within the space of the arch in synchrony with the virtuality of theatrical time. The crescent, as a symbol of the Islamic world, serves to contain that experience in the particular narrative context to which it is addressed.[153] The figure of Aladdin, standing in Wright's mind for the "human imagination," occupies the apex of the arch under the pinnacle of the crown, orchestrating the events by rubbing his "wonderful lamp" (figures 10.48–49).[154]

The fantasmatic character of the *Thousand and One Nights* was to suffuse the "crescent arch" so completely that it would be magically transformed—before our very eyes, one is tempted to say—into an illusion of paradise. The Islamic symbol representing the waxing moon would metamorphose, Wright noted on the drawings, into a "crescent rainbow" as an effect of the fountains cascading beneath the arch. Against the background of the southern sky, the rays of the sun would refract and reflect in the droplets of water spraying over the gilt bronze curve of the traceried arch. And through this rainbow would appear, over the annular wall of the ziggurat, a landscape representing the Garden of Eden (figure 10.44). Lushly planted along the Tigris, like the idealized landscape in the Bible, it contained statues of Adam and Eve under small water domes, like those in the Madison project. The image of paradise represented in abstract geometric terms in al-Mansur's original City of Peace was thus reconfigured, on the model of Genesis 2:6, through "a mist from the earth" that "watered the whole face of the ground."[155]

Wright's project for the Baghdad Opera House is a proscenium that transforms the architecture of the cultural center and its university campus into a performance art of synesthetic character and operatic scope. Sound becomes water; water, light; and light, story and image. Framed by the "crescent rainbow," the Isle of Edena, the Tigris River, and the city of Baghdad create a real-life setting for a play about themselves in which local citizens and tourists alike are invited to take part. The extravagant illusionism leads one into a realm of the imagination that is in many ways more "literary" than strictly "architectural." In its suggestive, near insubstantiality, the Opera House is almost like an image from the *Thousand and One Nights* itself.

Wright's Plan for Greater Baghdad stretches the limits of verisimilitude as it constantly changes temporal focal length. It offers an imaginary journey through a reconstructed past on nearly the same site where that past either actually or legendarily existed. History and memory are thus realized as a complex pattern of archaeological and literary representations.[156] The multiple images and layers in this vision cohere to form a well-orchestrated event celebrating the Hashimite monarchy it was intended to serve.[157] In reconstituting the historical dimensions of the site through his own form of archaeourbanism, Wright constructed a history for Faysal II that would celebrate him as a cultural leader in the eyes of his people.

The circular precinct of the University reestablished the determining context of the situation as the original foundation of Baghdad by the Abbasid Caliph al-Mansur, from whom Faysal could trace a direct line of descent.[158] The "rainbow crescent" arch of the Opera House, with its images of the *Thousand and One Nights*, joined with the statue of Harun al-Rashid to elaborate the cultural flowering of Baghdad under the Caliphate in its pre-Ottoman, pre-Western state of independence. The Garden of Eden, along with the foundational ziggurats of the Opera House and University, revealed the ancient, originary basis of Iraqi civilization, into which the minaret-like Sword of Muhammad infused new blood. The axis to Mecca clearly marked on almost all the plans indicated less a religious focus than a political connection between the current Hashimite king and his family lineage back to his grandfather, the Sharif Husayn, who was the custodian of the Islamic holy places in Mecca and Medina.

The two art museums, but especially the Opera House, provided evidence of the continuing beneficence to be derived from a constitutional monarchy that traced its roots back to such an august past. Looking like a medieval Islamic princely palace, as depicted in manuscript paintings or described in the *Thousand and One Nights*—surrounded by pools, fountains, and gardens and topped by an openwork metal dome representing nothing so much as a crown—the Opera House clearly defined the royal presence as the centering factor in Iraq's "development."[159] Not only was it Faysal II who gave the island to Wright—and thus to his city and nation—but it was the very successes of the first stage of the Development Board program under his reign, concentrating in particular on flood-control measures, that allowed Wright's scheme to become a possibility. Of all the international architects, Wright was the only one, shortsightedly as it turned out, to dedicate his project to the king and to acclaim that, while in modern times it may be "extremely decorative," "in IRAQ—monarchy has proved worthy."[160]

Throughout the last chapters of this book, most obviously in those devoted to Madison and Pittsburgh, the theatrical and the spectacular have played a critical role in Wright's urbanism. Wright shared this preoccupation with a central discourse of the period, enunciated most clearly by Sigfried Giedion in the mid-1940s. Wright's plan for a cultural center to anchor the development of West Baghdad, while certainly a part of this general trend, took it in a direction that was unique in both its narrative/representational content and its ascription to architecture of the purpose of reconstructing an urban history. Although both the idea of historical reconstruction and the adoption of a literary program to accomplish it would seem to have less to do with the principles and goals of modernism and more to do with the program of a theme park à la Disneyland (which opened in 1955, just two years prior to the Baghdad project), Wright's design could not be more different from the latter either.

The basic concept of the theme park, as brilliantly exploited by Disney and his team of "imagineers," was to construct a generic image of a place, like "Main Street, U.S.A.," that may never have existed and certainly not at the site of Disneyland. The purpose was commercial, purely and simply, and the means nostalgic and hyperrealistic. What appeared to look like the past, or another place, issued from a very subtle form of alienation and decontextualization. Wright's Baghdad project, by contrast, was all about integration, contextualization, and the specificity of place. The commercial was there merely to support a more important goal. This was to "rejuvenate," to use Wright's word, the historical context by the presence of images and signs reminding both local citizens and tourists alike of what was historically important about the environment and how a renewed awareness of that could become a functioning part of daily life. As a destination point meant to give significance to a much larger urban development scheme, Wright's Baghdad project has more to do with the kinds of cultural centers like New York's Lincoln Center, with which it was contemporary, or Paris's Centre Pompidou (1971–77) and Bilbao's Guggenheim Museum (1991–97), which followed it, than with Disneyland, which preceded it.

Still, the Plan for Greater Baghdad stands well apart from the cultural centers just mentioned, as indeed it does from the typical modern urban design of the period. Seen by most observers at the time, and since, as little more than an

"Arabian nights spectacular," as the critic for the *Christian Science Monitor* put it, the sui generis character of the project fundamentally caused it to be displaced from the history of modern urbanism and thus evacuated of any meaningful relationship with that history.[161] To see it otherwise necessitates viewing it not in the merely functional terms that it actually would so well have performed but rather in the more ambitious cultural terms it engaged.

Wright's Opera House and the larger Plan for Greater Baghdad it informed take architecture and urbanism into the problematic realm of wish fulfillment, where desire rather than need, as Louis Kahn would say, is the motivating force. At the very beginning of his effort, Wright told the Development Board that his intention was to appeal to their "imagination." The exaggeration of the purely decorative aspect of the architecture was certainly part of the history of the opera house typology. One need only think of Charles Garnier's Opéra in Paris (1861–75), since named the Palais Garnier, to appreciate this. But more than merely decorative, Wright's project embodied the very quality of the "operatic." And in doing so, it turned the building and its surroundings into a stage set for the performance of a historical drama at an urban scale. Neither a nostalgic recreation of a past that never was, nor an archaeological reconstruction of one long since disappeared, Wright's Baghdad scheme condensed a story about a cultural past into a limited spatiotemporal framework as only a theatrical performance can do. The urban dimension was to turn the theater inside out, as the opera's "crescent arch" did, so as to make the entire experience of the site an entertaining, potentially enlightening, and inspiring one for its visitors.

When thought about in this way, the Plan for Greater Baghdad was not that far removed from a certain type of city planning and urban design that we have seen more than once in this book. An imaginative, visionary conceit certainly underlay Ebenezer Howard's Garden City, as it did Le Corbusier's Contemporary City for the modern Machine Age (figures 3.31, 5.8). The almost imperceptible leap from the known to the unknown, from the quotidian to the fanciful drove the various projects for multilevel cities in the early part of the twentieth century as it did Wright's Pittsburgh ziggurat-coliseum of the later 1940s (figures 5.42, 9.39). And in the background of all this meditation on the form a city ideally might take, at least in terms of the scope of this book, is the Burnham and Bennett Plan of Chicago, which Wright

grew up with, so to speak (figure 3.24). One wonders whether, in designing Baghdad, Wright was not thinking of Burnham's famous, apocryphal words: "Make no little plans. They have no magic to stir men's blood and probably will themselves not be realized. Make big plans; aim high in hope and work, remembering that a noble, logical diagram once recorded will never die, but long after we are gone will be a living thing, asserting itself with ever-growing insistency."[162]

It certainly seems that Wright took a great risk in designing his Baghdad scheme as he did, first, by integrating into it much more than the original commission called for; and, second, by choosing a site that was still untested in terms of flood conditions.[163] One could speculate that at the age of ninety, and at the end of a long career, he was hardly interested in designing a single building in a country where he probably had little expectation of its ever being built. In this he would not have been far off the mark. Of the projects by the six international architects invited to design signature buildings, only one was built in its architect's lifetime and the other never completed. Both Ponti's Development Board and Ministry of Development Building and Gropius and TAC's Baghdad University were submitted and approved after the July 1958 revolution and thus had the imprimatur of the Qasim government from the outset. Neither the Aalto nor the Dudok nor the Corbusier project got off the drawing boards.[164] Nor did the Wright Post and Telegraph Building for that matter. But the Wright Plan for Greater Baghdad, unlike those by everyone but Gropius and TAC, added a work of unique conception and design to the architect's historical legacy. And unlike all the others, it remains a singularly challenging contribution to the history of modern urbanism.

CONCLUSION

This book has taken us on a long journey—from the suburbs of Chicago and the pages of the *Ladies' Home Journal*, through the central business district of Chicago, to downtown Madison, Washington, and Pittsburgh, and finally to the capital city of Iraq. Other places seen in passing have included Letchworth, Hampstead Garden Suburb, Forest Hills Gardens, Cleveland, Paris, and New York. At the very least, one can say initially, in this brief conclusion, that Broadacre City proved to be but a deviation revealing its unique place in Wright's urbanism as a polemical critique, purely theoretical construct, and sui generis proposition. Through its multiple case studies of designs for real conditions and sites, this book has shown how Wright's urbanism was a broad-ranging, continually evolving effort to enrich city life that cannot and should not be reduced to an exceptional vision for a utopian agrarian world of rural-like existence.

Wright's urban interventions are important both for what they tell us about his own intense involvement in the rethinking of the modern city and for what they reveal of the larger national and international contexts in which they were produced, to which they responded, and which they informed. The case-study method has allowed us to avoid easy answers and received opinion by forcing a close look at each specific program and site. The three-part division of Wright's urban designs stemmed from the nature of the work. At the same time it underscores the historical evolution of modern urbanism. The focus on residential communities in the inner-ring suburbs of the growing metropolitan areas of American cities was, in general, a prime concern of city planning in the period 1890–1914. The intense drive to build more and higher skyscrapers in central business districts during the Roaring Twenties was evident not only throughout the United States but in Europe as well. The reaction to the dispersion of populations and disembowelment of the downtown core, as a consequence of the automobile, inspired in the most forward-looking urban designers in the post–World War II period projects for revitalizing the "heart of the city." As we have seen, Wright's work over more than half a century was an integral part of these developments.

If the focus of Wright's urban thinking evolved in tune with the times, there were also significant constants, which he often shared with others, to be sure, but to which he gave unusual expression. The most important constant was the accommodation to means of circulation, beginning with the streetcar but soon dominated by the automobile, both moving and stationary. Another constant was the independent path he attempted to steer between a traditional idea of urban design grounded in City Beautiful principles of geometric order and symmetry and the picturesque-based approach of Garden City and Suburb proponents. In the City Club competition of 1912–13, he expressed this as an opposition to those who either "ape the academic Gaston or steal from 'My Lord.'" Wright's adherence to the grid preluded any semblance of conventional picturesque design—and thus any relationship with the Garden City or Suburb—while it allowed him to work easily and flexibly within the City Beautiful framework, be it Burnham and Bennett's in the early years, or Nolen's later on. Indeed, it was a lingering element of such classical thinking, indebted to the perimeter-block principle and axial organization, that became the counterweight to a more abstract, Corbusian modernism that determined the designs of Wright's third phase, namely, the civic and cultural centers for Madison, Pittsburgh, and Baghdad.

Aside from Broadacre City, which in its physical form represented only a fragment of a larger whole, Wright never designed a comprehensive city plan, nor did he seem to have the intellectual desire to do so. The closest he came was the development scheme for the expansion of West Baghdad. The second closest was the quarter section neighborhood of Chicago done for the City Club competition. More characteristic of his urbanism was, at first, a typical residential block diagram, then a downtown commercial multiblock concept, and, finally, a megastructure incorporating numerous functions in what Rem Koolhaas might call a "big building." Wright's first venture in urban design, the Roberts block scheme of 1896, indicated how his approach would evolve over the following two decades. Starting with the metropolitan Chicago grid as a practical principle of spacing, interrelationships, and modularity, Wright soon understood how an ideal solution based on the square could result in a new form of urban space — open, nonhierarchical, and interactive — with many of the attributes of picturesqueness but with none of its anticlassical dissonances and sense of the accidental or the nostalgic.

The Quadruple Block Plan became the DNA of Wright's residential design thinking, whether as the basis for communities of houses or of the design of the individual house itself. As such, it revealed how, from the very beginning of his career, an urban intention served as the framework for the conception and composition of individual buildings. The Prairie House was the direct outcome of the centering and pinwheeling process at the heart of the Quadruple Block Plan. And critical to the geometric construction of the Quadruple Block Plan was the city street pattern and the provision for separated pedestrian and vehicular access to each individual residence, with stables, and later garages, centered within the composition and becoming its pivot point.

With its dependence on the ubiquitous Midwestern grid and its avoidance of a Riverside-like curvilinearity, the Quadruple Block Plan gave Wright a means to define a completely original path through the planning conventions then in vogue. It allowed his 1912–13 City Club design to fit in seamlessly with the development of Chicago's outskirts along the lines of the recently published Burnham and Bennett plan. It also revealed how unusual Wright's urban thinking

was when seen in the context of the typically self-contained Garden City–derived projects of some of the competitors or the declaratively overinflated City Beautiful plans of others. Wright's acceptance and manipulation of the grid that was so much a part of American urban history and mythology grounded his work in a long tradition of American thought and practice.

The grid continued to inform Wright's urbanism into the late 1920s, during which time he used it to create a commercial, skyscraper version of its earlier, mainly residential applications. The Skyscraper Regulation project, in particular, conformed to a perimeter-block condition and followed from his adherence to zoning regulations that directed the slightly earlier National Life Insurance Company Building. The architect's willing submission to such restrictions as zoning undercuts another of the stereotypes of Wright. Both the acceptance of a perimeter-block footprint and the zoning regulations that devolved from it were typical of traditionalist skyscraper design of the period that Le Corbusier and others in Europe categorically rejected as outmoded and poorly adapted to the automobile and truck traffic beginning to overwhelm the city. Wright's move toward a multilevel street system incorporated within the building design was a solution more in tune with the classically inspired traditionalist approach of Harvey Wiley Corbett and Edward Bennett than that of the avant-garde Europeans who would influence Wright by the end of the decade.

Broadacre City was the direct result of Wright's awareness of European advances, in particular those made by Le Corbusier. Wright's immediate reaction was to counter Le Corbusier's centralizing *urbanisme* with a radically decentralized *ruralisme*. The frequent use of the French words by Wright made the confrontation with Le Corbusier explicit. While it still showed signs of an underlying grid, Broadacre City neither highlighted its presence nor accepted any of the urban manifestations to which the U.S. Rectangular Land Survey had historically given rise. It was, in effect, a wholesale rejection of urbanism as it had previously been practiced by architects and planners including Wright himself. While Wright remained attached to the Broadacre concept throughout the rest of his career, he was at first reluctant to draw in detail how it might actually manifest itself — or even build the model by which it came to be best known. Indeed, he almost immediately contravened its fundamental argument in the project for the Madison Civic Center that established the basis for his urban designs of the later thirties, forties, and fifties.

The civic centers for Madison and Pittsburgh and the commercial/residential complex for Washington, D.C., were premised on the very idea of centralization as a beneficial condition of modern life. None of the three projects proceeded from a desire to escape the city, as Broadacre City did; rather, all three embraced the city's dynamics and diversity in providing a forum for public gathering and communal activity. In each, as later in Baghdad, the metaphor of the city as stage and the building as theater played a crucial role. The spectacle was meant to engage users with the surrounding cityscape and landscape. The architecture incorporated landscape, engineering, and more traditional concepts of building into new megastructural forms that ran counter to the established perimeter-block downtown pattern. The automobile, both moving and stationary, had a uniquely decisive part to play in such designs, which predicted many of the methods used in post–World War II redevelopment projects both in America and in Europe.

Along with the cultural center for Baghdad, the Madison, Washington, and Pittsburgh projects represent an evolving notion of how to adapt to and control the impact of social, economic, and industrial change. The move from the openness of the plazas in Madison and Washington to the enclosed atrium space of Pittsburgh was just one sign of this. The development of an entirely new area of Baghdad as a destination point was another. The Pittsburgh ziggurat-coliseum signaled a new role for urban design as magnet and symbolic destination point, a role that would become increasingly recognized in the later twentieth century as critical to the revitalization of cities by means of similarly conspicuous and individuated "superforms." At the same time, the differences between the Madison, Washington, and Pittsburgh projects illustrate an evolution from a traditional City Beautiful notion of urban planning to a modernist one. The idea of simply extending the lines of classically defined blocks and spaces was transformed through the concept of the superblock into one that ultimately redefines the scale of the city in terms of the highway and the role of the building as a generator rather than merely a container of functions and activities. In Baghdad Wright expanded the scope of the operation to the city as a whole.

Wright's extension and transformation of the City Beautiful civic center and Rockefeller Center–type "city within the city" into fully modernist expressions of public space and form occurred at a critical moment in the history of twentieth-century architecture and urbanism, a crossroads one might say. In America, the Depression had put an end to the last remnants of the City Beautiful approach, except perhaps in Washington, D.C., where it hung on until the end of the war. European modernists, on the other hand, did not begin to think seriously about the "core of the city" and the civic center until the final years of the war. Wright's sequence of planning efforts thus fills an important gap and reveals key stages in the transition from traditionalism to modernism in architecture's attempt to deal with the city as a whole. The projects for Madison, Washington, Pittsburgh, and Baghdad help us to understand how what was called city planning in the late thirties came to be called urban design by the early fifties. The evolution from the first to the last also forcefully illustrates the arrival in the mid-forties of an entirely new word and idea in America, that is to say, redevelopment. Pittsburgh's Point Park was in fact the first such public-private initiative completed under the authority of the 1949 urban renewal statute.

But the most important connection between the premodern and the modern and the prewar and the postwar that Wright's urban projects effectuated was in the social meanings of architecture and urban design. The designs for Madison, Washington, Pittsburgh, and Baghdad consistently and spectacularly revived a sense of community space, festive atmosphere, and cultural symbolism about which Sigfried Giedion spoke so compellingly in his description of "The Need for a New Monumentality," published well after Wright's design for Madison's Civic Center. Giedion, as we read, declared that the civic center would once again take its proper place in modern urbanism "when cities are not regarded as mere agglomerations of jobs and traffic lights," but when "community life is closely connected with a sense for leisure and relaxation." "Those who govern," he added, "must know that spectacles, which will lead the people back to community life, must be re-incorporated into … newly created civic centres [that] should be the site for collective, emotional events, where the people play as important a role as the spectacle itself, and where a unity of the architectural background, the people and the symbols created by artists will arise again."[1]

From 1938 through 1958, Wright pursued this idea of the civic center as a place of community interaction and public spectacle, creating new symbolic forms for the urban and suburban dweller in the process, before ultimately expanding it into the recently created type of cultural center designed for Baghdad at the very end of his career. It would have been unthinkable at the time for Giedion to refer to these examples of Wright's work given his engagement with CIAM. Now it seems historically irresponsible not to do so. The projects for Madison, Washington, Pittsburgh, and Baghdad offer new perspectives on the decades that reoriented modernist thinking in architecture and urbanism just as Wright's work in the field of urbanism prior to 1930 allows one to rethink both the debate between the City Beautiful and the Garden City and the discourse of the skyscraper city of the 1920s. As part of the overall development of urbanism in the first half of the twentieth century, Wright's work stands out as contributory and as integral as it was visionary and extraordinary.

NOTES

Introduction

1. Frank Lloyd Wright, "'Broadacre City': An Architect's Vision," *NYT Magazine*, 20 March 1932, 8–9.
2. Kenneth T. Jackson, *Crabgrass Frontier: The Suburbanization of the United States* (New York: Oxford University Press, 1985), 115.
3. See, esp., Sigfried Giedion, "The Need for a New Monumentality," in *New Architecture and City Planning*, ed. Paul Zucker (New York: Philosophical Library, 1944), 549–68; and Giedion, José Luis Sert, and Fernand Léger, "Nine Points on Monumentality" (1943), repr. in Giedion, *Architecture, You and Me: A Diary of a Development* (Cambridge, Mass.: Harvard University Press, 1958), 48–51.
4. Nor will I deal with all of Wright's urbanistic projects. Two that I leave out, which have been studied by Donald Leslie Johnson, are the designs for the town and village of Bitter Root, Montana (1909). Neither is well enough documented to sustain careful analysis in my view. In addition, I seriously doubt Wright's full involvement in the design development of either given his impending departure for Europe in the early fall of 1909.
5. Ildefonso Cerdà, *Teoría general de la urbanizacíon y aplicacíon de sus principios y doctrinas a la reforma y ensanche de Barcelona*, 2 vols. (Madrid: Imprenta Española, 1867). See Françoise Choay, *The Rule and the Model: On the Theory of Architecture and Urbanism*, orig. pub. in French 1980, ed. Denise Bratton (Cambridge, Mass.: MIT Press, 1997).
6. Le Corbusier, *Manière de penser l urbanisme*, new and rev. ed. (1946; repr., Paris: Gonthier, 1966), 11–12.
7. Statement by José Luis Sert, in "Urban Design: Condensed Report of an Invitation Conference … [at the] Graduate School of Design, Harvard University, April 9–10, 1956," *Progressive Architecture* 37 (August 1956): 97. In the introduction to this report, it was stated that "'the sponsors have avoided the term Civic Design as having, in the minds of many, too specialized or too grandiose a connotation'" and instead have used the new term "'Urban Design.'" "Grandiose" was obviously a code word for the City Beautiful. In his remarks following directly on the introduction, Sert described the outdated "'city beautiful' approach" as "superficial" in having "ignored

the roots of the [urban] problems and attempted only window-dressing effects" (ibid.). The first program in Civic Design was instituted by Charles Herbert Reilly at the Liverpool School of Architecture in 1909 after visiting the United States to study the work of McKim, Mead & White, Daniel Burnham, and other examples of American Beaux-Arts classicism.
8. Jackson, *Crabgrass Frontier*, 71.
9. Robert Fishman, *Bourgeois Utopias: The Rise and Fall of Suburbia* (New York: Basic Books, 1987).
10. "Suburb and City," *Oak Leaves*, 6 February 1903.

One: Wright's First Urban Design Initiative: The Development Plan for the Roberts Block, 1896

1. Burnham and Bennett, 31; Adna Ferrin Weber, *The Growth of Cities in the Nineteenth Century: A Study in Statistics*, Studies in History, Economics and Public Law, vol. 11 (New York: Macmillan, 1899), 450; and Jackson, *Crabgrass Frontier*, 92. See also William Cronon, *Nature's Metropolis: Chicago and the Great West* (New York: Norton, 1991).
2. Comments by William E. Barton, minister of the First Congregational Church of Oak Park, in "Suburb and City."
3. *Our Suburbs: A Resumé of the Origin, Progress and Present Status of Chicago's Environs, Reprint from "The Chicago Times"* (Chicago: Blue Island Land and Building Company, [1873]), 3. The prefatory note states that "the subject matter of this book is a reproduction of the superb and exhaustive article which appeared in 'The Sunday Times,' of Chicago, on the 4th of May, 1873."
4. There has been some debate as to when Wright joined Sullivan's office. Robert Twombly, *Louis Sullivan: His Life and Work* (New York: Viking, 1986), 173, maintains that it was "probably early in 1888." It should be noted that Wright worked for Silsbee two separate times; in between, he did a short stint in the office of William W. Clay.
5. Jon A. Peterson, *The Birth of City Planning in the United States, 1840–1917* (Baltimore: Johns Hopkins University Press, 2003), 332.
6. See Frank Lloyd Wright, *An Autobiography*, orig. pub. 1932, repr. in *FLWCW* 2:187–88. Wright referred more elliptically to the event in "Daniel Hudson Burnham:

An Appreciation," *AR* 32 (August 1912): 184. A motive for Burnham's offer may have been the need to replace his chief designer, Charles B. Atwood, whose health was becoming increasingly compromised by a serious drug addiction. Atwood died in 1896 at the age of forty-six.
7. Peterson, *Birth of City Planning*, 123. The McMillan Commission plan was published in Charles Moore, ed., *The Improvement of the Park System of the District of Columbia*, pt. 1, *Report of the Senate Committee on the District of Columbia*; and pt. 2, *Report of the Park Commission*, 57th Congress, 1st sess., S. Rept. 166 (Washington, D.C.: Government Printing Office, 1902). The other members of the Senate Park Commission were Charles F. McKim and Augustus St. Gaudens. The Cleveland plan was published in Daniel H. Burnham, John M. Carrère, and Arnold W. Brunner, *The Group Plan of the Public Buildings of the City of Cleveland. Report Made to the Honorable Tom L. Johnson, Mayor, and to the Honorable Board of Public Service* (New York: Cheltenham Press, August 1903). The 1904–5 plans were published in Burnham, with Edward H. Bennett, *Report on a Plan for San Francisco* (San Francisco: By the City, 1905); and Burnham, *Report on Proposed Improvements at Manila, June 28, 1905*, Bureau of Insular Affairs, War Department, Report of the Philippine Commission, pt. 1 (Washington, D.C.: Government Printing Office, 1906).
8. Royal Institute of British Architects, *Town Planning Conference, London, 10–15 October 1910: Transactions* (London: Royal Institute of British Architects, 1911), 106–7, 368–78. Burnham's lecture was titled "A City of the Future under a Democratic Government." The Berlin exhibition, followed by one in Düsseldorf, was organized by the young urbanist Werner Hegemann.
9. The best account of Lake Forest's origins is Michael H. Ebner, *Creating Chicago's North Shore: A Suburban History* (Chicago: University of Chicago Press, 1988), 27–35 and passim. Ebner points out that there has been a debate over which Hotchkiss drew up the plan, although he seems to be convinced that it was Almerin rather than David or Jedediah, as others have suggested (243).
10. Although Jackson, *Crabgrass Frontier*, 76, calls Llewellyn Park "the world's first picturesque suburb," it has precedents in John Nash's Park Village East and

Park Village West of the early 1820s, which were part of London's Regent's Park development, and the Maisons-Lafitte subdivision outside Paris, begun in the 1830s.

11. See Walter L. Creese, *The Crowning of the American Landscape* (Princeton: Princeton University Press, 1985), 221–40; and Riverside Improvement Company, *Riverside in 1871, with a Description of Its Improvements Together with Some Engravings of Views and Buildings* (Chicago: D. and C. H. Blakeley, n.d.).

12. Olmsted, Vaux & Co., Landscape Architects, "Preliminary Report upon the Proposed Suburban Village at Riverside, Near Chicago," 1 September 1868, in *The Papers of Frederick Law Olmsted*, vol. 6, *The Years of Olmsted, Vaux & Company, 1865–1874*, ed. David Schuyler and Jane Turner Censer (Baltimore: Johns Hopkins University Press, 1992), 284, 273, 275.

13. Riverside Improvement Company, *Riverside in 1871*, 6. The combination of the advantages of the city and the country minus the disadvantages of each became a mantra for Ebenezer Howard in his Garden City proposition in *Tomorrow: A Peaceful Path to Real Reform*, published in 1898 and republished four years later as *Garden Cities of To-Morrow* (see chapter 3 below).

14. Riverside Improvement Company, *Riverside in 1871*, 19.

15. Olmsted, Vaux & Co., "Preliminary Report," 287.

16. Ibid., 288.

17. Ibid., 286, 275.

18. Ibid., 280, 286–87.

19. The most succinct and useful study of the subject is William D. Pattison, *Beginnings of the American Rectangular Land Survey System, 1784–1800*, Department of Geography Research Paper 50 (Chicago: University of Chicago Press, 1957). See also Payson Jackson Treat, *The National Land System, 1785–1820* (New York: E. B. Treat, 1910); Hildegard Binder Johnson, *Order upon the Land: The U.S. Rectangular Land Survey and the Upper Mississippi Country* (New York: Oxford University Press, 1976); and C. Albert White, *A History of the Rectangular Survey System* (Washington, D.C.: U.S. Department of the Interior, Bureau of Land Management, 1983).

20. Quoted in Pattison, *Beginnings of the American Rectangular Land Survey*, 3.

21. Ibid., 57.

22. André Corboz, "Les Dimensions culturelles de la grille territoriale américaine," in Corboz, *Le Territoire comme palimpseste et autres essais*, ed. Sébastien Marot (Besançon, France: Editions de l'Imprimeur, 2001), 172–84. For a similar interpretation, see Andro Linklater, *Measuring America: How an Untamed Wilderness Shaped the United States and Fulfilled the Promise of Democracy* (New York: Walker, 2002). Dell Upton, *Another City: Urban Life and Urban Spaces in the New American Republic* (New Haven: Yale University Press, 2008), esp. 113–79, offers an analogous reading of the grid in the earlier plans of eastern cities such as Philadelphia and Savannah.

23. In the case of the Coonley House there is an additional piece of evidence of Wright's unease with the suburb's picturesque planning that deserves mention. For the terrace that projects toward the Des Plaines River to the southwest, Wright designed a bronze plaque, inset in the concrete, that explicitly relates the house to the Chicago grid. The plaque displays the compass points of the north-south grid overlaid on the actual orientation of the plan so as to serve as a constant reminder of the larger framework within which the house exists.

24. On the history and culture of Oak Park, see Arthur Evans Le Gacy, "Improvers and Preservers: A History of Oak Park, Illinois, 1833–1940" (Ph.D. diss., University of Chicago, 1967); Kathryn Elizabeth Ratcliff, "The Making of a New Middle-Class Culture: Family and Community in a Midwest Suburb, 1890–1920" (Ph.D. diss., University of Minnesota, 1990); and David M. Sokol, *Oak Park: The Evolution of a Village* (Charleston, S.C.: History Press, 2011).

25. Sokol, *Oak Park*, 19, states that the subdivision was officially named in 1856.

26. The Lake Street line was at first horse-drawn and then powered by cable. It started at Pulaski and Madison Streets, traveled west on Madison to Harlem (at the border with River Forest), then north on Harlem to Lake, turned east on Lake to Cicero, where it went south to Madison and then back on Madison to Pulaski. The streetcar that crossed Oak Park on Chicago Avenue also started at Pulaski and Madison, but had a more complicated route than the first. I am grateful to William Jerousek, information services officer at the Oak Park Library, for this information. For newspaper accounts, see "One Great Gridiron: How the Street-Car Tracks Have Spread over the City," *CDT*, 23 August 1891; "Cicero to Have an Elevated Road," *CDT*, 11 February 1894; "Electric Lines Now Exceed in Extent All Other Lines of Transportation in Chicago," *CDT*, 19 May 1895; "Two Hundred Miles of Streets," *CDT*, 19 May 1895; and "Cicero's Network of Railways," *CDT*, 2 August 1895.

27. See Vincent J. Scully Jr., *The Shingle Style and the Stick Style: Architectural Theory from Downing to the Origins of Wright* (1955; rev. ed., New Haven: Yale University Press, 1971), 159. The two houses by Price to which Scully specifically refers are the Chandler and Kent Houses, both in Tuxedo Park, N.Y., and both published prior to Wright's design.

28. This is pointed out in Robert McCarter, *Frank Lloyd Wright, Architect* (London: Phaidon, 1997), 233.

29. Frank Lloyd Wright to [William] Norman Guthrie, 20 November 1928, in *Letters to Clients: Frank Lloyd Wright*, ed. Bruce Brooks Pfeiffer (Fresno: Press at California State University, 1986), 279. On Roberts, see "Death of Charles E. Roberts, Long Prominent Here," *Oak Leaves*, 29 March 1934; Leonard Eaton, *Two Chicago Architects and Their Clients: Frank Lloyd Wright and Howard Van Doren Shaw* (Cambridge, Mass.: MIT Press, 1969), 77–79; and Joseph Siry, *Unity Temple: Frank Lloyd Wright and Architecture for Liberal Religion* (Cambridge: Cambridge University Press, 1996), 72–73, 283–84. The Roberts family papers, to which Meryle Secrest had access for her biography of Wright (*Frank Lloyd Wright: A Biography* [New York: Knopf, 1992]), have been impossible to locate.

30. Roberts was one of the three clients Wright thanked in the Wasmuth portfolio of 1910, the other two being Darwin Martin, of Buffalo, and Francis Little, of Peoria.

31. *FLWM* 1:19. In his later *FLWCW/DG/OC* 1:37, Pfeiffer states that this "design was probably done for one of Roberts' [*sic*] housing projects for Oak Park," suggesting that it was not for Roberts's own family.

32. The block was originally platted in 1872 and then resubdivided to conform to its present condition in 1906. Recorder of Deeds Office, Cook County, Chicago.

33. The 1894 plat map, however, calls Fair Oaks, Scoville.

34. Village of Ridgeland, blocks 1–12, 39–13 Cook County—book 112, Recorder of Deeds Office, Cook County, Chicago. The western half of the block was purchased from Noah Porter, who had bought it from James W. Scoville in 1872. The eastern half of the block was purchased from Anson and Adelaide Hemmingway.

I am grateful to Heidi Galles for gathering this information for me.

The contiguous block 7 has a similar history. Scoville owned most of the block, which he began selling off between 1888 and 1899. The next set of transactions took place between 1903 and 1912. Block 9 saw little action until 1904. The major period of activity, however, did not occur until 1909–15. Village of Ridgeland, Recorder of Deeds Office, Cook County, Chicago.

35. The dimensions refer to the outside property lines and exclude everything from the sidewalk to the street curb.

36. The numbers of the drawings are 9608.001–046, and 9705.001–006. However, FLWFA 9608.038, which should have been the basement plan of House [5] was missing when I studied the drawings in the spring of 2002. However, *FLWCW/DG/OC* 1:81, 85, states that House [3] (FLWFA 9608.020–027) is "a problematic, if not questionable, part of the same project"; and that the Corner House (FLWFA 9705.001–005) is later than the others since, despite its marked similarity to Wright's own 1889 house, it "reveals a design far different and more mature than the houses of the 1896 project." Pfeiffer also includes the development plan for the block with the Corner House, dating it to 1897, while at the same time noting that "it is obvious that this tract of land was for the four Ridgeland houses of the previous year" (85). For more on the development plan, see note 38 below.

37. Except for the sketchier Corner House, the set of drawings for each house usually includes a basement plan, a first-floor plan, a second-floor plan, an attic/roof plan, a front elevation, two side elevations, a rear elevation, and a section through the hall and sitting room. A couple also include perspectives, which suggests that they all once did.

38. As noted above (note 36), the drawings in the group FLWFA 9705 were considered by the Wright Foundation Archives to be one year later than the other group. They are not dated, nor is there any supporting evidence for a later date. There has been great confusion over this project in the literature, much of which, I believe, stems from the fact that the development plan was not published, or even assumed to exist, until 2006 (see note 45 below). Following the description in *FLWM* 1:94–99, 109, Siry, *Unity Temple*, 283–84n91, states that "in 1896 Wright designed for [Roberts] five small … houses for lots in 'Ridgeland.' … In 1897 Wright planned an unbuilt house for Roberts, perhaps as a prototype for twenty-two houses on the block Roberts owned in Oak Park [*sic*]." McCarter, *Frank Lloyd Wright*, 234, likewise maintains that the project is actually two different designs, the first dating from 1896 and the second from the following year: "In 1896, Wright proposed his first suburban housing scheme, a modest set of five houses … for Charles Roberts.… The next year Wright designed another set of prototype houses for Roberts … [in which] he apparently intended the houses to be arranged four on each block, linked by service wings at their back and facing away from one another to assure privacy." Pfeiffer and McCarter clearly wanted the "Corner House" to be part of a scheme predicting the 1900–1901 Quadruple Block Plan (see chapter 2 below). Gwendolyn Wright, *Frank Lloyd Wright's Progressive Suburbia*, Geske Lectures (Lincoln: Hixson-Lied College of Fine and Performing Arts, University of Nebraska-Lincoln, 2010), 17, also erroneously states that the 1896 plan "introduced" the Quadruple Block Plan of four years later.

39. I thank John Thorpe for this information.

40. A version of House 2 was built for the Goodrich

family in Oak Park in 1896 using the porch arrangement of House 1. The very tall roof of House 1 recalls the Williams House in River Forest, built the year before.

41. The Tudor detailing recalls the house Wright built, opposite his own house, for the Moore family in 1895.

42. This plan, or one very much like it, was published in Robert C. Spencer Jr., "The Work of Frank Lloyd Wright," *Architectural Review* (Boston) 7 (June 1900): 66 (middle in group of three).

43. This plan was also published in ibid., 66 (top in group of three). It is very similar to the one used for the Peter Goan House built in La Grange, Ill., the previous year. A third plan reproduced in ibid. (bottom in group of three) relates to the ones for Roberts's Houses 4 and [5].

44. The band of four leaded windows in the gable on the side elevation (figure 1.25), so similar to the one in the front gable of Wright's own house, was initially designed to have a pointed rather than circular lunette window above the middle two. This was erased, but one can still see the traces.

45. The development plan was first published in Neil Levine, "*The Quadruple Block Plan*: l'obsession de Frank Lloyd Wright pour la grille/The Quadruple Block Plan and Frank Lloyd Wright's Obsession with the Grid," *EaV: La revue de l'école nationale supérieure d'architecture de Versailles/Versailles Architecture School Journal* 11 (2005/6): 66. Later versions of that essay include my "Making Community Out of the Grid: Wright's Quadruple Block Plan and the Origin of the Prairie House," in *Frank Lloyd Wright: From Within Outward*, ed. Richard Cleary et al. (New York: Skira Rizzoli, Guggenheim Museum, 2009), 58–73; "La Restructuration du lotissement résidentiel autour de 1900 et le schéma communautaire de Frank Lloyd Wright," in *Tony Garnier, la Cité Industrielle et l'Europe*, ed. Philippe Dufieux (Lyon: Conseil d'architecture, d'urbanisme et de l'environnement du Rhône, 2009), 78–89; and "The Late Eighteenth-Century U.S. Rectangular Land Survey and Frank Lloyd Wright's Recuperation of Its Enlightenment Ideal," in *Early Modern Urbanism and the Grid: Town Planning in the Low Countries in International Context. Exchanges in Theory and Practice, 1550–1800*, ed. Piet Lombaerde and Charles van den Heuvel, Architectura Moderna 10 (Turnhout, Belgium: Brepols, 2011), 187–206.

46. See Peter Collins, "The Origins of Graph Paper as an Influence on Architectural Design," *JSAH* 21 (1962): 159–62.

47. Jean-Nicolas-Louis Durand, *Précis of the Lectures on Architecture with Graphic Portion of the Lectures on Architecture*, orig. pub. 1802–5/1821; trans. David Britt, Texts & Documents, Getty Research Institute Publications Program (Los Angeles: Getty Research Institute, 2000), esp. text and accompanying plates of *Graphic Portion*.

48. Charles E. White Jr. to Walter R. B. Willcox, 13 May 1904, in "Letters, 1903–1906, by Charles E. White, Jr. from the Studio of Frank Lloyd Wright," ed. Nancy K. Morris Smith, *Journal of Architectural Education* 25 (Fall 1971): 105. According to Smith, White left Burlington, Vt., for Oak Park in 1903 to work for Wright. According to Paul Kruty, "At Work in the Oak Park Studio," *Arris: Journal of the Southeast Chapter of the Society of Architectural Historians* 14 (2003): 21, 29n20, he left Boston for Chicago in 1902 and began working for Wright in 1903. He married Alice May Roberts in 1901.

49. This was also true of the plans of the Martin House (1903–6), Ullman House project (1904), and Unity Temple (1905–8), all of which were redrawn for

publication in Frank Lloyd Wright, "In the Cause of Architecture, I: The Logic of the Plan," *AR* 63 (January 1928): 52–55.

50. White to Willcox, in "Letters, 1903–1906," 105. The "3-foot by 3-foot planning grid explicitly shown in red ink" on the drawing for the Gerts cottage is pointed out in McCarter, *Frank Lloyd Wright*, 46.

51. It is not known whether the replatting would have been acceptable to officials, since the project was never brought to a stage of completion requiring permitting.

52. The alley entering from Superior Street was planned to be only twelve rather than twenty feet wide. A corresponding alley, running south from the middle of the Chicago Avenue frontage, was initially drawn and then erased.

53. In his pamphlet *Nothing Gained by Overcrowding! How the Garden City Type of Development May Benefit Both Owner and Occupier* (London: Garden Cities & Town Planning Association, 1912), 4 (diagram I) and 9 (diagram III), the latter here illustrated in figure 1.37, Unwin famously contrasted a typical "by-law" development of row houses lining the street, with rear gardens and alleys between, to a plan "developed in accordance with the Garden City principles" in which superblocks are composed of a much reduced number of houses surrounding central communal park and recreation areas. Interestingly, in the Roberts-like design, the corners are treated differently from the rest of the block and have angled paths leading into the central communal space from the street. The design by George C. Cone for the O. C. Simonds firm for the Beloit Model Homes Company, in Beloit, Wis., done in 1913 or 1914, follows the same model but on a scale closer to the Wright precedent. It has an oval-shaped central garden and recreation area with pathways leading into it from each of the block's four sides. It was published in Yeomans, 36. This book documented the City Club competition for a Scheme of Development for a Quarter Section within Chicago, in which Cone was a participant and Wright a noncompeting contributor, that is the subject of chapter 4.

Two: The Quadruple Block Plan as the Framework for the Ladies' Home Journal "Home in a Prairie Town," 1900–1901

1. John Lloyd Wright Jr., *My Father Who Is on Earth*, ed. Narciso Menocal (1946; repr., Carbondale: Southern Illinois University Press, 1994), 22.

2. Sam Bass Warner Jr., *Streetcar Suburbs: The Process of Growth in Boston, 1870–1900* (1962; 2nd ed., Cambridge, Mass.: Harvard University Press, 1978).

3. Unfortunately virtually all the records of the Philadelphia-based Curtis Publishing Company, publisher of the *Ladies' Home Journal* (hereafter *LHJ*), were discarded or otherwise disappeared; and there is no correspondence in the Wright Foundation Archives relating to the commission. In an editorial in the July 1900 issue, Edward Bok, the magazine's editor, stated that a new series of architectural designs for "everybody who wishes to build a pretty country home at a moderate cost" would "include [plans by] the best and most distinguished talent of Philadelphia, Boston and New York." Edward Bok, "The American Man and the Country," *LHJ* 18 (July 1900): 14. By October, he added Chicago to the list, writing, in a note to the first published design, that "the foremost architects of New York, Philadelphia, Boston and Chicago will prepare the plans and estimates for these houses." Bruce Price, "A Georgian House for Seven Thousand Dollars," *LHJ* 17 (October 1900): 15.

Between the beginning of July and October, Bok had been in extended contact with Robert Spencer regarding a "Series of Good Practical Farmhouses at Moderate Cost" that Spencer would publish in the magazine in seven installments between October 1900 and June 1901. Spencer was not only a friend and colleague of Wright's, but also a great admirer of his work who published the first study of it in the Boston-based *Architectural Review* in June 1900. Spencer, "Work of Frank Lloyd Wright," 61–72. Spencer's advisory role would seem to be supported by the fact that the only other midwesterner included was Elmer Grey, who, like Spencer, was born in Milwaukee. Spencer's education at MIT and employment in Boston for a number of years may explain the further fact that of the fourteen firms included, more than a third were based in Boston.

4. On the *LHJ* series, see Kathryn Dethier, "The Spirit of Progressive Reform: The *Ladies' Home Journal* House Plans, 1900–1902," *Journal of Design History* 6 (1993): 247–61; and Leland M. Roth, "Getting the Houses to the People: Edward Bok, The *Ladies' Home Journal*, and the Ideal House," *Perspectives in Vernacular Architecture* 4 (1991): 187–96. I am grateful to Amanda Reeser Lawrence for numerous ideas contained in the paper she did for me on the subject in a course I taught at Harvard several years ago.

5. Frank Lloyd Wright, "A Home in a Prairie Town," *LHJ* 18 (February 1901): 17. The text minus the original illustrations and graphics was reprinted in *FLWCW* 1:73–75.

6. See Salme Harlu Steinberg, *Reformer in the Marketplace: Edward W. Bok and the Ladies' Home Journal* (Baton Rouge: Louisiana State University Press, 1979); Jennifer Scanlon, *Inarticulate Longings: The* Ladies' Home Journal, *Gender, and the Promise of Consumer Culture* (New York: Routledge, 1995); and Hans Krabbendam, *The Model Man: A Life of Edward William Bok, 1863–1930*, Amsterdam Monographs in American Studies 9 (Amsterdam: Rodopi, 2001).

7. Edward Bok, *The Americanization of Edward Bok: An Autobiography*, originally published in 1920 as *The Americanization of Edward Bok: An Autobiography of a Dutch Boy Fifty Years After* (Philadelphia: American Foundation, 1973), 300, 116–17.

8. Ibid., 180.

9. Ibid., 176, 178–79.

10. Ibid., 171–72. See also Gwendolyn Wright, *Moralism and the Model Home: Domestic Architecture and Cultural Conflict in Chicago, 1873–1913* (Chicago: University of Chicago Press, 1980), 136.

11. Quoted in Bok, *Americanization*, 179. Bok also notes that Stanford White, who originally "discouraged" him from starting the project, came around in the end to admitting its success. "'I firmly believe,'" White wrote, "'that Edward Bok has more completely influenced American domestic architecture for the better than any man in this generation'" (ibid., 174).

12. Ibid., 172.

13. W[illiam] L. Price, "A $3500 Suburban House," *LHJ* 13 (December 1895): 37. The design was republished in Price, *Model Houses for Little Money*, Ladies' Home Journal Household Library (Philadelphia: Curtis Publishing, 1898), as the frontispiece and the first example. The booklet included all the house designs Price had published anonymously in the magazine between July 1897 and March 1898 as "the Journal's Special Architect."

14. Ralph Adams Cram, "A $5000 Colonial House," *LHJ* 13 (February 1896): 17.

15. Edward T. Hapgood, "A $3500 Shingle House," *LHJ* 13 (March 1896): 19. The Bruce Price house, "A $5000 Dutch

Colonial," was published in April 1896; the Pickering shingled cottage "for $2000" in May 1896; the turreted "$3500" Handy house in July 1896; the small "$1500 Summer Cottage" by Pentecost in February 1897; and the three modest classical designs by Keith in March and April 1897.

16. These appeared in July, September, November, and December 1897 and in January, February, and March 1898. As noted above (note 13), they were reprinted in Price's booklet *Model Houses for Little Money*, which was published as part of the *LHJ Household Library*.

17. "The Gossip of the Editors: A Special Prize of $100.00 for Those Who Have Built the Journal's Model Homes," *LHJ* 15 (June 1898): 26; and "The Gossip of the Editors: The Journal's Houses Built in Egypt," *LHJ* 15 (July 1898): 27. The prize photographs were published in "The Journal's Prize Model House: Illustrations from Original Photographs," *LHJ* 16 (June 1899): 23. Photographs of four different houses were premiated and published.

18. Bok, "American Man and the Country."

19. Price, "Georgian House," 15; Charles Barton Keen and Frank E. Mead, "A Quaint, Old-Fashioned House for $6600," *LHJ* 17 (November 1900): 17.

20. The complete list of designs includes the following: Bruce Price, "A Georgian House for Seven Thousand Dollars," *LHJ* 17 (October 1900): 15; Charles Barton Keen and Frank E. Mead, "A Quaint, Old-Fashioned House for $6600," *LHJ* 17 (November 1900): 17; Milton Bennett Medary Jr. and Richard Littell Field, "An Old English Country House for $7000," *LHJ* 18 (December 1900): 21; Ralph Adams Cram, "A Country House of Moderate Cost," *LHJ* 18 (January 1901): 15; Frank Lloyd Wright, "A Home in a Prairie Town," *LHJ* 18 (February 1901): 17; Edwin J. Lewis Jr., "A Suburban House for $6500," *LHJ* 18 (March 1901): 15; William G. Rantoul, "A Stucco Country House for $7500," *LHJ* 18 (April 1901): 15; Arthur D. Pickering, "A Dutch Colonial House for $5000," *LHJ* 18 (May 1901): 15; Frank Lloyd Wright, "A Small House with 'Lots of Room in It,'" *LHJ* 18 (July 1901): 15; Albert Bayne Lawyer, "A $5000 House for a Family of Three," *LHJ* 18 (August 1901): 15; Elmer Grey, "An Old English House for $7000," *LHJ* 18 (September 1901): 15; Horace S. Frazer, "A Wood and Stone House for $6700," *LHJ* 18 (October 1901): 15; Wilson Eyre Jr., "A Country House on a Small Place," *LHJ* 18 (November 1901): 15; and George Edward Barton, "A $6000 House with a Garden," *LHJ* 19 (January 1902): 15. Although a prospectus in the December 1900 issue of the magazine announcing upcoming articles for 1901 noted that "there will be fully a dozen more" "Model Country Houses at a Small Cost" in addition to the three that "have [already] been given," only eleven appeared. "What the Ladies' Home Journal Will Give You in 1901," *LHJ* 18 (December 1900): 1.

21. Bok, *Americanization*, 173; and see figures 2.2–12 and 2.15–16.

22. Price, "Georgian House."

23. Medary and Field, "Old English Country House."

24. Grey, "Old English House."

25. Keen and Mead, "Quaint, Old-Fashioned House."

26. Cram, "Country House."

27. Lewis, "Suburban House."

28. Rantoul, "Stucco Country House."

29. Lawyer, "$5000 House."

30. Frazer, "Wood and Stone House."

31. Eyre, "Country House."

32. R. Clipston Sturgis, "Suburban Homes: A Plea for Privacy in Home Life," *Cosmopolitan: A Monthly Illustrated Magazine* 21 (June 1896): 182; and V[ernon] L.

Parrington, "On the Lack of Privacy in American Village Homes," *House Beautiful* 13 (January 1903): 109–12.

33. Medary and Field, "Old English Country House."

34. Lewis, "Suburban House."

35. Grey, "Old English House."

36. Keen and Mead, "Quaint, Old-Fashioned House."

37. Henry-Russell Hitchcock, *In the Nature of Materials: The Buildings of Frank Lloyd Wright, 1887–1941* (1942; repr., New York: Da Capo Press, 1975), 33. Grant Carpenter Manson, *Frank Lloyd Wright to 1910: The First Golden Age* (New York: Van Nostrand Reinhold, 1958), 103, says that in the two designs for the magazine, "Wright officially unveiled the Prairie House." H. Allen Brooks used the term "prototype" in his *Frank Lloyd Wright and the Prairie School* (New York: George Braziller, in association with Cooper-Hewitt Museum, 1984), 18–19.

38. Hitchcock, *Nature of Materials*, 34. Manson, *Frank Lloyd Wright to 1910*, 103, 207, does not even mention the overall plan until more than one hundred pages after discussing the house design. He then characterizes the Quadruple Block Plan as merely "background for the Ladies' Home Journal model houses in 1901." Robert C. Twombly, *Frank Lloyd Wright: His Life and His Architecture* (New York: John Wiley, 1979), 52–53, refers to the Quadruple Block Plan only when discussing a later project to implement it in Oak Park. Charles E. Aguar and Berdeanna Aguar, *Wrightscapes: Frank Lloyd Wright's Landscape Designs* (New York: McGraw-Hill, 2002), 49–56, follow the Hitchcock pattern but focus more on the overall planning scheme than the house itself. The authors, however, describe the Quadruple Block Plan as a design totally "separate" from that of the house, which was combined with the latter only in the magazine's layout. They acknowledge, however, that Wright's "interest at this point lay at least as much with the subdivision of the land and the manner of unitizing the houses on the land as with the design of the house itself" and that "his intent certainly seemed to be to promote the house and his Quadruple Block Plan as an entity" (51–52).

39. Wright, "Home in a Prairie Town."

40. Whereas none of the other five Wright drawings reproduced in the February 1901 article still exist, the perspective of a single house was either based on FLWFA 0007.001 or another version of it. The drawing in the Wright Foundation Archives, which is quite dark in tonality, almost as if seen in moonlight, varies from the published one in several respects: the shadow cast by the porte-cochere is missing; the chimney capstones do not project; there are no pavement scoring lines; and the foliage treatment is very different. In the signed red square at the middle left is the date 1900. Later annotations include a legend on the bottom that reads "DESIGN FOR 'PRAIRIE HOUSE' LADIES HOME JOURNAL 1900," followed by a square with a signature in it plus the abbreviation "del." and an inscription in the lower right-hand corner saying "For Richard Bock [*sic*?] Ladies Home Journal."

The perspective of "A Home in a Prairie Town" reproduced in Frank Lloyd Wright, *Ausgeführte Bauten und Entwürfe von Frank Lloyd Wright* (Berlin: Ernst Wasmuth, 1910[–11]), pl. 13, is similar to the one in the 1901 *LHJ*; the one used a few years later to illustrate the Quadruple Block Plan houses in his Scheme of Development for a Quarter Section within Chicago in Yeomans, 101 (see figure 4.30) is similar to the existing perspective.

41. Wright, "Home in a Prairie Town." Until Eyre's submission, which did not even include a budget, Wright's was the only one not to include the cost of the house in the article's title.

42. Ibid.

43. Ibid.

44. Ibid.

45. Ibid.

46. This drawing (FLWFA 0309.001) was misdated to 1903 (based on the later note in the lower right-hand corner) and filed in the Wright Foundation Archives with the 1903 scheme for Charles Roberts. It was published in *FLWM* 2:64, figure 112, as part of the later project. By contrast, there are a number of drawings filed with the *LHJ* Quadruple Block Plan that are part of the sequence of studies for the 1903 project. These include FLWFA 0019.001-002, 004-007, and 009. Aside from the perspective referred to in note 40 above, there are a number of drawings in the Wright Foundation Archives that are thought to be preliminary sketches or studies for the house itself (FLWFA 0007.002-008 and 010-011). A variant of the aerial perspective of the *LHJ* Quadruple Block Plan was published in Yeomans, 100 (see figure 4.34).

47. See, e.g., Unwin, *Nothing Gained by Overcrowding!*; Lawrence Veiller, "Buildings in Relation to Street and Site," in *Proceedings of the Third National Conference on City Planning, Philadelphia, Pennsylvania, May 15–17, 1911* (Boston, 1911), 80–96; and "Report of Conference Committee on 'Best Methods of Land Subdivision,'" appendix A, in *Proceedings of the Seventh National Conference on City Planning, Detroit, June 7–9, 1915* (Boston, 1915), 247–73.

48. Wright's attention to these framing elements can be seen in the sketch in figure 2.17, where the widths of sidewalk, parkway, and street are all indicated, the first being five feet, the second sixteen, and the third, thirty-three. I want to thank Brendan Fay for many of the insights he offered in a paper analyzing the Quadruple Block Plan done for a seminar at Harvard.

49. There is much confusion in the literature on this matter due to Wright's having published in the Wasmuth portfolio the perspective of the *LHJ* "Home in a Prairie Town" and the Quadruple Block Plan aerial perspective with the two plans from the 1903 project for Charles Roberts (to be discussed in chapter 3), neither of which has stables and one of which shows a completely different configuration of the four houses. Wright, *Ausgeführte Bauten*, pls. 13–13a.

Manson, *Frank Lloyd Wright to 1910*, 206, illustrates the Quadruple Block Plan with the perspective from the *LHJ* and a redrawn detail of the 1903 plan. G. Wright, *Moralism and the Model Home*, 139, incorrectly describes the house groupings as taking different forms, as they would in 1903. McCarter, *Frank Lloyd Wright*, 234–35, likewise, erroneously states that the *LHJ* overall plan proposed two "siting variants," only one of which had garages or stables. Again, this stems from a conflation with later schemes based on the 1900–1901 prototype.

The conflation of plans from earlier and later versions of the Quadruple Block Plan has led some authors to see a strong influence of Walter Burley Griffin on the design. Following the lead of James Birrell, *Walter Burley Griffin* (Queensland: University of Queensland Press, 1964), esp. 35–47, Donald Leslie Johnson, *The Architecture of Walter Burley Griffin* (Melbourne: Macmillan, 1977), 41, states that "the initial developmental work on the Quadruple Block Plans of Wright was given to Griffin." Aguar and Aguar, *Wrightscapes*, 55, agree. The only bases for this attribution are statements by Griffin's wife, Marion Mahony Griffin, made after she and her husband left the United States for Australia. These will be discussed in chapter 3 since they are not in fact relevant to the *LHJ* design but only to the later Roberts project. It should simply be noted here that Griffin was hired by Wright as a draftsman in June 1901, which means that he was not even working for Wright when the Quadruple Block Plan was developed.

50. An even closer parallel to the Quadruple Block Plan was produced by the progressive Beaux-Arts-trained architect Ernest Flagg (1857–1947) in 1894 in response to concerns for improving New York City tenements. His novel idea was to group the city's narrow lots into large square building blocks one hundred feet to a side. An open central court gave access to the two apartments in each of the four corners as well as light and ventilation to the interior units. The design, which Wright could have known, was published in Ernest Flagg, "The New York Tenement-House Evil and Its Cure," *Scribner's Magazine* 16 (July 1894): 112. A revised version of this plan won the 1896 competition sponsored by the Improved Dwelling Council; and in the following year the scheme was built by the philanthropic City and Suburban Homes Company. See David P. Handlin, *The American Home: Architecture and Society, 1815–1915* (Boston: Little, Brown, 1979), 202–5.

51. Norris Kelly Smith, *Frank Lloyd Wright: A Study in Architectural Content* (1966; rev. ed., Watkins Glen, N.Y.: American Life Foundation & Study Institute, 1979), 102, stressed the importance of the metropolitan grid in Wright's planning of the individual house between 1902 and 1909, noting that, through sharing this rectilinear framework, "[the houses] are bound together by the city itself."

52. Hitchcock, *Nature of Materials*, 30. Paul E. Sprague, "The Evolution of Wright's Long Narrow Hip Roofs," in Paul Kruty, *Prelude to the Prairie Style: Eight Models of Unbuilt Houses by Frank Lloyd Wright, 1893–1901* (Urbana-Champaign: School of Architecture, University of Illinois, 2005), 20, claims that the clubhouse was designed in January 1899.

53. To be fair, Hitchcock somewhat hedged on the subject, noting that "all the essential innovations appear in the first version as published in 1900, and most of them in the original front wing, presumably of 1898." Hitchcock, *Nature of Materials*, 30. Vincent Scully, *Frank Lloyd Wright* (New York: George Braziller, 1960), 16, noted that only "as completed," i.e., in 1901, did the clubhouse present "a clear cross-axial plan."

54. The front door of the house was originally located in the central bay, under the porch, directly opposite the main stairs. It was subsequently rubbed out and moved to the bay to the left. Paul E. Sprague, "Appendix: Documenting the Dates of Design of Eight Unbuilt Houses by Frank Lloyd Wright," in Kruty, *Prelude to the Prairie Style*, 28, claims that the house was "conceived by Wright at least three months before the March 1898 date on the drawings or about December 1897." Another pre-1900 example of Wright's deployment of a conventional, diagrammatic form of cross-axial composition is the Devin House project for Chicago (1896).

55. Wright, "Small House with 'Lots of Room in It.'" The text alone was reprinted in *FLWCW* 1:76–77.

56. One can point to an incipient but undeveloped form of pinwheeling in the plan of Wright's own Oak Park house as well as in the plan for the remodeling of the Waller River Forest House (1899) and the two schemes for the Lake Delavan Wallis Summer Cottage (1900).

57. The Willits House has traditionally been thought of as the first Prairie House. It is interesting that, even though we now know that it was designed only in 1902 and completed in 1903, it is often still misdated to 1901.

58. Almost two decades later, John Nolen, ed., *City Planning: A Series of Papers Presenting the Essential Elements of a City Plan*, National Municipal League Series (New York: Appleton, 1916), 39, 23, stated that although "land subdivision … has a very direct and important influence on housing—perhaps greater and more permanent than any other single influence," there are many reasons why it "has not been given more attention by city planners in this country." He posited the hope "that the investigation and study of land subdivision in connection with city planning … will bring great benefits—physical, financial, and sociological—in the land subdivision of the future" (44). One of the first articles to deal with the matter, which Nolen cited, was Veiller, "Buildings in Relation to Street and Site."

59. Johnson, *Architecture of Walter Burley Griffin*, 30.

60. Gwendolyn Wright, "Architectural Practice and Social Vision in Wright's Early Designs," *The Nature of Frank Lloyd Wright*, ed. Carol Bolon et al. (Chicago: University of Chicago Press, 1988), 108; and G. Wright, *Moralism and the Model Home*, 139.

61. N. K. Smith, *Frank Lloyd Wright*, 100; and Twombly, *Frank Lloyd Wright*, 223.

62. Manson, *Frank Lloyd Wright to 1910*, 207.

63. David G. De Long, "Frank Lloyd Wright and the Evolution of the Living City," in *Frank Lloyd Wright and the Living City*, ed. De Long (Weil am Rhein, Germany: Vitra Design Museum, 1998), 18.

64. McCarter, *Frank Lloyd Wright*, 235.

65. Gwendolyn Wright, "Frank Lloyd Wright and the Domestic Landscape," in *Frank Lloyd Wright, Architect*, ed. Terence Riley, with Peter Reed (New York: Museum of Modern Art, 1994), 90–91.

66. Rosalind Krauss, "Grids," 1979, repr. in Krauss, *The Originality of the Avant-Garde and Other Modernist Myths* (Cambridge, Mass.: MIT Press, 1985), 12.

67. Dell Upton suggested this in response to the initial presentation of this work in the talk titled "Frank Lloyd Wright's Quadruple Block Plan: A Framework for the Early Twentieth-Century Suburb" that I gave at a symposium on "Paris-Chicago: Parallels Morphological and Conceptual," organized by David Van Zanten and held in Chicago in September 2000.

68. Frederick Jackson Turner, "The Significance of the Frontier in American History," in *Annual Report of the American Historical Society for the Year 1893* (Washington, D.C.: Government Printing Office, 1894), 197–227.

Three: The Roberts Block Revisited, 1903–4, the City Beautiful, and the Garden City

1. It is unclear whether the phrase "two blocks" referred to two groups of four houses or to two Oak Park blocks. The former is much more likely given the size of the blocks in question and is what I assume to be the case. Block 7 had been platted for eight houses in 1894. Blocks 7 and 6 (which had been platted for twelve houses) were approximately the same size, i.e., 350 feet from street curb to street curb in the east-west direction and 575 feet in the north-south direction.

2. "New Idea for Suburbs. Plan of Frank Lloyd Wright," *Chicago Evening Post*, 12 July 1901; repr. in *Oak Park Reporter*, 18 July 1901.

3. It is unclear whether the terms "colony" and "settlement" were suggested by Wright. Wright never used them elsewhere in relation to the Quadruple Block Plan.

4. "New Idea," *Chicago Evening Post*.

5. Ibid.

6. The version in the *Oak Park Reporter* added the word "fence" to the sentence in the original publication.

7. "New Idea," *Chicago Evening Post*. The quotations from the *LHJ* text reflect the changes in punctuation and spelling in the *Post* and *Reporter* pieces.

8. Frank Lloyd Wright to S. T. Kendall, 10 September 1901, FLWFA.

9. Ibid.

10. An unsigned review under the heading "Chicago" in *American Architect and Building News* 76 (26 April 1902): 29 was scathingly critical of the exhibition for its "advertising" of a single architect's work, which it linked to "the semi-grotesque, the catchy."

11. "A Selection of Works Exhibited at the Art Institute in March of the Year One Thousand Nine Hundred and Two," in *Chicago Architectural Annual* (Chicago: Chicago Architectural Club, 1902), n.p. Although the "Small House with 'Lots of Room in It'" preceded the "Home in a Prairie Town," Wright mentioned the alternative site plans for it before discussing the house itself. He also noted that "the house is to be built at Riverside, Illinois." It was Wright who changed the original series title from "moderate cost" to "modern."

12. Ibid.

13. A letter from Charles E. White Jr., Roberts's son-in-law, who began working in Wright's office in 1903, to his former employer, Walter Willcox, states that "Father Roberts," who "resigned from the [American] Screw Company, and is gradually pulling out some of his interests," now "is thinking of going ahead with the Wright scheme of twenty [*sic*] houses on his block." White to Willcox, [20 May 1904], in "Letters, 1903–1906," 107.

14. The date of instrument for the transaction was 14 August 1906 and the date of filing, 23 August. Winterbotham proceeded to have the alley between Scoville and Elmwood Avenues vacated and, in September-October 1906, began the process of resubdividing the block to create the twenty lots, all facing east and west, that exist today. Village of Ridgeland, Blocks 1–12, 39–13 Cook County—Book 112, Recorder of Deeds Office, Cook County, Chicago. I am grateful to Heidi Galles for this information. Winterbotham sold off the lots over the next few years, and building permits for new construction were issued beginning in late 1906. Resubdivision of Block 8, Village of Ridgeland, Oak Park Village Hall, Oak Park, Ill. I am grateful to Sandra Sokol and Fred Zinke for providing me with access to these records.

15. Manson, *Frank Lloyd Wright to 1910*, 207. Manson states that "the houses were rather undistinguished two-story dwellings with hip roofs and stucco walls, but already completely recognizable as being within the Prairie House family" (ibid.). Manson confuses the earlier *LHJ* version of the project with the 1903–4 Roberts one, as Wright himself did in his *Ausgefürhte Bauten*, by publishing plans for the later scheme with the perspective of the earlier one (ibid., 206).

16. Wright to Kendall, 10 September 1901. I have substituted the word "although" for "and" in the final sentence quoted in order to clarify its meaning.

17. Ibid.

18. Of the houses that were built soon after Roberts sold the property in 1906, 434 and 436 N. Scoville, permitted in 1908, were estimated to cost $3,400; 431 Elmwood, permitted in 1906, was estimated at $3,000; 419 and 423 Elmwood, permitted in 1906, were estimated to cost $3,900; and 415 Elmwood, also permitted in 1906, was estimated at $4,000. Somewhat more expensive, 411 Elmwood, permitted in 1906, was estimated to cost

$5,000. The houses ranged in size from a little under six-teen hundred to nearly twenty-six hundred square feet. Resubdivision of Block 8, Village of Ridgeland.

19. Concrete sidewalks were approved on Superior between Scoville and Ogden and on Elmwood from Superior to South Lake in June 1903. Record B, Minutes of Village Meetings, Village of Oak Park, 5 March 1903–14 May 1904, Oak Park Village Hall. See also Record A, Minutes of Village Meetings, 2 January 1902–19 February 1903; and Record C, Minutes of Village Meetings, 2 June 1904–2 November 1905.

20. Four of the six are miscatalogued in the Wright Foundation Archives with the 1900 *LHJ* scheme as FLWFA 0019.002 (sketch house plan), 0019.006 (prelim-inary sketch perspective), 0019.007 (sketch perspective), and 0019.009 (house plan template). Two others, FLWFA 0019.004 (half-block plan with houses brought to street line) and 0019.005 (half-block plan with houses in center of lots), are similarly miscatalogued. The three presentation drawings with legend blocks are FLWFA 0309.012 (elevations), 0309.013 (partial site plan and sections), and 0309.014 (house plans). FLWFA 0309.011 may be a study for 0309.013, although it was more likely done later, for a related or even different project. The two half-block plans (FLWFA 0019.004 and 005) do not have the specific street names on them and were most likely done after the presentation drawings. *FLWM* 1:154–55, figures 324, 327–28, are for the 1903 Roberts project rather than the *LHJ* design; whereas *FLWM* 2:64, figure 112 is for the *LHJ* rather than the 1903–4 Roberts project and pp. 66–67, figures 117 and 119 are for the City Club competition of 1912–13 (see chapter 4). McCarter, *Frank Lloyd Wright*, 236 (bottom right), misidentifies one of the City Club plans as being for the 1903 Roberts project, thus assuming there was provi-sion for a garage in the latter. The catalogue of the 1994 MoMA exhibition, Riley, *Frank Lloyd Wright,* 324–25, also confuses the 192–13 City Club Quarter Section Scheme with the Roberts project as do Aguar and Aguar, *Wrightscapes*, 59.

21. The second sketch perspective, FLWFA 0019.006, is almost the same as the one illustrated in figure 3.9.

22. A handwritten note on figure 3.10, though very possibly later in date than the drawing, says "Low cost houses—no garage or stable."

23. The Larkin Building was commissioned in 1902, but was built from the revised design of April 1904. The Martin House was commissioned in 1903 and planned in 1904. The plan of the Martin House is literally a transla-tion of "A Home in a Prairie Town" into the disaggregated and abstracted forms of the Roberts type-house. Indeed, there can be little doubt that the Quadruple Block Plan was on Wright's mind while he was planning the Martin House complex, which includes two other houses plus a conservatory.

24. The depression also allowed for clerestory windows to let light into the basement laundry rooms.

25. For comparison's sake, the one-story Cheney House (1903–4) is approximately sixty-four by sixty feet and sits on a lot about one hundred by eighty-five feet. The Heurtley House (1902–3) is about seventy by fifty-five feet, whereas the Willits House is about one hundred forty by one hundred feet and sits on a lot approximately two hundred seventy by two hundred sixty feet.

26. Where the houses in the 1896 project averaged a little less than twenty-two hundred square feet, those in the 1903 plan were a little over twenty-five hundred square feet, excluding the half basement.

27. On the other hand, there may have been a miscom-munication between Wright and his draftsperson since the dimension for the overall Superior Street frontage is confused with that of Scoville Avenue, not to speak of the fact that the latter is called by its former name, Fair Oaks. I owe many of these observations regarding dimensions and orientation to Brendan Fay.

28. This idealized rendering of the Roberts block does not have the actual street names indicated. The same is true for its pendant illustrated in figure 3.10.

29. The plans in figures 3.9 and 3.10 are the ones that were misleadingly reproduced in Wright's *Ausgeführte Bauten* in conjunction with the perspective for the 1901 *LHJ* "Home in a Prairie Town" article. See chapter 2, notes 40 and 49.

30. Johnson, *Architecture of Walter Burley Griffin*, 41, claims that "the idea of pairing houses in a more pragmatic situation was Griffin's." Aguar and Aguar, *Wrightscapes*, 55–58, assume that Griffin designed both plans for the 1903–4 Roberts project. They base this as-sumption on an interview that Grant Carpenter Manson conducted with Marion Mahony Griffin in 1940 (Grant Carpenter Manson, "Records of F. L. Wright," handwrit-ten notes, Oak Park Library, Oak Park, Ill.). Quoting from Manson's notes out of context, the Aguars state that "[Mahony] alleged it was because 'Griffin at once showed a flair for town planning which incited Wright's jealous emulation' that Wright's 'so-called quadruple block plan' came about" (58). What Manson actually recorded is the following. First, he said, as a kind of disclaimer, that "[Mahony] is vague on actual details, perhaps purposely." More to the point, he noted that she "was unsympathetic to F.L.W." and "inclined to think that F.L.W. pirated designs and credit from everyone who worked for him, including herself" (card 1 recto). She maintained "that much of the production of the atelier after Griffin's arrival was his doing" (card 2 recto). As for the Quadruple Block Plan, Mahony distanced it from Griffin's way of thinking rather than associating it with him. Manson recorded at the very end of the interview that "she said Griffin at once showed a flair for town-planning, which incited F.L.W.'s jealous emulation—that the so-called 'Quadruple Block Plan' of F.L.W.'s was the result—but very bad, she thinks—entirely the wrong approach—the houses should not be placed toward the interior, but rather to-ward the exterior, off [*sic*: of] the block—and no alleys on [*sic*: or] driveways" (card 2 recto). She then drew a plan of what Griffin would have done, a quite conventional scheme with houses up to the street, rather than a plan showing the houses centered in their lots "as in Wright's scheme" (card 2 verso). In other words, rather than being the source of the Quadruple Block Plan, Griffin, at least according to his wife, was the author of the alternate design shown in figure 3.10. Mahony earlier ex-pressed this attribution to Griffin of the 1903–4 Roberts block variant in Marion Mahony Griffin, "Democratic Architecture—II. Its Development, Its Principles and Its Ideals," *Building* (Australia) 14 (12 August 1914): 91, where she vaunted its "practical gain" over Wright's "so-called idealistic method." Mahony's pronounced hatred for Wright comes clear in the 1914 article where she re-fuses even to mention him by name, referring to him only as "my architect employer." Mahony Griffin, "Democratic Architecture—I," *Building* 14 (12 June 1914): 101.

I thank William Jerousek for providing me with ac-cess to the Manson Papers at the Oak Park Library and Cammie McAtee for researching and transcribing the relevant materials.

31. Some of these have been published. Two were uncat-alogued in the Wright Foundation Archives as late as the spring of 2002 and were only then given the numbers FLWFA 0309.014 and 0309.015. The numbers of the others are FLWFA 0309.002–007. The group as a whole has never been identified as such. McCarter, *Frank Lloyd Wright*, 236–37, describes the plans illustrated in figures 3.16 and 3.19 as being for the Roberts block despite their being for very different length blocks. Aguar and Aguar, *Wrightscapes*, 57, not only mistakenly publish the same two drawings as part of the Roberts block project, they also assume that they are on the same sheet and thus were deliberately intended to draw a comparison between the two schemes represented. The misdating can be traced to *FLWM* 2:66–67, figures 116 and 118. *FLWCW/DG/OC* 1:204–5 perpetuates the confusion by publishing the two aforementioned plans as for the "Charles E. Roberts Block," which they do not match in size.

32. This drawing was first published in Levine, "*The Quadruple Block Plan*," 75. It was also published in a later version of the essay, Levine, "Making Community Out of the Grid," 70.

33. Where the width of the Roberts block was 364 feet, the width of these is 367.

34. The critical measurement indicating property lines is from the inner edge of one sidewalk to that of the other.

35. Related to the last is a drawing left unfinished due to errors in the indication of sidewalks and street curbs (FLWFA 0309.007).

36. See FLWFA 0309.004.

37. A premonition of such standardization can be seen in the perspective of the 1897 Heller House published in Spencer, "Work of Frank Lloyd Wright," pl. 35. The view looking up Woodlawn Avenue shows a replica of the house just to the north of the one that was built. The arrangement also predicts the Munkwitz and Richards Duplex Apartments, both built in Milwaukee in 1916.

38. Based on a confusion of this drawing with those for the Roberts block, Aguar and Aguar, *Wrightscapes*, 56, assume that it was intended "to convince Roberts of the feasibility of the [Quadruple Block Plan] concept and/or as a mechanism to use in marketing the concept to inves-tors." Even if this were the case, the question remains as to why Wright designed houses for only one side of the block.

39. As late as 1916, Nolen, *City Planning*, 19–44, bemoaned the lack of study of the subject of land subdivi-sion but could offer only slight alterations in lot sizes or a more picturesque manner of general layout à la Riverside as ways to ameliorate the existing state of affairs.

40. The phrase "Garden City and Garden Suburb," in-discriminately linking the two types, was a usual way of talking about the movement, even by its leaders and proponents. See, e.g., Raymond Unwin, "Discussion" of talk by Lawrence Veiller, "Buildings in Relation to Street and Site," 98; and *City Club Housing Exhibition, April 15 to June 1 [1913]: Guide to the Exhibition* [Chicago: City Club, 1913], 28.

41. William H. Wilson, *The City Beautiful Movement* (Baltimore: Johns Hopkins University Press, 1989), offers a more balanced understanding.

42. Burnham and Bennett, 4.

43. Ibid., 6–8; and Charles D. Norton, "The Merchants Club and the Plan of Chicago," in *The Merchants Club of Chicago, 1896–1906* (Chicago: Commercial Club of Chicago, 1922), 95–99. For the history of the Chicago plan, see Thomas S. Hines, *Burnham of Chicago: Architect and Planner* (New York: Oxford University Press, 1974), 312–45; and Carl Smith, *The Plan of Chicago:*

Daniel Burnham and the Remaking of the American City (Chicago: University of Chicago Press, 2006).

44. Burnham and Bennett, 43. The image serves as the book's frontispiece. "Chicago, the Metropolis of the Middle West" is the title of the first chapter describing the plan itself. That chapter is preceded by one devoted to the "Origin of the Plan of Chicago" and a second offering a history of "City Planning in Ancient and Modern Times."

45. Ibid., 99–118.

46. Ibid., 117, 116.

47. Ibid., 115.

48. Ibid., 80.

49. Ibid., 32, 37.

50. Ibid., 36–37.

51. Ibid., 34.

52. Ibid., 42, 34.

53. In the later chapter on "Streets within the City," Burnham wrote that "no rectilinear city is perfect without the diagonal streets." He called "straightness … a duty, and diagonals … a necessity." Furthermore, "if Chicago were to be relocated to-day, it would still be placed at the spot where it now is; and if the streets were again to be mapped, the same general system would be adopted, because the present rectilinear street system best comports with the line of the Lake front which nature has unalterably fixed. The rectilinear system certainly accords with the ideas of rightness inherent in the human mind; and also it involves a minimum waste of ground space." Ibid., 89–90.

54. Ibid., 36.

55. Ibid., 35.

56. Ibid., 41–42, 36, 35.

57. Ibid., 35.

58. Ibid., 43.

59. For Ebenezer Howard and the Garden City and Suburb, see Robert Fishman, *Urban Utopias in the 20th Century: Ebenezer Howard, Frank Lloyd Wright, Le Corbusier* (New York: Basic Books, 1977), 21–86; Walter L. Creese, *The Search for Environment: The Garden City—Before and After* (1966; rev. and enl. ed., Baltimore: Johns Hopkins University Press, 1992); and Stephen V. Ward, *The Garden City: Past, Present, and Future* (London: E. and F. N. Spon, 1992). For the movement as a whole, see now Robert A. M. Stern, David Fishman, and Jacob Tilove, *Planned Paradise: The Garden Suburb and the Modern City* (New York: Monacelli Press, 2013).

60. Ebenezer Howard, *Garden Cities of To-morrow (Being the Second Edition of "To-morrow: A Peaceful Path to Real Reform")* (London: Swan Sonnenschein, 1902), 14, 13, 18.

61. Ibid., 15–16.

62. Creese, *Crowning of the American Landscape*, 228. In *Search for Environment*, Creese wrote of Howard's having "observed Olmsted's suburban town of Riverside" while on the same page stating that "he [Howard] would have found considerable food for thought if he had taken the trouble to visit the suburb" (153), finally noting that "it could be assumed merely by virtue of Howard's residence in Chicago that he would be cognizant of Riverside" (155).

63. Howard, *Garden Cities*, 24.

64. Ibid., 130.

65. The most informative early history of Letchworth Garden City is C[harles] B[enjamin] Purdom, *The Garden City: A Study in the Development of a Modern Town* (London: J. M. Dent, 1913), esp. 37ff. See also Mervyn Miller, *Letchworth: The First Garden City*, 2nd ed. (Chichester, West Sussex: Phillimore, 2002).

66. Parker and Unwin won the job in a limited competition with the teams of Halsey Ricardo and William R. Lethaby and of Geoffry Lucas and Sydney Cranfield.

67. In the chapter "Of Formal and Informal Beauty" in his *Town Planning in Practice: An Introduction to the Art of Designing Cities and Suburbs* (1909; repr., New York: Princeton Architectural Press, 1994), 115–39, Unwin urged his readers to reject any categorical assumption of the value of the one form of beauty over the other and to search for ways to integrate the two. Two years later, he told an American audience in a "Discussion" of talk by Lawrence Veiller, "Buildings in Relation to Street and Site," 104, "curved roads and straight roads may both be used in a design. Curved roads may be treated formally just as straight roads may be extremely informal. Each type has a special beauty and affords its own opportunities." "A very beautiful and even picturesque town design may," he added, "be made … entirely of straight streets, provided that sufficient variety in the design itself is secured, and sufficient terminal features to close the street vista are provided."

68. Anthony Sutcliffe, *Towards the Planned City: Germany, Britain, the United States and France, 1780–1914*, Comparative Studies in Social and Economic History 3 (Oxford: Basil Blackwell, 1981), 67.

69. The size of the estate was increased to over four hundred acres within a decade. For the architects' intentions and early results, see Raymond Unwin and M. H. Baillie Scott, *Town Planning and Modern Architecture at the Hampstead Garden Suburb* (London: T. Fisher Unwin, 1909). See also Mervyn Miller, *Hampstead Garden Suburb: Arts and Crafts Utopia?* 2nd ed. (Chichester, West Sussex: Phillimore, 2006).

70. Frank Jackson, *Sir Raymond Unwin: Architect, Planner and Visionary*, Architects in Perspective (London: A. Zwemmer, 1985), 89–90, points out that Unwin learned of Sitte through his reading of T[homas] C[oglan] Horsfall, *The Improvement of the Dwellings and Surroundings of the People: The Example of Germany* (Manchester: University Press, 1904). The discredited French translation of Sitte by Camille Martin was published in 1902 as *L'Art de bâtir les villes* (Geneva: Ch. Eggiman, 1902).

Four: The Quadruple Block Plan Expanded into an Entire Neighborhood Scheme for the Chicago City Club Competition of 1912–13

1. "Pick Winners of Housing Prizes," *CST*, 23 March 1913, sec. 1.

2. Josef Stübben, *Der Städtebau*, 9th half vol. of pt. 4, *Entwerfen, Anlage und Einrichtung der Gebäude*, in *Handbuch der Architektur*, ed. Josef Durm et al. (Darmstadt: A. Bergsträsser 1890). A second, enlarged and revised edition was published by Alfred Kröner in Stuttgart in 1907.

3. For a summary of these developments and their impact on America, see George R. Collins and Christiane Crasemann Collins, *Camillo Sitte and the Birth of Modern City Planning*, Columbia University Studies in Art History and Archaeology 3 (New York: Random House, 1965).

4. See chapter 3, note 67.

5. Founded by Camillo Sitte and Theodor Goecke and published by Wasmuth in Berlin and Vienna, *Der Städtebau*'s subtitle was *Monatsschrift für die künstlerische Ausgestaltung der Städte nach ihren wirtschaftlichen, gesundheitlichen, und socialen Grundsätzen*. *Garden Cities & Town Planning: A Journal of Housing, Town Planning & Civic Improvement* was published in London as the official organ of the Garden Cities and Town Planning Association. *Der Städtebau* ceased publication in 1929; *Garden Cities & Town Planning* stopped in 1932.

6. The *American City* was published in Pittsfield, Mass., and appeared first in September 1909; it ceased publication in 1975. The *Town Planning Review* was published, beginning in April 1910, by the Department of Civic Design in the School of Architecture of the University of Liverpool. The *National Municipal Review* was founded by the National Municipal League and published by them from 1912 through 1958.

7. On the German events, see Collins and Collins, *Camillo Sitte*, 92–100 and passim; and Christiane Crasemann Collins, *Werner Hegemann and the Search for Universal Urbanism* (New York: Norton, 2005), 35–80. For the London event, see Royal Institute of British Architects, *Town Planning Conference*.

8. C. Collins, *Werner Hegemann*, 38, points out that while only photographs of the Chicago drawings were shown in Berlin, the actual drawings were exhibited in Düsseldorf and London.

9. "Object of the City Club," circular of 11 November 1903 announcing plans for the organization, in City Club of Chicago, *Ninth Year Book, May 1, 1912* (Chicago: [City Club], 1912), 22–23. The best source on the club and its role in the field of city planning is David P. Handlin, "The Context of the Modern City," *Harvard Architecture Review* 2 (Spring 1981): 76–89. See also James L. Merriner, *The City Club of Chicago: A Centennial History* (Chicago: City Club, 2003), 1–39; and Leslie Coburn, "Considering the People on the Back Streets: Urban Planning at the City Club of Chicago," in *Drawing the Future: Chicago Architecture on the International Stage, 1900–1925*, ed. David Van Zanten (Evanston: Mary and Leigh Block Museum of Art, Northwestern University Press, 2013), 84–106.

10. Handlin, "Context of the Modern City," 77–84. Collins and Collins, *Camillo Sitte*, 72, 154n86, refer to Hooker's encounter with Sitte and characterize Hooker as "an American member of his following" (47). The Collinses mention that Hooker had intended to translate Sitte's book *Der Städte-Bau* and that his name appeared on the masthead of the journal *Der Städtebau* that Sitte cofounded just before his death in late 1903. The George Ellsworth Hooker City Planning, Transportation and Housing Collection, 1882–1932, is housed in the Special Collections Research Center of the University of Chicago Library. It contains almost exclusively bound materials and has no correspondence or personal papers relating to the City Club Quarter Section competition.

11. George Ellsworth Hooker, *Through Routes for Chicago's Steam Railroads: The Best Means for Attaining Popular and Comfortable Travel for Chicago and Suburbs* (Chicago: City Club of Chicago, 1914). As the City Club's civic secretary, he also sponsored, in the previous year, the publication of *The Railway Terminal Problem of Chicago: A Series of Addresses before the City Club, June Third to Tenth, 1913, Dealing with the Proposed Re-organization of the Railway Terminals of Chicago, Including All Terminal Proposals Now before the City Council Committee on Railway Terminals* (Chicago: City Club of Chicago, September 1913).

12. George E. Hooker, "Cammillo [*sic*] Sitte, City Builder," *Chicago Record-Herald*, 15 January 1904; and Hooker, "The German Municipal Movement," *Chicago Record-Herald*, 30 January 1904. For Germany, see Sutcliffe, *Towards the Planned City*, 9–46; and Brian Ladd, *Urban Planning and Civic Order in Germany, 1860–1914* (Cambridge, Mass.: Harvard University Press, 1990).

13. Hooker, "German Municipal Movement."

14. Ibid.; and George E. Hooker, "Garden Cities," *Journal of the American Institute of Architects* 2 (February 1914): 81, 80. It was common practice to link the terms "Garden City" and "Garden Suburb" in the single phrase "Garden City and Garden Suburb," or simply "Garden City and Suburb." See chapter 3, note 40.

15. Hooker, "Garden Cities," 88, 91, 84. The article was originally delivered as a paper at the Third National Housing Conference held in Cincinnati in early December 1913 and reported on in the Chicago press in "Urges 'Garden Cities' as Check on Congestion," *CDT*, 4 December 1913. Hooker explicitly related such a "revolutionized land policy" to the German experience: "The necessity for such a revolution has been the strenuous contention for years of German students of housing conditions. Its necessity for clearing the path of city development was recognized in the so-called Lex Addicks [*sic*] … authorizing that city [Frankfurt], when particular urban areas needed to be re-arranged, to take possession of those areas, against the will of the owners if need be [in order to] replan them" (90).

16. Handlin, "Context of the Modern City," 83, says that Hooker's "work at the City Club after 1909 was in large part conceived in response to the [Burnham and Bennett] *Plan*'s shortcomings."

17. The Board of Directors Minutes record that in early February 1912 the "General Committee [of the City Club was] authorized to carry out the plans heretofore suggested for exhibiting in the Club rooms the Chicago plans of the Commercial Club." Board of Directors Minutes, 15 February 1912, box 2, subseries 1 — Board of Directors Minutes, 1912–16, General Files, 1903–1978, City Club of Chicago, CHM. I thank David Van Zanten for alerting me to the existence of the club's archives and helping me go through them.

The club's stated intention to exhibit the Burnham and Bennett plan certainly contradicts Donald Leslie Johnson's claim that the distaste for Burnham and Bennett's work was so great among socially concerned progressives that nothing could have convinced them to exhibit the project. Donald Leslie Johnson, "Origin of the Neighbourhood Unit," *Planning Perspectives* 17 (2002): 228–30; and Johnson, "Frank Lloyd Wright's Community Planning," *JPH* 3 (February 2004): 12–13.

18. George E. Hooker, "A Plan for Chicago," *Survey* 22 (4 September 1909): 778–90. He had previously given an address on the subject at the First National Conference on City Planning, held in Washington, D.C., in May 1909. It was published as "Report on City Planning in Chicago," in *City Planning. Hearing before the Committee on the District of Columbia, United States Senate, on the Subject of City Planning*, 61st Congress, 2nd Session, document 422, 11 March 1910 (Washington, D.C.: Government Printing Office, 1910), 96–98.

19. Hooker, "Plan for Chicago," 790, 786, 789.

20. Ibid., 780.

21. Ibid., 789–90.

22. Ibid., 790.

23. "The Vision of Greater Chicago," *Survey* 22 (4 September 1909): 735. In a talk on "The Housing Problem in Chicago" given at the City Club on 10 January 1910, the social reformer Jacob Riis described the Burnham and Bennett plan as "beautiful" and "splendid" but repeated, almost word for word, the "Volume I/Volume II" critique. He ascribed the characterization, however, to the philanthropist and social activist Anita (McCormick) Emmons Blaine. *CCB* 3 (12 January 1909 [*sic*]): 112.

24. See, e.g., George E. Hooker, opening comments, in "The City Club's Civic Exhibit," *CCB* 5 (31 January 191[2]): 1.

25. George E. Hooker to Jens Jensen, 27 April 1910, Correspondence—Committee on City Planning, box 11, folder 6, City Club of Chicago, CHM. I thank David Van Zanten for providing me with a copy of this.

26. George E. Hooker, "Discussion" of "City Planning Study" conducted by the National Conference on City Planning in 1912–13, in *Proceedings of the Fifth National Conference on City Planning, Chicago, Illinois, May 5–7, 1913* (Boston, 1913), 189. Hooker was claiming rightful priority for an idea that John Nolen and others at the National Conference had co-opted with their parallel "City Planning Study" competition.

27. As noted above (note 8), only photographs of the Chicago drawings were shown in Berlin.

28. Shortly before his European visit, Hooker spoke at the Second National Conference on City Planning on "Congestion and Its Causes in Chicago," in *Proceedings of the Second National Conference on City Planning and the Problems of Congestion, Rochester, New York, May 2–4, 1910* (Boston, 1910), 42–57. Earlier that year, he invited Jacob Riis to speak at the City Club on the "Housing Problem in Chicago" (see note 23 above) and Lawrence Veiller, director of the National Housing Association, to speak on "A Housing Reform Program," published in *CCB* 3 (27 April 1910): 287–93.

29. "Report of Committee on City Planning," *CCB* 5 (28 September 1912): 235. This survey may have been done in cooperation with the Chicago School of Civics and Philanthropy, whose director of its Extension and Reference Department, Edward L. Burchard, was an active member of the City Club and chair of its Civic Exhibit Committee. "Rooms in Stockyards District Too Tiny," *Survey* 27 (13 January 1912): 1568, reported that "the Chicago School of Civics and Philanthropy … has just devoted a year to a new inquiry into the housing conditions of the city."

30. "City Club, Chicago, Ill. Pond & Pond, Architects," *Brickbuilder* 21 (May 1912): pls. 57–59. The building on South Plymouth Court is no longer occupied by the City Club.

31. Edward L. Burchard, "Chicago City Club Opening," *National Municipal Review* 1 (April 1912): 248.

32. "Report of Committee on City Planning," 255.

33. Most of these talks were published in the club's *Bulletin*. See Thomas Adams, "The British Town Planning Act," *CCB* 4 (29 May 1911): 126–32; Raymond Unwin, "Garden Cities in England," *CCB* 4 (7 June 1911): 132–40; Thomas H. Mawson, "Town Planning in England," *CCB* 4 (21 November 1911): 263–69; and Henry Vivian, "Copartnership Housing and Garden Cities," *CCB* 5 (12 October 1912): 281–89.

34. *Forest Hills Gardens: The Suburban Land Development of the Russell Sage Foundation* (New York: Sage Foundation Homes, 1911). The promotional brochure featured brief articles by Robert W. De Forest, Alfred T. White, Frederick Law Olmsted Jr., Grosvenor Atterbury, William E. Harmon, and Edward H. Bouton. See also Susan L. Klaus, *A Modern Arcadia: Frederick Law Olmsted Jr. and the Plan for Forest Hills Gardens* (Amherst: University of Massachusetts Press, in association with Library of American Landscape History, 2002).

35. Hooker, opening comments, 1–2.

36. See note 17 above.

37. George E. Hooker, "Report of the Civic Secretary, Annual Meeting of the City Club, 19 April 1913," *CCB*

6 (28 June 1913): 198–99. Hooker added that "while the plans for the Housing Exhibition were being worked out it was decided to hold a competition for plans designed to encourage improved methods of laying out the now unbuilt areas in and around Chicago."

38. John Nolen, B. A. Haldeman, and George B. Ford, "Report of the Committee on the Proposed Study in City Planning, Business Session, 29 May 1912," in *Proceedings of the Fourth National Conference on City Planning, Boston, Massachusetts, May 27–29, 1912* (Boston, 1912), 222–25; and "City Planning Study," in *Proceedings of the Fifth National Conference on City Planning*, 163–211. The original five-member committee running the "Study," chaired by Nolen, was appointed in May 1912. Hooker was one of the six additional members, including A. F. Brinckerhoff, Arthur C. Comey, and Edward C. Whiting, appointed in January 1913. Two of the participants, Comey and the firm of Morell & Nichols, took part in the City Club competition.

39. Minutes of Committee on Housing Conditions, 28 October 1912, Civic Committees Minutes and Reports, box 14, subseries 2—Civic Committees Reports and Minutes, 1912–16, General Files, 1903–1978, City Club of Chicago, CHM.

40. Ernest Wreidt, "Report of the Housing Exhibit Committee," *CCB* 6 (28 June 1913): 201, stated that Burchard's trip occurred "last summer." Burchard described the trip in a talk at the City Club on 30 November 1912 published as "A Tour through Some European Social Experiments," *CCB* 5 (7 December 1912): 385–92. The following February, Burchard prepared a thirty-six-page bibliography, with 710 entries, of which well more than half were European, of "Housing and Its Associated Subjects: Literature in Central Chicago Libraries." In his preface he stated that the "list [was] prepared … in anticipation of the Housing Exhibition of March at the Chicago City Club." *Housing Literature in Central Chicago Libraries* (Chicago: Chicago School of Civics and Philanthropy, [1913]). He also published a bibliography on "The Housing Problem: Literature in Central Chicago Libraries" in July 1912.

41. Board of Directors Minutes, 21 November 1912.

42. George E. Hooker, *Program of a Competition with Cash Prizes for the Procuring of a Scheme of Development for a Quarter-Section of Land within the Limits of the City of Chicago, Illinois* ([Chicago]: City Club of Chicago, 21 December 1912). The program was bound into some editions of the final number of the *CCB* of 1912. It was published in *Architecture* 27 (15 January 1913): 18–19, and later included in Yeomans, 1–5.

43. Yeomans, 1. Announcements of plans for the exhibition and opening of the competition appeared in *Construction News*, 4 January 1913, and *AC*, 13 January 1913, 42, in addition to the issue of *Architecture* cited above.

44. Yeomans, 4.

45. "City Club Housing Show Will Be Opened March 17," *CDT*, 14 March 1913; "Plans Are Completed for Housing Show at City Club," *CDT*, 15 March 1913; and "Exhibit of Housing Conditions," *CST*, 16 March 1913, sec. 8.

46. "Pick Winners of Housing Prizes." Later reports in journals, however, almost invariably refer to 17 March as the opening date. Ernest Wreidt, "Report of the Housing Exhibit Committee." *CCB* 6 (28 June 1913): 201, gave the opening date as 17 March, as did the "Report of the Civic Secretary" by Hooker in ibid., 199.

47. The catalogue, *City Club Housing Exhibition*, has a later date for the opening on its cover as well as an earlier

date for the closing, which was to occur on 15 June. The catalogue did not appear until after 19 April. In his "Report of the Housing Exhibit Committee," delivered at the club's annual meeting on 19 April, Wreidt stated that "a fifty-six page catalogue of the exhibition is being printed." The late appearance of the catalogue no doubt explains the fact that the cover included a drawing of a cottage by Wilhelm Bernhard, the winner of the competition. Bernhard was probably also responsible for the cover's Secessionist-style graphic design.

48. There appears to have been some confusion in the naming of the jury and even misdirection or manipulation. Ten days after the competition was scheduled to close, the club's vice president reported that he had appointed "a jury to act as judges for the Competition plans consisting of Messrs. Walter Burley Griffin, Jens Jensen and C. D. Hill." Board of Directors Minutes, 13 March 1913. Both Jensen and Griffin were club members. Griffin was also the current chair of the Committee on City Planning, having replaced Jensen in that capacity. More important, he had entered a project in the competition, which he signed as a consultant. Whether the vice president had misunderstood the earlier directive or had simply acted on his own, a note of 10 June 1914 was attached to the 13 March 1913 minutes, stating the following: "Messrs. Griffin, Hill and Jensen were appointed to act jointly with a committee of three—Charles H. Prindeville, Arthur and P. J. Weber—appointed by the Illinois Chapter of the American Institute of Architects in selecting a jury to pass upon the sketches submitted in the competition for laying out a typical quarter-section in the outskirts of Chicago. The jury so selected later consisted of John C. Kennedy, Chairman, John W. Alvord, Jens Jensen, George W. Maher, and Arthur Woltersdorf." The note added that Edward H. Bouton, director of Baltimore's Roland Park, was invited to serve as a consultant by the other members of the jury.

49. "Housing Prize to Cowpath Artist: Wilhelm Bernhard of Berlin Wins City Club's Housing Award," *CDT*, 18 March 1913; "Pick Winners of Housing Prizes"; and "'Garden City' Plans Are Shown by Club," *Chicago Inter Ocean*, 23 March 1913, sec. 1. Later reports listing the winners and often illustrating one or more of them include "City Club Competition: Prize Awarded for Plans for Subdividing Typical Chicago Quarter Section for Residence Purposes," *Construction News* 35 (22 March 1913): 6–9; "Chicago City Club Competition: Prize Awarded for Plans for Sub-dividing Typical 160 Acre Plot," *WA* 19 (April 1913): 39–40; "Prize-Winning Plans for Laying Out a Quarter-Section of Urban Land," *AC* 8 (April 1913): 421–27; "Town Planning and Civic Improvement: Illinois Chapter," *Journal of the American Institute of Architects* 1 (June 1913): 266; and Graham R. Taylor, "Satellite Cities," *Survey* 30 (7 June 1913): 343–45.
50. *City Club Housing Exhibition*, 5–23. See also "City Club Housing Show"; John Ihlder, "Chicago City Club's Housing Exhibition," *National Municipal Review* 2 (April 1913): 498. According to the latter, Burchard directed the work of the two women's clubs.
51. *City Club Housing Exhibition*, 23–43.
52. Ihlder, "Chicago City Club's Housing Exhibition," 498. Ihlder and Ball were among the featured speakers in a series of nine "discussions" held at the City Club in connection with the exhibition between 17 March and 16 April. The complete schedule was published in "City Club of Chicago," *Municipal Journal* 34 (20 March 1913): 429.
53. See, e.g., "Prize-Winning Plans"; "City Club Competition," *Construction News*; and "City Club

Competition," *WA*. The article in the *CDT* announcing the opening, "City Club Housing Show," predicted that "possibly the most interesting feature of the whole exhibition to Chicagoans will be the collection of drawings submitted in the prize competition for laying out a typical quarter section in the outskirts of Chicago." Ihlder, "Chicago City Club's Housing Exhibition," went even further, describing the proposals for the quarter section as "the central feature of the exhibition" and the four-part documentary section as merely "a background for the [competition] plans."
54. Published reports differed widely, however, on how many architects submitted plans, the number ranging from thirty-one to over fifty. The high number was in "Plans Are Completed for Housing Show at City Club," *CDT*, 15 March 1913, the low number in "Pick Winners of Housing Prizes."
55. *City Club Housing Exhibition*, 44, 47. The checklist of exhibited drawings is on 43–47.
56. The jury report claimed that thirty-nine sets of plans were reviewed. Yeomans, 6. Little is known about Yeomans. He was born in Orange, New Jersey, in 1870 and graduated from Princeton University in 1891. Around 1902, he turned to landscape architecture. He moved to Chicago by 1911, where his two brothers, Edward and Charles, were members of the City Club and lived at Hull House. Charles served at one time as secretary and a director. Alfred was a member by early 1912 and began attending City Club events on a regular basis. He was later appointed to the club's Committee on Parks and Playgrounds. A fourth Yeomans, N. Tracy, was listed as a member of the club in its *Ninth Year Book*, 87.
57. Frank Lloyd Wright, "Plan by Frank Lloyd Wright," in Yeomans, 95–102. This is reprinted in *Wright: Collected Writings*, 1:139–43, but without all the original illustrations.
58. Hooker, "Report of the Civic Secretary," 199.
59. Only one account of the exhibition mentioned (or illustrated) any project other than the prize-winning ones. "'Garden City' Plans," *Chicago Inter Ocean*, reported that "Frank Lloyd Wright contributed a series of four carefully executed plans after the distinctive spirit of his work, but did not enter them for a prize." I thank Wilbert Hasbrouck for bringing this to my attention and providing me with a copy of it.
60. On the jury, see note 48 above. Pamela Hill, "Marion Mahony Griffin: The Chicago Years," in *Chicago Architecture: Histories, Revisions, Alternatives*, ed. Charles Waldheim and Katerina Rüedi Ray, Chicago Architecture and Urbanism (Chicago: University of Chicago Press, 2005), 155, describes the design submitted under Edgar H. Lawrence's name, with Griffin in an "advisory" role, as a "Griffin project" that the architect "is believed to have entered [in] this competition anonymously." Coburn, "Considering the People," 105n26, reports that Griffin republished the plan in Australia more than once, "suggesting that his role in its design may have extended beyond 'advisory.'"
61. Minutes of Committee on City Planning, 1 April 1913, Civic Committees' Minutes and Reports, box 14, subseries 2—Civic Committees' Reports and Minutes, 1912–16; and City Club of Chicago, *Tenth Year Book, July 1, 1913* (Chicago: [City Club], 1913), 6. In a vituperative article published one year after the competition, Frank Lloyd Wright, "In the Cause of Architecture, Second Paper: 'Style, Therefore Will Be the Man, It Is His. Let His Forms Alone,'" orig. pub. *AR*, May 1914; repr. in *FLWCW* 1:129, accused many of his former employees not only of

"half-baked imitative designs" and "utter prostitution" but also of a "total lack of any standard of artistic integrity" and ethical principles. One can assume that the involvement of Drummond and Griffin in the City Club competition was on his mind.
62. Frank Lloyd Wright, "In the Cause of Architecture," *AR* 23 (March 1908): 155–221.
63. Wright, *Ausgeführte Bauten*; and Frank Lloyd Wright, *Frank Lloyd Wright: Ausgeführte Bauten* (Berlin: Ernst Wasmuth, 1911).
64. Wright, *Autobiography*, in *FLWCW* 2:219–20.
65. For Wright's career between 1909 and 1914, see Levine, 58–111.
66. Ibid., 114–24; and Kathryn Smith, "Frank Lloyd Wright and the Imperial Hotel: A Postscript," *Art Bulletin* 67 (June 1985): 296–310.
67. Only four of the drawings were shown in the exhibition (figures 4.28–30 and 4.34). Their numbers in the catalogue checklist are 1370–73. The other three (figures 4.31–33), which were alternative site plans of Quadruple Block Plan arrangements, were published with the four others in Yeomans, 97–98, 100–101.
68. Albert Kelsey, "Aesthetic Review of the Plans," in ibid., 111.
69. Johnson, "Origin of the Neighbourhood Unit," 232; and Johnson, "Wright's Community Planning," 13.
70. Based on documents in the City Club Archives, David Van Zanten has informed me that the City Club's Executive Committee was told on 23 July 1914 that the then publisher R. R. Donnelly needed to be paid printing costs for the book but that the publishing fund was exhausted. Van Zanten to Neil Levine, email, 18 November 2011. My own earlier research showed that funds were voted for the publication only on 30 March 1916. On 25 May, it was decided to defer the publication until the "fall." Board of Directors Minutes, box 3, subseries 1—Board of Directors Minutes, 1912–16, General Files, 1903–1978, City Club of Chicago, CHM. The July 1914 date for the book's completion undermines the scenario proposed in Johnson, "Wright's Community Planning," 18, that, in 1916 for the publication, Wright redrew the two Quadruple Block Plans, added a third, and redrew the perspectives to "accompan[y] what was probably a freshly edited text."
71. The two manuscripts have the same number, MS 2401.431, FLWFA. The first, which is six single-spaced pages long, is titled "A NEW SYSTEM OF SUBDIVISION." The second, seven double-spaced pages, is titled "AUTHOR'S STATEMENT." The latter title was partially crossed out and written over by Yeomans to read "EXPLANATORY STATEMENT by Frank Lloyd Wright." In the published version the title is "Plan by Frank Lloyd Wright."
72. The title ultimately used, "Plan by Frank Lloyd Wright," is written along the right-hand edge of the page, perpendicular to the typed text.
73. It is unclear how well Wright and Hooker knew one another. G. Wright, "Architectural Practice and Social Vision," 114, claims that between 1908, when Wright was made a "charter member of the [City Club's] City Planning Committee" and 1911, "when Taliesin I was under construction [and] Wright retired from active participation," Wright "attended lectures about European planning reforms, zoning, industrialization, overcrowding, and improved housing" at the club. I have seen no evidence for this.
74. I thank David Van Zanten for this information gleaned from the City Club Archives.
75. As we shall see, the competition program required

a plan and a perspective only. The additional drawings by many of the architects and engineers published by Yeomans were not part of the competition. Three participants had only one drawing in the exhibition, two of whom were excluded from the competition for noncompliance, the third, Per Olof Hallman, having submitted only a sketch for his noncompeting participation. Bernhard, who drew his plan and perspective on the same sheet (figure 4.21), was allowed, as the first prize winner, to show several additional sketches not part of his competition entry.

76. Yeomans, 1.

77. Ibid.

78. This is a very different reading of the program's attitude toward the Burnham and Bennett plan from Johnson, "Origin of the Neighbourhood Unit," 228–31, and Johnson, "Wright's Community Planning," 12–13. As evidence of the practical orientation of the City Club's purposes, the program stated that it "hoped that some of the plans proposed in this competition may actually be adopted as the basis for developing some of the vacant quarter-sections in the outskirts of the city." Yeomans, 2.

79. Ibid., 1–2.

80. Ibid. Johnson, "Origin of the Neighbourhood Unit," 232, and Johnson, "Wright's Community Planning," 13, inexplicably locate the site "eight miles south of central Chicago," not southwest or northwest, and place streetcar lines on all four of its sides.

81. Yeomans, 4.

82. Ibid.

83. Ibid.

84. Ibid., preface (n.p.).

85. Although nothing was specifically said about the economic makeup of the residential community in the program, the jury report noted that "several" of the submitted plans "were not adapted to such a district as the one to be provided for according to the terms of the competition. The most common defect in these plans was an over-elaborate system of parks, boulevards, or public buildings which could not be maintained by working people with only moderate means." Yeomans, 6.

86. For the American side, one can cite the writings by John Nolen, Charles Mulford Robinson, and Lawrence Veiller.

87. George E. Hooker, "Literature," in Yeomans, 5.

88. Ibid.

89. The final four entries on the list were German publications: the German Garden City Society's *Die deutsche Gartenstadtbewegung: Zusammenfassende Darstellung über den heutigen Stand der Bewegung* (1911), Hans Eduard von Berlepsch-Valendàs's *Die Garten-Stadt München-Perlach* (1910), Berlepsch-Valendàs's *Bodenpolitik und gemeindliche wohnungsfürsorge der stadt Ulm an der Donau* (1912), and Albert Weiss's *Können die in den heutigen grossstädtichen Wohnverhältnissen liegenden Mängel und Schäden behoben werden?* (Berlin: Carl Heymanns, 1912).

90. The concurrent National Conference on City Planning Study produced very similar designs, with allowances made for the more detailed, nuts-and-bolts requirements laid out in their program intended more for a professional audience than the lay one Hooker had in mind.

91. The project with only one church was Robert Anderson Pope's; the one with ten was Edgar Lawrence and Walter Burley Griffin's.

92. "Report of the Jury," in Yeomans, 7.

93. Yeomans, 86.

94. Ibid., 45, 47.

95. Ibid., 35, 33, 32. For the Yeomans publication, Cone included a design he did for O. C. Simonds & Co. for a subdivision in Beloit, Wis., as "an application in actual practice of the fundamental innovation suggested" by his City Club project (36). In its grouping of single-family houses around a central oval court, planted with trees and offering recreation facilities for the homeowners, it closely resembles Wright's 1896 development plan for the Roberts block.

96. Ibid., 81.

97. Ibid., 50.

98. Ibid., 75.

99. Ibid., 24.

100. On Griffin's role, see note 48 above.

101. Yeomans, 60, 59. Reinforcing the connection with the Howard diagram, the Lawrence-Griffin text noted that, for the purpose of "community congregation," "the central functions are joined together by a protected passageway as a promenade for students and visitors, overlooking the public gardens setting off the pool with its central feature of an open pagoda designed as a music pavilion."

102. Ibid., 37–44, devoted eight pages to this ex post facto design, more space than allotted to anyone else. Whereas all the other projects were titled "Competitive Plan by … " or in Wright's case "Non-Competitive Plan by … ," the Drummond contribution was titled "Plan by William Drummond, Developed from a Sketch Submitted in Competition" (37). This project has garnered almost more interest than Wright's from later historians.

103. The Yeomans project, which was published under his name alone in the 1916 book, was listed in the 1913 exhibition catalogue as the joint product of Yeomans and the Chicago architect George Awsumb, then secretary of the Chicago Architectural Club.

104. The differing directions of the diagonal arteries can be explained by the quadrant in which the quarter section was to be located.

105. Yeomans, 64.

106. Ibid., 59.

107. Ibid., 25–26.

108. Ibid., 30, 28.

109. See Robert Anderson Pope, "Some of the Needs of City Planning in America," talk at First National Conference on Town Planning, 1909, in *City Planning. Hearing before the Committee on the District of Columbia*, 75; and Pope, "The Co-partnership Principle," in *Proceedings of the Second National Conference on City Planning*, 104–6.

110. Yeomans, 70, 69.

111. See note 48 above.

112. Yeomans, 6.

113. Ibid., 6–7.

114. Ibid.

115. Hooker, "German Municipal Movement." The Danish-born architect Alfred J. Roewade, who entered the competition but was excluded for not having supplied the required perspective, commented in a letter to the editor in *AC* that the "premiated plans" were all inappropriate to Chicago in completely ignoring "the common gridiron of our city lay-out." Instead of being "atomic parts of a pattern," he wrote, they form "individual independent villages with parks and building arrangements of local or exceptional nature" that are "useless and impossible for [the] systematic improvement of a city plan, and run up against almost every rule and practice of our street department." Alfred J. Roewade, "Taste and Knowledge in Town Planning," *AC* 8 (May 1913): 511.

116. The relationship with Forest Hills Gardens was pointed out in Kelsey, "Aesthetic Review," 109. Bernhard himself was more elliptical about his sources, stating only that the idea for such "an organically worked out community center" was "comparatively new but has proved a success in many rapidly growing and prosperous communities in this country." Yeomans, 12. Bernhard exhibited the premiated design in the 1913 Annual Exhibition of the Chicago Architectural Club. *Book of the Twenty Sixth Annual Exhibition of the Chicago Architectural Club 6 May–11 June 1913* (Chicago, 1913), nos. 41–42.

Bernhard, who later changed his first name to William, was a German national born in Petrograd, Russia. After arriving in the United States from Dresden in early 1910, he worked for Olmsted Jr. on the 1909–10 master plan for Pittsburgh, for which he designed the towered city hall (see chapter 9 and figure 9.5). After moving to Chicago, he was hired by Wright as a draftsman in late 1911 or early 1912. After 1913, he practiced in Chicago, for a time entering into partnership with Arthur Woltersdorf, who had served on the City Club competition jury. I thank Bill Whitaker for helping me piece together Bernhard's biography.

117. Yeomans, 10.

118. Bernhard studied and refined this part of the plan for the 1914 City Club Neighborhood Center competition. The later drawing, which revised the functions and placement of a number of the structures, was published in "The Problem of the Neighborhood," *CCB* 8 (23 March 1915): 81; and Fiske Kimball, "The Social Center. Part III—Civic Enterprises," *AR* 46 (July 1919): 44.

119. Yeomans, 12.

120. Ibid., 14.

121. Ibid., 14, 10.

122. "Housing Prize to Cowpath Artist."

123. Yeomans, 10.

124. Kelsey, "Aesthetic Review," 108, noted that "the one loop, circling through and bisecting lesser thoroughfares, is quite sufficient to give easy access to all quarters, to individualize the district, and to create pleasant, ever-changing perspectives."

125. Yeomans, 12, 14.

126. The captions for the school and church were mistakenly switched in ibid., 12–13.

127. Ibid, 12, 10, 14.

128. Ibid., 7.

129. "City Club Competition: Prize Awarded for Plans," 7.

130. William B. Faville, "Aesthetic Review of the Plans," in Yeomans, 105–6.

131. Irving K. Pond, "Aesthetic Review of the Plans," in Yeomans, 116. Bernhard's project was republished in 1916 in Nolen, *City Planning*, 21, 40, to make the larger point that picturesque design using curved streets can be applied just as well to flat as to hilly land.

132. Although a perspective was included in the exhibition, only the plan was published by Yeomans. See *City Club Housing Exhibition*, 46 (nos. 1302–3). Arthur Coleman Comey received his degree in landscape architecture from Harvard in 1907 and opened his own office as a consultant on city planning in Cambridge in 1911. He entered the Canberra competition in 1911 and prepared a city planning report for Houston in the following year. After 1913, his planning career took off. In addition to authoring numerous publications, he served, between 1928 and 1940, on the Harvard faculties of Landscape Architecture, City Planning, and Regional Planning.

133. Kelsey, "Aesthetic Review," 109.

134. "Report of the Jury," 8.

135. Yeomans, 16, 18.

136. "Report of the Jury," 8. Albert Lilienberg, who married Ingrid Wallberg in 1909, was an engineer by training who became a leading Swedish town planner of his generation. A follower of Camillo Sitte, he was appointed the first director of public works of Gothenburg in 1907 and was responsible, over the next twenty years (before being named city planning director of Stockholm), for a number of important Garden City–type town extensions. He was the only representative of Scandinavia to speak at the 1910 London Town Planning Conference, where he delivered a paper on "Town Planning and Legislation in Sweden during the Last Fifty Years," Royal Institute of British Architects, *Town Planning Conference*, 702–15. At the same conference, Raymond Unwin illustrated his talk on "The City Development Plan" with an image of the model of one of the Lilienbergs' first town extension schemes for Gothenburg (ibid., 249).

137. Yeomans, 20.

138. Kelsey, "Aesthetic Review," 110.

139. In his talk at the London Town Planning Conference two years before, Albert Lilienberg described the "'grid-iron' plans" that resulted from the Swedish Building Law for Towns of 1874 as "monotonous" and destructive of "many a beautiful or picturesque street or place." Lilienberg, "Town Planning," 706.

140. The perspective does not correspond with the plan in many significant respects. The foreshortening is such that many of the buildings, both civic and private, have been curtailed, altered, or even left out.

141. Much confusion exists in the literature about the five reused designs. The perspective of the single-family house (figure 4.30) is FLWFA 0007.001. See FLWR, pl. 13; and *FLWCW/DG/OC* 1:119 (see also chapter 2, note 40; and figure 2.16).

Plans B and C are dated to 1903 in *FLWM* 2: figures 117, 119, as part of the 1903 Roberts block project. They were numbered FLWFA 0309.009–010, at least until recently. They are drawn in a completely different style and by a different hand from the person or persons who did the 1903–4 Roberts block plans. The later drawings were done on linen mounted on board and are less precisely delineated than the earlier ones. The coloration is also entirely different. Where the interiors of the blocks in the earlier drawings are yellow and blue, these are gray. The property lines are not solid but dashed. The houses themselves are the same size in both sets. Plan B has a later legend that says "Quadruple Block Plan—(HOUS-ING[)]" with dates of 1904 and 1903 above it. Plan C has a later annotation that reads "QUADRUPLE BLOCK PLAN FOR THE PRAIRIE GRIDIRON" and is signed and dated "FLW 1911." Almost all publications of these plans have misdated them to 1903. Johnson, "Wright's Community Planning," 16, also states that only "five drawings [were] prepared" for the Yeomans book. Possibly not having seen the originals of the plans illustrated in figures 4.31–33, he must have thought that plans A, B, and C comprised a single drawing as they appear to in the book.

The aerial perspective of the Quadruple Block Plan published by Yeomans (figure 4.34) is different from the one in the 1901 *LHJ* that was republished in 1910 [–11] in Wright, *Ausgeführte Bauten*, pl. 13a, as "Quadruple Block Plan for a Prairie Community." It not only is drawn from a less raking angle, but also shows the beginnings of blocks to the right and to the rear. Like plans A, B, and C, it was most likely drawn in early 1913.

142. Wright, "Plan," 101, 99.

143. Handlin, *American Home*, 164, was the first to note Wright's independence from the two main European-derived traditions. Most scholars, however, have found it difficult to separate Wright from the picturesque Garden City/Suburb tradition. For example, Aguar and Aguar, *Wrightscapes*, 12, state that "Garden City theories formed the basis of the layouts Wright prepared for the City Club Competition in 1913."

144. Wright, "Plan," 96. The quotation is from bk. 2, chap. 9 ("The Everlasting Yea") of the work originally serialized in *Fraser's Magazine for Town and Country* in 1833–34. There are several errors in the transcription. The quotation should read "Fool! the Ideal is in thyself, the impediment too is in thyself: thy Condition is but the stuff thou art to shape that same Ideal out of." When it initially appeared in *Fraser's* in the April 1834 issue, the first letter of the word "impediment" was also capitalized.

145. Wright, "Plan," 101–2.

146. Ibid., 96.

147. Ibid.

148. The measurement is taken to the street center lines.

149. This idea was suggested by Robert Bruegmann.

150. Wright, "Plan," 96–97.

151. Ibid. In the preliminary draft of his text, Wright was even more adamant about the ecumenical character of the religious building. In "A NEW SYSTEM OF SUBDIVISION," 5, he wrote, "No sectarian churches planned—enough are already built elsewhere. A large auditorium is provided for union services and in connection therewith various club rooms for the work of the various secular or sectarian services."

152. Wright, "Plan," 96.

153. Ibid., 97, 99.

154. A precedent for the low-income row houses and the workmen's cottages on the north side of the development exists in Wright's project for Workmen's Cottages designed for the Larkin Company, Buffalo, in 1904. His involvement with the American System-Built Homes between 1911 and 1915 represents a more relevant connection. Two examples of the duplex, or "two-flat buildings," the Richards Company Duplex Apartments and the Munkwitz Duplex Apartments, were built in Milwaukee in 1916.

155. Ibid., 96.

156. Ibid., 99.

157. Ibid., 101, 99.

158. Ibid., 99 (italics are Wright's).

159. Ibid., 101.

160. The number of individuals given in Wright's "Statistical Data" in ibid., 98, reflects an editorial error. The publication lists " 4 Two and three room apartment buildings for women, accommodating 250 to 300" individuals. There are in fact only three such buildings shown on the plan. Furthermore, the list does not include the four similar-sized apartment buildings for men. (Each of these seven structures would have had either thirty-six or forty-two apartments.) In his preliminary draft of the text, "A NEW SYSTEM OF SUBDIVISION," 6, the correct information is given under the rubric "DISTRIBUTION OF POPULATION," where it is noted that there are "4 - 2 and 3 room apartment buildings [f]or men - accomodating [*sic*] 300–350" and " 3 - 2 and 3 room apartment buildings for women - Accomodating [*sic*] 250–300." The total was given as " 550 Individuals," not the 1,550 listed in the published "Statistical Data" (the number of 1,032 families remained the same). Without the corrective provided by the manuscript draft, historians have assumed that Wright planned for a population of between six and seven thousand people, an impossible number for such a site.

161. G. Wright, "Architectural Practice and Social Vision," 107, and G. Wright, "Frank Lloyd Wright and the Domestic Landscape," 91, make many of these same points. In the first, published in 1988, she says that "even the street pattern," meaning "the continuation of Chicago's grid," "stressed a distinctly urban conception," and "while Wright did try to ensure privacy for the well-to-do in a spacious, single-family 'Residence Park' . . . , he also encouraged social mixing between classes by concentrating the generous public spaces." In the second, published nearly ten years later, she was more declarative on this score, noting that Wright's "intricately woven landscape by no means ostracized a complex public realm." "This social vision went far beyond the competition's program," she continued: "While Wright certainly favored single-family houses, he recognized the need for apartments and commerce, asking how design could help incorporate them into a suburban neighborhood."

The appreciation of Wright as an urbanist reflects a major change in Gwendolyn Wright's opinion as well as a rethinking in the field as a whole. In 1980, she wrote in *Moralism and the Model Home*, 282, that in the City Club project "Wright stressed the separation of houses from one another. . . . Workers' apartments and semide-tached houses were on the periphery, almost exiled from the middle-class community which formed the core. . . . Here each family would be 'protected' from neighbors, as Wright put it, for there was only one dwelling on each side of a block. While he acknowledged the mix of incomes in the program, Wright's scheme favored the upper crust." Just a year earlier, Twombly, *Frank Lloyd Wright*, 225, criticized Wright for segregating the inhabitants by class and sex in a way that revealed his "conservative social thinking." One of the most ungrounded and tendentious readings of this sort was in Roger Cranshawe, "Wright's Progressive Utopia," *aaq: Architectural Association Quarterly* 10, no. 1 (1978): 9. The author describes the Wright project as a symptom of the class struggle wherein "the old class barriers were re-drawn." In what he unfairly characterizes as a "self-centered neighbourhood," the "less affluent and less fortunate members" were confined to less desirable quarters, and thereby subjected "(from both a class and an ethnic point of view) to a process of 'acculturisation [*sic*]'" that was "strictly tailored to fit in with the bourgeois world-image." None of these earlier critics compared Wright's design to those of the other competitors, nor did they take into account the requirements of the program.

162. Handlin, *American Home*, 165.

163. Kenneth Frampton, "Modernization and Mediation: Frank Lloyd Wright and the Impact of Technology," in Riley, *Frank Lloyd Wright*, 65; and Cranshawe, "Wright's Progressive Utopia," 9. McCarter, *Frank Lloyd Wright*, 239, following Frampton, calls Wright's quarter section scheme a "complete and viable neighbourhood or community," a "city-in-miniature, the kind of small-scale quarter for 5,000–7,000 residents [*sic*], where it would be possible to live and work, and where a true form of democracy could flourish." There was, of course, no provision for work because that was not part of the program. The concept of combining living and working in a single community environment was a driving force of the Garden City movement.

164. This was pointed out in Handlin, *American Home*, 165–66, and repeated in G. Wright, "Architectural Practice and Social Vision," 107, and G. Wright, "Wright and the Domestic Landscape," 91.

165. The only other design to emphasize only one main street, indeed, the east-west artery, was Fixmer's.

166. Cranshawe, "Wright's Progressive Utopia," 7, projects Wright's plan into a thirty-six-square-mile township-sized design based on Jefferson's idea for the U.S. Land Survey.

167. Kelsey, "Aesthetic Review," 111.

168. Ibid.

169. Ibid., 108, 109.

170. Robert Craik McLean, "City Residential Land Development: A Review of a Volume Presenting the Plans Submitted in a Competition by the City Club of Chicago," *WA* 25 (January 1917): 6–8, and 5 plates. The discussion of Wright's design is on p. 8.

171. According to H. Allen Brooks, *Prairie School Architecture: Studies from "The Western Architect"* (New York: Van Nostrand Reinhold, 1975), xii, "it seems likely that McLean nourished a personal, as well as professional, dislike for Wright."

172. Krauss, "Grids," 8–22.

173. Handlin, *American Home*, 166.

Five: Congestion and Its Remedies in the Skyscraper City of the 1920s

1. The most famous of these encomiums was in Louis H. Sullivan, "The *Chicago Tribune* Competition," *AR* 53 (February 1923): 151–57. The competition results were almost immediately published in *The International Competition for a New Administration Building for the Chicago Tribune MCMXII, Containing All the Designs Submitted in Response to the Chicago Tribune's $100,000 Offer Commemorating Its Seventy Fifth Anniversary, June 10, 1922* (Chicago: Tribune Company, 1923).

2. See John W. Stamper, *Chicago's North Michigan Avenue: Planning and Development, 1900–1930* (Chicago: University of Chicago Press, 1991).

3. Congestion had been isolated by Ebenezer Howard as a primary reason for his creation of the Garden City. It was also isolated as a major cause of the need for city planning in Benjamin Clarke Marsh, *An Introduction to City Planning: Democracy's Challenge to the American City* (1909; repr., New York: Arno, 1974), and was the theme of the 1910 annual meeting of the National Conference on City Planning. See chapter 3 and *Proceedings of the Second National Conference on City Planning*.

4. Eliel Saarinen, "Project for Lake Front Development of the City of Chicago," *AAAR* 124 (5 December 1923): 487–88.

5. Ibid., 488. The project was amply presented to the public in J. L. Jenkins, "Chicago Traffic Evils Attacked in Saarinen Plan: Depressed Boulevard and Underground Garage Proposed," Motordom, *CST*, 18 November 1923, pt. 2. Two of the very few discussions of the Saarinen project are Manfredo Tafuri, "The Disenchanted Mountain: The Skyscraper and the City," in *The American City: From the Civil War to the New Deal*, ed. Giorgio Ciucci et al., trans. Barbara Luigia La Penta (1973; Cambridge, Mass.: MIT Press, 1983), 417–31; and David G. De Long, "Eliel Saarinen and the Cranbrook Tradition in Architecture and Design," in *Design in America: The Cranbrook Vision, 1925–1950*, ed. Robert Judson Clark and Andrea P. A. Belloli (New York: Abrams, in association with Detroit Institute of Arts and Metropolitan Museum of Art, 1983), 49–50.

6. Saarinen, "Project for Lake Front Development," 491–92.

7. The Chicago Zoning Ordinance, to be discussed more fully below, was approved by the City Council on 5 April 1923 and went into effect on 5 May. Jenkins, "Chicago Traffic Evils Attacked," states that Saarinen worked on his design for "six months," which would place the beginning of the "study" right after the passage of the new law.

8. Le Corbusier, *The City of To-morrow and Its Planning*, trans. Frederick Etchells (1929; repr., New York: Dover, 1987), 117–18, 170; orig. pub. as *Urbanisme* (Paris: Editions G. Crès, 1925). The phrase "motor traffic" was Etchells's translation of *automobilisme*, which appears on p. 108 in the original French edition. The principle of limited-access, grade-separated, multilevel "express motor highway" construction was proposed to relieve the traffic congestion of Detroit's city streets by the Detroit Rapid Transit Commission in 1924. It included centrally placed rapid transit rail lines as part of the 204-foot-wide thoroughfare. Daniel L. Turner, "The Detroit Super-Highway Project," *AC* 32 (April 1925): 373–76.

9. Throughout *The City of To-morrow*, Le Corbusier gives the figure of three million as the population of Paris.

10. The Voisin Plan is discussed and illustrated in ibid., 277–89.

11. Ibid., 277.

12. These statistics are gleaned from a number of sources, including Automobile Manufacturers Association, *Facts and Figures of the Automobile Industry* 2 (New York: National Automobile Chamber of Commerce, 1921), 40–42; "U. S. Has 10,505,600 Motor Cars in Use: More than 83 Per Cent of Total World Output Operated in This Country," *WP*, 12 March 1922; Motor Vehicle Registration Report, R. H. Donnelly Corporation, 31 December 1924; Chicago Plan Commission, *Through Traffic Streets* (Chicago: City Council Committee on Efficiency, Economy and Rehabilitation, 1925); Miller McClintock, *Report and Recommendations of the Metropolitan Street Traffic Survey* (Chicago: Chicago Association of Commerce, 1926); Clifton R. Bechtel, *Our Traffic Problem* (Chicago: Chicago Real Estate Board, 1927); and Motor Vehicle Manufacturers Association of the United States, *World Motor Vehicle Data* (Washington, D.C.: American Automobile Manufacturers Association, 1982), 33.

In considering the context for which Le Corbusier was designing, it should be noted that France as a whole had only 202,500 cars in 1921, or 1 car for every 205 persons, as compared to the United States, which had 9,211,295 cars, or 1 per every 11 persons. This meant that the United States had forty-five times the number of automobiles as France in 1921. That number was cut in half by 1928, when France's figure rose to 1,115,800 and that of the United States reached 24,511,700.

13. T[heodore] C[ardwell] Barker, "The International History of Motor Transport," *Journal of Contemporary History* 20 (January 1985): 12–13.

14. McClintock, *Report and Recommendations*, 17–18. On McClintock and the nascent field of traffic analysis and planning, see Jeffrey Brown, "From Traffic Regulation to Limited Ways: The Effort to Build a Science of Transportation Planning," *JPH* 5 (February 2006): 3–34.

15. Cabinet Impérial, Bureau de la Statistique Générale, *Résumé statistique de l'empire du Japon*, 41st yr. (Tokyo, 1927), states that there were 3,663 private automobiles in Japan in 1918/19 and that the number rose to 8,265 by 1921/22. "U.S. Has 10,505,600 Motor Cars in Use" states that the combined number of all types of motor vehicles in Japan in 1918 was nearly 12,000.

16. McClintock, *Report and Recommendations*, 26.

17. Fishman, *Bourgeois Utopias*, 188. In an interview published in the early fall of 1923, Wright stated that, although he had established a studio in Hollywood, "in the future, he expects to have studios at Chicago, Hollywood and Tokio." William T. Evjue, "Wright Now Being Acclaimed as World Leader," *CT*, 18 October 1923.

18. "F. Lloyd Wright Coming Here to Build Factories," *CDT*, 26 November 1924. Despite the headline, it is doubtful that "factories" are what Wright meant by the word "industrial." Wright had used the same word a couple of years before in responding to a critique by H. P. Berlage of the romantic and highly personalized character of his recent work as evidenced in the Imperial Hotel and Hollyhock House, in Los Angeles (1918–21). In a letter to the Dutch architect, Wright said, "Yes—you are right.—I have been romancing—engaged upon a great Oriental Symphony—where my own people should have kept me at home busy with their own characteristic industrial problems—work which I would really prefer to do and to have done." Frank Lloyd Wright to H. P. Berlage, 30 November 1922, FLWFA.

Chicago would not be his exclusive place of residence or work. He clearly intended to divide his time between the city and south-central Wisconsin, where Taliesin is located and where he would, in fact, do much of his designing.

19. "Frank L. Wright, Architect, to Open Up Studio," *CDT*, 21 December 1924. The address was 19 East Cedar Street, which is on the block between North Lake Shore Drive (the continuation of North Michigan Avenue) and North State Street. After the fire at Taliesin in April 1925, Wright decided against renovating the East Cedar Street building, and the space was taken over by the Great Central Motor Club for its Chicago headquarters.

20. *ABC: Beiträge zum Bauen* 2d ser., no. 3 (1926): 5. See also note 72 below.

21. Board of Estimate and Apportionment, City of New York, *Building Zone Resolution (Adopted July 25, 1916)*, in Commission on Building Districts and Restrictions, *Final Report, June 2, 1916* (New York: Committee on the City Plan, Board of Estimate and Apportionment, 1916), appendix VII, 232–80.

22. Michael Holleran, "Boston's 'Sacred Sky Line': From Prohibiting to Sculpting Skyscrapers, 1891–1928," *Journal of Urban History* 22 (July 1996): 561–62; and Holleran, *Boston's "Changeful Times": Origins of Preservation and Planning in America* (Baltimore: Johns Hopkins University Press, 2001), 165–68. The Boston action was quickly reported in the Chicago press in "No More High Buildings in Boston," *CDT*, 11 October 1891.

23. See, e.g., "Want No Sky-scrapers," *CDT*, 7 October 1891; "That High Building Ordinance," *CDT*, 6 February 1892; "For Safe Buildings," *CDT*, 25 January 1893; "Meets with Favor," *CDT*, 26 January 1893; "Limit of Ten Stories," *CDT*, 9 March 1893; and "His Veto Unheeded," *CDT*, 14 March 1893. Sullivan's partner, Dankmar Adler, was the sole architect on the committee that drafted the law. For an overview of the implementation of the 1892–93 ordinance in the context of Chicago's history, see Carol Willis, *Form Follows Finance: Skyscrapers and Skylines in New York and Chicago* (New York: Princeton Architectural Press, 1995), 109–31; and Joseph P. Schwieterman and Dana M. Caspall, *The Politics of Place: A History of Zoning in Chicago*, ed. Jane Heron (Chicago: Lake Claremont Press, 2006), 79–95.

24. See chapter 8, esp. note 30.

25. See Thomas H. Logan, "The Americanization of German Zoning," *JAIP* 46 (October 1976): 377–85; and Holleran, "Boston's 'Sacred Sky Line,'" 566–67.

26. "Council Lifts Building Limit," *CDT*, 4 February 1902; "Change in Referendum," *CDT*, 25 February 1902. *An Ordinance Related to the Department of Buildings and Governing the Erection of Buildings, Etc. in the City of*

Chicago, Passed March 13, 1905 (Chicago, 1905), makes no reference to building height limits.

27. *Revised Building Ordinances of the City of Chicago, Passed December 5, 1910 with Amendments and Additions up to January 1, 1912* (Chicago: Francis D. Connery, City Clerk, December, 1911), sec. 598(c), 127; sec. 592, 125. Under pressure from real estate interests, the restriction became applicable only in September 1911. See, e.g., "Aldermen Vote 16 Story Limit on Skyscrapers," *CDT*, 2 December 1910; "Building Limit 200 Feet on Sept. 1," *CDT*, 5 January 1911; "Skyscraper Limit Begins Tomorrow," *CDT*, 30 August 1911.

28. *Revised Building Ordinances of the City of Chicago, with Amendments up to and Including May 26, 1920*, 8th ed. (Chicago: James T. Igoe, City Clerk, June 1920), sec. 583(c), 140; sec. 576, 137–38. See also Willis, *Form Follows Finance*, 111ff.

29. *Chicago Zoning Ordinance, Passed by the City Council of the City of Chicago on April 5, 1923* (Chicago: Al. F. Gorman, City Clerk, 1923).

30. Frank Lloyd Wright, "In the Cause of Architecture. VIII: Sheet Metal and a Modern Instance," *AR* 64 (October 1928): 338, 341.

31. "City Gets Right to Raise Head 60 Feet Higher," *CDT*, 19 March 1920.

32. "Aldermen Vote to Raise Limit on Skyscrapers," *CDT*, 5 March 1920.

33. "Chicago's Newest and Greatest," *CDT*, 5 January 1922.

34. Al Chase, "Huge Office Building for Shore Drive [*sic*]," *CDT*, 5 January 1922. For a discussion of the entire venture, including Wright's involvement, see Stamper, *Chicago's North Michigan Avenue*, 93–100. The information regarding the first Johnson initiative comes from John Zukowsky, ed., *Chicago Architecture 1872–1922: Birth of a Metropolis* (Munich: Prestel-Verlag, in association with Art Institute of Chicago, 1987), 464.

35. Chase, "Huge Office Building."

36. Although he may have known of Wright through his earlier business dealings in Chicago, Johnson more than likely was persuaded to commission Wright by Alfred MacArthur, a younger officer of the National Life Insurance Company. MacArthur was deeply impressed by Wright's architecture and tried to buy his Oak Park house in the 1910s with the intention of helping Wright out financially and, in the process, preserving the house. He and his family lived in the Oak Park house during that period of time as renters. By April 1924, MacArthur spoke of Wright to Darwin Martin as "the world's greatest architect." Alfred MacArthur to Darwin D. Martin, 16 April 1924, box 4, folder 14, MS 22.8, Frank Lloyd Wright–Darwin D. Martin Papers, University Archives, State University of New York, Buffalo.

37. A[lbert] M. Johnson to Frank Lloyd Wright, 19 July 1924, FLWFA; and *FLWCW* 2:290. Harvey Wiley Corbett, "Do We Want Three-Level Streets?" in *Housing Problems in America: Proceedings of the Tenth National Conference on Housing. Philadelphia, Jan. 28, 29, 30, 1929* (New York: National Housing Association, 1929), 244–46, devoted a section of his talk at the conference to "Dwellings on Top of Business Buildings," saying that he "look[ed] forward to a time when habitations will be made part of those same concentrated business centers that we now have" (244).

38. Wright, *Autobiography*, in *FLWCW* 2:293, 290.

39. Wright, "In the Cause: Sheet Metal," 342 (italics are mine).

40. Ibid. Wright wrote that he "had the good fortune to explain it [the design] in detail to … Louis H. Sullivan, some months before he died" (ibid.). The latter's death

occurred on 14 April 1924.

41. Robert L. Sweeney, "Frank Lloyd Wright Chronology 1922–1932," in *Frank Lloyd Wright: Designs for an American Landscape, 1922–1932*, ed. David G. De Long (New York: Abrams, in association with Canadian Center for Architecture, Library of Congress, and Frank Lloyd Wright Foundation, 1996), 189. In the list of buildings Evjue reported Wright told him he was working on in October 1923, the National Life, however, was not included. Evjue, "Wright Now Being Acclaimed."

42. Albert M. Johnson to Henry-Russell Hitchcock, 18 June 1941, U.S. Department of the Interior, National Park Service, Death Valley National Monument, Death Valley, Calif. For the Death Valley commission, see Levine, 173–89.

43. Dione Neutra to [Alfred and Lilly Mueller Niedermann], July 1924, in Dione Neutra, comp. and trans., *Richard Neutra: Promise and Fulfillment, 1919–1932, Selections from the Letters and Diaries of Richard and Dione Neutra* (Carbondale: Southern Illinois University Press, 1986), 126.

44. Johnson to Wright, 19 July 1924, FLWFA. It is curious that the contract specified the "proposed office building [to be] of undetermined height and undetermined cost." It also described the site as "all or a portion of the block lying between Pearson and Chestnut Streets and Michigan Avenue and the Quigley Memorial [Seminary] building," as if Johnson had not yet given up the possibility of acquiring the Palmer estate property north of the alley. A cover letter accompanying the contract letter said, "I shall be glad to hear from you as to what progress you are making, as I am intensely interested and everything seems to indicate that Upper [North] Michigan Avenue is going ahead very rapidly, even more so than some of us anticipated." Johnson ended by saying, "I shall endeavor to get in touch with you either at Taliesen [*sic*] or Chicago and talk over the situation." Johnson to Wright, 19 July 1924.

45. Wright, "In the Cause: Sheet Metal," 338–40, 342.

46. Ibid., 342. Wright explained in his *Autobiography*, in *FLWCW* 2:291–92, that "Johnson's fear of 'too much glass'" led him to "make the exterior area of this project about 1/4 of copper and 3/4 of glass," although that proportion could easily be altered to make the skyscraper an almost all glass-clad structure— "opalescent, iridescent, copper-bound glass."

47. Frank Lloyd Wright, *Modern Architecture: Being the Kahn Lectures for 1930*, Princeton Monographs in Art and Archaeology (1931; repr., Princeton: Princeton University Press, 2008), 83–98.

48. Frank Lloyd Wright, "Why the Skyscraper?" 8 September 1923, MS 2401.437, FLWFA; and Wright, *Experimenting with Human Lives*, 1923, repr. in *FLWCW* 1:169–74. The original manuscript was edited, but not in any substantive sense.

49. Ibid., 169–72, 174.

50. "F. L. Wright Has Scheme to End Bedlam in Loop: Would Slash Tops off Skyscrapers," *CDT*, 13 October 1923. This is precisely what the 1909 Burnham and Bennett *Plan of Chicago* proposed in its drawings of the Loop. Parts of the Chicago interview along with other information were printed in "Says Angeleno Shuns Crowd: Architect Sees Curse in Downtown Congestion," *Los Angeles Times*, 15 October 1923.

51. Evjue, "Wright Now Being Acclaimed."

52. "Divergent Views by Architects on City Planning and Skyscrapers," *NYT*, 31 October 1926, Real Estate sec.

53. Commission on Building Districts and Restrictions,

Final Report, 1–2. The commission acknowledged that the model for such "differential" treatment of districts had its source, in the United States, in Boston's 1904 law, and, more generally, in the laws enacted by German municipalities in the 1890s and 1900s, starting with the regulations adopted by Frankfurt in 1891 (59–72).

54. Ibid., 233–42. For a general account of the New York law, see Seymour I. Toll, *Zoned American* (New York: Grossman, 1969).

55. Louis H. Sullivan, "The High-Building Question," 1891, repr. in *Louis Sullivan: The Public Papers*, ed. Robert Twombly (Chicago: University of Chicago Press, 1988), 76–79, proposed a similar idea in a project certainly known to Wright. Sullivan's Chicago Fraternity (Odd Fellows') Temple design of 1891 was based on the same idea.

56. "A New Architecture from the Set-Back Zoning Law," *WA* 31 (July 1922): 82.

57. Harvey Wiley Corbett, "High Buildings on Narrow Streets: Being Extracts from a Paper Delivered Before the Fifty-Fourth Annual Convention of the American Institute of Architects," *AA* 119 (8 June 1921): 603–19. On Corbett, see Paul D. Stoller, "The Architecture of Harvey Wiley Corbett" (master's thesis, University of Wisconsin–Madison, 1995).

58. For a selection of these texts, see Hugh Ferriss, "The New Architecture," *NYT Book Review and Magazine*, 19 March 1922, 8–9, 27; Ferriss, "Civic Architecture of the Immediate Future: The Demands of American Civilization Have Compelled a Radical Change in Our Building Laws," *Arts and Decoration* 18 (November 1922): 12–13; Harvey Wiley Corbett, "The Influence of Zoning on New York's Skyline," *AAAR* 123 (3 January 1923): 1–4; Corbett, "Zoning and the Envelope of the Building," *Pencil Points* 4 (April 1923): 15–18; Corbett, "What the Architect Thinks of Zoning," *AAAR* 125 (13 February 1924): 149–50; Corbett, "New Stones for Old," *Saturday Evening Post* 198 (15 May 1926): 16–17, 175, 177–78; and Corbett, "New Heights in American Architecture," *Yale Review* 17 (July 1928): 690–701. Carol Willis has discussed this issue in "The Titan City: Forgotten Episodes in American Architecture," *Skyline*, October 1982, 26–27; "Zoning and *Zeitgeist*: The Skyscraper City in the 1920s," *JSAH* 45 (March 1986): 47–59; "Drawing Towards Metropolis," in Ferriss, *The Metropolis of Tomorrow* (1929; repr., Princeton: Princeton Architectural Press, 1986), 148–79; "Skyscraper Utopias: Visionary Urbanism in the 1920s," in *Imagining Tomorrow: History, Technology, and the American Future*, ed. Joseph J. Corn (Cambridge, Mass.: MIT Press, 1986), 164–87; and *Form Follows Finance*, esp. 67–79.

59. Willis, "Drawing Towards Metropolis," 157–58. The drawings were published in Ferriss, "New Architecture" (March 1922) and Corbett, "Zoning and the Envelope" (April 1923): 15–16, where the original four "stages" were supplemented by a fifth and "final" one, less abstract and overtly classical in its detailing and references. The five were republished by Corbett in "New Stones for Old," 16–17, where the "fifth stage" was captioned "the finished building," leaving no mistake about Corbett's adherence to the classical vocabulary of design.

60. See, e.g., "Woman 8 Hour Bill Killed … ," *CDT*, 21 June 1919; "Lowden Signs 69 Bills to Insure Greater Chicago," *CDT*, 30 June 1919; "Compromise Plan for Zoning Ready for Submission," *CDT*, 2 January 1920; "Mayor to Name Zone Body after Delay of Year," *CDT*, 2 July 1921; "Zoning Board to Study Plans of Other Cities," *CDT*, 29 July 1921.

61. Irving K. Pond, "Zoning and the Architecture of High

Buildings," *AF* 35 (October 1921): 132–33.

62. Irving K. Pond, "High Buildings and Beauty: Part I," *AF* 38 (February 1923): 44, 42; and Pond, "High Buildings and Beauty, Part II," *AF* 38 (April 1923): 182.

63. A draft, titled *Tentative Report and a Proposed Zoning Ordinance for the City of Chicago, January 5, 1923* (Chicago: Chicago Zoning Commission, 1923), circulated by the Chicago Zoning Commission three months prior to the approval by the City Council, was adopted by the commission on 8 December 1922. The *Tentative Report* served as the basis for serious criticism of the proposed height allowances by the Zoning Committee of the Chicago Real Estate Board, which published its counter-proposal in *Studies on Building Height Limitations in Large Cities with Special Reference to Conditions in Chicago*, comp. Charles M. Nichols (Chicago: Library, Chicago Real Estate Board, 1923).

64. George C. Nimmons, "The Passing of the Skyscraper," 1922, repr. in *Studies on Building Height Limitations*, 104–5.

65. Drafted by the Chicago Guarantee Survey Company, the plat is dated 12 December 1921, which means that it was probably originally done for the Graham, Anderson, Probst, and White project.

66. For the Sullivan article, see note 1 above.

67. This is indicated in a note on the drawing in the upper right-hand corner of the plan, which specifies shops, restaurants, stores, and salesrooms as occupying the lower three levels of the building.

68. The photograph in "Going Up and Coming Down—Wacker Drive in the Making," *CDT*, 25 October 1925, pt. 3, shows the two building operations going on concurrently. The parking was located on floors 2 through 22. The mechanical space for the lift mechanism was located on the 24th floor. The elevator's original purpose disappeared when the building was sold to the Pure Oil Company shortly after it opened. It remained operational despite significant mechanical problems until around 1940, when it was finally removed.

69. This made it the second-tallest building in Chicago at the time (the steeple of the Chicago Temple, built by Holabird and Roche in 1924, reached a height of 568 feet). Al Chase, "Jewelers' New $10,000,000 Bldg. Partly Garage," *CDT*, 16 April 1924; Chase, "Work to Start Soon on 547 Ft. Jewelers' Bldg.," *CDT*, 12 September 1924; and "Busch Gives O. K. to Plan for Big Jewel Building," *CDT*, 11 July 1925.

70. Wright, "In the Cause: Sheet Metal," 340. This recalls Le Corbusier's description of the sawtooth "set-back" glass walls (*façades à redents*) of the cruciform skyscrapers in the City of Three Million Inhabitants as "radiant prisms" (*radiateurs à lumière*). Le Corbusier, *City of Tomorrow*, 177–78; and Le Corbusier, *Urbanisme*, 181.

71. The plans include those of the ground floor, main floor, mezzanine floor, third through seventeenth and fifth through seventeenth floors, twenty-second through twenty-fifth and twenty-second through twenty-seventh floors, twenty-seventh floor, thirty-first floor, and thirty-second floor. In the letter of contract for the building, Johnson specified that he wanted "one-eighth (1/8th) inch scale plans showing general arrangement of all floors, together with sections and elevations to same scale or larger, showing general scheme of construction, also true perspective drawings based on mathematical projections, presenting the exterior truly and faithfully, according to the actual plans and elevations; also a plaster model of same, if owner shall deem same necessary, the owner to pay the actual contract cost of same, and the model and

all plans, elevations, and so forth, to be and remain the property of the owner." Johnson to Wright, 19 July 1924. There is no evidence that a model was ever made. Wright says in his *Autobiography*, in *FLWCW* 2:290, that Johnson took the drawings "to his house and put them in his own bedroom," specifying that at least one of them was "the color perspective" similar to the one in figure 5.17. It is not known whether Johnson ultimately held on to any of the drawings. Although Wright signed the contractual letter, it was not his practice to allow clients to keep drawings.

72. Labeled "Bürohaus in Chicago, Chicago 1924," the Moser design was published first in 1926 in *ABC* (see note 20 above) and later in "Design for Office Building, Chicago, Werner M. Moser, Architect," *AR* 68 (December 1930): 489.

73. By contrast, the multilevel plan and section of the May 1923 design reproduced in *AR* show a thirty-one-story building whose fin wings project five bays toward the south and only one toward the north. Thus the hall or corridor that runs east-west down the length of the slab is offset to the rear in the earlier design.

74. The thin projecting wings provided almost precisely what Corbett described as the ideal "depth of a well-lighted office" in terms of the "distance from windows to corridor." He said this should be "never over twice the clear ceiling height," with "twenty feet being better than twenty-five." Corbett, "New Stones for Old," 17. In presenting his general scheme for a setback skyscraper in "Zoning and the Envelope" in 1923 (figure 5.20), Corbett explained, "To conform to the fact that daylight does not penetrate in sufficient intensity for practical use more than two or three times the floor height, the architect must provide either an interior court or an exterior court. If he uses an interior court he takes the very heart out of his possible building for the slope of the step backs [in New York] applies on the court side as well as on the street side, but to a greater extent. So it becomes necessary to cut the court from the outside" (15, 18).

75. Aymar Embury, "New York's New Architecture," *AF* 35 (October 1921): 123, explained the reason for this in saying that, whereas in an office building "the total thickness of the mass may easily be 60 to 80 feet, … in hotels or apartment houses, where all rooms must have outside light, the thickness of any wing will be determined by the width of two rooms plus the necessary corridor and elevator space, etc. This will amount, as a rule, to not over 44 feet." Among the most well-known hotel buildings of this type are the William Penn Hotel, Pittsburgh (original part, Janssen and Abbott, 1914–16); Hotel Pennsylvania, New York (McKim, Mead & White, 1915–20); Statler Hotel, Buffalo (George Post and Sons, 1921–23); and the rebuilt Palmer House, Chicago (Holabird and Roche, 1922–27).

76. Louis Kahn, "Order in Architecture," 1957, repr. in *Louis I. Kahn: Writings, Lectures, Interviews*, ed. Alessandra Latour (New York: Rizzoli, 1991), 72.

77. There were three apartments on the west side of the thirty-first floor and two on the thirty-second. The east side, with the view over the lake, had a duplex apartment for Johnson and his wife.

78. Instead of the 12- to 12.5-foot floor height that was typical at the time and that formed the basis of the zoning calculations, the height in the National Life project was 10 feet, except for the ground floor, which was 14, and the top service floor, which was also more than 10.

79. Corbett earlier suggested such raised garden terraces for the skyscraper setbacks in his "Different Levels for Foot, Wheel and Rail," *AC* 31 (July 1924): 3. The Ferriss

drawing was previously published as the front-page illustration under the headline "New York's Towering Terraces: The New City of the Future Made Glorious with the Hanging Gardens of Old Babylon," in George MacAdam, "Vision of New York That May Be: A Forecast of Manhattan Transfigured by the Zoning Law," *NYT Magazine Section*, 25 May 1924, 1–2.

80. George Howe and William Lescaze repeated the National Life Building's disposition of elevators placed in a rear transverse bar in their Philadelphia Savings Fund Society Building in Philadelphia of 1928–32, which can be read as a transformation into International Style terms of one of the four vertical sections of the Wright project.

81. McClintock, *Report and Recommendations*, xiii, 2.

82. Ibid., 13–20.

83. Edward H. Bennett, "Subway Condemned as Loop Congestion Cure," *CHE*, 15 January 1926. This was the second article in a four-part series. The other three were "Loop Termed Key to Traffic Problem Solution," *CHE*, 14 January 1926; "Grade Separation Cure for Loop Congestion," *CHE*, 16 January 1926; and "Chicago's Advance to Bring Traffic Paths High in Air," *CHE*, 18 January 1926. Bennett later stated that the four articles were also printed in the *Chicago Evening Post*, but I have not seen them.

84. Bennett, "Chicago's Advance"; Bennett, "Subway Condemned"; Bennett, "Grade Separation Cure"; and Edward H. Bennett, *The Chicago Business Center and the Subway Question* ([Chicago]: By the Author, 15 April 1926), 5, 11.

85. Ibid. An excerpt of this booklet was published as "Raised Sidewalks and Traffic Separation Urged for Chicago," *AC* 35 (September 1926): 334–36.

86. See, e.g., Harvey Wiley Corbett, "Triple-Decked Streets for Traffic Relief," *NYT*, 3 February 1924, sec. 8; Corbett, "Different Levels for Foot, Wheel and Rail"; and MacAdam, "Vision of New York That May Be."

87. One Who Walks, "A Plea for Pedestrians," letter to the editor, *CDT*, 19 December 1922; "Unstrangling the Loop," editorial, *CDT*, 12 May 1923; and "Proposed Upper Level Sidewalks—East on Madison Street," *CDT*, 12 May 1923.

88. Wright predicted the need for "second-story sidewalks" to relieve automobile congestion in the fall of 1923 in "Says Angeleno Shuns Crowds." In an unpublished article written at least two to three years after the Skyscraper Regulation design, he reimagined the project's underlying conception in relation to a site not in the center of the city but slightly outside it. "Abandon further construction in all congested areas," he wrote. "Move aside to construct new centers, where the entire ground surface would be available for traffic parking area, and sub-basement garages: the second story level reserved for pedestrians, for commercial-display and entrances to buildings: Up and down connection to traffic to be had only at each corner of street intersections by way of traffic stations on roadways below." Frank Lloyd Wright, "The Tall Building. (Article to Popular Mechanic [*sic*]," 2, MS 2401.434A, FLWFA. Although this unpublished article is dated by the Wright Foundation Archives to 1927, it has to be at least two to three years later since it contains references to the Daily News Buildings in New York and Chicago as well as to Wright's own project for the St. Mark's Towers in New York, all of which date from 1929–31. The article and its reference to the Skyscraper Regulation project may well coincide with Wright's revisiting the project in 1930, when he made notations on photographs of some of the earlier drawings. See FLWFA 2603.008 (photograph of 2603.002), 2603.010 (photograph

of 2603.003), 2603.011 (photograph of 2603.005), and 2603.012 (photograph of 2603.006).

89. Without a doubt, the text displaying the greatest ignorance and misunderstanding of the project is Giorgio Ciucci, "The City in Agrarian Ideology and Frank Lloyd Wright: Origin and Development of Broadacres," in Ciucci et al., *American City*, 329, where it is described as "a design of a skyline for Chicago, intended as a counterproposal to the skyscrapers of New York and the city divided according to the grid of real-estate speculation."

90. According to Mark Reinberger, "The Sugarloaf Mountain Project and Frank Lloyd Wright's Vision of a New World," *JSAH* 43 (March 1984): 39, Alfred MacArthur, who introduced Johnson to Wright, was also responsible for bringing Strong to Taliesin to meet Wright and see the National Life drawings.

91. In addition to the article cited above, see Mark Reinberger, "The Sugarloaf Mountain Automobile Objective and Frank Lloyd Wright's Middle Years" (Ph.D. diss., Cornell University, 1982), esp. 4–8; "Executive Committeeman — Gordon Strong," *Bulletin of the National Association of Building Owners and Managers* 57 (July 1921): 9; and Earle Schultz and Walter Simmons, *Offices in the Sky* (Indianapolis: New Bobbs-Merrill, 1959), 82–127.

92. For Strong's very conservative defense of property rights regarding building heights, see *Studies on Building Height Limitations*, 85–86. For his support of the creation of "multiple level streets," see Gordon Strong, "Skyscraper Streets," *CDT*, letter to the editor, 24 September 1924; and Strong, "Three-Level Streets," *CDT*, 15 June 1925.

93. Notations by Wright on the sketch plan and elevation in figure 5.34. The architect described the idea a few years later as a system of "modified zoning laws" wherein "heights of buildings in the rank and file [would] match the width of streets" in contrast to more widely spaced skyscraper towers, whose "heights above the street width" would be specially taxed. Wright, "Tall Building," 2.

94. Though not actually entered in the competition, the Lönberg-Holm project was much vaunted in avant-garde circles. It was published in J.J.P. Oud, "Bij een Deensch Ontwerp voor de Chicago Tribune," *Bouwkundig Weekblad: Orgaan van de Maatschappij tot Bervordering der Bouwkunst Bond van Nederlandsche Architecten* 44th yr., no. 45 (10 November 1923): 456–58; "Projet de gratte-ciel pour le 'Chicago Tribune,'" *Architecture vivante*, Fall–Winter 1924, pls. 24–25; and Walter Gropius, *Internationale Architektur*, Bauhausbücher 1 (Munich: Albert Langen, 1925), 48. A good reason to assume Wright knew the issue in which the Oud piece appeared is that it contained an article on the Imperial Hotel as a follow-up to a spread on the building in the previous issue. See H[ermanus] G[erardus] J[acob] Schelling, "Het Imperial Hotel te Tokio," *Bouwkundig Weekblad: Orgaan van de Maatschappij tot Bervordering der Bouwkunst Bond van Nederlandsche Architecten* 44th yr., no. 45 (10 November 1923): 161. Lönberg-Holm emigrated to Chicago in 1924. He published Wright's desert camp Ocatilla, built in the South Phoenix Mountains in 1929, in "The Weekend Home," *AR* 68 (August 1930): 188–91.

95. The French architect and city planner Eugène Hénard offered various proposals for pedestrian overpasses and tunnels for mass transit in his *Etudes sur les transformations de Paris* (Paris: Librairies-Imprimeries Réunies, 1903). He presented some of the latter in "Les Villes d'avenir/The Cities of the Future," Royal Institute of British Architects, *Town Planning Conference*, 345–67. Burnham and Bennett cited Hénard's *Etudes sur les transformations*

as an important precedent in their *Plan of Chicago*, 17, 88–91.

96. A summary of the early stages in imagining such multilevel street systems is given in Jean-Louis Cohen, *Scenes of the World to Come: European Architecture and the American Challenge, 1893–1960*, trans. Kenneth Hylton (Paris: Flammarion; Montreal: Canadian Centre for Architecture, 1995), 31–37. See also Aldo de Poli, "Les Projets pour la métropole des années vingt: référents américains," in *Américanisme et modernité: l'idéal américain dans l'architecture,* ed. Jean-Louis Cohen and Hubert Damisch (Paris: EHESS, Flammarion, 1993), 229–38.

97. "Costly Street Widenings, as Manhattan Crowds Increase, Might Be Obviated by Planning This Kind of Thoroughfare" and "Sees Future New York," *New-York Tribune*, 16 January 1910. The similarity between this image and the one in Moses King is highlighted by the fact that the clock on the tower building on the right registers the same time in both.

98. Henry Harrison Suplee, "The Elevated Sidewalk," *Scientific American* 109 (26 July 1913): 67. The cover drawing was illustrated, without justification, in the section devoted to Harvey Wiley Corbett in Alison Sky and Michelle Stone, *Unbuilt America: Forgotten Architecture in the United States from Thomas Jefferson to the Space Age* (New York: McGraw-Hill, 1976), 74. It was then attributed, without clarification, to Corbett in Cohen, *Scenes of the World*, 19, 32, 216. Cohen also noted that the article and illustration were quickly republished (in translation) in "La Ville future — une solution hardie du problème de la circulation," *Illustration* 71st yr., no. 3676 (9 August 1913): 124; "La Circolazione futura e i grattanuvole a Nova York," *Illustrazione italiana* 40th yr., no. 35 (31 August 1913): 211; and *Vokrug Sveta*, no. 36 (1913): 592. I thank Carol Willis for her help on the Corbett misattribution.

99. The Perret project for an "Avenue des maisons-tours" between Paris and St. Germain-en-Laye was published in a drawing by Jacques Lambert in J. Labadié, "Les Cathédrales de la cité moderne," *Illustration* 54 (12 August 1922): 133, and *Wasmuths Monatshefte für Baukunst und Städtebau* 8, nos. 9–10 (1924): 315. The van Eesteren project for "part of the Business district of a modern city," done with Georges Pineau, was published in Cornelis van Eesteren, "Tien jaar 'Stijl.' Kunst, Techniek en Stedebouw," *De Stijl* 7, nos. 79–84 (1927): 93. Hilberseimer published his Hochhausstadt project first in *Grosstadtbauten*, Neue Architektur 1 (Hannover: Aposs, 1925), 12, 14, and then in *Groszstadtarchitektur*, Baubücher 3 (Stuttgart: Julius Hoffmann, 1927), 18–19. According to Cohen, none of these had any influence in the United States and rather were themselves influenced by a general culture of "Americanism." For Hilberseimer's reference to Corbett's work, see note 103 below.

100. Deborah Nevins, ed., *Grand Central Terminal: City within the City* (New York: Municipal Art Society of New York, 1982).

101. "To Relieve Traffic Congestion in New York," editorial, *AA* 119 (30 March 1921): 395. Brunner's plan unusually called for placing only "slow moving business traffic" on the existing street level and combining both "quicker moving [vehicles] and pedestrian traffic" on the new second-floor level. Brunner repeated this same disposition in "Coming City of Set-Back Skyscrapers: Diminishing Terraces Stretching Indefinitely Upward," *NYT Magazine*, 29 April 1923, 5, 10.

102. Richard E. Enright, "Second Story Tunnel as Solution of City's Growing Traffic Jam," *NYT*, 7 January 1923, sec. 8.

103. Corbett, "Triple-Decked Streets for Traffic Relief." In the same article, Corbett pointed out, as others later would, that the multilevel idea was "much older than most people imagine," citing Leonardo's project for "a double deck system of streets for Milan." The Corbett drawings in this article plus those published in the *American City* in July 1924 (as well as the relevant Leonardo sketch) were included in Werner Hegemann, "Das Hochhaus als Verkehrsstörer und der Wettbewerb der Chicago Tribune: Mittelalterliche Enge und Neuzeitliche Gotik," *Wasmuths Monatshefte für Baukunst und Städtebau* 8, nos. 9–10 (1924): 297–300. Ludwig Hilberseimer used some of the Corbett images from Hegemann's article to illustrate his *Groszstadtarchitektur*, 11 (pls. 10–14).

104. Corbett, "Triple-Decked Streets for Traffic Relief."

105. "900 in Conference on Traffic Solution," *NYT*, 21 May 1924.

106. The Ferriss drawing was previously published on the front page of the *NYT Magazine*, 25 May 1924, to illustrate the cover story, MacAdam, "Vision of New York That May Be."

107. Harvey Wiley Corbett, "Problem of Traffic Congestion, and a Solution," *AF* 46 (March 1927): 201–8. Corbett continued to push the idea as late as 1929 in a talk at the National Conference on Housing held in Philadelphia in January and published as "Do We Want Three-Level Streets?" 239–49.

108. One Who Walks, "A Plea for Pedestrians"; John H. Busse, "More Dollars for the Loop through Elevated Sidewalks," letter to the editor, *CDT*, 23 November 1923; W. S. Shields, "Put Elevated Sidewalks in Loop Alleys," letter to the editor, *CDT*, 29 November 1923; Strong, "Skyscraper Streets"; Cha[rle]s C. Wollers, "Two Story Streets," letter to the editor, *CDT*, 1 November 1924; and Bernard MacGillian, "Double Level Streets," letter to the editor, *CDT*, 25 February 1926.

109. "Unstrangling the Loop"; "Cut the Knot of Loop Traffic," editorial, *CDT*, 7 June 1923; "Elevated Sidewalks," editorial, *CDT*, 15 November 1923; "A Start toward Elevated Sidewalks," editorial, *CDT*, 9 March 1924; "One Story Streets and Four Story Cities," editorial, *CDT*, 14 September 1924; "Double Deck Streets Proposed Four Centuries Ago," editorial reprinted from the *Des Moines Capital*, *CDT*, 26 November 1924; "Three-Level Streets," editorial, *CDT*, 15 June 1925; "A Double Decked Loop," editorial, *CDT*, 27 July 1925; "The Automobile and the City," editorial, *CDT*, 1 October 1925; and "The Price of Invention," editorial, *CDT*, 5 December 1926.

110. "Unstrangling the Loop"; and "One Story Streets." The first reference was anonymous; the second mentioned Corbett by name.

111. The Chicago City Council seriously studied the idea of double-decking some if not all of the streets in the Loop in 1927 and even developed a plan by the fall, but nothing came of it.

112. Frank Lloyd Wright, "The Hillside Home School of Allied Arts," 10 December 1928, 16, box 5, folder 14, MS 22.8, Wright–Martin Papers. When Wright published an edited version of the prospectus in October 1931, Corbett's name was the only one of the group that was eliminated. One can surmise that this was a result of his role in the planning of the Century of Progress Exhibition, held in Chicago in 1933–34, in which Wright was not included.

113. Corbett, "Do We Want Three-Level Streets?" 243–44. Rem Koolhaas cast Corbett as the archetypal proponent of congestion in his *Delirious New York: A Retroactive*

Manifesto for Manhattan (1978; new ed., New York: Monacelli Press, 1994), 110ff.

114. See note 88 above.

Six: Decentralization versus Centralization: Broadacre City's Ruralist Alternative to Le Corbusier's Urbanism, 1929–35

1. Frank Lloyd Wright to E[arl] Baldwin Smith, 17 February 1930, FLWFA.

2. The most celebrated example of the latter case is Wright, "In the Cause of Architecture, Second Paper," 405–13.

3. Frank Lloyd Wright, "Towards a New Architecture," review of *Towards a New Architecture*, by Le Corbusier, *World Unity,* September 1928, repr. in *Wright: Collected Writings,* 1:317–18. Le Corbusier, *Towards a New Architecture,* was originally published as *Vers une architecture* (Paris: Editions G. Crès, 1923). It was translated into English by Frederick Etchells as *Towards a New Architecture* (New York: Payson & Clarke, 1927).

4. The series is conveniently reprinted in Frederick Gutheim, ed., *In the Cause of Architecture: Frank Lloyd Wright. Essays by Frank Lloyd Wright for Architectural Record with a Symposium on Architecture with and without Wright by Eight Who Knew Him* (New York: Architectural Record Books, 1975), 130–230. The republications in *FLWCW* 1:225–309; and Bruce Brooks Pfeiffer, ed., *The Essential Frank Lloyd Wright: Critical Writings on Architecture* (Princeton: Princeton University Press, 2008), 92–155, either lack the original illustrations or have different ones.

5. Frank Lloyd Wright, "~~In the Cause of Architecture:~~ The City," 29 September 1929, MS 2401.064 A, FLWFA. Gutheim, *In the Cause,* viii, states that "Wright always joked with the *Record* editors that he 'still owed them an article,' having supplied only fourteen of the fifteen contracted for." As indicated, the overall series title is crossed out in the manuscript. This may have been done when Wright reused the piece for the sixth of his Kahn Lectures at Princeton University in May 1930 that were published the following year as *Modern Architecture.* An edited version of the text also appeared as "The Usonian City" in the section immediately preceding "St. Mark's Tower" in the third (then final) book of the 1932 *Autobiography.*

In an essay otherwise full of errors and largely driven by unexamined biases, Ciucci, "City in Agrarian Ideology," 328, suggests that the architect's preliminary thoughts for Broadacre City went back to 1921. He then states that Wright's first "two unpublished attacks on the city [were] 'In Bondage' and 'The Usonian City.'" In a footnote (382n82), he claims that "these two essays probably became 'The Tyranny of the Skyscraper' and 'The City,' two of the six lectures given at Princeton University in 1930." First, there is no manuscript titled "In Bondage" in the Wright Foundation Archives checklist of manuscripts. Second, the text "The Usonian City," which appeared in the 1932 *Autobiography,* was an edited version of the sixth chapter of *Modern Architecture,* which itself was an edited version of the unpublished "~~In the Cause of Architecture:~~ The City."

6. See note 3 above. The Etchells translation appeared "at the close of 1927" according to Mardges Bacon, *Le Corbusier in America: Travels in the Land of the Timid* (Cambridge, Mass.: MIT Press, 2001), 16.

7. I disagree on this score with Hilary Ballon who, in "From New York to Bartlesville: The Pilgrimage of Wright's Skyscraper," in *Prairie Skyscraper: Frank Lloyd Wright's Price Tower,* ed. Anthony Alofsin (New York:

Rizzoli International, 2005), 105, describes the review as "scorching."

The first significant discussion of Wright as merely a precursor of the European modern movement is Henry-Russell Hitchcock Jr., "Modern Architecture. I: The Traditionalists and the New Tradition," *AR* 63 (April 1928): 337–49; and "Modern Architecture. II: The New Pioneers," *AR* 63 (May 1928): 453–60. A subsequent article by Douglas Haskell, "Organic Architecture: Frank Lloyd Wright," *Creative Art* 3 (November 1928): li–lvii, made much the same point regarding Wright's conservative position vis-à-vis the younger Europeans. Hitchcock repeated the argument regarding Wright's relationship to Le Corbusier and other European modernists in his *Modern Architecture: Romanticism and Reintegration* (1929; repr., New York: Hacker Art Books, 1970), 116–18 and passim. Wright responded to the Hitchcock and Haskell articles in "In the Cause of Architecture: Purely Personal," 1928, repr. in *FLWCW* 1:255–58; and Wright, "Surface and Mass,—Again!" *AR* 66 (July 1929), 324–28, repr. in *FLWCW* 1:93. The first of these two articles, unpublished at the time, was written "out of a desire," as Wright said, "to interrupt th[e] series and utter a few harsh, vain things" (1:255).

In his rebuttal of Hitchcock in "In the Cause of Architecture: Purely Personal," 257, Wright made it clear that in condemning the critic he was not condemning the architects the critic supported: "I respect and admire Otto Wagner, Berlage, Gropius, Olbrich, Oud, Wijdeveld, Dudok, Mendelsohn, Mallet-Stevens, Perret, Le Corbusier, and a score of their peers and compeers—all fine earnest men at work. We are one family in a great cause." For more on this debate in the period following the International Style exhibition and Wright's turn from a critique of the critics to a diatribe against the architecture they supported, see my introduction to Wright, *Modern Architecture,* esp. li–lv.

8. Wright, "Towards a New Architecture," 317–18.

9. Ibid., 317.

10. Ibid., 318.

11. See chapter 5 above.

12. Wright, "Towards a New Architecture," 317–18.

13. Frank Lloyd Wright, "The Hillside Home School of Allied Arts," 10 December 1928, 9, box 5, folder 14, MS 22.8, Wright–Martin Papers. The books by Viollet-le-Duc and Jones were the former's *Dictionnaire raisonné de l'architecture française du XIe au XVIe siècle* (1854–68) and the latter's *Grammar of Ornament* (1856). In the 1931 publication of the prospectus, the section on the school library, including mention of Le Corbusier's *Towards a New Architecture,* was left out. Le Corbusier, however, was retained on the list of visiting critics, as were all the others except Corbett. An edited version of the prospectus was reprinted in *FLWCW* 3:40–49.

14. For a sustained analysis of the influence of *Towards a New Architecture* on the text of Wright's 1930 Kahn Lectures, see my introduction to Wright, *Modern Architecture,* xxix–lv.

15. Catherine Bauer, "Machine-Age Mansions for Ultra-Moderns: French Builders Apply Ideas of the Steel and Concrete Era in Domestic Architecture," *NYT,* 15 April 1928. It was no doubt for reasons of transparency that the title of Le Corbusier's book *Urbanisme* was rendered as *The City of To-morrow and Its Planning* when it was translated into English in 1929.

16. Le Corbusier, *Towards a New Architecture,* 1923, trans. Frederick Etchells (1927; repr., New York: Holt, Rinehart and Winston, 1960), 54.

17. *The City of To-morrow and Its Planning* received positive reviews in R[obert] L[uther] Duffus, "A Vision of the Future City: Le Corbusier's Revolutionary Plan for the Modern Metropolis," *NYT Book Review,* 27 October 1929, 1; and John Nolen, "Cities Fit to Live In: Cogent Suggestions for the City of Tomorrow, a 'Machine à Habiter,'" *Technology Review* 32 (April 1930): 3–6. The *Times* followed up the Duffus review with an editorial praising the Corbusian idea of widely spaced skyscraper towers in "Not Quite Topless Towers," *NYT,* editorial, 1 December 1929. Over a year before, a *Times* editorial had described the "denser populations" in Le Corbusier's skyscraper cities as a solution for eliminating "congestion" and noted the "illogicality" of having to commute back and forth "every day" to the suburbs. "Cities on Stilts," *NYT,* editorial, 1 July 1928.

18. It is also more than likely that Wright knew Buckminster Fuller's 1928 design for highrise structures lifted off the ground with floors hung from a central mast as well as Raymond Hood's design for a highrise standing on a narrow, pedestal-like base.

19. Le Corbusier, *Towards a New Architecture,* 54, 56.

20. See my "Frank Lloyd Wright's Diagonal Planning Revisited," in *On and By Frank Lloyd Wright: A Primer of Architectural Principles,* ed. Robert McCarter (London: Phaidon Press, 2005), 232–63.

21. "St. Mark's Tower: St. Mark's in the Bouwerie, New York City," *AR* 67 (January 1930): 1.

22. Ballon, "From New York to Bartlesville," 104.

23. Wright, *Modern Architecture,* 92–93.

24. Ibid., 89; and Lewis Mumford, "The Fourth Migration," 1925, repr. in *Planning the Fourth Migration: The Neglected Vision of the Regional Planning Association of America,* ed. Carl Sussman (Cambridge, Mass.: MIT Press, 1976), 55–64. On the relationship between Mumford and Wright, see Bruce Brooks Pfeiffer and Robert Wojtowicz, *Frank Lloyd Wright and Lewis Mumford: Thirty Years of Correspondence* (New York: Princeton Architectural Press, 2001); and Wojtowicz, *Lewis Mumford and American Modernism: Eutopian Theories for Architecture and Urban Planning* (Cambridge: Cambridge University Press, 1996).

25. Wright, *Modern Architecture,* 91, 96, 89.

26. "F. L. Wright Has Scheme to End Bedlam in Loop."

27. Wright, *Experimenting with Human Lives,* in *FLWCW* 1:170.

28. The phrase comes from Edward Bellamy's 1888 utopian novel *Looking Backward, 2000–1887,* which Wright knew well.

29. Frank Lloyd Wright, "In the Cause of Architecture. V: The New World," *AR* 62 (October 1927): 322.

30. Frank Lloyd Wright, "The City of Tomorrow," [1931], 8, MS 2401.107; and Wright, "The Traffic Problem," 24 January 1932, 5, 1–2. MS 2401.114, FLWFA. This typescript of "The City of Tomorrow" is different from the eponymous article published in *Pictorial Review,* 1933, repr. in *FLWCW* 3:149–53. In that article, Wright spoke in the plural of "the Broadacre Cities of to-morrow" (152). The typescript of "The Traffic Problem" has a note on the top of the first page "Reprint from American Architect.–Jan. 24–1932. To Go into 'The Disappearing City.'" This is written over an erased notation "N. Y. Times of sunday." No article with this title was published in *AA,* nor was the text incorporated as such in Frank Lloyd Wright, *The Disappearing City* (New York: William Farquhar Payson, 1932). The text is different from Wright, "America Tomorrow: 'We Must Choose between the Automobile and the Vertical City,'" *AA* 141

(May 1932): 16–17, 76. It is also different from Wright, "'Broadacre City': An Architect's Vision," 8–9. Sections of "The Traffic Problem" were, however, used in the articles that appeared in *NYT Magazine* and *AA*. Wright also referred to his scheme as "the Broadacre City of tomorrow" in *Disappearing City*, 44. Because the illustrations of the last differ so markedly in its republication in *FLWCW* 3:70–112, I will not refer to the later version. The same is true for the republication in Pfeiffer, *Essential Frank Lloyd Wright*, 235–75.

31. Wright, *Autobiography*, in *FLWCW* 2:345; and Wright, "City of Tomorrow," in *FLWCW* 3:150. In *Modern Architecture*, 109, Wright wrote, "Ruralism as distinguished from Urbanism is American, and truly Democratic." In the unpublished manuscript "~~In the Cause of Architecture:~~ The City," 8, Wright wrote, "Ruralisme as distinguished from Urbanisme is American, and is truly Democratic." The sentence was added in pencil but, like the many other editorial changes, it is impossible to know when.

32. The bibliography of Broadacre City is extensive. Among the most significant publications are "Broadacre City: Frank Lloyd Wright, Architect," *AA* 146 (May 1935): 55–62; Meyer Schapiro, "Architect's Utopia," *Partisan Review* 4 (March 1938): 42–47; George R. Collins, "Broadacre City: Wright's Utopia Reconsidered," in *Four Great Makers of Modern Architecture: Gropius, Le Corbusier, Mies van der Rohe, Wright*, Verbatim Record of a Symposium Held at the School of Architecture, Columbia University, March–May 1961 (New York: Trustees of Columbia University, 1963), 55–74; Lionel March, "Imperial City of the Boundless West—Lionel March Describes the Impact of Chicago on the Work of Frank Lloyd Wright," *Listener* 83 (30 April 1970): 581–84; John Sergeant, *Frank Lloyd Wright's Usonian Houses: The Case for Organic Architecture* (New York: Watson-Guptill Publications, Whitney Library of Design, 1976), 121–36; Fishman, *Urban Utopias*, 91–160; Ciucci, "City in Agrarian Ideology"; L. March, "An Architect in Search of Democracy: Broadacre City," talks broadcast on BBC's *Third Programme* (7 and 15 January 1970), repr. in *Writings on Wright: Selected Comment on Frank Lloyd Wright*, ed. H. Allen Brooks (Cambridge, Mass.: MIT Press, 1981), 195–206; Herbert Muschamp, *Man About Town: Frank Lloyd Wright in New York City* (Cambridge, Mass.: MIT Press, 1983), esp. 45–87; Anthony Alofsin, "Broadacre City: The Reception of a Modernist Vision," in *Center: A Journal for Architecture in America*, vol. 5, *Modernist Visions and the Contemporary American City* (Austin: Center for the Study of American Architecture, School of Architecture, University of Texas, 1989), 8–43; Donald Leslie Johnson, *Frank Lloyd Wright versus America: The 1930s* (Cambridge, Mass.: MIT Press, 1990), 108–40; K. Paul Zygas, ed., *Frank Lloyd Wright: The Phoenix Papers*, vol. 1, *Broadacre City* (Tempe: Herberger Center for Design Excellence, College of Architecture and Environmental Design, Arizona State University, 1995); and De Long, *Frank Lloyd Wright and the Living City*.

Among Wright's numerous presentations of the project, the most important are "~~In the Cause of Architecture:~~ The City"; *Modern Architecture*, 100–15; "'Broadacre City': An Architect's Vision"; *Autobiography*, in *FLWCW* 2:340–49; *Disappearing City*; "Broadacre City: A New Community Plan," *AR* 77 (April 1935): 243–54; Frank Lloyd Wright, ed., "The New Frontier: Broadacre City," in *Taliesin: Taliesin Fellowship Publication* 1 (October 1940); "An Autobiography, Book Six: Broadacre City," 1943, repr. in ibid., 241–54; *When Democracy Builds* (Chicago:

University of Chicago Press, 1945); *The Living City* (1958; repr., New York: New American Library, 1970); and *The Industrial Revolution Runs Away* (New York: Horizon Press, 1969). The last is a posthumously published facsimile of the architect's handwritten editing of *The Disappearing* City accompanied by a newly typeset text.

33. There is an intriguing notation in Wright's hand of the date "1928" on the top right-hand corner of the 29 September typescript, "~~In the Cause of Architecture:~~ The City," possibly indicating when the first idea for, or draft of, the text originated. There are also many emendations, additions, and deletions in pencil. None are substantive. Most are editorial and/or meant to amplify meaning. One completely new addition to the version in *Modern Architecture* is the mention of Henry Ford's Muscle Shoals project (109). The eleven-page typescript constitutes four-fifths of the book's sixth chapter (101–12). A section of a little less than three and a half pages was added by way of conclusion to the book as a whole.

34. Alofsin, "Broadacre City," 8, for instance, states in his opening sentence, "Conceived in theoretical terms immediately after the Stock Market Crash of 1929, Broadacre City was Frank Lloyd Wright's project for a new way of living in the American landscape."

35. Wright, "'Broadacre City': An Architect's Vision," 8–9; and Le Corbusier, "A Noted Architect Dissects Our Cities: Le Corbusier Indicts Them as Cataclysms and Describes His Ideal Metropolis," *NYT Magazine*, 3 January 1932, 10–11, 19. Le Corbusier also published a synopsis of his ideas in Le Corbusier, "We Are Entering upon a New Era," *T-Square* 2 (February 1932): 14–17, 41–42. This was the same issue in which Wright wrote his diatribe against the International Style, "For All May Raise the Flowers Now, for All Have Got the Seed," 6–8.

A little over a month prior to the publication of his piece in the *Times*, Wright spoke of his idea for "broad acre city" in response to a question he was asked after a lecture on "An Architecture for the Individual" at the City Club of Chicago on 9 February 1932. "F. L. Wright to Speak at City Club Luncheon," *CDT*, 7 February 1932; and "Frank Lloyd Wright Tells of the Broad Acre City," *CCB* 25 (15 February 1932): 27, 29. Wright later sometimes referred to the project as "Broadacres," although this was much less common than "Broadacre City."

36. Although Wright never cited Mumford's "Fourth Migration" in anything I have come across, his thinking echoed it closely. Mumford wrote that the "basis" of the "fourth migration" was "the technological revolution" that "has made the existing layout of cities and the existing distribution of population out of square with our new opportunities." The key inventions leading to the ultimate "dispersal" of the population were, in his estimation, the automobile, the telephone, the radio, and "electric transmission." Mumford, "Fourth Migration," 61–63.

37. "~~In the Cause of Architecture:~~ The City," 1. In the fifth chapter of *Modern Architecture*, "The Tyranny of the Skyscraper," Wright continued to offer the idea of double-decking city streets, critical to his Skyscraper Regulation project, as a way of "taking pedestrians off the road-bed and so widening it" (93). By the time he published "'Broadacre City': An Architect's Vision" in March 1932, he had begun to question the usefulness of the idea: "Why deck or double-deck or triple-deck the city streets at a cost of billions of dollars, only to invite increase [of traffic] and invite inevitable defeat?" he asked. Instead, he suggested taking "the billions that decking would cost" and somehow providing the money to people to allow them "to buy more motor cars" so they could move to the

countryside (8). He repeated this in "America Tomorrow," 16.

38. "~~In the Cause of Architecture:~~ The City," 3, 7, 2.

39. Ibid., 2. The particular Ballard text I have in mind is the short story "Build-Up," originally published in 1957, repr. in J. G. Ballard, *The Best Short Stories of J. G. Ballard* (New York: Washington Square Press, 1985), 1–24.

40. "~~In the Cause of Architecture:~~ The City," 5–6. Wright was probably led astray by Etchells's translation, which mistakenly stated that the central cruciform towers were meant for housing as well as offices.

41. Ibid., 7.

42. Ibid., 5. In *Modern Architecture*, 109, Wright added the reference to Henry Ford's plans for Muscle Shoals, Alabama, as predicting a further "decentralization of industry."

43. "~~In the Cause of Architecture:~~ The City," 8.

44. Ibid., 8, 11, 7.

45. Ibid., 8. For the linear city and Broadacre City, see George R. Collins, "The Ciudad Lineal of Madrid," *JSAH* 18 (May 1959): 38–53; G. Collins, "Linear Planning throughout the World," *JSAH* 18 (October 1959): 74–93; and G. Collins, "Broadacre City," 60–65. For the Soviet type, see N[ikolai] A[leksandrovich] Miliutin, *Sotsgorod: The Problem of Building Socialist Cities*, 1930, trans. Arthur Sprague (Cambridge, Mass.: MIT Press, 1974).

46. "~~In the Cause of Architecture:~~ The City," 9.

47. Ibid., 10.

48. Ibid., 10, 8–9. The final words "of our own choosing" are difficult to read in the edited typescript and may be somewhat different. In *Modern Architecture*, 110, Wright changed the text to "in congenial company."

49. Ibid., 10.

50. Wright's first use of the acronymic Usonia to signify the United States of North America appears to be in Frank Lloyd Wright, "In the Cause of Architecture: The Third Dimension," *Wendingen* 7 (1925), repr. in *FLWCW* 1:211. The term is used a couple of times in "~~In the Cause of Architecture:~~ The City."

51. As I point out in my introduction to Wright's *Modern Architecture*, xlix, the townhouse design in question was antedated to 1912–13 and misidentified as a "Small Town Hall." The aerial perspective of the Strong project in figure 6.3 was, however, used by Wright to illustrate his *Two Lectures on Architecture* (Chicago: Art Institute, 1931), opp. 56, which appeared shortly after *Modern Architecture*. I also point out that Wright had no interest in illustrating the Princeton lectures with slides and that whatever slides were used were chosen by Princeton faculty members without Wright's foreknowledge.

52. Wright, *When Democracy Builds*, 58; and Wright, *Living City*, 122. Prior to settling on this phraseology, Wright used others such as "the city is nowhere or it is everywhere" ("'Broadacre City': Architect's Vision," 8) or that it is "everywhere or nowhere" (wording on panel of 1935 Broadacre City exhibition; see figure 6.8). While clearly deriving from the etymological meaning of the word "utopia," Wright's reference to "nowhere" can also be traced to the novels *Erewhon*, by Samuel Butler (1872), and *News from Nowhere*, by William Morris (1890). The best discussion of Broadacre City in the context of utopian thought remains Fishman, *Urban Utopias*, 91–160.

There was also an iconoclastic (Platonic?) streak in Wright that may have led him from the start to think that images might only diminish the power of the word. In 1927, in "In the Cause: New World," 324, he wrote to the "Young Man in Architecture":

Shall I too paint pictures for you
to show to you this new world? …
Would you not rather make them
yourself?
Because any picture I could make
would not serve you well.
A specific "picture" might betray
you. You might take it for the
thing itself—and so miss its merely symbolic value, for it could have
no other value.

53. Wright, "'Broadacre City': An Architect's Vision," 8.
In later presentations of Broadacre City, it was captioned
"A 'Close-up' of the Tall Building for Residence Where It
Belongs."

54. Wright, *Disappearing City*, 71. More sardonically, he
described such a residence as an "infirmary for the confirmed 'citified,'" to be inhabited by "those who have been
emasculated by the present city" (ibid.).

55. Wright, "In the Cause of Architecture: The City," 9;
and Wright, "'Broadacre City': An Architect's Vision," 9.

56. Ibid. 9. The reference to farms and markets probably
relates to the designs for Prefabricated Sheet-Metal Farm
Units and Wayside Markets that Wright was designing for
Walter V. Davidson for the New York and Philadelphia
areas in 1932–33. See Jack Quinan, *Frank Lloyd Wright's
Buffalo Venture: From the Larkin Building to Broadacre
City. A Catalogue of Buildings and Projects* (San Francisco:
Pomegranate, 2012), 188–98.

57. Wright, "'Broadacre City': An Architect's Vision," 9.

58. Le Corbusier, "A Noted Architect," 11; and Wright,
"'Broadacre City': An Architect's Vision," 8.

59. In the scheme as presented in 1935, the four-square-
mile area comprising 2,560 acres was to contain 1,400
families averaging five or more members each. Alofsin,
"Broadacre City," 8, gives the correct figures for the size of
the area and number of families but calculates the density
as "2.2 families per acre" rather than 2.2 persons per acre.

60. In *The Living City*, this image was eliminated and the
smoke-shrouded one that earlier served as the frontispiece
was recaptioned "Find the Citizen."

61. While it is intriguing to recall that Bruno Taut titled
the 1920 book in which he published his utopian scheme
for small settlements spread throughout the landscape
Die Auflösung der Städte (The Dissolution of Cities), there
is no evidence that Wright knew the work.

62. Wright, *Disappearing City*, 14, 8, 33.

63. The self-built, subsistence farm concept for improving
the housing conditions of the working class was devas-
tatingly and, in many ways, unfairly criticized from a
Marxist point of view in Meyer Schapiro, "Architect's
Utopia." It was earlier criticized in Lewis Mumford, "The
Sky Line: Mr. Wright's City—Downtown Dignity," *New
Yorker* 11 (27 April 1935): 80.

64. Wright, *Disappearing City*, 63, 65.

65. See note 56 above.

66. Wright, *Disappearing City*, 71–72.

67. Ibid., 73–76, 78.

68. Ibid., 70.

69. Ibid., 85.

70. Ibid., 48, 51, 66, 70.

71. Kathryn Smith to author, emails, 4 August 2008. In
a follow-up email of 24 February 2012, Smith said that it
was Karl E. Jensen, Wright's secretary and a draftsman
in his office, who, on visits to New York looking for work
for himself, connected up with people at the National
Alliance of Art and Industry, which eventually sponsored

the 1935 exhibition at Rockefeller Center. It may be significant that Robert Mosher, one of the Taliesin apprentices,
writing in the "At Taliesin" newspaper column for 9
December 1934, clearly differentiated between Wright's
authorship of the earlier Broadacre City text and that of
the model, for which he unusually credited the Fellowship
itself: "Two years ago Mr. Wright's *Disappearing City*
appeared from the press.… Early next year an important
New York exhibition sponsored by the characteristic 'big-
boys' will present Taliesin's pattern for a New America in
form of the Broadacre City." Randolph C. Henning, ed.,
*"At Taliesin": Newspaper Column by Frank Lloyd Wright
and the Taliesin Fellowship, 1934–1937* (Carbondale:
Southern Illinois University Press, 1992), 91.

72. One is reminded of the map-making episode in Lewis
Carroll, *Sylvie and Bruno Concluded* (London: Macmillan,
1893), 169, where Mein Herr speaks of making "a map
of the country, on the scale of *a mile to the mile*!" The
only problem was that "the farmers objected: they said it
would cover the whole country, and shut out the sunlight!
So we now use the country itself, as its own map, and I
assure you it does nearly as well."

73. Wright, "New Frontier," 22, indicates that there were
"ten smaller collateral models." I count at least eleven in
figure 6.8. There may have been a twelfth, if the highway
overpass illustrated in "Broadacre City: Frank Lloyd
Wright," 58, and in Wright, "Broadacre City: A New
Community Plan," 246, was exhibited as a separate item.

74. K. Paul Zygas, "Broadacre City as Artifact," in *Wright:
Phoenix Papers*, 1:20, says that the model is actually twelve
feet by twelve feet eight inches, the eight inches being the
additional piece to accommodate the highway. *FLWCW/
DG/OC* 2:237, however, states that the model "forms a
square twelve feet six inches on each side."

75. For more on Kaufmann Sr. and the circumstances
of his first contacts with Wright, see chapter 9. For the
building of the model, see John Meunier, "A Model for
the Decentralized City: An Interview with Cornelia
Brierly," in *Wright: Phoenix Papers*, 1:32–46; and Cornelia
Brierly, *Tales of Taliesin: A Memoir of Fellowship* (Tempe:
Herberger Center for Design Excellence, Arizona State
University, in collaboration with Frank Lloyd Wright
Foundation, 1999), 21–28.

76. For the New York venue, see "Architect Models New
Type of City," *NYT*, 27 March 1935; "Exhibit Model City,"
NYT, 14 April 1935, sec. 10; "An Architect Visualizes
'Broadacre City,'" *AC* 50 (April 1935): 85, 87; Mumford,
"Sky Line," 79–80; and Stephen Alexander, "Frank Lloyd
Wright's Utopia," *New Masses* 15 (18 June 1935): 28.
For Washington, D.C., see Laura Vutray, "Frank Lloyd
Wright's Famous Model of a 'Modern City' Comes to
Corcoran Gallery," *WP*, 30 June 1935. The exhibition at
the State Historical Society of Wisconsin took place be-
tween 4 June and 14 June. That at the Iowa County Fair
occurred between 7 September and 10 September. I thank
Mary Jane Hamilton for the information on Wisconsin.
For a lively narrative account of the venture, see Brierly,
Tales of Taliesin, 98–99. Wright's "Broadacre City: A New
Community Plan" and "Broadacre City: Frank Lloyd
Wright" were both published in connection with the
Rockefeller Center exhibition. Whereas the latter consists
solely of photographs, some with lengthy captions, the
former contains a seven-page text by Wright.

77. The note on the rear of the drawing (FLWFA 3402.001)
states that "no land of any kind less than one acre" could
serve as a building site and that all land would be "free
from speculative manipulation." It goes on to talk about
the co-optation of the railroad rights-of-way by the

double-deck highways, the construction of the integral
warehousing facilities and linked "mercantile distribution" centers and roadside markets. It also reiterates, as
Wright had stressed in *The Disappearing City*, that the
small farms and minimum one-acre houses with subsistence plots would be "part of the community life." Finally,
after noting the importance of county government as opposed to federal or village government, and specifying the
services such county government would provide, it mentions that one of the services would be radio broadcasts of
"popular programmes and news of a general character,"
the latter "taking over the functions of the newspaper."
Voting, overseen by the federal government, would be
done by mail, assured by the federal government but lo-
cally delivered from the county offices. Federal telephone
and telegraph service would be wireless.

78. As noted above (note 74), Zygas, "Broadacre City as
Artifact," states that the highway strip was an addition to
the four equal-sized elements.

79. I owe the information about the location of the plan to
Kathryn Smith, who is completing a book on Wright's exhibitions. She also pointed out that the text above the plan
forms the first part of that of the panel it adjoins, making
the two read: "A NEW FREEDOM FOR LIVING IN AMERICA." The
plan with numbers overlaid and a legend identifying the
various elements was published in Wright, "Broadacre
City: A New Community Plan," 250–51; and "Broadacre
City: Frank Lloyd Wright," 56–57. I characterize the plan
as schematic not only because of its graphic style but also
because it does not include a number of the buildings and
other elements shown in the model.

80. Zygas, "Broadacre City as Artifact," 29, erroneously
states that the density of Broadacre City was to have
been a "scandalously low" "500 people per square mile,"
or under 1 person per acre. His figures were based on
measurements taken from the model as refurbished and
changed over time. Disregarding Wright's own figure of
1,400 families averaging 5 members each, Zygas claims
the total population of the site depicted by the model was
to have been 2,283 people living in 761 units.

81. Wright, "Broadacre City: A New Community Plan,"
253. One view of the model shows only two levels,
however.

82. The design was based on the project for the *Capital
Journal* Building in Salem, Oregon (1931–32). Above
the double-height space for the printing presses and
offices were two floors of apartments for the owner and
employees.

83. The motor hotel was based on a design Wright had
done in 1929 for a motor inn for Albert Chandler, called
the San Marcos Water Gardens. It was to have been built
on the road leading into the town of Chandler, Ariz.,
where the San Marcos Hotel was located.

84. Wright, "Broadacre City: A New Community Plan,"
253.

85. See Richard Longstreth, *City Center to Regional
Mall: Architecture, the Automobile, and Retailing in Los
Angeles, 1920–1950* (Cambridge, Mass.: MIT Press, 1997);
and Longstreth, *The Drive-In, the Supermarket, and the
Transformation of Commercial Space in Los Angeles, 1914–
1941* (Cambridge, Mass.: MIT Press, 1999).

86. Wright, "Plan," 96.

87. Bullet point on exhibition panel titled "A NEW FREE-
DOM"; and Frank Lloyd Wright, "A New Freedom for
Living in America," radio broadcast at opening of
Rockefeller Center exhibition, April 1935, in Wright,
"New Frontier," 36 (the bolding is Wright's).

88. Wright, "New Frontier," 11, noted that a county

averaged from "thirty to fifty square miles."

89. Wright, "'Broadacre City': An Architect's Vision," 9.

90. Alofsin, "Broadacre City," 10, 8.

91. G. Collins, "Broadacre City," 67; and Meunier, "Model for the Decentralized City," 36. Later in the same interview, Brierly came back to this point, saying, "I would like to remind you that … Mr. Wright's ideas for Broadacre City were a direct result of the experiences of the Depression. Everyone at the time was trying desperately, not only architecturally, but politically and economically, to remedy a sick situation" (44).

92. Wright, "New Frontier," 35–36.

93. This has not deterred most critics and historians from citing such figures as being instrumental in Wright's formulation of the ideology that generated Broadacre City.

94. In 1932, Wright suggested that the money spent to double-deck and triple-deck streets would be better spent helping "citizens … buy motor cars" so they could get out of the city. Wright, "America Tomorrow," 16.

95. Ibid., 16, 76.

96. Le Corbusier, "Noted Architect," 10.

97. Wright, "New Frontier," 36.

98. Following from Georges Benoît-Lévy's writings, the French ordinarily used the phrase *cités-jardins* to mean "garden suburbs."

99. The first three of these projects were dealt with by me in "Frank Lloyd Wright urbaniste: Trois projets pour revitaliser la ville," *Revue urbanisme* 329 (March–April 2003): 82–89.

Seven: A Civic Center Megastructure for the Lakefront of Madison, Wisconsin, 1938

1. See Levine, 191–297.

2. "Usonian Architect," *Time* 30 (17 January 1938): cover, 29–32; "Frank Lloyd Wright," *AF* 68 (January 1938): 1–102 (paginated separately); "Frank Lloyd Wright," *AF* 88 (January 1948): 65–127; and "Frank Lloyd Wright: A Selection of Current Work," *AR* 123 (May 1958): 167–90.

3. Frank Lloyd Wright, *An Organic Architecture: The Architecture of Democracy*, Sir George Watson Lectures of the Sulgrave Manor Board for 1939 (London: Lund Humphries, 1939), 34–37. The republication in *FLWCW* 3:300–334 has a different set of illustrations.

4. The story of the project and its prehistory are extensively recounted in Mollenhoff and Hamilton. Mary Jane Hamilton, "The Olin Terraces and Monona Terrace Projects," in *Frank Lloyd Wright and Madison: Eight Decades of Artistic and Social Interaction*, ed. Paul E. Sprague (Madison: Elvehjem Museum of Art, University of Wisconsin–Madison, 1990), 195–206, previously detailed Wright's involvement and the changes in his design from 1938 through 1959. In the versions Wright produced in the 1950s, the government functions were eliminated and the plan was devoted exclusively to cultural activities and community recreational facilities. The major new element in the project designed by Taliesin Architects in 1989–94 and built in 1995–97 was a convention center.

5. Nolen earned his professional degree in 1905 from Harvard's Landscape Architecture program, where he studied with Olmsted Jr. and Arthur Shurtleff. With an office in Cambridge, Mass., he received his first two planning jobs in 1907, for Roanoke, Va., and San Diego. The latter established his reputation. On Nolen, see John Hancock, "John Nolen and the American City Planning Movement: A History of Cultural Change and Community Response, 1900–1940" (Ph.D. diss., University of Pennsylvania, 1964); and Hancock, "'Ciò che è giusto deve essere adatto': Disegni e piani di John Nolen, city planner americano/'What Is Fair Must Be Fit': Drawings and Plans by John Nolen, American City Planner," *Lotus International: Rivista trimestrale di architettura/Quarterly Architectural Review* 50, no. 2 (1986): 30–45.

6. The speech Olin gave to civic leaders in late January 1909 urging them, successfully as it turned out, to vote in favor of Nolen's appointment was published as "Looking Ahead—To Plan a City Beautiful," *Municipality: Devoted to the Interests of Town, County, Village and City Government* 9 (March 1909): 223–36. It echoes ideas he discussed with the landscape architect/planner over the previous months, which were eventually included in the Nolen report discussed below.

7. Nolen laid out the general principles of his approach to city planning in a lecture to the League of Wisconsin Municipalities later that spring. It was published as "City Making in Wisconsin," *Municipality: Devoted to the Interests of Town, County, Village and City Government* 10 (May 1910): 417–27.

8. John Nolen, *Madison: A Model City* (Boston, 1911). The date of August 1910 appears in the reproduction of Nolen's letter to the Madison Park and Pleasure Drive Association and the city's Citizen's Committee that accompanies the published report on p. 16 of the "Explanatory" introduction. A number of the drawings were finished by April 1910 and were exhibited in the 1910 Universal City-Building Exhibition in Berlin that opened in May. *Führer durch die Allgemeine Städtebau-Ausstellung in Berlin 1910* (Berlin: Ernst Wasmuth, 1910), 159 (nos. 1200–1207).

9. Hancock, "'Ciò che è giusto,'" 32; and Mel Scott, *American City Planning since 1890: A History Commemorating the Fiftieth Anniversary of the American Institute of Planners* (Berkeley: University of California Press, 1969), 110–33. Peterson, *Birth of City Planning*, 263, 265, astutely remarked that "the conventional historical labels used to interpret these years [1911–17], notably the shift from the City Beautiful to the City Practical … , fail to reveal much of the confusion and perplexity within the movement" and that, "in fact, the renunciation of the City Beautiful never expressed true repudiation" of the "park systems and civic centers—ideas at the heart of the City Beautiful plan making."

10. Nolen, *Madison*, 144.

11. Ibid., 31. To these first two, he added that "as a residence city it should be homelike, convenient, healthful and possess ample facilities for wholesome recreation."

12. Ibid., 89, 125.

13. Ibid., 146, 150.

14. Ibid., 90, 115, 118, 94–95, 113, 109.

15. Ibid., 124.

16. It was only in his detailed list of recommendations included in the final chapter of the report that Nolen added, in the sixteenth of seventeen suggestions, that the city "consider methods of improving the housing of people of small means" (ibid., 143).

17. Ibid., 143.

18. In the chapter dealing with residential areas of the city, the only models Nolen included were a photograph of a group of picturesque cottages at Bournville; two of his own plans for private subdivisions in upper-middle-class suburbs of Madison (Round Top Hill and Lakewood, both 1910); and the Olmsted-inspired plan for the suburban subdivision of Bellevue Park, Harrisburg, Pennsylvania.

19. Mollenhoff and Hamilton, 7, point out that, as early as 1905, James Huff Stout, who was chair of the Senate Committee on Capitol and Grounds, began lobbying for expanding the park surrounding the Capitol. In May 1907, he introduced a bill to authorize the state to buy the six blocks between it and Lake Monona. In fact, the previous month, a plan for a landscaped mall between the Capitol and the lake, with a series of public buildings flanking it, was published in the *WSJ* by Dr. Clarke Gapen, a Madison civic leader.

20. Burnham was a key member of the jury that chose the Post submission.

21. Wright, *Autobiography*, repr. in *FLWCW* 2:125.

22. Mollenhoff and Hamilton, 21.

23. Nolen, *Madison*, 37, 45.

24. John Nolen, lecture, Annual Meeting of Madison Park and Pleasure Drive Association, April 1909, *WSJ*, 28 April 1909, quoted in Mollenhoff and Hamilton, 15.

25. Mollenhoff and Hamilton, 244, state that the Wilson Street sidewalk is fifty-six feet above lake level; the William Kaeser drawing done for Ladislas Segoe (figure 7.11) shows the Olin Terrace extension of Wilson Street to be forty-five feet above the level of the lake.

26. Nolen, *Madison*, 43.

27. Ibid., 40.

28. Ibid., 40, 43; and Mollenhoff and Hamilton, 20.

29. Nolen, *Madison*, 43, 45.

30. Mollenhoff and Hamilton, 20–39.

31. The ordinance was upheld by the State Supreme Court in 1923.

32. Harland Bartholomew, *Madison, Wisconsin: Report on Major Streets, Transportation and Zoning* (St. Louis, 1922), 1. Bartholomew was apparently initially approached for the job in April 1921 and officially commissioned on 25 August. He submitted his final report on 26 October 1922.

33. Ibid., 7–8.

34. Bartholomew neither mentioned the Cleveland precedent in his report nor illustrated his adaptation of it.

35. Ibid., 40–41. Nolen's union station was located a number of blocks to the east of the mall and was to connect to it by way of a plaza and lake esplanade.

36. An article summarizing Bartholomew's recommendations on the elimination of grade crossings and the need for zoning appeared in "Bartholomew Outlines Plan for Grade Crossing Elimination," *WSJ*, 1 March 1927. The text of the new Zoning Ordinance accompanied by a "District Map … Showing the Districts for the Use, Height and Area Regulations," drawn by Bartholomew and dated 1927, was serialized in the same newspaper, 12–15 March 1927.

37. See Mollenhoff and Hamilton, 28–29.

38. According to ibid., 21–22, the site was purchased by the government in 1922. James A. Wetmore was the supervising architect.

39. In 1930 the county part of the combination was dropped and an auditorium–city hall was proposed, although nothing came of this idea.

40. Joseph W. Jackson to John Nolen, 5 June 1934, box 41, folder 24, Joseph W. Jackson Papers 919, WHS. Underlinings are the author's; italics are mine.

41. James R. Law to William V. Kaeser, 5 June 1934. I am grateful to Mary Jane Hamilton for supplying me with a copy of this letter. On Kaeser, see Anne E. Biebel, "William Kaeser's Fifty Year Plan for Madison," *Historic Madison* 13 (1996): 43–56.

42. Law to Kaeser, 7 December 1934. I am again grateful to Mary Jane Hamilton for providing me with a copy of this letter.

43. When Jackson wrote to Nolen on 5 June 1934 inviting him to lecture, he listed the things that had been accomplished since 1911 along with those that had not. He was

very ambiguous on the future of the Monona Avenue civic center, foreseeing its development limited to a plaza at lake level. "Your magnificent proposal for the State to acquire the six blocks from the Capitol Square to [Lake] Monona is probably for all time out of the realm of possibilities" due to the construction of the Madison Club, Capitol Annex, and Federal Building. What would "still be possible," however, was "to carry out your idea for a plaza development by filling in along the lake shore."

44. Explaining his project in *City Planning: A Discussion Outlining a System for the Design of a Master Plan of Madison, Wisconsin* (Madison: By the Author, 1935), 3, Kaeser wrote that "[Mayor] Law … provided me with invaluable information and suggestions for proposed projects" and that "I have incorporated projects which we have discussed." Kaeser's design was published in Roger Wade Sherman, "The Art of City Building," *AA* 147 (October 1935), 18–19. I thank Anne Biebel for this reference.

45. Kaeser, *City Planning*, 14.

46. See "Streamlined Madison: Kaeser Outlines System of Logic for Master Patternn [sic] of Future," *WSJ*, 18 March 1935.

47. I am indebted to Harry Miller for showing them to me and providing me with study images.

48. The city began a landfill operation along the lakeshore in 1934.

49. These issues are fully documented and analyzed in Mollenhoff and Hamilton, 23–39. See also Henry Noll, "City Ready to Start $7,800,000 Works Program, U.S. Told," *WSJ*, 17 February 1935.

50. Jackson to Nolen, 13 February 1937, box 41, folder 24, Jackson Papers 919, WHS.

51. From revised articles of incorporation, in "Madison and Wisconsin Foundation," [1937], 3, box 40, folder 14, Jackson Papers 919, WHS.

52. "Original 31-Point Program of the Madison and Wisconsin Foundation—1937," 2, 1, box 40, folder 14, Jackson Papers 919, WHS.

53. Jackson to Ladislas Segoe, 5 June 1937, box 28, Planning 1937–38, Dane Series 5, WHS. The suggestion to hire Segoe may have come from Clarence A. Dykstra, president of the University of Wisconsin and former city manager of Cincinnati. On Segoe, see David J. Edelman and David J. Allor, "Ladislas Segoe and the Emergence of the Professional Planning Consultant," *JPH* 2 (February 2003): 47–78.

54. The first visit and lecture took place in early July 1937; a second visit, which included an interview with the Madison Planning Trust, occurred on 17–18 March 1938. The Trust voted to hire Segoe on 30 March, and he was officially appointed on 9 May.

55. Ladislas Segoe, *Comprehensive Plan of Madison, Wisconsin, and Environs*, 2 vols. (Madison: Trustees of Madison Planning Trust, [1938–39]).

56. Ladislas Segoe to James R. Law, 6 December 1937, box 28: Planning 1937–38, Dane Series 5, WHS. After beginning work on the Madison job, Segoe wrote an official letter of support for the project to Law. Segoe to Law, 14 July 1938, box 3: Segoe Correspondence, Dane Series 228, WHS. Segoe's statement was published in "Segoe Asks for a Joint County, City Building," *CT*, 17 July 1938.

57. Paul O'Brien, "See County Board Approval of City Hall-Courthouse Plan as Committee Favors Building," *CT*, 21 July 1938.

58. The later design was published in "The County-City Dual Building," *WSJ*, 12 November 1938.

59. [Joseph Jackson], "Re: Lake Shore Community Development, General Proposal," 23 June 1938, [1], box 31, folder 1696, Dane Series 5, WHS. Jackson had earlier outlined his idea for an auditorium at the Mendota location in an article published in the *WSJ* in August 1936.

60. Wright's 1938 estimate was actually only $700,000 more than what the city-county building was slated to cost. When Wright re-presented the project in 1941, the estimate went up to $3.25 million.

61. Sprague, *Wright and Madison*.

62. Wright to P. B. Grove, 14 November 1938, FLWFA. Another version of the story is in "PWA Allots $186,000 for Dual Building: Wright Outlines Dream Civic Center at Lake Monona," *WSJ*, 2 November 1938. Mollenhoff and Hamilton, 282n3, state that it is far from clear "how many citizens joined Harloff to come up with Wright's $1,000 fee." They also claim that "Wright understood that Harloff, George Steinle … and five others (seven in all) had agreed to raise the money." Bruce Brooks Pfeiffer, *Treasures of Taliesin: Seventy-Six Unbuilt Designs* (Fresno: Press at California State University, 1985), n.p. (under figure 22b), earlier wrote that "P. B. Grove and the noted landscape architect Franz Aust of the University of Wisconsin went to Taliesin to suggest that Mr. Wright make some sketches for a civic center for Madison."

63. Mollenhoff and Hamilton, 92. The authors note that Harloff was the electrical contractor for Post's State Capitol building.

64. Wright to Grove, 14 November 1938.

65. Although Mollenhoff and Hamilton, 92, specify no date for the second request, Hamilton, "Olin Terraces and Monona Terrace," 195, earlier suggested that "Harloff approached Wright again about July 1938."

66. Paul F. Harloff, "Building for the Future," *CT*, letter to the editor, 31 July 1938. The letter is dated 29 July, meaning that it was written the day after the Kaeser Mendota auditorium-armory project was published and a week after the Starck, Sheldon, and Schneider city-county building design was published. George Steinle, one of Harloff's associates in commissioning the Wright design, was a part owner of the Monona Avenue site slated for the new dual building and thus would have stood to lose financially on the deal.

67. Ibid.

68. Paul F. Harloff, "Lake Site for City-County Building," *CT*, letter to the editor, 6 August 1938.

69. Paul F. Harloff, "Favors Lake Edge as City-County Building Site," *CT*, letter to the editor, 12 August 1938; and Harloff, "Mr. Harloff's Park Plan," *CT*, letter to the editor, 26 August 1938.

70. This last point comes out most forcefully in the final letter, Paul F. Harloff, "For Over-the-Lake Site for City-County Building," *CT*, letter to the editor, 9 September 1938.

71. Albert G. Michelson to Frank Lloyd Wright, 17 August 1938, FLWFA. Michelson, an officer of the Bank of Wisconsin, was the third vice president of the club and chair of its Program Committee. Rather than specifying a topic, he told Wright he could "give … a talk on any subject you might choose."

72. Eugene Masselink (Wright's secretary) to Michelson, 21 September 1938, FLWFA.

73. Despite the fact that at least one of the final drawings for the project is signed and dated July 1938 (figure 7.23), Mollenhoff and Hamilton, 93, date the first Wright sketches to September 1938.

74. Harloff to Wright, 22 September 1938, FLWFA.

75. Mollenhoff and Hamilton, 93.

76. Russell B. Pyre, "Wright Scorns 'Wrong' Buildings, Plans 'New Deal' Dual Structure," *WSJ*, 28 September 1938. The other report was Herbert Jacobs, "Wright Pleads for Civic Center on Lake Monona," *CT*, 28 September 1938. Pyre preceded the names of Nolen and Olin with that of James Stout, for whom see note 19 above.

77. Pyre, "Wright Scorns 'Wrong' Buildings."

78. Aware that word must have gotten back to Harloff that he never mentioned him in his talk, Wright wrote to him four days later with the following excuse: "I brought you up at the dinner the other day but in the report they left you out." He added, "I am working something up for you and you will have it soon. So cheer up." Wright to Harloff, 1 October 1938, FLWFA; and Paul F. Harloff Papers, in Harloff SC 193, WHS.

79. Pyre, "Wright Scorns 'Wrong' Buildings."

80. Wright to Harloff, 1 October 1938.

81. Masselink to Harloff, 18 October 1938, FLWFA; and Harloff SC 193, WHS.

82. Frank Lloyd Wright, "OLIN TERRACES. FACTS CONCERNING THE SCHEME: HANGING GARDENS CONSTRUCTED ABOVE THE LAKE," 15 October 1938, MSS 2401.226 D, E, FLWFA. A later typescript, "OLIN TERRACES. MADISON; WISCONSIN. FACTS CONCERNING THE SCHEME: HANGING GARDENS CONSTRUCTED ABOVE THE LAKE," is dated 4 November 1938, MSS 2401.226 C, I, FLWFA. Copies of both are in Harloff SC 193, WHS.

83. Mollenhoff and Hamilton, 95, 282n11, add that "Harloff showed the drawings to Frank Stewart, chairman of the county board, on November 1, 1938."

84. This was reported in "PWA Allots $186,000 for Dual Building."

85. "Stalling by 2 Supervisors Delays County Action on Proposed Dual Building," *CT*, 2 November 1938; and "Frank Lloyd Wright Offers Lake Monona Development Plan for Public Buildings," *CT*, 2 November 1938; and *Dane County Board of Supervisors Proceedings*, November Session, 2 November 1938, 10 A.M., 122–23.

86. While denying that he was paid by Harloff to appear before the board, Wright later acknowledged to board member Grove that it was at Harloff's suggestion that he went: "I was asked by Paul Harloff to go [to the meeting]—but I went on my own." Wright to Grove, 14 November 1938.

87. *Dane County Board of Supervisors Proceedings*, November Session, 2 November 1938, 3 P.M., 123–24. In response to the fifteen-minute time limit, Wright reportedly shot back, " 'Don't you think you're extravagant[?]' " J. Paul O'Brien, "Wright Attack Big Factor in Defeat of City-County Project," *CT*, 3 November 1938. Fred J. Curran, "City Officials Seek Revival Test Tonight," *WSJ*, 3 November 1938, described Wright as a "visionary … 'away ahead of his time,' " who "stood out like a red [communist] at a church meeting, as he told the county board members about living buildings, about beauty in buildings, about building for the future."

88. O'Brien, "Wright Attack Big Factor."

89. "Frank Lloyd Wright Offers Lake Monona Development Plan."

90. The two perspectives and the section were published the same day as the meeting in "PWA Allots $186,000 for Dual Building" and "Frank Lloyd Wright Offers Lake Monona Development Plan." Both articles also printed large excerpts from Wright's explanatory text, "OLIN TERRACES."

91. Curran, "City Officials Seek Revival Test Tonight."

92. Ibid.

93. Fred J. Curran, "Dual Building Killed, 42–40," *WSJ*, 4 November 1938.

94. O'Brien, "Wright Attack Big Factor"; and Curran,

"City Officials Seek Revival Test Tonight."

95. J. Paul O'Brien, "Death Blow Given to City-County Offices as Supervisors Fight," *CT*, 4 November 1938; and O'Brien, "Wright Attack Big Factor." See also *Proceedings of the Dane County Board of Supervisors*, November Session, 3 November 1938, 7:30 P.M., 134–38.

96. See, e.g., the front-page editorial, "Are They Going to Kiss $1,000,000 Goodbye?" *CT*, 25 November 1938.

97. *Proceedings of the Dane County Board of Supervisors*, November Session, 17 November 1938, 7 P.M., 165–69; and 25 November 1938, 2 P.M. and 7:30 P.M., 180–94. See also J. Paul O'Brien, "Board Votes Dual Building and the Monona Ave. Site Is O.K.'d," *CT*, 26 November 1938; and Fred J. Curran, "Dual Building Wins by 44–34 Vote," *WSJ*, 26 November 1938.

98. "PWA Acts to Cancel $939,600 Grant for Dual City-County Building Here," *CT*, 14 November 1938; and "PWA Funds for Dual Building Are Cancelled," *CT*, 5 December 1938.

99. This story is told in illuminating detail in Mollenhoff and Hamilton, 192–253.

100. This began the day after the city was informed that the PWA funding had been rescinded and the immediate prospects for the dual city-county building thus put on indefinite hold. In a lecture to an audience of more than three hundred that was broadcast over the local radio, Wright called upon Madisonians to "organize a citizens' committee and press politicians of the city and of Dane county for creation of a city-county civic center on Lake Monona at the foot of Monona ave." in accord with his plans. "Wright Urges Citizens to Push Civic Center Plan," *CT*, 5 December 1938.

101. Hamilton, "Olin Terraces," 198, describes it as a "megastructure," as do Mollenhoff and Hamilton, passim. Reyner Banham, *Megastructure: Urban Futures of the Recent Past* (New York: Harper & Row, Icon Editions, 1972), 7–8, cites Le Corbusier's 1931–32 Obus Plan for Algiers (figure 7.31) as the "most general ancestor" of modern megastructures and makes no mention of the Wright civic center project despite the fact that it perfectly fulfills the definition he gives of the concept.

102. Wright, "OLIN TERRACES," 1, 3, MS 2401.226 E. Expanding on this theme for a later version of the scheme, Wright wrote that "this immediate waterfront has been virtually cut off from this most important area by railroad tracks along the lake's edge." "The purpose of the Monona Terrace scheme is to recover the waterfront for urban use and make it as a part of the central avenue tributary to the capitol square and the Capitol itself." Frank Lloyd Wright, "The Monona Terrace Project," 6 August 1958, 1–2, MS 2401.395 A, FLWFA.

103. Mollenhoff and Hamilton, 94.

104. The two numbers given by the Wright Foundation Archives for the section and the plan, FLWFA 3909.024 and 3909.023, are misleading in that they imply there are two different sheets of paper rather than the recto and verso of the same sheet.

105. While Mollenhoff and Hamilton, 94, perceptively remark that the site plan sketch "shows how the concept was evolving in Wright's mind," the authors reproduce the drawing upside down, thereby denying much of what it was intended to show. The earlier Hamilton, "Olin Terraces," 197, reproduces it correctly.

106. Wright, "OLIN TERRACES," 1, MS 2401.226 E; and Frank Lloyd Wright, "MONONA TERRACES: CIVIC GARDENS CONSTRUCTED ABOVE THE LAKE, FACTS CONCERNING THE MONONA PROJECT," 28 May 1941, 1, MS 2401.248 A, FLWFA. In the 1938 text Wright described the project more simply as a

becoming foil for the capital [*sic*] building" (3).

107. Wright, "OLIN TERRACES," 1, MS 2401.226 E. Wright's explanatory text refers only to a drive extending to Olin Park on the south side of the lake. Nolen's plan, however, had called for the drive to encircle the lake, which is probably also what Wright had in mind.

108. In 1941 he reduced the estimated number of spaces to thirty-five hundred. Wright, "MONONA TERRACES," 3, MS 2401.248 A.

109. Wright used a similar water dome as the major feature of his campus plan for Florida Southern College in 1938, where it is contained by a theater-like arrangement of curved steps. It is not known if the Madison domes were to have had aluminum frames and Pyrex glass tubes as in the Johnson Wax building then in construction.

110. The redrawn section was published in "Frank Lloyd Wright's Revised Monona Ave. Development," *CT*, 4 June 1941; and "Wright Submits His Dream Plan for Auditorium," *WSJ*, 4 June 1941.

111. The seating capacity of the auditorium is given in Wright, "OLIN TERRACES," 1, MS 2401.226 E. Mollenhoff and Hamilton, 242, 245, state, without explanation, that the auditorium in the 1938 project was to have seated seventy-five hundred people. Based on this figure, they criticize the design, writing that it "would have been about three times bigger than the finest theaters in the world and would have produced complaints about unsatisfactory sight lines, extreme distances to the stage, and the lack of a stage house for dramatic and musical productions."

Wright was aware of the potential of noise from the trains below and claimed to have overcome the problem in his design. In 1938 he wrote that the "noise of trains cannot be heard on terraces." Wright, "OLIN TERRACES," 2, MS 2401.226 E. Three years later, he was less categorical, stating that "the noise of passing trains could not be easily heard on the various terraces" but "would not be heard at all within the sealed and insulated auditorium." Wright, "MONONA TERRACES," 3, MS 2401.248 A.

112. The shell, which is mentioned in Wright's explanatory text and is shown on the plans, is not, however, very perceptible in the perspective. It was probably simply a semicircular stage on the ground using the curved wall of the offices behind as the enclosing element.

113. Wright, "MONONA TERRACES," 2–3, MS 2401.248 A. In the 1938 text he was more succinct, writing only that "civic gardens with music shell, refectories, and tables are on same level as balcony foyer of auditorium area so they may be used in connection with auditorium events." Wright, "OLIN TERRACES," 2, MS 2401.226 E.

114. Mollenhoff and Hamilton, 242–45, offer a list of the "limitations" of Wright's various designs for the site.

115. The term "artificial sites" was given currency by Le Corbusier in *The Radiant City: Elements of a Doctrine of Urbanism to Be Used as the Basis for Our Machine Age Civilization*, trans. Pamela Knight, Eleanor Levieux, and Derek Coltman (1935; New York: Orion Press, 1967), 55–59.

116. Wright, "MONONA TERRACES," 1, MS 2401.248 A.

117. Hamilton, "Olin Terraces," 197, points out Wright's debt to the existing classical context, as do Mollenhoff and Hamilton, 98, 255. Mention should also be made of Wright's retention of Bartholomew's idea for an underground union station at the end of Monona Avenue.

118. Wright, "MONONA TERRACES," 1, MS 2401.248 A; and Wright, "OLIN TERRACES," 3, MS 2401.226 E. In a later description, Wright wrote that the design brings into being "a great syndrome consisting of the Capitol Square, the

Capitol itself, the central avenue from Dome to Terrace, the great balcony parking area over the lake below, and then the lake itself intensified in beauty by the architectural foreground." Frank Lloyd Wright, "THE GREATER MADISON MONONA TERRACE PROJECT, FRANK LLOYD WRIGHT, ARCHITECT," 21 August 1955, 8, MS 2401.349 B, FLWFA.

119. Hamilton, "Olin Terraces," 197, makes many of these same points.

120. The release of the report was detailed in "Monona Ave. Civic Center Proposed for Madison by Segoe, City Plan Expert," *CT*, 30 July 1939.

121. Kaeser's allocation of the block opposite the Federal Building to a new city hall (actually a city-county building) reflected Segoe's clients' hopes that the municipal building would eventually be built on the mall.

122. This amphitheater was in addition to a proposed auditorium-recreation center to be located on the Mendota lakefront. It thus represented an attempt to mimic the Wright plan and, at the same time, satisfy the continuing desire of Jackson and Law to have the auditorium complex distinct from the civic center.

123. Segoe, who attended the 2 November Dane County Board of Supervisors meeting, had, unlike his employee Kaeser, no interest in or appreciation of Wright's work. When asked in May 1939 what he thought of Wright's Olin Terraces project, "Segoe replied that he considered the Monona shore 'much too good for a glorified garage,' and that architecture is a failure 'if it cannot do better than bury itself in the ground.'" Herbert Jacobs, "Reveal 20-Year Plan for Greater Madison—'And How to Pay for It All,'" *CT*, 10 May 1939. In a somewhat less nasty tone, Segoe told a reporter for the same newspaper a month and a half later that "the Wright plan of bringing the railroad stations close to the central section of the city would merely increase congestion." Moreover, "since the height from the shore at the foot of Monona ave. is about 45 feet, only a three-story structure could be erected without blocking the view.... This would prevent any adequate development of an auditorium or recreation center in addition to the parking space Wright included in his plan." "Monona Ave. Civic Center Proposed for Madison by Segoe."

124. Wright, "MONONA TERRACES," 1–3, MS 2401.248 A.

125. Frank Lloyd Wright, "The Monona Terrace Project," 18 August 1953, 4, MS 2401.336 B, FLWFA.

126. Wright, "MONONA TERRACES," 4, MS 2401.248 A.

127. Mollenhoff and Hamilton, 29. The filled land was turned into a 630-car parking lot in the mid-1950s.

128. Ibid., 120, states that in 1953 it was reported that the downtown had suffered an 8 percent drop in retail sales. A study, "An Overall Parking Plan for Madison, Wisconsin," was released in June 1956. The city's first suburban shopping center, Madison East, opened in 1953.

129. Segoe, *Comprehensive Plan of Madison*, vol. 2, bk. 12, 12–31. The number of automobile registrations in the entire city as of 1937 was 17,270. Segoe calculated that 32,789 cars and trucks entered the city in a typical twelve-hour day in 1939. Although he felt that there was "no shortage of parking facilities in or near the Central Business District during any time of an average business day," he recommended the construction of new off-street parking and said that "of all the possibilities investigated, ... [the] area on the Monona Lake Front is by far the most desirable and most easily obtainable." "By filling in the lake," he wrote, "a parking area capable of accommodating some 650 cars could be created here without detriment to the appearance or ultimate use of this, the principal lake front of Madison" (85, 84).

130. Wright, "MONONA TERRACES," 4, 1, MS 2401.248 A.

131. Ibid., 4.

132. See chapter 9 and J[aqueline] Tyrwhitt, J[osé] L[uis] Sert, and E[rnesto] N. Rogers, *The Heart of the City: Towards the Humanisation of Urban Life*, CIAM 8 (New York: Pellegrini and Cudahy, 1952).

Eight: Crystal City: A Highrise, Mixed-use, Superblock Development for Washington, D.C., 1940

1. Sigfried Giedion, *Space, Time and Architecture: The Growth of a New Tradition*, 4th ed., enl. (1941; Cambridge, Mass.: Harvard University Press, 1962), 760–64. This is even more surprising since Giedion must have passed through Madison on his way to and from Taliesin when the project was very much in the public notice. The first visit to Wisconsin took place in January 1939, the one to Taliesin later that summer. [Sigfried] Giedion to Frank Lloyd Wright, 23 September 1938; Giedion to Wright, 17 June 1939; and Eugene Masselink to Giedion, 27 June 1939, FLWFA.

2. Giedion, *Space, Time and Architecture*, 744.

3. Ibid., 756, 751, 754. Skepticism of Giedion's civic center argument and stress on the commercial and corporate are found in William H. Jordy, *American Buildings and Their Architects*, vol. 4, *The Impact of European Modernism in the Mid-Twentieth Century* (Garden City, N.Y.: Anchor Books, 1972), 1–85; Tafuri, "Disenchanted Mountain," 461–87; Carol Herselle Krinsky, *Rockefeller Center* (Oxford: Oxford University Press, 1978); and Robert A. M. Stern, Gregory Gilmartin, and Thomas Mellins, *New York 1930: Architecture and Urbanism between the Wars* (New York: Rizzoli International, 1987), 616–71.

4. Giedion, *Space, Time and Architecture*, 757, 756, 747.

5. Ibid., 752–54.

6. Wright used the phrase "city within the city" to describe the complex in "Radio City," 21 June 1931, MS 2401.096, FLWFA. This was published, with the section referring to the "city within the city" excised, as Wright, "Architect Calls Radio City False," *New York Evening Post*, 30 June 1931. The full text, erroneously dated 1932 and without mention of the editorial changes made by the newspaper, is reprinted in *FLWCW* 3:61.

The phrase "city within the city" or "city within a city" goes back at least to 1913, when it was used to characterize the Grand Central Station complex in New York (see chapter 5 and figure 5.44). An advertisement in the Real Estate section of the *Daily News*, 15 February 1913, called the terminal "a wonderful city, within a city, built for the comfort and convenience of the traveling public." "This vast improvement," it continued, "is more than a great railway Terminal—it is a Terminal City, complete in itself. . . . It will embrace convention, amusement and exhibition halls, hotels, clubs and restaurants; post office, express offices, modern apartment and office buildings, and numerous stores and specialty shops." As the development neared completion in the 1920s, an editorial in the *NYT* reminded its readers of the history of the site and of how "this section [of midtown Manhattan] has well been called a 'city within a city.'" "A City within a City," *NYT*, 28 September 1924, sec. 2. The year after Grand Central opened, New York's mayor described the "mammoth" Equitable Building (Graham, Anderson, Probst, and White, 1912–15) as a "'city within a city.'" "New Equitable Office Building May Be Last of Huge Skyscrapers," *NYT*, 3 May 1914. In the following years, the phrase was applied to a number of large, self-contained complexes, even to the Federal Triangle in Washington, D.C. (1927–32; figure 8.15), which, as an "autonomous architectural unit" comparable to "Radio City in New York," was called a "classic city within a city." Eunice Fuller Barnard, "New Washington Rises," *NYT*, 6 September 1931. By the late 1930s Radio City/Rockefeller Center was certainly the example most commonly cited and the standard by which the concept was judged. I thank Danny Abramson for pointing me to Grand Central and the Equitable Building as early instances of the use of the phrase.

The original name for the Rockefeller development was Metropolitan Square, reflecting the fact that the Metropolitan Opera House was to be the prime tenant. When that fell through and the Radio Corporation of America took the opera's place, the development came to be known as Radio City. The name officially changed from Metropolitan Square to Rockefeller Center in late December 1931.

7. *WDN*, 9 August 1940. The story, "$12,000,000 'Radio City' Area Planned for D.C.," was printed on the following page.

8. "The Month in Building," *AF* 73 (October 1940): 2; and "Art: Wright Goes to Washington with a $15,000,000 Surprise," *Newsweek* 16 (18 November 1940): 48.

9. James M. Goode, *Best Addresses: A Century of Washington's Distinguished Apartment Houses* (Washington, D.C.: Smithsonian Press, 1988), 363.

10. Hitchcock, *Nature of Materials*, 101, caption figure 411.

11. It is quite likely that the later development took its name from the Wright project since its promoter, Morris Cafritz, had planned an office building for the Wright Crystal City site in 1952.

12. "$12,000,000 'Radio City' Area Planned for D.C.," *WDN*, 9 August 1940; "Dean Estate Developed," *WDN*, 9 August 1940; "Large Development on Temple Heights Forecast by Option," *ES*, 9 August 1940; "Syndicate Buys Dean Estate," *TH*, 10 August 1940; "$12,000,000 Project to Rise on Florida Ave.," *WP*, 10 August 1940; and "Work for Planners," editorial, *WP*, 11 August 1940.

13. "$12,000,000 'Radio City' Area Planned." In contrast to the *WDN*, which placed the Dean Tract in the downtown district, the *ES*, in "Large Development on Temple Heights," referred to the site as "close to the center of the downtown area," while the *WP*, in "$12,000,000 Project to Rise," described it as "near the downtown area." Zoning Commission of the District of Columbia (recorded by S. G. Lindholm), *Experiences with Zoning in Washington, D.C., 1920–1934* (Washington, D.C.: Zoning Commission, 1935), 15, gives the following definition of downtown Washington: "Down town is the common name for the section of Washington between North Capitol Street and Rock Creek, and between Constitution and Florida Avenues." With its southern boundary being Florida Avenue, this places the Dean Tract on the northern border of downtown.

14. "Work for Planners."

15. "$12,000,000 Project to Rise."

16. "$12,000,000 'Radio City' Area Planned." Goode, *Best Addresses*, 361, mistakenly dates the purchase of the option to April 1940. The report in the *ES* on the late September press conference in which Wright's plans were unveiled stated, contrary to the earlier report, that the syndicate "consisted of some 12 groups, most of them from out of town." "Wright Designs 'Crystal City' for Temple Heights," 24 September 1940. "$15,000,000 'Crystal Palace' to Rise on Connecticut," *TH*, 25 September 1940, also said the majority of the "financial backers" were "from out of town."

17. "Wright Designs 'Crystal City' for Temple Heights," *ES*, 24 September 1940.

18. The report was done by Stone's Mercantile Agency and was obtained for Wright from the Second National Bank by Wright's former secretary Karl E. Jensen, at the time senior administrative assistant of the National Youth Administration, Washington, D.C. The report, "Thurman, Roy S.," dated 5 September 1940, was sent by Jensen to Wright on 11 September 1940, FLWFA.

19. The biographical information is based on "Thurman, Roy S."; "Roy Sage Thurman, Business Consultant," obituary, *WP*, 9 August 1993; and recollections of C. Ford Peatross, who interviewed Thurman in the 1980s at the time the latter gave the materials on Crystal City to the Library of Congress. I am grateful to Ford Peatross, Susan Olsen, and Jennifer Beauregard, of Harvard University, for their help in piecing together Thurman's biography.

20. homelibraryfoundation.org, accessed 26 December 2011; and William A. McGarry, "How Not to Run a Business," *Nation's Business* 26 (February 1938): 76–77. The story in *Nation's Business* states that Mittell and Thurman convinced ten others to join them in creating their organization. On its advisory board in 1938 were Albert Einstein, Will Durant, James Truslow Adams, Havelock Ellis, Felix Frankfurter, and Senator Arthur Capper. Mittell, who was in the class of 1923 at Harvard but left a year before graduating, died at the age of thirty-eight in July 1942, shortly after being appointed assistant to Paul V. McNutt on the War Manpower Commission.

21. Peatross learned this from Thurman in his interview in the early 1980s. "Mittell Funeral Will Be Held at 2 P.M. Today," obituary, *WP*, 17 July 1942, stated that "the recently completed Longfellow Building . . . was one of Mr. Mittell's real estate ventures in this city." It did not mention Thurman's name. The building permit was issued on 17 April 1940.

A story about Thurman's later commissioning of the local architect Charles Goodman to design a modern townhouse on Eighteenth Street, "D.C.'s Most Unusual Town House Planned for 18th Street Site," *WP*, 8 June 1947, sec. 5, noted that Thurman was "one of the original developers of the Longfellow Building, . . . the District's most modernistic office building." I owe this reference to Ford Peatross.

22. "Thurman, Roy S." The cover letter from Jensen concluded that Thurman "has evidently not been a very successful operator!" Jensen to Wright, 11 September 1940.

23. According to Peatross, Thurman set his architectural sights much lower after Crystal City, focusing mainly on undistinguished row-house developments. He apparently served in the Canadian Army during World War II and, after the war, advised Japanese companies seeking to do business in the United States in the area of technology. He later became a consultant with the Mount Vernon Foundation and worked for the Galaxy consulting firm. He lived in Washington until 1991, when he moved to Dunedin, Fla.

24. The property was split into two parts and partially rezoned in the later 1940s or 1950s when T Street was cut through between Florida and Connecticut Avenues. The larger, upper portion became the site of the Washington Hilton Hotel in the 1960s; the lower part, rezoned as commercial, became office buildings.

25. The story was often repeated in news articles related to Wright's Crystal City project. See, e.g., "Large Development on Temple Heights"; Eugene Warner, "Wright's Blistering Tongue Is a Terrible Weapon," *TH*, 18 January 1941; John Clagett Proctor, "Old Temple Heights and the 'Widow's Mite,'" *Washington Sunday Star*, 21

January 1945, sec. C; and "Property Sale Revives Legend of Temple Heights Treaty Oak," *Washington and Vicinity*, 31 January 1945.

26. Wright labeled one of the early section drawings "Temple Heights" rather than "Crystal Heights" (figure 8.20). "Crystal Heights," however, appears in a handwritten note to the right of the main building mass.

27. The Marshall and Pierson commission is mentioned in Goode, *Best Addresses*, 77; the Wood project was pointed out to me by Ford Peatross. A perspective sketch by the latter, now in the Prints and Photographs Division, LC, shows a multicourt composition, based on Italian villa design, mounting up the hill slope to a towered central building.

28. I thank Sue Kohler, formerly of the CFA, and William Creech, of the NARA, for providing me with copies of the relevant documentation.

29. Corbett was named to the advisory board of architects for the New York project in February 1929 and took part in the so-called board symposium in May. His design, called an "Arts Center," was the one favored by the jury (figure 8.10). Corbett's firm was appointed consulting architects of Rockefeller Center in October of that year and made one of the three associated architects in February 1930. The United Masonic Temple project in figures 8.8–9 was submitted to the CFA for approval on 22 May 1929.

30. *Act to Regulate the Height of Buildings in the District of Columbia*, approved June 1, 1910, in *Statutes of the United States of America Passed at the Second Session of the Sixty-First Congress* 35, pt. 1, *Public Acts and Resolutions* (Washington, D.C.: Government Printing Office, 1910), chap. 263, 452–55. Special conditions were created for the north side of Pennsylvania Avenue, where 160 feet was allowed, and Union Station Plaza, where the limit was set at 80 feet.

31. *An Act to Regulate the Height, Area and Use of Buildings in the District of Columbia and to Create a Zoning Commission, and for Other Purposes*, approved March 1, 1920, in *The Statutes at Large of the United States of America from May, 1919, to March, 1921* 41, pt. 1, *Public Laws of the United States of America Passed by the Sixty-Sixth Congress, 1919–1921* (Washington, D.C.: Government Printing Office, 1921), chap. 92, 500–502.

32. Zoning Commission of the District of Columbia, *Zoning Regulations*, 30 August 1920 (Washington, D.C.: Government Printing Office, 1920).

33. Zoning Commission of the District of Columbia, *Zoning Regulations, Revised to August 1, 1930* (Washington, D.C.: Government Printing Office, 1930), 11–13. The setback was six inches for each foot over 110 feet.

34. Sue A. Kohler, *The Commission of Fine Arts: A Brief History, 1910–1990* (Washington, D.C.: Commission of Fine Arts, 1991), 1–7. The chairman of the CFA from 1915 to 1937 was Charles Moore. Moore, who had been Senator McMillan's aide and personal secretary, edited Burnham and Bennett's *Plan of Chicago* and wrote the first biographies of Burnham and Charles McKim.

35. Quoted in Frederick Gutheim and Antoinette J. Lee, *Worthy of the Nation: Washington, DC, from L'Enfant to the National Capital Planning Commission*, 2nd ed. (Baltimore: Johns Hopkins University Press, 2006), 170. The NCPPC grew out of the National Capital Park Commission that was created in 1924 on the recommendation of the Committee of 100 on the Federal City. It was chaired by Delano from 1923 through 1944. For a succinct statement of his view of the role and purpose of the successor commission, see Frederic A. Delano, "The Service

of the National Capital Park and Planning Commission," in *American Civic Annual*, vol. 5, ed. Harlean James (Washington, D.C.: American Civic Association, 1934), 63–65.

Delano started his career in Chicago, where he was general manager of the Chicago, Burlington, and Quincy Railroad from 1901 through 1905 and later president of the Wheeling and Lake Erie Railroad and the Wabash-Pitt Terminal Company. In 1904, he authored *Chicago Railway Terminals: A Suggested Solution for the Chicago Terminal Problem*, published in 1906, the same year he and Charles D. Norton, both members of the Merchants Club, convinced Burnham to undertake the project that would eventuate in the 1909 *Plan of Chicago*. While living and working in Washington in the 1920s and early 1930s, Delano also served as chair of the New York Regional Planning Committee. In 1933 he was appointed by President Roosevelt to chair the National Resources Board.

36. The block to the south of it, on the other side of Florida Avenue, was, however, zoned for commercial use.

37. Richard Longstreth, "The Neighborhood Shopping Center in Washington, D.C., 1930–1941," *JSAH* 51 (March 1992), 16, stresses the importance of this in Washington's unique pattern of urban development and, especially, its early adoption of the drive-in shopping center.

38. *To Amend an Act Regulating the Height of Buildings in the District of Columbia, Approved June 1, 1910*, 71st Cong., 1st sess., S. 686, 29 April 1929. A similar bill, H.R. 10528, was introduced in the House of Representatives on 5 March 1930 by Rep. Frederick H. Zihlman, chair of the House Committee on the District of Columbia and a member of the NCPPC.

39. Committee on the District of Columbia, *Amendment of District of Columbia Zoning Law to Permit Erection of United Masonic Temple*, 71st Cong., 2nd sess., 1930, S. Rept. 249 [to accompany S. 686], 1, submitted by Sen. [Arthur] Capper, 6 March 1930.

40. Herbert Hoover to Col[onel] U[lysses] S. Grant [III], 29 April 1930, folder 500-50 Dean Tract (Squares 2534–2535), box 500-50, Anacostia Park, Benning Heights, Benning Park, Dean Tract, Deanwood Playground, Land Acquisition Case Files, 1924–1961, Land Acquisition Records, Record Group (hereafter RG) 328, Records of the National Capital Planning Commission (hereafter RNCPC), NARA. Grant, who was the grandson of the eighteenth president, was vice chair of the NCPPC and director of Public Buildings and Public Parks of Washington, D.C. My thanks go to Caroline Spurry for correcting the NARA reference information, for this and subsequent notes, since it was changed for national security reasons following 9/11, after I completed my research.

41. Handwritten note by Delano attached to ibid. Delano consistently opposed the construction of tall buildings in the District and even came out against the amendment of 1927 permitting an increase in height from 110 to 130 feet for buildings in commercial districts. "This being the Nation's Capital," he wrote two years prior to the United Masonic Temple decision, "why shouldn't we err on the side of keeping the height of buildings down at least to the width of the street … ? I would go farther and establish a height not to go higher than eighty or eighty-five feet, which is the standard of European capitals." Frederic A. Delano, "The Nation's Interest in the Nation's Capital," in *Planning Problems of Town, City, and Region: Papers and Discussions at the Nineteenth National Conference on City Planning, Held at Washington, D.C., May 9 to 11, 1927* (Philadelphia: Wm. F. Fell, 1927), 221.

42. Handwritten note by Delano attached to Hoover to Grant, 29 April 1930. M[ilton] B. M[edary], J[r.], "Draft of Reply to the Board of Directors of the United Masonic Temple" [ca. 7 June 1929], noted that the NCPPC, in its initial review of the project, felt "it unfortunate that the elevated temple should so closely approximate, in design, proportions and dimensions, the Lincoln Memorial. While the whole design is a very distinguished conception, we believe that, when seen from a distance, the elevated temple would appear to the average visitor as a duplication of the Lincoln Memorial, and would be confusing to those who were familiar with this monument and its location only by photographs." Folder 500-50, Dean Tract (Squares 2534–2535), RG 328, NARA.

43. Handwritten note by Delano attached to the letter Hoover wrote to Grant III on 29 April 1930. It is not evident when the apartment buildings were added to the project. Clearly they were not seen by Capper when he framed his bill in April 1929. It is most likely that the additions were made between June and October of that year, for both the CFA and the NCPPC came out against the idea in November. It was also mooted, whether true or not, that the buildings were only temporary financial expedients that would be built of brick rather than stone and would be removed at some point in the future. In any event, once having been apprised of the fact that the Masons were intending to build more than just the temple, Rep. Louis C. Cramton, chair of the House Interior Department Committee and a member of the House Committee on Appropriations, introduced a bill in Congress to repeal the amendment passed the previous March.

44. The NCPPC officially requested the Commissioners of the District of Columbia on 7 June 1930 "to defer the issuance of any permit for building to be erected on this [Dean] tract until the design of the proposed building and the layout of the grounds shall have been submitted to and approved by the Fine Arts Commission and this Commission." Grant III to Commissioners of the District of Columbia, 7 June 1930, folder 500-50, Dean Tract (Squares 2534–2535), RG 328, NARA.

45. Harvey Wiley Corbett to Delano, 3 November 1930, folder 500-50, Dean Tract (Squares 2534–2535), RG 328, NARA.

46. The CFA gave its approval to the same truncated version of the project on 12 February 1931.

47. The reopening of the apartment house issue was mentioned as a possible option in a letter of 7 November 1931 from Grant III to Walter H. Newton, secretary to President Hoover, folder 500-50, Dean Tract (Squares 2534–2535), RG 328, NARA.

48. For a contemporaneous discussion of the major parking problem Washington faced and ideas for its solution, see Miller McClintock, Erskine Bureau, and Staff of the NCPPC, *A Report on the Parking and Garage Problem of the Central Business District of Washington, D.C.* (Washington, D.C.: Automobile Parking Committee of Washington, 1930).

49. "Wright's Lance Hurled at D.C.," *ES*, 26 October 1938. The Jefferson Memorial was also controversial due to the changes made to Pope's design, after he died, by Eggers and Higgins, his successor firm.

50. Joseph Hudnut, "Last of the Romans," *Magazine of Art* 34 (April 1941): 169, 173, 172.

51. The story is recounted in James D. Kornwolf, ed., *Modernism in America, 1937–1941. A Catalog and Exhibition of Four Architectural Competitions: Wheaton College, Goucher College, College of William and Mary,*

Smithsonian Institution (Williamsburg, Va.: Joseph and Margaret Muscarelle Museum of Art, College of William and Mary, 1985), 176–95.

52. In his criticism of skyscrapers and the 1927 amendment of the zoning regulations allowing for an increase from 110 to 130 feet for buildings in commercial areas, Delano often referred to European cities as the model. See, e.g., note 41 above.

53. Delano himself embodied this very contradiction. While noting that "the history of many American cities has shown that the widening of streets and the building of subways or elevated routes to reach the center has been costly but has proved to be only a palliative," he went on to say, "I am convinced that the City of Washington would be better off if we did not allow excessive heights in the downtown region, and allowed the business of the city to be spread out more evenly." Frederic A. Delano, "Statement before the Zoning Commission, December 4, 1940," 2–3, box 7, folder 4, Zoning Series 2, subseries 1: Nolen File NCPPC, MS 2193, John Nolen Jr. Papers, 1921–1986, Special Collections Research Center, George Washington University, Washington, D.C. I thank Amber Wiley for providing me with this and other documents from this collection.

54. Roy S. Thurman, "Crystal City, Washington, D.C.," n.p., secs. F and N, MS ADE-UNIT 2451 (Misc. supp.), Prints and Photographs Division, LC.

55. The LC has only a photocopy of the leather-covered ring binder that contains two aerial photographs of the site (figures 8.5–6), a topographical survey (figure 8.19), six drawings by Wright (figures 8.24–28 and a plan of a double-unit tower), and fourteen pages of text. The text pages are not numbered but are arranged in sections assigned the letters C, E–G, and N–P. The other letters are assigned to the illustrations. The brochure must date from around early January 1941 since the text refers to 1940 census figures and the project was canceled by early February 1941.

56. Thurman, "Crystal City," sec. F. One reason often given for this, though not by Thurman, was the growth in the federal bureaucracy under the New Deal. Thurman noted that the population in the District increased from 331,069 in 1910 to 437,571 in 1920 and 485,716 in 1930, before jumping to 663,152 by 1940. In addition, between 1930 and 1940, the population of Fairfax County doubled, that of Arlington more than doubled (from 20,000 to 56,500), while Montgomery County saw an increase from 50,000 in 1930 to 81,444 a decade later.

57. Ibid.

58. Ibid.

59. Ibid. The Shoreham, later taken over by Omni, was built in 1929–31 by Joseph Abel, an architect known for his large apartment houses in the northern Connecticut Avenue neighborhood. It was a combined transient hotel and apartment-hotel, the same model Thurman was to follow in the Crystal City project.

60. Ibid., secs. C, P, and O.

61. Ibid., sec. N.

62. Ibid.

63. Ibid.

64. Ibid., sec. E.

65. Ibid. It was in February, it should be recalled, that Thurman left his position with the National Home Library. One wonders if one of the professionals Thurman spoke with was the architect William Lescaze. Thurman, ibid., sec. N, mentioned his Longfellow Building as "the only new construction on Connecticut Avenue [that] … is now taking place," noting that it is "on a comparatively

small plot and will offer only several new shops." Thurman must certainly have spoken with his cousin, Mittell, who was also involved in real estate affairs.

66. Ibid., sec. G.

67. Ibid.

68. "$12,000,000 Project to Rise"; and "Syndicate Buys Dean Estate."

69. "Dean Estate Developed" and "Large Development on Temple Heights." It is interesting that the term "apartment-hotel" does not appear, even though the type had become rather common in large cities in the United States beginning in the late 1910s.

70. Longstreth, "Neighborhood Shopping Center," 11–17.

71. Thurman to Wright, 8 August 1940, FLWFA. I am indebted to Margo Stipe for bringing this to my attention. The article in the *WDN* that appeared on the evening of the announcement stated that "services of a nationally famous architect are being sought to supervise construction." The following January, however, Warner, "Wright's Blistering Tongue," claimed that well before the August press conference, "the purchasers had Frank Lloyd Wright in mind as their architect and indeed had consulted with him some two months prior to concluding their deal for the land." Warner went on to say that, at that time, "Mr. Wright had looked over the site and … had begun to form a vision." Warner's assumption is probably based on the testimony that Thurman's lawyer James C. Wilkes presented in the Zoning Commission's public hearing of 26 December 1940. Wilkes began by saying that "several months ago the Masonic Order entered into a contract with Roy Thurman and associates for the sale of this land [Dean Tract]," at which point "Mr. Thurman contacted … Mr. Wright, and got Mr. Wright to come to the city and go over the land and make [a] topographical study of the property, [and] study of the surroundings." As for the date of this supposed visit, Wilkes said, "When Mr. Wright made a study of this project …[he] suggested to Mr. Thurman that in June [*sic*: in June that] the floor plans for his Manhattan development [St. Mark's Towers] would be typical of the development he proposes." Minutes of Public Hearing, Zoning Commission of the District of Columbia, 26 December 1940, 2–3, Public Hearings and Orders, 1939–1940, Zoning Commission Record, District of Columbia Office of Zoning, Washington D.C. Not only is the June date impossible; Wright's Washington visit did not take place until after the project was designed. To compound the problem of when the project was initiated, a number of Wright's drawings are signed and dated "Dec. '39." The handwriting is his, but the reasons for his antedating the designs are baffling.

72. Thurman to Wright, Monday [12 August 1940], FLWFA. The letter is handwritten on Chicago's Drake Hotel stationary.

73. Thurman very possibly brought to Taliesin the previous weekend the topographical survey of the site done by Corbett, Harrison and MacMurray in February 1930 (figure 8.19).

74. According to Margo Stipe, the "Group Idea" note is located in the correspondence file just before Thurman's letter of 12 August, yet she feels "it doesn't really seem to belong there." In the Wright Foundation Archives photocopy file, it is with the memorandum Thurman sent to Wright on 16 August but, as she notes, "doesn't seem to belong there either." Bruce Pfeiffer could not identify the handwriting on the note, saying it is neither Wright's nor Eugene Masselink's, nor William Wesley Peters's, nor John Howe's. Stipe did not think it looked like Thurman's

either. She also said that "it seems an odd piece to mail—or maybe it did not get mailed?" Margo Stipe to the author, 5 January 2005.

75. Thurman to Wright, 16 August 1940, FLWFA.

76. He noted that "the 10% fee" he was to get "is substantially less than the sum paid for complete services in usual circumstances." Significantly, he began by saying that "there would be no use quibbling over terms as all the stake I have in this effort is the character and honor of one Roy S. Thurman.…Let's see what comes of the combination? I dare say it is not perfect but if sincerity is behind our purpose it may, probably will, work out to our mutual satisfaction and a great good." Wright to Thurman, 19 August 1940, FLWFA. It was probably around this time that Wright requested the confidential report on Thurman referred to above and in note 18.

77. Ibid.

78. Eugene Masselink to Thurman, 21 August 1940, FLWFA. There is no record of what Masselink "enclosed" with his note.

79. Wright to Thurman, 27 August 1940, FLWFA.

80. Pfeiffer, *Treasures of Taliesin*, n.p. (opp. figure 24a), claims that Wright did send "preliminary drawings" with the letter.

81. Developed by Fred R. French and designed by H. Douglas Ives, Tudor City was similar in size to Wright's project, with about two thousand apartment units in its seven buildings and 450 rooms in its thirty-two-story apartment hotel. It was aimed at a less upscale market, however. See T-Square, "The Sky Line: Arabian Night—Vistas and an Uptown Oasis," *New Yorker* 3 (21 January 1928): 56–58; "Tudor City: A Residential Center," *Architecture and Building* 61 (July 1929): 202, 219–22, 227; and H. Douglas Ives, "The Moderate Priced Apartment Hotel," *AF* 53 (September 1930): 309–12.

82. In Wright's description, seven stories of the towers were devoted to "medium size rooms" and seven to "large rooms." The St. Mark's Towers were 205 feet high. The overall height of twenty-three stories included nine levels of duplex apartments (eighteen floors) plus the ground floor and the thirty-five-foot-high, four-story, set-back central core. The interfloor height was only eight feet nine inches, which was much less than the typical building of the time. This was the same for Crystal City.

83. Wright to Thurman, 27 August 1940.

84. Ibid. The first underground parking garage was constructed on four levels under Union Square in San Francisco in 1941–43. It was designed by Timothy Pflueger beginning in 1939, and the idea for it went back at least to 1935. Wright would certainly have known it since he always stayed at the St. Francis Hotel, which overlooks the square.

85. Wright to Thurman, 27 August 1940.

86. As noted above, the preliminary section in figure 8.20 is uniquely labeled "Temple Heights."

87. Ibid. Wright remarked that although Thurman "promised it enthusiastically" when they met, he had "neglected" to put it "in the written memo" of 16 August and that it thus "might pass beyond your [Thurman's] control."

88. Thurman to Wright, 29 August 1940, FLWFA. Wright's response is penciled as draft on bottom of sheet.

89. Wright to Thurman, 5 September 1940, FLWFA. Wright dated his "layout" to 26 August in this note.

90. According to ibid., Wright was to have been in Washington on 20 September, no doubt for a Friday press conference to unveil the designs for the project. The press conference actually took place on 24 September,

a Tuesday. In his note of 5 September, Wright told Thurman that Loren Pope, a reporter for the *ES* for whom he was concurrently designing a house in Falls Church, Va., could be counted on for "good publicity."

91. Thurman to Wright, 6 September 1940, FLWFA.

92. Wright to Thurman, 7 September 1940, FLWFA; and Thurman to Wright, 9 September 1940, FLWFA.

93. Ibid.

94. Wright to Thurman, 11 September 1940, FLWFA.

95. Jensen to Wright, 11 September 1940.

96. Thurman to Wright, 18 September 1940, FLWFA. Aside from the originals, he wanted "at least six prints of each." Wright apparently did not send the prints until the end of the first week of October.

97. Ibid.

98. There is nothing to indicate that Wright brought any other than these two drawings with him to Washington at this time or that he had sent any in advance of his trip.

99. The inexplicable fact that a number of the drawings are dated to December 1939 is referred to in note 71 above.

100. The Library of Congress preserves more than seventy Diazo prints and blueprints of the drawings of Crystal City and St. Mark's Towers that were donated by Thurman. Nos. 1–74, ADE-UNIT 2451, LC. A couple have pencil notations by Wright (see, e.g., figure 8.31).

101. They are numbered FLWFA 4016.001–015 and 4016.020. One of the duplicates (FLWFA 4016.010) is an unfinished plan of the hotel mezzanine level. The prospectus Thurman put together has copies of six of these: the two perspectives, the three plans of the entire site, and the double-unit tower floor plan. Thurman, "Crystal City," secs. H–M.

102. It must have been acquired by Thurman and given by him to Wright. A copy of it is in Thurman, "Crystal City," sec. D.

103. As noted above, the fact that six of the drawings (FLWFA 4016.004–005 and 4016.010–014) are dated December 1939 is to be discounted.

104. Both perspectives were published in Una Franklin, "$15,000,000 'Crystal City' Planned for Temple Heights," *TH*, 24 September 1940; and Gerald G. Gross, "Architect Visions $15,000,000 City of Future on Temple Heights," *WP*, 25 September 1940. The aerial perspective alone was published in "$15,000,000 'Crystal City' Proposed on Conn-Av," *WDN*, 24 September 1940; and "Wright Designs 'Crystal City' for Temple Heights," *ES*, 24 September 1940. The Connecticut Avenue perspective alone was published in "Walls of Glass: Nary One Window in 'Crystal City,'" *WDN*, 25 September 1940.

105. Wright to Thurman, 10 October 1940, FLWFA; and Thurman to Wright, 12 October, 1940, FLWFA. Among the blueprints Wright sent to Thurman is a sheet on which the architect pasted the two perspectives and inscribed the following note:

> To Roy Thurman—with a great hope—
> Frank Lloyd Wright. Taliesin Oct 7, 40
> (No. 18, ADE-UNIT 2451, LC)

106. One must question the accuracy of Wilkes's statement to the Zoning Commission (see note 71 above) asserting an earlier visit by Wright, which was repeated in a number of later newspaper reports.

107. In a follow-up letter to the press conference, Thurman told Wright he was sending back the originals and photographic prints of the two drawings, while reminding Wright of the others he had previously requested. Thurman to Wright, 26 September 1940, FLWFA.

108. Franklin, "$15,000,000 'Crystal City'"; "Wright Designs 'Crystal City' for Temple Heights"; and Gross, "Architect Visions $15,000,000 City of Future." See also "$15,000,000 'Crystal City' Proposed on Conn-Av"; "Walls of Glass"; and "$15,000,000 'Crystal Palace.'"

109. Gross, "Architect Visions $15,000,000 City of Future." "$15,000,000 'Crystal Palace' to Rise" says that "the famed architect explained that the 21 buildings, all united, will be of different heights, the tallest rising 135 feet into the air."

110. "Wright Designs 'Crystal City'" says there are "some 2,500 rooms"; but Gross, "Architect Visions $15,000,000 City of Future" more accurately quotes Wright saying "'there will be some 2,500 dwelling units divided among the hotel and the apartment building.'"

111. "Wright Designs 'Crystal City.'"

112. The elevations in figures 8.29–30 show the heights quite clearly, although Wright did not include either the ground floor or the roof setbacks in the calculations marked on the buildings themselves. These are shown on the upper structural core as fourteen and sixteen stories for the lower towers and twenty (or twenty-four) for the tall one.

113. Although Wright sent prints of these drawings to Thurman in early October, they were not included in the developer's prospectus.

114. The present entrance to the Washington Hilton Hotel (where Ronald Reagan was shot) is more or less exactly where Wright's was.

115. Among the freestanding, purpose-built parking structures in Washington that serviced the downtown shopping and hotel area was the ten-story Capital Garage, designed by Arthur B. Heaton and constructed in 1926. Its capacity was thirteen hundred automobiles.

116. "Wright Designs 'Crystal City.'"

117. "$15,000,000 'Crystal Palace.'"

118. Ibid.; and "$15,000,000 'Crystal City' Planned."

119. Wright's statement about the design creating "'21 buildings in one'" is the only hint that he was already thinking of the issue and how it might be argued to the project's advantage.

120. Even late in life, when he was interviewed by Ford Peatross, Thurman claimed that zoning by itself was not the reason for the demise of the project. Rather, it was the time it took to overcome the objections of the authorities that caused his loans to expire. Peatross to author, in conversation, December 2004.

121. "$15,000,000 'Crystal City' Planned."

122. *An Act Providing for the Zoning of the District of Columbia and the Regulation of the Location, Height, Bulk, and Uses of Buildings and Other Structures and of the Uses of Land in the District of Columbia, and for Other Purposes*, approved June 20, 1938, *United States Statutes at Large Containing the Laws and Concurrent Resolutions Enacted during the Third Session of the Seventy-Fifth Congress of the United States of America, 1938* 52, *Public Laws* (Washington, D.C.: Government Printing Office, 1938), chap. 534, 797–802. The composition of the Zoning Commission was not affected by the 1938 act.

123. Ibid., 798.

124. Ibid., 799–800. The institution of the BZA was a response to the report three years earlier to the Zoning Commission on *Experiences with Zoning in Washington, D.C., 1920–1934*, 23, where it was stated that one of the most serious problems facing the commission was that of balancing "piecemeal rezoning," or spot zoning, with "a general rezoning" of an entire area. This presented the Zoning Commission with "the dilemma of either being

a party to speculative deals, or to rezoning all, or at least whole streets, of down town property." The even greater problem with adding a "'spot' on the zoning map" to allow for a nonconforming use was that such a use might change from a desirable to undesirable one over time. A mechanism to allow for "the grant of a specific use" with a "time limit set" could, according to the report, overcome this problem.

125. *Act Providing for the Zoning of the District of Columbia*, 797.

126. Thurman to Board of Commissioners of the District of Columbia, 1 October 1940, FLWFA.

127. The three-member Board of Commissioners of the District of Columbia was at the time composed of Melvin C. Hazen, president, John Russell Young, and McCoach. The five-member Zoning Commission was composed of McCoach, chair, Hazen, Young, David Lynn, and Newton B. Drury (at the time replaced by A. E. Demaray). S. G. Lindblom was the executive officer and secretary of the Zoning Commission.

128. Thurman to David McCoach Jr., 15 October 1940, FLWFA.

129. Wright to Thurman, 10 October 1940.

130. As noted above (note 105), Wright apparently also sent to Thurman at this time prints of the two perspectives (figures 8.29–30) that he had brought to Washington for the September press conference.

131. Wright to Thurman, 10 October 1940.

132. Ibid. The reference to the United Masonic Temple indicates that Thurman had informed his architect that there was no need to heed the zoning regulations to the letter.

133. Ibid. Wright also gave a political interpretation to the project, saying, "we have … planned to build the greatest building of modern times … at a time when the nation is jittery with fear. … This enterprise should do more to restore the nation's confidence in itself and keep it out of war than anything else anyone seems to be thinking of just now."

134. Thurman to McCoach, 15 October 1940. The blueprint is No. 40, MS ADE-UNIT 2451, LC.

135. Thurman to McCoach, 15 October 1940. Thurman added the caveat that, "as presently shown, Mr. Wright's sketches reflect four separate and independent units, this having been done for a special purpose, but should the regulations so require, no problem is involved in making them integral."

136. Extract from Minutes of the 154th Meeting of the NCPPC, Thursday & Friday, October 17–18, 1940, 14, par. 31, NCPPC Minutes, Volume 1940, Transcripts of the Proceedings and Minutes of Meetings, 1926–1976, General Records, RG 328, NARA.

137. Ibid.

138. McCoach to Delano, 29 October 1940, folder Planning, box Zoning: Subdivisions; Building Heights; Sewage; Flood Control; Pollution of Potomac, Office Files of Chairman Frederic A. Delano 1926–42, General Records, RG 328, NARA.

139. Thurman to Wright, 25 October 1940, FLWFA. Thurman may have been referring to Senator Capper, who served on the advisory board of the National Home Library Foundation. In the late 1920s, as a member of both the Committee on the District of Columbia and the NCPPC, he had pushed through Congress the 180-foot height allowance for the United Masonic Temple.

140. Ibid.

141. "Art: Wright Goes to Washington," 48.

142. John Nolen Jr. to Delano, 29 November 1940, Office

Files of Chairman Frederic A. Delano, 1926–1942, RG 328, NARA. Delano noted in hand on the letter the word "Bad" next to the first two paragraphs referring to "Wright's project" and explaining the request by "the promoters of this project to change the zoning from residential 90' height to commercial 110' height." He wrote at the bottom of the sheet: "Nothing higher than 130 ft any where [sic] in the district."

143. Minutes of Public Hearing, Zoning Commission of the District of Columbia, 4 December 1940, 18–19, Public Hearings and Orders, 1939–1940, Zoning Commission Record. The intervention of Wilkes, the lawyer representing Thurman, was highlighted in the coverage of the meeting in "Crystal City Group Fights Zone Plan," *WP*, 5 December 1940; "Decision on 110-Foot Over-All Height of Buildings Deferred," *ES*, 5 December 1940; and "Planning Group Asks Ban on 130-Foot Buildings," *WDN*, 5 December 1940. The NCPPC's case was prepared by Harland Bartholomew. Thurman informed Wright a few days later of Wilkes's success in getting the decision deferred. He also repeated his request to Wright for "a complete descriptive statement of your conception of 'Crystal City' emphasizing among other things the extreme practicality, the sound engineering principles involved and the obvious advantages of the design over the conventional buildings that could be erected within the present law to house some 9,000 families and which would create all kinds of public menaces in the way of congestion, traffic and parking problems, fire hazards and extreme ugliness." Thurman to Wright, 9 December 1940, FLWFA.

144. In a letter to the commission saying he would not be able to attend the meeting on 19–20 December, Delano stated his absolute opposition to "spot zoning," or "map amendments." "For the protection of zoning as an instrument for the welfare of the people of Washington," he wrote, "it is of the utmost importance that the practice of spot zoning be stopped." Delano to NCPPC, 18 December 1940, Appendix C, December 19–20, 1940, Meeting, Minutes of the 156th Meeting of the NCPPC, held on Thursday & Friday, December 19–20, 1940, NCPPC Minutes, Volume 1940, Transcripts of the Proceedings and Minutes of Meetings, 1926–1976, Volume 15 of 24, General Records, RG 328, NARA.

145. Minutes of the 156th Meeting of the NCPPC, 22–23.

146. According to J. Welles Henderson IV, "The Evolution of Washington's Paradigm: A Study of Frank Lloyd Wright's Crystal Heights Project and the Smithsonian Gallery of Art Competition, Washington, D.C., 1939–1941" (B.A. thesis, Harvard University, 2000), 34, Delano remained in close contact with Gilmore D. Clarke, chair of the CFA, who told him, on 15 December, that his group would not support the Wright project. Henderson also states that the following day T. S. Settle, the NCPPC's secretary, wrote to Delano suggesting that the commission push for the Dean Tract to be condemned so as to force the developers to sell and thus terminate the project (32).

147. Wright to Thurman, 19 December 1940, FLWFA. Thurman released this letter to the press in the final throes of his fight for approval of the project. It was published under the headline "A Genius Fights with the D.C. Government to Save His Crystal City," accompanied by Warner, "Wright's Blistering Tongue."

148. Wright to Thurman, 19 December 1940; and "Genius Fights with the D.C. Government."

149. Delano, "Statement before the Zoning Commission, December 4," 2. In their monthly meeting immediately following the defeat of the Crystal City project, the

NCPPC discussed a preliminary draft of an "Outline of General Principles for Providing Off-Street Parking Facilities in the District of Columbia," 20 February 1941, Appendix B; and Harland Bartholomew, "Memorandum on Relation of Building Heights to Automobile Parking in the Central Business District of Washington, D.C.," 29 January 1941, Appendix E, Minutes of the 158th Meeting of the NCPPC, held on Thursday & Friday, February 20–21, 1941, Minutes, Transcripts of the Proceedings and Minutes of Meetings, 1926–1976, Volume 16 of 24, General Records, Volume 1941, RG 328, NARA.

150. Wright to Thurman, 19 December 1940.

151. Minutes of Public Hearing, Zoning Commission, 26 December 1940, 2, 6, 3–4.

152. Ibid., 4, 3, 5

153. Ibid., 13–14.

154. Ibid., 15.

155. "Nolen Offers Plan to 'Save' Crystal City," *WP*, 27 December 1940.

156. "Zone Board Acts to Save Crystal City," *WP*, 3 January 1941. Nolen Jr. presented the draft proposal to the Zoning Commission at its 2 January meeting. Four days later, he wrote to Delano to say that McCoach eliminated from the proposal the advisory role the NCPPC would play in judging the applicability of any particular project for consideration. He also reduced the minimum area for a "community unit" from ten to seven and a half acres. Both these proposed changes were seen as detrimental by Nolen Jr. and Delano (and both were rescinded by McCoach in the final formulation of the amendment). Nolen Jr. to Delano, 6 January 1941, Office Files of Chairman Frederic A. Delano 1926–42, RG 328, NARA.

157. "Public Hearing Is Set on 'Community Unit' Zoning Classification," *ES*, 3 January 1941.

158. Minutes of the 157th Meeting of the NCPPC, held on Thursday & Friday, January 16–17, 1941, 26, NCPPC Minutes, Volume 1941, RG 328, NARA; and Minutes of Public Hearing, Zoning Commission of the District of Columbia, 6 February 1941, 34, Zoning Commission Record, Reports of the Zoning Advisory Council, January 1941 to December 1941, District of Columbia Office of Zoning, Washington, D.C.

159. Hilary Ballon, "Frank Lloyd Wright's Automobile Urbanism," Margaret Floyd Henderson Lecture, Tufts University, 16 October 2001. As noted, Peatross said that Thurman told him in the 1980s that it was not the zoning problems as such that killed the project but rather the resulting time delays that caused him to lose his financing.

160. "Planning Group Scored by Crystal City Head," *WDN*, 9 January 1941. The inflammatory nature of the charge was only exacerbated by the reporter's identification of Delano in the first three words of the article as "President Roosevelt's Uncle." Thurman also leaked the response from McCoach as well as his rejoinder to it. "D.C. Commissioner's Reply," *WDN*, 14 January 1941.

161. "Crystal City Denied Zone Change Plea," *WP*, 15 January 1941.

162. "Crystal City Plan Rejected by Zone Unit," *TH*, 17 January 1941.

163. Warner, "Wright's Blistering Tongue." Although nowhere in his letter did Wright specifically single out the NCPPC or Delano for criticism, Warner, no doubt picking up on Thurman's recent attack, wrote,

> Frank Lloyd Wright has been having fights all his life. …
> Now he is engaged in a fight with the various

masters of Washington's esthetic fate—the National [Capital] Park and Planning Commission, the District Commissioners, the Zoning Commission, and numerous other assorted dignitaries. …

> His most notable opponent is Frederick [sic] A. Delano, uncle of the President, and chairman of the National Capital Park and Planning Commission. Mr. Delano is an architect [sic] strongly devoted to the Graeco-Roman classical ideals, which Wright criticizes with his bitterest scorn.

In the regular monthly meeting of the NCPPC the day before the Wright letter and Warner article appeared, Nolen Jr. made a point of bringing to the "attention" of the commission, immediately following their vote to approve the "community unit" amendment, a newspaper "spread by Frank Lloyd Wright, in which he attacks scathingly the [National Capital Park and] Planning Commission for not permitting the development to go ahead." In addition, he accused the architect of "go[ing] into a city and stil[sic: stirring] up a fight with the city authorities about doing something that is not in accord with existing laws," Minutes of the 157th Meeting of the NCPPC, held on Thursday & Friday, January 16–17, 1941, 175, Minutes, 1941 Meetings 157–160, box 14, RG 328, RNCPC, NARA. In the edited Minutes of the 157th Meeting of the NCPPC, 27, NCPPC Minutes, Volume 1941, the word "scathingly" was left out as was the reference to the architect's "go[ing] into a city. …"

Did Nolen Jr. have an advance copy of the letter and Warner article? If so, he was confusing Warner's words with Wright's. If he did not, could he have been referring to Thurman's letter to McCoach quoted in the *WDN* of 9 January (see note 160 above). In either case, the substitution of Wright for Thurman as the source of a direct attack on the commission and Delano for their role in the Crystal City case is one of the very rare instances where something written into the record by Nolen Jr. or anyone else on the NCPPC allows one to think that an animus against Wright, in particular, and modern architecture, in general, may have played a part in their objections to the project.

164. Thurman to Wright, 18 January 1941, FLWFA. Thurman added that his "only consolation, and it is a great one, is that I have been honored with your affectionate and wholesome relationship." Thurman also noted that he was sending to Wright, under separate cover, the "leather-bound prospectus" referred to earlier. (I have seen no copy of this in the Wright Foundation Archives.) Wright responded to Thurman, telling him to stay on the case and not "give up." Wright to Thurman, 22 January, 1941, FLWFA.

165. Warner, "Wright's Blistering Tongue."

166. "Zoning Plan May Save Crystal City," *WP*, 7 February 1941, reported that Thurman "did send an observer" to the meeting.

167. "Board Defers Crystal City Zoning Action," *WP*, 12 February 1941.

168. "Temple Heights Plans Call for $2,500,000 Building Project," *ES*, 22 January 1945. The project was designed by the local firm of E. Burton Corning and Raymond G. Moore, in association with Pierre Ghent, in early November 1944 and submitted to the NCPPC for approval at the end of the month. It was approved by the commission with some changes in late January 1945. Pierre Ghent to NCPPC, 27 November 1944; and Extract from Minutes of the 202nd Meeting, NCPPC, held on Jan. 25–26, 1945, sec. 10, folder 500-50, Dean Tract (Squares

2534–2535), RG 328, NARA.

169. Giedion, *Space, Time and Architecture*, 744.

170. Wright to Thurman, 19 December 1940, in Wright, "A Genius Fights with the D.C. Government."

171. Cf. Krinsky, *Rockefeller Center*, 96.

172. Wright to Thurman, 10 October and 19 December 1940.

Nine: The Point Park Civic Center and Traffic Interchange for the Heart of Downtown Pittsburgh, 1947

1. Wright's projects have been documented and analyzed in Richard L. Cleary, "Edgar J. Kaufmann, Frank Lloyd Wright and the 'Pittsburgh Point Park Coney Island in Automobile Scale,'" *JSAH* 52 (June 1993), 139–58; Cleary, *Merchant Prince and Master Builder: Edgar J. Kaufmann and Frank Lloyd Wright* (Pittsburgh: Heinz Architectural Center, Carnegie Museum of Art, in association with University of Washington Press, 1999), 54–64, 144–61; and Cleary, "Beyond Fallingwater: Edgar J. Kaufmann, Frank Lloyd Wright and the Projects for Pittsburgh," in *Wright Studies*, vol. 2, *Fallingwater and Pittsburgh*, ed. Narciso G. Menocal (Carbondale: Southern Illinois University Press, 2000), 80–113 (hereafter Cleary [1993], Cleary [1999], and Cleary [2000]). For an earlier account of the site and its development, see Robert C. Alberts, *The Shaping of the Point: Pittsburgh's Renaissance Park* (Pittsburgh: University of Pittsburgh Press, 1980). One of the few critical discussions placing Wright's project in a larger planning context is in Tafuri, "Disenchanted Mountain," 483–93.

2. "Pittsburgh Renascent," *AF* 91 (November 1949): 59.

3. "Pittsburgh's New Powers," *Fortune* 35 (February 1947): 71.

4. The story of Pittsburgh's demise and redevelopment is told in Stefan Lorant, *Pittsburgh: The Story of an American City* (Garden City, N.Y.: Doubleday, 1964), commissioned and partially underwritten by Edgar J. Kaufmann, a leading figure, as shall be seen, in the city's postwar redevelopment. Three later, and more critical, accounts are Roy Lubove, *Twentieth-Century Pittsburgh: Government, Business, and Environmental Change* (New York: John Wiley, 1969); Joel A. Tarr, *Devastation and Renewal: An Environmental History of Pittsburgh and Its Region* (Pittsburgh: University of Pittsburgh Press, 2003); and John F. Bauman and Edward K. Muller, *Before Renaissance: Planning in Pittsburgh, 1889–1943* (Pittsburgh: University of Pittsburgh Press, 2006).

5. Park H. Martin, "Redevelopment of Pittsburgh's Golden Triangle," [3], [1954], published speech, VF NAC 1613g 27 Pit, Loeb Library, Graduate School of Design, Harvard University; Joel Tarr, interview with Park Martin, 17 November 1971, "Pittsburgh Renaissance: Transcriptions of Interviews on the Pittsburgh Renaissance; Part of an Oral History Program Financed by the Buhl Foundation," University of Pittsburgh, Graduate School of Public and International Affairs, 1973, vol. 4, 1325, PDCL; and Interview with John J. Grove, 16 September 1971, "Pittsburgh Renaissance: Transcriptions of Interviews," vol. 3, 784, PDCL. Martin was executive director of the ACCD, the prime mover in the Pittsburgh redevelopment process, from 1945 through 1958; Grove was hired as the public relations officer for the ACCD in 1947 and later became its assistant director and secretary of its PPC.

6. Interview with John Grove, 784.

7. [John W. Oliver], "Report of the Study Committee on the Historical Significance of the Point Park Project," [ACCD], 18 April 1946, 1, box 11, folder 4: PPC Minutes,

1945–1970, Series III: Point State Park, Robert C. Alberts Papers, 1812–1988, MS 37, Library and Archives Division, SJHHC; [Oliver], "Statement of a Basic Policy 're' Historical Significance of Point Park," [ACCD], 16 December 1952, 1, box 156, folder 13: Reports, 1945–53, Series XV: PPC (1937–1981), ACCD Records, 1920–1993, MS 285, SJHHC; and Oliver, "Historical Significance of Point Park, Pittsburgh, Pennsylvania," 18 May 1950, 6, talk given at Demolition Ceremony for Point State Park, box 156, folder 13: Reports, 1945–53, ACCD Records, SJHHC.

8. Alberts, *Shaping of the Point*, 37.

9. Frederick Law Olmsted [Jr.], *Pittsburgh: Main Thoroughfares and the Down Town District. Improvements Necessary to Meet the City's Present and Future Needs. A Report* (Pittsburgh: Pittsburgh Civic Commission, 1911), 1. Olmsted Jr. was commissioned by the Pittsburgh Civic Commission, whose advisory board included Daniel Burnham and Robert W. De Forest of the Russell Sage Foundation, which had underwritten the Pittsburgh Survey a few years before. See Bauman and Muller, *Before Renaissance,* 63–91. An earlier version appeared in their "The Olmsteds in Pittsburgh: (Part II) Shaping the Progressive City," *Pittsburgh History: A Magazine of the City and Its Region* 76 (Winter 1993/1994): 191–205. This was preceded by their study of the Olmsted Brothers' work in the mainly wealthy suburbs, "The Olmsteds in Pittsburgh: (Part I) Landscaping the Private City," *Pittsburgh History* 76 (fall 1993): 122–38.

10. Bauman and Muller, *Before Renaissance*, 76, however, seeks to interpret the Olmsted plan more as an expression of the City Practical than the City Beautiful.

11. Olmsted, *Pittsburgh*, 12, explained that his decision was mainly in response to the location of H. H. Richardson's Allegheny County Courthouse and Jail (1884–88).

12. Ibid., 29.

13. Ibid., 30, 29.

14. Ibid, 29.

15. "Art Commission Has Finished First Year," *PS*, 7 March 1913; and "Art Commission Provides for Obtaining Practical Scheme Quickly," *PD*, 22 October 1913.

16. "Chart of City's Territory at the Point," *PD*, 3 January 1914.

17. See Bauman and Muller, *Before Renaissance*, 102–93.

18. H. D. Sterick, "Proposed Improvements for Pittsburgh's Historic Point," 30 November 1929, box 7, folder 2: General Information, 1934–1974, Series III: Point State Park, Alberts Papers, SJHHC.

19. "U.S. Memorial Park Proposed at 'Point' Here," *PST*, 18 May 1930; and "National Park Proposed at Local 'Point,'" *PPG*, 19 May 1930. Cleary (1993), 143; (1999), 56; and (2000), 84, infer that the Bell project was done in 1935, based on its republication in *PST*, 27 October 1935.

20. "Point Lease for Exposition Hall Vetoed," *PPG*, 24 September 1934; and "Plans to Build Park at Point to Be Studied," *PPG*, 27 September 1934.

21. Bartholomew was no stranger to Pittsburgh. According to Bauman and Muller, *Before Renaissance*, 114–35, he developed a traffic plan and zoning regulations for the Citizens Committee on the City Plan between 1919 and 1923. On Bigger, see Bauman and Muller, "Planning Technician as Urban Visionary: Frederick Bigger and American Planning, 1881–1963," *JPH* 1 (May 2002): 124–53. Janssen and Cocken designed the Kaufmann House in Fox Hill, called "La Tourelle," 1924–25, and the interior renovations of Kaufmann's downtown Pittsburgh

Department Store, 1927–30.

22. *Progress Report of the Jefferson National Expansion Memorial* (St. Louis: Jefferson National Expansion Memorial Association, May 1940); Daniel Cox Fahey Jr., "Jefferson National Expansion Memorial: A Mississippi Waterfront Development in St. Louis," *Landscape Architecture* 31 (October 1940): 4–8. St. Louis began the process for creating a United States Territorial Expansion Memorial in the summer of 1933.

23. Historical Society of Western Pennsylvania, "Resolution," 27 April 1937, box 157, folder 2: Resolutions, Acts & Agreements, 1937–52, Series 15: PPC (1937–1981), ACCD Records, SJHHC. The Citizens Committee on the City Plan had apparently put forward the idea for a park at the Point centered around the Blockhouse in early 1935, but it was opposed by the City Planning Commission. This proposal, like the one by the HWSP published in early 1938, defined the eastern boundaries of the park as Short and Barbeau Streets. It also called for the elimination of the two bridges at the Point and their reconstruction upstream.

24. Ibid.

25. "Historic Park Plan at Point Moves Ahead," *PPG*, 28 January 1938, sec. 2.

26. "Proposed Plans for the Point," *PST*, 7 January 1938; and "Here's How Triangle Will Look If Plans Go Through," *PP*, 16 January 1938.

27. Lower Downtown Business Men's Association and Harland Bartholomew & Associates, "A Preliminary Study for the Proposed Development of the George Washington Memorial Park, Pittsburgh, Pennsylvania," prepared at request of Western Pennsylvania Historical Society, n.d. A photomontage showing the current Historical Society/Lower Downtown Business Men's Association plan was published in "Proposed Plan for Point National Park," *PST*, 12 March 1939, sec. 2. It is different from the one published in the Cocken-Bartholomew brochure in that it appears to include a total reconstruction of Fort Pitt.

28. The opposition of the City Planning Commission is documented in [Frederick T. Bigger], "Analysis and Recommendations re Proposals for Triangle Improvement and Routing of Lincoln-Wm. Penn Highways," 28 June 1938, box 8, folder 3: Point Park, 1938–1959, Series III, Alberts Papers, SJHHC.

29. Alberts, *Shaping of the Point*, 44–46.

30. Bauman and Muller, *Before Renaissance*, 252.

31. Robert Moses to Howard Heinz, 13 August 1939, in ibid., 253.

32. Robert Moses, with the assistance of Arthur E. Howland et al., *Arterial Plan for Pittsburgh*, prepared for the PRPA, November 1939.

33. Ibid., 3.

34. Ibid., 6.

35. Ibid.

36. Ibid., 6–7.

37. Ibid., 18.

38. Ibid., 7.

39. Ibid., 12.

40. Ibid.

41. Ibid., 12, 7.

42. Ibid., 7.

43. Ibid. Ralph E. Griswold, the landscape architect who was to be the lead designer on the Point Park project that was finally implemented in the late 1940s, disparaged Embury's shaft as a gratuitous "lighthouse sort of a phallic symbol" that "had no relation to anything that had ever been there before" and had "no reason" for being

"except that an architect didn't know what else to draw." Robert C. Alberts, interview with Ralph E. Griswold, February 1975, 35, box 9, folder 6: Ralph E. Griswold, 1945–1979, Series III: Point State Park, Alberts Papers, SJHHC.

44. Moses, *Arterial Plan*, 15.

45. Ibid., 11.

46. Ibid., 21–22.

47. Park H. Martin, "Review of Robert Moses Arterial Plan for Pittsburgh," 7 December 1939, 15, 2, 4, box 205, folder 4, Series XV: PPC (1937–1981), subseries 47: Planning/Allegheny County Planning Commission, ACCD Records, SJHHC. The dismissal of the Moses report by city and county authorities contradicts Tafuri's conclusion in "Disenchanted Mountain," 489, that "the influence of Moses's report was decisive."

48. According to William Froehlich, who succeeded Martin as chief planning engineer of the PRPA before becoming its executive director, "during the war when Mr. Mellon served in Harrisburg in charge of the [state's military] draft, he was pretty close to Governor [Edward] Martin. Governor Martin was telling him that they were going to rebuild a very historical landmark in Philadelphia, the Independence Mall. Mr. Mellon came back and said, 'We have a very important historical place in Pittsburgh, too, namely the Blockhouse.' It appealed to Mr. Martin, who was a military man himself, because the Point Park really was a battleground historically. That was when the Point Park idea was born." Nancy Mason, interview with William Froehlich, "Pittsburgh Renaissance: Transcriptions of Interviews," vol. 2, 678, PDCL. On Mellon's role in the Pittsburgh Renaissance in general, see, e.g., "Pittsburgh's New Powers," 73–77; "Mr. Mellon's Patch," *Time* 54 (3 October 1949): 11–14; and Karl Schriftgiesser, "The Pittsburgh Story," *Atlantic Monthly* 187 (May 1951): 66–69.

Also, during the war, the well-known German émigré architect Eric Mendelsohn (1887–1953) produced a design for a new "residential district" for the Point based on modernist planning principles of the 1920s, eschewing any historical or symbolic references. Although it was published in E. Mendelsohn, "Visions of an Architect," *Magazine of Art* 38 (December 1945): 308–9, it was never referred to either in the local press, meetings of the ACCD, or reports of the PRPA. See Hans Morgenthaler, "Pittsburgh's Golden Triangle: Opportunity Lost and Found?" *Avant-Garde: Journal of Theory and Criticism in Architecture and the Arts* 4 (Summer 1990): 58–71.

49. In March 1945, the executive committee of the PRPA, which included Kaufmann, authorized the organization's staff, under the direction of Richards, to prepare a Point Park Development Study. PRPA, "General Description: Point Park Development Study," 1, box 152, folder 7: Development Study, Executive Committee, 14 November 1945, Series XV: PPC (1937–1981), ACCD Records, SJHHC.

50. Ibid., 1–2.

51. Ibid., 2.

52. Ibid.

53. "Gov. Martin Announces: $57,000,000 Pittsburgh Plan," *PST*, 25 October 1945. For the workings of the design team and discussions with Richards and Mellon, see Alberts, interview with Griswold, 5–12; Ralph E. Griswold, "Point State Park: Notes for the Record," [2 December 1979], 1–4, Series III, box 9, folder 6, Alberts Papers, SJHHC; Alberts, interview with Charles Morse Stotz, 5 and 29 May 1975, 17–20, box 10, folder 2: Charles M. Stotz, 1975–1978, Series III, Alberts Papers, SJHHC;

and Alberts, interview with Donald McNeil, n.d., 1–17, box 9, folder 9: Donald McNeil, Alberts Papers, SJHHC.

54. The drawings for Scheme B are mainly dated October 1945; the ones for Scheme A date from October and November.

55. Charles M. Stotz, "Historical and Architectural Features," in PRPA, "General Description: Point Park Development Study," 7.

56. Ibid., 7–8.

57. Ralph E. Griswold, "General Description—Landscape Features," in ibid., 5.

58. Ibid., 6.

59. Ibid.

60. Ibid. The information regarding Mellon was supplied to me by Thomas Schmidt. He said that his father, Adolph W. Schmidt, an in-law of R. K. Mellon who served as chair of the ACCD and as president of the A. W. Mellon Educational and Charitable Trust, told him that Mellon always wanted a simple landscape treatment for the park and would never have approved of a design that disturbed the view from edge of downtown to the water.

61. Griswold, "General Description," 7.

62. Ibid., 5.

63. Ibid.

64. Ibid., 12–13; and Moses, *Arterial Plan*, 13, 16–17. Moses put the total cost of his entire package at $38 million (22). The breakdown for the Griswold-Stotz-McNeil-Richardson Scheme A was $1,703,271 for the park and $14,000,000 for the bridges and approaches.

65. "Million a Year from New Park, Scully Says," *PP*, 26 October 1945.

66. "Fort Pitt Restoration Urged for Point Park," *PST*, 26 October 1945 (ellipsis points in original).

67. "Point Park Details Told by Planners," *PP*, 15 November 1945; "Civic Leaders Tell Plans for Historic Point Shrine," *PST*, 15 November 1945; "Point Park Plans Taking Shape," *PPG*, 15 November 1945; and "How Park at Point May Look," *PPG Daily Magazine*, 15 November 1945. The estimated cost of $5–6 million given in most of these articles was exclusive of highway and bridge improvements.

The model made it particularly evident that the various elements of the highway interchange would create a visual barrier between the city and the park. At least one reporter remarked on this but noted that "it is maintained that, from ground level, they would not block views of the park from uptown." "Point Park Details."

68. "Point Park Plans"; and "Point Park Details." The latter also noted that "the park suggested by the Planning group would be basically simple, taking full advantage of the beauties of the site, yet with plenty to remind visitors of the world-changing events that transpired there."

69. "Pittsburgh-Allegheny Post-War Conference," 27 April 1943, n.p., box 39, folder 1: Executive Committee, 1943–49, Series VI: Executive Director (1934–1990), ACCD Records, SJHHC. The original idea for a name, Pittsburgh-Allegheny Post-War Conference, was put forward in the late April meeting. It was changed to Allegheny County Conference on Post-War Community Planning in July 1943. "Minutes of Meeting of Allegheny County Conference on Post-War Community Planning," 21 July 1943, box 39, folder 1, ACCD Records, SJHHC.

70. Ibid.; and Robert E. Doherty, "The Allegheny Conference Program," *Allegheny Conference Digest* 1 (July 1945): 1.

71. See, e.g., Park H. Martin, "Community Revitalization—by the Citizens," *AC* 60 (September 1945): 137; Martin, "The Allegheny

Conference—Planning in Action," *Proceedings of the American Society of Civil Engineers* 78, separate no. 131 (May 1952): 1–8; and P. Martin, "Pittsburgh's Redevelopment Plan," *Traffic Quarterly* 8 (April 1954): 148–60.

72. Minutes, First Meeting of PPC, ACCD, 27 December 1945, 1, box 11, folder 4, Series III, Alberts Papers, SJHHC.

73. The announcement was made on 14 November 1945. Wallace Richards, "A Fifty-Seven-Million-Dollar Program," *Allegheny County Digest* 1 (December 1945): 7.

74. Ibid.

75. Minutes, First Meeting of PPC, 2.

76. Minutes, Second Meeting of PPC, ACCD, 17 January 1946, 1, box 11, folder 4, Series III, Alberts Papers, SJHHC. Immediately appointed to Kaufmann's committee were Heinz and A. W. Robertson, chairman of the Board of Westinghouse Electric. Thomas E. Kilgallen, a member of the Pittsburgh City Council, and W. B. McFall were added by June.

77. Ibid., 2.

78. Ibid.

79. Griswold was aware of Kaufmann's displeasure with his team's project. He later recalled that Kaufmann "was not exactly a dissenter but a questioner whether Stotz and Griswold were advanced enough to do the right thing by this great project" and for this reason commissioned a counterproject from Wright. Alberts, interview with Griswold, 33.

80. Alberts, *Shaping of the Point*, 85–88; ACCD, "Highlights of the Point Redevelopment Project, Point Park and Gateway Center at the Forks of the Ohio: A Dramatic Story in Civic Achievement: A Major Feature of Pittsburgh's Renaissance," May 1950, box 7, folder 24: Chronology, 1950–74, subseries I: Miscellaneous Writings, Series II: Articles (1944–1987), ACCD Records, SJHHC; "Point Park Is Brought Nearer to Reality," *PPG*, 2 May 1946; and Minutes, Fourth Meeting of the PPC, ACCD, 7 November 1946, [2], box 11, folder 4, Series III, Alberts Papers, SJHHC.

81. See Park H. Martin, "Narrative of the Allegheny Conference on Community Development and the Pittsburgh Renaissance, 1943–1958," [March 1964], 13–16, box 10, folder 5: Miscellaneous Biographies, 1954–1972, Series III, Alberts Papers, SJHHC.

82. "Fine New Buildings Are Included in Giant Plan to Redevelop Area Adjacent to Park at the Point," *PP*, 26 May 1946; and "Redevelopment Group Tackles Point Project," *PP*, 1 June 1946. See also Marshall Stalley, "The Point Redevelopment Program," *Allegheny Conference Digest* 1 (September 1946): 8.

83. "Fine New Buildings"; and "New Authority Is Appointed by Lawrence," *PPG*, 21 November 1946.

84. Alberts, *Shaping of the Point*, 87, 102–7; and ACCD, "Highlights of the Point Redevelopment Project," 2–5.

85. Minutes, Second Meeting of PPC, 4.

86. "Reiner Proposes 'Point Art Center,'" *PST*, 31 October 1945.

87. "Point Park Plan Rushed," *PST*, 8 November 1946.

88. PRPA, "Parking Study of the Pittsburgh Central Business District," prepared for ACCD, 1945–46, 3, 4, 10.

89. Wallace Richards, "Memorandum of January 24, 1946," to Chairman Arthur B. Van Buskirk and Chairmen of Point Park Study Committees, 4, box 156, folder 1: Miscellaneous, 1945–57, ACCD Records, SJHHC.

90. "Statement by Mr. Edgar J. Kaufmann," Third Meeting of PPC, 18 April 1946, 1, box 11, folder 4, Series III, Alberts Papers, SJHHC.

91. Ibid., 1–2.

92. Ibid., 2.

93. Frank Lloyd Wright to E[dgar] J. [Kaufmann], 17 June 1946, FLWFA. Cleary (1993), 144–45; (1999), 56; and (2000), 84, confuse this initial overture to Wright with that made by Kaufmann the following year. Alberts, *Shaping of the Point*, 91, previously misstated that Wright's first meeting with the ACCD was in "the early summer of 1945." Cleary acknowledged in footnotes in his three articles that "the exact date of this meeting has not been confirmed" and "the year [1945] is certainly an error." The 1945 date, which Alberts proposed for Wright's commission, came from Martin's "Narrative of the Allegheny Conference" that Alberts relied on for his book. In that manuscript, completed in 1964, Martin claimed that "Wright came to Pittsburgh in the early summer of 1945 and met with the executive committee at a Saturday noon luncheon in the Duquesne Club. After some discussion Wright agreed to make a study for which he would receive a fee of $10,000 to be paid out of a grant Kaufmann would make to the Conference" (17). Both the date and the fee were incorrect. The events loosely described here will be returned to below.

94. Edgar J. Kaufmann to Mr. [Arthur] Van Buskirk and members of the Architectural Committee, 20 December 1946, box 156, folder 1, Series XV, ACCD Records, SJHHC. He said he got this phrase from the recent book by F.S.C. Northrop, *The Meeting of East and West: An Inquiry Concerning World Understanding* (New York: Macmillan, 1946). He urged the members of the committee to invite Northrop to Pittsburgh to discuss his ideas, but nothing came of this.

95. Kaufmann to Van Buskirk et al.

96. Kaufmann to Frank Lloyd Wright, 20 October 1934; Kaufmann to Wright, 4 December 1934; Kaufmann to Wright, 30 December 1934; and Kaufmann to Wright, 5 April 1935, FLWFA. See also Cleary (2000), 81–82; Bauman and Muller, *Before Renaissance*, 213–15; and Franklin Toker, *Fallingwater Rising: Frank Lloyd Wright, E. J. Kaufmann, and America's Most Extraordinary House* (New York: Knopf, 2003), 116–20.

97. Wright to Kaufmann, 26 December 1934, FLWFA.

98. Frank Lloyd Wright, "Broadacres to Pittsburgh," *PST*, 24 June 1935; and MS 2401.169 E, FLWFA (my quotations are from the latter). The paper's own editorial, "Pittsburgh Is Criticized," published the same day, was quite sympathetic in its response, acknowledging that "there is, of course, some truth in what Mr. Wright says," but also pointing out that "we are trying to correct" the "undesirable conditions of which he complains." While marginalizing Wright as an impractical dreamer, the response tried to justify its printing of the architect's critique by saying "his article will serve a useful purpose if it stimulates in Pittsburghers a desire to solve" the problems it exposes. Cleary (2000), 81–82, mistakenly places the Wright op-ed piece during his trip to Pittsburgh to close the Broadacre City exhibition, which only occurred several days later. This confuses the criticism with others Wright made in interviews when he was in the city. "Broadacres to Pittsburgh" was reprinted in Wright, "New Frontier," 30–32.

99. "City Target of Architect," *PPG*, 1 July 1935. Other Wright remarks of a similar sort were quoted in James A. Baubie, "Flings Sneers at Pittsburgh," *PST*, 30 June 1935.

100. "'Silly,' Replies Hornbostel to Architecture's Critic," *PPG*, 2 July 1935. A less well-known local architect, Edward J. Weber, added his criticism the next day in "Architect Strikes Back," *PPG*, 3 July 1935.

101. Frank Lloyd Wright, "Frank Lloyd Wright to Pittsburgh," 16 July 1935, 1–2, MS 2401.153B, FLWFA.

102. Kaufmann to Wright, 13 March 1947, FLWFA. For the precise date of this crucial visit (24 January), see telegram from Kaufmann to Wright, 22 January 1947, FLWFA, announcing his imminent departure from Palm Springs. Corroborating the discussion of the commission, Kaufmann's son wrote the following to Wright a little over a week later: "I hope that all the plans that you worked out with E. J. will prove worthwhile." Edgar Kaufmann Jr. to Frank Lloyd Wright, 4 February 1947, FLWFA. See note 93 above for the confusion of Alberts and Cleary on the date of commission. Neither refers to the late January meeting as the decisive moment.

103. Cf. Kaufmann to Wright, 7 February 1947, FLWFA.

104. Wallace Richards to Kaufmann, 31 January 1947, FLWFA.

105. Kaufmann later sent Wright a plan of the twenty-three-acre redevelopment area (FLWFA 4821.053) outlined in red, with indications of the heights of existing buildings. Kaufmann to Wright, 17 February 1947, FLWFA.

106. The visual material he sent, describing soil conditions, river elevation, and flood levels, included a map, two aerial photographs of the Point and Golden Triangle (one looking east and the other west [FLWFA 4821.065]), and two blueprints of the existing Point Bridge pier abutments. Kaufmann to Wright, 7 February 1947.

107. Ibid. On the same day this letter was mailed, Wright wrote to Kaufmann saying "the magnum opus is thrown up to scale on the big draughting board." This could only mean that the architect was about to begin work on the design based on his discussions with Kaufmann a couple of weeks before and that the letter was fundamentally a confirmation of the points addressed. On the other hand, the statement about beginning work may just have been a pretext for the request for a down payment of $10,000 on the $25,000 fee. Wright to Kaufmann, 7 February 1947.

108. Kaufmann to Wright, 12 February 1947, FLWFA. Five days later Kaufmann wrote to Wright saying that he had contacted the Pennsylvania Railroad "to give me a map" showing "where the spur comes along Duquesne and then crosses over the property between Fancourt and Barbeau Sts. into their freight warehouse." Kaufmann to Wright, 17 February 1947, FLWFA.

109. Wright responded several days later saying: "Your additional thoughts are now being digested in the general scheme." Wright to Kaufmann, 20 February 1947.

110. See note 107 above. Wright went to Pittsburgh from Princeton, where he lectured at the Architecture School on 6 March at a conference on "Planning Man's Physical Environment" in which Moses was one of the other featured speakers. Wright probably spoke with him about the Pittsburgh project at this time, for Moses sent the architect a copy of his 1939 *Arterial Report* soon thereafter. Wright later thanked him for "the extraordinary (and futile) report," saying it "lies on my board as I write" and adding, "How could you have left those goddam bridges where they are? No toothpick could save them." Wright to Robert Moses, 4 April 1947, FLWFA.

Wright's 8 March visit was reported several days later in "Frank Lloyd Wright to Aid Point Park," *PST*, 12 March 1947; "'Bad Boy' Architect to Help with Ideas for Point Park,'" *PP*, 12 March 1947; and "Expert Asked for New Park Suggestions," *PPG*, 13 March 1947. None of these are cited in Cleary (1993), (1999), or (2000), nor in Alberts, *Shaping of the Point*, where the visit is placed in "the early summer of 1945" (91). Cleary dated the beginning of

Wright's design work prior to his having received the program from Kaufmann. Cleary (2000), 85, stated that "by January 1947, Wright's studio had begun sustained work on the project." Wright, however, later wrote to Kaufmann about "the board I had met before I started to work." Wright to Kaufmann, 23 January 1950, FLWFA. He also later told a local newspaper reporter that he worked on the plans for "nine months," which is precisely the time that elapsed between mid-March and mid-December 1947, when he completed the drawings for the second, scaled-back scheme. David Felix, "Architect Reveals Plans for Point Park 'Fairyland,'" *PST*, 5 May 1949.

111. "Triangle Apartment Building Sites Surveyed by Insurance Heads," *PP*, 6 March 1947: "Despite Setback—Door Still Open for Developing Blighted Area," *PP*, 7 March 1947; and "Plan to Redevelop Big Triangle Area Is Jolted," *PPG*, 7 March 1947.

112. "Pittsburgh Renascent," 62. Wright was not told about the Dowling-Eken visit nor did he learn about their involvement until later. When he did, he was furious and exploded to Martin, saying that had he known, he never would have gotten involved in the project. "It is only recently," he said,

> that I have had a chance to see how "the game" was going.…Had I known a little more of Dowling and Eakins [*sic*] relationship to the project—the sketches would probably never have been made.…The two worst characters in the urban field today are Dowling and Eakin [*sic*]—both enemies of mine, made so by me deliberately. Had I known they were in this Point Park frame that alone would have warned me out and I would never have begun. (Wright to Martin, 21 January 1950, FLWFA.)

Martin later wrote in his "Narrative of the Allegheny Conference," 14, that "it had been our idea that … part of the area in the 23 acre tract … to be redeveloped … would be a desirable place for downtown apartment buildings facing the park.…However, after some study of the Triangle, [Equitable's] real estate advisors [Dowling and Eken] recommended that the Triangle needed a number of new modern office buildings and that the area would be a desirable one since it was large enough to permit the building of modern office buildings with plenty of open space in a park-like setting."

113. "'Bad Boy' Architect."

114. Ibid.

115. "Wright's Huge Point Dome a Renaissance Prophecy," *PP*, 29 January 1961. The quotation is unattributed, but the factual accuracy of the rest of the article leads one to believe it is from a reliable eyewitness.

116. Martin to Wright, 28 May 1947 and 15 July 1947, FLWFA.

117. Martin to Wright, 28 May 1947.

118. Kaufmann to Wright, 13 March 1947, FLWFA. There is a possibility that Kaufmann did not attend the lunch. We know that he was in town for Wright's visit and probably accompanied the architect around the city, since Wright spent the next day (Sunday) with Kaufmann at Fallingwater. Draft of response from Wright to Kaufmann on ibid.

119. Wright to Kaufmann, 27 June 1947, FLWFA. Cleary (1993), (1999), and (2000) assumed that the housing project was also for Mt. Washington. That is not clear and it could just as well have been for the North Side, which came up in later discussions between Wright and Martin. Cleary (1993), 145; (1999), 57; and (2000), 86, also used Wright's reference in this letter to the Point Park project

as a "Coney Island in automobile scale" to claim that Wright "entitled" the project this way. As far as I know, it is the only time he used the phrase. He never labeled any of the drawings this way, nor did he so title the project description submitted to the ACCD on 5 May 1947.

120. "'Bad Boy' Architect." "Wright to Aid Point Park" added that the retainer was to be paid by "a special contribution from the Edgar J. Kaufmann Charitable Trust."

121. Ibid.; and "'Bad Boy' Architect."

122. Wright to Kaufmann, 2 April 1947, FLWFA, suggested they come around 19 April, at which time they could make "suggestions" before the "final" drawings were done. Martin, "Narrative of the Allegheny Conference," 17, however, takes credit for the idea of a small group from the ACCD going to look at the drawings at Wright's studio. He said "he became concerned about what Wright might propose for the Point, knowing that Wright was a controversial figure and might suggest something that would cause dissension in the community." He "suggested to Kaufmann that he and Kaufmann should go to Wright's studio and look over the plan before it was brought to Pittsburgh." He said that "Kaufmann thought this was a good idea." It should be recalled that he remembered the trip as having taken place in the spring of 1946, following Wright's supposed visit to Pittsburgh and discussion with the ACCD committee members at the Duquesne Club during the previous summer. Ibid.

123. Kaufmann to Wright, 7 February 1947. Only the photograph looking west (FLWFA 4821.065) and the map of the redevelopment area (FLWFA 4821.053) are in the Wright Foundation Archives.

124. The Griswold-Stotz-McNeil-Richardson Scheme A plan for Point Park with a superimposed sketch by Wright is figure 9.22. A copy of this was submitted by Wright as part of his presentation to the ACCD. Frank Lloyd Wright, "For the Allegheny Conference, Frank Lloyd Wright, Architect: Cantilever development in automobile-scale of Point Park, Pittsburgh," 5 May 1947, [page following p. 10], box 156, folder 13: Reports, 1945–53, ACCD Records, SJHHC. There is a copy of the text in the Wright Foundation Archives as well as two preliminary drafts, one of which has the slightly different title "For the Allegheny Conference, Frank Lloyd Wright, Architect: Cantilever Development in Automobile-Scale of Pittsburgh Area Known as the Golden Triangle." All three carry the number MS 2401.534, FLWFA. I have also consulted the copy of the typescript that Wright gave John M. Rosenfield Jr., the art critic for the *Dallas Morning News*, kindly provided to me by his son and my late colleague John M. Rosenfield III.

The larger of the two Griswold-Stotz-McNeil-Richardson plans for the Triangle, with overlays by Wright, is figure 9.19; the smaller is figure 9.21. The version of the latter out of which Wright cut a piece and pasted over his own scheme is figure 9.24. The traffic flow map is figure 9.20. The flood chart and the plan of the Crosstown Thoroughfare were uncatalogued when I consulted them in the Wright Foundation Archives. The map of major highways projected in 1945 is FLWFA 4821.052.

One official document that Wright probably did not have was George Richardson's *Downtown Interchange, Penn-Lincoln Parkway East, Allegheny County, Pennsylvania: Engineering Report*, pt. 1, April 1947. This was commissioned by the Pennsylvania Department of Highways in August 1946. It had a short section on the Penn-Lincoln Parkway West and proposed new Point Bridge (13–14), which would have been relevant to Wright's study. "Downtown Interchange, Penn-Lincoln

Parkway East," 1947, box 189, folder 17, subseries 27: Highways/Bridges, Series XV, ACCD Records, SJHHC.

125. See note 110 above.

126. Wright, "For the Allegheny Conference," 3, 2.

127. Franklin Toker, *Pittsburgh: An Urban Portrait* (University Park: Pennsylvania State University Press, 1986), 25, states, contrary to the facts, that although the city "shied away from" building Wright's design, "it did adopt Wright's ideas for a colossal fountain at the Point and for twin bridges crossing the rivers close by." Cleary (2000), 86, states that "he [Wright] planned to clear the site, demolish the existing bridges, and build new quays along the rivers" without acknowledging the precedent of the Griswold-Stotz-McNeil-Richardson plan. This repeats Cleary (1999), 57, and (1993), 145.

128. The courtyard block may represent an early idea for government office space, although it also appears in the later perspectives (figure 9.26). There is also a faint indication of a second large circle, the same size and just to the east of the one indicating the megastructure.

129. See note 110 above.

130. Cleary (1999), 55 (caption figure 32), remarks on the parallel between the Moses oval (which he calls "circular") and the "circular" geometry of the final Wright plan. He says that the two "circular figure[s]" occupy "about the same area," which is not accurate since the Moses oval is only about seven hundred feet in its longest dimension whereas the diameter of Wright's final design for his circular megastructure is well over a thousand feet. Here, the circle has a diameter of at least fourteen hundred feet.

131. Wright, "For the Allegheny Conference," 1.

132. Ibid., 7.

133. Ibid., 1–2.

134. Ibid., 2–3, 8. In a later interview, after his project was shelved, Wright called his design "'a fairyland,'" "'a people's project.'" Felix, "Architect Reveals Plans."

135. Wright, "For the Allegheny Conference," 10. Wright said the 123,000 amounted to "a third of Pittsburgh's population" in Felix, "Architect Reveals Plans."

136. Wright, "For the Allegheny Conference," 10.

137. Based on the rather preliminary drawings we have, these measurements must remain approximate. Different drawings result in different estimates. Wright, "For the Allegheny Conference," 4, said that the "GRAND AUTO RAMP" was "4 1/2 miles in length, rising 175 feet above street level." Alberts, *Shaping of the Point*, 92, says the diameter of the ziggurat was one-fifth of a mile, i.e., 1,056 feet. He does not give a source for this nor indicate at what level the measurement was taken. Cleary, who apparently never saw Wright's "For the Allegheny Conference," relied on quotations in Alberts for information contained in the descriptive text. Cleary (1993), 145; (1999), 57; and (2000), 86, repeat Alberts in saying that the main building was "one-fifth of a mile in diameter."

138. Wright, "For the Allegheny Conference," 10.

139. The phrase "county fair" was employed in ibid., 8. The phrase "street fair" was notated on the preliminary section FLWFA 4821.002.

140. Although Kaufmann had spoken to Wright about a federal office building and a state office building back in February, Wright planned buildings for state, county, and municipal offices, but not for the federal government.

141. Ibid., 7.

142. Ibid., 6.

143. Cleary (1993), 145; (1999), 86; and (2000), 145, give the date of the visit as 6–7 May. The group actually left Pittsburgh on the 6th but only arrived after midnight. They spent the 7th and 8th with Wright and returned

to Pittsburgh on the morning of the 9th. Kaufmann to Wright, 25 April 1947, FLWFA, gives the itinerary.

144. Ibid. Alberts, *Shaping of the Point*, 92, states that Richardson was part of the group, but he was confusing this trip with a second one in January 1948. In his "Narrative of the Allegheny Conference," 17, Martin claimed that James McClain, the planning officer of the PRPA, rather than Richards, flew with Kaufmann and himself from Pittsburgh. There is no corroborating evidence for this. McClain did not join the staff of the ACCD until 1954, when he was appointed planning director.

145. Wright to Kaufmann, 21 April 1947, FLWFA.

146. Alberts, interview with Griswold, 33. John P. Robin, who was appointed as the first executive director of the new Urban Redevelopment Authority in 1948, where he would work closely with Kaufmann, supports the interpretation of Kaufmann's independence of action in Robert C. Alberts, interview with John P. Robin, 10 September 1975, 4–5, box 9, folder 12: John P. Robin, 1975–1979, Alberts Papers, SJHHC.

147. Martin, "Narrative of the Allegheny Conference," 17; and Lynda Waggoner to author, 1 February 2008, recalling the remark about Wright's being "a little crazy" from a conversation she and her husband, a relative of Martin, had in the early 1970s. Waggoner added that Martin "seemed to imply that it was a good thing the [Wright] Point Project was never realized."

148. Martin, "Narrative of the Allegheny Conference," 18.

149. Ralph Griswold, in Alberts, interview with Griswold, 33, used the term "embarras[s]ed." "When he [Kaufmann] received [i.e., saw] the drawings," Griswold said, "he realized he didn't dare show them even to the committee."

150. Martin to Wright, 28 May 1947, FLWFA. By about this time, some of the most important elements Wright had included in his design based on Kaufmann's program, notably the sports arena and convention center, were being considered by the PRPA for inclusion in a plan for redeveloping the Lower Hill, a slum on the eastern edge of the Golden Triangle, adjacent to the proposed Crosstown Thoroughfare. Gilbert Love, "Giant Center for Sports, Conventions Proposed for Pittsburgh of Tomorrow," *PP*, 30 October 1947.

151. Handwritten response on Martin to Wright, 28 May 1947. The earlier, unfinished draft, also on ibid., questioned whether the ACCD's opinion of his project "boils down solely to your own eye-view report" and, "if so it is easy to understand why Pittsburgh" is in the shape it is.

152. Wright to Kaufmann, 27 June 1947, FLWFA.

153. [Oliver], "Report of the Study Committee on Historical Significance," 1, 4. Martin sent the "Report" on 9 June, saying he was "sure that the thoughts contained in this document will provide sufficient material for a conception that will be impressive and outstanding." Martin to Wright, 9 June 1947, FLWFA.

154. Wright to Martin, 15 June 1947, box 151, folder 5: Correspondence, 1947–1958, Series XV, ACCD Records, SJHHC. The draft preserved in FLWFA has minor differences.

155. Cleary (1999), 58; and (2000), 92, state that "Kaufmann persuaded Martin to soften his position on the historical issues" but offer no evidence for this, nor have I seen any.

156. Martin to Wright, 15 July 1947, FLWFA. There is a draft in box 151, folder 5, Series XV, ACCD Records, SJHHC.

157. Kaufmann to Wright, 14 July 1947, FLWFA.

158. Handwritten draft on Martin to Wright, 15 July 1947; and Wright to Martin, 19 July 1947, FLWFA.

159. Wright to Kaufmann, 14 November 1947, FLWFA.

160. Kaufmann to Wright, 19 November 1947, FLWFA.

161. Martin to Wright, 9 December 1947; and Wright to Martin, 16 December 1947, FLWFA.

162. Martin to Wright, 2 January 1948, FLWFA.

163. Cleary (2000), 59.

164. Cleary (2000), and email to the author, 19 May 2008, state that the sequence went from this to the final second scheme mainly because it maintained the cantilevered bridges of the initial design.

165. Cleary (2000), 95–97, argues, quite compellingly, that Wright would have been introduced to the technology by the Polish émigré engineer Jarolslav Joseph Polivka (1886–1960), whom Wright hired as a consultant on the Guggenheim Museum in 1946.

166. Felix, "Architect Reveals Plans"; and Kaufmann to Richards, 9 February 1948, FLWFA. Cleary (1993), 149; (1999), 58; and (2000), 92, capitalize the word "bastion" and claim that it was the title Wright gave the project. I have seen no evidence for either.

167. Felix, "Architect Reveals Plans."

168. J. Cutler Andrews, interview with Arthur Van Buskirk, 28 October 1971, "Pittsburgh Renaissance: Transcriptions of Interviews," vol. 6, 2107, PDCL; Robert C. Alberts, interview with John Grove, 3 September 1975, 6, box 9, folder 7: John Grove 1975, Series III, Alberts Papers, SJHHC; and Wallace Richards to E[dgar] J. [Kaufmann], 20 January 1948, FLWFA. The Richards letter is a copy probably sent to Wright by Kaufmann.

169. Alberts, interview with John Grove, 6; Mason, interview with William Froehlich, 661; Alberts, interview with Griswold, 55; and Martin to Kaufmann, 15 January 1948, FLWFA. The Martin letter is a copy probably sent to Wright by Kaufmann.

170. Richards to Kaufmann, 20 January 1948. Kaufmann appreciated Richards's ability to see the artistic value and creativity of Wright's architecture. In response to his report on the January meeting (see below), Kaufmann wrote: "What you said, and how you expressed it, is indicative of your feeling for this type of creative architecture." Kaufmann to Richards, 9 February 1948, box 156, folder 1, ACCD Records, SJHHC.

171. Wright seems to have completely misread the situation. He wrote to Kaufmann that he was "surprised the Allegheny Conference didn't tell you how really enthusiastic they all were over Scheme II." Wright to Kaufmann, 23 January 1948, FLWFA.

172. Martin to Kaufmann, 15 January 1948; and Richards to Kaufmann, 20 January 1948.

173. Minutes, Fifth Meeting of the PPC, ACCD, 13 February 1948, 2, box 11, folder 4, Series III, Alberts Papers, SJHHC.

174. Martin to Kaufmann, 15 January 1948.

175. Ibid.

176. Richards to Kaufmann, 20 January 1948.

177. Martin to Kaufmann, 15 January 1948; and "Preliminary Report Dealing with Pittsburgh Point Park Development," n.d., [1, 4], box 156, folder 13, ACCD Records, SJHHC.

178. Richards to Kaufmann, 20 January 1948; and Martin to Kaufmann, 15 January 1948. Martin specified that it should be "a selected group from the Point Park Committee."

179. This is substantiated by remarks by Arthur Van Buskirk, chair of the PPC, to Kaufmann after having received a copy of Kaufmann's 9 February letter to Richards. "There are recent important developments bearing upon the timing of the Point Park program," he said, "which make it important, I think, to have a meeting when you return. This should include the Committee of Architecture and Design, Dr. Weidlein, Richards, Martin, and myself." Van Buskirk to Kaufmann, 27 February 1948, box 156, folder 1, ACCD Records, SJHHC.

180. Kaufmann to Richards, 9 February 1948. In order for Wright to do the drawings explaining "how bridges … will connect to the proposed downtown streets and the Penn-Lincoln Parkway" and thus "tie in with the State plans," Kaufmann asked Richards to send the architect "what the Highway Department has in mind."

181. Ibid.

182. Ibid.

183. Kaufmann to Wright, 3 March 1948, FLWFA. Kaufmann openly acknowledged at the outset of this final effort that he was "quite sure that the men which we have to deal with are full of skepticism, lack of understanding, fear of complications within the State political picture, and totally unaware of your true stature in the creative world; all accented by the possible costs involved in the two studies which you have already conceived and which are to be presented later on." As far as we know, Wright did no drawings for the project. By the end of June, Kaufmann confirmed that "there is no chance of building this auditorium at this place." Kaufmann to Wright, 30 June 1948, FLWFA.

184. At around this time, Wright received a visit from J. Lester Perry, president of Columbia Steel and former president of Carnegie-Illinois Steel, who was chair of the Area of Development Sub-Committee of the Point Redevelopment Committee of the PPC and a colleague of Kaufmann's on the board of Pittsburgh's Urban Redevelopment Authority. It is unclear who or what prompted the visit and who else came with Perry. Wright to Kaufmann, 21 February 1948, FLWFA, reported that "the Steel boys came. Perry seemed very pleased but God help us all—these men hard-boiled in business can't open up their minds between meum and tuum." In a later letter, he noted that he showed Perry the new "traffic distribution" as requested by Kaufmann. Wright to Kaufmann, 18 March 1948, FLWFA.

185. Martin to Wright, 9 August 1948, FLWFA. In asking for the drawings, he said that "our people feel that it would be desirable for us to have here in Pittsburgh the studies you made." When Wright refused to send the originals, as was his practice, and said that he would bring them with him "whenever they [the ACCD] choose to summon me officially," Kaufmann responded: "I really had asked Park to write to you for these drawings for my own personal files and not for the files of the Conference." Wright to Martin, 15 August 1948; and Kaufmann to Wright, 20 September 1948, FLWFA. Wright agreed to send the drawings if Kaufmann promised "to make no public use of [them] … without my consent and … regard them as a loan from their author to be returned on demand." Wright to Kaufmann, 27 September 1948, FLWFA.

This correspondence helps to clear up one of the often repeated stories about Kaufmann's secretiveness regarding the drawings. Alberts, *Shaping of the Point*, 96, quotes Griswold's chronologically muddled account:

> "Edgar [Kaufmann] had intended to spring a great surprise on the Point Park Committee with Wright's solution to the whole problem. When he saw the drawings he realized he didn't dare show them, even to the Committee. He rolled them up and put them under his desk. When Wright came to town to talk to Edgar about some other project, he asked, 'Whatever happened to those plans I did for the Point?' Poor Edgar was embarrassed—there they were rolled up under his desk. He had to bring them out and show them to Van Buskirk to satisfy Wright. Van took one look at the drawings and almost dropped dead in amazement. He said, 'Edgar, you'd better put them back under your desk.'"

This is not corroborated in Alberts, interview with Van Buskirk, done for *Shaping the Point*.

As usual, Martin took credit for what occurred. In his "Narrative of the Allegheny Conference," 18, he said that "following this meeting [in May 1947 in Arizona, which Kaufmann attended], Martin advised Kaufmann to have Wright send his drawings to the Conference and not to expose them to the public," his reasoning being that "Wright's proposal would have completely eliminated Point Park which the State by that time was committed to build. Wright agreed to send the plans to the Conference [*sic*]," Martin continued, but "because of their grandiose proportions, the plans never officially received the light of day."

186. Kaufmann to Wright, 13 October 1948, FLWFA. No such exhibition ever took place. Some of the drawings were exhibited at the Carnegie Institute of Technology in early May 1949 when Wright was invited to give a lecture there. In relation to the event, an interview with the architect, accompanied by reproductions of figures 9.25 and 9.57, was published in Felix, "Architect Reveals Plans."

187. Minutes, Sixth Meeting of the PPC, ACCD, 5 November 1948, 4, box 11, folder 4, Series III, Alberts Papers, SJHHC. Kaufmann was quoted as calling the overpass a "Chinese wall" in "Scenic View or Bridges at Point Park?" *PP*, 6 November 1948.

188. Rapuano's role is described in Alberts, interview with Griswold, 11–12.

189. "$50 Million Triangle Project to Be Most Modern in World," *PP*, 21 November 1950. The role of Dowling and Eken in the planning of the towers was emphasized in "Pittsburgh Renascent," 62–65. For Wright's opinion of Dowling and Eken, see note 112 above and pp. 330–31.

190. The history is detailed in Alberts, *Shaping of the Point*, 108–209.

191. Ralph E. Griswold, "From Fort Pitt to Point Park: A Landscape Architect's Viewpoint," n.d., 8, box 156, folder 1, ACCD Records, SJHHC; and Alberts, interview with Stotz, 16.

192. Griswold, "From Fort Pitt," 7, 4, 8.

193. Ibid., 11, 8.

194. Wright to Martin, 21 January 1950, FLWFA.

195. Alberts, interview with Griswold, 34.

196. Ibid., 29.

197. Griswold, "From Fort Pitt," 7.

198. Jane Jacobs, "Downtown Is for People," *Fortune* 57 (April 1958): 134, 133.

199. Ibid., 134.

200. While describing the first Wright scheme as "one of Wright's most fascinating urban projects," Tafuri, "Disenchanted Mountain," 493, called it "also one of his most absolutely antiurban."

201. Wright to Martin, 21 January 1950, FLWFA.

202. Felix, "Architect Reveals Plans." As noted previously, the main structure was planned to hold nearly 125,000 people.

203. Hugo's discussion of the Tower of Babel is in bk. V, chap. 2. One of Wright's earliest references to this is in Frank Lloyd Wright, "The Art and Craft of the Machine," 1901, repr. in *FLWCW* 1:61. As late as 1957

Wright described Hugo's discussion of architecture in *Notre-Dame de Paris* as "the most illuminating essay on architecture yet written." Frank Lloyd Wright, *A Testament* (New York: Bramhall House, 1957), 17.
204. The major document of this trend is Tyrwhitt, Sert, and Rogers, *Heart of the City*, published in 1952.
205. José Luis Sert to Lewis Mumford, 28 December 1940, in Eric Mumford, *The CIAM Discourse on Urbanism, 1928–1960* (Cambridge, Mass.: MIT Press, 2000), 133–34. The full reference for the Sert book is *Can Our Cities Survive? An ABC of Urban Problems, Their Analysis, Their Solutions, Based on the Proposals Formulated by the C.I.A.M., International Congresses for Modern Architecture, Congrès Internationaux d'Architecture Moderne* (Cambridge, Mass.: Harvard University Press, 1942).
206. Giedion, "Need for a New Monumentality," 568. A slightly earlier iteration of these ideas appeared in Giedion, Sert, and Léger, "Nine Points on Monumentality," 48–51.
207. Sigfried Giedion, in "In Search of a New Monumentality: A Symposium," by Gregory Paulsson et al., *Architectural Review* 104 (September 1948): 127.
208. Giedion, *Architecture, You and Me*, 39, 28.

Ten: Plan for the Expansion of Baghdad Anchored by a Cultural Center, 1957

1. Martin Mayer, *Bricks, Mortar and the Performing Arts: Report of the Twentieth Century Fund Task Force on Performing Arts Centers* (New York: Twentieth Century Fund, 1970), 1, noted that "173 arts centers and theaters were completed in the United States between 1962 and 1969, with another 179 on the drawing boards or in construction." One of the first to highlight the trend was Alvin Toffler, *The Culture Consumers: A Study of Art and Influence in America* (New York: St. Martin's, 1964), esp. 73–126.
2. Frank Lloyd Wright, "THE YOUTH OF AMERICA: THE POETIC PRINCIPLE (Monona Terrace, State of Wisconsin, Baghdad)," Talks to Taliesin Fellowship, 23 June 1957, reel 189, 1, 7, MS 1502.258, FLWFA.
3. Étienne de Vaumas, "Introduction géographique à l'étude de Bagdad," *Arabica* 9 (October 1962): 229–47.
4. K[eppel] A[rchibald] C[ameron] Creswell, *Early Muslim Architecture*, vol. 2, *Early 'Abbāsids, Umayyads of Cordova, Aghlabids, Tūlūnids, and Samānids, A.D. 751–905* (Oxford: Clarendon, 1940), 18.
5. The main literary sources for our knowledge of ancient Baghdad are the ninth-century accounts of Abu Ja'far Muhammed al-Tabari and Ahmad al-Ya'kubi, and the eleventh-century one of Al-Khatib al-Baghdadi. For the early history of Baghdad, see Guy Le Strange, *Baghdad during the Abbasid Caliphate, from Contemporary Arabic and Persian Sources* (Oxford: Clarendon, 1900); Friedrich Sarre and Ernst Herzfeld, *Archäologische Reise im Euphrat- und Tigris-Gebiet*, 4 vols. (Berlin: Dietrich Reiner/Ernst Vohsen, 1911–20), 2:94–202; Creswell, *Early Muslim Architecture*, 2:1–38; A[bdul] A[ziz] Duri, "Baghdād," in *The Encyclopaedia of Islam*, new ed. (Leiden: Brill, 1960, 1:894–908; Mustapha Jewad et al., eds., *Baghdad: An Illustrated History* (Baghdad: Iraqi Engineers Association, 1969) (in Arabic); Saleh Ahmad El-Ali, "The Foundation of Baghdad," 87–101 and Jacob Lassner, "The Caliph's Personal Domain: The City Plan of Baghdad Re-examined," 103–18, both in *The Islamic City: A Colloquium*, ed. A. H. Hourani and S. M. Stern (Oxford: Bruno Cassirer, 1970); and Lassner, *The Topography of Baghdad in the Early Middle Ages* (Detroit: Wayne State University Press, 1970).

6. Phebe Marr, *The Modern History of Iraq* (Boulder, Colo.: Westview, 1985), 21.
7. After the armistice of 1918, Faysal was initially given the Syrian throne in Damascus. When the French received the mandate over Syria in April 1920, conflict arose between them and Faysal, resulting in his expulsion. He was then offered the throne of Iraq by the British, with the understanding that a treaty of alliance (October 1922) would replace the mandate and thus ensure the new nation a certain degree of self-determination. The Iraqi constitution was instituted in 1924.
8. There is little documentation of the careers of Wilson and Mason. See "A Baghdad Diary," *IT*, 10 December 1954; Khalid Sultani, "Architecture in Iraq between the Two World Wars, 1920–1940," *UR: The International Magazine of Arab Culture* 2/3 (1982): 92–105; Mark Crinson, *Modern Architecture and the End of Empire* (Aldershot: Ashgate, 2003), 29–30, 62; Ihsan Fethi, "Protection et restauration de l'architecture coloniale à Bagdad: problèmes et enjeux," in *Architecture coloniale et patrimoine: expériences européennes. Actes de la table ronde organisée par l'Institut national du Patrimoine, … 2005* (Paris: Somogy/Institut national du patrimoine, 2006), 195–99; and Pauline Lavagne d'Ortigue, "Connaître l'architecture classique et l'urbanisme colonial: rêver d'une ville moderne et syncrétique: J. M. Wilson," in *Rêver d'Orient, connaître l'Orient: visions de l'Orient dans l'art et la littérature britanniques*, ed. Isabelle Gadoin and Marie-Élise Palmier-Chatelain (Lyon: ENS, 2008), 317–40.
9. The scant literature on twentieth-century Baghdad urbanism includes Kahtan A. J. Al-Madfai, "Baghdad," in *The New Metropolis in the Arab World*, ed. Morroe Berger (New Delhi: Allied, 1963), 39–63; John Gulick, "Baghdad: Portrait of a City in Physical and Cultural Change," *JAIP* 33 (July 1967): 246–55; Khalis H. al-Ashab, "The Urban Geography of Baghdad" (Ph.D. diss., Newcastle upon Tyne, 1974); Ihsan Fethi, "Contemporary Architecture in Baghdad: Its Roots and Traditions," *Process, Architecture* 59 (1985): 112–32; Caecilia Pieri, "La Formation d'une ville 'moderne': Bagdad à la période hachémite (1920–1958)," *Histoire de l'art: revue de recherche et d'information publiée sous l'égide de l'Association des professeurs d'archéologie et d'histoire de l'art des universités* 59 (October 2006): 107–16; Pieri, "Baghdad Architecture, 1921–1958: Reflections on History as a 'Strategy of Vigilance,'" *Bulletin of the Royal Institute of Inter-Faith Studies* 8 (2006): 1–25; Pieri, "Bagdad 1921–1937: entre tutelle coloniale et souveraineté nationale," in *Architecture coloniale et patrimoine*, 184–93; Ghada M. R. Al Siliq, "Baghdad: Images and Memories," in *Azara*, 49–72; Pieri, "Urbanism in Baghdad before the Planning: A Codification between the Fates of the Arbitrary and Urban Needs (1920–1950)," in *Azara*, 266–71; Pieri, "Modernity and Its Posts in Constructing an Arab Capital: Baghdad's Urban Space and Architecture, Contexts and Questions," *Middle East Studies Association Bulletin* 42 (Summer/Winter 2008): 32–39; Pieri, *Baghdad Arts Deco: Architectural Brickwork, 1920–1950*, trans. Yves Stranger and Wendy Parramoze (2008; Cairo: American University in Cairo Press, 2010); and Al Siliq, *City of Mirages* (Baghdad: Iraqi Cultural Support Association, 2011).
10. According to Pieri, "Urbanism in Baghdad," 268, Baghdad's first Building and Road Law was enacted in 1935. It included regulations for the layout of streets, setbacks, lot division, building heights, and construction permits. It apparently also instituted a schematic form of zoning. The first master plan for the city was apparently

done in late 1936 by the German engineering firm Brecks and Bronoweiner but was never implemented. M. B. al-Adhami, "A Comprehensive Approach to the Study of the Housing Sector in Iraq; with Special Reference to the Needs, Standards, Inputs, Density and Costs as Factors in the Analysis of Housing Problems in Baghdad" (Ph.D. diss., University of Nottingham, 1975), 566.
11. Zuhour Palace, at the southern tip of the Karadat Maryam section of the west bank, begun by Mason in 1933, replaced the earlier royal residence located at the northern edge of Rusafa. It became a VIP Guest House (Villa Harathiyat) when the new Royal Palace, designed by J. Brian Cooper, was built in the 1950s.
12. *Guide-Book to the Iraq Museum*, 3rd ed. (Baghdad: Ministry of Information, Directorate General of Antiquities, 1976); and Lamia al-Gailani Werr, "The Story of the Iraq Museum," in *The Destruction of Cultural Heritage in Iraq*, ed. Peter G. Stone and Joanne Farchakh Bajjaly (Woodbridge, Suffolk: Boydell Press, 2008), 25–30. I thank Amin Alsaden, a student in the seminar on Baghdad I gave at Harvard in the spring of 2013, for the latter reference and for much additional information on the history of the March project.
13. Cooper became Iraq's government architect in 1934 after designing the critically acclaimed Islamic-styled Mausoleum of King Faysal I in the previous year. As government architect, he later designed, in addition to the new Royal Palace, Nuri al-Said's house and the new Parliament Building (1951–57), both on riverside sites in Karadat Maryam. For the Parliament, see "The Consulting Engineer at Work Overseas," *Consulting Engineer*, January 1957, 2; and Board of Development and Ministry of Development, Government of Iraq, *Development of Iraq: Second Development Week* (Baghdad: Government of Iraq, 1957), [27, 32–33], W. M. Dudok Papers, DUDO 212 M.124, HNI. The Royal Palace was published in the *Builder*, 30 May 1958, 989; and Hamid 'al Hilali and Hamdi Alkyhayat, eds., *Iraq: A Pictorial Record* (Cologne-Deutz: Orient Mercur, in cooperation with Iraqi Commissariat of the World Exhibition, Brussels 1958, 1958), 90. Both the Royal Palace and Parliament were commissioned by Iraq's Development Board, created in 1950 (to be discussed below). For John Brian Cooper, see "Obituaries," *RIBA* [Royal Institute of British Architects] *Journal* 91 (March 1984): 93; and "Form of Application for Admission as a Fellow … to the Council of the Royal Institute of British Architects," 3 September 1940, MS 3796, Royal Institute of British Architects, London.
14. "Baghdad Railway Station. J. M. Wilson, A.R.I.B.A., and H. C. Mason, F.R.I.B.A., Architects," *Builder*, 29 April 1949, 521–23.
15. Ibid., 522. The formality of the Wilson-Mason design is underscored by the fact that the station was not aligned with the tracks and the tracks were not shifted southwest into the station until a number of years after the building was completed. The map of Baghdād, Series K 941, Sheet Baghdād No. 3, Edition 3-AMS, printed by the Army Map Service, Corps of Engineers, U.S. Army, Washington, D.C., in 1960 based on information compiled in 1958, identifies the building as "Government Offices" and shows no tracks entering it.
16. The plan in figure 10.5, which also shows the proposed Queen Aliyah Street, is among the documents that Le Corbusier acquired while designing his Olympic Stadium for Baghdad (see below).
17. "Baghdad West Growing Quickly—Significance Worthy of Ancient Times," *IT*, 7 July 1956. I thank Joseph

Siry for directing me to the issue of Baghdad West and for providing me with copies of relevant articles from the *IT*.

18. In Lord [Arthur] Salter, *The Development of Iraq: A Plan of Action* (Baghdad: Iraq Development Board, 1955), 126. In the original plan of May 1950, 100 percent of the revenue was targeted for development. The 30-percent reduction was a response to the enormous increase in revenues resulting from the even split in royalties negotiated in February 1952. For early accounts, see Hal Lehrman, "Iraq Tries 'Operation Bootstrap,'" *NYT Magazine*, 24 February 1957, 15, 35–36, 38; [Government of Iraq], *Development of Iraq* ([Baghdad]: Middle East Export Press, [1957]); and "Development in Iraq," *Economist*, no. 5939 (22 June 1957), special numbered sec., 1–4, 7–8, 11–14. The most useful studies are Fahim I. Qubain, *The Reconstruction of Iraq* (New York: Praeger, 1958); Stanley John Haberman, "The Iraq Development Board: Administration and Program," *Middle East Journal* 9 (Spring 1959): 179–86; Kathleen M. Langley, *The Industrialization of Iraq* (Cambridge, Mass.: Center for Middle Eastern Studies, Harvard University Press, 1961); Ferhang Jalal, *The Role of Government in the Industrialization of Iraq, 1950–65* (London: Frank Cass, 1972); and Edith and E. F. Penrose, *Iraq: International Relations and National Development* (London: Ernest Benn, 1978).

19. Salter, *Development of Iraq*, 140, 239–40, notes that significant funds were allocated for the Royal Palace, Parliament, and Iraq Museum for the years 1955–58, but these projects were all ones that had been under way for a number of years.

20. Nothing of substance has yet been written about the firm, nor has their role in Baghdad been well understood. It has been assumed that Minoprio & Spencely and P. W. Macfarlane were hired by the Development Board. See, e.g., Mina Marefat, "1950s Baghdad—Modern and International," *TAARII Newsletter*, no. 2–2 (Fall 2007): 1; and Lefteris Theodosis, "'Containing' Baghdad: Constantinos Doxiadis' Program for a Developing Nation," in Azara, 169. This was not the case. It was a municipal commission.

I thank most warmly Hugh Spencely and John Minoprio, two of the principals' sons, for their extremely generous help in piecing together the history of the firm and understanding the work's significance in Baghdad and elsewhere. Other invaluable resources have been the archives of the AAM, HNI, and FLC.

21. Minoprio, Spencely, and Macfarlane, 1, state that "on the 8th December, 1954, we were instructed to prepare the Master Plan." This must refer to an official letter of commission, for negotiations and consultations went back at least a month. "Baghdad Boundaries to Be Extended," *IT*, 4 November 1954, reported that, in a speech two days before, the lord mayor announced that the city government was "thinking of inviting the well-known British expert in town planning, Mr. Anthony Minoprio, to advise the authorities on projected plans to expand the boundaries of the capital." Two weeks later, it was reported that "Mr. Anthony Minoprio, … engaged by [the] Amanat al-Asimah [the municipality] to study the improvement of Baghdad, arrived" and "expected to stay about 10 days" in order "to suggest improvements" and complete "'his studies of what is needed'" before "'send[ing] a team of his engineers from England … [whose] job will be the preparation of specifications, maps and other detailed work before the improving of Baghdad starts.'" "British Town Planner Arrives in Baghdad," *IT*, 17 November 1954. "British Town Planner Ends Studies in Baghdad,"

IT, 29 November 1954, reported on Minoprio's departure after his having "completed his initial studies in Baghdad."

For the instrumental role of the lord mayor, see "Town-Planning for Baghdad: A Long-Term Scheme," *Times* (London), 30 December 1954; and "A Baghdad Diary," *IT*, 8 September 1956, where it is stated that "the Amin al-Asimah, Sayid Fakhruddin al-Fakhri, went into action on the measure [of planned development] soon after the Amanah mantle fell on his shoulders in early summer 1954. He engaged noted town planning consultants, Minoprio and Spencely and P. W. Macfarlane, of Britain, for the job on which the firm has been working over the past two years." It went on to say that "a final plan for the capital" plus "other plans and detailed reports [are] all now with … Sayid Fakhruddin al-Fakhri."

In all likelihood the lord mayor, or his predecessor, came to know the work of Minoprio, Spencely, and Macfarlane in early 1953 when Minoprio stopped in Baghdad, en route to Kuwait, and was invited by the British Council to lecture on "Recent Town Planning in Great Britain" at the British Institute Club in Waziriyah. "British Experts to Plan Baghdad," *Roads and Road Construction*, January 1955, noted that "Mr. Anthony Minoprio … was first approached on the matter [of a master plan for Baghdad] when lecturing for the British Council in Iraq in [February] 1953." It is surely not merely a coincidence that on the same day it ran the initial story on the mayor's speech announcing his intention to invite Minoprio to consult on Baghdad, the *IT* did a piece, datelined London, on the firm's ongoing work in Kuwait, "British Firm Entrusted with the Replanning of Kuwait," *IT*, 4 November 1954.

The 29 November 1954 *IT* story said that they were doing plans for Mosul and Basra at the time (the Mosul job eventually went to Raglan Squire and that of Basra to Max Lock). The firm was also active in plans for Tehran and Bahrein. They began working on a master plan for Dhaka in 1957–58. Their *Report on the Master Plan for Dacca, 1960*, done for the Dacca Improvement Trust, was completed in December 1959 and published the following year.

22. I know of only one copy of the *Report*, which is the one in the Doxiadis Archives, Athens. I thank Thomas Doxiadis, a student in my 1992 Baghdad seminar at Harvard, for providing me with a photocopy of it. I am grateful to Amin Alsaden for having provided me with a high-resolution scan of the plan itself.

23. During the year and a half they spent preparing the plan, Minoprio and/or Spencely and/or Macfarlane made three trips to Baghdad lasting anywhere from one to two weeks. After they submitted their plan in April 1956, the frequency of their visits increased. There were seven between May 1956 and December 1957, lasting from one week to a month. On the extended visit made by Minoprio and Macfarlane in May–June 1956, the planners made use of a helicopter and a municipal fire boat to view the city from the air and from the river. Although Minoprio informed Willem Dudok at the beginning of October 1958 that his own firm's contract had been terminated, he sent him a drawing of proposed road level changes dated November 1958. Anthony Minoprio to [Willem] Dudok, 2 October 1958, DUDO 212 M.124, HNI. A detailed chronicle of the firm's visits to Baghdad (as well as to Kuwait and Tehran) and their work on Baghdad's master plan from 15 June 1955 through 17 December 1957 is contained in the 280-page "Middle East Diary 1955" that Minoprio, Spencely, and Macfarlane kept. This bound document,

written by hand generally on the recto side only of foolscap-size paper, is now in a private collection.

The rare contemporaneous press reports of the architectural commissions include "Architects Build a Modern Baghdad," *Christian Science Monitor*, 2 April 1958, sec. 2; "New Lights for Aladdin," *Time* 71 (19 May 1958): 80; and "Suurtyö akateemikko Aallolle Bagdadista," *Ilta-Sanomat*, 26 September 1958. In Levine, 383–404, I first laid out the history of what took place in Iraq in the 1950s following the creation of the Development Board and its commissioning of a slate of internationally celebrated architects to design signature buildings for the capital city. A number of articles and essays have been published after this based on the framework I established and the analysis I proposed. Some deal almost exclusively with one or another of the architects involved and will be cited where relevant. The more synoptic studies include Marefat, "1950s Baghdad," 1–7; Azara; and Magnus T. Bernhardsson, "Visions of Iraq: Modernizing the Past in 1950s Baghdad," in *Modernism in the Middle East: Architecture and Politics in the Twentieth Century*, ed. Sandy Isenstadt and Kishwar Rizvi (Seattle: University of Washington Press, 2008), 81–96. Azara, which contains numerous contributions but also unfortunately many errors, was accompanied by an exhibition in Barcelona. A modified version of this formed a traveling exhibition.

24. Al-Madfai, "Baghdad," 61, stated in 1963 that despite the "proposal submitted by Doxiadis Associates," the earlier Minoprio-Spencely-Macfarlane plan was still "the official one." It remained so until the Miastoprojekt (Poleservice) plan of 1967. In fact, there is even a revised civic center plan by the British firm done in July 1959 (#454/86; private collection).

On Miastoprojekt's work, see Łukasz Stanek, "Miastoprojekt Goes Abroad: The Transfer of Architectural Labour from Socialist Poland to Iraq (1958–1989)," *Journal of Architecture* 17, no. 3 (2012): 361–86. For the short-lived Doxiadis initiative, see Panayiota Pyla, "Rebuilding Iraq: Modernist Housing, National Aspirations, and Global Ambitions," *Docomomo* 35 (September 2006): 71–77; Pyla, "Back to the Future: Doxiadis's Plans for Baghdad," *JPH* 7 (February 2008): 7–10; Pyla, "Baghdad's Urban Restructuring, 1958: Aesthetics and Politics of Nation Building," in Isenstadt and Rizvi, *Modernism in the Middle East*, esp. 97–102; and Theodosis, "'Containing' Baghdad," 17. For the even shorter-lived Sert involvement as the "new coordinator" of the civic center, see Nouraddin Muhiaddin to Dudok, 18 September 1960; Dudok to Muhiaddin, 18 October 1960; and Dudok to Ministry of Works and Housing, 20 December 1962, DUDO 212 M.124, HNI. The possibility of Sert's appointment was reported in "Harvard Dean Here to Design Civic Centre," *IT*, 13 January 1961. Khaled Al-Sultany, "The 'American Embassy' Building in Baghdad: The Architect and Architecture," in Azara, 109, 113, erroneously dates Sert's sketches for the civic center to 1955 based on the earlier misdating in Josep M. Rovira, *Sert, 1928–1979: Complete Work, Half a Century of Architecture* (Barcelona: Fundació Joan Miró, 2005), 218. The two Sert sketches in question are in the Sert Papers, Special Collections, Loeb Library, Graduate School of Design, Harvard University. I thank Mary Daniels and Inés Zaldundo for showing them to me.

25. Joseph Sharples, Alan Powers, and Michael Shippobottom, *Charles Reilly and the Liverpool School of Architecture, 1904–1933*, Catalogue of an Exhibition at the Walker Art Gallery, Liverpool, 25 October 1996–2 February 1997 (Liverpool: Liverpool University Press,

National Museums & Galleries on Merseyside, 1996), 175–77 and passim. On Minoprio, see "Obituary of Mr Anthony Minoprio," *Times* (London), no. 63020, 5 March 1988.

26. Hitchcock, "Modern Architecture. I."

27. Anthony Minoprio, *Chelmsford Planning Survey, 1945: A Survey and Plan for Chelmsford Borough and Rural District* (Chelmsford: Chelmsford Area Planning Group, 1945); and Ana Lescenko Fuller and Robert Home, *On the Planning History of Chelmsford*, Papers in Land Management, no. 9 (Cambridge: Anglia Ruskin University, 2007), esp. 14–18.

28. "A Baghdad Diary," *IT*, 14 February 1953, reporting on Minoprio's first visit to Baghdad and the lecture on "Recent Town Planning in Great Britain" that he was to give at the British Institute Club, noted that "he is author, and co-author with his partner, H.G.C. Spencely, of planning schemes for Chelmsford, Worcester, Shanlin, Slough, and the new town developments at Crawley and Cwmbran in Britain." Hugh Spencely confirmed to me that his father was equally involved with the design for Crawley.

29. For Crawley, see Anthony Minoprio, "Report on a Preliminary Outline Plan for Crawley New Town," 14 October 1947, Loeb Library, Graduate School of Design, Harvard University; Minoprio, "The Development of New Towns with Particular Reference to Crawley," *Papers of the National Housing and Town Planning Council* (1948): 8–10; Minoprio, "Crawley New Town," *Town and Country Planning* 16 (Winter 1948–49): 215–21; Minoprio, "The New Towns: No. 3, Crawley. Consultant Anthony Minoprio, M.A., F.R.I.B.A." *Journal of the Town Planning Institute* 35 (January–February 1949): 59–61; Minoprio, *A Master Plan for Crawley New Town* (London: By the Author, 1949); and John Goepel, *The Development of Crawley* (Crawley: Crawley Museum Society, 1993). For Cwmbran, see Minoprio & Spencely and P. W. Macfarlane, *Cwmbran New Town* (Cwmbran: Cwmbran Development Corporation, March 1951).

30. Minoprio, "Crawley New Town," 215.

31. Minoprio, "Development of New Towns," 9.

32. As the town was built out, the railway station was relocated eastward, more or less opposite where the monastery is shown in figure 10.10.

33. For Kuwait, see Minoprio & Spencely and P. W. Macfarlane, *Plan for the Town of Kuwait: Report to His Highness Shaikh Abdullah Assalim Assubah, C. I. E., The Amir of Kuwait* (November 1951); "Town Planning in Kuwait: Rebuilding a Middle East Capital," *Times Review of Industry*, new ser., 5, no. 57 (October 1951): 91; P[eter] W. Macfarlane, "Planning an Arab Town: Kuwait on the Persian Gulf," *Journal of the Town Planning Institute* 40 (April 1954): 110–13; Raglan Squire, ed., "Architecture in the Middle East," *Architectural Design* 27 (March 1957): 74–75; Stephen Gardiner, *Kuwait: The Making of a City* (Harlow, Essex: Longman, 1983), esp. 33–65; Richard Trench, ed., *Arab Gulf Cities*, vol. 2, *Kuwait City* ([Slough]: Archive Editions, 1994), esp. 550–65; Yasser Mahgoub, "Kuwait: Learning from a Globalized City," in *The Evolving Arab City: Tradition, Modernity, and Urban Development*, ed. Yasser Elsheshtawy (Abingdon: Routledge, 2008), esp. 154–60; Muhannad A. Albaqshi, "The Social Production of Space: Kuwait's Spatial History" (Ph.D. diss., Illinois Institute of Technology, December 2010), esp. 67–107. I want to express my gratitude to John Minoprio for the information he provided me on the Kuwait City project. I also want to thank Muhannad Albaqshi for providing me with a copy of the 1951 Minoprio, Spencely, and Macfarlane *Report*.

34. Minoprio, Spencely, and Macfarlane, 9. A summary of the main points of the *Report* is given in P[eter] W. Macfarlane, "The Plan for Baghdad—The Capital of Iraq," *Housing Centre Review* 5 (1956): 193–95.

35. Minoprio, Spencely, and Macfarlane, 1.

36. Ibid., 3, 2. Macfarlane, "Plan for Baghdad," 194, reiterated that he and his associates believed that "the human problem" was as great if not greater than the "mechanical problem" of providing "a road system adequate to allow the free movement of traffic." "The human problem," he stated, "meant providing housing, replacing slums, and allocating open space for children," which placed an "emphasis on the dignity of the individual and the importance of working for human happiness." The need for a more adequate housing supply was one of the main recommendations made by Salter in his report on the first five-year plan of the Development Board, *Development of Iraq*, esp. 79–82, 121. In May 1956, on their first trip to Baghdad after submitting the master plan, Minoprio and Macfarlane produced a separate report on their proposed neighborhood plan concept and a drawing of it. "Middle East Diary," 30 May 1956 (entry by Minoprio), 110.

37. Minoprio, Spencely, and Macfarlane, 4.

38. Ibid., 13.

39. Ibid., 4, 17.

40. Ibid., 6.

41. Ibid., 8, 18.

42. Ibid., 12.

43. Ibid., 13.

44. Ibid.

45. Ibid., 15–16.

46. "Middle East Diary," 28 June 1955 (entry by Minoprio), 8, 10.

47. Minoprio, Spencely, and Macfarlane, 16.

48. On 6 October 1956, Minoprio learned from the lord mayor that it had been decided that the university was "to go in the Karradah peninsula." "Middle East Diary," 128.

49. Minoprio, Spencely, and Macfarlane, 16, 22, 17.

50. Ibid., 18.

51. Ibid., 19.

52. The Minoprio-Spencely-Macfarlane master plan received little or no critical acclaim at the time, no doubt in large part due to its conservatism. The firm's rival in the Middle East, Raglan Squire, described their plans for Kuwait and Baghdad, in "Architecture in the Middle East," 74, as "represent[ing] a comparatively simple approach to the problem. They have accepted the situation as it exists; they have proposed a new road plan and attempted to do a certain amount of zoning." This, Squire contrasted to the "more difficult task" undertaken by Max Lock (in Basra, 1955–56) and his own firm (in Mosul, 1955–56) "of attempting to impose modern town-planning analyses on the ancient cities with which they have been dealing." Al-Madfai, "Baghdad," 61, characterized the plan "as a mere street-and-road system, with only the broadest possible hint at zoning." After the firm had been relieved of its "co-ordinating architects" role, Aalto, who was asked by the new Republican government to redesign at least part of the civic center, wrote that he thought it would be "a very pleasant thing to do." "I was not satisfied with the Surveyors Minoprio & Spencely & P.W. Macfarlane and their planning," he explained, "which was too monotonous and schematic and also lacking in the special character which is absolutely necessary to make the whole match with the new Centre of your town." Alvar Aalto to Hasan al-Jalili, 8 June 1959, Bagdad, Development Board, AA 43, AAM.

53. Squire, "Architecture in the Middle East," 74.

54. Minoprio, Spencely, and Macfarlane, 13.

55. In an "Eye-Witness" interview in early January 1955 on the BBC, Minoprio noted that "'the first city of Baghdad was built by Harun al-Rashid's grandfather in A.D. 762. The city was circular and was called the Abode of Peace, a most inappropriate name as it turned out.'" He ended by saying that, although "'wide streets, parks, and shopping centres must be planned in the old congested quarters, and model factory and housing areas on the fringe of the city where now are matting huts and herds of Indian buffaloes,'" he and his partners believed that "'at the same time we have to do this without destroying the Arab character of the town.'" "Did You Hear That?" *Listener*, 27 January 1955, 143. On his first visit to Baghdad after submitting the master plan, Minoprio noted in "Middle East Diary," 28 May 1956, 106, that he had just gone to the British Institute library where he "read K.E[*sic*].C. Creswell[']s 'History of Muslim Architecture' in two vols. written 1932 & 1940." He characterized it as "a most impressive work."

56. Minoprio, Spencely, and Macfarlane, 4, 9.

57. Ibid., 4.

58. Michael G. Ionides, a British irrigation expert, member of the Development Board, and fellow Harovian, told Minoprio on 3 June 1957 that he "thought that [the] expansion of [the] city would be almost exclusively westwards … and thought that if the cost of acquiring the Civic Centre east of Aliyah St. was too high, the southern end of the airport, next to the station, might be considered." This, in Minoprio's view, "would involve [the] complete separation of the C[ivic] C[entre] from the existing commercial centre" and would thus be unacceptable. "It should however be recognized," Minoprio continued, "that several big changes have taken place since March 1956 when the Master Plan was made, notably the airport, the University & the Washash housing sites. New bridges would also eliminate to a large extent the barrier effect of the River Tigris & access between both banks would be easy. It could happen," Minoprio concluded, "that the easier development of the west side of the town together with the above factors would result in the shifting of the city centre from Rusafa to the south end of the airport site." "Middle East Diary," 224, 226.

59. The plans for Rusafa (figure 10.17) and Karkh are dated January 1957 and April 1957, respectively. The plans for Khadimain and Adhamiya were submitted to the municipality on 2 June 1957. "Middle East Diary," 2 June 1957, 222 (entry by Minoprio). There are at least thirteen different plans for the civic center, showing either the entire site or a part, in the Aalto Foundation Archives, Dudok Papers, and private collections dating from April 1956 through November 1958. There is also an early perspective of the civic center, dated September 1955. The perspective does not correspond with any plan I have seen. It hung in the lord mayor's office.

60. Langley, *Industrialization of Iraq*, 103ff.; and Jalal, *Role of Government*, 33. The report produced by Salter in 1955 was commissioned by the government in response to political pressures. For a summary of progress through 1957, see Waldo G. Bowman, "Iraq's Operation Bootstrap," pt. 1, "A Modern Mesopotamia Is Molded"; and pt. 2, "Big Dams Instead of Hanging Gardens," *Engineering News Record* 159 (12 December 1957): 34–36, 38, 40, 45–46, 48, 50, 52, 54; and (26 December 1957): 32–34, 37–38, 40.

61. Salter, *Development of Iraq*, 118.

62. It is unclear why and how the change in Development Board thinking regarding architectural hires occurred. For Levine, I interviewed Rifat Chadirji and Ellen

Jawdat, young foreign-educated architects then living in Baghdad, who claimed that they were part of a group that influenced the board's decisions. In a lecture given in my 1992 Baghdad seminar at Harvard, Chadirji stated that, after seeing the names of architects being proposed by the Development Board, he and the others went to the minister of development in 1952 to complain. He said that they were asked to draw up a list of better candidates, which they did by the "end of 1952." This list, which the board subsequently adopted, he said, included Gropius, Wright, Aalto, Ponti, and Oscar Niemeyer (but left out Le Corbusier). Marefat, "1950s Baghdad," 6, repeats the same story, adding that Chadirji was appointed to the Technical Division of the Development Board in 1952. In an interview in July 2012, Mohammed Makiya, one of the other young architects supposedly involved in educating the board, told me that as far as he remembers there were never anything more than some informal discussions, if that. In any event, aside from much later oral history, there is no documentary evidence on the matter. In an entry in "Middle East Diary," 21 November 1955, 38, Minoprio identifies Chadirji as "architect to Awkaf," the religious endowment administration. The diary never mentions Chadirji in the context of the Development Board.

In what could be considered a trial run for the Development Board's program, Ellen Jawdat managed an invited international competition for "European architects" to design the Rusafa headquarters of the National Bank of Iraq. The competition, which was not sponsored by the Development Board, opened in November 1954 and closed in March 1955. The winner was the Zurich-based (ETH) William Dunkel. Both Aalto and Ponti entered unsuccessful designs. The other invitees who competed were Palle Suenson, Werner March, Peter Celsing and Nils Tesch, Sep Ruf, Gordon Tait, D. Roosenberg, and Pierre Bailleau. Herbert J. Rowse did not make the deadline, while André Leconte, Jean Lurçat, and Marcello Piacentini decided not to enter drawings. Dunkel's design was built in 1955–56. Documentation of the competition and Aalto's part in it is contained in the National Bank of Iraq material, AAM. Aalto visited Baghdad in December 1954 in preparing the project.
63. Nadim al-Pachachi to Le Corbusier, 22 June 1955; al-Pachachi to Le Corbusier, 23 July 1956; and al-Pachachi to Le Corbusier, 28 July 1956, FLC. For Le Corbusier's project, see H. Allen Brooks, gen. ed., *The Le Corbusier Archive*, vol. 27, *Le Corbusier: Projet pour un Stade Olympique, Baghdad, and Other Buildings and Projects, 1953* (New York: Garland; and Paris: Fondation Le Corbusier, 1984), 101–514; Rémi Baudouï, "To Build a Stadium: Le Corbusier's Project for Baghdad, 1955–1973," in Azara, 271–80; Mina Marefat, "Mise au Point for Le Corbusier's Baghdad Stadium," *Docomomo* 41 (September 2009): 30–40; and Marefat, *The Le Corbusier Gymnasium in Baghdad* (Paris: Editions du patrimoine, Centre des monuments nationaux, 2014).
64. For more on this, see below.
65. See Government of Iraq, Development Board—Ministry of Development, Doxiadis Associates, *The Housing Program of Iraq* (Baghdad, March 1957); Government of Iraq, Doxiadis Associates, *Housing in Baghdad* (Baghdad, March 1957); Doxiadis Associates, *Progress of the Housing Program*, Monthly Report No. 46, May 1959, prepared for the Government of the Republic of Iraq, Development Board and Ministry of Development (Baghdad and Athens, May 1959); Pyla, "Back to the Future," 3–19; Pyla, "Baghdad's Urban

Restructuring," 97–115; and "Sector 10 of the Partial Plan for Western Baghdad (Plan and Partial Construction: 1957–1958). Neighborhood of Al-Thawra ('Sadr City'), Part of the Partial Plan for Eastern Baghdad (Plan: 1958; Construction: 1961–63)," in Azara, 304–6.
66. Dhia Jafar to Le Corbusier, 25 December 1956, FLC.
67. On the Wright project, see Levine, 386–404; Mina Marefat, "Wright's Baghdad," in *Frank Lloyd Wright: Europe and Beyond*, ed. Anthony Alofsin (Berkeley: University of California Press, 1999), 184–213; Joseph Siry, "Wright's Baghdad Opera House and Gammage Auditorium: In Search of Regional Identity," *Art Bulletin* 87 (June 2005): 265–81; Marefat, "Wright's Baghdad: Ziggurats and Green Visions," in Azara, 145–55; "Plan for Greater Baghdad (1957–1959), in ibid., 298–300; and Marefat, "Wright in Baghdad: Urban Life More Beautiful," in Cleary et al., *Frank Lloyd Wright*, 74–91.

On the Aalto project, see Elissa Aalto and Karl Fleig, *Alvar Aalto*, vol. 3, *Projects and Final Buildings* (Zurich: Verlag für Architektur Artemis, 1978), 150–53; and Alvar and Aino Aalto, "Project for the Fine Arts Museum in Baghdad (Civic Center) (1957–1963)," in Azara, 302–3.
68. Dhia Jafar to Frank Lloyd Wright, 15 January 1957; and Wright to Minister of Development [Jafar], 24 January 1957, MS 1502.258, FLWFA (only pages 1 and 3 of Wright's response have been preserved in this file). Dhia Jafar to Messrs. Alvar Aalto Firm of Architects, 15 January 1957, Bagdad, Development Board, 1957–1958, AA 4; and Secretary to Aalto to Development Board and Minister of Development, 5 April 1957, Bagdad, Development Board, AA 43, AAM. I have been unable to track down the Niemeyer correspondence and thus have no idea what building he was asked to design. We can be sure of the approximate date, since a note in Le Corbusier's sketchbooks, his first on the subject of Baghdad, reads: "January 9, 1956[*sic*: should be 1957]; // Goutail from Baghdad they have called on Wright Oscar Niemeyer Aalto//USA—Sert." Françoise de Franclieu, ed., *Le Corbusier Sketchbooks*, vol. 3, *1954–1957* (New York: Architectural History Foundation, 1982), K 45/812. The Sert reference is to his American Embassy, built between 1955 and 1961. It was obviously not a Development Board commission.
69. Dhia Jafar to William [*sic*] Dudok, 2 February 1957; and Dudok to Minister of Development, 14 February 1957, DUDO 212 M.124, HNI. On the Dudok project, see "Police Headquarters, Palace of Justice, Property Register (Civic Center) (1957–1959). Willem Marinus Dudok," in Azara, 301–2. When I wrote my *Architecture of Frank Lloyd Wright*, I was unaware of the Dudok commission. It came to light only with the Azara publication. Contemporaneous articles about the Development Board program failed to mention his contribution.
70. In an article published in 1960, Ponti stated that the Development Board "simultaneously" commissioned Aalto, Wright, Le Corbusier, and himself. Gio Ponti, "Progetto per l'edificio del 'Development Board' in Baghdad," *Domus* 370 (September 1960): 1. The *IT*, however, reported on 27 February 1957 that his selection by the Development Board took place the previous day. "Baghdad to Have New Opera House," *IT*, 27 February 1957. On the Ponti building, see "Headquarters for the Development Board and the Ministry of Planning (1958). Gio Ponti in Collaboration with Antonio Fornaroli and Alberto Rosselli, and Giuseppe Valtolina and Egidio Dell'Orto," in Azara, 304. See also Lisa Licitra Ponti, *Gio Ponti: The Complete Work, 1923–1978* (Cambridge, Mass.: MIT Press, 1990), 202. The Ponti Archives in

Milan contain only photographs of the project and completed structure.
71. Gropius and his wife visited the Jawdats in Baghdad in the summer of 1954. Following that visit, Ellen Jawdat wrote to them, "We are more than ever convinced that we must find some way for you to make your contribution to this country." Ellen Jawdat to "Gropiuses both," 3 October 1954, Walter Gropius Papers, 1925–1969, b MS ger 208, 956, Houghton Library, Harvard University. The following year, she added, "The university scheme is temporarily halted until the English firm of Minoprio & Spencely have made their recommendations for the Baghdad City plan and have settled on the site for the university center. So it still simmers, and we keep talking. Reginald Squire … are blatantly publicizing themselves for the job." E. Jawdat to Gropiuses [prob. mid-1955], Houghton Library. I am grateful to Elizabeth Dean Hermann, a student in my 1992 Baghdad seminar, for bringing these letters to my attention.
72. "Board Decisions," *IT*, 9 September 1957, states that the Development Board decision was made on 7 September. The *Three-Monthly Economic Review: Iraq and Arabian Peninsula* recorded in its January 1958 issue that "Iraq has added to the great names of Frank Lloyd Wright (who has now produced preliminary drawings for the Opera House), Le Corbusier, and Gio Ponti that of Gropius, whose firm was invited during the autumn to discuss the planning of Baghdad University" (no. 8, p. 8). See also Reginald R. Isaacs, *Walter Gropius: Der Mensch und sein Werk*, 2 vols. (Berlin: Gebrüder Mann, 1984) 2:1040–42.

On the university, see "Planning a University," *Christian Science Monitor*, 2 April 1958, sec. 2; [The Architects Collaborative], *Report on the University of Baghdad Designed by The Architects Collaborative, Cambridge, Massachusetts, U.S.A.*, n.d.; "TAC: The Architects Collaborative," pt. 1, "The University of Baghdad," *AR* 125 (April 1959): 147–55; "The Architects Collaborative International Limited: La città universitaria di Baghdad," *Casabella continuità* 242 (August 1960): 1–31; "Planning the University of Baghdad," *AR* 129 (February 1961): 107–22; Walter Gropius et al., *The Architects Collaborative, 1945–1965* (New York: Architectural Book Publishing, 1966), 119–37; and John C. Harkness, ed., *The Walter Gropius Archive*, vol. 4, *1945–1969: The Work of the Architects Collaborative* (New York: Garland, 1991), 189–238. For recent accounts, see Mina Marefat, "Bauhaus in Baghdad: Walter Gropius Master Project for Baghdad University," *Docomomo* 35 (September 2006): 78–86; Marefat, "The Universal University: How Bauhaus Came to Baghdad," in Azara, 157–66; and "University Campus of Baghdad (1957–). Walter Gropius, TAC and Hisham A. Munir," in Azara, 300–301.
73. He was invited to come in late March in order to be present during the Second Development Week, but had to postpone the visit until May. Dhia Jafar to Wright, 9 March 1957, MS 1502.258, FLWFA. For the aborted March trip, see "Wright Going to Iraq to Design Opera House," *NYT*, 27 January 1957; "Opera House for Baghdad," *NYT*, editorial, 28 January 1957; and "Wright to Design Baghdad Opera: Opera and Poetry," *AF* 106 (March 1957): 97. For the May trip, see "Architect Wright en Route Here," *IT*, 20 May 1957; "Wright in Baghdad," *IT*, 21 May 1957; "A Baghdad Diary," *IT*, 22 May 1957; and "Mr. Lloyd [*sic*] Wright in Baghdad," *IT*, 29 May 1957. Dudok kept clippings of the "Wright in Baghdad" and "Mr. Lloyd [*sic*] Wright in Baghdad" pieces, the latter of

which had a photograph of Wright and Dhia Jafar sitting and conversing in the Khayam Hotel. DUDO, 212 M. 125, HNI.

74. Aalto to Dhya [sic] Jafar, 2 July 1957; and Aalto to Mahmud Hasan, 18 July 1957, Bagdad, Development Board, AA 43, AAM.

75. "Board Building Discussed," IT, 14 August 1957. His upcoming trip was announced in "Board's Designer Arriving Soon," IT, 25 July 1957. "Headquarters for the Development Board," 304, however, states that "Ponti himself was never in Baghdad."

76. See "Middle East Diary," 5–12 October 1957 (entries by Spencely and Minoprio), 240–52; and Dudok to Minister of Development, 19 November 1957, DUDO 212 M. 124, HNI.

77. Although Gropius's visit attracted no notice in the IT, Le Corbusier's was reported on three occasions: "A Baghdad Diary," IT, 8 November 1957; "Corbusier to Give Lecture," IT, 11 November 1957; and "A Baghdad Diary," IT, 12 November 1957. Franclieu, Le Corbusier Sketchbooks, 3: L 50/1056–73, documents the visit.

78. Both "Wright to Design G.P.O.," IT, 27 May 1957; and "Mr. Lloyd [sic] Wright in Baghdad" referred to the additional building as a "General Post Office." M. Hasan to Frank Lloyd Wright, 3 March 1958, DUDO 212 M.124, HNI, referred to the building as the "Telegraph & Telephone Building," which was its official name. In this same letter, he differentiated it from the "Directorate General of Posts and Telegraph Building in the Civic Centre," which was being designed by Aalto. In other official correspondence, the Wright building was referred to as the Telegraphs & Telephones Building in contradistinction to the Aalto Telegraphs & Posts Building. Aalto, for his part, labeled his May 1958 drawings "G.P.O.," for General Post Office (see figure 10.26), which is how the program was described by Minoprio, Spencely, and Macfarlane in their updated civic center plans. For Wright, see also the reference in Three-Monthly Economic Review of Iraq and Arabian Peninsula, no. 6 (July 1957):6.

79. "Wright, 88, to Design Iraqi Cultural Center," NYT, 8 June 1957; and Frank Lloyd Wright, "To the Minister and his Development Board, City of Baghdad, Iraq" (draft), n.d. [1957], MS 2401.379 BB, FLWFA. The Three-Monthly Economic Review (July 1957): 6, reported "the appointment of Mr. Frank Lloyd Wright to draw the plans for a central post office and a cultural centre, which will include a university building."

80. For the Aalto Directorate General of Posts and Telegraph Building, see Alvar Aalto, Architect, vol. 20, Maison Louis Carré 1956–1963, ed. Esa Laaksoren and Ásdis Ólafsdóttir (Helsinki: Alvar Aalto Foundation, Alvar Aalto Academy, 2008), 175.

81. Discussions about reducing the size of the civic center and eliminating many of its government buildings began as early as the fall of 1956 and took effect by the following February. Newspaper reports in July 1957 ascribe the economic reason to the decrease in funds from oil exports. See "Civic Centre Must Be Studied Now," IT, 4 July 1957; and "Not Enough Funds to Build Civic Centre," IT, 20 July 1957.

82. Dudok to Minister of Development, 19 November 1957, DUDO 212 M.124, HNI.

83. Minoprio to Aalto, 19 August 1957, Minoprio, Anthony, AA 24, AAM.

84. On the Aalto side, boxes AA 9, 24, 44, and 49, AAM, contain approximately twenty-five letters. For Dudok, the number is more significant. There are about thirty-five letters in DUDO 212 M.124, HNI.

85. For documentation of this, see notes 118–22 below.

86. For Dudok, see Dudok to Minister of Development, 17 April 1958; and Dudok to Director General of Public Buildings, 17 April 1958, DUDO 212 M.124, HNI. He did not immediately go to Baghdad and continued to work on the design through September, when his "Report and Building Programmes of the Courts of Justice, Directorate General of Land Settlement and TAPU Department, and Police Buildings to Be Built at the Civic Centre in Baghdad" is dated. DUDO 212 M.125 and 212 PF.60, HNI. For Aalto, see Aalto to Ministry of Development, 22 April 1958; and Aalto to Hazim Namuq, Director General of Public Buildings, 19 May 1958, Bagdad, Directorate General of Buildings, AA 43, AAM. For Le Corbusier, see Le Corbusier to M. Hasan, 9 May 1958 and 6 June 1958; and [Le Corbusier], "The Olympic Stadium Baghdad: Provisional Presentation of the Project Dated May 31st 1958," FLC.

87. Dudok's is in DUDO 212 M.124; Aalto's, of which only the left half is preserved, is in an uncatalogued folder, AAM. Both are black-and-white photographic reproductions.

88. "Baghdad Civic Centre: Report on Draft Plan, Prepared by the Co-ordinating Consultants (Drawings 454/44A and 46)," 3 September 1957, 1–2. Minoprio, Anthony, AA 24, AAM.

89. Dudok to Minister of Development, September 1958, DUDO 212 M.125, HNI. A number of sketches in DUDO 212 K.39, HNI, like the one reproduced in figure 10.23, reveal these material and coloristic intentions more than do the rather sober, rendered drawings.

90. In the notes explaining his use of similar tiles in his 1954–55 competition entry for the National Bank of Iraq, which would have been located at the corner of Rashid and Bank Streets, just a few blocks northwest of the civic center, Aalto said, "Fortunately there is an exceptional finish material available in the outstanding ceramics of the Orient and North Africa. Among the most ~~attractive and~~ [crossed out] durable of these is the china blue ceramic." [Alvar Aalto], undated note, 2, National Bank of Iraq, AAM.

91. The source of the Baghdad design was the project for the Art Gallery at Reval (now Tallinn), Estonia (1936). Aalto reused the design for his entry in the 1958 Aalborg Museum competition (Denmark), built in 1969–73.

92. The colored master plan is FLC 29554; the black-and-white stadium site plan is FLC 29566. The former was dated "LC–16–11–57" by Le Corbusier in the lower margin; the same date is inscribed in the Atelier Le Corbusier stamp in the upper right corner. The latter is not dated and has the following addition in pencil at the bottom left: "James Cubitt & Partners, 2 February 1956." Cubitt did not do the drawing but may have supplied the information on which it was based. There are a few notes on the master plan as well as a very sketchy indication of the stadium site.

93. "Middle East Diary," 29 May 1956, 106, 108 (entries by Minoprio).

94. In Franclieu, Le Corbusier Sketchbooks, 3: L 50/1062, Le Corbusier notes, "Attention le plan d'Urb mirifique en couleur n'est pas exact // Stade."

95. Ibid., L50/1072: "12 nov 57 // L-C pourquoi pas Stade ouvrant sur le fleuve près de Ponti (le Pont Neuf) et eau pénétrant dans stade jeunesse."

96. [Le Corbusier], "Olympic Stadium Baghdad," 6.

97. Le Corbusier, My Work, trans. James Palmes (London: Architectural Press, 1960), 132. As in Baghdad, the earlier project also included an extensive sports complex. Among

the various possible locations were the Bois de Vincennes, Gennevilliers, Gentilly, and the Bois de Boulogne.

98. Ponti, "Progetto," 1, 6.

99. Ibid., 6.

100. "Middle East Diary," 6 October 1956, 128 (entry by Minoprio); and 26 February 1957, 194 (entry by Macfarlane). The start of expropriation was reported in Board of Development, Development of Iraq: Second Development Week, 28.

101. "TAC: The Architects Collaborative," 148.

102. Ibid.

103. The Baghdad auditorium-theater was directly based on the arcaded, multiuse civic auditorium Gropius and TAC designed for the Tallahassee, Florida, civic center in 1956 (see figure 10.51).

104. The regionalist discourse of the 1940s and 1950s can be dated to the publication of Lewis Mumford's The South in Architecture, The Drancy Lectures, Alabama College, 1941 (New York: Harcourt, Brace, 1941), esp. 79–110; and his "The Sky Line: Status Quo," New Yorker 34 (11 October 1947): esp. 106, 108–9. The latter raised the issue as a critique of International Style "functionalism" by its "free yet unobtrusive expression of the terrain, the climate, and the way of life" (110). The article's impact was so great that in February 1948 the Museum of Modern Art organized a symposium to discuss its implications. "What Is Happening to Modern Architecture? A Symposium at the Museum of Modern Art," Museum of Modern Art Bulletin 15 (Spring 1948): 4–20. Two significant articles that followed were Sigfried Giedion, "The State of Contemporary Architecture: 1. The Regionalist Approach," AR 115 (January 1954): 132–37; and Pietro Belluschi, "The Meaning of Regionalism in Architecture," AR 118 (December 1955): 131–39. The debate continued well into the 1970s, 1980s, and 1990s. See Kenneth Frampton, "Towards a Critical Regionalism: Six Points for an Architecture of Resistance," in The Anti-Aesthetic: Essays on Postmodern Culture, ed. Hal Foster (Port Townsend, Wash.: Bay Press, 1983), 16–30; and Alan Colquhoun, "The Concept of Regionalism," in Postcolonial Space(s), ed. Gülsüm Baydar Nalbantoğlu and Wong Chong Thai (New York: Princeton Architectural Press, 1997), 13–23. A useful compendium is Architectural Regionalism: Collected Writings on Place, Identity, Modernity, and Tradition, ed. Vincent B. Canizaro (New York: Princeton Architectural Press, 2007).

105. "Middle East Diary," 11 June 1957, 232 (Minoprio entry); 30 September 1957, 234 (Spencely entry); and 3 October 1957, 238 (Spencely entry). I have not seen a copy of this "draft letter."

106. In Levine, 383–404, I laid out the basis for the discussion of both these aspects of Wright's contribution to the Development Board's program but focused more on the historicizing than I will here. Few other scholars or critics following my original study have stressed the uniqueness of Wright's project as an urban intervention. Two that come to mind are Khaled Al-Sultany, "Half a Century after the Creation of the 'Wright' Projects in Baghdad: Plans for the Imagined Architecture," in Azara, 131–44; and Marefat, "Wright in Baghdad," 74–91. Al-Sultany stated that the Wright contribution was "an urban project" and not "a lonely building" (139) and astutely compared it to the Pittsburgh Point design (143). For whatever reason, Marefat compared the Baghdad project to Wright's Crystal City design, in which she saw a "parking ziggurat" as underpinning the design (91).

107. "Wright Going to Iraq"; and "Wright to Design Baghdad Opera." The original commission letter specified

only that the site would be "about 9000 sq.m." but did not give the location. Jafar to Wright, 15 January 1957. Nine thousand square meters is indeed just a little over two acres. Although he was right that the site was "in the middle of the city," how and when Wright came to this understanding is not known. A major problem with the documentation of Wright's Baghdad commission(s) is that the archival material was moved to the Taliesin Associated Architects Archives after Wright died and has since gone missing. The only pieces that were found for me are the two letters referred to in note 68 above plus a third, Jafar to Wright, 9 March 1957, MS 1502.258, FLWFA, confirming Wright's 24 January letter accepting the commission. The three letters were at that time reincorporated in the Wright Foundation Archives. Based on the correspondence and reports that exist in the Dudok Papers and Aalto Foundation Archives, one must assume that a treasure trove awaits future scholarship.

108. In Levine, 386, I incorrectly assumed that "middle of the city" meant the civic center. Siry, "Wright's Baghdad Opera House," 270, accepted what I said but added that, because of "shortfalls in Iraqi oil exports … expropriation costs for the civic center proved prohibitively high, and many of its component buildings, including the opera house, were relocated in subsequent plans." He ultimately correctly placed the site on the Trade Fair grounds. On the 1954 Trade Fair and its site, see "How to See All the Attractions," *IT. Special Number: British Trade Fair, Oct. 25–Nov. 8, 1954*, October 1954; and British Overseas Fairs Limited, for Federation of British Industries, London, *British Trade Fair. Baghdad 1954. October 25—November 8* (includes site plan on last page).

109. "Middle East Diary," 23 November 1955, 40 (entry by Minoprio); 10 October 1956, 136 (entry by Minoprio); 12 February 195[7], 178, 180 (entry by Macfarlane); and 24 February 1957, 190 (entry by Macfarlane).

110. "Wright in Baghdad."

111. There are two copies of the master plan and a collage of two Hunting Aerosurveys aerial photos in the Wright Foundation Archives (FLWFA 5733.001; 5733.002; and 5733.003; figures 10.35–37).

112. Soon after returning to the United States, Wright told the Taliesin Fellowship that "flying over [the city] I saw an island, unoccupied, practically in the heart of the city. … And I wondered—well, when I came down and looked at the map there was that island with nothing on it whatever. And in figuring out where to build the opera house and develop the cultural center, I saw that they had allocated the university on the ground opposite the island, and the island was a cleavage right between the city and the university. So I went after that island." There is no indication of when the flight occurred. "Mr. Wright—June 16, 1957: Bagdad [*sic*]," 5, reel 188, FLWFA. The talk was published, with minor variations, in Bruce Brooks Pfeiffer, ed., *Frank Lloyd Wright: His Living Voice* (Fresno: Press at California State University, 1987), 51. In an interview recorded in 1989, Nezam Amery, a former apprentice at Taliesin who spent time with Wright in Baghdad during the May visit, stated that "FLLW didn't like the opera house site, so he went to see the King who told him, 'All Baghdad is yours!' and lent him his plane so that he could see the land. When Mr. Wright came back he had chosen an island." Indira Berndtson, "Video Interview with Nezam and Shenda Amery, September 13, 1989," 2, VHS/DVD 2070.032, FLWFA. Although he accompanied Wright on the plane flight to Baghdad, William Wesley Peters made no mention of the island incident but did describe Wright's having chosen the

site later, when "I wasn't there." Indira Berndtson et al., "Video Interview with William Wesley Peters, February 13, 1991," 3, audiotape 2050s; VHS 2070s, FLWFA. The suggestion that the discovery of the site occurred on the arrival flight into Baghdad first appeared in "New Lights for Aladdin," 80, where it is stated that "Wright found his site the Wright way. Circling in over Baghdad by airplane, he spotted a long narrow island in the middle of the Tigris … and went straight to King Feisal II" to request it for his project. In an interview with me in 1993, Ellen Jawdat, who said she was detailed to pick Wright up at the airport, told me that Wright came off the plane saying he had already finished the design for the island cultural center based on the *Thousand and One Nights* and the Tower of Babylon. She also said that when she told Wright that the island site was reserved for Aalto, who was to design a library for it, Wright replied, "Aalto and I are friends and he'll give me the island" (in conversation, 3 July 1993). This part of the story corresponds with nothing else I have ever come across.

113. "Mr. Wright—June 16, 1957," 5–6; and Berndtson, "Video Interview with William Wesley Peters," 1–3. Wright to Walter Bimson, 11 June 1957, told the Phoenix banker that "IRAQ turned out to be fabulous but real. King Faisal has given me a sizable island in the Tigris on which to put the cultural buildings of the State: Opera, Art Gallery, the University—and broad bridges connecting the city on one side and the university on the other." MS 1502.258, FLWFA.

It should be emphasized that Wright's meetings with the king were extraordinary. None of the other international architects were apparently accorded the privilege. Peters reported that Wright and his wife, Olgivanna, who also accompanied him on the trip, were given presents by the king, including elegant robes. Berndtson, "Video Interview with William Wesley Peters," 6–7. Aside from visits to the Khadimain Mosque, an early sixteenth-century residence, and the historical downtown *suks*, or markets, we do not know what else they saw other than what the *IT* reported. Berndtson, "Video Interview with William Wesley Peters," 1–5; and E. Jawdat, in conversation.

114. The event was reported in "A Baghdad Diary," *IT*, 22 May 1957.

115. A transcript of a tape recording of the talk is preserved as MS 2401.377–78 C, FLWFA. It has deletions and additions that are reflected in revised MS 2401.377–78 D, FLWFA. Further revisions are contained in MSS 2401.377 A and B; and MSS 2401.377–78 E and G, FLWFA. Wright probably edited the transcript in view of the fact that, as he claimed, the text was "printed … and distributed … all through Iraq." "Mr. Wright—June 16, 1957," 2. I have encountered no evidence of such dissemination. In order to convey a sense of what the Iraqi audience actually heard, I quote exclusively from the unedited typescript of the talk. This means including words that were crossed out but allowing for changes in spelling, etc.

116. "Transcript of Tape Recording of Mr. Wright's Speech," MS 2401.377–78 C, 1–2, 5–7.

117. Ibid., 6–7, 2. "Frank Lloyd Wright Designs for Baghdad," *AF* 108 (May 1958): 91, reported that there were thirty thousand cars in Baghdad in 1958. This represented a sixfold increase over the previous decade.

118. Wright, "To the Minister and His Development Board," 1.

119. Ibid., 1–2. The thoughts in this letter were already expressed by Wright on 23 June, three days after signing and dating the first, and largest, group of drawings, in

response to a question regarding the reshaping of the island in a talk to Taliesin Fellowship: "Well, anyhow, I do not know that there is very much hope for the Baghdad project. This is really my proposition to them. The King gave me the island that I asked for, but I do not have the slightest idea in the world what I am going to do with it. And so, I am in a great haste to pull it all together and let them have it, before it is too late. But it is pretty late already, because they have already spent almost all of the money they have on bad buildings and a post office I am going to do, and various other structures scattered all over town, a stadium. I sort of came in on the tail end of things [*sic*], so what impression I can make now, I do not know—but I am going to try." Wright, "YOUTH OF AMERICA," 6–7.

120. The drawings in the Wright Foundation Archives are in the series 5733–34, 5748–52, and 5759. There are eighty-five on the Archives list. In addition, there are eight prints (including one of a lost drawing) and one photograph.

121. A "List of Drawings Actually Sent to Iraqui [*sic*] Government in Baghdad," prepared on 18 November 1963, itemizes forty-eight colored prints and "photo-murals," seven working drawings (of the Post and Telegraph Building), and an unspecified number of black-and-white prints of the aerial perspective of the opera house (figure 10.44) to be used for publicity purposes. MS 1502.258, FLWFA.

122. The cover letter and all the versions of the different parts of the text are in MS 2401.379, FLWFA. The article in *AF* appeared as "Frank Lloyd Wright Designs for Baghdad," 89–101. An exhibition of Wright's drawings for the Baghdad project opened at the Iraqi Consulate in New York on 2 May 1958. The occasion was a diplomatic reception, which Wright and about six hundred others attended, marking Faysal II's twenty-third birthday. "Wright's Plans for Baghdad Cultural Center Shown," *NYT*, 3 May 1958.

123. Frank Lloyd Wright, "Proposed—This Nine-Year Plan for the Cultural Center of Greater Baghdad," June–July 1957, 3–4, MS 2401.379 M, FLWFA.

124. "Baghdad West Growing Quickly."

125. See "Washash to Be Main Centre of Recreation," *IT*, 21 October 1957.

126. Minoprio, Spencely, and Macfarlane, 10, stated that "should a Government decision be made to move the airport, we recommend that the present site should be retained as an open space and that much of it should be intensively planted with trees. This would provide a green lung and cool down the hot winds that blow across the desert to Karkh."

On the Washash Channel, Minoprio, Spencely, and Macfarlane, 18, stated, "We have indicated the Washash Channel as an open space throughout its whole length from the Tigris to the northern boundary of the area proposed for development, and terminating at the present Municipal gardens, with a spur eastwards across the Mosul road to the river. Though this watercourse is blocked at several points, it still exists as a pleasant feature that could be much enhanced by tree-planting. It should certainly be retained open, even if no longer required as a watercourse."

127. Although Le Corbusier and Aalto both had sheets of the Hunting aerial photographs, only Le Corbusier made notations on them.

128. Wright, "Preface," [June–July 1957], 4, 7, MS 2401.379 GG, FLWFA.

129. Wright, "Proposed—This Nine-Year Plan," 2, 4; and

Wright, "Preface," 5, 6.

130. A hard-line half-plan drawing of this was done (FLWFA 5733.036).

131. Minoprio, Spencely, and Macfarlane, 14.

132. Wright, however, did some very large-scale drawings of the area, at least one of which has survived in FLWFA 5733.035. It is approximately three by six feet.

133. "Baghdad West Growing Quickly."

134. Wright, "Proposed—This Nine-Year Plan," 3; and Wright, "To the Minister and His Development Board," 2.

135. The Round City was first discussed in detail and reconstructed, based purely on literary sources, in Le Strange, *Baghdad* (1900; see figure 10.1). The two most significant publications following that were Sarre and Herzfeld, *Archäologische Reise*, vol. 2 (1920; see figure 10.3), and Creswell, *Early Muslim Architecture*, vol. 2 (1940). While not inconceivable, it is unlikely that Wright consulted these works. The Round City was not included in any general survey of architectural history until Spiro Kostof's *History of Architecture: Settings and Rituals* of 1985. When in 1951, however, the Iraqi historian Ahmed Sousa published a map of Baghdad with the Round City superimposed on the modern city (*Baghdad qadiman wa-hadlithan* [Baghdad: Majma al-limi al Iraqi]), followed a year later by his *Atlas Baghdad* (Baghdad: Mudiriyat al-Misahah al-Ammah, 1952), in which the Round City was overlaid on a map of medieval Baghdad, the plan of the original settlement seems to have entered the popular imagination of Iraqi artists, intellectuals, and others. Just a few days after Wright's talk to the Society of Engineers, in which he did not mention the Round City, the local historian and writer Memdouh Zeki published a piece in the *IT* that talked about the Round City as the foundation of Baghdad's long history of urban development and current expansion. M. Zeki, "Baghdad Is Changing Now as It Did 11 Centuries Ago," *IT*, 25 May 1957. Zeki followed this in late August with a three-part series on the history of Baghdad, of which the second one in particular focused on the Round City. Zeki, "Life Revolves Round Palace, Home, and Market," *IT*, 24 August 1957.

As for Wright's attribution of the plan to Harun al-Rashid, it should be recalled that, in his reference to the Round City in his BBC radio interview in January 1955, Minoprio described its author not as al-Mansur but as "Harun al-Rashid's grandfather" (see note 55 above). I thank Mark Warren, a student in my 2013 Baghdad seminar, for providing me with a detailed historiography of the Round City.

136. Wright, "Proposed—This Nine-Year Plan," 2.

137. [Wright], "The University of Baghdad," [June–July 1957], [3], MS 2401.379 II, FLWFA.

138. "Wright Designs for Baghdad," 98. John Rattenbury, who was responsible for the rendering of the University, told me that Wright drew the mosque himself but later whited it out (in conversation, 26 August 1993).

139. For Iraq's education system, see Reeva S. Simon, *Iraq between the Two Wars: The Creation and Implementation of a Nationalist Ideology* (New York: Columbia University Press, 1986).

140. There was a gradual shift during the 1940s and 1950s from the pan-Arabism of Faysal I to a more "separatist" position emphasizing the unique heritage of Iraqi culture. This was particularly true among the more progressive artists and writers, something Wright may have become aware of during his visit. Government propaganda, at the international level at least, stressed the dual heritage of Iraq's past, i.e., its pre-Islamic ancient civilizations and

its Islamic medieval and modern cultures. For instance, *An Introduction to the Past and Present of the Kingdom of Iraq*, published in English by a Committee of Officials in 1946, devoted about two-thirds of its section on pre-twentieth-century history to ancient Mesopotamia and the remaining third to the Islamic period. The purpose of the brochure *Iraq Today ...*, produced by the Directorate-General of Propaganda and published by the Ministry of Interior in May 1953, when Faysal II acceded to the throne, was to provide an overview "of the various phases of development now taking place in this modern kingdom that stands on such ancient foundations" (3). The later Ba'thist regime followed a similar pattern of relating medieval and modern Islamic traditions to Iraq's ancient, pre-Islamic past. See Amatzia Baram, *Culture, History and Ideology in the Formation of Ba'thist Iraq, 1968–89* (New York: St. Martin's, 1991); and Samir al-Khalil [Kanan Makiya], *The Monument: Art, Vulgarity and Responsibility in Iraq* (Berkeley: University of California Press, 1991). For a review of the debate in terms of Iraq's archaeological investigations, see Magnus T. Bernhardsson, *Reclaiming a Plundered Past: Archaeology and Nation Building in Modern Iraq* (Austin: University of Texas Press, 2005).

141. Wright referred to this often in his descriptions of the project: "The Garden of Eden was located at an old city named Edena which was on the great canal taken from the Tigris and the Euphrates ... south of Baghdad. So we are calling this little island ... the Isle of Edena, and we are going to make a big feature of Adam and Eve when we do the building." See, e.g., "Mr. Wright–June 16, 1957," 3–4.

142. Bernhardsson, "Visions of Iraq," 88–90, deals with the multicultural referencing to some extent.

143. Richard Ettinghausen and Oleg Grabar, *The Art and Architecture of Islam: 650–1250* (Harmondsworth: Penguin, 1987), 86–88.

144. Gulick, "Baghdad," 254, discusses the importance of the riverfront *kazinu* in the social life of Baghdad.

145. The Iraqi Symphony Orchestra was created in 1941, and Western classical music became a significant interest of middle- and upper-class residents of Baghdad by the mid-fifties. According to Chadirji, the key supporter of the opera house project was Fadil al-Jamali, who was minister of foreign affairs in the late 1940s, then director general of education in the early 1950s, and prime minister in 1954. Rifat Chadirji, lecture, Baghdad seminar, Harvard University, 1992.

146. The stated capacity of the house differs considerably from one Wright text to the next. *FLWPS*, 218, maintains that "the auditorium ... was created to seat 3,000." In "Wright Designs for Baghdad," 95, the architect wrote that in addition to "a 1,600-seat opera auditorium ... 3,700 seats [were] available for conventions or patriotic celebrations." The expanded civic auditorium idea may not have been Wright's alone, but there are no records of his discussions with the Development Board concerning the matter.

147. In order to eliminate the need for a fly loft, the revolving circular stage was designed to be lowered for scenery changes.

148. Frank Lloyd Wright, "The Crescent Opera and Civic Auditorium," 1–2, MS 2401.378 II, FLWFA.

149. Wright certainly would have seen the article on the Tallahassee project in G[eorge] E[verard] Kidder Smith, "Beethoven and Basketball," *AF* 106 (March 1957): 114–17 since news of his commission for the Baghdad Opera House ("Wright to Design Baghdad Opera") appeared in the same issue of the magazine.

150. Wright, "Crescent Opera," 2.

151. The results of the Sydney competition (opened 1955; judged late January 1957) were widely published in February–April 1957. An article appeared in *AF* in March and another in *AR* in April. According to Sigfried Giedion, "Jörn Utzon and the Third Generation," *Zodiac* 14 (1965): 38, "in 1949 a scholarship took him [Utzon] first to the USA and then to Mexico. He spent a short time with Frank Lloyd Wright in Taliesin West and Taliesin East." Utzon, however, was never formally a member of the Taliesin Fellowship.

152. Wright, "Crescent Opera," 1. One of Wright's first references to the tales was the mural in his Oak Park house playroom (1895). The "Transcript of Tape Recording of Mr. Wright Speech" begins with a reference to the tales: "I am one of the 'subjects' of Harun Al-Rashid by the way of the 'Arabian Nights' and I know nearly every tale of the Arabian Nights today by heart even [as] I had them as a boy" (1). The framing character of the arch not only relates to the framing narrative of Shahrazad and Shahrayar but also physically frames the procession through the spaces. This processional aspect becomes even more pronounced when one takes into account the fact that the crescent arch was to be built not perpendicular to the ground but tilted back, so as to embrace the visitor's movement in depth (see figure 10.47).

153. The crescent (*hilal*) in Islamic culture represents the new or waxing moon. It is important in the Islamic calendar, which is lunar rather than solar. Its appearance determines the date of pilgrimage to Mecca (*hajj*) as well as the beginning and end of Ramadan. Used as a military and religious symbol by the Turks during the Ottoman Empire, it became in the nineteenth century a sign of Islam and was adopted by many Arab countries in the twentieth century for their national flags.

Wright may also have had in mind the early Sassanid arch of the Palace at Ctesiphon (the capital of Mesopotamia just prior to the construction of the Round City), which remained an important symbol of Iraqi culture. Frank Lloyd Wright and Iovanna Lloyd Wright, *Architecture: Man in Possession of His Earth*, ed. Patricia Coyle Nicholson (Garden City, N.Y.: Doubleday, 1962), 77, noted that, "the arch was first used in this land between the Tigris and the Euphrates because wide openings had to be spanned with units no larger than brick. The evolution from the Sumerian architecture of great ramps, terraces and roadways to the more delicately ornamented arched and domed architecture of the Persians has created a lasting wealth of architectural ideas."

154. Wright "Crescent Opera," 2. The tale of Aladdin was not part of the *Thousand and One Nights* when the stories were recorded in the late thirteenth and fourteenth centuries. It first appeared in Antoine Galland's early eighteenth-century French translation, although it soon became one of the most famous of the tales. Wright apparently owned and read Richard Burton's late nineteenth-century translation.

155. Without specifically referring to the Baghdad project, N. K. Smith, *Frank Lloyd Wright*, 175ff., noted the general significance of Edenic imagery in Wright's work.

156. Wright thought of Baghdad as being almost midway between the biblical and ancient sites to which he referred: "The Garden of Eden is only sixty miles away, and the Tower of Babylon is only about forty miles away." Response to question after talk to Michigan Society of Architects, 21 October 1957, in Patrick J. Meehan, *Truth Against the World: Frank Lloyd Wright Speaks for an Organic Architecture* (New York: John Wiley, 1987), 155.

157. This was probably a major reason for the project's rejection by the successor military regime (another being the regime's stated desire for explicitly "modern" representations of its industrial base).

158. A significant argument for the legitimacy of the Hashimites was their supposed descent from Fatima, the Prophet Muhammad's daughter. The propagandistic *Introduction to the Past and Present of the Kingdom of Iraq*, 3, stressed that "by choosing a Hashimite as head of the State she [Iraq] also restored to the throne the very family from which the Abbasid Caliphs themselves had sprung."

159. I thank my colleague Gülru Necipoğlu for pointing out the relationship between the Opera House and literary descriptions of palaces and pavilions in the *Thousand and One Nights*. She also noted that Wright's device of backlighting a fountain to create a rainbow effect has its parallel in a number of Mughal palaces, where candles were placed in niches behind fountains.

160. Wright, "Proposed—This Nine-Year Plan," 1; and "Transcript of Tape Recording of Mr. Wright's Speech," 8. The dedication also included the crown prince, Abd al-Illah.

161. "Architects Build a Modern Baghdad."

162. Quoted in Charles Moore, *Daniel H. Burnham: Architect, Planner of Cities*, 2 vols. (Boston: Houghton Mifflin, 1921), 2:147.

163. "Architects Build a Modern Baghdad" noted that Wright's "whole" project "may be delayed pending the completion of hydrological studies on the flow of the Tigris." "Surveying for Tigris Corniche," *IT*, 1 March 1958, reported on one of such studies. As Minoprio, Spencely, and Macfarlane suspected, the flood-prevention measures put in place in the mid-1950s were insufficient, and major flooding of the city occurred in 1971 and 1988.

164. The last communication in the Aalto Foundation Archives is a letter informing him that the General Post Office and the "Fine Arts Institute ... [were] not abandoned for the present time," although nothing ever happened on either building. Director General of Buildings to Aalto, 3 July 1963, Bagdad, Directorate General of Building, AA 5, AAM. Dudok traveled to Baghdad in September 1959 at which time he submitted a final version of his project. The last communication in the Dudok Papers is a letter from the architect complaining about the nonpayment of fees in which he notes that the "project has reached a deadlock." Dudok to Ministry of Works and Housing, 20 December 1962, DUDO 212 M.124, HNI.

The Le Corbusier Stadium and sports complex fared much better. It was continually discussed and revised up through the architect's death in 1965, the most important revision occurring following a change in site in late 1960 that relocated the project to East Baghdad. Correspondence continued in the later 1960s, and the project was partially revived in 1973, when the small, enclosed sports hall was built by Le Corbusier's former associate Georges-Marc Présenté on yet a third site. It was completed in 1983 as the Saddam Hussein Gymnasium. See Suzanne Taj-Eldin and Stanislaus von Moos, "Nach Plänen von ... : Eine Gymnastikhalle von Le Corbusier in Baghdad," *Archithèse* 3 (May–June 1983): 39–44; Taj-Eldin, "Baghdad: Box of Miracles," *Architectural Review* 181 (January 1987): 78–83; "Saddam Hussein Sports Complex (1955–1965, 1979–1983: Le Corbusier and George Marc [*sic*] Présenté," in Azara, 296–97; and Marefat, *The Le Corbusier Gymnasium*.

The Ponti Development Ministry and Board Building was sent out for bids in August 1960 (as the Ministry of Planning and Economic Planning Board Building) and was completed in 1962. The initial plans for Baghdad University, done in 1958, were presented to General Qasim in early 1959. Changes were requested, and a significantly different final scheme was approved the following year. Construction was begun in 1962 but never fully realized.

Because the materials in the Taliesin Associated Architects Archives concerning Baghdad have not been located, it is impossible to state with any degree of certainty how and when the Wright project evaporated. What we do know is the following. Probably sometime in May 1958, Ellen Jawdat wrote to Ise Gropius of Wright's "Opera House having been consigned forever, we hope, to a dusty shelf," Walter Gropius Papers. Wright himself, as we read, had doubts about the government's will and ability to carry through with the project from quite early on. Following a year of considerable turmoil and realignment of government agencies after the July 1958 revolution, during which time Wright died, the earlier Development Board program was reviewed. Most of the projects were kept on the books, except for Wright's. Republic of Iraq, *The Five-Years Detailed Economic Plan (1961–62)–(1965–66)* (Baghdad: Ministry of Guidance, 1961), 463–512.

Wright's design was much more tied to the Hashimite dynasty in terms of expression than the other projects. Their adherence to a stricter functionalist form of expression allowed them to appear more in tune with Qasim's socialist-revolutionary aims. Nevertheless, the Qasim regime, despite early rhetoric to the contrary, completed and made use of the Royal Palace and Parliament. By the end of 1959, Qasim decided not only to develop a zoo at the scale of London's Kew Gardens but to do it on Wright's island site. Abdul Karim Qasim, *Objectives of Iraq's Revolution*, press conference, 2 December 1959 (Baghdad: Ministry of Guidance, 1959), 77. Gropius informed his wife on 26 February 1960 that his own reputation was "sky-high in Baghdad" and that it looked as if the opera house was also to be given to him, adding, "F. L. Wright would turn over in his grave." Quoted in Isaacs, *Walter Gropius*, 2:1044. An international competition for an opera house was announced in November 1962, but nothing came of it.

Conclusion

1. Giedion, in "In Search of a New Monumentality," 127.

An Act Providing for the Zoning of the District of Columbia and the Regulation of the Location, Height, Bulk, and Uses of Buildings and Other Structures and of the Uses of Land in the District of Columbia, and for Other Purposes. Approved June 20, 1938. In *Public Laws*, vol. 52 of *United States Statutes at Large Containing the Laws and Concurrent Resolutions Enacted during the Third Session of the Seventy-Fifth Congress of the United States of America, 1938*, chap. 534, 797–802. Washington, D.C.: Government Printing Office, 1938.

An Act to Regulate the Height, Area and Use of Buildings in the District of Columbia and to Create a Zoning Commission, and for Other Purposes. Approved March 1, 1920. In *Public Laws of the United States of America Passed by the Sixty-Sixth Congress, 1919–1921*, vol. 41, pt. 1 of *The Statutes at Large of the United States of America from May, 1919, to March, 1921*, chap. 92, 500–502. Washington, D.C.: Government Printing Office, 1921.

An Act to Regulate the Height of Buildings in the District of Columbia. Approved June 1, 1910. In *Public Acts and Resolutions*, vol. 35, pt. 1 of *Statutes of the United States of America Passed at the Second Session of the Sixty-First Congress*, chap. 263, 452–55. Washington, D.C.: Government Printing Office, 1910.

Aguar, Charles E., and Berdeanna Aguar. *Wrightscapes: Frank Lloyd Wright's Landscape Designs.* New York: McGraw-Hill, 2002.

Alberts, Robert C. *The Shaping of the Point: Pittsburgh's Renaissance Park.* Pittsburgh: University of Pittsburgh Press, 1980.

Alexander, Stephen. "Frank Lloyd Wright's Utopia." *New Masses* 15 (18 June 1935): 28.

El-Ali, Saleh Ahmad. "The Foundation of Baghdad." In *The Islamic City: A Colloquium*, edited by A. H. Hourani and S. M. Stern, 87–101. Oxford: Bruno Cassirer, 1970.

Alofsin, Anthony. "Broadacre City: The Reception of a Modernist Vision." In *Modernist Visions and the Contemporary American City*, vol. 5 of *Center: A Journal for Architecture in America*, 8–43. Austin: Center for the Study of American Architecture, School of Architecture, University of Texas, 1989.

[The Architects Collaborative]. *Report on the University of Baghdad Designed by The Architects Collaborative, Cambridge, Massachusetts, U.S.A.*, n.d.

Architecture coloniale et patrimoine: expériences européennes. Actes de la table ronde organisée par l'Institut national du Patrimoine, . . . 2005. Paris: Somogy/Institut national du patrimoine, 2006.

al-Ashab, Khalis H. "The Urban Geography of Baghdad." Ph.D. diss., Newcastle upon Tyne, 1974.

Azara, Pedro, ed. *Ciudad del espejismo: Bagdad, de Wright a Venturi/City of Mirages: Baghdad, from Wright to Venturi.* Barcelona: Departament de Composició Arquitectònica, Universitat Politècnica de Catalunya, 2008.

Bacon, Mardges. *Le Corbusier in America: Travels in the Land of the Timid.* Cambridge, Mass.: MIT Press, 2001.

Ballon, Hilary. "From New York to Bartlesville: The Pilgrimage of Wright's Skyscraper." In *Prairie Skyscraper: Frank Lloyd Wright's Price Tower*, edited by Anthony Alofsin, 100–111. New York: Rizzoli International, 2005.

Banham, Reyner. *Megastructure: Urban Futures of the Recent Past.* New York: Harper & Row, 1972.

Barker, T[heodore] C[ardwell]. "The International History of Motor Transport." *Journal of Contemporary History* 20 (January 1985): 3–19.

Bartholomew, Harland. *Madison, Wisconsin: Report on Major Streets, Transportation and Zoning.* N.p., 1922.

Barton, George Edward. "A $6000 House with a Garden." *LHJ* 19 (January 1902): 15.

Batatu, Hanna. *The Old Social Classes and the Revolutionary Movements of Iraq: A Study of Iraq's Old Landed and Commercial Classes and of Its Communists, Ba'thists, and Free Officers.* Princeton: Princeton University Press, 1978.

Bauman, John F., and Edward K. Muller. *Before Renaissance: Planning in Pittsburgh, 1889–1943.* Pittsburgh: University of Pittsburgh Press, 2006.

———. "The Olmsteds in Pittsburgh: (Part I) Landscaping the Private City." *Pittsburgh History: A Magazine of the City and Its Region* 76 (Fall 1993): 122–38.

———. "The Olmsteds in Pittsburgh: (Part II) Shaping the Progressive City." *Pittsburgh History: A Magazine of the City and Its Region* 76 (Winter 1993/94): 191–205.

Bechtel, Clifton R. *Our Traffic Problem.* Chicago: Chicago Real Estate Board, 1927.

Belluschi, Pietro. "The Meaning of Regionalism in Architecture." *AR* 118 (December 1955): 131–39.

Bennett, Edward H. *The Chicago Business Center and the Subway Question.* [Chicago]: By the Author, 15 April 1926.

———. "Chicago's Advance to Bring Traffic Paths High in Air." *CHE*, 18 January 1926.

———. "Grade Separation Cure for Loop Congestion." *CHE*, 16 January 1926.

———. "Loop Termed Key to Traffic Problem Solution." *CHE*, 14 January 1926.

———. "Raised Sidewalks and Traffic Separation Urged for Chicago." *AC* 35 (September 1926): 334–36.

———. "Subway Condemned as Loop Congestion Cure." *CHE*, 15 January 1926.

Bernhardsson, Magnus T. *Reclaiming a Plundered Past: Archaeology and Nation Building in Modern Iraq.* Austin: University of Texas Press, 2005.

Biebel, Anne E. "William Kaeser's Fifty Year Plan for Madison." *Historic Madison* 13 (1996): 43–56.

Board of Development and Ministry of Development, Government of Iraq. *Development of Iraq: Second Development Week.* Baghdad: Government of Iraq, 1957.

Board of Estimate and Apportionment, City of New York. *Building Zone Resolution (Adopted July 25, 1916).* In Commission on Building Districts and Restrictions, *Final Report, June 2, 1916*, appendix VII, 232–80. New York: Committee on the City Plan, Board of Estimate and Apportionment, 1916.

Bok, Edward. *The Americanization of Edward Bok: An Autobiography.* Originally published in 1920 as *The Americanization of Edward Bok: An Autobiography of a Dutch Boy Fifty Years After.* Reprint, Philadelphia: American Foundation, 1973.

Boyer, M. Christine. *Dreaming the Rational City: The Myth of American City Planning.* Cambridge, Mass.: MIT Press, 1983.

Brierly, Cornelia. *Tales of Taliesin: A Memoir of Fellowship.* Tempe: Herberger Center for Design Excellence, Arizona State University, in collaboration with Frank Lloyd Wright Foundation, 1999.

"Broadacre City: Frank Lloyd Wright, Architect." *AA* 146 (May 1935): 55–62.

Brooks, H. Allen. *Frank Lloyd Wright and the Prairie School.* New York: George Braziller, in association with Cooper-Hewitt Museum, 1984.

———, gen. ed. *Le Corbusier: Projet pour un Stade Olympique, Baghdad, and Other Buildings and Projects, 1953*, vol. 27 of *The Le Corbusier Archive*, 101–514. New York: Garland, 1984.

Brown, Jeffrey. "From Traffic Regulation to Limited Ways: The Effort to Build a Science of Transportation Planning." *JPH* 5 (February 2006): 3–34.

Brunner, Arnold. "Coming City of Set-Back Skyscrapers: Diminishing Terraces Stretching Indefinitely Upward." *NYT Magazine*, 29 April 1923, 5, 10.

Burnham, Daniel H., and Edward H. Bennett. *Plan of Chicago*. Edited by Charles Moore. Originally published 1909. Reprint, New York: Princeton Architectural Press, 1993.

Burnham, Daniel H., with Edward H. Bennett. *Report on a Plan for San Francisco*. San Francisco: By the City, 1905.

Burnham, Daniel H., John M. Carrère, and Arnold W. Brunner. *The Group Plan of the Public Buildings of the City of Cleveland. Report Made to the Honorable Tom L. Johnson, Mayor, and to the Honorable Board of Public Service*. New York: Cheltenham Press, August 1903.

Caemmerer, H. P. *Washington: The National Capital*. Senate Document no. 332, 71st Congress, 3d Session. Washington, D.C.: Government Printing Office, 1932.

Cerdà, Ildefonso. *Teoría general de la urbanizacíon y aplicacíon de sus principios y doctrinas a la reforma y ensanche de Barcelona*. 2 vols. Madrid: Imprenta Española, 1867.

Chicago Plan Commission. *Through Traffic Streets*. Chicago: City Council Committee on Efficiency, Economy and Rehabilitation, 1925.

Chicago Zoning Ordinance, Passed by the City Council of the City of Chicago on April 5, 1923. Chicago: Al. F. Gorman, City Clerk, 1923.

Choay, Françoise. *The Rule and the Model: On the Theory of Architecture and Urbanism*. Originally published in French 1980. Edited by Denise Bratton. Cambridge, Mass.: MIT Press, 1997.

City Club Housing Exhibition, April 15 to June 1 [1913]: Guide to the Exhibition. [Chicago: City Club, 1913].

"City Planning Study." In *Proceedings of the Fifth National Conference on City Planning, Chicago, Illinois, May 5–7, 1913*, 163–211. Boston, 1913.

Ciucci, Giorgio, et al. *The American City: From the Civil War to the New Deal*. Originally published 1973. Translated from the Italian by Barbara Luigia La Penta. Cambridge, Mass.: MIT Press, 1983.

Cleary, Richard, et al. *Frank Lloyd Wright: From Within Outward*. New York: Skira Rizzoli, Guggenheim Museum, 2009.

Cleary, Richard L. "Beyond Fallingwater: Edgar J. Kaufmann, Frank Lloyd Wright and the Projects for Pittsburgh." In *Fallingwater and Pittsburgh*, vol. 2 of *Wright Studies*, edited by Narciso G. Menocal, 80–113. Carbondale: Southern Illinois University Press, 2000.

———. "Edgar J. Kaufmann, Frank Lloyd Wright and the 'Pittsburgh Point Park Coney Island in Automobile Scale.'" *JSAH* 52 (June 1993): 139–58.

———. *Merchant Prince and Master Builder: Edgar J. Kaufmann and Frank Lloyd Wright*. Pittsburgh: Heinz Architectural Center, Carnegie Museum of Art, in association with University of Washington Press, 1999.

Cohen, Jean-Louis. *Scenes of the World to Come: European Architecture and the American Challenge, 1893–1960*. Translated from the French by Kenneth Hylton. Paris: Flammarion; Montreal: Canadian Centre for Architecture, 1995.

Collins, Christiane Crasemann. *Werner Hegemann and the Search for Universal Urbanism*. New York: Norton, 2005.

Collins, George R. "Broadacre City: Wright's Utopia Reconsidered." In *Four Great Makers of Modern Architecture: Gropius, Le Corbusier, Mies van der Rohe, Wright*, Verbatim Record of a Symposium Held at the School of Architecture, Columbia University, March–May 1961, 55–74. New York: Trustees of Columbia University, 1963.

———. "The Ciudad Lineal of Madrid." *JSAH* 18 (May 1959): 38–53.

———. "Linear Planning throughout the World." *JSAH* 18 (October 1959): 74–93.

Collins, George R., and Christiane Crasemann Collins. *Camillo Sitte and the Birth of Modern City Planning*. Columbia University Studies in Art History and Archaeology 3. New York: Random House, 1965.

Collins, Peter. "The Origins of Graph Paper as an Influence on Architectural Design." *JSAH* 21 (1962): 159–62.

Corbett, Harvey Wiley. "Do We Want Three-Level Streets?" In *Housing Problems in America: Proceedings of the Tenth National Conference on Housing. Philadelphia, Jan. 28, 29, 30, 1929*, 244–46. New York: National Housing Association, 1929.

———. "High Buildings on Narrow Streets: Being Extracts from a Paper Delivered Before the Fifty-Fourth Annual Convention of the American Institute of Architects." *AA* 119 (8 June 1921): 603–19.

———. "The Influence of Zoning on New York's Skyline." *AAAR* 123 (3 January 1923): 1–4.

———. "New Heights in American Architecture." *Yale Review* 17 (July 1928): 690–701.

———. "New Stones for Old." *Saturday Evening Post* 198 (15 May 1926): 16–17, 175, 177–78.

———. "What the Architect Thinks of Zoning." *AAAR* 125 (13 February 1924): 149–50.

———. "Zoning and the Envelope of the Building." *Pencil Points* 4 (April 1923): 15–18.

Corboz, André. "Les Dimensions culturelles de la grille territoriale américaine." In *Le Territoire comme palimpseste et autres essais*, edited by Sébastien Marot, 172–84. Besançon, France: Editions de l'Imprimeur, 2001.

Cram, Ralph Adams. "A Country House of Moderate Cost." *LHJ* 18 (January 1901): 5.

Cranshawe, Roger. "Wright's Progressive Utopia." *aaq: Architectural Association Quarterly* 10, no. 1 (1978): 3–9.

Creese, Walter L. *The Crowning of the American Landscape*. Princeton: Princeton University Press, 1985.

———. *The Search for Environment: The Garden City — Before and After*. Originally published 1966. Rev. and enl. ed. Baltimore: Johns Hopkins University Press, 1992.

Creswell, K[eppel] A[rchibald] C[ameron]. *Early 'Abbāsids, Umayyads of Cordova, Aghlabids, Tūlūnids, and Samānids, A.D. 751–905*. Vol. 2 of *Early Muslim Architecture*. Oxford: Clarendon, 1940.

Crinson, Mark. *Modern Architecture and the End of Empire*. Aldershot: Ashgate, 2003.

Cronon, William. *Nature's Metropolis: Chicago and the Great West*. New York: Norton, 1991.

Delano, Frederic A. "The Nation's Interest in the Nation's Capital." In *Planning Problems of Town, City, and Region: Papers and Discussions at the Nineteenth National Conference on City Planning, Held at Washington, D.C., May 9 to 11, 1927*, 221. Philadelphia: Wm. F. Fell, 1927.

———. "The Service of the National Capital Park and Planning Commission." In *American Civic Annual*, vol. 5, ed. Harlean James, 63–65. Washington, D.C.: American Civic Association, 1934.

De Long, David G. "Eliel Saarinen and the Cranbrook Tradition in Architecture and Design." In *Design in America: The Cranbrook Vision, 1925–1950*, edited by Robert Judson Clark and Andrea P. A. Belloli, 46–89. New York: Abrams, in association with Detroit Institute of Arts and Metropolitan Museum of Art, 1983.

———, ed. *Frank Lloyd Wright and the Living City*. Weil am Rhein, Germany: Vitra Design Museum, 1998.

Dethier, Kathryn. "The Spirit of Progressive Reform: The *Ladies' Home Journal* House Plans, 1900–1902." *Journal of Design History* 6 (1993): 247–61.

Doxiadis Associates. *Progress of the Housing Program*. Monthly Report No. 46, May 1959. Prepared for the Government of the Republic of Iraq, Development Board and Ministry of Development. Baghdad and Athens, May 1959.

Duffus, R[obert] L[uther]. "A Vision of the Future City: Le Corbusier's Revolutionary Plan for the Modern Metropolis." *NYT Book Review*, 27 October 1929, 1.

Duri, A[bdul] A[ziz]. "Baghdād." In *The Encyclopaedia of Islam*. Vol. 1, new ed. Leiden: Brill, 1960.

Eaton, Leonard. *Two Chicago Architects and Their Clients: Frank Lloyd Wright and Howard Van Doren Shaw*. Cambridge, Mass.: MIT Press, 1969.

Ebner, Michael H. *Creating Chicago's North Shore: A Suburban History*. Chicago: University of Chicago Press, 1988.

Edelman, David J., and David J. Allor. "Ladislas Segoe and the Emergence of the Professional Planning Consultant." *JPH* 2 (February 2003): 47–78.

Eesteren, Cornelis van. *Het idee van de functionele stad/The Idea of the Functional City: Een lazing met lichtbeelden, 1928/A Lecture with Slides, 1928*. Introduction by Vincent van Rossem. Rotterdam: NAi Uitgevers, 1997.

Embury, Aymar. "New York's New Architecture." *AF* 35 (October 1921): 119–24.

Eyre, Wilson, Jr. "A Country House on a Small Place." *LHJ* 18 (November 1901): 15.

Fahey, Daniel Cox, Jr. "Jefferson National Expansion Memorial: A Mississippi Waterfront Development in St. Louis." *Landscape Architecture* 31 (October 1940): 4–8.

Ferriss, Hugh. "Civic Architecture of the Immediate Future: The Demands of American Civilization Have Compelled a Radical Change in Our Building Laws." *Arts and Decoration* 18 (November 1922): 12–13.

———. "The New Architecture." *NYT Book Review and Magazine*, 19 March 1922, 8–9, 27.

Fethi, Ihsan. "Contemporary Architecture in Baghdad: Its Roots and Traditions." *Process, Architecture* 59 (1985): 112–32.

Fishman, Robert. *Bourgeois Utopias: The Rise and Fall of Suburbia*. New York: Basic Books, 1987.

———. *Urban Utopias in the 20th Century: Ebenezer Howard, Frank Lloyd Wright, Le Corbusier*. New York: Basic Books, 1977.

Flagg, Ernest. "The New York Tenement-House Evil and Its Cure." *Scribner's Magazine* 16 (July 1894): 108–17.

Fogelson, Robert M. *Downtown: Its Rise and Fall, 1880–1950*. New Haven: Yale University Press, 2001.

Forest Hills Gardens: The Suburban Land Development of the Russell Sage Foundation. New York: Sage Foundation Homes, 1911.

Foster, Mark S. *From Streetcar to Superhighway: American City Planners and Urban Transportation, 1900–1940*. Technology and Urban Growth. Philadelphia: Temple University Press, 1981.

Frampton, Kenneth. "Towards a Critical Regionalism: Six Points for an Architecture of Resistance." In *The*

Anti-Aesthetic: Essays on Postmodern Culture, edited by Hal Foster, 16–30. Port Townsend, Wash.: Bay Press, 1983.

Franclieu, Françoise de, ed. *1954–1957*. Vol. 3 of *Le Corbusier Sketchbooks*. New York: Architectural History Foundation, 1982.

Frazer, Horace S. "A Wood and Stone House for $6700." *LHJ* 18 (October 1901): 15.

Gardiner, Stephen. *Kuwait: The Making of a City*. Harlow, Essex: Longman, 1983.

Giedion, Sigfried. In "In Search of a New Monumentality: A Symposium by Gregor Paulsson [et al.]." *Architectural Review* 104 (September 1948): 117–28.

———. "The Need for a New Monumentality." In *New Architecture and City Planning*, edited by Paul Zucker, 549–68. New York: Philosophical Library, 1944.

———. *Space, Time and Architecture: The Growth of a New Tradition*. Originally published 1941. 4th ed., enl. Cambridge, Mass.: Harvard University Press, 1962.

———. "The State of Contemporary Architecture: 1. The Regionalist Approach." *AR* 115 (January 1954): 132–37.

Giedion, Sigfried, José Luis Sert, and Fernand Léger. "Nine Points on Monumentality" (1943). In *Architecture, You and Me: A Diary of a Development*, 48–51. Cambridge, Mass.: Harvard University Press, 1958.

Goode, James M. *Best Addresses: A Century of Washington's Distinguished Apartment Houses*. Washington, D.C.: Smithsonian Press, 1988.

Government of Iraq, Development Board—Ministry of Development and Doxiadis Associates. *The Housing Program of Iraq*. Baghdad, March 1957.

Government of Iraq and Doxiadis Associates. *Housing in Baghdad*. Baghdad, March 1957.

Grey, Elmer. "An Old English House for $7000." *LHJ* 18 (September 1901): 15.

Griffin, Marion Mahony. "Democratic Architecture. Its Development, Its Principles and Its Ideals." Parts 1 and 2. *Building* (Australia) 14 (12 June and 12 August 1914): 101–2 and 88–91.

Gulick, John. "Baghdad: Portrait of a City in Physical and Cultural Change." *JAIP* 33 (July 1967): 246–55.

Gutheim, Frederick, ed. *In the Cause of Architecture: Frank Lloyd Wright. Essays by Frank Lloyd Wright for Architectural Record with a Symposium on Architecture with and without Wright by Eight Who Knew Him*. New York: Architectural Record Books, 1975.

Gutheim, Frederick, and Antoinette J. Lee. *Worthy of the Nation: Washington, DC, from L'Enfant to the National Capital Planning Commission*. 2nd ed. Baltimore: Johns Hopkins University Press, 2006.

Haberman, Stanley John. "The Iraq Development Board: Administration and Program." *Middle East Journal* 9 (Spring 1959): 179–86.

Hall, Peter. *Cities of Tomorrow: An Intellectual History of Urban Planning and Design in the Twentieth Century*. Originally published 1988. Reprint, Oxford: Basil Blackwell, 1990.

Hamilton, Mary Jane. "The Olin Terraces and Monona Terrace Projects." In *Frank Lloyd Wright and Madison: Eight Decades of Artistic and Social Interaction*, edited by Paul E. Sprague, 195–206. Madison: Elvehjem Museum of Art, University of Wisconsin–Madison, 1990.

Hancock, John. "'Ciò che è giusto deve essere adatto': Disegni e piani di John Nolen, city planner americano/'What Is Fair Must Be Fit': Drawings and Plans by John Nolen, American City Planner." *Lotus International: Rivista trimestrale di architettura/Quarterly Architectural Review* 50, no. 2 (1986): 30–45.

———. "John Nolen and the American City Planning Movement: A History of Cultural Change and Community Response, 1900–1940." Ph.D. diss., University of Pennsylvania, 1964.

Handlin, David P. *The American Home: Architecture and Society, 1815–1915*. Boston: Little, Brown, 1979.

———. "The Context of the Modern City." *Harvard Architecture Review* 2 (Spring 1981): 76–89.

Harkness, John C., ed. *1945–1969: The Work of the Architects Collaborative*. Vol. 4 of *The Walter Gropius Archive*. New York: Garland, 1991.

Harloff, Paul F. "Building for the Future." *CT*, letter to the editor, 31 July 1938.

———. "Favors Lake Edge as City-County Building Site." *CT*, letter to the editor, 12 August 1938.

———. "For Over-the-Lake Site for City-County Building." *CT*, letter to the editor, 9 September 1938.

———. "Lake Site for City-County Building." *CT*, letter to the editor, 6 August 1938.

———. "Mr. Harloff's Park Plan." *CT*, letter to the editor, 26 August 1938.

Hegemann, Werner. "Das Hochhaus als Verkehrsstörer und der Wettbewerb der Chicago Tribune: Mittelalterliche Enge und Neuzeitliche Gotik." *Wasmuths Monatshefte für Baukunst und Städtebau* 8, nos. 9–10 (1924): 297–300.

Hegemann, Werner, and Elbert Peets. *The American Vitruvius: An Architect's Handbook of Civic Art*. Originally published 1922. Edited by Alan J. Plattus. New York: Princeton Architectural Press, 1988.

Hénard, Eugène. *Etudes sur les transformations de Paris*. Paris: Libraries-Imprimeries Réunies, 1903.

Henderson, J. Welles, IV. "The Evolution of Washington's Paradigm: A Study of Frank Lloyd Wright's Crystal Heights Project and the Smithsonian Gallery of Art Competition, Washington, D.C., 1939–1941." B.A. thesis, Harvard University, 2000.

Hilberseimer, Ludwig. *Groszstadtarchitektur*. Baubücher 3. Stuttgart: Julius Hoffmann, 1927.

———. *Grosstadtbauten*. Neue Architektur 1. Hannover: Aposs, 1925.

Hill, Pamela. "Marion Mahony Griffin: The Chicago Years." In *Chicago Architecture: Histories, Revisions, Alternatives*, edited by Charles Waldheim and Katerina Rüedi Ray, 143–62. Chicago Architecture and Urbanism. Chicago: University of Chicago Press, 2005.

Hines, Thomas S. *Burnham of Chicago: Architect and Planner*. New York: Oxford University Press, 1974.

Hitchcock, Henry-Russell. *In the Nature of Materials: The Buildings of Frank Lloyd Wright, 1887–1941*. Originally published 1942. Reprint, New York: Da Capo Press, 1975.

Holleran, Michael. *Boston's "Changeful Times": Origins of Preservation and Planning in America*. Originally published 1988. Reprint, Baltimore: Johns Hopkins University Press, 2001.

———. "Boston's 'Sacred Sky Line': From Prohibiting to Sculpting Skyscrapers, 1891–1928." *Journal of Urban History* 22 (July 1996): 552–85.

Hooker, George E. "Cammillo [sic] Sitte, City Builder." *Chicago Record-Herald*, 15 January 1904.

———. "Congestion and Its Causes in Chicago." In *Proceedings of the Second National Conference on City Planning and the Problems of Congestion, Rochester, New York, May 2–4, 1910*, 42–57. Boston, 1910.

———. "Garden Cities." *Journal of the American Institute of Architects* 2 (February 1914): 80–91.

———. "The German Municipal Movement." *Chicago Record-Herald*, 30 January 1904.

———. "A Plan for Chicago." *Survey* 22 (4 September 1909): 778–90.

———. "Report on City Planning in Chicago." In *City Planning. Hearing before the Committee on the District of Columbia, United States Senate, on the Subject of City Planning*. 61st Congress, 2d Session, Document No. 422, 11 March 1910, 96–98. Washington, D.C.: Government Printing Office, 1910.

———. *Through Routes for Chicago's Steam Railroads: The Best Means for Attaining Popular and Comfortable Travel for Chicago and Suburbs*. Chicago: City Club of Chicago, 1914.

Horsfall, T[homas] C[oglan]. *The Improvement of the Dwellings and Surroundings of the People: The Example of Germany*. Manchester: University Press, 1904.

Howard, Ebenezer. *Garden Cities of To-morrow (Being the Second Edition of "To-morrow: A Peaceful Path to Real Reform")*. London: Swan Sonnenschein, 1902.

———. *Tomorrow: A Peaceful Path to Real Reform*. Original ed. with new commentary by Peter Hall, Dennis Hardy, and Colin Ward. London: Routledge, 2003.

Hudnut, Joseph. "Last of the Romans." *Magazine of Art* 34 (April 1941): 169–73.

The International Competition for a New Administration Building for the Chicago Tribune MCMXII, Containing All the Designs Submitted in Response to the Chicago Tribune's $100,000 Offer Commemorating Its Seventy Fifth Anniversary, June 10, 1922. Chicago: Tribune Company, 1923.

Isaacs, Reginald R. *Walter Gropius: Der Mensch und sein Werk*. Vol. 2. Berlin: Gebrüder Mann, 1984.

Isenstadt, Sandy, and Kishwar Rizvi, eds. *Modernism in the Middle East: Architecture and Politics in the Twentieth Century*. Seattle: University of Washington Press, 2008.

Ives, H. Douglas. "The Moderate Priced Apartment Hotel." *AF* 53 (September 1930): 309–12.

Jackson, Frank. *Sir Raymond Unwin: Architect, Planner and Visionary*. Architects in Perspective. London: A. Zwemmer, 1985.

Jackson, Kenneth T. *Crabgrass Frontier: The Suburbanization of the United States*. New York: Oxford University Press, 1985.

Jacobs, Jane. "Downtown Is for People." *Fortune* 57 (April 1958): 133–40, 236, 238.

Jakle, John, A., and Keith A. Sculle. *Lots of Parking: Land Use in a Car Culture*. Charlottesville: University of Virginia Press, 2004.

Jalal, Ferhang. *The Role of Government in the Industrialization of Iraq, 1950–65*. London: Frank Cass, 1972.

Jewad, Mustapha, et al., eds. *Baghdad: An Illustrated History*. Baghdad: Iraqi Engineers Association, 1969 (in Arabic).

Johnson, Donald Leslie. "Frank Lloyd Wright's Community Planning." *JPH* 3 (February 2004): 3–28.

———. *Frank Lloyd Wright versus America: The 1930s*. Cambridge, Mass.: MIT Press, 1990.

———. "Origin of the Neighbourhood Unit." *Planning Perspectives* 17 (2002): 227–45.

Johnson, Hildegard Binder. *Order Upon the Land: The U.S. Rectangular Land Survey and the Upper Mississippi Country*. New York: Oxford University Press, 1976.

Jordy, William H. *The Impact of European Modernism in the Mid-Twentieth Century*. Vol. 4 of *American Buildings and Their Architects*. Garden City, N.Y.: Anchor Books, Anchor Press/Doubleday, 1972.

Kaeser, William V. *City Planning: A Discussion Outlining a System for the Design of a Master Plan of Madison, Wisconsin*. [Madison: By the Author, 1935].

Keating, Ann Durkin. *Building Chicago: Suburban Developers and the Creation of a Divided Metropolis.* Originally published 1988. Reprint, Urbana: University of Illinois Press, 2002.

Keen, Charles Barton, and Frank E. Mead. "A Quaint, Old-Fashioned House for $6600." *LHJ* 17 (November 1900): 17.

Klaus, Susan L. *A Modern Arcadia: Frederick Law Olmsted Jr. and the Plan for Forest Hills Gardens.* Amherst: University of Massachusetts Press, in association with Library of American Landscape History, 2002.

Kohler, Sue A. *The Commission of Fine Arts: A Brief History, 1910–1990.* Washington, D.C.: Commission of Fine Arts, 1991.

Koolhaas, Rem. *Delirious New York: A Retroactive Manifesto for Manhattan.* Originally published 1978. New ed. New York: Monacelli Press, 1994.

Kornwolf, James D., ed. *Modernism in America, 1937–1941. A Catalog and Exhibition of Four Architectural Competitions: Wheaton College, Goucher College, College of William and Mary, Smithsonian Institution.* Williamsburg: Joseph and Margaret Muscarelle Museum of Art, College of William and Mary, 1985.

Krabbendam, Hans. *The Model Man: A Life of Edward William Bok, 1863–1930.* Amsterdam Monographs in American Studies 9. Amsterdam: Rodopi, 2001.

Krauss, Rosalind. "Grids." Originally published 1979. In *The Originality of the Avant-Garde and Other Modernist Myths,* 8–22. Cambridge, Mass.: MIT Press, 1985.

Krinsky, Carol Herselle. *Rockefeller Center.* Oxford: Oxford University Press, 1978.

Krueckeberg, Donald A., ed. *Introduction to Planning History in the United States.* New Brunswick, N.J.: Center for Urban Policy Research, Rutgers University, 1983.

Kruty, Paul. *Prelude to the Prairie Style: Eight Models of Unbuilt Houses by Frank Lloyd Wright, 1893–1901.* Urbana-Champaign: School of Architecture, University of Illinois, 2005.

———. "At Work in the Oak Park Studio." *Arris: Journal of the Southeast Chapter of the Society of Architectural Historians* 14 (2003): 17–31.

Ladd, Brian. *Urban Planning and Civic Order in Germany, 1860–1914.* Cambridge, Mass.: Harvard University Press, 1990.

Langley, Kathleen M. *The Industrialization of Iraq.* Cambridge, Mass.: Center for Middle Eastern Studies, Harvard University Press, 1961.

Lassner, Jacob. "The Caliph's Personal Domain: The City Plan of Baghdad Re-Examined." In *The Islamic City: A Colloquium,* edited by A. H. Hourani and S. M. Stern, 103–18. Oxford: Bruno Cassirer, 1970.

———. *The Topography of Baghdad in the Early Middle Ages.* Detroit: Wayne State University Press, 1970.

Lavagne d'Ortigue, Pauline. "Connaître l'architecture classique et l'urbanisme colonial; rêver d'une ville moderne et syncrétique: J. M. Wilson." In *Rêver d'Orient, connaître l'Orient: visions de l'Orient dans l'art et la littérature britanniques,* edited by Isabelle Gadoin and Marie-Élise Palmier-Chatelain, 317–40. Lyon: ENS, 2008.

Lawyer, Albert Bayne. "A $5000 House for a Family of Three." *LHJ* 18 (August 1901): 15.

Le Corbusier. *The City of To-morrow and Its Planning.* Originally published 1925. Translated from the French by Frederick Etchells 1929. New York: Dover, 1987.

———. *Manière de penser l'urbanisme.* Originally published 1946. New and rev. ed. Paris: Gonthier, 1966.

———. "A Noted Architect Dissects Our Cities: Le Corbusier Indicts Them as Cataclysms and Describes His Ideal Metropolis." *NYT Magazine,* 3 January 1932, 10–11, 19.

———. *The Radiant City: Elements of a Doctrine of Urbanism to Be Used as the Basis for Our Machine Age Civilization.* Originally published 1935. Translated from the French by Pamela Knight, Eleanor Levieux, and Derek Coltman. New York: Orion Press, 1967.

———. *Towards a New Architecture.* Originally published 1923. Translated from the French by Frederick Etchells. New York: Payson & Clarke, 1927.

———. "We Are Entering upon a New Era." *T-Square* 2 (February 1932): 14–17, 41–42.

Le Gacy, Arthur Evans. "Improvers and Preservers: A History of Oak Park, Illinois, 1833–1940." Ph.D. diss., University of Chicago, 1967.

Le Strange, Guy. *Baghdad during the Abbasid Caliphate, from Contemporary Arabic and Persian Sources.* Oxford: Clarendon, 1900.

Levine, Neil. *The Architecture of Frank Lloyd Wright.* Princeton: Princeton University Press, 1996.

———. "Frank Lloyd Wright urbaniste: Trois projets pour revitaliser la ville." *Revue urbanisme* 329 (March–April 2003): 82–89.

———. Introduction to *Modern Architecture: Being the Kahn Lectures for 1930,* by Frank Lloyd Wright, ix–lxxi. Princeton Monographs in Art and Archaeology. Originally published 1931. Reprint, Princeton: Princeton University Press, 2008.

———. "La Restructuration du lotissement résidentiel autour de 1900 et le schéma communautaire de Frank Lloyd Wright." In *Tony Garnier, la Cité Industrielle et l'Europe,* edited by Philippe Dufieux, 78–89. Lyon: Conseil d'architecture, d'urbanisme et de l'environnement du Rhône, 2009.

———. "The Late Eighteenth-Century U.S. Rectangular Land Survey and Frank Lloyd Wright's Recuperation of Its Enlightenment Ideal." In *Early Modern Urbanism and the Grid: Town Planning in the Low Countries in International Context. Exchanges in Theory and Practice, 1550–1800,* edited by Piet Lombaerde and Charles van den Heuvel, 187–206. Architectura Moderna 10. Turnhout, Belgium: Brepols, 2011.

———. *"The Quadruple Block Plan*: l'obsession de Frank Lloyd Wright pour la grille/The Quadruple Block Plan and Frank Lloyd Wright's Obsession with the Grid." *EaV: La revue de l'école nationale supérieure d'architecture de Versailles/Versailles Architecture School Journal* 11 (2005/6): 62–84.

Levitan, Stuart D. *Madison: The Illustrated Sesquicentennial History, Volume 1: 1885–1931.* Madison: University of Wisconsin Press, 2006.

Lewis, Edwin J., Jr. "A Suburban House for $6500." *LHJ* 18 (March 1901): 15.

Linklater, Andro. *Measuring America: How an Untamed Wilderness Shaped the United States and Fulfilled the Promise of Democracy.* New York: Walker, 2002.

Logan, Thomas H. "The Americanization of German Zoning." *JAIP* 46 (October 1976): 377–85.

Longstreth, Richard. *City Center to Regional Mall: Architecture, the Automobile, and Retailing in Los Angeles, 1920–1950.* Cambridge, Mass.: MIT Press, 1997.

———. *The Drive-In, the Supermarket, and the Transformation of Commercial Space in Los Angeles, 1914–1941.* Cambridge, Mass.: MIT Press, 1999.

———. "The Neighborhood Shopping Center in Washington, D.C., 1930–1941." *JSAH* 51 (March 1992): 5–34.

Lorant, Stefan. *Pittsburgh: The Story of an American City.* Garden City, N.Y.: Doubleday, 1964.

Lower Downtown Business Men's Association and Harland Bartholomew & Associates. "A Preliminary Study for the Proposed Development of the George Washington Memorial Park, Pittsburgh, Pennsylvania." Pittsburgh: Western Pennsylvania Historical Society, n.d.

Lubove, Roy. *Twentieth-Century Pittsburgh: Government, Business, and Environmental Change.* New York: John Wiley, 1969.

MacAdam, George. "Vision of New York That May Be: A Forecast of Manhattan Transfigured by the Zoning Law." *NYT Magazine,* 25 May 1924, 1–2.

Macfarlane, P[eter] W. "The Plan for Baghdad—The Capital of Iraq." *Housing Centre Review* 5 (1956): 193–95.

———. "Planning an Arab Town: Kuwait on the Persian Gulf." *Journal of the Town Planning Institute* 40 (April 1954): 110–13.

Al-Madfai, Kahtan A. J. "Baghdad." In *The New Metropolis in the Arab World,* edited by Morroe Berger, 39–63. New Delhi: Allied, 1963.

Manson, Grant Carpenter. *Frank Lloyd Wright to 1910: The First Golden Age.* New York: Van Nostrand Reinhold, 1958.

March, Lionel. "An Architect in Search of Democracy: Broadacre City." Talks originally broadcast on BBC, 7 and 15 January 1970. In *Writings on Wright: Selected Comment on Frank Lloyd Wright,* edited by H. Allen Brooks, 195–206. Cambridge, Mass.: MIT Press, 1981.

———. "Imperial City of the Boundless West—Lionel March Describes the Impact of Chicago on the Work of Frank Lloyd Wright." *Listener* 83 (30 April 1970): 581–84.

Marefat, Mina. "Bauhaus in Baghdad: Walter Gropius Master Project for Baghdad University." *Docomomo* 35 (September 2006): 78–86.

———. *The Le Corbusier Gymnasium in Baghdad.* Paris: Editions du patrimoine, Centre des monuments nationaux, 2014.

———. "Mise au Point for Le Corbusier's Baghdad Stadium." *Docomomo* 41 (September 2009): 30–40.

———. "1950s Baghdad—Modern and International." *TAARII Newsletter,* no. 2–2 (Fall 2007): 1–7.

———. "Wright's Baghdad." In *Frank Lloyd Wright: Europe and Beyond,* edited by Anthony Alofsin, 184–213. Berkeley: University of California Press, 1999.

Marr, Phebe. *The Modern History of Iraq.* Boulder, Colo.: Westview, 1985.

Marsh, Benjamin Clarke. *An Introduction to City Planning: Democracy's Challenge to the American City.* Originally published 1909. Reprint, New York: Arno, 1974.

Martin, Park H. "The Allegheny Conference—Planning in Action." *Proceedings of the American Society of Civil Engineers* 78, separate no. 131 (May 1952): 1–8.

———. "Pittsburgh's Comprehensive Improvement Program." Paper no. 2825. *American Society of Civil Engineers Transactions* 121 (1956): 885–98.

———. "Pittsburgh's Redevelopment Plan." *Traffic Quarterly* 8 (April 1954): 148–60.

Mayer, Martin. *Bricks, Mortar and the Performing Arts: Report of the Twentieth Century Fund Task Force on Performing Arts Centers.* New York: Twentieth Century Fund, 1970.

McCarter, Robert. *Frank Lloyd Wright, Architect.* London: Phaidon, 1997.

McClintock, Miller. *Report and Recommendations of the Metropolitan Street Traffic Survey.* Chicago: Chicago Association of Commerce, 1926.

McClintock, Miller, Erskine Bureau, and Staff of the NCPPC. *A Report on the Parking and Garage Problem of the Central Business District of Washington, D.C.* Washington, D.C.: Automobile Parking Committee of Washington, 1930.

McLean, Robert Craik. "City Residential Land Development: A Review of a Volume Presenting the Plans Submitted in a Competition by the City Club of Chicago." *WA* 25 (January 1917): 6–8.

Mead, Frank E. "A Quaint, Old-Fashioned House for $6600." *LHJ* 17 (November 1900): 17.

Medary, Milton Bennett, Jr., and Richard Littell Field. "An Old English Country House for $7000." *LHJ* 18 (December 1900): 21.

Merriner, James L. *The City Club of Chicago: A Centennial History.* Chicago: City Club, 2003.

Miliutin, N[ikolai] A[leksandrovich]. *Sotsgorod: The Problem of Building Socialist Cities.* Originally published 1930. Translated from the Russian by Arthur Sprague. Cambridge, Mass.: MIT Press, 1974.

Miller, Mervyn. *Hampstead Garden Suburb: Arts and Crafts Utopia?* 2nd ed. Chichester, West Sussex: Phillimore, 2006.

———. *Letchworth: The First Garden City.* 2nd ed. Chichester, West Sussex: Phillimore, 2002.

Minoprio, Anthony. *Chelmsford Planning Survey, 1945: A Survey and Plan for Chelmsford Borough and Rural District.* Chelmsford: Chelmsford Area Planning Group, 1945.

———. "Crawley New Town." *Town and Country Planning* 16 (Winter 1948–49): 215–21.

———. "The Development of New Towns with Particular Reference to Crawley." *Papers of the National Housing and Town Planning Council* (1948): 8–10.

———. *A Master Plan for Crawley New Town.* London: By the Author, 1949.

———. "The New Towns: No. 3, Crawley. Consultant Anthony Minoprio, M.A., F.R.I.B.A." *Journal of the Town Planning Institute* 35 (January–February 1949): 59–61.

Minoprio, [Anthony], [Greville] Spencely and P[eter] W. Macfarlane. *Cwmbran New Town.* Cwmbran: Cwmbran Development Corporation, March 1951.

———. *The Master Plan for the City of Baghdad, 1956: Report.* N.p., 1956.

———. *Plan for the Town of Kuwait: Report to His Highness Shaikh Abdullah Assalim Assubah, C. I. E., The Amir of Kuwait.* N.p., November 1951.

Mollenhoff, David V., and Mary Jane Hamilton. *Frank Lloyd Wright's Monona Terrace: The Enduring Power of a Civic Vision.* Madison: University of Wisconsin Press, 1999.

Moore, Charles. *Daniel H. Burnham: Architect, Planner of Cities.* 2 vols. Boston: Houghton Mifflin, 1921.

———, ed. *The Improvement of the Park System of the District of Columbia.* Pts. 1 and 2 of *Report of the Senate Committee on the District of Columbia.* 57th Congress, 1st sess., S. Rept. 166. Washington, D.C.: Government Printing Office, 1902.

Morgenthaler, Hans. "Pittsburgh's Golden Triangle: Opportunity Lost and Found?" *Avant-Garde: Journal of Theory and Criticism in Architecture and the Arts* 4 (Summer 1990): 58–71.

Moses, Robert, with the assistance of Arthur E. Howland et al. *Arterial Plan for Pittsburgh.* Pittsburgh: PRPA, November 1939.

Mumford, Eric. *The CIAM Discourse on Urbanism, 1928–1960.* Cambridge, Mass.: MIT Press, 2000.

———. *Defining Urban Design: CIAM Architects and the Formation of a Discipline, 1937–69.* New Haven: Yale University Press, 2009.

Mumford, Lewis. *The Culture of Cities.* Originally published 1938. Reprint, New York: Harcourt Brace Jovanovich, 1970.

———. "The Fourth Migration." Originally published 1925. In *Planning the Fourth Migration: The Neglected Vision of the Regional Planning Association of America,* edited by Carl Sussman, 55–64. Cambridge, Mass.: MIT Press, 1976.

———. "The Sky Line: Mr. Wright's City—Downtown Dignity." *New Yorker* 11 (27 April 1935): 79–81.

———. "The Sky Line: *Status Quo.*" *New Yorker* 34 (11 October 1947): 104–6, 108–9.

———. *The South in Architecture.* The Drancy Lectures, Alabama College, 1941. New York: Harcourt, Brace, 1941.

Muschamp, Herbert. *Man About Town: Frank Lloyd Wright in New York City.* Cambridge, Mass.: MIT Press, 1983.

Neutra, Dione, comp. and trans. *Richard Neutra: Promise and Fulfillment, 1919–1932, Selections from the Letters and Diaries of Richard and Dione Neutra.* Carbondale: Southern Illinois University Press, 1986.

Nevins, Deborah, ed. *Grand Central Terminal: City within the City.* New York: Municipal Art Society of New York, 1982.

Nichols, Charles M., comp. *Studies on Building Height Limitations in Large Cities with Special Reference to Conditions in Chicago.* Chicago: Library, Chicago Real Estate Board, 1923.

Nolen, John. "Cities Fit to Live In: Cogent Suggestions for the City of Tomorrow, a 'Machine à Habiter.'" *Technology Review* 32 (April 1930): 3–6.

———. "City Making in Wisconsin." *Municipality: Devoted to the Interests of Town, County, Village and City Government* 10 (May 1910): 417–27.

———, ed. *City Planning: A Series of Papers Presenting the Essential Elements of a City Plan.* National Municipal League Series. New York: D. Appleton, 1916.

———. *Madison: A Model City.* Boston, 1911.

Norton, Charles D. "The Merchants Club and the Plan of Chicago." In *The Merchants Club of Chicago, 1896–1906,* 95–99. Chicago: Commercial Club of Chicago, 1922.

Olin, John. "Looking Ahead—To Plan a City Beautiful." *Municipality: Devoted to the Interests of Town, County, Village and City Government* 9 (March 1909): 223–36.

Olmsted, Frederick Law, [Jr.]. *Pittsburgh: Main Thoroughfares and the Down Town District. Improvements Necessary to Meet the City's Present and Future Needs. A Report.* Pittsburgh: Pittsburgh Civic Commission, 1911.

Olmsted, Vaux & Co., Landscape Architects. "Preliminary Report upon the Proposed Suburban Village at Riverside, Near Chicago." 1 September 1868. In *The Years of Olmsted, Vaux & Company, 1865–1874,* edited by David Schuyler and Jane Turner Censer, 273–90. Vol. 6 of *The Papers of Frederick Law Olmsted.* Baltimore: Johns Hopkins University Press, 1992.

An Ordinance Related to the Department of Buildings and Governing the Erection of Buildings, Etc. in the City of Chicago, Passed March 13, 1905. Chicago, 1905.

Oud, J.J.P. "Bij een Deensch Ontwerp voor de Chicago Tribune." *Bouwkundig Weekblad: Orgaan van de Maatschappij tot Bevrordering der Bouwkunst Bond van Nederlandsche Architecten* 44th yr., no. 45 (10 November 1923): 456–58.

Our Suburbs: A Resumé of the Origin, Progress and Present Status of Chicago's Environs, Reprint from "The Chicago Times." Chicago: Blue Island Land and Building Company, [1873].

Park, Robert E., and Ernest W. Burgess. *The City: Suggestions for Investigation of Human Behavior in the Urban Environment.* The Heritage of Sociology. Originally published 1925. Reprint, Chicago: University of Chicago Press, Midway, 1984.

Parrington, V[ernon] L. "On the Lack of Privacy in American Village Homes." *House Beautiful* 13 (January 1903): 109–12.

Pattison, William D. *Beginnings of the American Rectangular Land Survey System, 1784–1800.* Department of Geography Research Paper 50. Chicago: University of Chicago Press, 1957.

Penrose, Edith, and E. F. Penrose. *Iraq: International Relations and National Development.* London: Ernest Benn, 1978.

Peterson, Jon A. *The Birth of City Planning in the United States, 1840–1917.* Baltimore: Johns Hopkins University Press, 2003.

Pfeiffer, Bruce Brooks. *The Essential Frank Lloyd Wright: Critical Writings on Architecture.* Princeton: Princeton University Press, 2008.

———. *Frank Lloyd Wright: Collected Writings.* 5 vols. New York: Rizzoli, in association with Frank Lloyd Wright Foundation, 1992–95.

———. *Frank Lloyd Wright: The Complete Work/Das Gesamtwerk/L'oeuvre complète.* 3 vols. Cologne: Taschen, 2009–11.

———, ed. *Letters to Clients: Frank Lloyd Wright.* Fresno: Press at California State University, 1986.

Pfeiffer, Bruce Brooks, and Yukio Futagawa, eds. *Frank Lloyd Wright.* 12 vols. Tokyo: A.D.A. EDITA, 1984–88. Vols. 1–8, *Monograph*; vols. 9–11, *Preliminary Studies*; vol. 12, *In His Renderings.*

Pfeiffer, Bruce Brooks, and Robert Wojtowicz. *Frank Lloyd Wright and Lewis Mumford: Thirty Years of Correspondence.* New York: Princeton Architectural Press, 2001.

Pickering, Arthur D. "A Dutch Colonial House for $5000." *LHJ* 18 (May 1901): 15.

Pieri, Caecilia. "Baghdad Architecture, 1921–1958: Reflections on History as a 'Strategy of Vigilance.'" *Bulletin of the Royal Institute of Inter-Faith Studies* 8 (2006): 1–25.

———. *Baghdad Arts Deco: Architectural Brickwork, 1920–1950.* Originally published 2008. Translated from the French by Yves Stranger and Wendy Parramore. Cairo: American University in Cairo Press, 2010.

———. "La Formation d'une ville 'moderne': Bagdad à la période hachémite (1920–1958)." *Histoire de l'art: revue de recherche et d'information publiée sous l'égide de l'Association des professeurs d'archéologie et d'histoire de l'art des universités* 59 (October 2006): 107–16.

———. "Modernity and Its Posts in Constructing an Arab Capital: Baghdad's Urban Space and Architecture, Contexts and Questions." *Middle East Studies Association Bulletin* 42 (Summer/Winter 2008): 32–39.

"Pittsburgh Renascent." *AF* 91 (November 1949): 59–73, 110, 112.

"Planning the University of Baghdad." *AR* 129 (February 1961): 107–22.

Poli, Aldo de. "Les Projets pour la métropole des années vingt: référents américains." In *Américanisme et modernité: l'idéal américain dans l'architecture,* edited by Jean-Louis Cohen and Hubert Damisch, 229–38. Paris: EHESS, Flammarion, 1993.

Pond, Irving K. "High Buildings and Beauty." Parts 1 and 2. *AF* 38 (February and April 1923): 44 and 179–82.

———. "Zoning and the Architecture of High Buildings." *AF* 35 (October 1921): 132–33.

Ponti, Gio. "Progetto per l'edificio del 'Development Board' in Baghdad." *Domus* 370 (September 1960): 1–6.

Price, Bruce. "A Georgian House for Seven Thousand Dollars." *LHJ* 17 (October 1900): 15.

Price, W[illiam] L. *Model Houses for Little Money*. Ladies' Home Journal Household Library. Philadelphia: Curtis Publishing, 1898.

Progress Report of the Jefferson National Expansion Memorial. St. Louis: Jefferson National Expansion Memorial Association, May 1940.

Purdom, C[harles] B[enjamin]. *The Garden City: A Study in the Development of a Modern Town*. London: J. M. Dent, 1913.

Pyla, Panayiota. "Back to the Future: Doxiadis's Plans for Baghdad." *JPH* 7 (February 2008): 7–10.

———. "Rebuilding Iraq: Modernist Housing, National Aspirations, and Global Ambitions." *Docomomo* 35 (September 2006): 71–77.

Qubain, Fahim I. *The Reconstruction of Iraq*. New York: Praeger, 1958.

Quinan, Jack. *Frank Lloyd Wright's Buffalo Venture: From the Larkin Building to Broadacre City. A Catalogue of Buildings and Projects*. San Francisco: Pomegranate, 2012.

The Railway Terminal Problem of Chicago: A Series of Addresses before the City Club, June Third to Tenth, 1913, Dealing with the Proposed Re-organization of the Railway Terminals of Chicago, Including All Terminal Proposals Now before the City Council Committee on Railway Terminals. Chicago: City Club of Chicago, September 1913.

Rantoul, William G. "A Stucco Country House for $7500." *LHJ* 18 (April 1901): 15.

Ratcliff, Kathryn Elizabeth. "The Making of a New Middle-Class Culture: Family and Community in a Midwest Suburb, 1890–1920." Ph.D. diss., University of Minnesota, 1990.

Reinberger, Mark. "The Sugarloaf Mountain Automobile Objective and Frank Lloyd Wright's Middle Years." Ph.D. diss., Cornell University, 1982.

———. "The Sugarloaf Mountain Project and Frank Lloyd Wright's Vision of a New World." *JSAH* 43 (March 1984): 38–52.

"A Report of Conference Committee on 'Best Methods of Land Subdivision.'" Appendix A. In *Proceedings of the Seventh National Conference on City Planning, Detroit, June 7–9, 1915*, 247–73. Boston, 1915.

Reps, John W. *The Making of Urban America: A History of City Planning in the United States*. Princeton: Princeton University Press, 1965.

———. *Monumental Washington: The Planning and Development of the Capital Center*. Princeton: Princeton University Press, 1967.

Revised Building Ordinances of the City of Chicago, Passed December 5, 1910 with Amendments and Additions up to January 1, 1912. Chicago: Francis D. Connery, City Clerk, December, 1911.

Revised Building Ordinances of the City of Chicago, with Amendments up to and Including May 26, 1920. 8th ed. Chicago: James T. Igoe, City Clerk, June 1920.

Riley, Terence, with Peter Reed, eds. *Frank Lloyd Wright, Architect*. New York: Museum of Modern Art, 1994.

Riverside Improvement Company. *Riverside in 1871, with a Description of Its Improvements Together with Some Engravings of Views and Buildings*. Chicago: D. and C. H. Blakeley, n.d.

Roth, Leland M. "Getting the Houses to the People: Edward Bok, The *Ladies' Home Journal*, and the Ideal House." *Perspectives in Vernacular Architecture* 4 (1991): 187–96.

Rowe, Colin. "Chicago Frame." Originally published 1956. In *The Mathematics of the Ideal Villa and Other Essays*, 89–107. Cambridge, Mass.: MIT Press, 1976.

Royal Institute of British Architects. *Town Planning Conference, London, 10–15 October 1910: Transactions*. London: Royal Institute of British Architects, 1911.

Saarinen, Eliel. "Project for Lake Front Development of the City of Chicago." *AAAR* 124 (5 December 1923): 487–88.

Salter, Lord [Arthur]. *The Development of Iraq: A Plan of Action*. Baghdad: Iraq Development Board, 1955.

Scanlon, Jennifer. *Inarticulate Longings: The Ladies' Home Journal, Gender, and the Promise of Consumer Culture*. New York: Routledge, 1995.

Schapiro, Meyer. "Architect's Utopia." *Partisan Review* 4 (March 1938): 42–47.

Schriftgiesser, Karl. "The Pittsburgh Story." *Atlantic Monthly* 187 (May 1951): 66–69.

Schultz, Earle, and Walter Simmons. *Offices in the Sky*. Indianapolis: New Bobbs-Merrill, 1959.

Schwieterman, Joseph P., and Dana M. Caspall. *The Politics of Place: A History of Zoning in Chicago*. Edited by Jane Heron. Chicago: Lake Claremont Press, 2006.

Scott, Mel. *American City Planning since 1890: A History Commemorating the Fiftieth Anniversary of the American Institute of Planners*. Berkeley: University of California Press, 1969.

Scully, Vincent J. *Frank Lloyd Wright*. New York: George Braziller, 1960.

———. *The Shingle Style and the Stick Style: Architectural Theory from Downing to the Origins of Wright*. Originally published 1955. Rev. ed. New Haven: Yale University Press, 1971.

Secrest, Meryle. *Frank Lloyd Wright: A Biography*. New York: Knopf, 1992.

Segoe, Ladislas. *Comprehensive Plan of Madison, Wisconsin, and Environs*. 2 vols. Madison: Trustees of Madison Planning Trust, [1938–39].

"A Selection of Works Exhibited at the Art Institute in March of the Year One Thousand Nine Hundred and Two." *Chicago Architectural Annual* (1902).

Sergeant, John. *Frank Lloyd Wright's Usonian Houses: The Case for Organic Architecture*. New York: Watson-Guptill Publications, Whitney Library of Design, 1976.

Sert, José Luis. *Can Our Cities Survive? An ABC of Urban Problems, Their Analysis, Their Solutions, Based on the Proposals Formulated by the C.I.A.M., International Congresses for Modern Architecture, Congrès Internationaux d'Architecture Moderne*. Cambridge, Mass.: Harvard University Press, 1942.

Sharples, Joseph, Alan Powers, and Michael Shippobottom. *Charles Reilly and the Liverpool School of Architecture, 1904–1933*. Catalogue of an Exhibition at the Walker Art Gallery, Liverpool, 25 October 1996–2 February 1997. Liverpool: Liverpool University Press, National Museums & Galleries on Merseyside, 1996.

Sherman, Roger Wade. "The Art of City Building." *AA* 147 (October 1935): 13–20.

Simon, Reeva S. *Iraq between the Two Wars: The Creation and Implementation of a Nationalist Ideology*. New York: Columbia University Press, 1986.

Siry, Joseph. *Unity Temple: Frank Lloyd Wright and Architecture for Liberal Religion*. Cambridge: Cambridge University Press, 1996.

———. "Wright's Baghdad Opera House and Gammage Auditorium: In Search of Regional Identity." *Art Bulletin* 87 (June 2005): 265–81.

Sitte, Camillo. *Der Städte-Bau nach seinen künstlerischen Grundsätzen: ein Beitrag zur Lösung modernster Fragen der Architektur und monumentalen Plastik unter besonderer Beziehung auf Wien*. Vienna: Carl Graeser, 1889.

Smith, Carl. *The Plan of Chicago: Daniel Burnham and the Remaking of the American City*. Chicago: University of Chicago Press, 2006.

Smith, Kathryn. "Frank Lloyd Wright and the Imperial Hotel: A Postscript." *Art Bulletin* 67 (June 1985): 296–310.

Smith, Nancy K. Morris, ed. "Letters, 1903–1906, by Charles E. White, Jr. from the Studio of Frank Lloyd Wright." *Journal of Architectural Education* 25 (Fall 1971): 104–12.

Smith, Norris Kelly. *Frank Lloyd Wright: A Study in Architectural Content*. Originally published 1966. Rev. ed. Watkins Glen, N.Y.: American Life Foundation & Study Institute, 1979.

Sokol, David M. *Oak Park: The Evolution of a Village*. Charleston, S.C.: History Press, 2011.

Sousa, Ahmed. *Atlas Baghdad*. Baghdad: Mudiriyat al-Misahah al-Ammah, 1952.

Spencer, Robert C., Jr. "The Work of Frank Lloyd Wright." *Architectural Review* (Boston) 7 (June 1900): 61–72.

Squire, Raglan, ed. "Architecture in the Middle East." *Architectural Design* 27 (March 1957): 72–108.

Stamper, John W. *Chicago's North Michigan Avenue: Planning and Development, 1900–1930*. Chicago: University of Chicago Press, 1991.

Stanek, Łukasz. "Miastoprojekt Goes Abroad: The Transfer of Architectural Labour from Socialist Poland to Iraq (1958–1989)." *Journal of Architecture* 17, no. 3 (2012): 361–86.

Steinberg, Salme Harlu. *Reformer in the Marketplace: Edward W. Bok and the Ladies' Home Journal*. Baton Rouge: Louisiana State University Press, 1979.

Stern, Robert A. M., David Fishman, and Jacob Tilove. *Planned Paradise: The Garden Suburb and the Modern City*. New York: Monacelli Press, 2013.

Stern, Robert A. M., Gregory Gilmartin, and Thomas Mellins. *New York 1930: Architecture and Urbanism between the Wars*. New York: Rizzoli International, 1987.

"St. Mark's Tower: St. Mark's in the Bouwerie, New York City." *AR* 67 (January 1930): 1–4.

Stoller, Paul D. "The Architecture of Harvey Wiley Corbett." Master's thesis, University of Wisconsin-Madison, 1995.

Stübben, Josef. *Der Städtebau*. 9th half-vol. of pt. 4 of *Entwerfen, Anlage und Einrichtung der Gebäude*. In *Handbuch der Architektur*, edited by Josef Durm et al. Darmstadt: A. Bergsträsser, 1890.

Sturgis, R. Clipston. "Suburban Homes: A Plea for Privacy in Home Life." *Cosmopolitan: A Monthly Illustrated Magazine* 21 (June 1896): 180–90.

Sullivan, Louis H. "The *Chicago Tribune* Competition." *AR* 53 (February 1923): 151–57.

———. "The High-Building Question." Originally published 1891. In *Louis Sullivan: The Public Papers*, edited by Robert Twombly, 76–79. Chicago: University of Chicago Press, 1988.

Sultani, Khalid. "Architecture in Iraq between the Two World Wars, 1920–1940." *UR: The International Magazine of Arab Culture* 2/3 (1982): 92–105.

Suplee, Henry Harrison. "The Elevated Sidewalk." *Scientific American* 109 (26 July 1913): 67 and cover.

Sutcliffe, Anthony. *Towards the Planned City: Germany, Britain, the United States and France, 1780–1914*. Comparative Studies in Social and Economic History 3. Oxford: Basil Blackwell, 1981.

Sweeney, Robert L. "Frank Lloyd Wright Chronology, 1922–1932." In *Frank Lloyd Wright: Designs for an American Landscape, 1922–1932*, edited by David G. De Long, 185–200. New York: Abrams, in association with

Canadian Center for Architecture, Library of Congress, and Frank Lloyd Wright Foundation, 1996.

Tafuri, Manfredo, and Francesco Dal Co. *Modern Architecture*. Originally published 1976. Translated from the Italian by Robert Erich Wolf. New York: Abrams, 1979.

Taj-Eldin, Suzanne, and Stanislaus von Moos. "Nach Plänen von . . . : Eine Gymnastikhalle von Le Corbusier in Baghdad." *Archithèse* 3 (May–June 1983): 39–44.

Tarr, Joel A. *Devastation and Renewal: An Environmental History of Pittsburgh and Its Region*. Pittsburgh: University of Pittsburgh Press, 2003.

Taut, Bruno. *Die Auflösung der Städte*. Hagen: Folkwang-Verlag, 1920.

Tentative Report and a Proposed Zoning Ordinance for the City of Chicago, January 5, 1923. Chicago: Chicago Zoning Commission, 1923.

Toffler, Alvin. *The Culture Consumers: A Study of Art and Influence in America*. New York: St. Martin's, 1964.

Toker, Franklin. *Pittsburgh: An Urban Portrait*. University Park: Pennsylvania State University Press, 1986.

Toll, Seymour I. *Zoned American*. New York: Grossman, 1969.

Treat, Payson Jackson. *The National Land System, 1785–1820*. New York: E. B. Treat, 1910.

Trench, Richard, ed. *Kuwait City*. Vol. 2 of *Arab Gulf Cities*. [Slough]: Archive Editions, 1994.

Turner, Frederick Jackson. "The Significance of the Frontier in American History." In *Annual Report of the American Historical Society for the Year 1893*, 197–227. Washington, D.C.: Government Printing Office, 1894.

Twombly, Robert C. *Frank Lloyd Wright: His Life and His Architecture*. New York: John Wiley, 1979.

———. "Undoing the City: Frank Lloyd Wright's Planned Communities." *American Quarterly* 24 (October 1972): 538–49.

Tyrwhitt, J[aqueline], J[osé] L[uis] Sert, and E[rnesto] N. Rogers. *The Heart of the City: Towards the Humanisation of Urban Life*. CIAM 8. New York: Pellegrini and Cudahy, 1952.

"The University of Baghdad." Pt. 1 of "TAC: The Architects Collaborative." *AR* 125 (April 1959): 147–55.

Unwin, Raymond. *Nothing Gained by Overcrowding! How the Garden City Type of Development May Benefit Both Owner and Occupier*. London: Garden Cities & Town Planning Association, 1912.

———. *Town Planning in Practice: An Introduction to the Art of Designing Cities and Suburbs*. Originally published 1909. Reprint, New York: Princeton Architectural Press, 1994.

Unwin, Raymond, and M. H. Baillie Scott. *Town Planning and Modern Architecture at the Hampstead Garden Suburb*. London: T. Fisher Unwin, 1909.

Upton, Dell. *Another City: Urban Life and Urban Spaces in the New American Republic*. New Haven: Yale University Press, 2008.

"Urban Design." *Progressive Architecture* 37 (August 1956): 97–112.

Van Zanten, David, Ashley Elizabeth Dunn, and Leslie Coburn. *Drawing the Future: Chicago Architecture on the International Stage, 1900–1925*. Evanston: Mary and Leigh Block Museum of Art, Northwestern University Press, 2013.

Vaumas, Étienne de. "Introduction géographique à l'étude de Bagdad." *Arabica* 9 (October 1962): 229–47.

Veiller, Lawrence. "Buildings in Relation to Street and Site." In *Proceedings of the Third National Conference on City Planning, Philadelphia, Pennsylvania, May 15–17, 1911*, 80–96. Boston, 1911.

Ward, Stephen V. *The Garden City: Past, Present, and Future*. London: E. and F. N. Spon, 1992.

Warner, Sam Bass, Jr. *Streetcar Suburbs: The Process of Growth in Boston, 1870–1900*. Originally published 1962. 2nd ed. Cambridge, Mass.: Harvard University Press, 1978.

Weber, Adna Ferrin. *The Growth of Cities in the Nineteenth Century: A Study in Statistics*. Studies in History, Economics and Public Law, vol. 11. New York: Macmillan, for Columbia University, 1899.

"What Is Happening to Modern Architecture? A Symposium at the Museum of Modern Art." *Museum of Modern Art Bulletin* 15 (Spring 1948): 4–20.

White, C. Albert. *A History of the Rectangular Survey System*. Washington, D.C.: U.S. Department of the Interior, Bureau of Land Management, 1983.

Willis, Carol. "Drawing towards Metropolis." In *The Metropolis of Tomorrow*, by Hugh Ferriss (1929), 148–79. Princeton: Princeton Architectural Press, 1986.

———. *Form Follows Finance: Skyscrapers and Skylines in New York and Chicago*. Princeton: Princeton Architectural Press, 1995.

———. "Skyscraper Utopias: Visionary Urbanism in the 1920s." In *Imagining Tomorrow: History, Technology, and the American Future*, edited by Joseph J. Corn, 164–87. Cambridge, Mass.: MIT Press, 1986.

———. "The Titan City: Forgotten Episodes in American Architecture." *Skyline* (October 1982): 26–27.

———. "Zoning and *Zeitgeist*: The Skyscraper City in the 1920s." *JSAH* 45 (March 1986): 47–59.

Wilson, William H. *The City Beautiful Movement*. Baltimore: Johns Hopkins University Press, 1989.

Wirth, Louis. "Urbanism as a Way of Life." *American Journal of Sociology* 44 (July 1938): 1–24.

Wojtowicz, Robert. *Lewis Mumford and American Modernism: Eutopian Theories for Architecture and Urban Planning*. Cambridge: Cambridge University Press, 1996.

Wright, Frank Lloyd. "America Tomorrow: 'We Must Choose between the Automobile and the Vertical City.'" *AA* 141 (May 1932): 16–17, 76.

———. *Ausgeführte Bauten und Entwürfe von Frank Lloyd Wright*. Berlin: Wasmuth, 1910[–11].

———. "'Broadacre City': An Architect's Vision." *NYT Magazine*, 20 March 1932, 8–9.

———. "Broadacre City: A New Community Plan." *AR* 77 (April 1935): 243–54.

———. "Broadacres to Pittsburgh." Originally published 1935. In *The New Frontier: Broadacre City*. Vol. 1 of *Taliesin: Taliesin Fellowship Publication* (1 October 1940): 30–32.

———. "Daniel Hudson Burnham: An Appreciation." *AR* 32 (August 1912): 184.

———. *The Disappearing City*. New York: William Farquhar Payson, 1932.

———. *Frank Lloyd Wright: Ausgeführte Bauten*. Berlin: Ernst Wasmuth, 1911.

———. "A Home in a Prairie Town." *LHJ* 18 (February 1901): 17.

———. "In the Cause of Architecture." *AR* 23 (March 1908): 155–221.

———. "In the Cause of Architecture, I: The Logic of the Plan." *AR* 63 (January 1928): 52–55.

———. "In the Cause of Architecture, Second Paper: 'Style, Therefore, Will Be the Man, It Is His. Let His Forms Alone.'" *AR* 35 (May 1914): 405–13.

———. "In the Cause of Architecture, V: The New World." *AR* 62 (October 1927): 322–24.

———. "In the Cause of Architecture, VIII: Sheet Metal and a Modern Instance." *AR* 64 (October 1928): 334–42.

———. *The Industrial Revolution Runs Away*. New York: Horizon Press, 1969.

———. *The Living City*. Originally published 1958. Reprint, New York: New American Library/Times Mirror, Meridian Book, 1970.

———. *Modern Architecture: Being the Kahn Lectures for 1930*. Princeton Monographs in Art and Archaeology. Originally published 1931. Reprint, Princeton: Princeton University Press, 2008.

———. *An Organic Architecture: The Architecture of Democracy*. Sir George Watson Lectures of the Sulgrave Manor Board for 1939. London: Lund Humphries, 1939.

———. "A Small House with 'Lots of Room in It.'" *LHJ* 18 (July 1901): 15.

———. "Towards a New Architecture." Review of *Towards a New Architecture*, by Le Corbusier. *World Unity* 2 (September 1928): 393–95.

———. *When Democracy Builds*. Chicago: University of Chicago Press, 1945.

Wright, Gwendolyn. "Architectural Practice and Social Vision in Wright's Early Designs." In *The Nature of Frank Lloyd Wright*, edited by Carol Bolon et al., 98–124. Chicago: University of Chicago Press, 1988.

———. *Frank Lloyd Wright's Progressive Suburbia*. Geske Lectures. Lincoln: Hixson-Lied College of Fine and Performing Arts, University of Nebraska-Lincoln, 2010.

———. *Moralism and the Model Home: Domestic Architecture and Cultural Conflict in Chicago, 1873–1913*. Chicago: University of Chicago Press, 1980.

Yeomans, Alfred B[eaver], ed. *City Residential Land Development: Studies in Planning. Competitive Plans for Subdividing a Typical Quarter Section of Land in the Outskirts of Chicago*. Publications of the City Club of Chicago. Chicago: University of Chicago Press, December 1916.

Zoning Commission of the District of Columbia. *Zoning Regulations, Revised to August 1, 1930*. Washington, D.C.: Government Printing Office, 1930.

———. *Zoning Regulations, 30 August 1920*. Washington, D.C.: Government Printing Office, 1920.

Zoning Commission of the District of Columbia (recorded by S. G. Lindholm). *Experiences with Zoning in Washington, D.C., 1920–1934*. [Washington, D.C.: Zoning Commission, 1935].

Zukowsky, John, ed. *Chicago Architecture 1872–1922: Birth of a Metropolis*. Munich: Prestel-Verlag, in association with Art Institute of Chicago, 1987.

Zygas, K. Paul, ed. *Broadacre City*. Vol. 1 of *Frank Lloyd Wright: The Phoenix Papers*. Tempe: Herberger Center for Design Excellence, College of Architecture and Environmental Design, Arizona State University, 1995.

INDEX